CONTEMPORARY BEHAVIORAL THERAPY

CONTEMPORARY BEHAVIORAL THERAPY

Michael D. Spiegler

Providence College

MAYFIELD PUBLISHING COMPANY

First Edition

Library of Congress Catalog Card Number: 82-073738
International Standard Book Number: 0-87484-350-2

Manufactured in the United States of America
Mayfield Publishing Company
285 Hamilton Avenue
Palo Alto, California 94301

Sponsoring editor: C. Lansing Hays
Manuscript editor: Linda Purrington
Managing editor: Pat Herbst
Art director: Nancy Sears
Designer: Marie Carluccio
Illustrator: Pat Rogondino
Production manager: Cathy Willkie
Compositor: Computer Typesetting Services, Inc.
Printer and binder: Bookcrafters

CREDITS

P. 47 From *Behavior Therapy and Beyond* by A. A. Lazarus. Copyright © 1971 by McGraw-Hill Book Company. Reprinted by permission of McGraw-Hill Book Company.

P. 75 From *Behavior Therapy Techniques: A Guide to the Treatment of Neurosis* by J. Wolpe and A. A. Lazarus. Pergamon Press, 1966. Reprinted by permission.

P. 77 From "The Use of Humor in the Counterconditioning of Anger Responses: A Case Study" by R. E. Smith, *Behavior Therapy*, 1973, 4, pp. 576–580. Reprinted by permission of Academic Press and the author.

P. 85 Reprinted from *Insight vs. Desensitization in Psychotherapy* by Gordon L. Paul with the permission of the publishers, Stanford University Press. © 1966 by the Board of Trustees of the Leland Stanford Junior University.

P. 90 Reprinted with permission from *Journal of Behavior Therapy and Experimental Psychiatry*, 4, E. B. Nesbitt, "An Escalator Phobia Overcome in One Session of Flooding *In Vivo*." Copyright © 1966 by Pergamon Press, Ltd.

P. 100 From "A Modified Shame Aversion Therapy for Compulsive Obscene Telephone Calling" by P. A. Boudewyns, V. L. Tanna, and D. J. Fleischman, *Behavior Therapy*, 1975, 6, pp. 704–707. Reprinted by permission of Academic Press and the authors.

P. 103 From case report by G. C. Davison, "Elimination of a Sadistic Fantasy by a Client-Controlled Counter-Conditioning Technique," *Journal of Abnormal Psychology*, 1968, 73, pp. 84–90.

P. 106 Reprinted with permission from *Journal of Behavior Therapy and Experimental Psychiatry*, 5, B. S. Lubetkin and S. T. Fishman, "Electrical Aversion Therapy with a Chronic Heroin User." Copyright © 1974 by Pergamon Press, Ltd.

P. 119 From "The Use of Social Reinforcement in a Case of Conversion Reaction" by W. M. Kallman, M. Hersen, and D. H. O'Toole, *Behavior Therapy*, 1975, 6, pp. 411–413. Reprinted by permission of Academic Press and the authors.

Continued on page 457

For
Barbara

Case Studies and Participation Exercises

CASE STUDIES

PARTICIPATION EXERCISES

Preface

Thank you for reading this preface. My impression is that few people read prefaces, and so I want to reinforce your exceptional behavior by answering one of the questions you are likely to ask: What makes this book different from other introductions to behavioral therapy?

The unique feature of *Contemporary Behavioral Therapy* is its *operational approach:* discussing behavioral therapy in terms of *how* it functions and *what* it accomplishes (rather than in terms of theoretical explanations of *why* it works). As far as I know, this is the first full-scale *operational* account of behavioral therapy, although I am certainly not the first to point out the merits of this strategy (which are discussed in the first chapter).

Describing behavioral therapy operationally differs from the traditional approach, which describes behavioral therapy in terms of learning theory. It is important to note, however, that learning *theory* (i.e., hypothetical explanations of underlying mechanisms) is here distinguished from learning *principles, procedures,* or *processes.* Behavioral therapy can be understood and practiced without recourse to learning theory, as indeed it often is. For example, reinforcement procedures that are so effective in changing behavior work perfectly well without taking into account any theoretical explanation of their possible physiological or cognitive mechanisms. Furthermore, the role of learning (processes) in the development, the maintenance, and especially the change of abnormal behavior is fully acknowledged in this book. It could not be otherwise because *Contemporary Behavioral Therapy* is consistently written from the behavioral perspective in which learning and environmental factors play prominent roles.

One pedagogical advantage of an operational approach is that readers need have no prior knowledge of learning theory (or other psychological concepts). That makes this book appropriate for students in many disciplines. Although behavioral therapy is most strongly rooted in psychology, its procedures and principles have become increasingly important in other fields, including education, social work, rehabilitation, medicine, nursing, health education, business and industry, and physical education. Accordingly, *Contemporary Behavioral Therapy* has been written for readers with diverse backgrounds and interests. Psychological concepts are presented, but psychological jargon is avoided. All necessary technical terms directly related to behavioral therapy are printed in boldface type when they are defined; technical terms indirectly related are printed in italics initially. Additionally, the case examples were chosen to illustrate a variety of problem behaviors, client populations, and treatment settings.

Three closely related goals guided my writing of *Contemporary Behavioral Therapy*, and they are products of my experiences with behavioral therapy as a teacher, researcher, and therapist. First, I wanted this to be a "teaching book," one from which students would easily learn. Second, I thought it important to stress the general principles underlying the behavioral approach to therapy and then to illustrate their application while describing the gamut of behavioral therapies used to treat a wide variety of problem behaviors. Third, I wanted to present an accurate and realistic picture of contemporary behavioral therapy and, in doing so, to dispel the common myths about it.

In teaching behavioral therapy, I have realized the necessity of stressing underlying principles (and this seems equally important for beginning and for advanced students). Without such postulates firmly in mind, the theory and the practice of behavioral therapy are likely to appear little more than a hodgepodge of unrelated therapeutic techniques. On the other hand, appreciation of the basic elements of behavioral therapy explains how procedurally divergent, but conceptually convergent treatment procedures—such as systematic desensitization and flooding, token economies and participant modeling—are all behavioral therapies. Furthermore, because no single, succinct definition of behavioral therapy exists, it is its fundamental principles that define behavioral therapy and differentiate it from other approaches to psychotherapy. Finally, broad concepts are more likely to be remembered than a catalogue of "facts." For all these reasons, the guiding principles of behavioral therapy are given substantial treatment in the first three chapters, and then their application is illustrated in the remainder of the book as behavioral therapies are described.

I have tried various ways of presenting behavioral therapy to my students, and I have incorporated the most successful of these into *Contemporary Behavioral Therapy*. To promote active learning, I have designed and pretested "participation exercises" from which readers can learn experientially. One of the criteria for selecting case examples was to maximize student interest and involvement by making them relevant to students' experiences. The cases are totally integrated with the text material. Specifically, they appear at the points where they are needed to illustrate a procedure or concept, and they are introduced beforehand, discussed afterward, and referred to subsequently in the text. One other example of the student focus of *Contemporary Behavioral Therapy* concerns the format used for references. Because most students find the typical parenthetical style of referencing burdensome (hurdles to be jumped, both literally and figuratively), the references are designated unobtrusively by superscript numbers that correspond to reference notes at the end of each chapter.

As a researcher (and as a behavioral therapist), I appreciate the importance of empirically validating therapeutic procedures. I believe that students being introduced to behavioral therapy should comprehend the necessity for empirically testing and that they should become aware of the general findings concerning the efficacy of behavioral therapy. However, beginning students usually do not have sufficient understanding of research methodology to critically evaluate studies and are not familiar enough with the extant research literature to draw informed conclusions. Accordingly, I have chosen to summarize the available research evidence and to describe in detail selected studies to acquaint students with the types of investigations typically performed. Evaluative comments are included in the discussion of each behavioral therapy, and an overall appraisal of the current status of behavioral therapy is presented in a separate chapter at the end of the book.

Being a behavioral therapist, I find clinical practice both challenging and rewarding. Challenge comes from such tasks as helping clients presenting broad, amorphous problems to select specific, clear-cut target behaviors to change in therapy; carefully observing clients to ascertain the probable maintaining conditions of their target behaviors; and planning treatment strategies that have the greatest chance of success for each individual client. Rewards come from such tasks as teaching clients therapeutic skills and having clients successfully implement them on their own; seeing objective evidence of desired changes in target behaviors (often relatively quickly); and knowing that I have helped clients deal with significant problems in their lives and contributed to alleviating their suffering and enhancing their well-being. To me, the process and outcome of behavioral therapy constitute a most human endeavor. I have tried to impart this flavor of the practice of behavioral therapy in what I have written.

These, then, are my goals for *Contemporary Behavioral Therapy* and the strategies I have used to implement them. You will be the judge of how successful my efforts have been, and I would like to know what you think after you have read this book. I would be grateful for your feedback and comments, which can be sent to me c/o Mayfield Publishing Company, 285 Hamilton Avenue, Palo Alto, CA 94301.

Many undergraduate and graduate students have challenged my ideas, have forced me to clarify concepts and issues to enhance their (and my) comprehension, and have taught me by sharing their thoughts and experiences. I hope some of them will read this book to which they have contributed and accept my sincere thanks. Stimulating dialogues about behavioral therapy with colleagues (and friends) and their critical comments on drafts of the book have substantially added to my knowledge of behavioral therapy; foremost among these people are Eric Cooley, Kathryn Ford, LaNelle Ford, Howard Prince, Mary Puckett, Stephen Puckett, Judith Skenazy, and Leonard Ullmann. Formal, and helpful, reviews of the manuscript were written by Hal Arkowitz of the University of Arizona; Carol A. Saslow of Oregon State University at Corvallis; Donald L. Tasto, a psychologist working in Palo Alto, California; and Leonard P. Ullmann of the University of Houston. My association through the years with Haig Agigian, David Fisher, and John Marquis, three outstanding behavioral therapists, has had untold influence on my learning the subtleties of the clinical practice of behavioral therapy, and I would like to formally tell them so. I appreciate the support and patience of my two editors at Mayfield, Lansing Hays and Robert Erhart. Linda Purrington, my copy editor, helped me clarify my writing as well as my ideas. Catherine Jahn assisted with compiling references, and Kristina Hanson aided the indexing.

Robert Edwards provided warm encouragement when the writing was going slower than. . . . As always and in all ways, the love and acceptance of my parents, Julius and Lillian Spiegler, made my work easier and, I believe, the final product better.

One person deserves special thanks. David Guevremont, my assistant for three years, was always available, totally reliable, and completely dedicated. He truly contributed to every phase of writing *Contemporary Behavioral Therapy*. Moreover, I am deeply grateful for his support and friendship.

M.D.S.

Siphnos, Greece
August 1982

CONTEMPORARY BEHAVIORAL THERAPY

CHAPTER 1 Introduction

For many people, opening to the first page of a textbook is like walking into a psychotherapist's office for the first time. The reader or client usually has only a vague notion concerning the specifics of what is about to happen, but in most cases he or she has some general expectations about the process. Most readers assume that the author will *teach* something and that their role is to read and comprehend the words. Similarly, most people participating in psychotherapy for the first time expect that they will be cured of their problems by the therapist's advice and that their role is to listen to and follow the advice. But to be taught and to be cured are passive processes, and therein lies an unfortunate misconception many people have about reading textbooks and being in psychotherapy (as well as other educational endeavors). For either process to be maximally effective, student or client must assume much of the responsibility for the effort and ultimate success.

The analogy between educational and therapeutic processes is fitting, because behavioral therapy is very much an educational and an active endeavor. Accordingly, the educational process about behavioral therapy begins by actively involving you in it. On page 2, you will find the first of a number of participation exercises that appear in this book to help you experience ideas, concepts, and procedures firsthand. Do the participation exercises at the points at which they occur in the text (unless the instructions state otherwise), in order to benefit fully from them.

PARTICIPATION EXERCISE 1-1
Thoughts About Behavioral Therapy

You have no doubt heard about behavioral therapy—or behavior therapy or behavior modification—and before reading this book it would be useful to assess how accurate your information is. Read each of the following statements and note in the margin whether you think it is primarily ***true*** or primarily ***false***. Do this before reading any further.

1. Behavioral therapy is the application of well-established laws of learning.
2. Behavioral therapy directly treats symptoms.
3. A trusting relationship between client and therapist is not important in behavioral therapy.
4. Behavioral therapy does not deal with problems of feelings, such as depression and low self-esteem.
5. There is generally little verbal interchange between therapist and client in behavioral therapy.
6. The cooperation of a client is not necessary for successful behavioral therapy.
7. Most patients in behavioral therapy can be successfully treated in less than five sessions.
8. Behavioral therapy is not applicable to problems that involve cognitions, such as obsessional thoughts and undesirable attitudes.
9. Positive reinforcement works better with naive children than with sophisticated adults.
10. Behavioral therapy has been adopted as the primary mode of treatment in most psychiatric hospitals and mental health centers.
11. Behavioral therapists do not use assessment techniques but rather focus immediately on treatment.
12. Much behavioral therapy involves the use of painful or aversive stimulation.
13. Behavioral therapy cannot begin until the client has well-defined goals for therapy.
14. Behavioral therapy is primarily applicable to dealing with relatively simple problem behaviors, such as phobias (e.g., fear of snakes) or undesirable habits (e.g., smoking).
15. Behavioral therapy often uses biological treatments such as drugs and psychosurgery (e.g., lobotomies).
16. In behavioral therapy, the therapist determines the goals for the client.
17. In behavioral therapy, the therapist is directly responsible for the success of therapy.

How many of those statements did you consider false? As will become clear at various points in this book, ***all*** the statements are predominantly false; they are all misconceptions or myths.

DEFINING BEHAVIORAL THERAPY

If the statements in Participation Exercise 1-1 reveal some of what behavioral therapy is *not*, then just what *is* behavioral therapy? Unfortunately a concise definition is not possible. The field is both diverse and evolving, which means that there is no single, agreed-on definition.[1] Behavioral therapists themselves have a hard time concisely defining the work they do.

The basic aim of behavioral therapy is to alleviate human suffering and to enhance human functioning, a goal shared with many other forms of treatment. "Human suffering" here refers to personal or psychological problems that have been called *abnormal behavior* (the term used in this book), *psychopathology*, *emotional disturbance*, or *mental illness*. Common examples of abnormal behavior include feeling anxious, being depressed, having interpersonal difficulties, experiencing problems with sexual adjustment, feeling overwhelmed by upsetting recurrent thoughts, exhibiting bizarre behaviors (e.g., hearing voices that do not exist), having various psychophysiological difficulties (e.g., insomnia and tension headaches), and being unable to cope with the everyday demands of living.

What distinguishes behavioral therapy from other forms of treatment for such problems is the general approach to and specific techniques for dealing with psychological and living problems. The following list presents the core characteristics of behavioral therapy and a brief explanation of each. These characteristics are explained more fully later and are illustrated in the applications of behavioral therapy described throughout the book. The term *client*, rather than *patient*, will be used for the most part to refer to the recipient of behavioral therapy because *patient* connotes someone who has a medical problem, which is inappropriate in most cases of behavioral therapy.

1. *Behavioral therapy deals with a client's behavior*. It focuses on behaviors that can be directly observed by others and also deals with behaviors of which only the client is aware (e.g., thoughts and feelings). The emphasis on behavior implies that hypothetical processes, such as unconscious impulses and personality traits, play little or no role in behavioral therapy.

2. *Behavioral therapy takes a scientific approach*. It aims for precision in specifying treatment goals and therapy procedures and advocates a commitment to objectively evaluating the effectiveness of behavioral therapy procedures in general and the specific therapy procedures used with each individual client.

3. *Behavioral therapy primarily focuses on the present—the client's current problems and the factors influencing them*. This focus is to be contrasted with that of other forms of psychotherapy, most notably psychoanalysis, which relies heavily on post hoc analysis of possible historical determinants.

4. *Continuous assessment (i.e., measurement) of the problem behaviors and the conditions that are currently maintaining them is an essential element of behavioral therapy*. In order to implement change procedures, it is necessary to know the dimensions of the problem behavior (such as how often it occurs, when and where it occurs most and least frequently) and of the specific conditions that are influencing the problem behavior. The measurement must be continuous because both the nature of the problem behavior and its maintaining conditions are expected to change during the course of therapy, as a result of the therapy.

5. *Behavioral therapy is principally educational in nature*. The client learns adaptive behaviors that are aimed at changing aspects of the client's

behavior (e.g., maladaptive lifestyles or habits) or at modifying conditions in the client's everyday environment in order to alleviate the client's problems. Behavioral therapy does *not* involve directly changing bodily processes by biological interventions such as the use of drugs.

6. *Often behavioral therapy takes place in the client's everyday environment or where the problem is occurring.* The therapeutic changes in the client's actions, feelings, and outlook are relevant to the problem situation and not, for example, to the therapist's office. Therefore, actually implementing therapy in the client's home environment where the difficulties occur is most efficient (i.e., learning is most effective if it takes place in the setting in which it is to be applied).

7. *There is an emphasis on providing clients with self-control skills,* and *the client is responsible for carrying out much of the therapy.* This practice follows from the previous one (Item 6). If therapy is to be implemented in the client's everyday environment, the client is often the most appropriate therapeutic agent (after all, no one else is always around, as clients themselves are).

8. *Behavioral therapy is action oriented.* Clients engage in specific behaviors in order to actively create needed changes in their lives. They do more than just talk about their problems.

9. *Behavioral therapy is individualized for each client.* Although there are standard therapy procedures, each is tailored to the unique problem of each individual client.

10. *Client and behavioral therapist usually enter into a contractual agreement regarding the goals and methods of therapy.* This practice assures that the client and the therapist are working toward the same goal for the client and that the client understands what will be done in order to effect the desired changes. It also assures that the client as well as the therapist will be aware of progress (or lack of it) toward the goal and when the goal has been met.

Even from this sketchy enumeration of core characteristics, you can begin to get an idea about how behavioral therapy differs from (as well as resembles) other forms of psychotherapy. The list also sheds light on some reasons why the statements in Participation Exercise 1-1 are myths.

The Many Varieties of Behavioral Therapy

Behavioral therapy is not a single technique. There are many different forms of behavioral therapy, which is to say that there actually are many behavioral therapies. An adherence to a common set of principles, which is called the *behavioral approach* to human behavior, groups all these behavioral therapies together. To illustrate some of the variety in behavioral therapy, the following brief descriptions of behavioral therapy cases are presented. The name of the behavioral therapy procedure employed and the chapter(s) in which it principally is covered in this book precede each description.

Positive reinforcement, Chapter 6: A college student was failing four of his five courses because he was studying only about 15 minutes a day. He was able to begin studying (and passing all of his courses) by allowing himself to visit friends, have an evening snack, and watch television only after doing predetermined amounts of studying.

Modeling and behavior rehearsal, Chapter 10: A woman was intimidated by her boss and consequently was unable to speak to him about important grievances she had concerning her work situation. She learned to appropriately express her desires to her boss (and other people in authority) by observing a behavioral therapist demonstrate a variety of ways to politely, yet forcefully, tell superiors about dissatisfactions and personal preferences. Then she practiced these behaviors, initially with the therapist, and later with less threatening people than her boss, and finally with her boss.

Response cost, Chapter 7: A 10-year-old boy, who was big for his age, frequently bullied smaller children. The incidents of bullying rapidly declined when his teacher instituted a rule that the boy would miss recess or gym, his favorite school activities, each time he was caught fighting.

Cognitive restructuring, Chapter 11: In order to increase her self-esteem, a woman regularly substituted positive, self-enhancing thoughts (e.g., "I look nice today" or "I'm doing a good job") for habitually negative, self-effacing ideas (e.g., "I look like a mess today" or "I can't do anything right").

Participant modeling, Chapter 10: A teenager who had an intense fear of riding in elevators learned to overcome this fear by spending increasing amounts of time in elevators with her therapist. The therapist provided a model of someone who was comfortable being in elevators and gave her physical and emotional support while on the elevator.

Shaping, Chapter 6: A mentally retarded girl was taught to dress herself by rewarding her with bites of her favorite food for each of the sequential behaviors involved in dressing oneself (e.g., putting each arm in a sleeve of a blouse, buttoning it, and tucking it into her skirt).

Systematic desensitization, Chapter 4: A bright student was doing poorly in school because she "choked up" during important examinations. By visualizing the anxiety-evoking situations (e.g., entering the examination room, reading over the questions) while remaining calm and relaxed, her test anxiety declined to the point where she was able to function well during examinations.

Covert sensitization, Chapter 5, and *stress inoculation*, Chapter 12: A business executive was drinking excessively when he arrived home each evening after a frustrating day at the office. In order to make drinking after work aversive to the man, the behavioral therapist instructed him to imagine a very upsetting scene (e.g., his boss telling him that he was being fired because of his excessive drinking) whenever he went to get a drink after work. This procedure reduced the man's desire to drink. The man was also helped to deal with his frustration by teaching him appropriate coping skills (e.g., deep muscle relaxation) and then having him practice using the coping skills in simulated frustrating situations.

Stimulus control, Chapter 12: An overweight teenage girl was able to significantly reduce the amount of food she ate by establishing and following a rule that she was not to go into the kitchen except during designated mealtimes.

Behavioral Therapy: What's in a Name?

Behavioral therapy is also referred to by other names—principally *behavior therapy* and *behavior modification*. For most purposes, the terms have the same meanings and can be used interchangeably. However, professionals in the field sometimes make distinctions among them (especially between *behavior therapy* and *behavior modification*), although unfortunately the distinctions are not standard.[2] The term *behavioral therapy* is used in this book because both professionals and lay people use it less frequently than they use the other two terms. Thus it carries less excess baggage, so to speak, in the form of idiosyncratic meanings and pejorative connotations. Some of the recent criticism and fear of behavioral therapy procedures is the result of a misunderstanding of what "behavioral therapy" is. One reason is that the term *behavior modification* has frequently been confused with all possible procedures that modify behavior, including psychosurgery, drug therapy, and electroconvulsive shock therapy—none of which is a behavioral therapy. Finally, besides referring to a definite focus on a client's behavior (as opposed to hypothetical states), the term *behavioral therapy* refers to psychological intervention procedures that are based on the behavioral approach discussed in the next chapter.

THE HISTORICAL ROOTS OF BEHAVIORAL THERAPY

How old is behavioral therapy? It has been said that behavioral therapy has "a long past but a short history."[3] In rudimentary forms, it is very old, but the systematic application of behavioral principles to dealing with people's personal problems is less than 30 years old. There is little doubt that humans have been employing behavioral principles to modify behavior for thousands of years (e.g., parents rewarding children for doing chores). For the most part, however, such individual applications have been haphazard.

A number of documented cases (in the past) of the treatment of abnormal behavior closely resemble contemporary behavioral therapies. The eighteenth-century philosopher Jean Jacques Rousseau, for instance, recommended certain procedures for dealing with children's behavioral problems, such as crying and temper tantrums, which he believed were caused by the social attention of adults.[4] These procedures included withholding adult attention for the child's crying, attending to the child for not crying, and temporarily removing the opportunity to interact with adults for temper tantrums. These procedures are remarkably similar to standard modern behavioral therapies, namely extinction, reinforcement, and time out from positive reinforcement (discussed later in this book). Although Rousseau probably did not implement any of his own suggestions, his ideas did influence Jean-Marc-Gaspard Itard, who attempted to socialize the "Wild Boy of Aveyron," a child who grew up without human contact.[5] To teach the boy language, Itard made extensive use of modeling procedures that closely resemble contemporary modeling therapies for teaching language to autistic children.[6] Alexander Maconochie, who was a captain in the Royal Navy during the early years of the nineteenth century, had the dubious distinction of being in charge of one of the worst British penal colonies, on Norfolk Island, in Australia.[7] To rehabilitate the prisoners, he established a point system that allowed each prisoner to redeem himself by performing appropriate tasks and social behaviors. In Maconochie's words, "When a man keeps the key of his own prison, he is soon persuaded to fit it into the lock." Despite the apparent success of this early token economy, Maconochie's superiors disapproved of his innovative methods and denounced their effectiveness.[8]

Another example comes to us through a paper presented to the Royal Academy of Medicine in Paris in 1845. A physician named François Leuret treated a 30-year-old wine merchant for his obsessional thoughts by having him memorize and then recite song lyrics, a behavior that was incompatible with the disturbing, repetitive thoughts.[9] This procedure is remarkably similar to systematic desensitization. Finally, a very early example of aversion therapy was developed by Pliny the Elder, a first-century Roman scholar, who created an aversion to alcohol by putting putrid spiders in the bottom of the problem drinker's glass.[10] Although these therapeutic endeavors have historical significance and interest, such isolated incidents had no influence on the development of contemporary behavioral therapy.[11]

Early Experimental Work

The inspiration for contemporary behavioral therapy came from experimental work on learning done at the beginning of this century by physiologists such as Ivan Pavlov and Vladimir Bechterev in Russia and psychologists such as Edward Thorndike in the United States. Pavlov is credited with the first systematic account of what has come to be called "classical (or Pavlovian) conditioning." In brief, *classical conditioning* is a form of learning in which a neutral stimulus (one that elicits no particular response) is repeatedly presented along with a stimulus that reflexively elicits a particular response. The result is that the neutral stimulus alone eventually elicits the response. In Pavlov's well-known experiments with dogs, a neutral stimulus such as a tone or light was paired with meat powder, a stimulus that naturally produced salivation in the dog. After repeated pairings of these two stimuli, the neutral stimulus itself came to elicit salivation. Thorndike was concerned with a form of learning that has become known as "operant (or instrumental) conditioning." Basically, *operant conditioning* involves increasing or decreasing a behavior by systematically varying its consequences (e.g., rewards).

Besides their important laboratory experiments with animals, both Pavlov and Bechterev wrote about the application of learning procedures and theory to treating abnormal behavior.[12] Moreover, Pavlov's work had a definite influence on the U.S. experimental psychologist John B. Watson, who is known as the father of *behaviorism*—the philosophical school of thought on which behavioral therapy is largely based. Watson's classic statement of the behavioristic approach stressed the importance of studying behavior objectively by dealing only with observable responses. He forcefully rejected the use of any mentalistic concepts, such as consciousness, mind, will, and imagery.[13]

The feasibility of adhering to these philosophical tenets in practical applications of psychology was demonstrated by Mary Cover Jones, one of Watson's students. In 1924, she successfully treated a three-year-old boy named Peter, who had an intense fear of rabbits.[14] The therapy consisted of two basic procedures. First, she showed Peter that rabbits were not necessarily frightening, by having Peter watch other children enjoying their play with a rabbit. The other procedure involved exposing Peter to the rabbit without his being frightened. While Peter ate one of his favorite foods, Jones placed a caged rabbit in the room at a sufficient distance so that its presence did not interfere with Peter's eating and did not upset him. Gradually, over a period of days, Jones brought the rabbit closer to Peter, although she always kept it at a distance with which Peter was comfortable. Eventually Jones took the rabbit out of the cage and again, in a gradual manner, brought it closer and closer to Peter. After this treatment, Peter was able to comfortably hold and play with the rabbit. Many years later, Jones's two therapy procedures—modeling and systematic desensitization—were refined and became widely used behavioral therapy procedures for the treatment of fears.

Hobart and Molly Mowrer were also influenced by Pavlov's classical conditioning principles. In 1938, they developed a highly successful behavioral therapy procedure for enuresis (bedwetting).[15] Their procedure involved placing a special pad under the child's bedsheet so that when the child began to urinate at night a buzzer would sound and awaken the child. Eventually the child came to associate a full bladder with awakening. After repeated pairing of these two events, a full bladder would awaken the child, thereby eliminating the need for the buzzer. The technique proved to be highly successful and is still in use.

Despite the effectiveness of these early behavioral therapies and several dozen others,[16] contemporary behavioral therapy did not begin in earnest until the 1950s. Before examining what happened at that time, it is necessary to appreciate the nature and status of the treatment of abnormal behavior during the first half of this century. The treatment of abnormal behavior was the province of psychiatry, a specialized field of medicine. With few exceptions, psychiatrists believed that abnormal behaviors that did not have an identifiable physical cause, such as a brain tumor or an infection, were caused by unconscious intrapsychic (within the mind) conflicts. According to this Freudian or psychoanalytic point of view, treatment involved a lengthy series of therapy sessions in which the patient's childhood memories and current dreams, for example, were analyzed and interpreted to reveal the nature of the intrapsychic conflicts. Psychoanalysis was the only major approach to treating abnormal behavior during the first half of the twentieth century.

Growing Discontent with Psychoanalysis

After World War II, doubts about the effectiveness of psychoanalysis as a general treatment method began to mount, especially among clinical psychologists who were committed to evaluating treatment procedures through empirical research. During the war, it had become increasingly clear that the length of psychoanalytic psychotherapy (often several years) rendered it unsuitable to treating the large numbers of patients that were being seen as a result of the war.

This growing discontent with traditional psychoanalytic psychotherapy received a major impetus from a retrospective study by English psychologist Hans Eysenck, published in 1952.[17] After examining a large amount of data from existing sources such as hospital and insurance company records, Eysenck concluded that people with neurotic problems* (the vast majority of cases treated by traditional psychotherapy) were probably no more likely to improve after receiving traditional psychotherapy than if they had not received psychotherapy. Although the indictment against traditional psychotherapy turns out to be less clear-cut than Eysenck's original conclusion,[18] this study did influence professionals who studied and treated abnormal behavior to seriously question the benefits of traditional psychotherapy and to seek more effective alternatives. One of those alternatives was behavioral therapy.

Formal Beginnings of Contemporary Behavioral Therapy

The formal beginnings of contemporary behavioral therapy occurred in the 1950s, in three different countries. In the United States, a number of psychologists were starting to apply the principles of operant conditioning to clinical problems. B. F. Skinner's extensive laboratory experimentation with nonhuman animals served as the basis for this work. Although Skinner, like Pavlov and Bechterev, had written about the applied use of learning principles,[19] it remained for his students and followers to actually implement and refine such therapeutic procedures. In the early 1950s, Ogden Lindsley, then a graduate student of Skinner's at Harvard, directed a series of studies to determine the feasibility of using operant conditioning procedures with adult psychiatric patients.[20] Incidentally, in the midst of this work, Lindsley appears to have been the first person to formally use the term *behavior therapy* to describe attempts to change abnormal behavior.[21] In the same decade, Sidney Bijou, who had been a colleague of Skinner's when they were both on the faculty of Indiana University, began to apply operant principles to the understanding and treatment of children's problem behavior.[22] Also of note in the late 1950s is the work of Teodoro Ayllon, who performed now-classic demonstrations of the effectiveness of operant principles in modifying psychotic behavior† of patients at the Saskatchewan Hospital in Canada.[23] Several years later, in 1961, Ayllon teamed up with Nathan Azrin, another of Skinner's former students, to develop the first full-fledged token economy at Anna State Hospital in Illinois. This program paved the way for the widespread use of this important treatment method.[24]

**Neurotic behavior* is characterized by much anxiety, with which the person has difficulty coping, and by abnormal behaviors such as irrational fears (phobias), obsessional thoughts, and compulsions to carry out particular acts.

†*Psychotic behavior* is characterized by the deterioration of normal intellectual and social functioning. A psychotic person seems to be out of contact with objective reality and sometimes exhibits highly inapproriate or exaggerated emotions and odd or bizarre behaviors such as confused and highly individualized thinking, as well as hearing and talking to imaginary voices.

In South Africa, psychiatrist Joseph Wolpe had become disenchanted with psychoanalytic methods of treatment. He developed several procedures, most notably systematic desensitization and assertive training, for treating neurotic problems such as irrational fears and social inhibitions. Wolpe's treatment approach basically involved replacing debilitating anxiety, which people feel in stressful life situations, with more adaptive reactions such as deep muscle relaxation and assertive behavior. Wolpe explained his procedures in terms of learning theory that could be traced to Pavlov's classical conditioning and neurophysiological concepts.[25]

The third major origin of contemporary behavioral therapy in the 1950s occurred in England. It was spearheaded by Eysenck, whose critique of psychoanalysis has already been mentioned, and by M. B. Shapiro,[26] both of the Institute of Psychiatry at the University of London. Of particular note is Shapiro's emphasis, as director of the Clinical-Teaching Section, on the intensive study of individual cases,[27] the same position as that advocated by Skinner and his associates. This emphasis is but one commonality among the early behavioral therapists in the United States, England, and South Africa. As is often the case in the history of science (and other ideas), this simultaneous development of similar approaches apparently occurred independently. None of the three groups were aware of the work of their colleagues in different countries. There were also some significant differences in their approaches. For instance, Wolpe's use of systematic desensitization to reduce neurotic anxiety and Lindsley's application of reinforcement procedures to modify psychotic behavior are quite different in many respects (as will become evident later). But both procedures are examples of behavioral therapy because they share many of the core characteristics of the behavioral approach to therapy that were listed earlier in the chapter. Thus, despite arising independently on different continents and having some idiosyncratic differences, the three schools of behavioral therapy that arose in the United States, South Africa, and England in the 1950s represented a strong and moderately unified alternative to traditional psychoanalytic therapy.

Not surprisingly, traditional psychotherapists, who comprised the vast majority of psychotherapists in the 1960s, did not take too kindly to the intrusion of the radically different behavioral therapies into their well-established and comfortable domain. In the 1960s, there were few behavioral therapists in private practice, and behavioral therapists in psychiatric hospitals and outpatient facilities met resistance from traditional psychotherapists. Even in academic settings, which are among the most accepting and nurturing atmospheres for new ideas and innovations, behavioral therapists were often isolated because their colleagues viewed behavioral therapy as too radical a departure from mainstream psychology.

Growth and Acceptance of Behavioral Therapy

To overcome these barriers to growth and acceptance, behavioral therapists in the late 1950s and early 1960s spent considerable time gathering evidence that behavioral therapy was a viable alternative to traditional psychotherapy. This effort included the publication of many demonstration projects. These case studies clearly showed that a wide array of clinical problems could be successfully treated in a relatively brief period of time using behavioral therapy techniques.[28] For example, in one such demonstration Ayllon taught nurses to reinforce (primarily with social attention) a psychiatric patient's nonviolent behaviors on the ward in order to decrease the high frequency of violent acts, such as attacking other patients and staff, in which the patient typically engaged.[29] Because of the opposition by traditional psychotherapists, the patients whom behavioral therapists were allowed to treat were frequently people with whom all forms of traditional treatment had failed. As it turned out, this situation was a gift in disguise, because when the demonstration cases were treated successfully with behavioral therapy the results were especially impressive.

Along with demonstrating the wide application of behavioral therapy, behavioral therapists in the 1960s worked on refining established behavioral therapy procedures, such as systematic desensitization. Also during the 1960s, another major school of behavioral therapy evolved. Psychologists Albert Bandura and Richard Walters at Stanford University developed a comprehensive approach that combined the perspective and procedures initiated by Wolpe and by Lindsley and Skinner in the previous decade.[30] In addition, their **social learning theory** emphasized the critical role that imitation, cognitions (thoughts, images, and expectations), and self-regulatory processes (e.g., setting standards for oneself and postponing immediate rewards for long-term rewards) played in psychological functioning, and could potentially play in understanding and treating abnormal behavior. Proponents of social learning theory take a broad approach to behavioral therapy, as shown, for example, by their recognizing the existence and importance of cognitive processes in the development and modification of human behavior.

Recall that early behaviorists vehemently rejected any concepts suggestive of "mentalism," and advocated dealing only with directly observable behavior. This "radical" position was no doubt important in the early history of behavioral therapy, in order to counter the strongly entrenched psychoanalytic approach. However, many contemporary behavioral therapists have argued that dealing only with directly observable behaviors is too restrictive. Humans *do* think, expect, plan, and imagine, and these cognitive processes have a definite influence on how people behave. However, despite the obvious validity of this statement, the role of cognitive processes and other nonobservable behaviors in behavioral therapy is still hotly debated.

The 1960s was a crucial time for the emerging field of behavioral therapy. By the end of that decade, behavioral therapy was acknowledged by most professionals as an acceptable alternative form of treatment. A professional organization, the Association for Advancement of Behavior Therapy, had been established in 1966 in the United States, and by 1970 four major professional journals were devoted exclusively to behavioral therapy (see Table 1-1). Still, some skeptical critics voiced the opinion that behavioral therapy would soon fade into oblivion, along with a host of other types of therapy that arose in the 1960s. However, the events of the 1970s clearly indicated that behavioral therapy was much more than a passing fancy.

TABLE 1-1 *Professional Journals Devoted Exclusively to Behavioral Therapy*

TITLE	YEAR FOUNDED
Behaviour Research and Therapy	1963
Journal of Applied Behavior Analysis	1968
Behavior Therapy	1970
Journal of Behavior Therapy and Experimental Psychiatry	1970
Biofeedback and Self-Regulation	1975
European Journal of Behavioural Analysis and Modification (ceased publication 1981)	1975
Revista Mexicana de Análisis de la Conducta (Mexican Journal of Behavior Analysis)	1975
Advances in Behaviour Research and Therapy	1977
Behavior Modification	1977
Behavioral Analysis and Modification	1977
Cognitive Therapy and Research	1977
the Behavior Therapist	1978
Journal of Behavioral Medicine	1978
Behavioral Assessment	1979
Child and Family Behavior Therapy (formerly *Child Behavior Therapy)*	1979
Clinical Behavior Therapy Review	1979
Journal of Behavioral Assessment	1979
Behavioural Psychotherapy	1981

Emergence of Behavioral Therapy as a Major Force

In the 1970s, behavioral therapy became a major force in psychology and education and made a significant impact in psychiatry[31] and social work. The principles and techniques of behavioral therapy began to enhance the normal functioning of people in areas as diverse as business and industry,[32] child rearing,[33] ecology,[34] and the arts.[35] On an individual level, examples include improving athletic performance,[36] increasing people's willingness to adhere to medical regimes such as taking prescribed medications,[37] enhancing the quality of life of nursing home residents and geriatric patients,[38] and teaching young children to play musical instruments more efficiently than through conventional methods of instruction.[39] On a larger scale, behavioral therapy techniques have been employed to promote energy conservation,[40] to prevent crimes,[41] to provide individual instruction for large college classes,[42] and to influence entire communities to engage in behaviors that may lower the risk of cardiovascular diseases.[43]

A number of new forms or subfields of behavioral therapy evolved during the 1970s. Most prominent among these has been (1) an increased emphasis on self-control procedures that allow clients to perform much of their therapy on their own and (2) the development of cognitive behavioral therapies to directly deal with subjective events such as thoughts and attitudes.

By 1982, the Association for Advancement of Behavior Therapy had grown in membership from 18 in 1966 to more than 3,300. Other influential behavioral therapy societies had been founded in nations around the world, including England, France, Germany, Israel, Japan, Mexico, the Netherlands, South America, and Sweden.[44] Seventeen major journals devoted solely to behavioral therapy had been established (see Table 1-1), and articles dealing with behavioral therapy (primarily empirical research studies) filled the leading clinical psychology journals as well as many prestigious publications in social work, education, and psychiatry.

One indication of the increasing maturity of the field of behavioral therapy is the fact that during the 1970s its strongest critics came from its proponents rather than from its opponents. In effect, the field of behavioral therapy had reached the point where convincing outsiders and doubters of its merits was no longer a priority. Instead, behavioral therapists began to carefully scrutinize their own treatment methods and the impact the therapies were having on the people the therapists were serving and on society as a whole.[45]

AN OPERATIONAL APPROACH TO BEHAVIORAL THERAPY

The historical origins of contemporary behavioral therapy lie, for the most part, in applied work that stemmed from the experimental study of learning (particularly with nonhuman animals) and theories of learning, as discussed in the previous section.

> Learning theory was an obvious choice: first, because there is a history of suggested therapeutic applications of learning principles, from Thorndike and Pavlov through Mowrer and Guthrie; and second, because the heart of any *psycho*therapy is changing people's behavior without changing their body structure or gross functions—which means, in plain language, teaching them and getting them to learn.[46]

However, existing learning theories provide inadequate explanations of most behavioral therapies.[47] Most learning theories are based on findings from experimentation with nonhuman animals, whose learning bears only a partial resemblance to the learning of humans. For example, much human learning is mediated by complex cognitive processes, including language, which is not the case for animals.[48] Moreover, there is considerable controversy concerning the relationship between learning theories and actual clinical treatment procedures.[49] In many cases, multiple and highly divergent explanations of why a behavioral therapy is effective have been proposed.[50] As is shown in succeeding chapters, there is little doubt that many behavioral therapies are powerful procedures for ameliorating abnormal behaviors. Yet there is little agreement among behavioral therapists as to why these useful therapies work.

Today many behavioral therapies are developed and refined *empirically*—that is, by observing which procedures are effective and which are not and then adopting the former and rejecting the latter. Such a "seat-of-the-pants" strategy for developing therapeutic procedures has a compelling justification: it addresses "immediate practical problems that require solutions in fact, not in principle."[51] More often than not, theoretical explanations in terms of learning or other psychological processes are sought *after* the therapy procedures have been developed. True, these theoretical explanations may prove useful in refining the therapeutic procedures as well as in helping behavioral therapists choose the best therapies for their clients. But most contemporary behavioral therapies were not derived from existing psychological theories. Furthermore, even in those instances in which an existing theory leads to the ideas for a therapeutic procedure, subsequent empirical testing of the procedures is likely to result in their modification because of practical rather than theoretical considerations. Still, behavioral therapists have long been referring to theories of learning to explain why their therapy procedures work. This practice is still widely adhered to, and most textbooks in the field categorize and describe behavioral therapies in terms of various forms of learning (e.g., classical and operant conditioning).

The point of explaining this state of affairs is that the practice of describing behavioral therapies in terms of learning theories is *not* the approach taken in this book. Instead, this book introduces the reader to behavioral therapy *operationally* by describing how behavioral therapies operate rather than by giving hypothetical and often controversial explanations of why they are effective. Behavioral therapies are here grouped into three broad categories that describe the fundamental ways in which they work: (1) **substitution therapies,** in which a normal, adaptive behavior is substituted for an abnormal, maladaptive behavior (Chapters 4–5); (2) **consequential therapies,** in which the events that follow a behavior—its consequences—are changed in order to increase or decrease how often a behavior is performed (Chapters 6–9); and (3) **modeling therapies,** in which appropriate examples of behaviors and the consequences for performing them help clients change their own behavior in adaptive ways (Chapter 10). Also examined are **cognitive behavioral therapies** (Chapter 11) and **self-control therapies** (Chapter 12), which involve a combination of the three major categories of behavioral therapy just enumerated and which are at the forefront of behavioral therapy today.

Because this book takes an operational approach in describing behavioral therapy, learning theories are not discussed specifically. However, various behavioral therapies are considered direct applications of *principles* of learning (e.g., reinforcement and extinction). Much of behavioral therapy involves learning new adaptive behaviors to replace old maladaptive habits. Such principles are fully explained in nontechnical language, so the reader need not have any background in learning theory to be able to appreciate and understand the practice of contemporary behavioral therapy.

Besides more accurately reflecting the actual state of affairs regarding the development and practice of behavioral therapies, the operational approach adopted here is objective in the sense that the therapeutic procedures are viewed in terms of how they work and what they do rather than in terms of how they should (theoretically) work and what they should do. Because objectivity is one of the hallmarks of behavioral therapy, it is fitting to introduce the field operationally.

A NOTE ON THE PURPOSE OF THIS BOOK

The aim of this book is to introduce contemporary behavioral therapy by presenting its general principles and describing its wide array of treatment procedures. Readers can expect to learn what behavioral therapy is, but *not* how to do it. Certainly you are likely to find various principles and procedures described in this book that you can use to deal with minor problems in your everyday life. However, if a major problem in your life should arise and you think that you could benefit from behavioral therapy, you should consult with a professional behavioral therapist. If this occurs, consult Appendix A, which presents guidelines for choosing a behavioral therapist.

SUMMARY

The field of behavioral therapy can be defined by examining its core characteristics: behavior therapy (1) deals with behavior, (2) is scientific, (3) is present-oriented, (4) requires continuous assessment, (5) is educational, (6) takes place in the client's everyday environment, (7) involves clients as their own change agents, (8) is action-oriented, (9) is individualized, and (10) involves a client-therapist contract regarding goals and therapy procedures. The term *behavioral therapy* (or *behavior therapy* or *behavior modification*) refers to a large variety of procedures rather than to a single type of therapy.

Although historically there have been examples of therapeutic procedures very similar to contemporary behavioral therapies, the systematic application of behavioral principles to deal with human problems is less than 30 years old. Contemporary behavioral therapy has direct roots in early-twentieth-century laboratory studies of learning. It was spurred on by a growing disillusionment with psychoanalytic therapy; independently and simultaneously developed in the United States, South Africa, and Great Britain; and recently has emerged as a major force.

An *operational approach* to behavioral therapy is used in this book: behavioral therapy is explained in terms of how it works and what it does (its operations), rather than in terms of hypothetical and controversial theoretical explanations of why it is effective.

REFERENCE NOTES*

1. Kazdin & Wilson, 1978.
2. Wilson, 1978b.
3. Franks & Wilson, 1973.
4. Risley, 1969.
5. Itard, 1962.
6. Lovaas, 1977.

*Throughout this book, reference dates are the publication dates of the actual sources used and thus do not always correspond to the original publication dates of the works cited.

7. Kazdin, 1978.
8. Pitts, 1976.
9. Stewart, 1961.
10. Franks, 1963.
11. Franks, 1969b.
12. Kazdin, 1978.
13. Watson, 1914.
14. Jones, 1924.
15. Mowrer & Mowrer, 1938.
16. Yates, 1970.
17. Eysenck, 1952.
18. For example, Cartwright, 1955; Luborsky, 1954; Smith & Glass, 1977.
19. Skinner, 1953.
20. Lindsley, 1956, 1960, 1963; Skinner, 1954; Skinner, Solomon, & Lindsley, 1953; Skinner, Solomon, Lindsley, & Richards, 1954.
21. Skinner, Solomon, & Lindsley, 1953.
22. For example, Bijou, 1957a, 1957b, 1958; Bijou & Oblinger, 1960; Bijou & Orlando, 1961.
23. For example, Ayllon, 1963, 1965.
24. Ayllon & Azrin, 1968b.
25. Wolpe, 1958.
26. For example, Shapiro, 1951, 1952, 1957.
27. For example, Shapiro, 1961a, 1961b, 1966.
28. Ullmann & Krasner, 1965.
29. Ayllon & Michael, 1959.
30. Bandura, 1969, 1977b; Bandura & Walters, 1963.
31. Liberman, 1978.
32. Hermann, deMontes, Dominguez, Montes, & Hopkins, 1973; "New Tool," 1971; Pedalino & Gamboa, 1974.
33. For example, Becker, 1971; Christophersen, 1977; Patterson, 1975; Patterson & Gullion, 1976.
34. Kazdin, 1977a.
35. Madsen, Greer, & Madsen, 1975.
36. For example, Rushall & Siedentop, 1972.
37. For example, Epstein & Masek, 1978; Lowe & Lutzker, 1979.
38. For example, Libb & Clements, 1969; Sachs, 1975.
39. Madsen, Greer, & Madsen, 1975.
40. Kazdin, 1977a.
41. For example, McNees, Egli, Marshall, Schnelle, Schnelle, & Risley, 1976; Schnelle, Kirchner, Macrae, McNees, Eck, Snodgrass, Casey, & Uselton, 1978; Schnelle, Kirchner, McNees, & Lawler, 1975.
42. For example, Keller, 1968.
43. Maccoby, Farquhar, Wood, & Alexander, 1977.
44. Kazdin, 1978.
45. For example, Kazdin & Wilson, 1978; Krasner, 1976; Stolz & Associates, 1978.
46. London, 1972, p. 914.
47. Erwin, 1978.
48. Bandura, 1969.
49. For example, London, 1972.
50. Kazdin & Wilson, 1978.
51. London, 1972, p. 914.

CHAPTER 2 The Behavioral Model

Behavioral therapy is much more than the sum of specific therapeutic procedures. To appreciate the nature of behavioral therapy, one must understand the model of human behavior on which it is based. Because of an enduring commitment to employing therapies that are effective, specific behavioral therapy procedures have changed over the preceding two decades. However, the underlying philosophy and fundamental principles on which behavioral therapy rests have remained relatively stable. This chapter describes the general model of human behavior that forms the basis of behavioral therapy. The next chapter discusses the principles of behavioral therapy derived from this model. These two chapters are probably the most important in the book because, to a large degree, "all the rest is commentary." In other words, the majority of the book is devoted to description and discussion of the wide range of behavioral therapies currently in use, and all these therapies may be viewed as illustrating the application of the basic principles introduced in the first three chapters.

WHO OR WHAT ARE WE?

Each of us is a unique individual, and we all know many different people, each of whom is unique. But what makes us unique? How do we define what a person is? Think of someone you know well. How would you describe that person? Before reading any further, take just three minutes to write a brief description of one of your close friends or relatives. Write your description so that someone who did not know the person would get a good picture of what he or she is like. Then put the description aside and continue reading.

A person can be identified or defined in various ways. For example, an individual can be defined in terms of physical characteristics—height, build, hair and eye color, and other distinctive physical attributes. Such a definition might help us pick out the person if he or she were standing in a group of people, but it would tell us very little about how the person would act, what it would be like to spend time with him or her, and so on.

Another way to define a person is in terms of personality characteristics or *traits* that we attribute to people from observing their behavior. In fact, this is the most common way that people describe one another. In answer to the question "What's your roommate Kathryn like?" Michele might reply, "Oh, she's really nice. She's friendly, and considerate, and helpful. Kathryn is very smart and conscientious. She's a lot of fun, too. I think she's interesting. She's really straightforward and honest." This description of Kathryn may be similar in style to the one you wrote of your close acquaintance. Michele has listed a number of personality traits in describing her roommate: *nice, friendly, considerate, helpful, smart, conscientious, fun, interesting, straightforward, honest.*

Personality traits do not actually exist, in contrast to physical characteristics, such as height or hair color; they are *convenient* ways of describing people and integrating observations of their behavior, and they exist only in the viewer's thoughts. Thus, it may be a fact that John frequently telephones his friends, drops them notes, and invites them to his house, but how valid is it to conclude that John is "friendly"? One might be just as likely to view John as "lonely," given the same observations of his behavior toward his friends. This example reveals the speculative nature of ascribing personality traits to people.

Describing someone by using personality traits allows us to use few words to *presumably* communicate much information. The single words *honest, conscientious, smart,* or *fun* seem to give us a great deal of information about Kathryn. Actually, these and other trait descriptions may be telling us very little. For one thing, we each have our own definitions of these broad descriptive terms. Some people consider "conscientiousness" to mean that people do what is required of them. Others would add the criterion of meeting requirements on schedule or doing exceptional work or expending considerable effort. What did Michele mean when she described Kathryn as "conscientious"? It is not clear from merely the trait name *conscientious.* If Michele defined conscientiousness for us, that would help.

However, there would still be questions of the frequency and regularity of Kathryn's conscientiousness. Is Kathryn conscientious all the time, in all her endeavors? Is Kathryn likely to be more conscientious in some situations (e.g., in her schoolwork) than in others (e.g., in keeping her car in good condition)? It is highly unlikely that Kathryn is always conscientious, which raises the important question of when she can be counted on to be conscientious and when she is not likely to be conscientious. To answer this question, Michele would probably describe situations in which she has seen Kathryn act conscientiously. Michele might explain that Kathryn studies at least four hours a day, plans her work carefully, and usually finishes her assignments a day or two before they are due.

Note that to clarify Kathryn's "conscientiousness," Michele has now de-

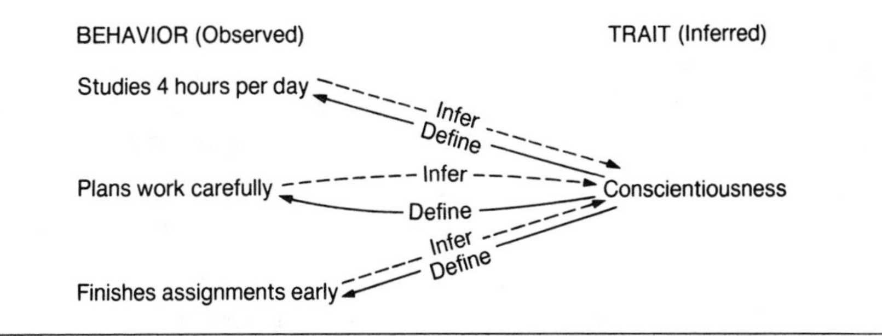

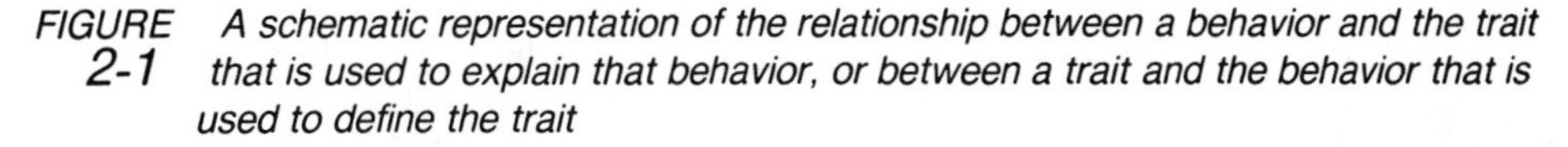

FIGURE 2-1 *A schematic representation of the relationship between a behavior and the trait that is used to explain that behavior, or between a trait and the behavior that is used to define the trait*

scribed Kathryn's *behavior,* the same behavior that Michele had observed in order to describe her as "conscientious." From her observations of Kathryn's actions, Michele has summarized her behavior by the term *conscientiousness* and has inferred that it is the result of a general trait of conscientiousness. This three-step process is illustrated schematically in Figure 2-1. First, we make an initial observation of someone's behavior. Second, we attempt to summarize and explain the behavior by a personality trait. Third, we go back to the initial behavioral observations in order to clarify the meaning of the personality trait.

Because this three-step process begins and ends with the same observations of someone's behavior, isn't it possible to stop with the behavioral observations, thereby eliminating two of the three steps? It most certainly is possible, and that is the behavioral approach: *direct observations of behavior are used as the primary source of information about a person.* In the behavioral model, inferences are minimized. This approach increases the chances that what is reported about the person is accurate, because making an inference (such as from a behavior to a trait) always involves some degree of conjecture and often one or more assumptions. The price paid for greater accuracy is a longer description. Michele's inferred trait description of Kathryn consisted of a single word *(conscientious),* in contrast to her direct behavioral description, which was a sentence long ("studies at least four hours a day, plans her work carefully, and usually finishes her assignments a day or two before they are due"). It is important to clearly understand the distinction between behaviors and traits, and Participation Exercise 2-1 can help you do so.

PARTICIPATION EXERCISE 2-1

Distinguishing Between Traits and Behaviors

People frequently view others in terms of personality traits rather than in terms of their behavior. It is important to recognize when we are referring to traits and when to behaviors. As a general rule, descriptions that concern what a person ***does*** refer to behaviors, while descriptions that concern what the person *"is"* or characteristics that he or she ***"has"*** (possesses) refer to traits. See if you can differentiate between the two types of descriptions in the following paragraph. On a sheet of paper, number blank lines from 1 to 20, and write the letter "T" (for ***trait***) or "B" (for ***behavior***) for each of the numbered statements.

(1) Dulie is extremely perceptive. (2) He notices even small changes in others' emotions and (3) accurately describes to other people how they are feeling. (4) He reads a great deal and (5) is very knowledgeable about many topics. (6) He is very intelligent, and (7) he can recall facts he learned years ago. (8) Dulie is a warm, sincere, good-natured individual. (9) He is a good friend, (10) goes out of his way to help other people, and (11) is generous with his friends. (12) He always dresses neatly. (13) Dulie works hard, and (14) he is dedicated to his work. (15) He is a good athlete. (16) He swims during the summer and ice skates during the winter. (17) He is an active person (18) who is very energetic. (19) Although he is gregarious, (20) he often spends his time alone.

Now check your answers with the correct ones in Appendix B. Look at the descriptions you mislabeled and apply the following rule: ***does*** means behavior, ***is*** or ***has*** means a trait.

Now that you have begun to recognize the differences between a behavioral and a trait description of a person, the next step is to translate trait descriptions into behavior. Behavioral therapists frequently must do this because their clients usually describe themselves and the problems that bring them to therapy in trait terms (e.g., "I'm shy and withdrawn"). Participation Exercise 2-2 shows you how to make such translations.

PARTICIPATION EXERCISE 2-2

Translating Trait Descriptions into Behaviors

In this participation exercise, you will translate trait descriptions into behaviors. In other words, you'll be finding behaviors that could be indicative of particular traits. This process was illustrated earlier in the text by Michele's trait description of Kathryn. Let's look at a few more examples before you attempt the process yourself.

Trait	*Behaviors That Might Indicate the Trait*
Happy	Smiling; laughing; talking about feelings of joy
Depressed	Crying; sitting alone; moving slowly; saying that one is depressed ("down," unhappy)
Friendly	Greeting people; smiling at others
Trustworthy	Coming on time to appointments; carrying out assigned tasks; keeping secrets
Generous	Volunteering to help others; frequently paying for the check when dining with others

Note that there is some overlap in the behaviors that indicate different traits. Overlap is one reason why trait descriptions are imprecise, and it is often necessary to describe the behavioral examples that led to the inference of the trait to get a clear idea of what the person is like.

On a sheet of paper, list several behaviors that might help describe individuals with the following traits:

1. Sociable
2. Hostile
3. Helpful
4. Thrifty
5. Dependable
6. Smart
7. Patient
8. Healthy

Examples of behaviors you might have listed for each trait can be found in Appendix B. Your responses need not be the same as those given in Appendix B, but they should be activities people *do* (i.e., behaviors) and ones that people generally would agree could be indicative of the particular trait.

People "Are" What They Do

All approaches to understanding the "essence" of an individual start by observing what a person does—that is, behavior. The approaches diverge, however, in terms of what they do with the observations of behavior once they have been made. Many approaches to personality, such as psychoanalytic and trait theories, are concerned with behavior only insofar as behavior indicates something about the deep, underlying structure of personality. In direct contrast, in the behavioral approach behavior is examined for its own sake because it is assumed that "people are what they do."[1]

Another important characteristic of the behavioral approach is that at any one time, relatively small and discrete behaviors are examined in depth, rather than studying an individual's whole personality. No prior assumptions are made about the interrelationship among behaviors. This is not to say that a person's behaviors are totally independent of one another but only that a relationship is not assumed until it has been demonstrated. Such a stance has an important implication for behavioral therapy because it makes it possible to treat clients' problems without *necessarily* delving into other aspects of their lives. For instance, a couple who seeks help with their inability to communicate with each other without arguing could be treated for this specific problem behavior without reference to their sexual interactions (unless there were a clear-cut connection between the two sets of behaviors). Such a straightforward treatment strategy would not be employed in other approaches to therapy that begin with basic, universal assumptions about human behavior. In psychoanalysis, for example, communications problems between men and women of any sort would be assumed to be related to sexual interactions, because the sexual drive plays a prominent role in psychoanalytic personality theory.[2]

Overt and Covert Behavior

Two classes of behavior can be distinguished: overt and covert. **Overt behavior** refers to actions that can be directly observed by other people—public behavior, so to speak. Examples include eating, walking, talking, kissing, driving a car, writing a sentence, hanging one's coat, cooking, laughing, singing . . . you can easily continue the list by enumerating actions you can *see* someone do.

Obviously, many of our behaviors cannot be directly observed by other people. Such private or **covert behaviors,** such as our thoughts and feelings, make up the second category of behavior. Covert behaviors are known to others only indirectly and always in terms of some overt behavior. Frequently we first learn about others' covert behaviors when they tell us about such behavior. "Speaking" is an overt behavior, and in fact verbal self-reports are important and sometimes the only means of learning about people's covert behaviors. Physical responses, such as muscle tension and heart rate, can be assessed by others indirectly by using various instruments and procedures (e.g., a polygraph).

Assessing another person's covert behavior always involves an inference—that is, judging that some overt behavior is indicative of a covert behavior. For instance, smiling and laughing are usually, but not always, signs of a person feeling happy. There is an important difference between (1) inferring traits from overt behavior and (2) inferring covert behaviors from overt behaviors. In both cases, it is necessary to make a deduction—that is, to go beyond the observation itself and to draw some conclusions about it. However, the *degree* of deduction, or how far one must go from the data, is less when covert *behavior* is inferred from overt *behavior,* because the observation (overt behavior) and that which is inferred from it (covert behavior) are both behaviors. This jump is less of an inferential leap than going from an overt behavior to a trait (which is not a behavior, but an abstraction). Participation Exercise 2-3 can help you distinguish between overt and covert behavior.

PARTICIPATION EXERCISE 2-3
Distinguishing Between Overt and Covert Behavior

Can you distinguish between overt (public) and covert (private) behavior? Below are 20 examples of behaviors. For each, ask yourself whether or not you could ***directly observe*** the behavior. If you could, the behavior is overt; if you could not, the behavior is covert. Number 1 to 20 on a piece of paper, and write "O" for overt behaviors and "C" for covert behaviors. Then check the answers in Appendix B.

1. Singing
2. Thinking
3. Smiling
4. Learning
5. Eating
6. Remembering
7. Liking
8. Staring
9. Enjoying
10. Writing
11. Listening
12. Observing

13. Speaking	16. Smoking	19. Concentrating
14. Dreaming	17. Hoping	20. Sighing
15. Drinking	18. Touching	

One reason why overt behavior plays such a prominent role in behavioral therapy is that it is often desirable to have observations of a client's behavior made by other people (which means that overt behavior is being directly assessed). There are at least three advantages to assessment being made by other people. First, observations of behavior must be reliable to be useful. The **reliability** of observations refers to their consistency and repeatability; generally reliability is assessed by measuring the agreement among two or more independent observers. The more often they agree that a particular behavior has occurred, the more reliable are the observations. Second, other people usually make more objective observations because they tend to be less involved and emotionally invested in the behaviors. Third, when people observe their own behavior, their attention is divided between behaving and observing, whereas outside observers potentially can fully attend to observing, thus producing more accurate observations.

Covert behavior is no less important than overt behavior. Indeed, many behaviors that supposedly set us apart from our distant "relatives" in the animal kingdom are covert, including complex thinking and reasoning. However, recall that the early proponents of the behavioral approach, such as Watson and Skinner, insisted that only overt behavior was legitimate subject matter, because it was directly observable. Although the behavioral approach has been broadened considerably so that covert behavior is explicitly studied, the early emphasis on objectivity regarding behavior is still very evident in the behavioral approach. First, covert behaviors are *operationalized*—that is, they are explicitly and unambiguously defined in terms of the operations employed to measure them. Second, whenever possible, covert behaviors are directly *anchored to overt behaviors.*[3] For example, "imagining" might be defined as "that behavior in which an individual engages and later reports when asked to imagine something." The operations in this case are the instructions to imagine, and the overt behavior is the individual's verbal report of the subjective experience. An all-too-familiar example to students is the way in which "learning," another covert behavior, is typically defined in school; namely, by one's "performance on a test covering the material to be learned." Here the operations are the examination questions, and the overt behavior is the student's written answers. Behavioral therapists deal with a client's covert problem behaviors (e.g., feeling depressed) by working with the client to operationalize the private behaviors and to find overt behaviors that will indicate to the therapist and other people in the client's life that the covert behaviors are occurring. For example, "depressive behavior" might be defined as "any self-deprecating or self-critical verbal statements a client makes." Participation Exercise 2-4 deals with anchoring covert behaviors to overt behaviors.

PARTICIPATION EXERCISE 2-4
Thinking Overt Behavior

The following list shows six common covert behaviors. For each, think of one or more overt behavioral anchors—that is, ***observable*** behaviors that people will agree are likely to indicate that the covert behavior is or was occurring.

In this participation exercise you are being asked to perform a covert behavior; namely, to ***think*** of overt behavioral anchors. How will your instructor (or anyone else) know if you have done the participation exercise? It would be better to suggest an overt behavioral anchor for "thinking." So ***write down*** one or more overt behavioral anchors for each of the following covert behaviors:

1. Silent reading
2. Worrying
3. Feeling happy
4. Being interested (in a particular topic)
5. Listening (to a speaker)
6. Liking (a particular person)

Examples of overt behavioral anchors for these covert behaviors are given in Appendix B.

The Reciprocal Relationship Between Overt and Covert Behavior

We are all familiar with the fact that our covert behaviors influence our overt behaviors. Thinking about being overweight may lead to initiating a diet, and feeling in love often results in our being physically affectionate. It seems natural for our thoughts and emotions to dictate the way we overtly behave.

What about the reverse order? Do our overt actions change our ideas and attitudes or make us feel a particular emotion? Yes, overt behaviors definitely can influence our covert behaviors. For instance, a college student whose parents expect her to write home regularly may feel good whenever she writes home and may feel guilty when she hasn't written home in a month. Similarly, our attitudes and beliefs are frequently a result of our explicit actions. What we do affects what we think (just as what we think influences what we do). In fact, one of the best ways to change an attitude or belief is to *act* in a way consistent with the new attitude or belief. The following true story illustrates this process.

To say that Mark did not like his father-in-law, Fred, is an understatement. Mark readily admitted that he could not stand Fred and avoided interacting with him as much as possible. Not surprisingly this situation created family problems, especially for Mark's wife, Lynn, who wanted to keep in contact with both her parents. When Mark and Lynn had their first child, Lynn felt that it was especially important for there to be some reconciliation between Mark and her father so that their son could spend time with his grandfather. Lynn had always believed that Mark had never given her father a "fair chance," although Mark repeatedly denied that. Nonetheless, with the arrival of their new family member, Mark agreed that something needed to be done about his relationship (or lack of it) with his father-in-law. Lynn suggested that

Mark try one more time to like her father. But Mark said he just couldn't do that. The best he could ever hope to do, he claimed, was put on a good act. Realizing that this was probably better than nothing, Lynn got Mark to promise to at least *act as if he liked her father* during an extended weekend visit the new grandparents would be making to Mark and Lynn's home. And he kept his promise. To begin with, he added a brief note to a letter Lynn had written to her father saying that he was looking forward to their visit. He went with Lynn to the airport to pick up his in-laws, and on the way home he suggested that they stop for lunch at a barbecue restaurant because he knew that Fred especially liked barbecue. During the course of the weekend, Mark continued to act as if he liked his father-in-law by spending time with him, asking him about his business and by doing little things he thought Fred might appreciate. By the end of the visit, Mark was quite relieved that his acting role was over. Nevertheless, several days later he admitted to Lynn that he did not feel as negative about her father as he used to, although he quickly added that he still didn't particularly like him. Lynn was pleased, because in her mind there had been a definite improvement, albeit a small one, in Mark's attitude toward her father.

Such examples of attitude change brought about by changing one's behavior are really quite common, although people tend to be skeptical about this approach—especially in the case of trying to change negative attitudes toward another person. You might want to do a little experiment to test this technique for yourself. Think of a person you do not particularly like (not your worst enemy!) and with whom you interact on a regular basis. Over the course of a week or more, behave toward this person in the same way as you would to someone that you especially liked. It is essential that you *consistently* act toward the person as if you liked him or her. To be able to do this effectively, you will have to plan in advance how you will specifically act with the person (it will not just magically occur). Furthermore, you should not expect your interactions with the person to feel particularly spontaneous or natural. Do not attempt to assess whether your attitude is changing during the "acting period." In fact, it may be best if you wait a few days after the "acting period" to reassess your feelings toward the person. Finally, do not expect miracles, as you are not likely to discover a "best friend." However, you may surprise yourself and find that your attitude has become a bit more favorable. (Obviously, part of this effect may be due to your pleasant actions toward the other person making the other person act more nicely toward you.)

WHY DO WE BEHAVE THE WAY WE DO?

How often have you asked, "Why did I do that?" or "Why did so-and-so act that way?" Questions concerning *why* people behave the way they do are among the most fascinating questions we ask. When we ask such "why" questions about behavior, we may be seeking information on one of two levels. We may be interested in the factors that originally caused the behavior, or we may be interested in the current factors that account for the behavior. In either case, it is never

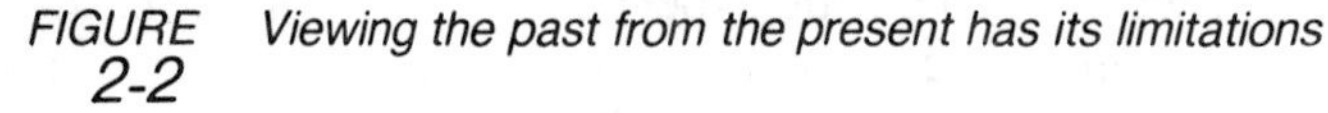

FIGURE 2-2 *Viewing the past from the present has its limitations*

possible to definitively answer questions about why we behave, because the factors that determine human behavior are multiple and complex. This problem is more pronounced when we try to answer questions concerning the factors associated with the origin of the behavior, because such questions require us to go back in time. At best we can come up with some reasonable hypotheses about the causes of our actions, but because they are retrospective the hypotheses can never be tested (see Figure 2-2).

In contrast, the *current* factors that are influencing the way we behave are considerably easier to assess. First, they are occurring in the present, so gathering the needed information is more feasible. Second, because the factors are currently active, it is possible to systematically alter them and observe the effects on the behavior, thereby testing out hypotheses about the current maintaining conditions of behavior.

To take a simple example, if you think that drinking coffee in the evening might be contributing to your inability to fall asleep when you get into bed, you could eliminate the evening coffee for a period of time and then see whether you were falling asleep more quickly. If you did fall asleep more easily, then you could conclude that one of the factors that *might* have been contributing to your inability to fall asleep was the coffee. Unless you also accounted for all other possible factors, you could never be absolutely sure that the coffee was the culprit. But because you were able to alter the situation and observe a change you could have more confidence in your hypothesis about what was influencing your behavior than if the factors were in the past and if you therefore could not have made such a test. (In terms of alleviating an actual problem, if you are now falling asleep more quickly, having eliminated evening coffee, then the question of whether the coffee was the critical factor may be unimportant.)

Many theories have been developed to explain "why" people behave the way they do. According to the behavioral model, a person's *behavior is influenced by actual events that surround the performance of the behavior.* Specifically, these events are (1) the relevant **antecedents** that occur or are present before the behavior is performed and (2) the relevant **consequences** that occur after the behavior has been performed and as a direct result of the behavior. These antecedents and consequences are *current,* taking place in close temporal proximity to the behavior. Many of these antecedents and consequences are presumed to be part of the *external environment* in which the behavior is performed. Finally, the behavioral model includes the assumption that most complex human behavior develops, continues, and changes as a direct result of *learning* (rather than as a result of hereditary, maturational, or other biological factors).

The Maintaining Conditions of Behavior: The ABC Model

The **ABC model** refers to the temporal sequence of *a*ntecedents, *b*ehavior, and *c*onsequences. The relevant antecedents and consequences of a behavior are called its **maintaining conditions.** In other words, certain events that precede and follow a behavior maintain that behavior. Note that not all the antecedents and consequences of a behavior are maintaining conditions of the behavior.

The maintaining functions of antecedents and consequences are different. *Antecedents set the stage for the behavior to occur*—they indicate when it is appropriate to perform the behavior. In this capacity, antecedents are stimuli or cues that indicate that the time and place and general circumstances are right for performing a particular behavior. For instance, when it is noon and you are walking past a restaurant and your stomach begins to "grumble," you are likely to eat. If you were unaware of the time, not near a restaurant or other source of food, and your stomach had not been actively conversing with you, the chances are you would not eat—unless, of course, some other cues associated with eating were present (e.g., a friend asking you to lunch). Behaviors that are strongly influenced by cues are said to be under **stimulus control,** and many of our everyday behaviors tend to be under stimulus control (e.g., sleeping, answering the telephone, stopping for a traffic light, paying attention in class).

Antecedents also include all the prerequisites that are required to perform a particular behavior, including the necessary knowledge, skills, and resources. For example, "going to the movies" requires knowing where the theater is located and what time the movie starts, being able to get to the theater, having enough money to pay for a ticket (unless one sneaks in through an exit door), buying a ticket, and finally finding a seat. (If these antecedents appear trivial, consider whether you could see a movie without them.)

The consequences of performing a behavior refer to all the relevant events that occur after and as a direct result of the behavior being performed. The consequences include what happens directly to the behaver as well as how other people respond to the behaver. They include what happens to other people and to the physical environment as a result of the act. Consequences can be either immediate or long-term.

Whereas antecedents signal that it is appropriate to perform a behavior, and provide the person with the requisites for doing so, *consequences determine whether the behavior will occur again* (see Figure 2-3). In general, when a behavior results in favorable consequences (e.g., lunch at the restaurant was good), the chances are that in the future the individual will repeat it or a similar behavior (e.g., eating at the restaurant again or trying another restaurant). When the consequences of a behavior are unfavorable (e.g., the food or service was bad), the individual will be less likely to repeat the behavior.

Obviously the actual consequences of a behavior can only influence its future occurrence, because the consequences take place after the behavior has been performed. However, *expectations* about the probable consequences, which are *antecedents*, influence whether the behavior will be performed in the present (see Figure 2-3). A person's prediction about what is likely to happen as a result of performing a particular behavior is one factor that determines if the conditions are "right" for performing the behavior. Our expectations about the consequences of our actions are largely a product of the consequences we have received for similar behaviors in the past.

A simple example will help clarify what is meant by antecedents and consequences and their role in determining behavior. Consider the behavior you

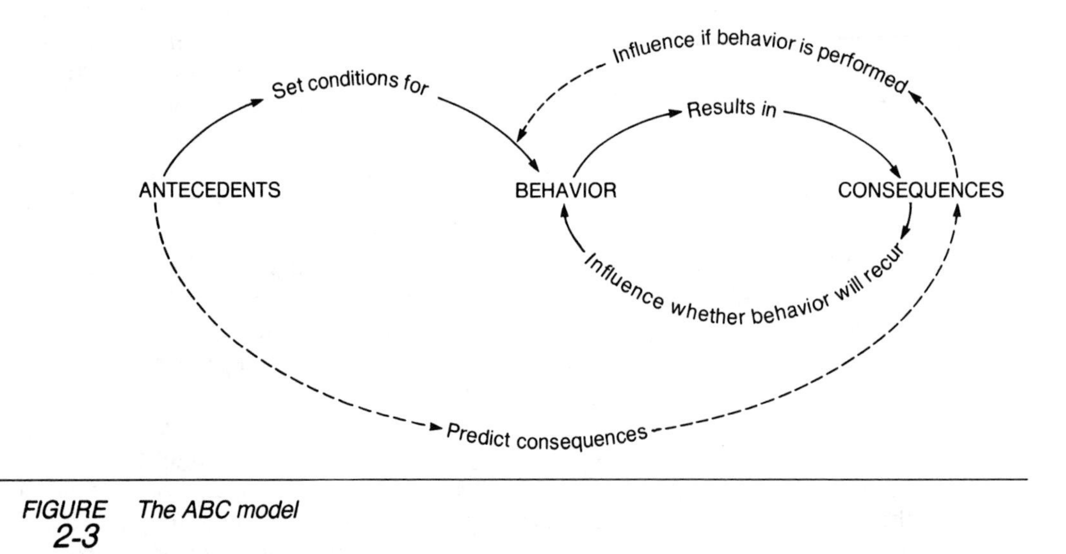

FIGURE 2-3 *The ABC model*

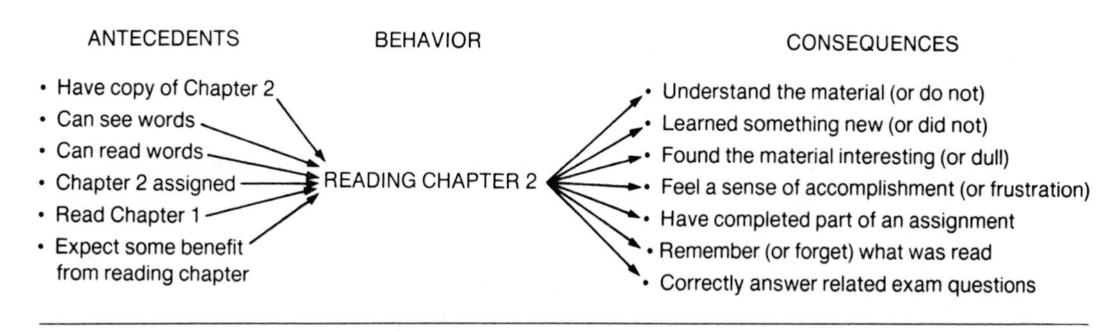

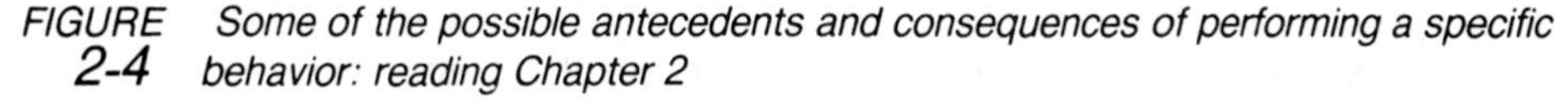

FIGURE 2-4 Some of the possible antecedents and consequences of performing a specific behavior: reading Chapter 2

are engaging in right now; namely, "reading Chapter 2." What preceded this behavior? Figure 2-4 suggests a few of the probable antecedents. It is absolutely necessary, for example, that you have a copy of the chapter, that you can see the words (e.g., you need enough light and if you require glasses to read, you must wear them), and that you are able to read and comprehend at the level at which the chapter is written. It is highly probable that you were assigned to read the chapter by your instructor (assuming this is a text for a course), that you have read the previous chapter, and that you expect to somehow benefit from reading this chapter. As mundane as each of these antecedent conditions may appear, most of them are the necessary conditions that set the stage for your reading this chapter. You can check out whether these antecedents existed for you and what additional ones were present, because you are reading Chapter 2 right now.

What are some of the possible consequences of reading Chapter 2? You may have understood the material, learned something new, found the material interesting, and felt that you accomplished something. Or, it is possible that you did not understand the points being made, learned nothing new, found the reading boring, and felt frustrated (I hope not). You probably have completed a class assignment by reading the chapter. Possible long-term consequences include your remembering (or forgetting) what you have read and your being able to answer questions on an examination covering Chapter 2. The better able you were to understand, learn, enjoy, remember, feel satisfied, and do well on an exam, the more likely it is that you will continue to read chapters in this book (and perhaps other books). When you actually finish reading this chapter, think about the actual consequences for you of reading it.

Identifying the probable maintaining conditions of a behavior is the first step in developing a treatment plan in behavioral therapy because changing the maintaining conditions of problem behaviors is, in a nutshell, how behavioral therapies operate. Accordingly, an appreciation of the process of assessing the antecedents and consequences of behavior is important, and Participation Exercise 2-5 will help you gain this.

PARTICIPATION EXERCISE 2-5

Identifying Antecedents and Consequences of Behaviors

In this exercise you will find a list of 10 behaviors and a short story about each. Read the story and write down the antecedents and the consequences of the behavior indicated. Include all the antecedents and consequences that are actually contained in the story and *only* those that are in the story. When you have finished, check what you've found with the antecedents and consequences listed in Appendix B.

Behavior 1: Running. Charles was a middle-aged man who wanted to lose a few pounds. He had heard of the health benefits of running and saw his neighbors run daily. His doctor had also recommended it to him for his breathing. After running for three months, Charles had lost 12 pounds, and his breathing had improved substantially. He reported feeling more energetic and better able to concentrate at work. His wife was so impressed that she began running too.

Behavior 2: Calling the Police. One hot summer evening, Mrs. Hudson sat in her second-floor apartment. As she looked out the window, she saw two young men violently attack an elderly woman and then run off with the woman's purse. She immediately called the police and reported the attack. The police thanked her and then rushed to the scene of the crime.

Behavior 3: Attending a Party. Chris received an invitation to his cousin's graduation party, and he quickly accepted. When he attended the party, he saw many old friends to whom he hadn't spoken in years. He also met several interesting new people, and by the end of the party he had even found himself a Saturday morning golf partner.

Behavior 4: Going to a Play. Jackie read about a new play in town. It had received especially good reviews, and she decided to get a student pass to go see it. By attending it, she could earn extra credit for her English class. As it turned out, she was disappointed in the play and felt it was a waste of time. The extra credit, however, did help boost her grade.

Behavior 5: Getting Up Too Late. Al did not go to bed until after 3 A.M. He was so drunk that he forgot to set his alarm clock. He woke up two hours late the next morning and found he had missed the last bus to the office. When he finally got to work, he discovered that he had missed two important clients.

Behavior 6: Cooking a Fancy Meal. Barbara's parents were coming for a visit, and she really wanted to make a good impression. It was the perfect opportunity for her to try out a new recipe, and besides, she enjoyed preparing an occasional fancy meal. Although her efforts turned the kitchen into a complete disaster area, the dish itself was a success, and her parents enjoyed the meal immensely. Barbara enjoyed it as well and felt very satisfied about the evening as a whole.

Behavior 7: Writing a Letter. Donna's parents asked her to reply to her brother's letter. She got out some stationery, looked up his current address, and wrote the long-overdue letter. She felt relieved to have finally gotten it out of the way. She suspected that he would be pleased to receive it. She hoped that it might possibly alleviate a long-term family dispute. Two weeks later she received a letter from her brother confirming these beliefs.

Behavior 8: Joining a Car Pool. Mr. Johnson saw an ad in the newspaper about car pools, and two weeks later he joined one. He found it a necessity, given the rising price of gas and the condition of his own car. In addition, he learned that a car pool is a good way to conserve energy and reduce pollution.

Behavior 9: Shopping for New Clothes. Jane badly needed new clothes. She had saved enough money during the summer to go shopping, so she got directions to the new shopping mall and took the family car. She bought a comfortable and stylish new wardrobe, and she felt good about her new clothes. Jane's mother and friends all commented that they made her look good.

Behavior 10: Pulling a Fire Alarm. Tom spotted a fire alarm box at the corner. He wanted to impress his friends and thought of all the excitement that would occur if he pulled the alarm. After reading the instructions and looking to see that no one was around, he pulled the alarm and ran. Fire trucks raced to the scene within minutes. A crowd quickly gathered. The angry fire chief announced that it was a false alarm. An investigation followed, while the crowd slowly dispersed and the fire trucks returned to the station.

Maintenance Versus Origin of Behavior

The distinction between the events that account for initially learning a behavior (i.e., at some time in the past) and the events that account for its continued performance (i.e., in the present) is critical because a fundamental axiom of the behavioral approach and behavioral therapy is that *the maintaining conditions of a behavior are always in the present.*

Much of our adult behavior may have originated in rudimentary form in childhood. However, if we still engage in that behavior, or very similar behavior, today, then it is a safe assumption that the behavior is presently occurring for reasons different from the initial reasons. Many factors that influence our behavior are to be found in our environments, and naturally our present life conditions are likely to be different from those in our past. According to the behavioral perspective, the influence of past events on present behavior is minimal and indirect. For example, as a child one may learn to cry as a reaction to frustration, perhaps by observing a parent react that way, and perhaps because of the adult attention one received for crying. Such crying will persist in adulthood, however, only if *present* circumstances support the crying; for example, if one's spouse responds with concern and sympathy to such crying.

Past events can have an indirect influence on current behavior, as when the *memory* of previous maintaining conditions affects one's current behavior. Thus, recalling how pleasant it was to be comforted by one's mother for crying when frustrated can help to maintain that behavior years after that sympathy was actually received. However, note that the maintaining conditions— "memories of being comforted"—are occurring in the present.

Behavioral therapists look primarily at conditions in a client's present situation to find the maintaining conditions of the client's present problem behavior. Past history may account for originally learning the behavior and may facilitate performing the behavior because it is a long-standing habit, but particular circumstances in the past are assumed to have little *direct* influence on current behavior unless they continue in the present—which, of course, makes them present as well as past.

The External Environment as a Primary Source of Maintaining Conditions

Given that the behavioral approach assumes that the primary factors influencing our behavior are occurring in the present, the next question becomes "Where do we find them?" According to the behavioral model, the most efficient place to look is in a person's external environment, which includes interpersonal interactions as well as the actual physical environment. The emphasis on seeking the maintaining conditions of behavior primarily (although not exclusively) in the external environment is based on three premises. First, abundant evidence shows that environmental factors significantly influence human behavior.[4] Second, it is generally easier to observe and measure external events than internal events. Third, it is often possible to modify external events, whereas it is usually difficult to alter many internal events—with obvious implications for behavioral therapy. Thus, the emphasis on identifying and dealing directly with environmental influences on people's behaviors is primarily utilitarian.

Of course, internal factors—such as genetic endowment, biological needs, and especially a host of important covert events—*do* influence behavior. However, because external factors are more accessible for observation and modification, they have been made the primary focus of efforts to understand and change human behavior. This pragmatic line of reasoning is basically the same as that used to support the greater emphasis on overt behavior than on covert behavior.

Although our behavior is maintained by factors located in the external environment, we, as active beings, can influence those factors. This concept is known as **reciprocal determinism:** the environment affects our behavior, and we behave in ways that affect the environment.[5] Thus, people are only "victims" of external circumstances to the extent that they relinquish their power to shape those circumstances.

The advantages of dealing with environmental events rather than with hypothetical psychological states, as well as the nature of reciprocal determinism, are illustrated by contrasting the traditional and behavioral views of self-control.[6] "Willpower" is a hypothetical state that people often invoke to supposedly explain their ability to be disciplined or exhibit "self-control." Whether "willpower" actually exists or not is less important than how useful that concept is in helping us gain control over our behavior. The problem with relying on willpower to create self-control is that no one has yet discovered a successful way of increasing "willpower." Standard advice such as "Just use your willpower" or "You've got to buckle down and have some willpower" tends to be quite unsatisfactory as more than a momentary source of inspiration.

In contrast, the behavioral approach to self-control provides people with specific actions they can take in order to accomplish their aims. The behavioral model of self-control involves setting up environmental events (both antecedents and consequences) to maximize the chances of our behaving as we would like to.

Consider the case of overeating. Rather than attribute a person's lack of restraint in eating to an absence of willpower, it is more *useful* to examine the environmental events that may be maintaining overeating, such as food in front of us (or in the kitchen or down the street) and people who encourage and reward our eating (e.g., often mothers or motherly people). The latter view is more useful because it is possible to change those possible maintaining conditions (e.g., sit in a room without food, do not keep attractive foods in the house, avoid the company of "bad influences" when trying to lose weight). People often view environmental conditions as beyond their control, whereas only a little ingenuity and assertive behavior is required to modify most environmental circumstances that appear to "run" our lives. For instance, just because particularly tasty foods have *always* been kept in your house does not mean they cannot be removed during those times you are attempting to lose weight.

The Situation-Specific Nature of Behavior

An important corollary of the emphasis on environmental factors is the proposition that people are best understood in terms of what they do in *particular situations.* Much behavior is influenced by socially accepted demands and expectations—which are often implicit rather than explicit—about how to act in specific situations. The "situation" includes where we are, who is there, and our status relative to the situation and other people. Also important are our personal expectations about appropriate behavior in the situation, based on our previous experiences with it or similar situations.

The position that "how people act is largely determined by the situations in which they find themselves" is referred to as **situational specificity.**[7] It implies that people's behavior tends to *vary* from situation to situation and to be *consistent* within the same general situation. A simple example will illustrate what is meant by behavior being situation-specific.

If we were to observe a hypothetical college student named Carl, we might find that he generally sits quietly in his lecture classes, usually talks at a moderate volume when having meals with friends at the cafeteria, and often "yells his head off" at football and basketball games. In each instance, how loudly Carl speaks is influenced by the social expectations and restrictions associated with the specific context in which the speaking occurs. Carl's speaking is consistent in similar situations, but it changes in different situations. For example, Carl may sit quietly in all of his lecture classes, but he often speaks up in other campus activities, including classes that are seminars or discussion sections where the demands are different than in lectures. Thus, to classify Carl as "quiet" would be as misleading as to call him "talkative." Carl is neither type of person; he engages in both behaviors in different contexts. (Once again, the impreciseness of the trait approach contrasts with the greater accuracy of the behavioral approach to describing and understanding people's behavior.)

Learning and Human Behavior

Implicit in the argument that behavior is primarily affected by environmental factors is another basic assumption: that behavior develops, is maintained, and is modified primarily (although not exclusively) by learning. Essentially, learning is the process by which environmental factors influence behavior.

According to the behavioral model, heredity and biological factors set broad limits on a person's behavior. These limits are most obvious in the case of physical characteristics. Some physical characteristics, such as eye color, are unchangeable, but many others are modifiable, at least to some degree. Physical size is partially determined by the relevant genes we receive from our parents and partially by diet and exercise. However, no amount of environmental intervention can make a genetic midget into a seven-foot basketball player.

Some psychological characteristics are also broadly limited by one's heredity. Considerable evidence shows that intelligence has a definite genetic component.[8] However, within the broad limits established by one's genes, intelligence can be substantially increased (as by an enriched intellectual environment) or decreased (as by minimal intellectual stimulation).[9] Similarly, very soon after birth, it is possible to assess an infant's general level of activity, and this activity level is a good predictor of the degree to which a person engages in active behaviors in adult life.[10] However, environmental factors also contribute to how active people tend to be, as the following hypothetical example illustrates.

Let us say that Hyman has a high activity level at birth, and Lois has a low activity level at birth. Let us assume that they are reared in very similar ways and have very similar experiences during childhood. When Hyman grows up, we would expect to see him doing things quickly, involved in many activities, and always "on the go," seeming never to tire. On the other hand, we would anticipate that adult Lois would generally move slowly, engage in fewer activities, and spend more time in sedentary behaviors. However, if Hyman were raised by parents who modeled and encouraged a slow-paced life, such as always avoiding "overdoing," and the reverse were true for Lois, their general levels of activity as adults could be similar. However, Lois would never engage in the very high level of activity that Hyman could potentially engage in given his genetic endowment and given environmental conditions conducive to a highly active lifestyle.

All that has been said here about hereditary factors also holds true for biological factors that are not inherited. Disease and poor health or a lack of disease and good health certainly play a role in one's potential and actual behavior. But usually that role can be influenced by environmental and psychological factors. The fact that most behaviors can be influenced by learning and thus can change even though they may be strongly influenced by hereditary or biological factors is critical in treating certain types of abnormal behavior that appear to have a substantial biological component (e.g., autistic and hyperactive behaviors in children, and schizophrenic and some types of depressive behaviors in adults[11]).

To summarize the behavioral view of the role of heredity and biology in determining human behavior: these factors set wide boundaries for behavior, and within these limitations environmental factors play the major role in influencing behavior.

SUMMARY

We commonly describe people in terms of their traits (hypothetical, relatively stable personality characteristics), and traits are always inferred from behavior. *In contrast*, the behavioral model deals directly with behavior.

The two major classes of behavior are (1) overt behavior, which is directly observable by others, and (2) covert behavior, which is private behavior such as thoughts and feelings. Whenever possible, behavioral therapists work directly with overt behavior. Covert behavior is frequently dealt with by finding overt behaviors that indicate that the covert behavior is occurring. There is a reciprocal relationship between overt and covert behavior: each affects and is affected by the other.

According to the behavioral model, behavior is determined by conditions that exist in the present, and these maintaining conditions are looked for in the antecedents and consequences of the behavior, which are primarily in the environment. It is important to distinguish between the originating and the maintaining conditions of behavior, because the originating conditions are often not the same as the (current) maintaining conditions. Another basic tenet of the behavioral model is that behavior is heavily influenced by the situation in which it is performed. Finally, the behavioral model assumes that much of our behavior is learned, and that hereditary and biological factors play a minor role in adult human behavior, in that they set broad limits within which the person is capable of acting.

REFERENCE NOTES

1. Liebert & Spiegler, 1982.
2. Liebert & Spiegler, 1982.
3. Craighead, Kazdin, & Mahoney, 1976.
4. For example, Bandura, 1969; Krasner & Ullmann, 1973; Skinner, 1953.
5. Bandura, 1977b.
6. Spiegler, 1981.
7. Mischel, 1968, 1973.
8. Willerman, 1979.
9. For example, Lee, 1951; Skeels, 1966.
10. For example, Buss, Plomin, & Willerman, 1973; Scarr, 1966; Willerman, 1973; Willerman & Plomin, 1973.
11. O'Leary & Wilson, 1975.

CHAPTER 3 Behavioral Therapy

How is the behavioral model discussed in the previous chapter applied to the treatment of abnormal behavior? The following case concerns a boy who was intensely afraid of going to school and was successfully treated by behavioral therapy (Case 3-1). This case is especially instructive because it involves several behavioral therapy procedures and illustrates a number of the core characteristics of behavioral therapy listed in Chapter 1.

CASE 3-1

*Treatment of a Child's Fear of School by Behavioral Therapy**

BACKGROUND

When he was referred for therapy Paul, age 9, had been absent from school for three weeks. The summer vacation had ended six weeks previously, and on entering the fourth grade, Paul avoided the classroom situation. He was often found hiding in the cloakroom and subsequently began spending less time at school each day. Thereafter, neither threats, bribes, nor punishments could induce him to reenter school.

*Reprinted from Lazarus, Davison, & Polefka (1965), pp. 225–227, 229.

Paul's history revealed a series of similar episodes. During his first day of kindergarten, he succeeded in climbing over an extremely high wall and fled home. His first-grade teacher considered him to be "disturbed." Serious difficulties regarding school attendance were first exhibited when Paul entered the second grade of a parochial school. It was alleged that the second-grade teacher . . . generally intimidated the children and was very free with physical punishment. . . . At this stage he became progressively more reluctant to enter the school and finally refused entirely. A psychiatrist was consulted and is reported to have advised the parents to use coercion, whereupon Paul was literally dragged screaming to school by a truant officer. Paul was especially bitter about his experience with the psychiatrist. In the third grade Paul was transferred to the neighborhood public school where he spent a trouble-free year at the hands of an exceedingly kind teacher.

Paul was the fourth of eight children, the first boy in a devout, orthodox Roman Catholic family. . . . The father was a moody, anxiously ambitious electronics engineer. . . . A harsh disciplinarian— "I run a tight ship"—he impulsively meted out punishment for any act [that] deviated even slightly from his perfectionistic standards. . . .

The mother, although openly affectionate and less rigid and demanding than her husband . . . stressed . . . that "Paul touches my nerve center," and stated that they frequently quarreled in the father's absence. She had always found Paul "less cuddlesome" than his siblings. When he was 2 years old, she would lock him out of the house, "so as to develop his independence." . . . In general, she was inclined to be inconsistent when administering rewards and punishment. . . . Testing suggested that Paul was uncertain whether a given response would meet with criticism and rejection or kind attention from his mother. It was nevertheless evident that Paul was eager to receive a greater share of his mother's highly rationed time.

The lad himself was somewhat small and frail-looking. Although reticent, essentially aloof and somewhat withdrawn, he was capable of unexpected vigor and self-assertion when he chose to participate in sporting activities. From the outset, the therapists noted his labile and expressive reactions to all stressful stimuli. The extent of his subjective discomfort was easily gauged by clearly discernible responses. As the magnitude of anxiety increased, there was a concomitant progression of overt signs—increased reticence, a postural stoop, a general constriction of movement, tear-filled eyes, mild trembling, pronounced blanching, culminating in sobbing and immobility. . . . These emotional indices were crucial in selecting appropriate therapeutic strategies.

A series of specific traumatic events commenced with his near-drowning when 5 years old. Toward the end of his third grade, he underwent a serious appendectomy with critical complications, which was followed by painful postoperative experiences in a doctor's consulting room. During one of these examinations, as Paul bitterly recounted, he had been left alone by his parents. Shortly after his recovery from surgery, he witnessed a drowning [that] upset him considerably. Following his entry into the fourth grade, the sudden death of a 12-year-old girl, who had been a close friend of his elder sister, profoundly affected the entire family. It is also noteworthy that Paul's father experienced personal stress in his work situation during the child's turbulent second grade, as well as immediately preceding fourth grade. Finally, Paul seemed to have been intimidated by a warning from his eldest sister that fourth-grade schoolwork was particularly difficult.

TREATMENT PLAN

After the initial interview, it was evident that Paul's school phobia was the most disruptive response pattern of a generally bewildered and intimidated child. Although subsequent interviews revealed the plethora of familial tensions, situational crises, and specific traumatic events [just] outlined . . . the initial therapeutic objective was to reinstate normal school attendance. . . .

The school was situated two and one-half blocks away from the home. The routine was for Paul to leave for school at 8:30 A.M. in order to arrive by 8:40. The first recess was from 10:00–10:30, lunch break from 12:00–1:00, and classes ended at 3:30 P.M. [Highly specific details regarding the circumstances surrounding the problem behavior, such as the exact times noted here, are typical of behavioral assessment.] At the time when therapy was initiated, the boy was extremely surly and dejected in the mornings (as reported by the parents), refused breakfast, rarely dressed himself, and became noticeably more fearful toward 8:30. Parental attempts at reassurance, coaxing, or coercion elicited only sobbing and further withdrawal.

Accordingly, the boy was exposed to the following increasingly difficult steps along the main dimensions of his school phobia:

1. On a Sunday afternoon, accompanied by the therapists, he walked from his house to the school. The therapists were able to allay Paul's anxiety by means of distraction and humor, so that his initial exposure was relatively pleasant. [Multiple therapists are sometimes used in behavioral therapy. They were used in this case because of the number of hours during which it was necessary for a therapist to be with Paul.]

2. On the next two days at 8:30 A.M., accompanied by one of the therapists, he walked from his house into the schoolyard. Again, Paul's feelings of anxiety were reduced by means of coaxing, encouragement, relaxation, and the use of "emotive imagery" (i.e., the deliberate picturing of subjectively pleasant images such as Christmas and a visit to Disneyland while relating them to the school situation). . . . [Emotive imagery* is an example of a substitution behavioral therapy similar to systematic desensitization.] Approximately 15 minutes were spent roaming around the school grounds, after which Paul returned home.

3. After school was over for the day, the therapist was able to persuade the boy to enter the classroom and sit down at his desk. Part of the normal school routine was then playfully enacted.

4. On the following three mornings, the therapist accompanied the boy into the classroom with the other children. They chatted with the teacher, and left immediately after the opening exercises.

5. A week after beginning this program, Paul spent the entire morning in class. The therapist sat in the classroom and smiled approvingly at Paul whenever he interacted with his classmates or the teacher. After eating his lunch, he participated in an active ball game, and returned to his house with the therapist at 12:30. (Since parent-teacher conferences were held during that entire week, afternoon classes were discontinued.)

6. Two days later when Paul and the therapist arrived at school, the boy lined up with

*Lazarus & Abramovitz (1962).

the other children and allowed the therapist to wait for him inside the classroom. This was the first time that Paul had not insisted on having the therapist in constant view.

7. Thereafter, the therapist sat in the school library adjoining the classroom.

8. It was then agreed that the therapist would leave at 2:30 P.M. while Paul remained for the last hour of school.

9. On the following day, Paul remained alone at school from 1:45 P.M. until 2:45 P.M. (Earlier that day, the therapist had unsuccessfully attempted to leave the boy alone from 10 until noon.)

10. Instead of fetching the boy at his home, the therapist arranged to meet him at the school gate at 8:30 A.M. Paul also agreed to remain alone at school from 10:45 A.M. until noon provided that the therapist return to eat lunch with him. At 1:45 P.M. the therapist left again with the promise that if the boy remained until school ended (3:30 P.M.) he would visit Paul that evening and play the guitar for him.

11. Occasional setbacks made it necessary to instruct the lad's mother not to allow the boy into the house during school hours. In addition, the teacher was asked to provide special jobs for the boy so as to increase his active participation and make school more attractive. . . .

12. After meeting the boy in the mornings, the therapist gradually left him alone at school for progressively longer periods of time. After six days of this procedure, the therapist was able to leave at 10 A.M.

13. The boy was assured that the therapist would be in the faculty room until 10 A.M., if needed. Thus, he came to school knowing the therapist was present, but not actually seeing him.

14. With Paul's consent the therapist arrived at school shortly *after* the boy entered the classroom at 8:40 A.M.

15. School attendance independent of the therapist's presence was achieved by means of specific rewards (a comic book, and variously colored tokens [that] would eventually procure a baseball glove) contingent upon his entering school and remaining there alone. He was at liberty to telephone the therapist in the morning if he wanted him at school, in which event he would forfeit his rewards for that day.

16. Since the therapist's presence seemed to have at least as much reward value as the comic books and tokens, it was necessary to enlist the mother's cooperation to effect the therapist's final withdrawal. The overall diminution of the boy's anxieties, together with the general gains [that] had accrued to his home situation, made it therapeutically feasible for the mother to emphasize the fact that school attendance was compulsory, and that social agencies beyond the control of both therapists and parents would enforce this requirement eventually.

17. Approximately three weeks later, Paul had accumulated enough tokens to procure his baseball glove. He then agreed with his parents that rewards of this kind were no longer necessary.

TREATMENT OUTCOME

[The treatment program just described was carried out over four and a half months, during which there were a number of setbacks. At the end of treatment, Paul was not only attending school regularly but, according to his mother's reports, his behavior had improved outside of school.] She referred to his marked decrease in moodiness, his increased willingness to participate in household chores, more congenial relationships with his peers, and general gains in self-sufficiency.

Ten months after the termination of therapy, a follow-up inquiry revealed that Paul had not only maintained his gains, but had made further progress.

Many features of the treatment used for Paul's school-phobic behavior are typical of behavioral therapy in general. To begin with, although Paul's problem is summarily referred to as a "school phobia," the targets of treatment were Paul's truancy (i.e., staying away from school) and his school attendance—two *overt behaviors.* His intense fear of the school situation was considered to be the primary *maintaining condition* of his truancy, and thus the therapy was directly aimed at changing his fear. Although the therapists had access to abundant information related to the first instances in which Paul avoided school, they concentrated instead on factors that were *current.* The therapy involved Paul in *actively doing* things that would alter the maintaining conditions of the problem, rather than just in talking about them. These procedures were carried out *in the situation* in which the problem was occurring and with the help of nonprofessional therapeutic agents, namely Paul's mother and teacher. Although standard therapeutic procedures were employed, they were *individualized* to fit Paul's unique case. Finally, Paul was made an active partner in his therapy, both in terms of his *assuming responsibility* for carrying out procedures and in terms of his entering into *contractual agreements* with the therapists concerning the specific details of the treatment.

TARGET BEHAVIORS

In behavioral therapy, a client's problems are treated by changing relatively small and discrete behaviors called **target behaviors.** The problem behaviors that clients typically present on entering therapy tend to be broad and amorphous. In contrast, target behaviors are clearly and narrowly defined so that they can be easily measured and so that changes in the target behaviors—the index of progress in behavioral therapy—can be assessed. Paul's parents probably told the therapists that Paul had "a school phobia" or was afraid to go to school. This presenting problem was translated into the operational terms of a target behavior, such as "the amount of time that Paul spent out of school from 8:40 A.M. to 3:30 P.M. on weekdays." Essentially this behavior is truancy or time away from school, but note that the target behavior has been defined unambiguously and much more precisely. Furthermore, the target behavior has been quantified (i.e., "amount of time"), to allow comparisons of Paul's performance at various stages. Because time can be broken down into very small units, very small changes can be recorded. With such a clearly defined target behavior, it is possible to specify an unambiguous treatment goal. Therefore, both therapist *and* client know when the therapy goal has been achieved.

Like most clients who come to therapy, Paul had more than one problem. The therapists chose to treat one problem rather than attempting to deal with many problems at once or with his "overall personality adjustment" (which was relatively poor, as the background information about Paul clearly indicates). In behavioral therapy, usually one target behavior is worked on at a time, although a number of target behaviors may have been established. Occasionally several target behaviors may be treated simultaneously, especially if they are in different areas of the client's life, but rarely are more than three treated at the same time. The decision as to which target behavior is worked on first depends on such factors as the following:

1. Severity and immediacy (as with Paul)
2. Centrality (e.g., one particular target behavior may be contributing to other target behaviors)
3. Efficiency (sometimes therapy begins by treating a target behavior that is relatively easy to change, which provides the client with some immediate relief as well as with a success experience to serve as a basis for dealing with target behaviors that are more resistant to change)
4. A combination of these criteria

When one target behavior has been changed, therapy then focuses on another target behavior. Thus, multiple problems are handled in behavioral therapy sequentially rather than simultaneously.

There are several advantages to the strategy of treating a single target behavior. First, it is frequently easier for clients to focus their attention on one task than on several. Second, dealing with a single target behavior usually brings about some change in the client's problem(s) relatively quickly, which may motivate the client to continue working on other problems. Third, problems usually are related to one another, so that improvement in one problem may reduce or even eliminate other problems (as apparently was the case with Paul). Thus, treating one target behavior at a time is often an efficient approach in the long run.

Once a target behavior has been selected, the next task is to divide it into its sequential components and to progressively work with each component until the entire target behavior has been treated. This approach is illustrated by the therapist's step-wise shaping of Paul's school attendance. The major component behaviors, in the order in which they were treated, are summarized in Figure 3-1.

Acceleration and Deceleration Target Behaviors

Two classes of target behaviors can be distinguished. **Acceleration target behaviors** are those that the client wishes to increase—they are adaptive behaviors that the client is not performing often enough, long enough, or intensely enough. For example, acceleration target behaviors would be indicated

1. Walking from the house to the school with the therapist on a nonschool day
2. Walking from the house to the schoolyard with the therapist at an appropriate time (i.e., 8:30 A.M.) on a school day
3. Spending 15 minutes in the schoolyard with the therapist
4. Entering the classroom and sitting at a desk with the therapist present after school hours
5. "Playing school" in the classroom with the therapist after school hours
6. Entering the classroom and talking with the teacher in the presence of the therapist
7. Spending the morning in the classroom with the therapist present
8. Spending the day at school without the therapist in sight (but available in the school building)
9. Walking to school alone
10. Spending all day in school with the therapist unavailable part of the day
11. Spending all day in school with the therapist unavailable (i.e., normal school attendance—the total target behavior)

FIGURE 3-1 *The component behaviors of Paul's school attendance, in the order in which they were treated*

in the case of a woman who rarely speaks up for her rights, or who says something assertive but gives up as soon as she meets any resistance, or who tells others what she wants but so timidly that she is not taken seriously. **Deceleration target behaviors** are those which the client wishes to decrease—they are maladaptive behaviors that the client performs too frequently, for too long a time, or too intensely. For example, deceleration target behaviors would be indicated in the case of a man who gets angry at the slightest provocation, who stays angry for hours or even days, or who often gets into physical fights.

Acceleration target behaviors are dealt with in a straightforward manner. Behavioral therapy procedures are implemented to directly increase the behavior. In the case of deceleration target behaviors, three possible tactics are employed. First, therapy can focus on directly decreasing the target behavior. Second, therapy can focus on accelerating a behavior that is an alternative to the deceleration target behavior. This acceleration target behavior would have to fulfill the same general function that the deceleration target behavior was fulfilling, and obviously it should be a more adaptive behavior. Optimally, the acceleration and deceleration target behaviors will be *incompatible:* they cannot both occur at the same time. Thus, if the client is performing the acceleration target behavior, she or he cannot be performing the deceleration target behavior. In Case 3-1, the deceleration target behavior was "time spent *outside* of school during school hours," and the acceleration target behavior was "time spent *in* school during school hours." Dealing with the acceleration target behavior was sufficient in this instance because if Paul were attending school he could not simultaneously be away from school. Other examples of deceleration target behaviors and suitable incompatible acceleration target behaviors for

TABLE 3-1 Examples of Incompatible Acceleration Target Behaviors for Deceleration Target Behaviors

DECELERATION TARGET BEHAVIOR	INCOMPATIBLE ACCELERATION TARGET BEHAVIOR
Studying in front of the television	Studying in the library
Biting one's fingernails	Keeping one's hands in one's pockets or at one's sides
Driving home from parties drunk	Taking a taxi home
Staying up until 3 A.M.	Getting into bed and turning out the lights at 1 A.M.
Talking to "voices" (i.e., hallucinating)	Talking to other people
Criticizing others	Praising others

them are given in Table 3-1. The third and most potent strategy for treating a deceleration target behavior is to simultaneously both decrease the unwanted deceleration target behavior and increase the alternative acceleration target behavior.

When a problem behavior is eliminated or substantially decreased, a void is created in the person's life. No matter how unpleasant or maladaptive the problem behavior was, it served a function and accounted for periods of time in the person's life. When one behavior is eliminated, another inevitably takes its place, because as long as we are alive, we are constantly behaving. Even staring out the window, sitting motionless, and sleeping are behaviors. If no explicit steps are taken to fill the void with an appropriate adaptive behavior (as an alternative to the maladaptive behavior that has been decelerated), another maladaptive behavior may take its place or the individual may eventually return to the old maladaptive habit. To prevent this, it is standard practice in behavioral therapy to include an acceleration target behavior in any treatment plan that has a deceleration target behavior. In other words, at the same time that a maladaptive behavior is being decelerated, an appropriate substitute behavior is being accelerated. For example, along with therapy procedures directly aimed at decreasing a client's excessive drinking of alcohol, therapy procedures that increased an alternative and more adaptive behavior would be instituted. If the client's drinking were being maintained by its ability to relax and help the client "unwind" from tensions created at work, then the acceleration target behavior would have to serve the same function, such as a program of regular physical exercise after work.

Including an acceleration target behavior in all treatment plans has the added advantage that an acceleration target behavior tells the client what to do, in contrast to a deceleration target behavior that merely indicates what the client is *not* to do. This important consideration is embodied in the **dead person rule:** *Never have a client "do" something a dead person can "do."* Only dead people are capable of *not* behaving! Applying the dead person rule makes target behaviors *active* rather than passive. Thus, it would be more useful for a teacher to ask a student who is disrupting class activities to "sit and work on your math assignment" than to ask the student to "sit quietly." A dead person cannot do math problems, but a dead person can (with minimal assistance) sit very quietly! The dead person rule has pragmatic value in that it provides a check that the target behavior is an action rather than the absence of an action. It is interesting to note, however, that the dead person rule violates the dead person rule! The principle could be incorporated into a "live person rule": Always have a client do something only a live person can do. Participation Exercise 3-1 can help you find acceleration target behaviors that are incompatible with deceleration target behaviors.

PARTICIPATION EXERCISE 3-1

Finding Acceleration Target Behaviors That Are Incompatible with Deceleration Target Behaviors

Behavioral therapists frequently must find an appropriate acceleration target behavior that is incompatible or opposite to a deceleration target behavior. This participation exercise gives you a chance to try that for yourself, giving you actual experience in an important behavioral therapy skill. This particular skill may also help you set personal goals to decrease undesirable behaviors by concentrating on more desirable activities that are incompatible with the behaviors you wish to eliminate.

For each deceleration target behavior in the following list, write down one or more ***acceleration*** target behaviors (i.e., behaviors that are to be increased) that, when performed, make it impossible (or highly unlikely) for the deceleration target behavior to occur. For example, if the deceleration target behavior were "exceeding the speed limit," then an appropriate incompatible acceleration target behavior would be "driving below the speed limit," because one cannot do both at the same time. Other examples appear in Table 3-1.

The acceleration target behaviors you think of should be both incompatible and appropriate. You will know if you have identified an incompatible acceleration target behavior if a person cannot reasonably perform it and the deceleration target behavior at the same time. In other words, engaging in the acceleration target behavior precludes engaging in the deceleration target behavior. The acceleration target behavior should also be ***appropriate*** to the problem. For example, although walking (instead of using a car) would be an incompatible acceleration target behavior for speeding, it is not likely to be an appropriate alternative given the distances that most people need to travel. Finally, be sure that you do not list any dead person behaviors.

1. Eating "junk" foods between meals
2. Cramming for exams
3. "Blowing" an entire paycheck
4. Using foul language
5. Leaving the lights on (when not in use)
6. Wasting time
7. Being late for class
8. Speeding on the highway
9. Procrastinating in paying bills
10. Littering

Examples of appropriate and incompatible acceleration target behaviors are given in Appendix B. You need not have the same acceleration target behaviors as those listed in Appendix B as long as each meets the two requirements mentioned.

CHARACTERISTICS OF BEHAVIORAL THERAPY

The key concepts of target behaviors and maintaining conditions having been discussed, it is now possible to discuss in detail several of the salient characteristics of behavioral therapy that were introduced in Chapter 1.

Behavioral Therapy Treats Maintaining Conditions

Once a target behavior has been selected, the next step in behavioral therapy is to discover the conditions influencing the behavior and then to change them. Recall that the behavioral approach assumes that behavior is directly influenced by *present* antecedents and consequences (the maintaining conditions). Thus, *behavioral therapy directly treats the maintaining conditions of the target behavior*. Contrary to the popular myth, behavioral therapy does *not* directly treat symptoms (behavior).

This critical point was illustrated in the case of Paul's school-phobic behavior. Paul's truancy, the deceleration target behavior, was thought to be maintained primarily by anxiety or feelings of extreme discomfort that he experienced in school. Much of the therapy involved reducing Paul's anxiety in school by exposing him, in progressive steps, to the school situation while he was relaxed and otherwise feeling positive emotions (see Steps 1 and 2 in Figure 3-1). School attendance (the acceleration target behavior) seemed to be at a low level because there were not enough positive consequences for being in school and there was an abundance of negative consequences associated with his attending school, notably the negative feelings he experienced while there. Thus, the acceleration target behavior was treated by providing Paul with many positive consequences for attending school, such as the support and friendship of the therapists, and specific tangible rewards.

Given Paul's stormy childhood, it would not be difficult to compile a list of factors in his past that may have contributed to his present school-phobic behavior. It is very likely, for example, that Paul's feelings of insecurity in stressful situations, such as school, were fostered by the negative or at least ambivalent treatment he received from his parents. There were also the series of traumatic events (e.g., experiences with drowning, a surgical operation, being left alone in a doctor's office, and the death of a close friend) that could easily have sensitized Paul to being left alone at school. Although these circumstances, as well as others, may have contributed to Paul's present problem, because they occurred in the past they are assumed, in the behavioral approach, to be of secondary importance. Moreover, because they occurred in the past, little can be done to change them. In contrast, the intense anxiety that Paul was experiencing in the present could be directly alleviated.

Past circumstances are likely to affect present behavior *only* when they also exist in the present. In behavioral therapy, examination of the client's remote past history is usually not essential but can be helpful if it points to the importance of particular circumstances that existed in the past and that *currently* exist as maintaining conditions of the problem behavior. In Case 3-2, the client's presenting problem to the therapist was a fear of crossing bridges. The objective of this initial behavioral assessment interview was to identify the probable maintaining conditions of the problem (fear of crossing bridges), because those events and conditions would be directly treated in therapy. As this actual therapist-patient dialogue shows, a behavioral therapist must be sensitive and alert to the subtle details surrounding a patient's problem. (The therapist was Arnold Lazarus, who was one of the first behavioral therapists and, coincidently, was the senior therapist for Paul in Case 3-1.)

CASE 3-2

Behavioral Assessment Interview for Fear of Crossing Bridges*

Patient: I have a fear of crossing bridges.
Therapist: Do you have any other fears or difficulties?
Patient: Only the complications arising from my fear of bridges.
Therapist: Well, in what way has it affected your life?
Patient: I had to quit an excellent job in Berkeley.
Therapist: Where do you live?
Patient: San Francisco.
Therapist: So why didn't you move to Berkeley?
Patient: I prefer living in the city.
Therapist: To get to this institute, you had to cross the Golden Gate.†
Patient: Yes, I was seeing a doctor in San Francisco. He tried to desensitize me but it didn't help so he said I should see you because you know more about this kind of treatment. It's not so bad when I have my wife and kids with me. But even then, the Golden Gate, which is about one mile long, is my upper limit. I was wondering whether you ever consult in the city?
Therapist: No. But tell me, how long have you had this problem?
Patient: Oh, about four years, I'd say. It just happened suddenly. I was coming home from work and the Bay Bridge was awfully slow. I just suddenly panicked for no reason at all. I mean, nothing like this had ever happened to me before. I felt that I would crash into the other cars. Once I even had a feeling that the bridge would cave in.

*Lazarus (1971). Quotations are from pp. 33–36.

†Berkeley, California, lies east of San Francisco, separated by San Francisco Bay; the Bay Bridge (about 8 miles long) crosses between Oakland and San Francisco. The Golden Gate Bridge (1 mile long) links San Francisco to Sausalito in the north, where Lazarus's Behavior Therapy Institute was located.

Therapist: Let's get back to that first panic experience about four years ago. You said that you were coming home from work. Had anything happened at work?

Patient: Nothing unusual.

Therapist: Were you happy at work?

Patient: Sure! Huh! I was even due for promotion.

Therapist: What would that have entailed?

Patient: An extra $3,000 a year.

Therapist: I mean in the way of having to do different work.

Patient: Well, I would have been a supervisor. I would have had more than 50 men working under me.

Therapist: How did you feel about that?

Patient: What do you mean?

Therapist: I mean how did you feel about the added responsibility? Did you feel that you were up to it, that you could cope with it?

Patient: Gee! My wife was expecting our first kid. We both welcomed the extra money.

Therapist: So round about the time that you were about to become a father, you were to be promoted to supervisor. So you would face two new and challenging roles. You'd be a daddy at home and also Big Daddy at work. And this was when you began to panic on the bridge, and I guess you never did wind up as a supervisor.

Patient: No. I had to ask for a transfer to the city.

Therapist: Now, please think very carefully about this question. Have you ever been involved in any accident on or near a bridge, or have you ever witnessed any serious accident on or near a bridge?

Patient: Not that I can think of.

Therapist: Do you still work for the same company?

Patient: No. I got a better offer, more money, from another company in the city. I've been with them for almost 1½ years now.

Therapist: Are you earning more money or less money than you would have gotten in Berkeley?

Patient: About the same. But prices have gone up, so it adds up to less.

Therapist: If you hadn't developed the bridge phobia and had become foreman in Berkeley at $3,000 more, where do you think you would be today?

Patient: Still in Berkeley.

Therapist: Still supervisor? More money?

Patient: Oh hell! Who knows? (laughs) Maybe I would have been vice-president.

Therapist: And what would that have entailed?

Patient: I'm only kidding. But actually it could have happened.

Further interviewing revealed "a history in which the patient, the youngest of five siblings, tended to accept his mother's evaluation that, unlike his brilliant older brothers, he would never amount to anything." Although it is not possible to definitively reconstruct past events, the following sequence of events may have resulted in the beginning of the patient's fear of crossing bridges. Shortly before the patient was to assume two major responsibilities, becoming a father and a supervisor at work, he was driving home from work (from Berkeley to San Francisco) on the Bay Bridge. On that day he had ample time to think about the added responsibilities he was to assume, because the bridge traffic was moving very slowly. It is a reasonable hunch that the panic he felt on the bridge was precipitated by these thoughts as well as by his long-standing notions that he was inadequate and would never succeed at anything. Thus, the panic was probably *not directly* related to being on the bridge. (If the patient had been stuck on a stalled train, he might have developed a fear of riding on trains.) Nonetheless, an association may well have been established between his intense thoughts and feelings of panic, and his being on the bridge. Although this sequence of events may account for the *origin* of his fear of crossing bridges, it does not account for its persistence over the next four years. It is very possible that his fear of crossing bridges served the important function of reducing his anxiety about his competence and achievements. In other words, because he was afraid to cross the Bay Bridge he was unable to accept the supervisory position with its added responsibility and chance to fail (if you don't try, you can't fail). If this reasoning is valid, then the maintaining conditions of the patient's fear of crossing bridges lay in his feelings of inadequacy, and treating them should alleviate his fear of bridges. In fact, that is exactly what occurred.

The patient was desensitized to his thoughts about his inadequacies so that they no longer were hurtful to him or resulted in self-defeating behaviors (e.g., avoiding opportunities for success). He was also taught to behave more assertively. These therapy procedures, which will be discussed in detail later, were aimed at eliminating the probable maintaining conditions of the patient's fear of crossing bridges. They were successful: "As he gained confidence in his own capabilities, his bridge phobia vanished as suddenly as it had appeared."

Behavioral Therapy Is a Scientific Endeavor

A commitment to a scientific approach is at the core of behavioral therapy. The goal of using scientific principles, methods, and findings to alleviate human suffering and enhance human functioning guides the practice of behavioral therapy. What are the major ways in which this commitment to science influences behavioral therapy?

The goals of behavioral therapy are specified in precise, unambiguous terms, which has at least two distinct advantages. One is that both the client and the therapist can assess progress and success. This point is significant, because in many other forms of psychotherapy the success of the treatment is determined only by the therapist's subjective opinion.[1] Having clear-cut therapeutic goals also makes it possible to obtain a detailed (and often quantitative) assessment of the target behavior and its maintaining conditions, which provides objective information about the course of therapy. Behavioral assessment and behavioral therapy are closely integrated and mutually dependent.[2]

Precision and objectivity are also employed in specifying behavioral therapy procedures. Clients are informed of exactly what will be going on in therapy. Also, precision and objectivity make it possible to accurately evaluate the effectiveness of treatment procedures and to use the same procedures again if they are effective.

The commitment to evaluation and accountability influences the course of treatment for individual clients as well as the general use of behavioral therapy procedures. Ongoing assessment of target behaviors makes it possible to monitor the effects of therapy procedures, which can then be modified or even changed completely when indicated. The course of behavioral therapy parallels the steps of a scientific investigation. First a target behavior is defined, and an assessment is made of the baseline (pretherapy) level of the target behavior and of the possible maintaining conditions of the target behavior. Next a hypothesis is formulated stating that certain antecedents and consequences are influencing the target behavior. This hypothesis is then tested by appropriately modifying the hypothesized maintaining conditions. If the target behavior changes in the desired direction, then the hypothesis is supported; in practical terms, this outcome indicates that the therapy has been successful. A clear example of this sequence of events in therapy was shown in the case of the man who was afraid of crossing bridges (Case 3-2). If the target behavior does not change in the desired direction, the hypothesis is not supported and the treatment is not successful. Then the maintaining conditions must be reassessed, and the resulting new hypothesis about the factors affecting the target behavior must be tested. The analogy between behavioral therapy and a scientific experiment is detailed in Table 3-2.

The effectiveness of behavioral therapies is evaluated empirically through scientific investigations. However logical or theoretically sound a therapeutic

TABLE 3-2 The Parallel Between Behavioral Therapy and a Scientific Experiment

STEP	BEHAVIORAL THERAPY	SCIENTIFIC EXPERIMENT
1. Define what is to be changed	Target behavior (TB)	Dependent variable (DV)[a]
2. Assess baseline	Pretherapy measurement of TB	Pretest measurement of DV
3. Search for influential factors	Assess critical antecedents and consequences of TB	Decide on important independent variable (IV)[a]
4. Formulate hypothesis	"If correct maintaining conditions (MCs) have been assessed, then modifying them will change the TB"	"If IV does affect the DV, then varying the IV will result in the DV covarying"
5. Test hypothesis	Implement therapy (i.e., modify MCs)	Carry out experiment (i.e., vary IV)
6. Examine outcome	Posttherapy measurement of TB	Posttest measurement of DV
7. Draw conclusions when		
a. Change is in expected direction	Therapy successful	Hypothesis confirmed
b. Change is in unexpected direction	Reassess MCs (i.e., return to Step 3)	Find other IV (i.e., return to Step 3)

[a]In a scientific experiment, the condition that is directly varied is called the *independent variable*. The object of an experiment is to observe the influence of the independent variable on subjects' behavior. The specific behavior under investigation is called the *dependent variable* because it is hypothesized to depend on or be influenced by the condition varied by the experimenter (i.e., the independent variable).

technique seems to be, it is necessary to demonstrate through appropriate scientific methods that the technique results in therapeutic changes. Literally hundreds of research studies on behavioral therapies are performed every year.[3] Many are **analogue studies,** so named because one or more elements of the study are only similar (not identical) to the conditions in actual clinical practice. For example, the subjects in an analogue study might be people who have the same type of problem as actual clients who seek help in therapy but for whom the problem is much less severe. Such an individual may experience minor difficulties in heterosexual relations in contrast to a client who has so much difficulty interacting with members of the opposite sex that he or she completely avoids them. Much clinical research is in the form of case studies, which may not have the same rigorous scientific controls as experimental studies.[4] And there is also a sizable minority of controlled scientific investigations that deal specifically with actual clinical problems and clients. The heavy reliance on analogue investigations and case studies of behavioral therapy may be less than ideal, because the evidence they provide is less substantial than evidence from well-controlled experiments with actual clients.[5] Taken together, however, they constitute an impressive and continually growing body of data concerning the process and effectiveness of behavioral therapies.[6]

There is a close relationship between research and the clinical practice of behavioral therapy: much of behavioral therapy includes or is part of a research endeavor. Most behavioral therapy procedures are developed and initially evaluated in research settings by individuals who are both behavioral therapists and researchers (e.g., in academic departments of psychology). Usually the primary aim of such studies is to gather broadly applicable information about particular therapies; for example, will Therapy X help people with a particular problem behavior, or is Therapy X more effective than Therapy Y? Secondarily, the client-subjects who participate in these therapy studies benefit from the therapy they receive.

It is now standard practice for client-subjects who receive a less adequate treatment (as determined by the results of the investigation) by virtue of the experimental condition to which they were assigned to be offered the most effective therapy procedure after the research has been completed. Many of the case examples that appear in this book were part of a joint research-therapy venture, but they were chosen to represent actual clinical practice as well. Purely clinical cases, which have no broad research component or implication, tend to not be reported publicly in professional journals. They would be found only in therapists' files, which are confidential.

Behavioral Therapy Takes Place in the Client's Environment

Whenever possible, behavioral therapy takes place in the setting in which the problem behavior is occurring. Behavioral therapy is an educational process in which clients learn skills and develop new modes of behavior. And learning is best retained when it is carried out in the setting in which it is ultimately to be practiced; in terms of behavioral therapy, this is where the client's problem is experienced. Obviously, clients' problems do not occur in a therapist's office, so that is not the optimal setting for behavioral therapy.

There are three major ways in which behavioral therapy is enacted in the problem environment. The most obvious procedure is for the therapist to work directly with the client in the problem environment, as in Paul's case. This approach usually requires too much therapist time, but sometimes it is the most efficient procedure because it can reduce treatment duration and can rapidly relieve the client's problem.

A second major way in which behavioral therapy is implemented in the client's natural environment is for the therapist to train people in the client's life to act as nonprofessional change agents. Such training is done with parents, teachers, spouses, and friends, and sometimes employers and other people who have frequent contact with the client and who are willing to participate in the client's therapy. Recall that Paul's mother and teacher were recruited to carry out specific aspects of Paul's treatment.

A third approach to effecting behavioral therapy in the problem environment is for clients themselves to carry out the therapy procedures. The therapist is a teacher and consultant regarding behavioral therapy techniques, and the client is a student who learns the appropriate techniques for changing target behaviors. Behavioral therapists explicitly share their expertise with clients and avoid the "professional mystique" wherein the psychotherapist has special abilities to which the client is not privy. The therapy *sessions*—the actual time the client spends with the therapist—are used to teach the client behavioral therapy techniques by direct instruction, modeling, and behavior rehearsal (role playing). Clients are given specific tasks to carry out between therapy sessions in the problem environment. They then report back to the therapist on their progress.

In effect, clients learn to become the major change agents (or, in a sense, their own behavioral therapists) for specific target behaviors worked on in therapy. One advantage of this approach is that clients who are able to generalize what they learn in dealing with specific target behaviors may be able to cope with *similar* problems in the future without seeking professional help. Furthermore, some behavioral therapy skills and much of the general approach of behavioral therapy to understanding and changing human behavior can be applied by clients in their daily lives. For example, clients are active participants in assessing the maintaining conditions of their problem behaviors by examining, with the behavioral therapist, the relevant antecedents and consequences. This practice may make it possible for clients to employ these same skills to understanding and constructively coping with the myriad of minor, everyday problems that all people encounter.

Examples of each of these three approaches to implementing behavioral therapy in the client's natural environment are given in later chapters. In most cases, the approach of teaching clients to carry out therapy procedures on their own is the most effective. Accordingly, such *self-control* therapies are being used more and more.[7] Thus an entire chapter (Chapter 12) is devoted to them, and examples of this approach appear throughout the book.

When it is not feasible to directly implement treatment procedures in the problem environment, behavioral therapists use techniques that simulate the conditions in which the problem behavior is occurring. For example, this approach may involve practicing adaptive behaviors by role playing or by imagining. Consider the case of a client who gets extremely angry whenever she has to discipline her teenage son. With the therapist assuming the role of the client's child, the client could practice reprimanding her son while remaining calm. Or the therapist might help the client vividly imagine scenes in which she was calmly disciplining her son—a kind of mental rehearsal.

Behavioral Therapy Is Action-Oriented

Behavioral therapy is an active process that requires clients to perform specific overt actions, such as observing and recording their own behaviors, practicing skills, rewarding themselves for appropriate acts, trying out new behaviors, and setting up conditions that are conducive for adaptive behavior. Clients in behavioral therapy *act* rather than merely talk or think about acting.

Traditionally, psychotherapy has been synonymous with "talking treatment," in which the verbal dialogue between client and therapist is the major means by which therapeutic changes occur. In psychoanalytic therapy, for example, patients free-associate, recall dreams, and relate their childhood experiences; the analyst makes verbal interpretations of this material; and the patient gradually gains insight (understanding) about personal problems. In contrast, verbal communication between client and therapist in behavioral therapy plays the important but minor role of exchanging information. The actual therapeutic processes involve much more than talk as in Paul's case. Rather than talking about Paul's fear of going to school, the therapists involved Paul in active procedures that helped to reduce his fear and to increase his attending school and his positive feelings about being in school.

Homework assignments, specific therapeutic tasks that clients perform in their everyday environments, are an integral part of behavioral therapy. Clients implement much of their therapy outside the therapy session. This approach should be contrasted with many verbal psychotherapies in which all significant therapeutic endeavors occur in the therapy hour.

This difference between the fundamental formats of behavioral therapy and verbal psychotherapy may account in part for the fact that behavioral therapies tend to bring about significant changes in clients' problems in a shorter *overall* time span than do most verbal psychotherapies. However, the total time spent in therapeutic endeavors may actually be greater for behavioral therapy in some cases. For example, when the bulk of treatment is done by clients at home, the number of therapy sessions per se is drastically reduced, although the actual number of hours of therapy—in and particularly out of the sessions—may be substantial.

Behavioral Therapy Is Individualized

In the behavioral approach, no universal assumptions—those that hold for all people—are made about the factors that influence people's behavior (although certainly there are some commonalities). This approach may be contrasted with many views of human behavior in which it is assumed that all people are affected by certain universally occurring personality dispositions or life events, such as a need for positive regard, a striving for power, or an Oedipus complex.[8] Behavioral therapy begins with an individual assessment of a client's specific problems in order to identify the unique set of conditions that are maintaining them. For changing these maintaining conditions, behavioral therapies are selected that are best suited to the specific problem and the unique characteristics of the client and her or his life situation. Not only are some behavioral therapies appropriate for some clients and not for others, but the specific details of the therapy procedures applied also must be customized for each client. For example, therapy proceeds at an optimal rate for each client, as in the step-wise progression of Paul's treatment.

A Contract Is Made Between Client and Therapist

The goals for therapy, as well as the behavioral therapies that will be employed, are agreed on by the client and the behavioral therapist before treatment begins. Often a written contract is formalized between the therapist and the client. Sometimes the contract also includes one or more significant other people in the client's life who will be involved in the therapy. The contract designates the roles and responsibilities of all parties involved and may also include specific consequences that the client will receive for fulfilling or failing to fulfill the terms of the contract.

As a general rule, the behavioral therapist and the client work out the goals of therapy together, with the client having the "final say." The exception to this rule occurs with **nonvoluntary clients**: people whom society deems incapable of making responsible decisions about their own welfare. Minors and legally committed psychiatric patients are the two major categories of nonvoluntary clients. In the case of a nonvoluntary client, the goals of therapy are frequently determined by the people legally responsible for the client (e.g., Paul's parents).

BEHAVIORAL ASSESSMENT

The assessment of a client's target behaviors and their maintaining conditions is an indispensible part of behavioral therapy. As is true of behavioral therapy, the principles and orientation of behavioral assessment, much more than its methods, define and elucidate its nature.[9] Accordingly, the basic characteristics of behavioral assessment will be examined before some specific assessment procedures are described.

Characteristics of Behavioral Assessment

There are five salient characteristics of behavioral assessment. First, assessment and therapy are very much interdependent processes. Second, behavioral assessment procedures are individualized for each client. Third, the assessment proceeds by collecting data on representative samples of the client's problem behaviors. Fourth, behavioral assessment covers only limited areas of a client's life. Fifth, behavioral assessment is concerned with events that are occurring in the present.

Behavioral Assessment and Therapy Are Closely Related

Behavioral assessment is an integral and continuous part of therapy, and it is often difficult (and practically unnecessary) to distinguish between the two.[10] Behavioral assessment is the initial step in behavioral therapy and continues during therapy and after therapy. The first step in behavioral therapy is to define a target behavior, which requires a detailed description, including information about its frequency and circumstances. Next, the maintaining conditions of the target behavior must be assessed. Based on this information, a treatment plan is devised and implemented. Measurements of the target behavior are made periodically during therapy to determine if the treatment plan is effective. This information indicates when the goals of therapy have been reached and when treatment can be terminated. Finally, whenever feasible, periodic follow-up assessments are made to assure that the effects of therapy are being maintained over time (e.g., at one month, six months, and one year).

The close interrelationship of assessment and therapy is illustrated in the case of a mother who sought professional help because her son was "too demanding."[11] For example, the boy frequently informed his mother, "Now we'll play this" and "You go over there, and I'll stay here." The interactions between the mother and child were observed in a playroom from behind a one-way mirror. From these observations, it was hypothesized that the mother's complying with her son's demands was probably the maintaining condition of the child's behavior. To test this hypothesis, the mother was instructed to ignore the child's inappropriate demands (the deceleration target behavior) and to reward him with attention for his cooperative behavior (the acceleration target behavior). These procedures were effective in decreasing the child's demanding behavior and increasing his cooperative behavior. Thus, the assessment of the maintaining conditions of the problem behavior was correct, and the therapy was successful.

Behavioral Assessment Is Individualized

The purpose of behavioral assessment is to obtain information to design a treatment plan and to measure its effectiveness. In other words, behavioral assessment as a clinical endeavor is totally related to therapy. In contrast, many traditional forms of personality assessment typically have as their goal assigning the client to a diagnostic category (e.g., "phobic reaction" or "neurotic depression") on the basis of characteristics the client is presumed to share with other people who fit the same diagnosis. Behavioral assessment does not involve comparison with other people.[12] Rather, a detailed analysis is made of the client's specific problem behavior and the conditions maintaining it. Thus, like behavioral therapy, behavioral assessment is individualized.

Behavioral Assessment Samples Relevant Behavior

In behavioral assessment, samples of a client's behavior are taken to provide a picture of the client's typical mode of behaving. The observations of behavior made are used directly; no inferences beyond the level of behavior are made. In the previous example, how the mother and son interacted in the playroom in the therapist's office was considered a sample of their interactions in other similar settings (e.g., playing at home in the living room). In behavioral assessment, behavior is *not* used as a sign or indication of personality characteristics such as traits or hypothetical states (e.g., unconscious conflicts in the mind).[13] For example, the mother's acquiescing to her son's unreasonable demands was taken at face value, rather than as an indication that she had a general trait of "compliance."

When actual observations of behavior are not feasible, verbal or written reports of typical behavior are sought. The mother, in the previous example, could have been asked to describe the way she responded to her son's verbal demands. Similarly, a number of commonly used self-report inventories (questionnaires) in behavioral therapy are used as efficient means of obtaining information about a client's behavior. For instance, the Fear Survey Schedule[14] asks the client to rate the degree to which he or she is afraid or uncomfortable in various common situations (e.g., going to the dentist) or in the presence of common objects (e.g., snakes) on a five-point scale ranging from "Not at all" to "Very much." In these instances, although the actual behavior is not observed, the client is asked to report *directly* about the behavior of interest.[15] This approach should be contrasted with the traditional nonbehavioral approach to personality assessment, which involves indirectly gathering information about a person's behavior. Consider the well-known Rorschach inkblots, which consist of a set of ambiguous shapes. A person is asked to say what she or he sees in the shapes, and these responses are *interpreted* (i.e., an inference is made beyond the actual responses) as indicating the individual's unconscious motives, desires, fears, and conflicts. Seeing dangerous snakes in an inkblot might be interpreted as a sign of castration anxiety (in the psychoanalytic tradition, a snake is a symbol for a penis) rather than merely a fear of snakes.

Behavioral Assessment Is Limited

Behavioral assessment involves an evaluation of limited areas of the client's life and of discrete behaviors, not of the client's total personality. This characteristic is consistent with the circumscribed nature of behavioral therapy, which deals with specific target behaviors rather than working toward overall personality or major lifestyle changes.

The circumscribed nature of behavioral assessment is also consistent with the behavioral practice of not making any prior assumptions about relationships among an individual's behaviors. For example, as mentioned earlier, it is not assumed that all interpersonal difficulties between spouses have a sexual basis or even are related to sexual behavior. Thus, it would be feasible and legitimate to assess a couple's interactions around handling household chores or disciplining the children without delving into their sex life. (Of course, if their sexual behavior seems to be a maintaining condition of the target behavior, then an evaluation would be made of their sexual behavior.)

Behavioral Assessment Focuses on the Present

Behavioral assessment primarily deals with current factors in the client's life—that is, with the details of the problem as they presently affect the client. Information about the client's past, especially early childhood, is not emphasized (e.g., Paul in Case 3-1), although it may be gathered if such information seems related to the client's current functioning (e.g., the man who was afraid of crossing bridges, in Case 3-2).

Methods of Behavioral Assessment

The salient characteristics of behavioral assessment having been enumerated, some of the specific procedures used in behavioral assessment will now be described. A recent survey of 353 behavioral therapists revealed that a variety of behavioral assessment procedures, as well as some traditional assessment procedures, are used in behavioral therapy.[16] Table 3-3 lists the 10 most frequently

TABLE 3-3 *The 10 Most Common Assessment Procedures Used by Behavioral Therapists*

ASSESSMENT PROCEDURE	PERCENT OF USE
Interview with client	89%
Client self-monitoring	51
Interview with client's significant others	49
Direct observation of target behaviors	40
Information from consulting professionals	40
Role playing	34
Behavioral self-report measures	27
Demographic questionnaires	20
Personality inventories (tests)	20
Projective techniques	10

SOURCE: Data from Swan & MacDonald (1978).

used assessment procedures employed by behavioral therapists and the percentage of clients with which each is used. The following discussion focuses on five frequently used behavioral assessment procedures: interview, self-recording, direct observation by others, role playing, and direct self-report inventories.

Keep in mind that it is the way an assessment procedure is used that defines it as behavioral assessment, rather than the procedure itself. For example, interviews are the most common form of assessment of clients' problems in all forms of therapy, and thus the interview is hardly unique to behavioral therapy. On the other hand, the emphases of a behavioral interview are generally different from the emphases of interviews in other types of therapy (e.g., behavioral interviews focus on present circumstances rather than on past events).

The Behavioral Interview

An interview is usually the first assessment procedure used in behavioral therapy.[17] The behavioral therapist's goals for the first interview are (1) to establish rapport with the client, (2) to gather some basic information about the client, and (3) to delineate the problem for which the client is seeking help. Because the client reveals personal and sometimes stressful information to the therapist, the client must feel comfortable talking to the therapist and trust the therapist enough to be open and candid. Thus, one task of the initial interview(s) is for the therapist to build rapport with the client, such as by listening attentively and dispassionately to the client (e.g., not making value judgments about the client's behavior) and by making it clear to the client that the therapeutic relationship is confidential.[18] Also, in the first interview the therapist gathers some necessary demographic information (such as age, marital status, education level, and occupation) by direct questioning.

Next, the therapist asks the client to describe what has brought her or him to therapy—that is, the nature of the problem. Clients typically describe their problems in general and often vague terms, and the therapist must ask questions to reveal the specific details of the problem. In particular, a behavioral therapist will want to know answers to the following:

1. When did the problem begin?
2. How often does it occur?
3. When does it occur?
4. In what circumstances does it occur?
5. What tends to occur before the problem (i.e., its antecedents)?
6. What tends to occur after the problem (i.e., its consequences)?
7. What does the client think about when the problem is occurring?
8. How does the problem affect the client's life?
9. What steps have already been taken to alleviate the problem, and with what results?

The behavioral interview focuses on "what," "when," "where," and "how often," and avoids "why" questions. Also, the interview emphasizes the present rather than the past.

Once the problem has been clearly delineated, the therapist inquires about the client's strengths or assets. Such questioning not only reveals important considerations for designing a treatment plan, but also helps a distressed client recall some positive aspects of his or her life, which helps to build up the client's confidence. Although the initial interview focuses on the client's "presenting complaint," the therapist also inquires about other problems in the client's life because they may be related to the problem that the client considers primary.[19]

Much important information can be gathered through an interview, but it is also frequently necessary to obtain additional information through other methods of behavioral assessment. For example, the client may not have been able to answer some of the therapist's questions about the problem, such as the circumstances surrounding its occurrence. If so, the client may be given a homework assignment: to carefully note the antecedents and consequences of the problem and to write them down for the therapist. It also may be valuable to cross-validate the information gathered from the client's verbal reports in the interview by collecting information in other ways. For example, a client's spouse might be asked to count how often the problem occurs, to see if the client has an accurate picture of its frequency.

In addition to interviewing the client, it is often useful for the therapist to interview significant people in the client's life to corroborate the client's view of the problem, to assess how people close to the client affect the problem, and to obtain information that the client cannot provide. The same guiding principles for interviewing the client are followed when significant others are interviewed (e.g., building rapport and asking specific detailed questions).

Self-Recording

Clients' recordings of their own behavior are one of the most convenient sources of vital information about problems. Self-recording, in contrast to observation and recording done by other people, has at least four advantages. First, clients are almost always available to observe their own behavior, whereas it is frequently inconvenient, impractical, and time consuming for other people to make the observations. Second, because the client is always present, the client is able to assess infrequently occurring behavior (e.g., seizures). Third, only clients themselves can directly assess covert behaviors. Fourth, clients' privacy is not invaded when they observe their own behavior.

Self-recording the frequency of behaviors need not require any elaborate equipment. One of the simplest procedures is for the client to make a checkmark, on an index card that is conveniently carried in a pocket, each time a target behavior occurs. When the behavior occurs very often, an inexpensive golf-counter, which the client wears like a wristwatch, can be used.[20] Specialized and more elaborate electronic and mechanical recording devices have been also developed,[21] such as a cigarette pack that records the number of cigarettes removed.[22]

Self-recording, like recording by others, varies in accuracy according to how attentive, careful, and truthful the client is. As a general procedure, the reliability of self-recording is occasionally spot-checked by outside observers.

When people record their own behavior, the frequency of the behavior may change *because* it is being recorded, a phenomena called **reactivity.**[23] Self-recording is not always reactive, and some measures tend to be more reactive than others. For instance, self-recording caloric intake may result in some weight loss, but self-recording of eating habits is not likely to be associated with any loss in weight.[24] Obviously, it may be advantageous for the target behavior to change in the desirable direction simply by measuring it, and self-monitoring as a therapy procedure is discussed in Chapter 12. On the other hand, if it is important to obtain an accurate assessment of a client's behavior before any treatment is begun (e.g., so that posttherapy comparisons can be made), which is often the case, then the self-recording should be as nonreactive as possible. When this is not possible, other methods of behavioral assessment must be employed (e.g., unobtrusive observations by others).

Participation Exercise 3-2 can help you experience what it is like for clients to self-record their behavior, including some of the inevitable problems that arise with this method of behavioral assessment. Because this participation exercise must be done over the course of several days, you will not be able to do it before continuing your reading. However, you may want to read over the participation exercise now (and carry it out in the coming week) because some of the details involved in self-recording are discussed in the instructions.

*PARTICIPATION EXERCISE 3-2**
Self-Recording of Behavior

The following steps are involved in this participation exercise:

1. Select a target behavior that you will observe and record.
2. Define the unit of behavior (e.g., number of pages read or cigarettes smoked).
3. Define the unit of time (e.g., hours, days).
4. Make a convenient recording device (e.g., a 3 x 5 index card marked off in time units). You may also want to keep brief notes on your daily activities.
5. Observe and record the target behavior.
6. Plot the frequency of responses each day.

SELECTING A TARGET BEHAVIOR

Exercise Table 3-2A contains a list of behaviors that are particularly applicable to the participation exercise, but you can select another response. The response should be relatively

*Based on Liebert & Spiegler (1982).

EXERCISE TABLE 3-2A

Examples of Target Behaviors to Observe and Record

BEHAVIOR	UNIT OF BEHAVIOR	UNIT OF TIME
Reading	Pages	Day or hour
Writing	Lines	Day or hour
Jogging	Quarter-miles	Day
Swimming	Laps in a pool	Day
Tardiness	Times late	Day
Daydreaming	Minutes spent	Day or hour
Talking on the telephone	Minutes spent	Day or hour
Swearing	Curse words	Day or hour
Studying	Minutes spent	Day
Bull sessions	Minutes spent	Day
Drinking		Day or hour
Coffee	Cups	
Beer	Ounces	
Smoking	Cigarettes	Day or hour

easy to observe and record without disrupting the behavior and without taking very much of your time. If the response is emitted at too rapid a rate (e.g., eyeblinks), it may prove difficult to record. On the other hand, it should occur with reasonable frequency in your life so that it can be observed and recorded.

OBSERVATION AND RECORDING

The next step is to observe the target behavior and keep a record of its frequency. Mark off a 3 x 5 index card in time intervals, and then simply make a checkmark each time you perform the behavior, as is shown in Exercise Figure 3-2A. At the end of each day (or other unit of time you are using), calculate the total number of marks; this becomes your rate for the day (e.g., 26 pages read per day). You should also keep brief notes about the events in your life over the course of your recording in order to help you isolate the conditions that may be maintaining the target behavior.

GRAPHING THE RESULTS OF OBSERVATION

Then plot each day's rate on a graph to facilitate inspection of the data. As illustrated in Exercise Figure 3-2B, mark off the horizontal axis of the graph in time intervals, such as days or hours. The vertical axis represents the number of responses per unit of time.

As can be seen from the graph, the person read approximately the same number of pages (i.e., between 26 and 28) for the first three days. On Thursday the number of pages nearly doubled, and it remained the same on Friday. On Saturday, the number of pages dropped to approximately the Monday-through-Wednesday rate, perhaps because of the interference of a Saturday evening social engagement. And on the seventh day no pages were read, perhaps because the person rested.

		Total Per Day
Mon.	𝍸 𝍸 𝍸 𝍸 𝍸 /	26
Tues.	𝍸 𝍸 𝍸 𝍸 𝍸 ///	28
Wed.	𝍸 𝍸 𝍸 𝍸 𝍸 ///	28
Thurs.	𝍸 𝍸 𝍸 𝍸 𝍸 𝍸 𝍸 𝍸 𝍸 𝍸 𝍸 /	56
Fri.	𝍸 𝍸 𝍸 𝍸 𝍸 𝍸 𝍸 𝍸 𝍸 𝍸 𝍸 //	57
Sat.	𝍸 𝍸 𝍸 𝍸 𝍸 𝍸	30
Sun.		0
Sat. night big date		
Sunday slept till 1:30 P.M.		

EXERCISE FIGURE 3-2A

Example of an index card record of pages read in a week

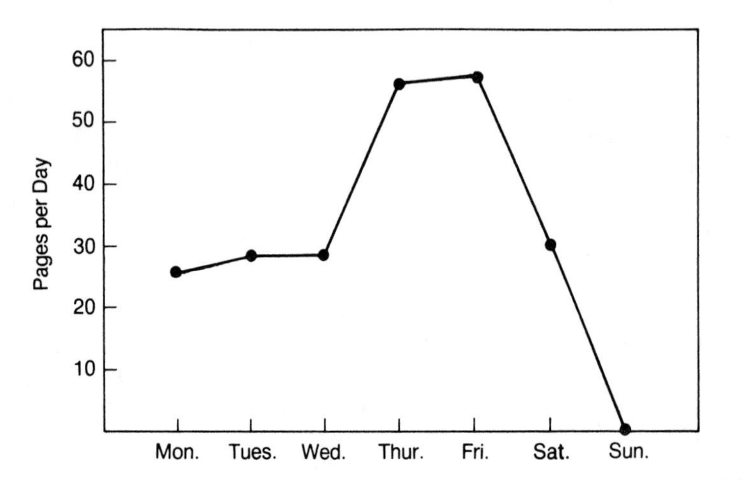

EXERCISE FIGURE 3-2B

Graph of a week's reading behavior

Direct Observation *In Vivo*

One of the best ways to assess a client's overt behavior is for another person to observe the client in the setting in which the behavior naturally occurs. The term ***in vivo*** (literally "in a life situation") refers to any procedure (assessment or therapy) that takes place in a client's natural environment. *In vivo* observation of behavior is the hallmark of behavioral assessment; it is the one procedure that is closest to being uniquely behavioral. Such observations can potentially provide the most representative and otherwise valid sample of the client's behavior. *In vivo* observations have proved very useful in a variety of settings, including private homes, schools, and psychiatric hospitals.[25]

To make *in vivo* observations of a client's behavior, it is first necessary to define the behavior that is to be observed in simple, unambiguous terms so that observers can quickly determine if the behavior has occurred or not. The following definition of "physically negative behavior," as might be seen in a classroom, meets this requirement: "A person attacks or attempts to attack another person with the possibility of inflicting pain. Examples include slapping, spanking, kicking, biting, throwing objects at someone, and so on." Note that this definition specifies the *possibility* of inflicting pain, which can be objectively determined—not the intention of inflicting pain, which an observer can never ascertain (unless the person tells the observer, "I want to hurt so-and-so").

The next step is to train observers. The observers must become very familiar with the definitions of the behavior categories they will be recording. They must also practice making observations until they can use the specific procedures with high accuracy, which is measured by comparing their observations with observations of the same behaviors made by others. When this **interobserver reliability**, or agreement among observers, is considered sufficiently high, the observers are ready to make the actual observations of the client's behaviors. Before they begin, however, the the observers may spend some time in the client's natural environment (e.g., sitting in the back of a classroom) so that the client will become accustomed to the observers being there and will be more likely to act naturally (i.e., as if the observers were not present). Finally, as with self-recording, periodic checks are made of the observers' accuracy by other independent observers.

The three most critical limitations of *in vivo* observation are *observer bias*, *reactivity*, and *impracticality*. There are many ways in which an observer may not be entirely objective in making observations.[26] For example, if the observer is interested in decreasing the frequency of a client's maladaptive target behavior, the observer may "overlook" some genuine occurrence of the behavior, or the observer may rate borderline behaviors as the absence of the target behavior. Generally, observer bias can be substantially reduced when the behaviors to be observed are narrowly defined and discrete and when the observations are made in small time samples (e.g., once every 90 seconds).

The problem of reactivity was introduced with respect to self-recording in the previous section. Similarly, clients also tend to change their behavior (usually in the desired or expected direction) when they know that they are being observed. For example, when families are observed at home, children may be less disruptive when observers are present. Such reactivity appears to decrease with time, so providing an adaptation period before actual observations are made is likely to improve the validity of the observations.[27]

In vivo observations may be impractical for a number of reasons. They are generally very costly, especially in terms of observers' time. Observers must be trained, and they must travel to and spend time in the client's natural environment. If the target behavior is performed infrequently, the observers may spend considerable time waiting for it to occur. Furthermore, for reasons of privacy or propriety, it may not be possible to make direct observations in the client's natural environment (e.g., in a client's bedroom or professional office). When these practical limitations make *in vivo* observation impractical, self-observation or role playing may be a suitable alternative.

Role Playing

As an assessment procedure, **role playing** involves a client enacting a problem situation, with the therapist and sometimes other people assuming the roles of various important people who are involved in the client's problem. (When such procedures are used to provide clients with an opportunity to practice how they will act in actual situations [i.e., as in therapy], the technique is referred to as *behavior rehearsal.*) In the case of a woman client who has difficulty talking politely to anyone who refuses her requests, she would be instructed to ask the therapist to do things and the therapist would refuse the requests. Role playing can provide the therapist with considerable information about a client's interpersonal skills (or lack of them).[28]

For role playing to be effective as an assessment procedure, the client must be able to act in role playing much as he or she does in the actual situation. This requirement means that the client must get over any uneasiness about "play-acting" and become emotionally involved in the role playing, behaving *as if* it were the real situation. In turn, the therapist must be able to realistically play the roles of critical people in the client's life. To do this, the therapist needs to have a *specific* knowledge of how these people behave (e.g., not the stereotype of "how fathers react to daughters"), which is usually gained through interviews with the client and the critical others in the client's life. Role playing has proved particularly useful in assessing social skills such as assertive behavior.[29]

Direct Self-Report Inventories

Self-report inventories are paper-and-pencil questionnaires that consist of a number of brief statements or questions to which a client responds. Many self-report inventories *indirectly* assess information about a respondent in the sense that the way the individual responds to the items is used to *infer* something about his or her personality (e.g., traits that might characterize the person). In contrast, behavioral self-report inventories *directly* inquire about a client's specific behaviors.[30] Earlier, the use of the Fear Survey Schedule to assess the degree of fear or discomfort a client experiences in various situations (e.g., while talking to members of the opposite sex or during a thunderstorm) was mentioned. Besides fear and anxiety,[31] depressive behavior[32] and assertive behavior[33] are other broad categories of behavior often assessed by direct self-report inventories (as well as other assessment procedures). For example, the Rathus Assertiveness Schedule[34] contains 30 statements that clients rate on a six-point scale to indicate the degree to which each describes their typical behavior. Two of the statements on the Rathus Assertiveness Schedule are:

> If a couple near me in the theater or at a lecture were conversing rather loudly, I would ask them to be quiet or to take their conversation elsewhere.
>
> When the food served at a restaurant is not done to my satisfaction, I complain about it to the waiter or waitress.

Direct self-report inventories can efficiently provide information about the client's behavior in a broad range of situations. However, they rarely provide the specific details required to assess the unique nature of a client's problem, and thus self-report inventories are most useful as initial screening devices or as adjuncts to other behavioral assessment procedures. Furthermore, they are subject to a variety of biases, which are less problematic with other methods of behavioral assessment such as direct observation. For instance, clients might indicate on a self-report inventory that they are more assertive in a particular situation than they actually are, either because they want their behavior to appear more acceptable (normal) than it actually is or because they overestimate the degree of assertion they actually exhibit in the particular situation.

Physiological Measurements

In addition to observation and self-report, behavioral therapists occasionally use physiological measurements,[35] such as heart rate, blood pressure, and skin resistance (galvanic skin response, typically abbreviated GSR) as typical physical responses related to fear,[36] and vaginal blood flow and penile erection as physiological indices of sexual arousal.[37] Such measurements are primarily used in behavioral therapy research and in biofeedback therapy, where the target behavior is an actual physiological response. The high cost of the elaborate instrumentation required to obtain accurate physiological measures precludes their general use in most clinics or behavioral therapists' private offices.[38]

The Relationship Among Behavioral Assessment Procedures

Behavioral assessment procedures tap three different modes of behavior: overt behavior, self-report, and physiological reactions. Unfortunately, measurements of these three modes of behavior may not be highly correlated.[39] For example, it is not uncommon to find a client who claims to be very upset or anxious while performing a particular overt behavior but is still able to perform the required actions flawlessly (e.g., the speaker who appears perfectly relaxed to the audience but reports feeling stage fright). Moreover, no one of the three basic assessment modes is more valid than any other. However, one is likely to be more relevant in an individual case, depending on the nature of the problem.[40] For example, if the client's primary complaint is feeling nervous while speaking in public, then self-report assessment takes precedence over observations of speaking behavior and physiological measurement of heart rate, sweating, and so on. If the client's problem involves inadequate performance as a speaker, however, then observation of overt behavior is more important.

SUMMARY

Behavioral therapy deals with specific, well-defined target behaviors, which may be acceleration target behaviors (behaviors to be increased) or deceleration target behaviors (behaviors to be decreased). Although it is possible to directly decelerate a target behavior, behavioral therapy usually accelerates an incompatible target behavior simultaneously. Behavioral therapy directly treats the maintaining conditions of target behaviors.

Behavioral therapy is a scientific endeavor: it emphasizes precision and objectivity and empirically validates procedures through scientific investigations. In fact, the procedures of behavioral therapy closely parallel those of a scientific experiment.

Much behavioral therapy takes place in clients' home environments; sometimes the therapist is present but more often significant others assist clients with the therapy or clients act as their own therapeutic agents. Clients in behavioral therapy play an active role in their therapy; for example, engaging in specific homework tasks.

The assessment procedures used for behaviors and their maintaining conditions are an essential part of behavioral therapy. Behavioral assessment is individualized, proceeds by sampling relevant behaviors, is limited in its scope, and is present-oriented. Five frequently used behavioral assessment procedures are interviews, self-recordings, direct observations by others, role playing, and physiological measurements. Each of these methods has its uses, depending on the nature of the target behavior and practical considerations.

REFERENCE NOTES

1. Bergin & Lambert, 1978.
2. Goldfried & Kent, 1972; Goldfried & Sprafkin, 1974.
3. For example, Franks & Wilson, 1973–1979.
4. Borkovec & Rachman, 1979.
5. Lazarus & Davison, 1971; see also Paul, 1969a.
6. Kazdin & Wilson, 1978; Rachman & Wilson, 1980.
7. For example, Goldfried & Merbaum, 1973; Mahoney & Thoresen, 1974.

8. Liebert & Spiegler, 1982.
9. Goldfried & Kent, 1972.
10. Goldfried & Sprafkin, 1974.
11. Wahler, Winkel, Peterson, & Morrison, 1965.
12. Goldfried & Sprafkin, 1974.
13. Mischel, 1968.
14. Wolpe & Lazarus, 1966.
15. Liebert & Spiegler, 1978.
16. Swan & MacDonald, 1978.
17. Morganstern, 1976.
18. Marquis, 1973; Peterson, 1968; Rimm & Masters, 1974.
19. Goldfried & Davison, 1976.
20. Lindsley, 1968.
21. Schwitzgebel, 1968; Schwitzgebel & Schwitzgebel, 1973.
22. Azrin & Powell, 1968.
23. Johnson & Bolstad, 1973.
24. Green, 1978.
25. Kent & Foster, 1977; Paul & Lentz, 1977.
26. Kent & Foster, 1977; Rosenthal, 1969.
27. For example, Dubey, Kent, O'Leary, Broderick, & O'Leary, 1977; Hagen, Craighead, & Paul, 1975; Mercatoris & Craighead, 1974; Nelson, Kapust, & Dorsey, 1978.
28. For example, Arkowitz, Lichtenstein, McGovern, & Hines, 1975; Eisler, Hersen, Miller, & Blanchard, 1975.
29. For example, Eisler, Hersen, Miller, & Blanchard, 1975; McFall & Marston, 1970; Prince, 1975.
30. Liebert & Spiegler, 1982.
31. For example, Geer, 1965; Watson & Friend, 1969.
32. For example, Beck, 1972; Beck, Ward, Mendelson, Mock, & Erbaugh, 1961; Lewinsohn & Graf, 1973; Lewinsohn & Libet, 1972; Lubin, 1967.
33. For example, Galassi, DeLo, Galassi, & Bastien, 1974; Gambrill & Richey, 1975; Rathus, 1973.
34. Rathus, 1973.
35. Epstein, 1976.
36. Lick & Katkin, 1976.
37. Schumacher & Lloyd, 1976.
38. Epstein, 1976; Lang, 1971.
39. For example, Lang, 1977.
40. For example, Barlow, 1977.

CHAPTER

4 Substitution Behavioral Therapies: Systematic Desensitization and Related Therapies

The first major category of behavioral therapies described in this book is called *substitution therapies*, because they directly substitute an adaptive behavior or reaction for a maladaptive behavior or reaction. This chapter examines by far the most frequently used substitution therapy: systematic desensitization, developed by Wolpe[1] to treat problem behaviors maintained by anxiety. Systematic desensitization essentially replaces a negative reaction (e.g., anxiety or disgust) to a particular class of situations with a positive reaction (e.g., relaxation, calm, or control). This chapter also briefly describes flooding and implosive therapy, which treat anxiety-related problems in a somewhat different manner. The next chapter discusses behavioral therapies that substitute negative responses for pleasurable but maladaptive behaviors such as drug addiction or deviant sexual behaviors.

One of the most common problems for which people seek therapy involves unrealistic and exaggerated negative reactions to objectively neutral, or even positive, situations or objects. The negative emotional reactions can be anxiety, fear, tension, disgust, and loss of control as well as other unpleasant feelings. However, anxiety or fear is most common, and these two emotional reactions will be emphasized in this chapter. The most typical overt behavior associated with anxiety and fear is *avoiding* the events that result in the unpleasant feelings. Examples include a straight-"A" student who feels anxious when taking tests, a person who fears crossing the street so badly that she will not venture from her apartment, a man who is "turned off" by women and thus cannot form heterosexual relationships, and a woman who avoids going to a physician because she fears that she will be told that she has cancer. Systematic desensitization is the most frequently used behavioral therapy for overcoming such anxiety or fear reactions.

SYSTEMATIC DESENSITIZATION

In **systematic desensitization**, the client is gradually (*systematically*) exposed to successively more anxiety-arousing situations while engaged in adaptive behavior that is incompatible with anxiety. The client learns to react, with an adaptive response other than anxiety, to a situation that previously evoked anxiety. The client thus becomes less sensitive, or *desensitized*, to the situation.

Systematic desensitization is an appropriate treatment for anxiety reactions that are (1) basically unrealistic and (2) are not the result of not knowing how to behave in an anxiety-arousing situation. Certain fears are realistic and adaptive, such as the fear of walking alone at night in high-crime neighborhoods. However, it is both unrealistic and maladaptive to be afraid of leaving one's home when the conditions are reasonably safe. A person who lacks the requisite skills to behave appropriately in the situations that evoke anxiety must first learn and practice the necessary behaviors. For example, people who do not possess the social skills needed to interact with members of the opposite sex (e.g., making casual conversation) must learn them before any treatment, such as systematic desensitization, designed to reduce anxiety would bring about the desired change—that is, to feel comfortable interacting with members of the opposite sex.

Systematic desensitization involves three sets of operations. First, the client is taught a response that is incompatible with anxiety. Second, specific details of the client's anxiety or other negative emotional reaction are assessed and an anxiety hierarchy is constructed. Once these preliminary procedures have been completed, the actual systematic desensitization is implemented. This process involves the repeated pairing of (1) the response that is incompatible with anxiety and (2) the anxiety-evoking events.

Substitute Responses for Anxiety

A variety of responses have been taught to clients as substitute ways of reacting to events that typically evoke anxiety. These substitutes include relaxation, sexual arousal, assertive behavior, anger, eating, humor, and pleasant thoughts. By far the most frequently employed substitute response is *deep muscle relaxation.*[2] The physiological concomitants of anxiety, such as increased heart rate, breathing, and shaking, are for the most part incompatible with deep muscle relaxation. People usually do not report being both nervous and relaxed at the same time.

Training in deep muscle relaxation proceeds in a systematic fashion, covering each of the various skeletal muscle groups—arms, face, neck, shoulders, chest, abdomen, and legs. Clients learn to differentiate between muscular relaxation and tension by first tensing and then relaxing each set of muscles. Later in training, clients work on creating deeper and deeper states of relaxation in their muscles without first tensing them. Clients usually sit in a comfortable armchair, such as a recliner, close their eyes, and follow the therapist's relaxation instructions. The following excerpt gives an idea of what these relaxation instructions are like:

> Close your eyes, settle back comfortably, and we'll begin. Let's start with your right hand. I want you to clench your right hand into a fist, clench it very tightly and study those tensions, hold it . . . (5-second pause) and now relax. Relax your right hand and let it rest comfortably. Just let it relax . . . (15-second pause). Once again now, clench your right hand . . . clench it very tightly, study those tensions . . . (5-second pause) and now relax. Relax your hand and once again note the very pleasant contrast between tension and relaxation.

The number of sessions needed to teach deep muscle relaxation varies from individual to individual, but usually less than six sessions are required if the client practices the technique at home in between sessions. (Participation Exercise 12-1 provides instructions for learning deep muscle relaxation on your own.)

Constructing an Anxiety Hierarchy

An **anxiety hierarchy** is a list of events that elicit anxiety, ranked in terms of increasing amounts of anxiety. The hierarchy starts with an event that evokes very little anxiety and ends with one that is extremely anxiety provoking for the client.

To construct an anxiety hierarchy, a detailed and highly specific accounting is made of those events that elicit anxiety. Sometimes a person will come to a therapist with a well-defined fear of a particular class of events, such as fear of driving or of going to the dentist. More often, however, people feel anxious at various times but are not aware of the conditions that precipitate the feeling. It is the therapist's task to discover, by detailed questioning, the situations that elicit anxiety. To facilitate this process, therapists may use a list of situations and objects that frequently make people anxious. Clients indicate the degree of discomfort they feel for each item. A portion of one **fear survey schedule,** the name typically given to these self-report inventories,[3] appears in Table 4-1.

When the stimuli that elicit anxiety have been listed, the therapist helps the client order them according to the degree of anxiety each evokes. Clients are frequently asked to rate each anxiety-evoking event using the **Subjective Units of Disturbance scale.** The units of this scale are called **SUDs** and range from 0 to 100, with 0 representing total relaxation and 100 representing the highest level of anxiety the client can imagine.[4] As the word *subjective* implies, SUDs are specific to each individual, and it is not possible to compare individuals' SUDs ratings. In other words, no assumptions are made that people who rate a situation at the same SUDs level are experiencing equivalent degrees or qualities of discomfort. For the particular person, however, it is possible to get rough estimates of the individual's states of discomfort in various situations and at different times.

The anxiety-provoking stimuli are often, but not always, categorized in terms of common themes before they are put in hierarchical order. For instance, fear of speaking in public and fear of being interviewed share a common theme of "evaluation of one's performance." If a client is anxious about several different situations, as is often the case, multiple anxiety hierarchies are

TABLE 4-1 *A Portion of a Fear Survey Schedule*

Instructions: The items in this questionnaire are objects, experiences, or ideas that may cause fear, anxiety, or other unpleasant feelings. Using the scale below, write the appropriate number after each item to describe the degree to which the item causes you to feel fear, anxiety, or other unpleasant feelings.

1 = Not at all
2 = A little
3 = A moderate amount
4 = Much
5 = Very much

1. Open wounds	25. Blood
2. Being alone	26. Enclosed places
3. Speaking in public	27. Flying in airplanes
4. Falling	28. Darkness
5. Automobiles	29. Lightning
6. Being teased	30. Doctors
7. Dentists	31. Losing control
8. Thunder	32. Making mistakes
9. Failure	33. Older people
10. High places	34. Going blind
11. Receiving injections	35. Drowning
12. Strangers	36. Examinations
13. Feeling angry	37. Cancer
14. Insects	38. Fog
15. Sudden noises	39. Being lost
16. Crowds	40. Police
17. Large open spaces	41. Talking on the telephone
18. Cats	42. Death of a loved one
19. Being watched while working	43. Pain
20. Dirt	44. Suicide
21. Dogs	45. War
22. Sick people	46. Going insane
23. Fire	47. Violence
24. Mice	48. Psychologists

SOURCE: Developed by Spiegler & Liebert (1970).

constructed and used in systematic desensitization. Examples of three anxiety hierarchies are found in Table 4-2. The items in the hierarchy are listed with the most anxiety-evoking one at the top and the least anxiety-evoking one at the bottom. The client's SUDs rating for each item is also given.

The items appearing in the hierarchies in Table 4-2 contain only the bare outline of each *scene* that will be used in the desensitization process. The client must provide the therapist with sufficient details so that the therapist is able to describe each scene in specific and idiosyncratic terms to enable the client to

TABLE 4-2 *Examples of Anxiety Hierarchies*

ITEM	SUDs
Dating	
10. Initially greeting date	95
9. Saying goodnight	85
8. Being on the date	75
7. Driving to pick up date	65
6. Getting ready to go on date	55
5. Calling someone for date	45
4. Asking for potential date's telephone number	35
3. Talking to potential date in class	30
2. Meeting an attractive member of the opposite sex	20
1. Thinking about going on date next weekend	10
Death	
19. Death of a close friend or loved one	100
18. Death of strangers in a dramatic fashion	85
17. Watching horror movies	80
16. Seeing others in dangerous situations	75
15. Hearing about a fatal and especially gruesome disease	70
14. Being around guns	60
13. Swimming in the ocean at night	55
12. Riding as a passenger in a car on the highway	50
11. Flying in an airplane	48
10. Driving a car on the highway	45
9. Thoughts of fire	43
8. Climbing on high objects	40
7. Being alone in a house at night	38
6. Thinking about auto crashes	35
5. Thoughts of earthquakes	25
4. Thinking of witches and ghosts	20
3. Swimming in a pool at night	15
2. Seeing a snake	10
1. Hearing a siren	5
Flying	
20. Plane is flying in rough weather	100
19. Plane touching down on runway	95
18. Pilot turns on seatbelt sign and announces turbulence ahead	90
17. Plane is banking toward your side of the plane	85
16. Plane is descending for landing	80
15. Announcement of preparation for final descent and landing	75
14. Plane is taking off	65

(Continued)

TABLE 4-2 *(Continued)*

	ITEM	SUDs
13.	Plane is taxiing to the runway	60
12.	Plane is climbing to cruising altitude	55
11.	Plane is cruising in good weather	50
10.	Sitting down and fastening seatbelt	45
9.	Announcement that the plane is ready for boarding	40
8.	Boarding the plane	35
7.	Waiting to be boarded	30
6.	Checking in at the airport	25
5.	Driving to the airport	22
4.	Calling the airport to find out if the flight is on time	20
3.	Packing for the trip	15
2.	Purchasing ticket 10 days before flight	10
1.	Making reservations 3 weeks before flight	5

vividly imagine him- or herself in the situation during desensitization. For example, the top item in the dating hierarchy in Table 4-2, "Initially greeting date," might be expanded in the following way: "You arrive at your date's apartment, knock on the door, and your date opens the door, smiles, and says, 'Hi!' "

The rank order of anxiety-evoking situations is a highly individual matter. As is apparent from the hierarchies in Table 4-2, the scenes might be ranked differently by another person. Constructing anxiety hierarchies is usually done concurrently with relaxation training.

The Desensitization Process

Relaxation training and construction of appropriate anxiety hierarchies are prerequisites for the actual procedure of desensitizing the events associated with anxiety. In the desensitization procedure, the client is instructed to relax his or her muscles and then to *imagine* scenes from the anxiety hierarchy, starting with the least anxiety-provoking situation (i.e., the lowest item on each anxiety hierarchy). Most people have the capacity to vividly imagine themselves in a situation and to experience many of the same emotional responses that they would feel if they were actually in the situation. (To help the client imagine scenes clearly, practice sessions in imagining scenes are sometimes employed before the desensitization process begins.[5]) Imagining an aversive situation during systematic desensitization can serve as a practical alternative to actually being in the situation, which is one way of simulating in the therapist's office the conditions under which a problem behavior naturally occurs.

Each scene is imagined for a few seconds at a time. The client is instructed to signal the therapist (usually by raising a finger) whenever any anxiety is felt, at which point the therapist immediately tells the client to stop visualizing the scene and to just concentrate on relaxing and experiencing the pleasant sensations that come from deep muscle relaxation. Thus, the client visualizes scenes from the anxiety hierarchy only when he or she is relaxing or engaging in another behavior that is incompatible with experiencing anxiety. The objective is for relaxation to replace the tension usually associated with the scene. Each scene is repeated until the client reports experiencing virtually no discomfort while visualizing it. Then the next highest scene in the hierarchy is visualized. To illustrate the desensitization procedure, a verbatim account of the presentation of scenes during an initial desensitization session is presented in Case 4-1.

CASE 4-1

*Excerpt from a Session of Systematic Desensitization**

A 24-year-old female art student requested treatment of examination anxiety, which had caused her to fail a number of tests. When she discussed her anxiety with the therapist, it was discovered that other situations also made her anxious. Thus, four different anxiety hierarchies were constructed; the themes of the hierarchies were "taking examinations," "discord between other people," "being scrutinized by others," and "being devalued by others."

After the client was placed in a state of deep muscle relaxation by following the therapist's relaxation instructions, the therapist proceeded with the first session of desensitization. Note that the client was first asked to visualize a neutral scene, one that was not expected to elicit any anxiety, so that the therapist could be sure that the client was totally relaxed.

> I am now going to ask you to imagine a number of scenes. You will imagine them clearly and they will generally interfere little, if at all, with your state of relaxation. If, however, at any time you feel disturbed or worried and want to attract my attention, you will be able to do so by raising your left index finger. First I want you to imagine that you are standing at a familiar streetcorner on a pleasant morning watching the traffic go by. You see cars, motorcycles, trucks, bicycles, people and traffic lights; and you can hear the sounds associated with all these things. *(Pause of about 15 sec.)* Now stop imagining that scene and give all your attention once again to relaxing. If the scene you imagined disturbed you even in the slightest degree, I want you to raise your left index finger *now. (Patient does not raise finger.)* Now imagine that you are at home studying in the evening. It is the twentieth of May, exactly a month before your examination. *(Pause of 5 sec.)* Now stop imagining the scene. Go on relaxing. *(Pause of 10 sec.)* Now imagine the same scene again—a month before your examination. *(Pause of 5 sec.)* Stop imagining the scene and just think of your muscles.

*Wolpe & Lazarus (1966). Quotation is from p. 81.

Let go, and enjoy your state of calm. *(Pause of 15 sec.)* Now again imagine that you are studying at home a month before your examination. *(Pause of 5 sec.)* Stop the scene, and now think of nothing but your own body. *(Pause of 5 sec.)* If you felt any disturbance whatsoever to the last scene, raise your left index finger now. *(Patient raises finger.)* If the amount of disturbance decreased from the first presentation to the third, do nothing; otherwise, again raise your finger. *(Patient does not raise finger.)* Just keep on relaxing. *(Pause of 15 sec.)* Imagine that you are sitting on a bench at a bus stop and across the road are two strange men whose voices are raised in argument. *(Pause of 10 sec.)* Stop imagining the scene and just relax. *(Pause of 10 sec.)* Now again imagine the scene of these two men arguing across the road. *(Pause of 10 sec.)* Stop the scene and relax. Now I am going to count up to 5, and you will open your eyes, feeling very calm and refreshed.

A total of 17 desensitization sessions were required for the client to report no anxiety while visualizing the highest scene on each anxiety hierarchy. Most importantly, the anxiety reduction transferred from the imagined scenes to the actual situations, so that the client was able to successfully take and pass her examinations.

The procedure of gradually exposing the client to increasingly more anxiety-evoking situations is an example of the general principle of *step-wise progression* that is used in many forms of behavioral therapy (i.e., "not going too far too fast"). Dealing with one or two relatively circumscribed target behaviors is an application of this principle. Another example of the principle was the step-wise fashion in which Paul's therapists shaped his school attendance (Case 3-1). As can be seen in Figure 3-1 (p. 43), the components of the target behavior (normal school attendance) form a hierarchy. The least anxiety-provoking and/or easiest tasks were practiced before more upsetting and more difficult tasks were attempted.

Group Systematic Desensitization

The procedures just described for systematic desensitization are for individual clients, but systematic desensitization can also be done with groups of clients, with a few minor procedural changes.[6] The obvious advantage of group systematic desensitization is that more clients can be treated by a single therapist. Other benefits include those typically found in any type of group therapy, such as sharing of similar problems and solutions among clients.

In group systematic desensitization, deep muscle relaxation is simultaneously taught to the entire group. If the clients share some common problem(s), then it is possible to construct *group hierarchies* by compiling information about the situations that evoke anxiety in each client and the degree of discomfort created.[7] During desensitization, the therapist verbally presents the scenes in the same manner as with an individual client except that the therapist must proceed up the hierarchy at the pace of the "slowest" group member.[8] In other words, if one or more clients signal anxiety for a given scene, all the group members are asked to visualize the scene again. Although this procedure may be inefficient for some "fast" group members, it does not decrease the effectiveness of the treatment and, in fact, may be beneficial because the repetition reinforces the effect. Individual anxiety hierarchies can also be used in group systematic desensitization, as is necessary if a group hierarchy cannot be constructed. In this case, clients are visualizing different scenes each time the therapist instructs the group to imagine a scene. The hierarchy items can be written on cards for each client so that clients can refer to their individual items during desensitization.

Systematic Desensitization as a General Treatment Model

Systematic desensitization is most frequently used to reduce anxiety by substituting a more adaptive emotional reaction (usually relaxation) for it. Systematic desensitization as a general model of treatment—substituting a positive emotional reaction for a negative emotional reaction—is applicable to a variety of target behaviors including anger,[9] asthmatic attacks,[10] insomnia,[11] motion sickness,[12] nightmares,[13] problem drinking,[14] sleepwalking,[15] speech disorders,[16] and even racial prejudice.[17] With many of these target behaviors and for a majority of clients, relaxation is often a suitable substitute behavior, but in some instances other substitute behaviors are more appropriate. Children, for example, may not easily learn deep muscle relaxation, so thoughts of pleasant experiences may be used as the substitute response. This procedure, called **emotive imagery**,[18] was used as part of the treatment of Paul's school-phobic behavior in Case 3-1.

Case 4-2 illustrates the use of systematic desensitization to anger, substituting humor as an emotional reaction. As with anxiety and relaxation, common sense dictates that one usually cannot laugh or otherwise appreciate humor and be angry at the same time.

CASE 4-2

*Substituting Humor for Anger Through Systematic Desensitization**

The patient was a 22-year-old female who referred herself for treatment because of a reported lack of ability to control extreme anger responses within her relationships with her husband and with her 3-year-old son. The latter was described as a very active child whose almost constant misbehavior appeared to be attempts to antagonize his mother and gain her attention. Behavioral observations of the mother interacting with her child supported her description of the situation. The patient reported that she generally reacted to the child's misbehavior with extreme rage responses which consisted of screaming at the top of her voice, jumping up and down, smashing things, and physically attacking her child. She described her rage responses as so "automatic" as to be beyond her control. Her relationship

*Reprinted from Smith (1973), pp. 577–578.

with her husband was also marked by interpersonal strife. The patient reported that when she became angry with her husband she screamed at and berated him, and he occasionally became the target of thrown objects and physical assaults. Acquaintances and relatives attributed [her] family problems to a "violent temper" which had been a disruptive factor in her relationships since childhood. At the time she referred herself for treatment, the patient reported that she had been contemplating suicide because "my temper makes everyone, including me, miserable."

In the initial phase of treatment, standard systematic desensitization procedures were employed. The patient was trained in deep muscular relaxation, and two 10-item hierarchies of anger-inducing scenes were constructed, one primarily involving interactions with her son, the other with her husband. In the treatment sessions, a deep state of relaxation was induced and the patient was instructed to imagine the anger-evoking scenes and to signal the therapist if a scene resulted in anger arousal. In addition, the patient's GSRs [galvanic skin responses] were monitored by means of a portable Keeler polygraph.

After seven sessions of desensitization with relaxation, negligible progress had been made. The strength and explosive quality of the patient's anger responses rendered her incapable of imagining any but the most innocuous scenes involving her husband or son without experiencing anger. The lack of success with relaxation resulted in the search for another potential competing response. On the basis of empirical evidence that humor can have anger-reducing properties . . . each item in the hierarchies was embellished with as much humorous content as possible. The insertion of humorous content into the items generally took the form of what might best be termed slapstick comedy. For example, an item concerned with her son's engaging in mischievous behavior while the patient is driving was presented in the following form:

> As you're driving to the supermarket, little Pascal the Rascal begins to get restless. Suddenly he drops from his position on the ceiling and trampolines off the rear seat onto the rear view mirror. From this precarious position, he amuses himself by flashing obscene hand gestures at shocked pedestrians. As you begin to turn into the supermarket parking lot, Pascal alights from his perch and lands with both feet on the accelerator. As the car careens through the parking lot, you hear Pascal observe, "Hmm, . . . 25–80 in 2 sec. . . . not bad." But right now your main concern is the two elderly and matronly women that you're bearing down upon. You can see them very clearly, limping toward the door of the supermarket clutching their little bargain coupons. One, who is clutching a prayer book in her other hand, turns and, upon seeing your car approaching at 70 mph, utters a string of profanities, throws her coupons into the air, and lays a strip of Neolite as she sprints out of the way and does a swan dive into a nearby open manhole. The other, moving equally as fast, nimbly eludes your car and takes refuge in a nearby shopping cart, which picks up speed as it rolls downhill across the parking lot with Robert Ironside in hot pursuit.

As in the relaxation phase, the patient was asked to signal the therapist if a scene evoked anger. The treatment strategy called for the therapist to focus on and emphasize some humorous aspect of the situation being described on such occasions.

Whereas no visible progress was achieved during the relaxation phase of treatment, the introduction of humor proved to be highly effective. During the first humor session, it was possible to present all of the scenes in both hierarchies without the patient's experiencing anger. During the eight treatment sessions which followed, she generally reacted to the scenes with laughter and amusement, and seldom reported anger arousal. As treatment continued, she began to report major reductions in the frequency and intensity of her anger responses in her interactions with her son and husband. After three sessions, she reported that relatives had noted a marked improvement in her "temper."... Behavioral observations of playroom interactions before and after treatment were consistent with the patient's reports of positive changes in her response to noxious behaviors on [her son's] part. She likewise reported that her anger responses to her husband had markedly decreased and that she was able to remain calm in the face of situations which had previously infuriated her. The patient stated that her depressive episodes and suicidal ideation had ceased.

Laughter has also been used as an incompatible response to anxiety and has the advantage over deep muscle relaxation that it does not have to be learned by the client. This advantage made it possible, for example, to provide brief "emergency" therapy for a 20-year-old woman who requested a special appointment with a behavioral therapist because she was distressed about having to attend a banquet that same evening, at which she feared that she might be embarrassed by her former male friend and his new woman friend.[19] The client and the therapist constructed an anxiety hierarchy of potential humiliating situations that might arise at the banquet. The scenes were presented to the woman with details to elicit laughter. For example, in describing the hierarchy scene in which the woman pictures herself sitting at the banquet and seeing her old male friend enter the room, the therapist added that the friend was dressed in leotards. The woman found the scenes humorous, was able to complete the hierarchy, and attended the banquet that evening with only minor discomfort.

In Vivo Systematic Desensitization

***In vivo* systematic desensitization**[20] involves a client actually engaging in increasingly more anxiety-evoking behaviors while simultaneously engaging in behavior that is incompatible with anxiety. Before describing how this variant of systematic desensitization works, it would be useful to briefly contrast the advantages and limitations of systematic desensitization in imagination and *in vivo.*

Imagining an anxiety-evoking situation has several advantages over actually being in the situation. First, consistent with the general principle of gradually exposing the client to threatening events, imagining scenes usually produces less anxiety than actually being in the situation. Second, it is possible to visualize scenes that would be impractical or even impossible to reproduce in therapy—for example, being in an earthquake or contracting a fatal disease.

A more common example was seen in Case 4-2; it could have been dangerous for the woman to physically assault or hurl objects at her son or husband. A third advantage of systematic desensitization in imagination is a great savings in time for both client and therapist.

However, systematic desensitization in imagination does have some problems. First, some people have difficulty clearly visualizing scenes. Second, the therapist must rely exclusively on the client's self-report concerning the content and vividness of what he or she is imagining, and in some cases this self-report may not be accurate. For example, clients are sometimes reluctant to tell the therapists when they are not "getting into" a scene because clearly visualizing the scene is too disturbing for them. A third limitation of imaginal systematic desensitization concerns the transfer of effect from the imagined scene to the real-life situation. Although at least some transfer usually occurs, some effect is always lost because the imagined and real-life scenes are similar but not equivalent. Thinking about a visit to the dentist may be distressing, but it is not likely to be as disturbing as being in the dentist's chair! Thus, in terms of the rapidity with which negative reactions to a situation can be desensitized, imaginal desensitization is apt to be slower than *in vivo* desensitization.

The most frequently used incompatible behavior for *in vivo* systematic desensitization of anxiety reactions is muscle relaxation. However, because the client is using a variety of muscles to perform the anxiety-evoking behaviors, obviously the client cannot be asked to relax completely. It is possible, though, to relax all muscles that are not essential to the behaviors performed. This procedure is called **differential relaxation.**[21] For example, if a client were standing in a crowded elevator, the client would have to have some tension in the muscles that support the body (e.g., neck, back, and leg muscles). But the client's facial, arm, chest, and abdominal muscles need not be tensed. Furthermore, even the muscles essential to the ongoing behavior need not be contracted (tensed) any more than is necessary to perform their function.

Anxiety hierarchies for *in vivo* desensitization are constructed in the same way as for imaginal desensitization. In the desensitization phase, the client and the therapist venture into the problem situations. Before actually encountering an anxiety-evoking situation, the client uses differential relaxation to create an overall calm and relaxed feeling. Then the client, in the presence of the therapist, goes through as many items in the hierarchy as he or she feels comfortable doing. The client determines how far up the hierarchy to proceed in each *in vivo* session and terminates the session when he or she is too uncomfortable to continue.

In vivo systematic desensitization may also involve the use of behaviors other than differential relaxation as substitutes for anxiety. Recall that part of the treatment of Paul's truancy (Case 3-1) was essentially an *in vivo* desensitization procedure in which Paul's anxiety while walking to school with the therapist was allayed with such incompatible behaviors as humor and pleasant images (e.g., being at Disneyland).

The general procedure of *in vivo* systematic desensitization using differential relaxation is illustrated in Case 4-3.

CASE 4-3*

Treatment of Fear of Leaving the Hospital Grounds by In Vivo *Systematic Desensitization**

A 36-year-old male psychiatric patient who had been hospitalized for seven years was intensely afraid of venturing outside the hospital. "Spending increasing amounts of time outside the hospital" was established as the acceleration target behavior for the patient, and the first phase of the therapy involved *in vivo* systematic desensitization.

> After several relaxation sessions in the office, the relaxation sessions were continued while the patient was seated in an automobile. Each week the automobile was driven by the therapist closer to the gate of the hospital grounds, and then farther and farther away from the hospital, until a five-mile drive took place during the third session in the car. During each trip outside the hospital, the patient was let out of the car for increasing lengths of time, going from one minute to a half-hour in three weeks. Concomitant with therapy sessions outside the hospital grounds, the patient was encouraged to go on trips with other patients. By the seventh week, the patient had been to a country fair in the neighboring state, an art show across the river, a local fireman's carnival, and a fishing trip. The art show was the only trip on which the therapist accompanied the patient, and even then, he was alone for half the two-hour show. After the seventh session it was no longer necessary to encourage the patient to go out on day passes, since he signed up for passes and outside activities on his own. At the end of seven *in vivo* desensitization sessions, the patient felt comfortable enough to venture outside the hospital without the support of the therapist [or other patients]. At this point it was possible to use other forms of behavioral therapy to increase and maintain the patient's activities in the community.

Specifically, the patient was taught social skills through behavior rehearsal, and he reinforced himself for practicing them at home by engaging in activities that he did only after he had performed some socially appropriate behaviors.

Because *in vivo* desensitization takes place directly in the client's everyday environment, clients can often carry out the desensitization on their own, following the therapist's instructions and with the regular consultation of the therapist regarding progress and problems. A word of caution about clients carrying out *in vivo* systematic desensitization on their own is in order. There is a danger that clients will attempt to perform hierarchy items beyond their present capabilities. The result can be a setback in therapy: the client may become very anxious not only about the attempted anxiety hierarchy item but also about other items in the hierarchy that have already been desensitized. In short, it is critical that a client does not proceed up a hierarchy to the next item before feeling very comfortable with the preceding item. Furthermore, sometimes the jump from one hierarchy item to the next is more than the client can handle, in which case intermediate items would be introduced. All these poten-

*Weidner (1970). Quotation is from p. 80.

tial problems are generally taken care of when clients perform the *in vivo* desensitization under direct therapist supervision.

Client-implemented *in vivo* desensitization is particularly conducive to treating sexual dysfunctions, such as impotence and frigidity, and is an important aspect of Masters and Johnson's well-known treatment procedures.[22] *In vivo* desensitization uses sexual arousal (which, interestingly, is the very response that the individual is having difficulty making) as a substitute for the debilitating anxiety that is often a critical maintaining condition of the client's sexual dysfunction. (Pairs of clients are usually treated for sexual dysfunctions. Optimally the client will have a sexual partner who is willing to cooperate in the therapy in order for the client to overcome the sexual problems. For clients who do not have sexual partners, "surrogate partners" have occasionally been employed.[23] Furthermore, in all cases where there is a primary sexual partner [e.g., a spouse] the sexual problem is assumed to involve an *interaction* between the two parties, rather than to be the "fault" of one of them.[24]) Basically, the *in vivo* desensitization treatment requires that the clients engage in intimate physical contact only to the point where they begin to experience anxiety. The physical contact evokes some sexual response, and while experiencing it the clients proceed up an anxiety hierarchy, stopping when anxiety begins and sexual arousal starts to diminish. After both clients feel perfectly comfortable engaging in a particular behavior, the next behavior in the hierarchy is attempted. The anxiety hierarchy consists of increasingly more anxiety-producing sexual behaviors. For example, at the bottom of the hierarchy might be "sustained lip kissing," and at the top of the hierarchy might be "sexual intercourse to orgasm."

Clients are also instructed to follow the rule that pleasurable physical contact, rather than sexual performance, is the goal of each *in vivo* desensitization session.[25] Partners are not to demand of themselves or of the other partner that any particular sexual behavior to be engaged in. For example, intercourse and orgasms are never goals of a therapy session. In such a *nondemand situation*, clients are able to learn to enjoy sexual activity by gradually coming to feel comfortable and sexually aroused with each other instead of experiencing anxiety and negative self-evaluations.

Sexual arousal can also be used as an incompatible response to other forms of anxiety, as is illustrated in the case of the college professor who successfully used *in vivo* systematic desensitization to overcome his fear of flying in airplanes.[26] By sitting in an aisle seat, the professor was able to direct his attention to one of the airline stewardesses whenever he began to experience fear. The mild sexual arousal he experienced by watching the stewardess, coupled with sexual fantasies about her, eventually became a substitute reaction for his fear of flying.*

A final example of the versatility of *in vivo* systematic desensitization is provided by Case 4-4.

*The author is grateful to Carol Smith for reminding him of the possible sexist nature of this example. However, because it is a novel application of *in vivo* desensitization, it is worth noting.

CASE 4-4

Client-Administered In Vivo *Systematic Desensitization for Fear of Dogs**

A man sought the help of a behavioral therapist to deal with his intense fear of dogs. Between the first and second therapy sessions, a fortunate incident occurred. A friend told the client that his dog had just had puppies, and he jokingly asked the client if he wanted one of them. In consultation with his therapist, the client decided to take one of the puppies. The man believed that he could tolerate a baby dog in his home (i.e., that situation would be low on his anxiety hierarchy). The situation contained all the essential ingredients for *in vivo* desensitization. The client would be gradually exposed to a dog of increasing size as the puppy grew. Moreover, his exposure to the dog would be in the context of happy interactions involving his children, and this pleasure would serve as a substitute for his anxiety about dogs. After six months of raising the puppy in his home, the client reported no more fear of dogs.

Evaluation of Systematic Desensitization

Systematic desensitization has been the most frequently used behavioral therapy for problem behaviors that are maintained primarily by excessive anxiety or fear. The general model of treatment provided by systematic desensitization is also useful for treating a variety of problems that are maintained by other negative and maladaptive emotional reactions, such as anger. Clients generally consider systematic desensitization a very "acceptable" form of treatment, perhaps because it is "painless": clients are exposed to situations that evoke unpleasant emotional reactions only to the degree to which they feel comfortable. This factor explains why systematic desensitization is a widely applicable and often used treatment procedure.

Systematic desensitization should not be considered a general panacea, or "cure-all." If the initial assessment of the target behavior indicates that the maintaining conditions are not negative emotional reactions, then systematic desensitization would not be the appropriate treatment. In many cases in which a person experiences anxiety or fear concerning a particular situation, these emotions and the person's concomitant overt maladaptive behaviors are maintained by a skill deficit—that is, not knowing how to properly behave in the situation. Dating anxiety, for example, is often maintained primarily by ignorance of how to act appropriately in a dating situation. In such cases, anxiety is not the primary maintaining condition of the problem but is a by-product of the skill deficit. Generally when the person learns how to behave on dates, he or she no longer experiences excessive anxiety.

*Goldfried & Davison (1976).

The Efficiency of Systematic Desensitization

As a treatment for problems maintained by negative emotional reactions, systematic desensitization has much to recommend it. Systematic desensitization is extremely *efficient*, especially when clients are exposed to the troublesome situations in their imaginations. As noted, the procedures are also applicable to groups of clients. Compared to traditional psychotherapies that treat anxiety-related problems, systematic desensitization requires relatively few sessions. Furthermore, under some circumstances systematic desensitization can be effective in an automated form[27] (typically through tape-recorded instructions) or self-administered (by having clients follow written instructions).[28] Such procedures are obviously more efficient than treatment by a live therapist, and in some instances are as effective.[29] However, automated and self-administered treatments have their limitations, especially with clients who are highly anxious or who present particular problems for treatment (e.g., difficulty in relaxing).[30] When the therapist directly administers the treatment, he or she can modify standard procedures to meet unexpected problems that arise (e.g., encountering too much of a "jump" from one hierarchy item to the next) and can provide support and encouragement.[31]

The Effectiveness of Systematic Desensitization

Most importantly, there is no doubt that systematic desensitization is an *effective* procedure for treating a wide variety of problems that are maintained by anxiety. It is possible to make such a strong statement because literally hundreds of studies on the effectiveness of systematic desensitization have been performed over the past 20 years, and their findings are overwhelmingly positive.[32] For example, a 1969 review of the controlled outcome studies of systematic desensitization concluded that "for the first time in the history of psychological treatments, a specific treatment package reliably produced measurable benefits for clients across a broad range of distressing problems in which anxiety was of fundamental importance."[33] Seven years and many studies later, another comprehensive review of the existing research literature concluded that "Systematic desensitization is demonstrably more effective than both no treatment and [than] every psychotherapy variant with which it has so far been compared."[34]

An Illustrative Study

A classic study by Gordon Paul[35] illustrates both the evidence for the efficacy of systematic desensitization as well as the type of controlled experimentation that has validated behavioral therapies. The subjects in the study were college students enrolled in a public speaking class who volunteered to receive help with their anxiety about speaking in public. The comprehensive pretreatment assessment consisted of self-report, physiological, and overt behavioral measures of public speaking anxiety. The self-report measures asked subjects to rate the amount of anxiety they experienced in various situations related to public speaking. The physiological measures were of pulse rate and amount of

TIMED BEHAVIORAL CHECKLIST FOR
PERFORMANCE ANXIETY

Rater____________________ Name____________________

Date____________ Speech No.____________ I.D.____________

BEHAVIOR OBSERVED	TIME PERIOD								
	1	2	3	4	5	6	7	8	Sum
1. Paces									
2. Sways									
3. Shuffles feet									
4. Knees tremble									
5. Extraneous arm and hand movement (swings, scratches, toys, etc.)									
6. Arms rigid									
7. Hands restrained (in pockets, behind back, clasped)									
8. Hand tremors									
9. No eye contact									
10. Face muscles tense (drawn, tics, grimaces)									
11. Face "deadpan"									
12. Face pale									
13. Face flushed (blushes)									
14. Moistens lips									
15. Swallows									
16. Clears throat									
17. Breathes heavily									
18. Perspires (face, hands, armpits)									
19. Voice quivers									
20. Speech blocks or stammers									

Comments: Grand Total

FIGURE 4-1 *The checklist used by observers in Paul's study to rate subjects' overt behaviors indicating anxiety while giving a speech* SOURCE: *Adapted from Paul (1966), p. 109.*

sweat on the palms of their hands. As the subjects gave impromptu four-minute speeches, trained observers in the audience rated their visible (overt behavioral) signs of anxiety.

The checklist used by the observers is reproduced in Figure 4-1 (p. 85). The observers rated whether each of the 20 behaviors that indicate speech anxiety was either present or absent in successive 30-second time periods during the speech. The behavioral measure of anxiety for each subject was derived from the pooled ratings of the four observers. The manner and extent to which the observers were trained is noteworthy because it is a good example of thorough preparation, which is necessary for accurate and reliable behavioral observations. The four advanced graduate students in clinical psychology who served as observers were trained together for six hours to detect and record the 20 behaviors by observing both live and videotaped speakers. The observers were cautioned not to make judgments of "anxiety," but just to rate the presence or absence of the behaviors on the checklist. The success of this training is indicated by the 95 percent agreement obtained among the observers after their training.

The students were randomly assigned to one of four conditions: (1) systematic desensitization, (2) insight-oriented psychotherapy, (3) attention placebo, or (4) no treatment. The insight-oriented psychotherapy involved a verbal interchange between therapist and subject that emphasized subjects' gaining self-understanding and insight about the origins of their speech anxiety. In order to assess the effects of social interaction with the therapist and subjects' positive expectations of improvement, subjects in the attention placebo condition were given what they believed to be a "fast-acting tranquilizer" (actually, a capsule containing sodium bicarbonate). They were led to believe that the "tranquilizer" would reduce their anxiety during bogus stressful tasks they performed during their "therapy" sessions. To determine what changes would take place without any treatment, students in the no-treatment control condition merely participated in the pre- and posttreatment assessment procedures.

The therapy was limited to five sessions over a six-week period. Five experienced psychotherapists, who practiced predominantly insight-oriented psychotherapy, individually treated clients in the three therapy conditions. The therapists were unfamiliar with systematic desensitization and had to be trained in the procedures.

After the last therapy session, the subjects were again administered the self-report, physiological, and behavioral measures. The results shown in Figure 4-2 indicate a clear superiority of systematic desensitization over the insight-oriented therapy and the two control conditions. Furthermore, follow-up assessments based on the subjects' self-reported public speaking anxiety six weeks[36] and two years[37] after therapy indicated the same pattern of results.

Critics of this study have argued that five sessions is hardly enough time for insight-oriented therapy to be effective.[38] For example, the relationship between the therapist and the client is generally considered an important factor in insight-oriented therapy, and five sessions would be an insufficient time for

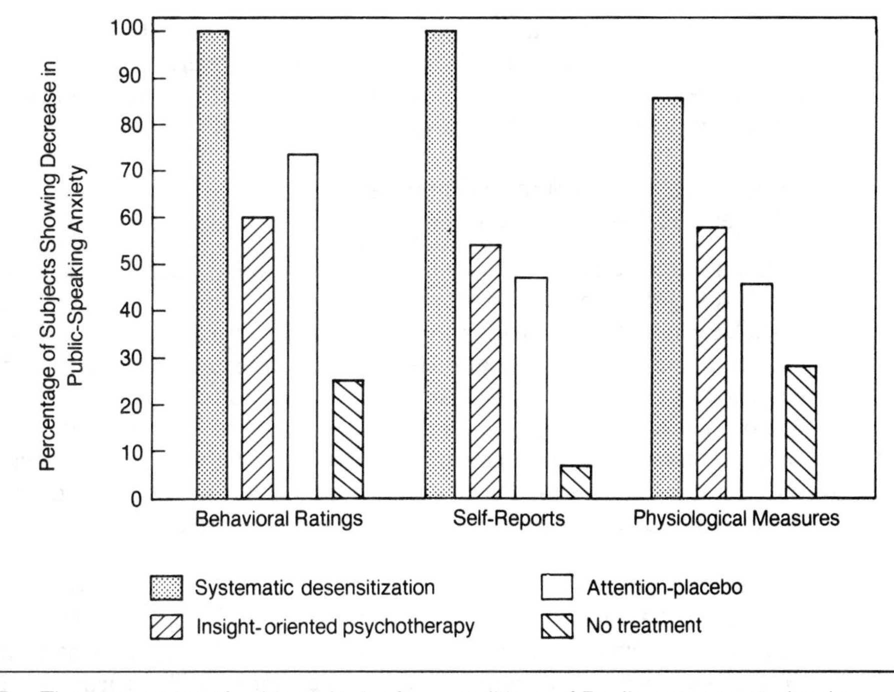

FIGURE 4-2 *The percentage of subjects in the four conditions of Paul's outcome study who showed a decrease in anxiety immediately after treatment, on behavioral, self-report, and psychological measures* SOURCE: *Data from Paul (1966).*

adequate rapport to be established. Nonetheless, even if it is accepted that insight-oriented psychotherapy was not given a fair test, the greater efficiency of systematic desensitization *may* be sufficient grounds for concluding that it is a superior treatment for specific anxieties.

None of the students successfully treated by systematic desensitization for their speech anxiety developed any deviant substitute behaviors. This possibility—formally called *symptom substitution*[39]—would be predicted from psychoanalytic theory, which holds that if a problem behavior (symptom) is eliminated without specifically dealing with its origin or its hypothesized underlying "cause" (e.g., an intrapsychic conflict that began in early childhood), then another deviant behavior (symptom) will replace the eliminated behavior. One early criticism of behavioral therapy was that behavioral therapy, because it eliminates behaviors, not underlying "causes," would result in symptom substitution. This study, which was carried out in the mid-1960s when the criticism was quite prevalent, specifically looked for symptom substitution. However, Paul found no evidence for symptom substitution. In fact, there is virtually no empirical evidence for behavioral therapy resulting in symptom substitution,[40] which essentially renders the criticism invalid. ("Symptom substitution" is being distinguished here from negative side effects of a therapeutic procedure; the latter is certainly a potential problem relevant to all types of therapy, including behavioral therapy.[41]) Note that the symptom substitution argument is based on the *mistaken* premise that behavioral therapy "treats symptoms," whereas behavioral therapy in fact treats the maintaining conditions (causes) of problem behaviors (symptoms).

The Essential and Facilitative Components of Systematic Desensitization

In addition to the outcome research just mentioned, there has also been extensive investigation of the process of systematic desensitization (i.e., *how* it works). Systematic desensitization is a complex therapy composed of a number of components. For practical reasons, it is important to know which components constitute the necessary and sufficient conditions for successful desensitization. Researchers have addressed this question by systematically omitting components and by then comparing the abbreviated treatment with the full treatment.[42] Using this dismantling strategy, if an abbreviated treatment is shown to be as effective as the complete one, then the component omitted is not essential.

Neither gradual exposure to anxiety-evoking situations nor engaging in a substitute behavior during the exposure seems to be an *essential* ingredient of successful systematic desensitization, although both may well be important *facilitative* components, as will be shown in a moment. The former conclusion is based on studies demonstrating that it is not necessary to expose clients to the anxiety scenes in ascending hierarchical order. In fact, desensitization can be effective when exposure occurs in descending order (i.e., beginning with the most anxiety-provoking item in the hierarchy).[43] Research has also demonstrated that desensitization with and without relaxation training can be equally effective.[44] The critical component in systematic desensitization appears to be *exposure to situations that evoke anxiety* (in imagination or *in vivo*) *without the client actually experiencing any negative consequences.*[45] (This would be the case, for example, if a man who is afraid to ride in a car either imagines himself riding in a car or actually rides in one, and no disastrous consequences, such as having an accident, befall him.)

In many cases, however, more than the essential components of systematic desensitization may be required for successful treatment. For example, clients who are repeatedly asked to expose themselves to situations that evoke high levels of anxiety may drop out of therapy because the treatment is too painful for them. In such cases, a variety of facilitative, although nonessential, components of systematic desensitization—such as gradually proceeding up a hierarchy and exposure to anxiety-evoking situations while relaxed or engaged in another substitute behavior—may be critical for successful treatment.[46] Furthermore, many factors other than the essential components may make the therapy more efficient and even more effective in actual clinical practice. For instance, clients typically expect to have positive interactions with their therapists (not an essential component of systematic desensitization), and when these expectations have been met clients may more diligently follow therapists' instructions.

FLOODING AND IMPLOSIVE THERAPY

Systematic desensitization has been discussed at length because of its proven efficacy and frequent use. Two other behavioral therapies for reducing anxiety are looked at briefly here: flooding and implosive therapy. Both procedures first increase the client's anxiety level in order to reduce it.

Flooding

Flooding involves exposing the client, usually *in vivo*, to a highly anxiety-evoking situation for a prolonged period of time without the feared negative consequences occurring. In contrast to systematic desensitization, during flooding the extent and duration of exposure to the anxiety-evoking situation is determined by the therapist (with the client's prior consent) rather than by the client. Furthermore, in flooding no substitute response for anxiety is employed. Cases 4-5 and 4-6 illustrate the basic procedures used in flooding.

CASE 4-5

*Fear of Loud Noises Treated by Flooding**

Bill was an 11-year-old boy who was intensely afraid of loud noises such as balloons bursting and capguns being fired. As a consequence, he did not attend children's parties, where balloons are frequently used as decorations, and he did not play with his peers, who often had noisy toys. At school, Bill was terrified that someone would set off a capbomb in back of him. His parents complained that he spent much time sulking and he believed people were against him. *In vivo* systematic desensitization was first employed, using a combination of relaxation, conversation, and eating as substitute responses, but this treatment was only successful in reducing his specific aversion to capguns. Nine months later, Bill was still afraid of balloons bursting, and he was worried that the boys in his new school would discover this. At this point flooding was attempted, in an effort to quickly alleviate the problem.

> The therapist explained that the treatment would be unpleasant for a short time, but despite this Bill wanted to try it. After settling him in a very small room, the door was opened and about 50 fully inflated balloons were taken in. He was obviously scared by this. He cowered into his chair, started to sweat and shake, and put his fingers into his ears. He refused to burst any balloons himself, so the therapist immediately burst half a dozen. In the confined space, the noise was unpleasant. Bill started to cry, but the therapist continued bursting balloons until he (Bill) no longer flinched.
>
> After much persuasion, Bill used his feet to push balloons against a nail held by the therapist. In rapid succession, 20 were burst in this fashion, and Bill no longer flinched. Next, following further verbal pressure, he agreed to burst one by hand, whilst keeping the other hand covering one ear. Immediately, about 30

*Yule, Sacks, & Hersov (1974). Quotation is from pp. 209–210.

more were presented in quick succession. Lastly, he was persuaded to burst about six, while both ears were uncovered.

At this stage, the first session was terminated. In one and a half hours, approximately 220 balloons had been burst. The patient was a little shaken by the experience, but agreed to return the next afternoon for a second session.

The second session was started by surrounding Bill with 100 to 150 balloons, and telling him to burst them. Initially he was still anxious, but energetic verbal persuasion coupled with actual prompting (i.e., moving his hand to the balloon, and gradually withdrawing adult pressure) soon had him bursting the balloons with occasional signs that he was actually enjoying the experience.

This session lasted 45 minutes, and by the end of it he was bursting balloons next to his uncovered ears, bursting them with his bare hands, and stamping on them in a determined fashion.

At the end of these two brief flooding sessions, Bill was no longer fearful of the noise made by bursting balloons, and none of the noises that previously bothered him were a problem for him at the follow-up assessment 25 months after the flooding. Furthermore, it appeared that Bill was now happier and had more friends at school.

CASE 4-6

*Fear of Riding on Escalators Treated by Flooding**

The patient was a 24-year-old female student with an intense fear and aversion of escalators. She had developed this phobia about seven years previously. She had ascended an escalator with some of her immediate family with relative ease, but had expressed fear of descending because of the apparent height. The relatives had jokingly forced her on to the escalator, and ever since she had experienced an aversion toward escalators, always taking the stairs or the elevator in preference. On one occasion she had unexpectedly come upon an escalator while shopping, and had become so overwhelmed with anxiety that it was only with great difficulty that she had prevented herself from vomiting. Whenever she was in the company of anyone who proposed riding an escalator to another floor, she would experience a quickening of the pulse and would bluntly refuse. Before the therapeutic session, she had made some unsuccessful attempts to overcome the fear by attempting, in the company of friends, to get on to an escalator. On those occasions when she could bring herself to stand at the foot of the escalator, she would not step on for fear that by holding on to the hand rail she would be pulled downward and so miss her step.

At the single session during which the history of the disorder was obtained, the *in vivo* flooding procedure was explained to the patient. She was told that the technique had been successfully employed in the treatment of numerous phobias and was almost certain to work in her case. She was also informed that she would experience some emotional distress but was assured that [the therapist] would be with her throughout the experience to ensure no resulting adverse effects. [The therapist] then arranged to meet her at a large department store with four levels of escalators.

*Reprinted from Nesbitt (1973), pp. 405–406.

Initially, the patient manifested an intense anxiety reaction when requested to approach the escalator, and it was only through much coaxing, reassurance, and a little physical force from [the therapist] that she finally stepped on to it. She then threatened to vomit and seemed at the verge of tears, all the time clinging tightly to [the therapist's] shirt. Getting on to the second flight of the escalator was much easier, but she still manifested the same signs of anxiety. After 27 minutes of riding up and down the escalator, she was approaching it with increasing readiness and reported a dramatic decrease in anxiety. She was then instructed to ride the escalator alone, and did so with relative ease. When she felt that there was no need for further treatment the session was terminated, after 29 minutes. Six months later the patient reported that she still experienced no anxiety on escalators except on rare occasions when descending.

Both cases illustrate the essential characteristics of successful flooding: *a client is exposed to a highly aversive situation long enough so that his or her discomfort reaches a maximum and then starts to decline.* The clients in both cases obviously experienced considerable initial anxiety during the flooding procedures, followed by a relatively quick decrease in anxiety. Flooding is sometimes referred to as **response prevention** because clients are prevented from performing their typical avoidance behaviors. Clients are "forced" to remain in the feared situation until the anxiety peaks and then declines, a process that often involves verbal and mild physical persuasion by the therapist. They are "compensated" for their intense, although relatively short, discomfort by the dramatically rapid improvement that can occur with flooding. It is important to note that clients are told about the unpleasant nature of the flooding ahead of time, and they must consent to the treatment before it begins.

The presence of the therapist during flooding may be an important facilitating factor in much the same way as a substitute response facilitates systematic desensitization. The therapist encourages the client to engage in the feared behavior, in some cases models the appropriate nonfearful response, and, perhaps most importantly, reassures the client that nothing catastrophic will occur.

Implosive Therapy

Implosive therapy is similar to flooding, but the client is always exposed to the anxiety-evoking situation in imagination.[47] In implosive therapy, the client visualizes the feared situation, which is described by the therapist in exaggerated and often fantasylike details (to maximize the client's anxiety), which is the major difference between implosive therapy and flooding. For example, a client who was afraid of flying insects might be asked to imagine being in a situation such as the following:

> Insects are flying around your head, first there is one, then a few, then dozens. They just keep flying around you, more and more of them, until you are surrounded by hundreds of flying insects. And

> they are getting bigger and bigger by the moment. Huge bugs, the size of birds, are flying so close to you that you can feel the vibrations of their wings against your skin. And now they begin to touch your skin, to bite you while moving up from your ankles and legs toward your groin and at the same time more insects are moving up your hands and arms toward your face, biting into your skin. And now they are boring into you, from all directions, all over your body. They are flying into your mouth and down your esophagus and you can feel them flying inside your stomach, bouncing off the walls of the stomach and tearing up your insides.

As with flooding, implosive therapy involves prolonged and intense exposure to the feared situation without any actual aversive consequences. The exaggerated scene description, such as the one just presented, may help the client realize that his or her worst fears are absurd and could not really happen. Implosive therapy has been used to treat the same type of target behaviors as those treated by flooding, although implosive therapy is used less frequently.

Evaluation of Flooding and Implosive Therapy

Research findings regarding the effectiveness of flooding and implosive therapy are equivocal, in marked contrast to the generally consistent finding that systematic desensitization is an effective behavioral therapy. Reports of successful treatment using flooding and implosive therapy are opposed by reports of unsuccessful treatment, although, of the two procedures, flooding clearly has a better "batting average." Part of the problem in evaluating these two procedures empirically is that early studies on both therapies had methodological weaknesses, making clear conclusions difficult.[48] In recent years, however, evidence has been increasing for the efficacy of flooding as a treatment for anxiety-related problems, and some studies have shown that flooding can be more effective than systematic desensitization.[49]

Both flooding and implosive therapy have some practical drawbacks. Obviously, these therapies are unpleasant for the client and sometimes for the therapist as well. The client is safeguarded by being informed prior to treatment about the nature of the therapy and by being given the clear option of deciding whether to undergo the procedures. Nonetheless, the unpleasant nature of flooding and implosive therapy is a limitation, because clients may well decline such treatment. The most serious *potential* danger of flooding and implosive therapy is that the prolonged and intense exposure to the feared situation will make clients even more fearful than before therapy. This possibility exists because both flooding and implosive therapy actually induce anxiety in order to reduce it. Fortunately, there seems to be little evidence of serious negative side effects. In a recent survey of behavioral therapists who had used flooding or implosive therapy, serious negative side effects were reported in 0.26 percent of the clients treated (9 out of 3,493).[50] Still, as a general rule, flooding and implosive therapy are probably best considered for treating anxiety or fear when more proven and particularly less negative and more conservative forms of therapy, such as systematic desensitization, have been found to be ineffective.

SUMMARY

Substitution therapies directly substitute an adaptive behavior or reaction for a maladaptive behavior or reaction. Systematic desensitization is the most frequently used therapy that substitutes a positive, adaptive response for a negative, maladaptive response (usually anxiety). In systematic desensitization, the client is gradually exposed to successively more anxiety-evoking (or otherwise negative) situations while engaged in an adaptive behavior that is more or less incompatible with anxiety. It involves three procedures: (1) learning a substitute response, which is most often deep muscle relaxation; (2) constructing an anxiety hierarchy, a list of situations that elicit anxiety in order of increasing anxiety; and (3) imagining being in an anxiety-evoking situation while making the substitute response. Systematic desensitization can be done with groups of clients as well as with individual clients.

In vivo systematic desensitization involves the client actually being in anxiety-evoking situations (rather than imagining them) while substituting adaptive responses for anxiety. The treatment of sexual dysfunction with couples often includes *in vivo* desensitization in which sexual arousal is the incompatible response substituted for anxiety about sexual performance.

Systematic desensitization is an efficient therapy that has been demonstrated to be effective and has been used widely. Gordon Paul's classic study on public speaking anxiety illustrates the type of research that has provided the evidence for the efficacy of systematic desensitization. A distinction is made between the essential and facilitative components of systematic desensitization; the critical component seems to be exposure to anxiety without experiencing negative consequences.

Flooding and implosive therapy are alternative therapies for treating anxiety-related problems. Both involve inducing intense anxiety in order to reduce it. The evidence for the effectiveness of flooding and implosive therapy is somewhat equivocal, although their use to bring about rapid decrease in anxiety has been documented in many case studies.

REFERENCE NOTES

1. Wolpe, 1958.
2. Jacobson, 1938.
3. For example, Geer, 1965; Spiegler & Liebert, 1970; Wolpe & Lang, 1964.
4. Wolpe & Lazarus, 1966; see also Spiegler & Agigian, 1977, p. 100.
5. Goldfried & Davison, 1976.

6. For example, Anton, 1976; Lazarus, 1961; Paul & Shannon, 1966; Rachman, 1966a, 1966b; Taylor, 1971.
7. For example, Spiegler, Cooley, Marshall, Prince, Puckett, & Skenazy, 1976; Wright, 1976; Zemore, 1975.
8. For example, Sue, 1975; Zemore, 1975.
9. For example, Rimm, deGroot, Boord, Heiman, & Dillow, 1971.
10. For example, Moore, 1965.
11. For example, Steinmark & Borkovec, 1974.
12. Saunders, 1976.
13. For example, Shorkey & Himle, 1974.
14. For example, Hedberg & Campbell, 1974.
15. For example, Meyer, 1975.
16. For example, Walton & Mather, 1963.
17. For example, Cotharin & Mikulas, 1975.
18. Lazarus & Abramovitz, 1962.
19. Ventis, 1973.
20. Goldfried & Davison, 1976.
21. Goldfried & Davison, 1976.
22. Masters & Johnson, 1970.
23. Masters & Johnson, 1970.
24. For example, Kaplan, 1974, 1975; Masters & Johnson, 1970; Wolpe & Lazarus, 1966.
25. Jacobs, Thompson, & Truxaw, 1975; Malamuth, Wanderer, Sayner, & Durrell, 1976.
26. Davison, 1982.
27. For example, Donner & Guerney, 1969; Evans & Kellam, 1973; Lang, Melamed, & Hart, 1970.
28. For example, Rosen, Glasgow, & Barrera, 1976.
29. For example, Evans & Kellam, 1973; Rosen, Glasgow, & Barrera, 1976.
30. For example, Bernstein & Borkovec, 1973; Marquis, Morgan, & Piaget, 1971.
31. For example, Goldfried & Davison, 1976; Walker, Hedberg, Clement, & Wright, 1981.
32. For example, Kazdin & Wilcoxon, 1976; Kazdin & Wilson, 1978.
33. Paul, 1969b, p. 159.
34. Leitenberg, 1976a, p. 131.
35. Paul, 1966.
36. Paul, 1966.
37. Paul, 1967.
38. Strupp, 1966.
39. Cahoon, 1968; Ullmann & Krasner, 1965.
40. For example, Bandura, 1969; Kazdin & Wilson, 1978; Sloane, Staples, Cristol, Yorkston, & Whipple, 1975.
41. See Kazdin & Wilson, 1978, p. 101.
42. Lang, 1969.
43. For example, Krapfl, 1967; Richardson & Suinn, 1973.
44. For example, Miller & Nawas, 1970; Nawas, Welsch, & Fishman, 1970.
45. Bandura, 1969; Lang, 1969.
46. Schubot, 1966; Wilson & Davison, 1971.
47. Stampfl & Levis, 1967, 1973.
48. Morganstern, 1973.
49. Leitenberg, 1976a; Marks, 1978; Rachman & Hodgson, 1980.
50. Shipley & Boudewyns, 1980.

CHAPTER 5 Substitution Behavioral Therapies: Aversion Therapies

This chapter continues the examination of substitution behavioral therapies. The previous chapter noted that systematic desensitization substituted positive reactions such as muscle relaxation for negative reactions such as anxiety. In contrast, the therapies discussed in this chapter substitute negative reactions, such as nausea, pain, or disgust, for "positive" reactions that are socially inappropriate and/or personally maladaptive, such as drug addiction. These procedures are called **aversion therapies** because they create an aversion in the client to performing the deviant behavior.

Harmful addictive behaviors (e.g., to alcohol, heroin, and tobacco) and various sexually abnormal behaviors (e.g., exhibitionistic and fetishistic behavior) constitute the major deceleration target behaviors treated by aversion therapies. Engaging in either target behavior usually results in *immediate* consequences that are highly positive or pleasant for the individual; negative consequences come later and may affect other people as well as the individual. Drinking alcoholic beverages excessively, for example, may at first make a person feel good; a sense of calmness and well-being results, anxiety is temporarily alleviated, and physical and psychological pain are anesthetized. But addictive drugs have long-term harmful effects on one's body, tend to make one withdraw from interactions with other people, and may lead to loss of one's job, alienation of one's family and friends, and criminal behavior to secure illegal drugs. Is the price of these serious long-range negative consequences worth the short-lived pleasure and comfort derived from the drug? Apparently the answer is yes for some individuals who do not have other satisfactions to substitute for the feelings created by the drugs. It is also important to realize that some feeling states associated with addictive drugs are extremely positive. Simply put, in order to give up the addictive behavior, the person wants or needs an alternative behavior that is at least as rewarding as the addictive behavior, and such an alternative is often very difficult to find. Similarly, the sexual pleasure derived from aberrant sexual practices is often very strong—sexual pleasure of any kind is one of the most powerful incentives for human beings. Because deviant sexual and addictive behaviors result in such highly pleasurable immediate consequences, and because the negative consequences occur at a later time, such behaviors are very difficult to eliminate. Behavioral therapies have been among the most successful interventions for some of these problem behaviors, but the duration of treatment effects is much less, and the number of people whose problem behaviors are successfully eliminated is much lower, than with many other target behaviors that are less rewarding and therefore are more amenable to change.[1]

Although addictive and sexually aberrant behaviors are the most common targets for aversion therapies, they are not the only appropriate target behaviors. In general, aversion therapy procedures are applicable for any persistent habits a client wishes to eliminate. Usually these behaviors are harmful to the individual (e.g., self-induced seizures) or to others (e.g., compulsively setting fires). Substituting a negative response for a positive one involves associating the presently pleasurable behavior with an aversive event so that the behavior elicits a negative reaction and the person's desire to engage in it diminishes. The chapter first examines examples of behavioral therapies that just create an aversion to performing a problem behavior and then turns to therapies that, in addition to eliminating the problem behavior by making it noxious, also help the person develop an alternative behavior for the one being eliminated.

AVERSION THERAPIES: BASIC PROCEDURES

In aversion therapy, the negative emotional response to be associated with the maladaptive habit can be created by pairing the habit with any event or stimulus that is specifically and sufficiently aversive to the individual client—that is, any event that is unpleasant, revolting, distasteful, or painful to the client.

Mild electric shock is the most frequently employed aversive event. Mild shock is a particularly useful aversive stimulus because most people find it aversive. Also, it can be turned on and off instantaneously so that it can be precisely associated with the undesirable behavior. Because many people have an "automatic aversion" to the use of mild electric shock as a therapeutic technique, it is important to place its use in proper perspective. First, although the mild shocks are painful, they are *not* at all dangerous, and they do *not* cause any lasting tissue damage (e.g., the skin is not burned). The mild shock used as a painful stimulus in aversion therapy should not be confused with electroconvulsive shock treatment, which (1) is a medical treatment for severe depression; (2) involves passing high-voltage electrical currents through the brain while the patient is sedated, a process that leads to a convulsion, temporary unconsciousness, and amnesia for the experience; and (3) most importantly is *not* a behavioral therapy.

Second, it is necessary to keep in mind the purpose of employing mild shock, or any other painful or unpleasant event, in aversion therapy—namely, to rid a person of a maladaptive and unwanted problem behavior. (More will be said about ethical and moral objections to aversion therapy later in the chapter.) Other examples of aversive events used in aversion therapy include noxious odors, hot air and smoke (to decelerate cigarette smoking), feelings of humiliation, and unpleasant thoughts.

The specific aversive event used depends on the nature of the deceleration target behavior. For example, aversion therapy for alcohol addiction is generally more effective when the aversive event is nausea rather than mild shock.[2] Furthermore, the strength of the aversive event varies for each individual client. Only the client can determine if the event is intense enough to create an aversion; the client's motivation to change undesirable behavior is a key factor in the success of aversion therapy. Desire to change is always important in therapy, but because aversion therapy is unpleasant and sometimes painful, clients must be especially motivated to succeed.

Aversion therapy requires that the deceleration target behavior and the aversive event occur simultaneously, so that the client will come to associate the two, thereby creating an aversion to performing the target behavior. In practice, this goal is accomplished in one of three ways. The aversive event may be presented (1) as the client is actually engaging in the target behavior, (2) as the client is exposed symbolically to various cues surrounding the behavior (e.g., pictures and verbal descriptions of the client engaging in the behavior), or (3) as the client imagines performing the behavior. The first two procedures are illustrated by Cases 5-1 and 5-2, respectively, and the third is seen in the discussion of covert sensitization later in the chapter.

CASE 5-1

*Elimination of Chronic Ruminative Vomiting Through Aversion Therapy**

Mark was a 9-month-old infant who was hospitalized for malnutrition and weight loss caused by ruminative vomiting, a potentially fatal condition characterized by regurgitating, chewing, and reswallowing food. Mark began vomiting after meals when he was 6 months old. A series of medical and psychological treatments were tried over the next three and a half months with no success. Because Mark's condition was considered critical, aversion therapy was instituted.

Mild shocks were administered for half-second intervals each time ruminative vomiting occurred and were terminated as soon as Mark stopped vomiting. The electrodes were strapped lightly to Mark's calf, and the shock was activated by a remote hand switch. This arrangement made it possible for Mark to move freely during the treatment. The therapy is described as follows.

*Cunningham & Linscheid (1976). Quotations are from pp. 232 and 233.

Treatment was initially conducted in Mark's hospital room with a series of observers present. Mark was placed in his bed, a feeding chair, walker, or allowed to play freely on the floor. On several occasions, Mark was left alone and observed via a closed circuit monitor. On Days 6 through 8, treatment was conducted in the ward day room, and on Day 9 in a simulated home environment. Finally, to facilitate transition from the hospital, Mark and his mother were monitored alone under circumstances approximating those in the home.

After two weeks of aversion therapy, Mark's ruminative vomiting ceased completely, he had gained almost three pounds, and his social behavior had generally improved (e.g., he cried less frequently and started babbling again). Interestingly, "Observers noted that mouthing movements formerly preceding ruminating, now produced the word *Mama*, a response resulting in considerable social attention." At a six-month follow-up assessment, ruminative vomiting had not recurred, Mark continued to gain weight, and his parents reported no further problems.

One limitation of aversion therapy (as well as of many other therapies) is that its treatment effects may remain specific to the therapy situation. In other words, the client may find it aversive to perform the target behavior only in the setting in which the aversion therapy was carried out. One way to increase the likelihood that the effects of therapy will *generalize* to the client's natural environment is to administer the treatment in a variety of situations, especially those in which the client is likely to be after treatment. Such generalization procedures were part of Mark's therapy (in the case just described), and may have been one of the factors that accounted for the successful treatment.

The next case of aversion therapy to be examined differs considerably from Case 5-1. Whereas Mark's behavior was clearly harmful, Case 5-2 concerns an adult who desired to change a sexual habit that, in fact, was not harmful to himself or others although it probably caused some problems in his life, or he would not have sought help in eliminating it. This case also illustrates the procedures of symbolically exposing the client to the target behavior, and the use of drug-induced nausea as the aversive event.

CASE 5-2

Treatment of Transvestic (Cross-dressing) Behavior by Aversion Therapy*

A 22-year-old married truckdriver reported that he had experienced the desire to dress as a woman since the age of 8. From the age of 15 and through his military service and marriage, he had derived erotic satisfaction from dressing in female clothes and viewing himself in the mirror. At the same time, he had maintained a good sexual relationship with his wife.

*Lavin, Thorpe, Barker, Blakemore, & Conway (1961).

The therapist prepared 35-mm slides of the client in various stages of female dress and had the client prepare an audiotape in which he described the same activities that were photographed. It was then determined that the presentation of the slides and tape in fact induced sexual excitement in the client.

The treatment involved pairing the transvestic experience with nausea, produced pharmacologically by injection of the drug apomorphine. As soon as the injection began to take effect, the slides and tape were presented, and these symbolic representations of the target behavior were terminated only after the client began to vomit. This treatment was administered every two hours for six days, a regimen that proved sufficient to completely eliminate the client's desire to don female attire. Systematic follow-up over a six-month period, including interviews with both the client and his wife, suggested that the client no longer engaged in transvestic behavior.

SHAME AVERSION THERAPY

Michael Serber accidently "discovered" shame aversion therapy while taking photographs of a male client cross-dressing.[3] The photographs were to be used as the symbolic stimuli to be shocked in aversion therapy. However, the client experienced the photographing as so aversive (presumably humiliating) that no further treatment was necessary. **Shame aversion therapy** capitalizes on religious or moral aversive procedures that have been practiced for centuries to inhibit "bad" behaviors. The client performs the undesirable behavior (usually a sexually deviant act) in the presence of several observers. Obviously, for the technique to work, the client must feel ashamed, embarrassed, humiliated, or guilty. Not surprisingly, shame aversion therapy has been found to be particularly effective with morally conservative individuals.[4]

Exhibitionistic behavior (a male exposing his genitals in public to a female) is one of the most frequent target behaviors for shame aversion therapy.[5] The client exposes himself to a woman who has been instructed to respond in a passive manner so as not to reinforce the exhibiting behavior by acting shocked or embarrassed. (The exhibiting male obtains gratification from observing the woman's reaction, which is generally one of surprise, fear, disgust, and embarrassment.)[6] Sometimes the shame aversion sessions are recorded and later played back to the client and other observers. Shame aversion therapy has also been used to treat pedophilic behavior (obtaining sexual gratification through contact with children),[7] fetishistic behavior (reliance on inanimate objects or on parts of the body for sexual arousal),[8] and transvestic behavior.[9]

Shame aversion therapy has not been widely employed, nor has its effectiveness been systematically evaluated. However, there are a number of encouraging case reports of its successfully creating a negative emotional response to sexually aberrant behavior in just a few sessions.[10] Case 5-3 illustrates one adaptation of shame aversion therapy to decelerate obscene telephone calls.

CASE 5-3

Compulsive Obscene Telephone Calling Treated by Shame Aversion Therapy*

Mr. A. was a 32-year-old, married, white, rural-area police officer. . . . The patient described himself as being "hypersexual" because he masturbated frequently (about twice a day) even though he was married and had a responsive wife.

In the two months prior to admission, the patient made numerous obscene phone calls to various young, adult women in his community. At the onset the frequency of the calls was one or two per week but later increased to 15 to 20 per week. He would masturbate while telephoning. If the victim hung up before he reached orgasm, he would continue masturbating to orgasm. He considered this behavior morally wrong, but felt he could not control it. He always felt remorseful, depressed, and ashamed after making the calls. He became increasingly careless and indiscriminate in his calling behavior, stating that he probably wanted to get caught. Three or four days before admission, he called a woman who knew him. She recognized his voice and notified the county sheriff's office. When apprehended and confronted with the complaint, Mr. A. confessed immediately. He lost his job, but was told no charges would be made if he would seek psychiatric help. This ultimatum precipitated his admission to a local hospital.

Over a three-week period, Mr. A. was given three "live" therapy sessions and subsequently listened to the audiotape of the first two. Each 20-minute session consisted of Mr. A. making a call to a female surrogate victim in another office. The two surrogates . . . would have been appropriate real victims for Mr. A. (i.e., young, attractive, adult females). Mr. A. was instructed to pick up the phone, and with the therapist present, visualize the surrogate whom he had met earlier. He was instructed to make the call saying exactly what he had said on previous occasions. The surrogate was instructed to listen to his statements and answer questions in a passive but noncomplying manner. She was instructed not to hang up first. The first call lasted 25 seconds before Mr. A. hung up. In the second and third sessions he was encouraged to continue the "conversation" for a longer period of time. These calls lasted about 2 minutes each. His emotional response to all the sessions was anxiety and embarrassment. Immediately after the call, the patient and the surrogate were asked to discuss their feelings with one another, with the therapist present. In these postcall sessions Mr. A. appeared embarrassed by the confrontations and reported experiencing only negative feelings both then and during the call. It was apparent that Mr. A. found the therapy extremely aversive.

At a one-month follow-up, the patient reported that he had not experienced any desire to make an obscene call since his discharge. In fact, he reported feeling anxious when using the telephone for any reason. At a three-month follow-up session, Mr. A. stated that he had had a couple of fleeting "thoughts about making an obscene call," but there was no "compulsion" to do so. At six- and nine-month follow-ups, Mr. A. again reported that he had not felt any strong urges to make a call, nor had there been any reports of such calls by authorities in his community. At this time he did report that he felt he still had to be careful of his sexual fantasies lest they lead to "trouble." He continued his satisfactory sexual relations with his wife on a regular basis and used heterosexual pornography as a stimulant for masturbation, the frequency of which he reported to have decreased to two or three times per week.

---

*Reprinted from Boudewyns, Tanna, & Fleischman (1975), pp. 705–706.

Earlier the potential problem that treatment effects may not generalize sufficiently from the therapy setting to the client's natural environment was discussed. In aversion therapy, another potential problem may arise from *too much* generalization. In some cases, the negative emotional response created in aversion therapy becomes associated with more than just the undesirable behavior and its specific cues. For example, Mr. A. (Case 5-3) came to feel anxious whenever he made *any* telephone call, not just when he made an obscene call. In such instances, it is necessary to increase *discrimination* (the opposite of generalization) between the inappropriate target behavior and similar, but appropriate, behaviors so that the aversive event is associated only with the inappropriate behavior. This goal is difficult to attain when the presentation of the noxious event cannot be precisely controlled, as with shame aversion and nausea-producing drugs. As mentioned previously, one advantage of using mild shock as the aversive event is that its presentation can be precisely controlled.

Because there are some ethical and moral objections to the use of physically aversive events (e.g., mild shock and nausea) in treatment, shame aversion therapy may be an attractive alternative in that the aversive event used in such therapy is only a "mental state." The same feature holds for the next aversion therapy to be discussed—covert sensitization.

COVERT SENSITIZATION

In **covert sensitization,** the aversive event (such as nausea and disgust) and the deceleration target behavior are associated completely in the client's imagination. Developed by Joseph Cautela,[11] covert sensitization has been used to treat problems such as sexually deviant behavior,[12] overeating,[13] alcohol addiction,[14] and smoking.[15] The following instructions were given to a client who wished to stop smoking and illustrate how covert sensitization works.

> I am going to ask you to imagine this scene as vividly as you can. I don't want you to imagine that you are seeing yourself in these situations. I want you to imagine that you're actually in the situations. Do not only try to visualize the scenes but try to feel, for example, the cigarette in your hand, or the back of the chair in which you are sitting. Try to use all your senses as though you were actually there. The scenes that I pick will be concerned with situations in which you are about to smoke. It is very important that you visualize the scenes as clearly as possible and try to actually feel yourself in the situation.
>
> You are sitting at your desk in the office preparing your lectures for class. There is a pack of cigarettes to your right. While you are writing, you put down your pencil and start to reach for a cigarette. As soon as you start reaching for the cigarette, you get a nauseated feeling in your stomach. You begin to feel sick to your stomach, like you are about to vomit. You touch the pack of cigarettes and bitter spit comes into your mouth; when you take the cigarette out of the pack some pieces of food come into your throat. Now you feel sick

and have stomach cramps. As you are about to put the cigarette in your mouth, you puke all over the pack of cigarettes. The cigarette in your hand is very soggy and full of green vomit. There is a stink coming from the vomit. Snot is coming from your nose. Your hands feel all slimy and full of vomit. The whole desk is a mess. Your clothes are all full of puke. You get up from your desk and turn away from the vomit and cigarettes. You immediately begin to feel better being away from the vomit and the cigarettes. You go to the bathroom and wash up and feel great being away from the vomit and the cigarettes.[16]

The effectiveness of covert sensitization partially depends on the client's ability to clearly visualize the scenes described and to experience negative emotional reactions from a verbal description of aversive events. Although nausea and vomiting are the most common aversive events used in covert sensitization, potentially any verbal description that can induce a negative reaction in the client will work. For example, covert sensitization was used to treat a 52-year-old man who had been engaging in incest with his 17-year-old daughter for five years.[17] Verbal descriptions of the man feeling nauseated and vomiting while having sexual relations with his daughter failed to prove aversive to the client. So the scene was changed to one in which the man was discovered in his deviant behavior by his wife, his father-in-law, or his family priest, which the client did experience as aversive.

Covert sensitization has several advantages over other aversion therapies. First, no equipment, such as a shock apparatus, is required. Second, unlike some drug-induced aversion procedures, covert sensitization can be safely carried out in the therapist's office without any medical assistance. Third, an aversive image is "portable," making it possible for the client to self-administer covert sensitization at home (if the client is able and willing to conjure up the aversive imagery without the therapist's assistance). *In vivo* covert sensitization is also possible. Whenever and wherever clients find themselves thinking about performing the maladaptive behavior or actually engaging in it, they can immediately "switch on" the aversive imagery to inhibit the undesirable behavior. A final advantage of covert sensitization compared to the other aversive therapies is that clients may consider it to be a more acceptable form of treatment because imagining an aversive event is less distasteful than actually experiencing the aversive event. Accordingly, clients may be more motivated to continue in therapy. For example, one study found that the dropout rate was lower for clients receiving covert sensitization than for those receiving aversive therapy using mild shock for the treatment of excessive drinking.[18]

In the clinical practice of behavioral therapy, treatment often involves a combination of several therapies used concurrently or sequentially. Recall that the treatment of Paul's truant behavior (Case 3-1) consisted of a number of different behavioral therapies. As you proceed through this book, you will increasingly encounter examples of **treatment packages**, as such multiple-therapy interventions are called. In Case 5-4, covert sensitization was combined with a specialized substitution behavioral therapy called *orgasmic reconditioning* to eliminate a young man's disturbing sadistic fantasies.

Orgasmic reconditioning is used in cases where an adult is sexually aroused by socially inappropriate sexual stimuli (e.g., children, fetishistic objects, or disturbing fantasies).[19] The therapy changes the antecedents of sexual arousal and behavior by substituting appropriate sexual stimuli for inappropriate ones. (Note that orgasmic reconditioning substitutes a positive for a negative response and is therefore *not* an aversion therapy.) The procedures in orgasmic reconditioning are as follows. The client masturbates in private by using *any* imagined scene that is sexually arousing. Generally the client uses his or her usual deviant sexual fantasies because these have become the primary means of becoming sexually aroused for the client. Just before orgasm, the client looks at a picture of an *appropriate* sexual stimulus. The purpose of this procedure is to have the intense pleasure of orgasm associated with an appropriate sexual stimulus. The shift of the client's attention to the appropriate sexual stimulus is gradually introduced earlier and earlier in masturbation. Initially pictures of the appropriate sexual stimulus are used to increase the likelihood that the client is thinking about the appropriate sexual stimulus when orgasm occurs. Over the course of therapy, the client is gradually shifted from pictures of appropriate stimuli to mental images of them. Finally, the client is instructed to apply the reoriented sexual interest to his or her personal sex life. Although orgasmic reconditioning appears to be used frequently in clinical practice,[20] there are few controlled studies of the efficacy of this procedure[21] and so its status cannot be evaluated at this time.

CASE 5-4

*Treatment of Sadistic Sexual Fantasies by Orgasmic Reconditioning and Covert Sensitization**

A college student sought treatment because he was troubled by sadistic sexual fantasies. He masturbated about five times a week, always to thoughts of torturing women. The behavioral therapist taught the client to use orgasmic reconditioning on his own to alter the sadistic mental images that led to sexual arousal.

> When assured of privacy in his dormitory room (primarily on the weekend), he was first to obtain an erection by whatever means possible—undoubtedly with a sadistic fantasy, as he indicated. He was then to begin to masturbate while looking at a picture of a sexy, nude woman (the "target" sexual stimulus); *Playboy* magazine was suggested to him as a good source. If he began losing the erection, he was to switch back to his sadistic fantasy until he could begin masturbating effectively again. Concentrating again on the *Playboy* picture, he was to continue masturbating, using the fantasy only to regain erection. As orgasm was approaching, he was at all costs to focus on the *Playboy* picture, even if sadistic fantasies began to intrude. It was impressed on him that gains would ensue only when sexual arousal was associated with the picture, and that he need not worry about indulging in sadistic fantasies at this point.

*Davison (1968). Quotations are from pp. 85, 86, and 89.

The first few sessions of therapy went well (e.g., the client was able to masturbate successfully three times over the weekend to a *Playboy* picture without using sadistic fantasies). However, the client was still reluctant to ask women for dates and to give up his sadistic fantasies entirely. A form of covert sensitization was then instituted. Specifically, the client was instructed to close his eyes and

> imagine a typical sadistic scene, a pretty girl tied to stakes on the ground and struggling tearfully to extricate herself. While looking at the girl, he was told to imagine someone bringing a branding iron toward his eyes, ultimately searing his eyebrows. A second image was attempted when this proved abortive, namely, being kicked in the groin by a ferocious-looking karate expert. When he reported himself indifferent to this image as well, the therapist depicted to him a large bowl of "soup," composed of steaming urine with reeking fecal boli bobbing around on top. His grimaces, contortions, and groans indicated that an effective image had been found, and the following five minutes were spent portraying his drinking from the bowl, with accompanying nausea, at all times while peering over the floating debris at the struggling girl. After opening his eyes at the end of the imaginal ordeal, he reported spontaneously that he felt quite nauseated, and some time was spent in casual conversation in order to dispel the mood.

Within five sessions the client had given up masturbating to sadistic fantasies entirely—he even had difficulty producing such thoughts—and was using thoughts of women and heterosexual scenes to masturbate. Some time after the termination of therapy, he began to date women. Even more impressive, when a relapse occurred, he was able to treat it himself, as may be seen from the following passage from a letter he wrote to the therapist describing the incident and his present state:

> I bought an issue of *Playboy* and proceeded to give myself the treatment again. Once again, it worked like a charm. In two weeks, I was back in my reformed state, where I am now. . . . I have no need for sadistic fantasies. . . . I have [also] been pursuing a vigorous (well, vigorous for *me*) program of dating. In this way, I have gotten to know a lot of girls of whose existence I was previously only peripherally aware. As you probably know, I was very shy with girls before; well now I am not one-fifth as shy as I used to be. In fact, by my old standards, I have become a regular rake!

This case illustrates several noteworthy points about behavioral therapy in general. First, successful treatment often requires a treatment package consisting of two or more therapies. Second, each client requires slightly different treatment procedures, even when the same basic therapy is employed. Third, modifications are often made in the procedures as therapy proceeds; for example, the therapist in Case 5-4 had to experiment with mental images that would be aversive to the client.

Finally, just as clients are unique individuals, behavioral therapists also vary considerably in their abilities and inclinations regarding different behavioral therapies. For example, behavioral therapies that involve creating vivid imagery, such as covert sensitization and systematic desensitization, require that the therapist be good at expressively depicting detailed scenes and scenarios for the client. Also, in the case of therapies in which the imagery is distinctly distasteful, as in covert sensitization, and sometimes in implosive therapy, the therapist must also have the "stomach" to tolerate noxious images. Obviously, some therapists are therefore more likely than others to employ such behavioral therapies. Therapists also may specialize in treating particular types of problems (e.g., sexual dysfunctions or problem behaviors of children) due to the therapists' individual abilities and interests (which, in turn, is one factor that determines the particular therapies they use most often). Therapists have an ethical obligation to refer a client to another therapist if for any reason they are not capable of adequately dealing with the specific client, the particular target behavior, or the optimal therapy for the client's problem.

Covert sensitization appears to be used relatively frequently despite the fact that controlled studies are equivocal concerning its efficacy.[22] The popularity of covert sensitization, then, seems to stem more from its practical advantages (as outlined earlier) than from its proven efficacy. The procedure is most effective in treating deviant sexual behavior,[23] and generally is less effective in dealing with drinking problems, overeating, and smoking—the other target behaviors to which covert sensitization has most often been applied. The moderate overall success rate of covert sensitization should be viewed in the light of the fact that all four of the problem behaviors most frequently treated by covert sensitization are among the most difficult to treat by any procedures. In the final analysis, effective treatment of these problem behaviors is likely to involve a combination of therapies. A recent study reported the treatment of exhibitionistic behavior in 186 clients by a treatment package in which the major component was covert sensitization. Up to 86 percent success was achieved, with follow-ups at periods of more than eight years later.[24]

AVERSION-RELIEF THERAPY

Aversion therapy, particularly when physically noxious events are employed, frequently makes clients highly anxious. This consequence is both expected and necessary for the treatment to be effective. At the end of each aversion therapy session, there is usually a marked decrease in the client's anxiety, which naturally is a pleasant experience. **Aversion-relief therapy** uses the relief that follows the end of the aversive event to substitute an adaptive behavior for the undesirable behavior.[25]

Aversion-relief therapy merely adds a "relief" phase to the standard aversion therapy procedure, as illustrated in Figure 5-1. When the client is thinking about (or actually engaging in) the deceleration target behavior, the noxious event is administered for a time and then terminated. At the point when the aversive event is terminated, the client focuses his or her attention on an alternative adaptive behavior. In this way the adaptive behavior becomes associated with a positive emotional feeling (relief from the aversive event) and becomes a substitute for the maladaptive behavior. An aversion-relief procedure was in-

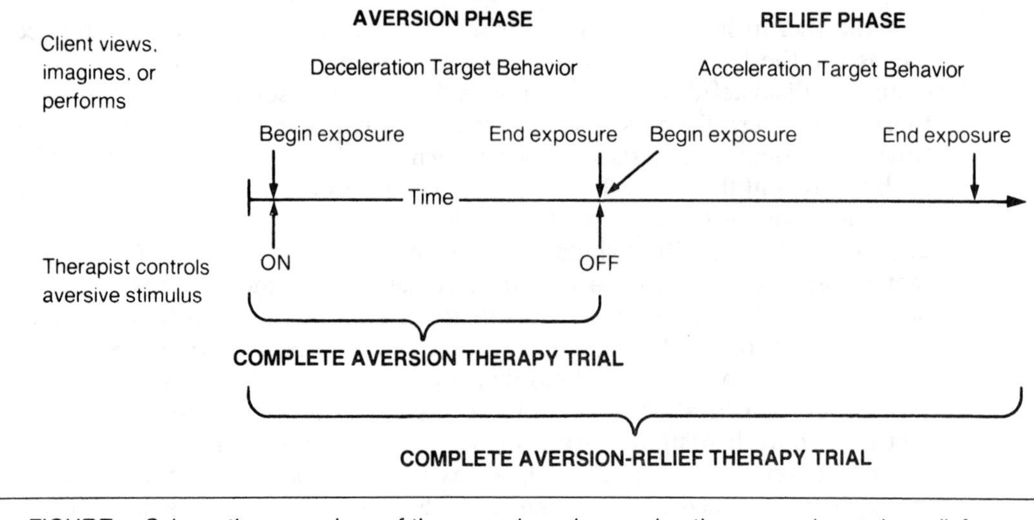

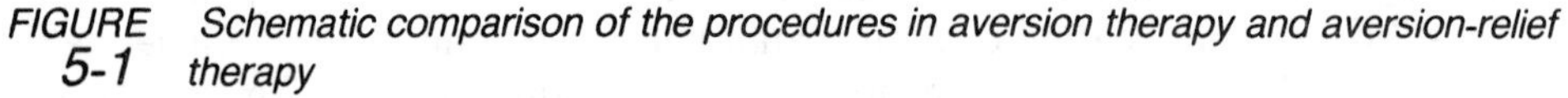

FIGURE 5-1 *Schematic comparison of the procedures in aversion therapy and aversion-relief therapy*

cluded in the therapist's instructions for covert sensitization of cigarette smoking presented earlier. Specifically, the client was told that as he turned away from the vomit and cigarettes, he would begin to feel better.

Various deviant sexual practices have been the primary target behaviors for aversion-relief therapy.[26] Mild shock is the most common aversive event, although other noxious stimuli, such as verbal descriptions of nausea and vomiting, have also been used.[27] Case 5-5 provides an example of aversion-relief therapy and is noteworthy because it is one of the few attempts to control heroin use using behavioral therapy.

CASE 5-5

*Chronic Heroin Use Treated by Aversion-Relief Therapy**

Mr. M. was a 23-year-old married graduate student.

For approximately three years before seeking treatment, Mr. M. had been taking heroin by injection into the arm on an average of two to three times per week. Periodically he abstained for as long as seven or eight days, but would invariably return to the two- to three-day pattern. By never using heroin on more than two successive days, he maintained some tenuous control over the habit. However, tolerance for the drug had been increasing steadily, requiring more frequent administrations at higher dosage. His drug usage had put his marriage in danger of dissolution, and his academic productiveness had fallen.

Because of the gravity of his situation, he volunteered for electric aversion treatment.

*Reprinted from Lubetkin & Fishman (1974), pp. 193–194.

The procedures were described to him in detail, and he was given the option of terminating whenever he desired.

Aversion treatment was carried out in twenty 20-minute sessions over approximately 2½ months. The client was seated comfortably in a Barca Lounger Chair. The shock intensity was set at a level described as painful but not unbearable. . . .

The client was asked to imagine and verbally describe the behavior sequence leading up to and including heroin intake. . . .

Throughout these verbalizations, he was encouraged to imagine the situations as clearly as possible and to try to capture the feelings involved. Randomly, during these descriptions the therapist would deliver a shock to his arm and simultaneously say, "Stop." Mr. M. was asked to continue his description until the shock became intolerable and then was to alter his fantasy and describe a socially adaptive and drug-free situation. Usually the client switched to a scene where he and his wife were on an outing, planning a trip or conversing. At the indication of scene change, the therapist immediately terminated the shock.

Throughout treatment Mr. M. abstained from heroin except that after the fifteenth . . . session he reported sniffing a small amount of the drug. He stated that he was "curious" about its effects after having abstained. However, his experience with it was negative.

As treatment progressed, Mr. M. reported the development of increasing ambivalence in his attitude toward heroin. There was no evidence of "symptom substitution" in any form. His relationship with his wife improved markedly, as did his academic performance. He was offered and accepted an opportunity to pursue advanced graduate work at another institution. An eight-month follow-up by correspondence, corroborated by his wife, confirmed that Mr. M. had remained drug-free.

Case 5-5 illustrates two important general features of behavioral therapies. First, the therapist explained the therapy procedures to the client in detail, and the client was specifically made aware of his option to terminate therapy at any time. Such preparation by the behavioral therapist is especially important with aversion therapies, which are always, at the very least, unpleasant for the client. Second, the case presents a clear example of how treating one target behavior—in this instance the most urgent and perhaps most central problem in Mr. M.'s life—is likely to have carryover effects to other problem behaviors (e.g., Mr. M.'s poor marriage and academic performance).

EVALUATION OF AVERSION THERAPIES

Overall, aversion therapies have been moderately successful at decelerating the two major categories of target behaviors for which they have been employed: aberrant sexual behaviors and addictive behaviors.[28] However, the percentage of clients who have been helped is lower than the percentage helped by other combinations of therapy and target behavior (e.g., systematic desensitization and phobic behavior).[29] One reason for the modest success rate is that both categories of target behaviors are extremely resistant to treatment of any kind.

Undoubtedly two reasons for their extreme intractability are that they immediately lead to very pleasant consequences and their negative consequences generally occur some time after the behavior. Such maintaining conditions not only make it very difficult to change the behavior but also make recurrence of the maladaptive behavior very probable. Other reasons for the modest success of aversion therapies in decelerating abnormal sexual behaviors and addictive behaviors lie in the limitations of aversion therapies.

First, one restriction on aversion therapies is that they cannot always be employed. In most cases, the client needs to be highly motivated to get rid of the maladaptive behavior. Not only does the person need to forego the immediate pleasure that follows the behavior, such as the euphoria created by some drugs, but to do so the person must endure noxious stimulation. Many clients do not want to be treated by aversion therapy and either decline such treatment at the outset or drop out of therapy prematurely.[30]

Second, ethical and moral considerations also may preclude the use of aversion therapy. Many people believe that it is unethical or immoral to subject clients to any physical or psychological discomfort as part of treatment. Simply put, the argument is that the ends do not justify the means. Whether this position is valid or not is irrelevant to the fact that people who hold it will object to aversion therapies for themselves and others. Obviously this argument means that factors other than the effectiveness of aversion therapies are being used to determine if these treatment procedures are employed. Similar issues are relevant to several other forms of behavioral therapy, and a general discussion of them appears later in the book after the gamut of behavioral therapies has been explored. Readers would do well to consider their own views regarding the ethicality and morality of using (as well as *not* using) unpleasant and perhaps painful therapeutic techniques in order to alleviate serious problem behaviors that often have major negative consequences for clients.

Third, a relatively minor issue that sometimes restricts the use of aversion therapies involves the possibility that therapists may be unable to tolerate administering them. For example, therapists may become nauseated themselves from their description of aversive images such as "a large bowl of 'soup,' composed of steaming urine."

Fourth, another limitation of aversion therapies is that their effectiveness in substantially reducing or eliminating behavior is often *only temporary.* One way of dealing with this problem is to provide the client with supplementary aversion treatments. Such **booster treatments** (like booster shots for continued immunization for certain diseases) can be administered on a regular basis as well as on an as-needed basis (e.g., when the maladaptive behavior recurs).[31] For example, in treating alcohol addiction with aversion therapies, the "abstinence rates are extremely high in the period immediately following treatment; the incidence of reversion to drinking is greatest between 6 and 12 months; therafter abstinence declines gradually with increasing duration."[32] Thus, in the case of alcohol addiction, the year following aversion therapy is critical, and booster treatments during this time period greatly increase the chances that the client will continue to abstain from drinking.[33] Furthermore, the odds become more favorable the greater the number of supplementary aversion sessions clients receive.[34] There is also some indication that the effects of aversion therapy may be more durable when the therapy sessions are scheduled over a relatively long period of time.[35] Probably the single most important way to prevent relapse of behaviors suppressed by aversion therapy is to supplement the aversion therapy with treatment procedures that accelerate an acceptable alternative behavior.[36]

Fifth, the fact that aversion therapies only *decelerate* maladaptive behaviors is another limitation. Assuring that the client will engage in appropriate alternative behaviors is critical for the typical deceleration target behaviors modified by aversion therapy. A person who no longer uses drugs to cope with frustration at work or home must have a new appropriate means of handling day-to-day problems, just as the man who is no longer sexually aroused by exposing himself in public wants sexual pleasure and therefore needs to be "turned on" in more socially acceptable ways. Case 5-4 illustrated the strategy of including both acceleration and deceleration behavioral therapy techniques—orgasmic reconditioning to provide new antecedent conditions for sexual arousal and behavior (normal fantasies of women), and covert sensitization to eliminate the client's sadistic fantasies. Aversion-relief therapy simultaneously accelerates an alternative behavior for the one being decelerated.

It should be noted that aversion therapies are almost always used as a last resort—that is, after other nonaversive treatments have been tried and have failed. This general precaution is exercised because aversion therapies always involve discomfort and often pain for the client. It is also important to emphasize that the target behaviors for which aversion therapies are employed are generally severe enough to warrant temporary unpleasantness and mild pain for the client. These important issues will be raised again in Chapter 7, which presents another major strategy for decelerating maladaptive behaviors—namely, by changing the consequences of the target behavior.

Aversion therapies, while sometimes highly effective, are used less frequently than other behavioral therapies, not only because they are generally less potent than other therapies but also because of the practical and ethical limitations just discussed. Furthermore, in most cases long-lasting deceleration of abnormal behaviors, especially those involving addiction and sexual deviation, require concomitant acceleration of alternative, adaptive behaviors. In fact, the most important contribution of aversion therapies (as well as the use of aversive consequences) is to rapidly decelerate maladaptive behaviors so that adaptive alternative behaviors can be accelerated. The next chapter deals with specific behavioral therapies that are used to establish such behaviors.

SUMMARY

Substitution behavioral therapies that substitute negative reactions for positive but socially inappropriate or otherwise maladaptive behaviors (e.g., addictive and sexually deviant behaviors) are typically called *aversion therapies*. They create an aversion in the client toward performing the maladaptive behavior.

Mild electric shock is the most typical aversive event used and has the advantage that its presentation and termination can be precisely controlled to coincide with the deceleration target behavior. Other aversive events include nausea, unpleasant thoughts, and humiliation. The aversive event can be presented while the client is actually engaging in the target behavior, while the client is exposed to cues related to performing the target behavior, or while the client is imagining engaging in the target behavior.

In shame aversion therapy, the client engages in the target behavior in the presence of observers, which results in the client feeling humiliated or guilty. In covert sensitization, both the aversive event and the target behavior are imagined by the client. Aversion-relief therapy capitalizes on the relief that clients experience when an aversive event is terminated by associating that relief with an alternative, adaptive target behavior.

Aversion therapies in general have been moderately successful in temporarily decelerating maladaptive behaviors, especially when alternative, adaptive target behaviors are simultaneously accelerated. There are a number of ethical and moral objections to the use of aversion therapies that sometimes preclude their use in practice.

REFERENCE NOTES

1. Bandura, 1969.
2. Nathan, 1976.
3. Serber, 1970.
4. Wickramasekera, 1976.
5. Serber, 1970, 1972; Wickramasekera, 1976.
6. Katchadourian & Lunde, 1972.
7. Serber, 1972.
8. Serber, 1972.
9. Serber, 1970, 1972.
10. Serber, 1970; 1972; Wickramasekera, 1976.
11. Cautela, 1966, 1967.
12. For example, Barlow, Leitenberg, & Agras, 1969; Gershman, 1970; Kolvin, 1967; Maletzky, 1974.
13. For example, Cautela, 1966; Janda & Rimm, 1972; Stuart, 1967.
14. For example, Anant, 1968; Ashem & Donner, 1968; Cautela, 1967, 1970, 1971; Cautela & Wisocki, 1969; Hedberg & Campbell, 1974; Smith & Gregory, 1976.
15. For example, Lawson & May, 1970; Sipich, Russell, & Tobias, 1974; Tooley & Pratt, 1967; Wagner & Bragg, 1970.
16. Cautela, 1972, pp. 88–89.
17. Harbert, Barlow, Hersen, & Austin, 1974.
18. Wilson & Tracy, 1976.
19. Marquis, 1970.
20. Conrad & Wincze, 1976; Rachman & Wilson, 1980.
21. Conrad & Wincze, 1976.
22. Rachman & Wilson, 1980.
23. For example, Barlow, Leitenberg, & Agras, 1969; Callahan & Leitenberg, 1972; Harbert, Barlow, Hersen & Austin, 1974.

24. Maletzky, 1980.
25. Thorpe, Schmidt, Brown, & Castell, 1964.
26. Rachman & Teasdale, 1969; Rachman & Wilson, 1980.
27. Barlow & Abel, 1981; Rachman & Teasdale, 1969; Rachman & Wilson, 1980.
28. Rachman & Wilson, 1980.
29. Kazdin & Wilson, 1978.
30. For example, Wilson & Tracy, 1976.
31. Rachman & Teasdale, 1969.
32. Bandura, 1969, p. 542.
33. Voegtlin, Lemere, Broz, & O'Hollaren, 1941.
34. Bandura, 1969.
35. Rachman & Teasdale, 1969.
36. For example, Barlow, 1973.

CHAPTER 6 Consequential Therapies: Accelerating Adaptive Behaviors

The previous two chapters considered a variety of behavioral therapies that substitute adaptive behaviors for maladaptive behaviors. The procedures described dealt primarily with the methods by which the substitution behaviors were instigated. The issue of how the adaptive responses were maintained—that is, what accounts for their continued substitution for the previous maladaptive behaviors—was not addressed. Recall that the conditions that maintain behaviors are primarily found in events that follow the performance of the behaviors—that is, in their *consequences*. Substitution behaviors are maintained for one of two reasons. First, they lead to desirable consequences: they allow clients to function successfully in situations that previously were difficult for them. For example, once learned, muscle relaxation becomes a more attractive alternative to the client than muscle tension, because the former is more pleasant and provides a means of effectively coping with anxiety. Second, substitution behaviors also may allow the person to successfully avoid undesirable consequences. For instance, aversion to alcohol is an adaptive reaction in that it helps the individual avoid negative consequences such as loss of family and job.

We now turn to the issue of how consequences influence behavior, and how they can be systematically changed to modify target behaviors. This chapter presents the basic principles of behavioral therapies that accelerate adaptive behaviors by providing clients with attractive consequences for learning and practicing them. Chapter 7 covers the fundamentals of behavioral therapies that make the consequences of performing maladaptive behaviors unattractive for the client, in an effort to decelerate them. Chapters 8 and 9 discuss in detail two specific areas of application of the consequential behavioral therapy procedures outlined in Chapters 6 and 7; namely, token economies (Chapter 8) and behavioral medicine (Chapter 9).

REINFORCEMENT: INCREASING THE FREQUENCY OF BEHAVIOR

To reinforce is to strengthen, and the term *reinforcement* refers to strengthening a behavior, in the sense that it will be likely to recur. The strength of a behavior is measured by its frequency of occurrence. Reinforcement as a behavioral therapy technique involves arranging the consequences of a behavior so that they will motivate the individual to perform the behavior again (and again and again).

We are all familiar with the use of reinforcement. Parents get their children to do their homework by allowing them to watch television or to engage in some other enjoyable pastime after they have finished their homework. Workers continue to show up at their jobs because they receive a paycheck each week. Teachers reward their students' good work with high grades or by exempting them from a required exam or assignment. Diners get good service from a favorite waiter by giving him large tips. In fact, dozens of times each day all of us are under the influence of reinforcers. New behaviors are learned and become strengthened—that is, more likely to recur—because we are reinforced for performing them. And old behaviors continue to be performed because they were reinforced in the past and continue to be periodically reinforced in the present.

An Empirical Definition of Reinforcement

Reinforcement *occurs whenever an event that follows a behavior increases the likelihood that it will recur.* This definition is *empirical* because reinforcement is said to have occurred only when an increase in the frequency of the behavior has been *observed.* An event that is a consequence of a behavior and that results in reinforcement is called a **reinforcer**. This relationship between a behavior and a reinforcer is often stated in terms of the reinforcer being *contingent on* the behavior. In other words, the person has to perform the behavior *before* receiving the reinforcer.

Generally, but not always, reinforcers are pleasurable or desirable events. However, reinforcers are defined in terms of their acceleration effects on the behavior, not in terms of their subjective desirability to the individual. It is possible that a particular consequence of a behavior could strengthen the behavior even though the person might not say that the consequence was pleasurable or desirable and might even say that it was unpleasant or undesirable. This is usually the case when the consequence of engaging in a behavior is not particularly enjoyable, but is the "lesser of two evils." For example, using dental floss may be a chore, but it is better than having to have dental work done.

TYPES OF REINFORCERS

Reinforcement can be classified into two broad categories. In **positive reinforcement,** the frequency of a behavior is increased when it is followed by the *presentation* of some event. The event the individual receives for performing the behavior is called a **positive reinforcer.** For example, a man wears a particular outfit more often because he often is told how handsome he looks in it. Or, a door-to-door salesperson keeps knocking on doors because she is making sales and earning money. We are all very familiar with positive reinforcement. Our everyday behavior is largely governed by it, and we frequently attempt to increase other people's behavior by providing them with various events we think will act as reinforcers. Positive reinforcement is probably the most extensively used procedure in behavioral therapy.

Negative reinforcement, the second category of reinforcement, refers to the increase in the frequency of a behavior when the behavior is followed by the *removal* or *avoidance* of an event. The event is called a **negative reinforcer,** and usually the client finds it aversive, unpleasant, or otherwise undesirable. For example, new parents quickly learn to attend to their infant's needs when doing so makes the baby stop crying. "Attending to the baby" increases because the parents thus stop or avoid the unpleasantness of listening to their baby crying.

Note that reinforcement, whether positive or negative, always refers to the acceleration of a target behavior. The terms *positive* and *negative* merely indicate whether the reinforcer is *added* in positive reinforcement (think of a plus sign in arithmetic) or *subtracted* in negative reinforcement (think of a minus sign) to increase the occurrence of the behavior.

Positive reinforcement is used much more frequently in behavioral therapy because it is more convenient and feasible to administer and has fewer potential problems. It is generally simpler to provide a client with an event for performing a desired behavior (positive reinforcement) than to remove an event (negative reinforcement), because the latter requires that the event be present while the person is performing the behavior. Furthermore, because negative reinforcement usually involves an aversive event, the procedure has some of the drawbacks associated with aversion therapies, as was discussed in the previous chapter. For these reasons, negative reinforcement is used relatively infrequently to accelerate adaptive behaviors in behavioral therapy, and this book's coverage of reinforcement deals primarily with positive reinforcement.

Positive Reinforcers

A variety of events serve as positive reinforcers. Before these are enumerated, take a few minutes to jot down as many specific reinforcers, or what are commonly called "rewards," as you can. What events do you find reinforcing? Do this before reading any further, and save this list, because you will use it later in conjunction with Participation Exercise 6-1.

Five major categories of reinforcers are discussed here: commodities, activities, social reinforcers, feedback, and token reinforcers.

Commodities

Probably a substantial number of reinforcers you listed were commodities, or material items, that have some worth to you and to other people. Favorite foods, fashionable and/or comfortable clothes, toys, books, jewelry, records, and recreational equipment are common examples of commodities that are likely to be reinforcers for many people in our society. When asked to name some potential reinforcers for themselves, most people mention primarily objects, but they constitute only one category of reinforcers.

Activities

Access to activities is a second major category of positive reinforcers, and you may have included a number of pleasurable or desirable activities in your list of reinforcers. Some activities that are reinforcers for many people are listening to music, going shopping, playing games, reading, taking naps, going to parties, talking to friends, cooking, dancing, getting dressed up, eating good foods, traveling, kissing, smoking, drinking, and giving gifts to people.

Although the activities that serve as reinforcers are often pleasurable for the person, they need not be. Many activities that a person does frequently, whether or not the person considers them pleasurable, can serve as reinforcers for behaviors that are performed infrequently. This basic idea is embodied in the **Premack principle**[1] (discovered by David Premack): when two behaviors are typically performed at different frequencies, *the lower-frequency behavior will increase when performing the higher-frequency behavior is made contingent on performing the lower-frequency behavior.* In other words, the higher-frequency behavior follows and functions as a reinforcer for the lower-frequency behavior. The person agrees to perform a specified amount of the low-probability behavior in order to be able to spend a specified amount of time engaging in the higher-probability behavior. For instance, students who study little could increase their studying by making a higher-probability activity (e.g., one that occurs more frequently) contingent on a specified amount of studying (e.g., talking on the telephone for 5 minutes only after 15 minutes of studying has been completed). An intriguing use of the Premack principle involved a married couple's increasing the frequency of their lovemaking by using their frequent visits to the beauty and barber shop as reinforcers for their low-frequency sexual activity.[2]

The Premack principle is a relatively simple and flexible procedure and also has the advantage that naturally occurring activities can be used as reinforcers by merely arranging them in an appropriate temporal order. Case 6-1 illustrates use of the Premack principle to accelerate the social interaction of a withdrawn psychiatric patient.

CASE 6-1

*Increasing Social Interaction by the Premack Principle**

A patient in a psychiatric hospital was socially isolated from her fellow patients and the hospital staff. She rarely interacted with others, the only exception being to follow instructions from a staff member or to nod her head in answer to a simple question. A variety of

*From the author's files.

strategies were tried to get her to be more sociable, including having volunteers take her on walks and short trips, repeatedly encouraging her to take part in activities with other patients, and attempting to engage her in casual conversation during meals (the only time that she spent with the other patients). None of these interventions changed her social behavior.

The ward staff members had never observed the patient enjoying any activities. In fact, she spent almost all her waking hours sitting in a specific chair in the day room of the ward, although she showed none of the usual signs of enjoyment (e.g., smiling, verbally expressing pleasure) while engaged in this solitary activity. Yet because sitting in her favorite chair was a high-frequency behavior, it was potentially a reinforcer for social interaction, which was a low-frequency behavior.

The patient was informed by a staff member that she would be permitted to sit in her favorite chair only after she had spent time in an activity with one or more of the patients or staff members. Specifically, the initial treatment plan established the criterion that the patient could sit in the chair for 30 minutes after she had spent two minutes interacting with others. This plan was explained to the patient, and she nodded that she understood. Because this interchange with the staff member took several minutes, the patient was immediately allowed to sit in the chair for a 30-minute period. (This contingency was directly explained to the patient by the staff member.) At the end of the first 30-minute period, a staff member approached the patient and suggested that they have a cup of coffee together, reminding the patient that she had to spend two minutes interacting with others in order to sit in the chair. With some reluctance, the patient assented to the staff member's invitation. For the rest of the day one of the ward staff would approach the patient after each 30-minute period of sitting and suggest some minimal social activity that would fulfill the requirement for continued sitting.

On successive days, the number of minutes of social interaction required for 30 minutes of sitting was gradually increased so that by the end of the second week the patient was spending 15 minutes interacting with others for every 30 minutes that she spent sitting. At the same time, the staff's suggestions for social interaction were faded (gradually eliminated), and the patient chose how she wanted to spend time with others from the examples the staff had provided for her in the first few days. Toward the end of the second week, the patient began to get up from the chair when 30 minutes had elapsed without having to be reminded by a staff member. As a direct consequence of the treatment plan, the patient was spending considerable time each day engaged in minimal social interactions. Furthermore, as time passed, she actually began spending more than the required time with others and less than her earned time sitting. For example, one way that she frequently chose to socialize was to play dominoes with a particular patient. The first few times she played she would get up in the middle of the game and walk to her chair as soon as she had accumulated enough social time to sit in her chair. After a while, however, she would first finish a game, which required a half-hour or more. Eventually the patient was spending the major portion of each day in some activity with others and was only occasionally observed sitting alone.

In using the Premack principle to accelerate the patient's social behavior, the ward staff made no assumptions that the patient enjoyed sitting in the chair; it was only known that sitting in the chair was a frequent behavior that occurred much more often than social behavior. Apparently "sitting in the chair" was a reinforcer for the patient because her interactions with others increased when social contact was followed by sitting in the chair.

Social Reinforcers

Social reinforcers involve various forms of interpersonal interaction and constitute the third category of positive reinforcers. Common examples include praise, approval of others, friendly gestures (e.g., smiling), physical contact (e.g., firm handshake, hug, pat on the back), and frequently just attention (e.g., talking to a person, maintaining eye contact).

Social consequences have several distinct advantages over commodities and activities as reinforcers. Social reinforcers are easy to administer: little time is required, and the **reinforcing agent**—the person administering the reinforcer—carries around a near-limitless supply at all times. Social reinforcers can often be given immediately after the target behavior has been performed, an advantage that will be discussed later. Furthermore, social reinforcers usually can be administered without interrupting the client's ongoing activities. For example, if social reinforcement had been part of the treatment plan for the female psychiatric patient in Case 6-1, a staff member could easily have smiled at the patient and given her some verbal encouragement, such as "It's good to see you playing dominoes," while the patient continued to play the game. Another advantage of social reinforcement is that it easily generalizes from the therapy situation to the client's everyday life. Social reinforcers are **naturally occurring reinforcers**—that is, consequences that people receive as a regular part of their daily lives. Thus, using social reinforcers during therapy to accelerate adaptive behaviors increases the chances that those behaviors will be maintained after therapy has ended.

Social reinforcers are frequently used in conjunction with other types of reinforcers to facilitate a shift from "contrived" reinforcers to naturally occurring reinforcers. To use the example of the patient in Case 6-1, offering verbal praise and attention along with access to sitting in her favorite chair might have made it possible to gradually decrease the woman's solitary sitting behavior while continuing to maintain her interpersonal behavior with social reinforcers alone.

Social reinforcers, even when used by themselves, are often among the most powerful consequences for accelerating behavior. Human beings frequently seek out and rely on other people's approval, praise, and attention to maintain their everyday behaviors. For example, our clothes are often dictated by what our close acquaintances think is attractive ("How does this outfit look, or should I wear the red one?"), not to mention the social pressure to conform to the "in" styles.

The potency of social reinforcement in behavioral therapy is illustrated in Case 6-2. Here, social reinforcement was the major component used to treat a patient whose legs were paralyzed although no physical factors could be found to account for the dysfunction (such disorders are called *conversion reactions*).

CASE 6-2

*Treatment of a Conversion Reaction by Social Reinforcement**

The patient, a 42-year-old white, married male, was admitted in a wheelchair to the Psychiatry Service of the Veterans Administration Center, Jackson, Mississippi. When admitted he was bent forward at the waist (45-degree angle) and unable to straighten his body or move his legs. For the past 15 years, he had consistently complained of lumbosacral [lower back] pain. On two occasions (12 and 5 years prior to admission) he underwent orthopedic surgery; however, complaints of pain persisted. In the last five years, the patient had numerous episodes of being totally unable to walk. These episodes, referred to by the patient as "drawing over," typically lasted 10–14 days and occurred every four to six weeks. The patient was frequently hospitalized and treated with heat applications and muscle relaxants. Five years prior to this admission, the patient had retired on Social Security benefits and assumed all household duties, as his wife was compelled to support the family.

Orthopedic and neurological evaluations failed to reveal contributory causes. An assessment of the patient's family life revealed that there were numerous stresses coinciding with onset of "drawing over" episodes. Included were the patient's recent discharge from the National Guard after 20 years of service, difficulties with his son and youngest daughter, and "guilt" feelings about the role reversal he and his wife had assumed. Moreover, it was clear that the patient received considerable social reinforcement from family members when he presented with symptoms of "illness" (e.g., receiving breakfast in bed [and] being relieved of household chores). . . .

In all phases of treatment, an attractive young female . . . assistant visited the patient in his room three times daily. Ten minutes were allotted for each visit, during which time she spoke to the patient about topics unrelated to his psychiatric disorder. At the conclusion of each 10-minute visit, the patient was asked to leave his wheelchair and instructed to stand and walk as far as possible. Length of time standing, number of steps taken, and distance walked were recorded.

In the first phase (Reinforce Standing), social reinforcement for standing was administered (e.g., "You're standing very well today," "You're standing straighter now," [and] "I'm very proud of you") but no comments were offered with respect to attempts at walking. Examination of data in [Case Figure 6-2A] shows that few attempts at walking were made during this phase. However, when social reinforcement for walking was added in Phase 2 (Reinforce Standing and Walking), a linear increase in walking was observed over Days 4–6. In Phase 3 reinforcement for walking was discontinued, resulting in no further increases in walking with the exception of Day 11. When reinforcement for walking was reinstated in Phase 4 (Reinforce Walking and Standing), a still further increase in walking was noted. On Days 15 and 16, the patient's wheelchair was replaced with a walker, and on Days 17 and 18 the walker was withdrawn. By Day 18 the patient was walking normally and was discharged from inpatient status. A four-week follow-up indicated that his gains had been maintained (was able to walk 350 yards).

Immediately following the four-week follow-up the patient experienced a severe episode of "drawing over," and was readmitted to the Psychiatry Service unable to walk. During this episode the patient's family once again had reinforced "sick" role behaviors by

*Reprinted from Kallmann, Hersen, and O'Toole (1975), pp. 411–412.

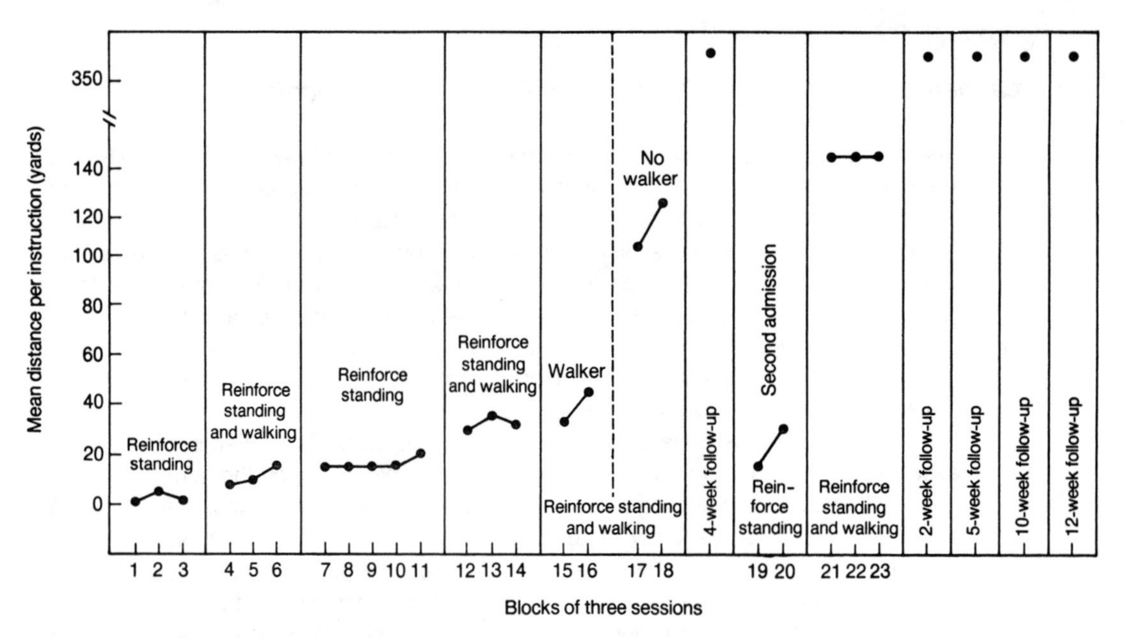

CASE FIGURE 6-2A

Mean distance walked by the patient during all phases of treatment and follow-up

SOURCE: Kallmann, Hersen, & O'Toole (1975), p. 412.

giving him a considerable amount of attention. Therefore, during the patient's second admission a family retraining program was also incorporated in the treatment.

First, social reinforcement procedures during Days 19–22 rapidly led to the patient's resumption of normal walking. *Second,* during the last phase of treatment (Reinforce Standing and Walking) two family therapy sessions were held. In the first session the patient and his family were videotaped while interacting with one another. Analysis of this videotape confirmed that family members were generally ignoring his positive initiatives. In the second session, the family was instructed to ignore the patient's presentation of complaints and to praise him for all positive efforts, including walking normally. In addition, social reinforcement procedures used by the . . . assistant during . . . treatment were modeled for the family. Subsequent 2, 6, 10, and 12-week follow-ups indicated that the patient was walking normally.

Feedback

Feedback, or information about one's behavior, can serve as a reinforcer. If clients know that they are performing an acceleration target behavior correctly, this knowledge by itself sometimes leads to an increase in the target behavior. In fact, all reinforcers provide a person with some feedback—minimally that a desirable behavior has occurred—although more precise feedback would include information about how well it was performed. For example, praise following the correct performance of a target behavior may function as both a social reinforcer and feedback. Feedback by itself and in conjunction with other therapeutic procedures has been successfully used to treat a variety of problem behaviors, including speech dysfunctions,[3] phobic behavior,[4] tics,[5] lack of assertiveness,[6] encopretic behavior (involuntary defecation),[7] and poor posture.[8] Also, bodily functions such as tension[9] and blood pressure[10] are beginning to be modified clinically via biofeedback. The use of feedback to treat tension headaches is illustrated in Case 6-3.

CASE 6-3

*Tension Headaches Treated by Feedback**

A 39-year-old male machinist was admitted to a hospital for treatment of chronic tension headaches. No physical causes were found, and a behavioral assessment indicated that the tension headaches probably were being elicited by pressures at home and at work. Because tension headaches are associated with contraction of the forehead muscles, relaxing these muscles was chosen as the acceleration target behavior.

During the treatment, the patient was seated in a comfortable overstuffed chair. Electrodes were placed above each eyebrow and connected to an electromyograph to monitor the tension level in his forehead muscles. After baseline recording of the patient's normal tension level, a maximum tension level was set as a criterion. Whenever the patient was below the criterion, a tape-recorder played music. Thus the music was the feedback indicating to the patient that his forehead muscles were sufficiently relaxed. The patient was instructed to "keep the music playing." The music stopped whenever the maximum level of tension was exceeded.

In 12 feedback sessions, the patient demonstrated that he could keep his forehead muscles below the criterion of tension, and he reported that his tension headaches were under control. At this point the patient was discharged from the hospital. However, when the patient returned to the situations that elicited the headaches (i.e., his normal home and work environments), the headaches returned. The patient was given four booster feedback sessions, and he was instructed to apply the self-control techniques he had learned in the hospital at home. Specifically, when he had a headache at home he was to sit in a comfortable chair and try to relax his forehead muscles. Both the booster treatments and his home practice appeared to help reduce his tension headaches and maintain this reduction. At a 66-day follow-up, the patient reported that he had experienced tension headaches on only two days.

Token Reinforcers

Token reinforcers, another major category of positive reinforcers, have no intrinsic value themselves but nonetheless are valued because of what they can

*Epstein, Hersen, & Hemphill (1974).

be exchanged for or because of what they stand for. The most familiar token reinforcer in our society is money. Money has little worth in itself (even to the most creative individual), but it can be exchanged for material goods and access to activities. In token economies, tokens in the form of plastic chips or points are given to clients when they perform acceleration target behaviors. The tokens, like money, can later be exchanged for various reinforcing events. Examples of token reinforcers that are valued by virtue of what they signify include a good grade, a trophy, a varsity letter, and a college diploma.

Identifying Reinforcers

Reinforcers must be individualized for each client. Although there certainly are events that tend to be reinforcing for many people, such as social attention, there are enough exceptions so that it cannot be assumed that any event will serve to increase *every* person's behavior in *all* situations. In each instance, one must test whether an event is indeed a reinforcer by seeing if it increases the behavior it follows. A variety of procedures are employed to find *potential* reinforcers for clients, including direct questioning, observation of the client's typical behaviors, and exposure to generalized reinforcers.

Direct Questioning

The easiest and most frequently used method of discovering potential positive reinforcers is for the therapist to simply ask the client concrete questions such as "What do you like to do in the evenings? On weekends?" or "If you had some extra money, what would you buy with it?" or "Where would you like to go if you had a day off?" The way the questions are phrased varies with the client being questioned. Simpler language is used with children, people with low intelligence or little education, and individuals who have language difficulties. In the case of clients who have not been exposed to reinforcers for long periods of time, as is often true for chronic psychiatric patients and prisoners, the questions are often more meaningfully phrased in the past tense (e.g., "What activities *did* you enjoy doing before you came to the hospital?"). Sometimes a therapist will ask future-oriented questions with clients who find it difficult to think of anything pleasant or rewarding in their present or even past lives, as with depressed clients (e.g., "What would you like to do when you leave the hospital?").

The information obtained must be specific and detailed. If a client merely says, "I enjoy sports," the therapist needs to know what type of sport (e.g., baseball, swimming, or horseback riding) and whether the client prefers participating or being a spectator. Besides asking clients themselves about events that may be reinforcing to them, sometimes therapists question people who know the clients well.

To identify possible negative reinforcers, the therapist asks about events in the client's life that are aversive (unpleasant or a nuisance) and can be terminated. For example, "What do you do regularly that you find bothersome and want to finish as quickly as possible?"

Although asking direct questions to obtain information about potential reinforcers is usually the most efficient method, clients may provide inaccurate or inadequate information. Some clients respond with socially desirable answers rather than accurate information about their particular interests and sources of pleasure. At a football-oriented school, for instance, it is socially desirable for students to say that they like football. Clients who are not verbally expressive (e.g., young children, mentally retarded individuals, or mute patients) often provide little or no useful information in response to direct questioning. These potential problems are circumvented when direct observations of the client's overt behaviors are made to identify reinforcers for the client.

Direct Observation of Overt Behavior

Observing how people spend their time is one of the most productive means of determining events that may serve as reinforcers for their behavior. As a general rule, behaviors that a person engages in frequently can be considered potential reinforcers. Following an assessment of the frequency of a client's daily activities, the Premack principle can be applied to accelerate desirable but infrequently occurring behaviors.

It is important to note that, with relatively few exceptions, all (living) people are constantly behaving. Consider a typical scene on a psychiatric ward. On entering the day room, one sees some patients standing and looking out the window, several pacing back and forth, a couple sleeping in chairs, and others chain-smoking cigarettes. In a sense, these people seem to be doing "nothing." But even from this sketchy description of the patients in the day room, we can begin to list those activities that are being engaged in frequently and that therefore might serve as reinforcers—namely, looking out the window, pacing, sleeping in a chair, and smoking.[11]

Exposure to Generalized Reinforcers

Events that tend to be reinforcing for many different people in a wide variety of situations are called **generalized reinforcers,**[12] and they can serve as a starting point for finding individualized reinforcers for a client. It is most useful to speak of generalized reinforcers for a specific category of people. For example, two boys of approximately the same age would likely have more common generalized reinforcers than a boy and girl of the same age. In identifying generalized reinforcers, the therapist must consider such factors as age, sex, socioeconomic level, cultural background, and educational level.

When clients are exposed to a representative sample of generalized reinforcers, they can often identify particular events that could serve as reinforcers for them. A child might be taken to a toy store and asked to pick out several toys he or she would really like to have, or an adult might be asked to look over a merchandise catalogue or the entertainment section of the Sunday newspaper in order to choose potential reinforcers.

A number of standardized lists of generalized reinforcers have been developed to facilitate identifying reinforcers for clients. The Reinforcement Survey Schedule[13] is a direct self-report inventory that asks clients to rate the degree to which they enjoy having or consuming certain commodities and engaging in common activities. Examples of items on the Reinforcement Survey Schedule appear in Table 6-1. One recently developed children's reinforcement survey schedule provides the therapist with a list of generalized reinforcers for children; the therapist checks off those items that the child especially values (see Table 6-2).[14] With the Pleasant Events Schedule,[15] the client rates an extensive list of behaviors in terms of how enjoyable they are, as well as how frequently the client has engaged in them in the past month. You will have a chance to fill out part of the Pleasant Events Schedule in Participation Exercise 6-1. Reinforcement menus, like the one in Figure 6-1, have been prepared for children who cannot read but can recognize the generalized reinforcing events depicted in the pictures and can point to the ones they enjoy.[16]

Participation Exercise 6-1 (p. 128) will give you a chance to try out two of the basic procedures used to find potential reinforcers for clients and also will make you aware of your own reinforcers. Because it will take you a while to do Participation Exercise 6-1, you may want to do it when you have finished reading the chapter, although it is appropriate to do at this time.

Alternatives to Identifying Reinforcers

A therapist is not always successful at identifying reinforcers for a client, and in such instances one alternative is to use generalized reinforcers that are appropriate for the particular client. The odds are good that some of the generalized reinforcers will turn out to be reinforcers for the client. This strategy is used in token economies by providing a large list of generalized reinforcers from which clients choose the reinforcers they wish to purchase with the

TABLE 6-1 Sample Items on the Reinforcement Survey Schedule

SECTION I: OBJECTS AND ACTIVITIES	*Not at All*	*A Little*	*A Fair Amount*	*Much*	*Very Much*
Eating					
Ice cream	_____	_____	_____	_____	_____
Fruit	_____	_____	_____	_____	_____
Cookies	_____	_____	_____	_____	_____
Beverages					
Milk	_____	_____	_____	_____	_____
Soft drink	_____	_____	_____	_____	_____
Solving problems					
Crossword puzzles	_____	_____	_____	_____	_____
Figuring out how something works	_____	_____	_____	_____	_____

SOURCE: Cautela & Kastenbaum (1967), pp. 1118–1122.

	Not at All	A Little	A Fair Amount	Much	Very Much
Nude men	____	____	____	____	____
Nude women	____	____	____	____	____
Watching sports					
Football	____	____	____	____	____
Baseball	____	____	____	____	____
Golf	____	____	____	____	____
Reading					
Adventure	____	____	____	____	____
Mystery	____	____	____	____	____
Sexy	____	____	____	____	____
Looking at beautiful scenery	____	____	____	____	____
Television, movies, or radio	____	____	____	____	____
Shopping					
Clothes	____	____	____	____	____
Auto parts and supplies	____	____	____	____	____
Gardening	____	____	____	____	____
Sleeping	____	____	____	____	____
Being right					
In an argument	____	____	____	____	____
About your work	____	____	____	____	____
Being praised					
About your appearance	____	____	____	____	____
About your work	____	____	____	____	____
Being in church or temple	____	____	____	____	____
Peace and quiet	____	____	____	____	____

SECTION II: SITUATIONS I WOULD LIKE TO BE IN

How much would you enjoy being in each of the following situations?

You have just led your team to victory. An old friend comes over and says, "You played a terrific game. Let me treat you to dinner and drinks."

Not at all ( ) A little ( ) A fair amount ( ) Much ( ) Very much ( )

You are sitting by the fireplace with your loved one. Music is playing softly. . . . Your loved one gives you a tender glance, and you respond with a kiss. You think to yourself how wonderful it is to care for someone and have someone care for you.

Not at all ( ) A little ( ) A fair amount ( ) Much ( ) Very much ( )

SECTION III: ACTIVITY OR PREFERENCE FREQUENCIES

List the things you do or think about more than:

5	10	15	20 times a day
____	____	____	____
____	____	____	____
____	____	____	____

TABLE 6-2 *Examples of Generalized Reinforcers Appearing on the Children's Reinforcement Survey Schedule*

Check off valued reinforcers according to child's report:

- Food
  - Candy (what kind?)
  - Ice cream (favorite flavor?)
  - Potato chips
- Toys
  - Racing cars
  - Dolls
- Entertainment
  - Television (favorite program?)
  - Movies (what kind: western, horror, etc.?)
- Sports and games
  - Playing football
    - with other kids
    - with your father
  - Swimming
  - Tennis
  - Checkers
  - Fishing
- Music, arts and crafts
  - Playing a musical instrument (what kind?)
  - Building models
  - Working with clay
  - Singing
- Excursions
  - Ride in the car
  - Visit to the seashore
  - A family picnic
  - An airplane ride
  - Visiting a friend
- Social
  - Playing with friends
  - Being praised (by whom: father, mother, etc.?)
  - Being hugged or kissed
  - Girl Scouts, Boy Scouts, or other clubs
- Learning
  - A new language
  - Piano lessons
- Schoolwork
  - Reading
  - Science
  - Gym
- Helping around the house
  - Setting the table
  - Making the bed
  - Going on errands
- Personal appearance
  - Getting new clothes
  - Getting a haircut
  - Dressing up in a costume

SOURCE: Phillips, Fischer, & Singh (1977), pp. 131–132.

tokens they have earned. A **token economy** is a structured environment in which clients earn token reinforcers (e.g., in the form of mock money) for performing specified adaptive behaviors. The tokens can be exchanged for desired commodities, activities, or services. The token economy will be discussed in detail in a later chapter.

Another possibility is to build in reinforcers by making various commodities or activities desirable so that they will become reinforcers. **Reinforcer sampling**[17] is a procedure in which clients are first given a particular commodity (e.g., candy) or allowed to do a specific activity (e.g., watch a movie) without having to do anything to obtain it. The object is to "hook" the client on the event, and then when it has acquired some value—that is, the individual begins to enjoy it and wants more of it—the client is required to do something to earn it. For example, psychiatric patients in a token economy program were

FIGURE 6-1 *Example of a reinforcement menu used to identify potential reinforcers for young children by having children point to the pictures of events they enjoy*
SOURCE: Daley (1969), p. 44.

PARTICIPATION EXERCISE 6-1
Identifying Your Own Reinforcers

Earlier in the chapter, you were asked to make a list of your reinforcers. Now that you have learned about some of the procedures behavioral therapists use to identify potential reinforcers for a client, you can compile a much more extensive list of your own potential reinforcers. As you proceed through this participation exercise, keep a running list of the events you identify as your potential reinforcers. When you have finished the exercise, compare the list of potential reinforcers you have identified with the list you made earlier.

PART 1. DIRECT QUESTIONING

Think about the different types of reinforcers discussed in the text, and then ask yourself questions to elicit a list of events that may be reinforcers for you. The following is a partial list of questions you can ask yourself:

Commodities

1. What things do I like to use? Buy? Consume (e.g., food)?
2. What possessions are most valuable to me?
3. What would I like as a gift?

Activities

4. What activities do I enjoy?
5. What do I like to do in my spare time?
6. What do I like to do most in my work?
7. What type of social events do I like?
8. What do I consider a fun night out? Night at home? Weekend? Vacation?

Social Reinforcers

9. What type of social interactions do I enjoy?
10. What do I like other people to do for me? Say to me?
11. How do I like to spend my time with other people?*

Feedback

12. What makes me feel happy? Alive? Useful? Good? Important?
13. What accomplishments give me satisfaction?

Negative Reinforcers

14. What events in my life do I look forward to ending? Want to finish as quickly as possible?

PART 2. PLEASANT EVENTS SCHEDULE

In this part of the participation exercise, you will be responding to a portion of the Pleasant Events Schedule. Exercise Table 6-1A contains a sample of the items that appear on the

*Question 11 essentially restates Question 9. Such "planned redundancy" can be a useful technique for obtaining information, because minor rephrasing of questions may elicit different responses.

Pleasant Events Schedule. Go over the list twice, first rating each event as to how often it has occurred during the past month, and then rating each event in terms of how pleasant it has been for you. There are no right or wrong answers.

Write the numbers 1 to 100 on a lined sheet of paper, leaving room for three columns (at least one-half inch wide) after each number. Go through the list of events in Exercise Table 6-1A and for each event ask yourself the question ***"How often has the event happened in my life during the past month?"*** Answer this question by rating each event using the following scale:

1 = This has ***not*** happened in the past 30 days.

2 = This has happened ***a few times*** (1–6) in the past 30 days.

3 = This has happened ***often*** (7 or more) in the past 30 days.

Write the appropriate number (1, 2, or 3) in the first column after the number corresponding to the event. Go through the list quickly, because you are not being asked to make fine discriminations.

Once you have gone through all the events and rated them in terms of their frequency of occurrence during the past month, you are ready to rate the items as to their pleasantness. This time you will be asking yourself the question ***"How pleasant, enjoyable, or rewarding was the event during the past month?"*** Answer this question by rating each event on the following scale:

1. This was ***not*** pleasant. (It was either unpleasant or neutral).
2. This was ***somewhat*** pleasant. (It was mildly or moderately pleasant.)
3. This was ***very*** pleasant. (It was strongly or extremely pleasant.)

Write the appropriate number (1, 2, or 3) in the ***second*** column after the number corresponding to the event. Again, go through the list quickly. ***Important:*** If an event has occurred more than once during the past month, put down an average pleasantness rating. If an event has ***not*** occurred during the past month, rate it according to how enjoyable you think it would have been.

When you have finished going through the list of events twice, multiply the two ratings for each event and put this cross-product in the ***third*** column. The cross-products should give a rough estimate of events that are most likely to serve as reinforcers for you. The products can range from "1," which indicates that the event has not happened in your life recently and that your estimate of its pleasantness is very low, to "9," which indicates that the event has occurred frequently and has been very enjoyable for you. Thus, the higher the cross-product for each event, the greater its potential to serve as a reinforcer for you.

At this point you should have a sizable list of events that might serve as reinforcers for you—events that you enjoy and/or participate in frequently. Whether a given event actually is a reinforcer is an empirical question that you can answer by making it contingent on engaging in some behavior you would like to increase. Suppose you identified that writing letters to friends is a potential reinforcer for you, and suppose that you would like to keep your room much neater than it generally is. First you need to establish some criteria for having a neat room (e.g., bed made, desk top clear, clothes in drawers and in closet), and then you need to set up some contingency for being able to write letters (e.g., "If my bed, desk, and clothes are in order before I leave my room in the morning, then I will write one letter to a friend that evening"). If you follow the contingency (e.g., you do write a letter each time your room is "neat," but only when it is "neat") and you find that your room is neater, then "writing letters to friends" is a reinforcer for your keeping your room neat and perhaps in other situations as well.

EXERCISE TABLE 6-1A
Pleasant Events That Are Potential Reinforcers

1. Going to the movies
2. Doing volunteer work; working on community service projects
3. Sleeping late
4. Attending a concert, opera, or ballet
5. Shopping
6. Being with my parents
7. Doing "odd jobs" around the house
8. Being in the country
9. Talking about my job or school
10. Doing housework or laundry; cleaning things
11. Learning to do something new
12. Doing craft work (pottery, jewelry, leather, beads, weaving, etc.)
13. Seeing old friends
14. Teaching someone
15. Playing board games (Monopoly, Scrabble, etc.)
16. Smoking marijuana
17. Having friends come to visit
18. Dating, courting, etc.
19. Social drinking
20. Getting up early in the morning
21. Wearing informal clothes
22. Listening to music
23. Writing letters, cards, or notes
24. Working with others as a team
25. Reading stories, novels, poems, or plays
26. Writing papers, essays, articles, reports, memos, etc.
27. Saying prayers
28. Dancing
29. Arguing
30. Talking about my hobby or special interest
31. Going to a museum or exhibit
32. Counseling someone
33. Winning a competition
34. Playing in a sporting competition
35. Hearing jokes
36. Brushing my teeth
37. Taking a shower
38. Going to a restaurant
39. Playing Frisbee or catch
40. Singing to myself
41. Playing a musical instrument
42. Repairing things
43. Going to the library
44. Swimming
45. Taking a walk
46. Traveling
47. Getting massages or backrubs
48. Going to a sports event
49. Sewing
50. Playing golf
51. Thinking about an interesting question
52. Crying
53. Doing artwork (painting, sculpture, drawing, movie making, etc.)
54. Taking a nap
55. Having someone agree with me
56. Bowling
57. Watching people
58. Hiking
59. Combing or brushing my hair
60. Cooking meals
61. Thinking about something good in the future
62. Complimenting or praising someone
63. Telling people what to do

SOURCE: MacPhillamy & Lewinsohn (1971).

64. Just sitting and thinking
65. Playing with pets
66. Boating (canoeing, kayaking, motor-boating, sailing, etc.)
67. Gardening, landscaping, or doing yard work
68. Going to service, civic, or social club meetings
69. Pleasing my parents
70. Helping someone
71. Reminiscing, talking about old times
72. Giving gifts
73. Writing stories, novels, plays, or poetry
74. Eating snacks
75. Staying up late
76. Solving a problem, puzzle, crosswords, etc.
77. Kissing
78. Reading maps
79. Being downtown
80. Buying things for myself
81. Reading essays or technical, academic, or professional literature
82. Woodworking, carpentry
83. Being complimented or told I have done well
84. Being asked for my help or advice
85. Talking on the telephone
86. Writing in a diary
87. Meeting someone new of the opposite sex
88. Seeing beautiful scenery
89. Going to a party
90. Reading the newspaper
91. Seeing good things happen to my family or friends
92. Going to lectures or hearing speakers
93. Having houseguests
94. Watching television
95. Going to a fair, carnival, circus, zoo, or amusement park
96. Rearranging or redecorating my room or house
97. Playing tennis
98. Being alone
99. Going to a rock concert
100. Talking about sports

---

encouraged to attend the first five minutes of a movie and then were charged tokens only if they stayed to see the remainder of the film.[18]

Even if commodities or activities are provided gratis, people may not avail themselves of them. A useful technique employed in another token economy is first to pay a patient with tokens for doing an activity, and later to require that the patient spend tokens to engage in the activity. For example, one patient who was afraid to travel on buses was paid a large number of tokens to attend his first field trip, which involved going by bus. He enjoyed the trip and decided to attend others, for which he then *paid* tokens.[19]

A potential reinforcer can also be made more attractive to a client by exposing the client to other people (models) who are partaking of the reinforcer and who clearly are enjoying themselves. For example, one token economy program set up a "reinforcement room" that contained a store for purchasing attractive commodities and recreational equipment for engaging in pleasurable activities.[20] Many events that appear to be "intrinsic" reinforcers, in fact have acquired reinforcing properties through imitation. Specifically, what we find enjoyable and valuable is determined in part by what other people find enjoyable and valuable. Humor is a good example. We often consider funny what we have seen others laugh at. Canned laughter used on television shows is a form of modeling that the audience often imitates.

ADMINISTERING REINFORCERS

Once reinforcers have been identified for a client, arrangements must be made for their being administered when the client performs the appropriate target behavior. The next two sections describe the alternative sources of reinforcers and specific guidelines for administering reinforcers for maximum effectiveness.

Sources of Reinforcers

Reinforcers may be administered (1) by other people, (2) by clients themselves, and (3) as a natural consequence of the behavior. Clients most often receive reinforcers from other people. Adults, such as parents and teachers, frequently are enlisted by a therapist to dispense reinforcers to their children, and spouses and close friends sometimes assume this role for other adults.[21] Occasionally children serve as reinforcing agents for other children, as in a classroom setting or at home with siblings.[22] And once in a while a child is asked to help an adult (usually a parent or teacher) develop an adaptive behavior by systematically providing reinforcers for the adult.[23]

Clients themselves may also serve as their own reinforcing agents. The major advantage of **self-reinforcement** is that the reinforcing agent is always around when the target behavior is performed. With some target behaviors, especially covert behaviors, only the client can know if they have occurred. Self-reinforcement allows clients to assume a critical role in their treatment and also provides them with a useful skill that they can apply in many situations. Any type of reinforcer can be self-administered: clients can give themselves appropriate "gifts" (commodities), permit themselves to engage in enjoyable activities, acknowledge that they have behaved appropriately and feel good about it (feedback and covert social reinforcement), or dispense their own token reinforcers, such as recording points they have earned.

The major drawback to self-reinforcement is that clients may not administer the reinforcers as prescribed by the treatment plan. For example, clients may give themselves reinforcers even though they have not earned them, or may fail to give themselves reinforcers for performing the target behavior (often because they believe that just acting appropriately should be a sufficient reinforcer). In the latter instance, clients may fail to appreciate the fact that if merely performing the target behavior had been a sufficient reinforcer, no reinforcement procedures to accelerate the target behavior would have been necessary.

A third source of reinforcers comes as a "natural" consequence of performing an adaptive behavior. For example, clients who are practicing asserting their right to ask for something to which they are entitled may be reinforced by getting what they ask for. Similarly, completing one's work ahead of time provides a person with free time as well as relief from the burden of having to complete the work.

Guidelines for Administering Reinforcers

Behavior therapists use a number of general guidelines for the proper administration of reinforcers to most effectively and efficiently accelerate a target behavior. The following is a list of some of the most important guidelines.

1. *The reinforcer must follow the target behavior.* Receiving a reinforcer must be *contingent on* performing the target behavior: *if* the target behavior occurs, *then* the client is entitled to the reinforcer. If a reinforcer is dispensed at other times, it has little or no effect on the target behavior. For example, if you decide to reinforce yourself for completing your assignments for the next day's classes by going to a movie, you cannot go to the movie before doing the assignments—that is, if you want to accelerate completing your next day's assignments on time. Benjamin Franklin was aware of this essential guideline, as the following passage demonstrates.[24]

> We had for our chaplain a zealous Presbyterian minister, Mr. Beatty, who complained to me that the men did not generally attend his prayers and exhortations. When they enlisted, they were promised, besides pay and provisions, a gill of rum a day, which was punctually serv'd out to them, half in the morning, and the other half in the evening; and I observ'd they were as punctual in attending to receive it; upon which I said to Mr. Beatty: "It is, perhaps, below the dignity of your profession to act as steward of the rum, but if you were to deal it out and only just after prayers, you would have them all about you." He liked the tho't, undertook the office, and, with the help of a few hands to measure out the liquor, executed it to satisfaction, and never were prayers more generally and more punctually attended; so that I thought this method preferable to the punishment inflicted by some military laws for nonattendance on divine service.

2. *The client should be aware that the reinforcer is a consequence of the target behavior.* This guideline is especially important if the client has performed several behaviors in close succession. One of the easiest and most powerful ways to make the client aware of the contingency is for the person administering the reinforcer to state the relationship between the reinforcer and the target behavior. For example, suppose a teacher is attempting to increase a student's correcting her own grammatical mistakes. When the student says, "I *ain't* finished with the test . . . I mean I am *not* finished with it," the teacher might reinforce the *correction*, but not the mistake, by saying, "You corrected your own mistake, Linda; that's very good." If the teacher had not made it clear to Linda what the praise was for, Linda could have mistakenly associated it with the incorrect grammatical construction or with some unrelated behavior such as telling the teacher that she had not completed the test.

3. *The reinforcer should be administered immediately after the target behavior has been performed.* Immediate reinforcement is generally more effective than delayed reinforcement in accelerating behavior.[25] However, reinforcement is often delayed for some time after the target behavior has been performed, because of practical limitations. For example, no one is around to

administer the reinforcer, or immediate reinforcement would disrupt ongoing behaviors of the client or other people. In such cases token reinforcers can be administered as soon as possible after the target behavior occurs, and later the tokens can be exchanged for a desirable commodity or activity. Social reinforcement, in the form of brief verbal praise that does not interrupt the ongoing behavior, may also be used. Administering a reinforcer immediately after the target behavior occurs also helps clarify the contingency between the target behavior and the reinforcer.

4. *Continuous reinforcement should be used first and then followed by intermittent reinforcement.* The term **continuous reinforcement** refers to the case in which a client receives a reinforcer each and every time he or she performs the target behavior (or, practically, each time it is observed by the reinforcing agent). The term **intermittent reinforcement** refers to providing a reinforcer for some, but not all, of the instances in which the target behavior occurs (e.g., on the average of every tenth time the client engages in the target behavior, or after each five-minute period in which the client engages in the target behavior). Continuous reinforcement is generally superior to intermittent reinforcement for initially accelerating a target behavior. However, once the client is performing the target behavior with some frequency, intermittent reinforcement effectively keeps the client performing the target behavior.

5. *Reinforcers should be kept potent.* The strength of a reinforcer varies as related conditions change, and behavioral therapists use several techniques to maintain the potency of the reinforcers. One procedure is to set up conditions so that the reinforcer used to accelerate a target behavior is only available to the client as a direct consequence of having performed the target behavior. For example, if completing a specified amount of work each day is being reinforced by watching television but, in fact, the client can watch television at any time, the effectiveness of television as a reinforcer will be weakened.

Another technique for maintaining the potency of a reinforcer involves temporarily depriving the client of the reinforcer (consistent with the popular adage "Absence makes the heart grow fonder"). If watching television is going to be used to reinforce a target behavior, then the client might be asked not to watch any television for a week before the treatment plan begins.

Conversely, even the most desirable reinforcer can lose its strength if it is administered too often or in too large a quantity. (For example, although my craving for ice cream seems endless, I find that five trips for Bud's bittersweet chocolate in one day substantially diminishes my interest in ice cream, albeit temporarily!) Administering a reinforcer in *small amounts* helps to avoid satiation (e.g., spoonfuls of ice cream rather than bowlfuls; listening to one song rather than a whole record). Another tactic is to use reinforcers that people tend to satiate on less easily—for example, social or token reinforcers, rather than physiological reinforcers such as food. Using several different reinforcers to accelerate a target behavior also reduces the problem of satiation.

6. *Naturally occurring reinforcers are preferable to "contrived" reinforcers.* When therapy has been completed, adaptive behaviors that have been accelerated through reinforcement procedures will be maintained only if they con-

tinue to be reinforced in the client's natural environment. Reinforcement, unlike a vaccine, is not a one-shot treatment; if a person is not reinforced for engaging in a particular behavior, at least every once in a while (i.e., intermittent reinforcement), the person will eventually stop performing that behavior. (This fact has obvious implications for decelerating behavior, as is shown in the discussion of extinction in the next chapter.)

To facilitate long-term maintenance of target behaviors, whenever possible the same (or at least similar) reinforcers that the client will receive in her or his natural environment should be used in therapy to accelerate the target behavior. Thus the typical strategy used in behavioral therapy is either (1) to employ naturally occurring reinforcers to accelerate target behaviors from the outset or (2) to gradually introduce naturally occurring reinforcers in conjunction with "contrived" reinforcers, which are then faded from the treatment program.

For example, two-year-old Jonathan has not yet learned to respond to social reinforcers, but good-tasting foods and access to his favorite form of play are usually effective reinforcers for him. A typical treatment plan to accelerate a target behavior in such a young child would involve reinforcing the child both with food (or play) and with social reinforcers. For example, as the child is given a bite of food as a reinforcer for performing the target behavior, the therapist would say something like "Very good, Jonathan. I'm proud of you." After the target behavior is occurring at an acceptable rate, the food reinforcer can be administered intermittently and eventually completely dropped. Meanwhile, the therapist's praise, which has become a reinforcer by association with food, takes over as the main reinforcer. In the child's home environment, the target behavior will most likely be maintained by similar social reinforcers.

7. *Reinforcement should be administered consistently.* Effective reinforcement requires consistency in following the details for administering reinforcers established by the therapist and client as well as consistency among reinforcing agents (if there is more than one) in following the treatment plan. Recall that a reinforcer always serves as feedback to the client that she or he is acting appropriately. In the case of a target behavior that occurs very infrequently and is initially being accelerated by continuous reinforcement, it is critical to reinforce every occurrence of the target behavior so the client gets the right "message" about the appropriateness of performing the target behavior. Reinforcement from one reinforcing agent but not from another for the same behavior is also likely to confuse a client, especially when the client is on a continuous reinforcement schedule. It is also important to prevent the inadvertent reinforcement of a deceleration target behavior. Consider a frequent sequence of events when a young child misbehaves: parent spanks child, child cries, and parent hugs and comforts child with words such as "Everything is OK; I love you." The parent's affection reinforces the child's misbehavior, which was instrumental in obtaining the affection. To assure that reinforcers will be administered consistently and properly (i.e., following the other guidelines), the therapist trains all the people who will be reinforcing the client and establishes procedures for coordinating their efforts.

ELICITING THE TARGET BEHAVIOR

In order to use reinforcement to accelerate a target behavior, the behavior must occur so that it can be reinforced. Sometimes the behavior occurs naturally, but frequently the reinforcing agent must wait a long time for the client to perform the target behavior unless specific procedures for eliciting the target behavior are instituted. Two of these procedures are prompting and shaping.

Prompting

As the name implies, **prompting** involves instructions or a reminder to perform the target behavior. **Verbal prompts** state what the client is expected to do, such as reminding the patient in Case 6-1 to interact with other people. **Physical prompts** involve someone guiding a client through a behavior—for example, teaching a retarded child to write by holding the child's hand and making the required movements. **Environmental prompts** include signs (e.g., "Turn Off Lights" and "STOP"), advertisements (e.g., "Run for Your Life"), and other environmental cues that remind people to perform various behaviors (e.g., an alarm clock). Prompts may come from other people, from clients themselves, or directly from the environment.

A prompt is used to initiate a behavior, but the behavior will continue to be performed only if it is reinforced. Generally, the need to use a prompt to elicit a target behavior diminishes as the behavior begins to be maintained by reinforcement. When a target behavior is occurring with enough frequency so that it can be adequately reinforced, the prompt is gradually withdrawn. This process is called **fading.**

Considerable prompting, which is then faded, is frequently involved in teaching language skills to *autistic children* (who suffer from a serious psychotic disorder characterized by social isolation, lack of interpersonal skills, mutism or repetitive speech, and intolerance for change in routine).[26] To teach the names of objects, a therapist will point to the object and say, "What is this? *Pencil.*" As the child begins to imitate the prompt "pencil," the therapist says the prompt at successively lower volumes so that eventually the therapist is whispering the prompt, then merely mouthing the prompt, and finally asking the child "What is this?" without any prompt.

Shaping

Shaping is the process of reinforcing progressively closer approximations of a complex behavior and is used to elicit acceleration target behaviors. In shaping, complex behaviors are broken down into their logical steps and then each of these steps is reinforced until the full behavior is occurring (see Figure 6-2). Shaping was used to accelerate the social interaction of the female psychiatric patient in Case 6-1 by gradually increasing the amount of time she was required to spend interacting with others in order to be reinforced. A common example of shaping is the children's game of "Hot and Cold," in which one child has to locate a particular object in a room while a playmate directs the child toward the object, saying "Hot" as the child gets closer and "Cold" when

FIGURE 6-2 *Shaping involves reinforcing successive steps required for a complex behavior*

the child starts to move farther away.[27] The process of shaping is illustrated schematically in Figure 6-3.

Shaping is a major component of treatment plans used to teach language and speech to such clients as autistic children, mentally retarded individuals, and mute psychotic patients. The procedure is illustrated in Case 6-4.

CASE 6-4

*Instituting Speech in a Mute Psychiatric Patient by Shaping**

[A 40-year-old male psychiatric patient who had been completely mute during 19 years of hospitalization served as the subject of this experimental therapy. (Although shaping is often used today, when this patient was treated 25 years ago, the procedures were innovative.)]

The S [subject] was brought to a group therapy session with other chronic schizophrenics (who were verbal), but he sat in the position in which he was placed and continued the withdrawal behaviors [that] characterized him. He remained impassive and stared ahead even when cigarettes, which other members accepted, were offered to him and were waved before his face. At one session, when E [experimenter] removed cigarettes from his pocket, a package of chewing gum accidentally fell out. The S's eyes moved toward the gum and then returned to their usual position. This response was chosen by E as one with which he would start to work. . . .

The S met individually with E three times a week. Group sessions also continued. The following sequence of procedures was introduced in the private sessions. Although the weeks are numbered consecutively, they did not follow at regular intervals since other duties kept E from seeing S every week.

Weeks 1, 2. A stick of gum was held before S's face, and E waited until S's eyes moved toward it. When this response occurred, E as a consequence gave him the gum. By

*Reprinted from Isaacs, Thomas, & Goldiamond (1960), pp. 9–10.

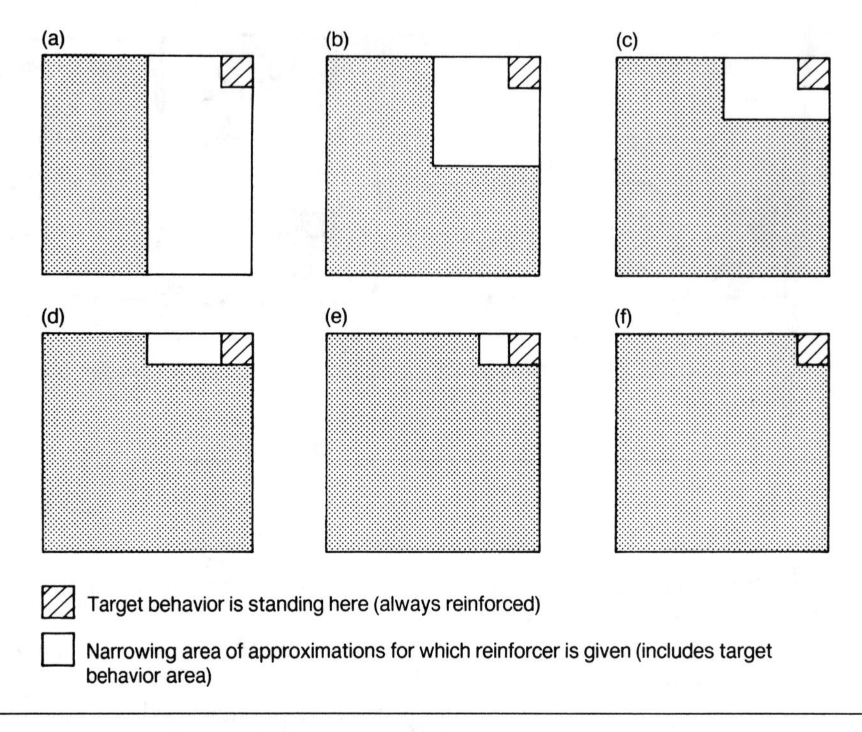

FIGURE 6-3 *A diagram representing the principle of shaping. The ultimate target behavior is "standing in the small (cross-hatched) square in the upper right." The person would be reinforced first for standing anywhere in the right half of the area, then for standing anywhere in the upper right quarter of the area, and so on.*
SOURCE: Adapted from Liebert & Spiegler (1978), p. 479.

the end of the second week, response probability in the presence of the gum was increased to such an extent that S's eyes moved toward the gum as soon as it was held up.

Weeks 3, 4. The E now held the gum before S, waiting until he noticed movement in S's lips before giving it to him. Toward the end of the first session of the third week, a lip movement spontaneously occurred, which E promptly reinforced. By the end of this week, both lip movement and eye movement occurred when the gum was held up. The E then withheld giving S the gum until S spontaneously made a vocalization, at which time E gave S the gum. By the end of this week, holding up the gum readily occasioned eye movement toward it, lip movement, and a vocalization resembling a croak.

Weeks 5, 6. The E held up the gum and said, "Say *gum, gum,*" repeating these words each time S vocalized. Giving S the gum was made contingent upon vocalizations increasingly approximating *gum.* At the sixth session (at the end of Week 6), when E said, "Say *gum, gum,*" S suddenly said, "*Gum,* please." This response was accompanied by reinstatement of other responses of this class; that is, S answered questions regarding his name and age.

Thereafter, he responded to questions by E both in individual sessions and in group sessions, but answered no one else. Responses to the discriminative stimuli of the room generalized to E on the ward; he greeted E on two occasions in the group room. He read from signs in E's office upon request by E.

Since the response now seemed to be under the strong stimulus control of E, the person, attempt was made to generalize the stimulus to other people. Accordingly, a nurse was brought into the private room; S smiled at her. After a month, he began answering her questions. Later, when he brought his coat to a volunteer worker on the ward, she interpreted the gesture as a desire to go outdoors and conducted him there. Upon informing E of the incident, she was instructed to obey S only as a consequence of explicit verbal requests by him. The S thereafter vocalized requests. These instructions have now been given to other hospital personnel, and S regularly initiates verbal requests when nonverbal requests have no reinforcing consequences.

Shaping can also be used to reduce anxiety or other negative reactions to particular events by accelerating successively more anxiety-evoking approach behaviors. Take the example of a college student who is afraid to talk to his professors (especially those he considers hostile) about his exams or assignments when he thinks that he deserves a higher grade than he received. A hierarchy of increasingly more anxiety-evoking approach behaviors would be constructed. At the bottom of the hierarchy might be such items as "Saying 'Good morning' to a friendly professor," "Saying 'Good morning' to a hostile professor," and "Asking a friendly professor the date of the next exam." These behaviors are successive approximations of the ultimate target behavior, "Discussing a disputed grade with a hostile professor." After performing each step, the student would be reinforced (e.g., buying himself an ice cream cone). This procedure is similar to *in vivo* systematic desensitization except that reinforcers are provided for successfully performing increasingly more anxiety-evoking or difficult aspects of the target behavior (rather than having the client engage in a substitute response for anxiety while performing the steps in the anxiety hierarchy).

An innovative application of shaping to change a woman's negative reaction to her husband-to-be's snoring is described in Case 6-5. You will note that there is no specific mention of the reinforcer used to shape successive approximations of the target behavior, "becoming less sensitive to snoring." After reading Case 6-5, see if you can state what the reinforcer was and whether it was an instance of positive or negative reinforcement.

CASE 6-5

*Increasing Tolerance to Snoring by Shaping**

Betty was a 20-year-old unmarried undergraduate student. Betty planned to marry and was greatly disturbed by the fact that her future husband was a heavy snorer. During past exposure to snorers, Betty reported severe agitation and tension to which she had been un-

*Reprinted from Koebel & Crist (1977), pp. 94–95.

able to adapt, even after extended exposures to snoring. During the period of their engagement, Betty and her fiance had spent an occasional weekend together. His snoring was so aversive that she was unable to fall asleep when close to him, and she would have to move to another room in order to fall asleep. Betty was highly motivated to seek a solution to her aversion to snoring for she felt it would become a sore-spot during her marriage and that she might come to blame her husband for her constant fatigue after a sleepless night.

A 12-minute recording was made of snoring. That recording was taken to a media specialist who reproduced it into a 60-minute recording with constant volume. The 60-minute tape was placed at the bedside of Betty and played each night as she retired. Before playing the tape Betty was reminded that the tape was at no time to be played at a volume that was aversive to her. Betty was given complete control of the volume. The range of volumes used was from Setting 1 to Setting 6 on the tape recorder. At Setting 6, the snoring was clearly audible and was similar to the sound of normal snoring.

During the first three nights, only the sound of the tape recorder was present. (The tape recorder turned off automatically after 60 minutes.) From nights 4 through 10, the volume was at Setting 1. That first setting seemed to be the most difficult for Betty to go beyond. At this setting the snoring was barely perceptible, but when she moved to Setting 2 the snoring was distinct enough to be annoying. Several times she moved the volume from Setting 1 to Setting 2 but found it too aversive and had to return to Setting 1 before she could fall asleep. Betty was somewhat disturbed when she was unable to tolerate Setting 2 and it was necessary to assure her that everything was working well and that it took time to change behavior of long standing.

Betty did raise the volume to Setting 2 on the eleventh night and was successful in falling asleep at that level of snoring. At the end of the thirty-second night Betty had increased the volume to Setting 6 and was successful in falling asleep to what could be called normal snoring. Betty was more than satisfied with her performance and felt quite confident that her future husband's snoring would not be aversive and that she would be able to sleep without distress.

As indicated, one troublesome part of the [therapy] occurred when Betty [reported that she was] unable to increase the volume from the Setting 1 to Setting 2. This might have been avoided if the volume had been [shaped] along a continuum rather than the discrete steps that were actually used. The reason for the discrete steps was that Betty had to set the volume herself, and it would have created too much confusion for her to make the minuscule changes in volume settings that a continuous ... process would have demanded.

Thirteen weeks after the final session, Betty was married. She had not slept in the presence of her fiance during those 13 weeks, and prior to the marriage she was fearful that the effects of the treatment might have worn off and that his snoring might evoke the tension and anger she had previously experienced.

During the first week of marriage Betty found her husband's snoring aversive. She reported, however, that the annoyance experienced at that time was not nearly as severe as that experienced in previous situations. Instead of being "forced" to sleep somewhere other than with her husband, she was able to fall asleep within 45 minutes and remained asleep throughout the rest of the night. This behavior lasted approximately a week, during which time the annoyance gradually decreased. By the second week of marriage she reported that her husband's snoring no longer annoyed her, and she was able to fall asleep with no interference from his snoring.

Interestingly, the reinforcer that Betty obtained for each successive approximation of the target behavior can be construed as either positive or negative reinforcement, either falling asleep or the termination of lying awake in bed while tired, respectively. Note also how similar this application of shaping is to *in vivo* systematic desensitization. Betty progressed to the next louder level of snoring only when she had been able to fall asleep with the previous volume.

Participation Exercise 6-2 will allow you to try your hand at shaping. Both you and the person whose behavior you shape should find it a challenging and enjoyable experience. As with Participation Exercise 6-1, this exercise will take more than a few minutes, so you may want to return to it at a later time.

PARTICIPATION EXERCISE 6-2

Shaping Behavior

Shaping is a skill that takes practice to do well. If you'd like to give it a try, enlist the aid of a friend who has about 30 minutes of free time.

SELECTING A TARGET BEHAVIOR

The first step is to select a behavior to shape. It should be a ***relatively simple*** one for your first attempt at shaping, but it must be one that can be ***easily broken down into components*** or steps. Examples of suitable behaviors are opening and closing a book; taking off the top of a pen and replacing it; standing up and sitting down; walking to the window, opening it, closing it, and then returning to the starting position; talking about a particular topic (e.g., schoolwork or the weather); and criticizing.

The behavior you choose to shape should meet three additional requirements. First, it should ***terminate fairly quickly*** so that it can be reinforced. Second, the behavior should ***end where it began.*** That is, when the behavior is completed, the subject should be able to immediately perform the same behavior again without having to rearrange the situation. For example, you would not want to shape "opening a book," because this would necessitate closing the book before the subject opened it again. Closing the book might give the person a clue concerning the desired behavior, and the object of this participation exercise is to get the person to perform the behavior by shaping alone. (In clinical practice, the client would be given complete information concerning the desired behavior including the therapist's describing and modeling the behavior.) Finally, the behavior should normally ***occur at a speed that makes counting feasible.*** Finger tapping, for instance, would be a poor choice.

You will need to observe your friend very closely so that you can determine if a particular behavior should be reinforced. The objective of shaping is to reinforce successive steps to the total behavior. To do this, you reinforce the first step initially and continue to reinforce it until it seems to be learned—that is, your friend performs it several times in a row. Then you look for a slight change in or addition to the first step, which is the second step. Once the second step occurs, you immediately reinforce it and continue to reinforce it, being careful not to reinforce just the first step. You may need to make fine discriminations about the person's behavior if there is only a slight difference between the two steps. Continue to reinforce the second step until it seems to be learned, and then look for the third step to appear. Repeat this sequence until all the steps have been learned.

If your friend seems to be experiencing difficulty going from one step to the next, you may not have divided the target behavior into small-enough steps. Should this occur during shaping, you will have to add an intermediate step(s). Your friend's behavior may give you a hint as to what one might be; other ideas can come from the nature of the behavior itself; and you can always begin by reinforcing the next movement or utterance after the previous component has been performed.

DIVIDING THE TARGET BEHAVIOR INTO LOGICAL STEPS

To shape the behavior you have chosen, you must first break down the total behavior into logical component parts. For example, suppose that you were going to shape "opening and closing a book." You would first reinforce (reinforcement procedures are discussed later) the first movement made, because this will start your friend moving about. The first movement your friend makes can be the initial component of any motor response, and the first utterance he or she makes can be the initial component of any verbal response. Next, you might reinforce (1) ***movement of either hand,*** (2) ***movement of either hand toward the book,*** then (3) ***touching the book,*** (4) ***opening it partway,*** (5) ***opening it fully,*** and finally, (6) ***closing the book.*** Similarly, the successive approximations of "verbal criticism" might be: (1) ***any verbal utterance,*** (2) ***any statement*** (i.e., as opposed to a question), (3) ***any negative statement,*** and finally, (4) ***any negative statement that is a criticism.*** If your friend combines any of the successive steps, the shaping will be more rapid, because one or more intermediate steps will not have to be reinforced.

REINFORCEMENT

Each time your friend makes an approximation of the behavior, you will say the word ***point.*** He or she should be able to see a record of the points earned. You can instruct your friend to make a checkmark on a sheet of paper each time you say ***point.*** An alternative procedure, preferable only if recording points will interrupt the behavior, is for you to record the points on a record sheet that is clearly visible to your friend.

The immediate and accurate administration of the token reinforcer ("point") is critical to successful shaping. If the reinforcer is not administered promptly, then one or more other behaviors will probably occur between the termination of the component behavior and reinforcement. This interference will make it difficult for your friend to discriminate the specific behavior for which the reinforcer was given. Thus, the reinforcer should be given immediately after a correct approximation of the target behavior is made.

PROCEDURE

Before your friend arrives, arrange the room so that he or she will be sitting facing you. Place any objects needed to perform the target behavior close by. If you are using a room with which your friend is familiar, be sure that the arrangement of the critical objects does not look out of the ordinary, lest this "give away" the target behavior.

When your friend arrives, explain that you are doing a project for one of your classes. Then give the following instructions: "Your job is to earn points. I will tell you each time you earn a point, and you (I) will record it immediately on this sheet of paper by making a tally mark for each point you receive. Try to get as many points as you can." Do not give any further instructions. If your friend asks you a question, merely say, "I'm sorry, but I'm not permitted to answer any questions. Just work for points and earn as many as you can."

After the instructions are given, your friend may sit motionless and say nothing for several minutes. Sooner or later, however, he or she will do something that you will be able to reinforce. Although this initial period of inactivity may be somewhat frustrating for both of you, do ***not*** try to alleviate the silence or awkward social situation.

Once you have given your friend the instructions, your task is to observe her or his behavior carefully and to reinforce successive approximations of the target behavior. Continue until he or she performs the total target behavior. At that point you should tell your friend that you are through with your project and explain what you have been doing. He or she may have some enlightening comments and questions that will give you further insight into the process of shaping.

EVALUATION OF REINFORCEMENT TO ACCELERATE ADAPTIVE BEHAVIORS

There is little doubt that reinforcement procedures, when properly applied (e.g., according to the principles of administration discussed earlier), are consistently effective behavioral therapies.[28] If the reinforcers are chosen individually for the client and if they are potent incentives, then most target behaviors dealt with in behavioral therapy can be accelerated. Reinforcement therapies have been successfully employed with the gamut of possible clients to accelerate a wide variety of adaptive target behaviors ranging from relatively simple, minor problem behaviors (such as increasing students' study time) to complex, severe problem behaviors (such as teaching language and social skills to chronic schizophrenic patients). In fact, reinforcement of adaptive behaviors has been by far the most successful psychological treatment in dealing with the immense deficits in socially appropriate and adaptive behaviors of psychotic, brain injured, and mentally retarded clients. Such people generally do not respond to other forms of psychotherapy, such as insight psychotherapy.[29]

Transferring the target behavior to the client's natural environment and maintaining the behavior over the long run (i.e., after therapy has ended) are more difficult than initially accelerating a target behavior and constitute the major obstacles to the successful use of reinforcement therapies. Some specific procedures that behavioral therapists use to enhance transfer and long-term maintenance of target behaviors have already been mentioned, including (1) employing naturally occurring and generalized reinforcers, (2) having clients reinforce their own behavior (i.e., self-reinforcement), (3) training other people in the client's home environment to provide reinforcers, and (4) administering reinforcers intermittently. The first three procedures have a common aim: assuring that the target behavior will continue to be reinforced. It cannot be overemphasized that behavior must be reinforced if it is to be maintained. Fortunately, intermittent reinforcement is generally sufficient, and often the reinforcers can be given quite far apart in time. Therefore, a person may continue to engage in a behavior even though it is reinforced infrequently, but the person will eventually stop engaging in the behavior if *no* reinforcers are received.

Because reinforcement procedures are so effective, questions sometimes arise regarding their misuse. In the context of behavioral therapy, a variety of safeguards have been established to substantially reduce the risk of misuse. First there is the contractual agreement made between the client and the behavioral therapist, in which the client has the major say about the goals of therapy and veto power concerning the specific therapy employed. Two additional safeguards to clients' being unduly influenced to act in particular ways are inherent in reinforcement therapies. One is that reinforcement procedures are most effective when the client is fully aware of the reinforcement contingency; frequently the procedures will not work unless the client is aware of the contingency.[30] Second, clients are not automatons who are at the mercy of others' actions, and they can easily subvert therapy procedures if they wish to, such as by failing to carry out homework assignments. (Recall the discussion of reciprocal determinism in Chapter 2.) Issues concerning safeguarding clients' personal rights and freedom are discussed at length in a later chapter. Concerns are also raised about the use of powerful reinforcement procedures on a mass scale (e.g., by government) to control people's behavior, such as is depicted in the novels *1984* and *Brave New World*. Although these issues are beyond the scope of behavioral therapy, they are addressed to some degree later in this book.

Another common objection to the use of reinforcers to accelerate socially adaptive and desirable behaviors is that clients *should* perform these behaviors because of their intrinsic value and not because they are "bribed" to do so. The major fallacy in this argument is the notion that some behaviors are intrinsically good, worthwhile, or rewarding. Except for behaviors that satisfy our physiological needs (e.g., obtaining food), the values of all human behaviors are determined through learning. Behaviors acquire particular values because those values are indicated by other people ("society"). But *if* the myriad of socially appropriate behaviors that are acceleration target behaviors in therapy were intrinsically rewarding, then why don't clients engage in them? Extrinsic reinforcers are often required to motivate a person to perform certain behaviors because there is, in fact, nothing intrinsically reinforcing about the behaviors.

As to the issue of extrinsic reinforcers being a form of bribery, the word *bribery* generally refers to offering something, such as money or a favor, in order to influence someone to act dishonestly or illegally. Reinforcers are not used in behavioral therapy to accelerate dishonest or illegal behaviors. Furthermore, bribes are usually given *before* the act is performed, while reinforcers are always given afterward. Providing reinforcers for engaging in appropriate or adaptive behavior is no more bribery than receiving a salary for a day's work.

Reinforcement is not a panacea, but it does have diverse applicability and virtually no limitations. Accelerating desirable behaviors by reinforcement has no major negative side effects and raises few objections among critics of behavioral therapy. By providing clients with new, adaptive behaviors that are often realistic alternatives to their maladaptive problem behaviors, reinforcement therapies help clients become freer (less restrained) and enhance their dignity as human beings.

SUMMARY

Reinforcers—events that increase behaviors—can be positive (the addition of an event) or negative (the termination of an event). Positive reinforcers are used more frequently. Reinforcers may be commodities, activities, social reinforcers, feedback, or token reinforcers. They must be individually identified for each client through direct questioning, direct observation of overt behavior, or exposure to generalized (common) reinforcers. Specific procedures and instruments for assessing a client's potential reinforcer have been developed. Often frequently performed activities can be used to accelerate less frequently performed behaviors (the Premack principle). Reinforcers are administered by other people, by the clients themselves, or as a "natural" consequence of performing a target behavior.

Effective use of reinforcement requires following certain important guidelines, including administering reinforcers immediately after the target behavior has been performed, making the client aware of the contingency, using continuous reinforcement initially and then intermittent reinforcement, keeping reinforcers potent, using naturally occurring reinforcers whenever possible, and administering reinforcers consistently.

Sometimes it is necessary to elicit the behaviors to be reinforced, by prompting (cueing the behaviors) or shaping procedures. Shaping, or reinforcing successive approximations of the complete target behavior, is often necessary with complex behaviors.

Reinforcement procedures are widely used and are highly effective in accelerating target behaviors. Maintaining these behaviors over long periods of time is more difficult and requires periodic reinforcement.

REFERENCE NOTES

1. Premack, 1965.
2. Goldiamond, 1965.
3. For example, Pineda, Barlow, & Turner, 1971.

4. For example, Leitenberg, Agras, Thomson, & Wright, 1968.
5. For example, Barrett, 1962.
6. For example, Eisler, Hersen, & Miller, 1974; Hersen & Bellack, 1976a, 1976b.
7. For example, Kohlenberg, 1973.
8. For example, Azrin, Rubin, O'Brien, Ayllon, & Roll, 1968; O'Brien & Azrin, 1970.
9. For example, Epstein, Hersen, & Hemphill, 1974.
10. For example, Patel, 1973, 1975a, 1975b; Patel & North, 1975.
11. Spiegler & Agigian, 1977.
12. Bandura, 1969.
13. Cautela & Kastenbaum, 1967.
14. Phillips, Fischer, & Singh, 1977.
15. MacPhillamy & Lewinsohn, 1971.
16. Daley, 1969; Homme, 1971.
17. Ayllon & Azrin, 1968a, 1968b.
18. Ayllon & Azrin, 1968a.
19. Spiegler & Agigian, 1977.
20. Spiegler & Agigian, 1977.
21. For example, Thomas, Becker, & Armstrong, 1968; Wahler, 1969.
22. For example, Solomon & Wahler, 1973.
23. For example, Graubard, Rosenberg, & Miller, 1974.
24. Franklin, 1969, p. 247.
25. Bandura, 1969.
26. Lovaas, 1977.
27. Morgan, 1974.
28. Kazdin & Wilson, 1978.
29. Rachman & Wilson, 1980.
30. Bandura, 1969.

CHAPTER

7 Consequential Therapies: Decelerating Maladaptive Behaviors

This chapter continues the discussion of consequential behavioral therapies, treatments that ameliorate clients' problems by changing the consequences of relevant target behaviors. The previous chapter described behavioral therapies that alleviate **behavioral deficits,** adaptive behaviors that clients perform too infrequently, too weakly, or too briefly. This chapter examines behavioral therapies that deal with **behavioral excesses,** maladaptive behaviors in which the client is engaging too frequently, too intensely, or for too long a time. Common examples of behavioral excesses include spending hours "wasting time," eating too much, interrupting others during conversations, and being late for appointments.

A major strategy for reducing the frequency of undesirable behaviors has already been introduced—namely, using reinforcement procedures to accelerate target behaviors that are incompatible with the deceleration target behaviors. This strategy is preferred for decelerating undesirable behaviors because it provides the client with an active adaptive behavior to take the place of the maladaptive deceleration target behavior. However, there is a place for therapies that directly decelerate maladaptive behaviors, especially in cases of certain maladaptive behaviors that have serious immediate consequences. A prime example is self-destructive behavior, as is sometimes observed in children and adults who are diagnosed as psychotic. This may involve such acts as head-banging, scratching, pinching, hitting, or slapping oneself to the point of serious open wounds and even profuse bleeding. Obviously, it is necessary to employ therapy procedures that will very quickly eliminate such behaviors.

Furthermore, when the deceleration target behavior is occurring very frequently it may be practically infeasible to accelerate alternative adaptive behaviors before the maladaptive behaviors have been drastically reduced. In less serious cases, the most effective treatment plan for eliminating a maladaptive behavior usually involves simultaneously decelerating the maladaptive behavior and accelerating an incompatible adaptive behavior (e.g., reducing disruptive classroom behavior while increasing attention to the assigned lesson).

EXTINCTION

Many behaviors are maintained by reinforcement, and withdrawing the reinforcers that are maintaining a behavior eventually eliminates it. The process of withholding or withdrawing reinforcers is called **extinction.** (The term *extinction* also refers to the elimination of a behavior. For example, it would be correct to say, "The target behavior was *extinguished* after *extinction* was employed.") Perhaps the most frequent use of extinction is to decelerate behaviors that are maintained by social attention. Extinction in this case merely involves ignoring the client when he or she performs the undesirable behavior. However, ignoring and extinguishing are *not* necessarily equivalent. Only when the deceleration target behavior is being maintained by social attention does extinction involve ignoring the person when he or she performs the target behavior. For example, Julie's leaving dirty dishes in the sink is being maintained by her roommate Susan's washing the dishes. Therefore, to extinguish Julie's habit Susan must stop washing the dishes whenever Julie leaves them in the sink. Case 7-1 provides a straightforward example of extinction.

CASE 7-1
*Bedtime Temper Tantrums Eliminated by Extinction**

The client was a 21-month-old child who was put to bed each night by one of his parents or an aunt who lived with the family. Frequently the boy screamed and cried when the adult tried to leave the room before he fell asleep. Thus, the person who put the child to bed was "forced" to remain in the room until the child fell asleep (a period ranging from one-half hour to two hours). It appeared, then, that the child's temper tantrums were being maintained by the adult's attention (i.e., attention was reinforcing the tantrums). Interestingly, the parents remarked that their son appeared to enjoy the control he had over their behavior.

To decelerate the child's temper tantrums, the hypothesized reinforcer was withdrawn: the child was placed in his bed as usual each night and shortly thereafter the adult left the room and did not return even when the child cried. Looking at the solid line in Case Figure 7-1A, it can be seen that in the first attempt to decelerate the temper tantrums the child cried for 45 minutes the first time, did not cry at all the second time (it is possible that he was exhausted by the previous crying bout), cried for 10 minutes the third time, and

*Williams (1959).

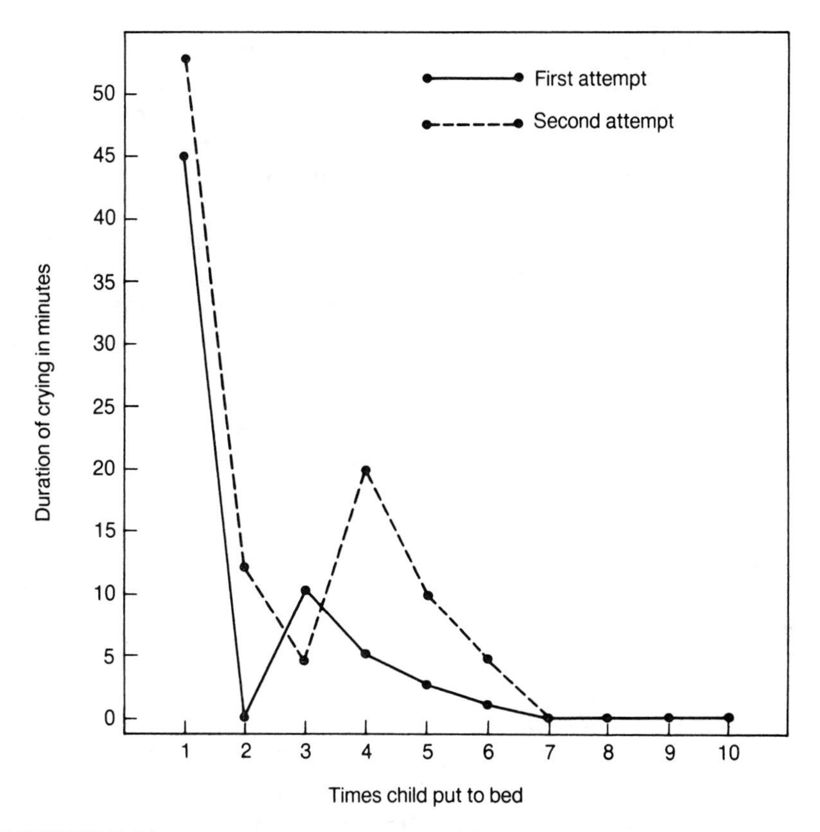

CASE FIGURE 7-1A

The results of two attempts to eliminate, through extinction, bedtime temper tantrums in a 21-month-old child SOURCE: *Adapted from Williams (1959), p. 269.*

thereafter gradually decreased to no crying. By the tenth night the child even smiled when the adult left the bedroom.

A week later the child cried when his aunt put him to bed, and she stayed in the child's bedroom until he went to sleep, which reinforced the tantrum behavior that had been eliminated. In fact, this single reinforcer was all that was needed to increase the child's rate of crying to its pretreatment level, which necessitated a second attempt to extinguish the target behavior. The broken line in Case Figure 7-1A indicates that the child's rate of crying reached zero by the seventh night of the second extinction series. This second attempt was successful, because the boy's parents reported that no additional bedtime temper tantrums occurred during the following two-year period.

Although extinction can be employed by itself to decelerate maladaptive behaviors, it is often used in conjunction with other procedures (which are discussed in this chapter) because extinction has a number of limitations. First, one must precisely assess the consequences that are maintaining the deceleration target behavior, and this precision is sometimes difficult to achieve. Obviously, if the "wrong" consequences are withdrawn, the behavior will not extinguish. Second, the reinforcers maintaining the target behavior must be *completely* withheld for extinction to be effective. Thus, all the potential reinforcing agents must consistently withhold reinforcers for the target behavior. This requirement is critical, because a single, isolated exception can reinstate the target behavior and, most importantly, can maintain it for a considerable time thereafter, as in Case 7-1. Third, extinction is a relatively slow procedure, and in some cases, such as self-abusive behavior, a rapid means of decelerating a maladaptive behavior is required, as discussed earlier.[1] A related problem is that extinction sometimes results in an initial increase in the target behavior before it begins to decrease.[2] Fourth, the effects of extinction may be so situation-specific that they do not generalize to other circumstances than those in which the extinction is carried out. This specificity may have accounted for the child in Case 7-1 crying when his aunt put him to bed, rather than his parents.

The discussion now turns to some more active consequential therapy procedures for decelerating maladaptive behaviors. For ease in learning, they are discussed one at a time, but in practice two or more of these procedures are frequently combined.

TIME OUT FROM POSITIVE REINFORCEMENT

Time out from positive reinforcement (or **time out,** for short) involves temporarily withdrawing a client's access to positive reinforcers immediately after the client performs the deceleration target behavior. Time out from positive reinforcement can be thought of as time-limited extinction.

Usually time out is implemented by having the client leave the situation in which the undesirable behavior occurred and having him or her spend a specified time in a **time-out room,** a physical location that does not allow access to any reinforcers. For example, when time-out procedures are employed in a classroom to decelerate disruptive behavior, the child is typically taken to a small room that lacks generalized reinforcers. The room has no windows, so the child cannot observe interesting happenings outside, nor any absorbing objects, such as books, pictures, and supplies. By way of contrast, sitting in the school office—a traditional disciplinary action for misbehavior in the classroom—is not an effective time-out procedure for most children. First, sitting in the office is likely to provide positive reinforcers because the school office is often a hub of activity with many fascinating events to observe (e.g., a kid with a nosebleed or a teacher being bawled out by the principal). Second, to the extent that the child is removed from an unpleasant situation, such as having to study in the classroom, sitting in the office will be a negative reinforcer.

The time-out period is always for a specified amount of time, and the client is made aware of the duration. In the case of an ongoing deceleration target behavior, such as a temper tantrum, the total time-out period includes a specified length of time during which the client must not have performed the target behavior before the time out is terminated. This provision ensures that the deceleration target behavior is not negatively reinforced by termination of time out and is positively reinforced by again having access to reinforcers. For example, a child in a nursery school may begin to scream whenever she does not get her way while playing with other children. Her teacher decides to employ time out from positive reinforcement by putting her in a bare corner of the room for two minutes each time she has a temper tantrum. As soon as she is placed in the corner, the child stops screaming for a short while and then resumes screaming until the two minutes are over. This means that when the teacher comes to take the child from the time-out corner, the child is screaming. Thus, the child's screaming is reinforced by the teacher's attention (a positive reinforcer) and by being taken out of the corner (a negative reinforcer).

Time-out periods are relatively short. For instance, time-out periods of as little as 15 seconds have been successfully applied to reduce inappropriate eating behavior and table manners in institutionalized mentally retarded children.[3] Not only are relatively short periods of time out (5–20 minutes) effective, but lengthening the time period does not necessarily increase the efficacy of the procedure.[4]

Time out from positive reinforcement needs to be distinguished from isolation (or seclusion), which is *not* a behavioral therapy procedure. The major difference is that the duration of time out tends to be relatively brief and is always clearly specified, whereas isolation is often for a long, indeterminate period of time. One problem with this long duration of isolation is that the contingency between the undesirable behavior and isolation may not remain apparent to the client, reducing the effectiveness of the isolation to decelerate the behavior.

Time out need not involve removing the client from the situation in which the undesirable behavior is performed (although it often does) as long as the client does not have access to positive reinforcers for the time-out period.[5] For example, a time-out procedure could involve the reinforcing agent (e.g., a teacher working individually with a student) turning away and refraining from reinforcing the client for the specified time-out period whenever the client engaged in the deceleration target behavior (e.g., making distracting comments during the lesson).

The time-out procedure has been used to decelerate a variety of maladaptive target behaviors in both children and adults, including the self-injurious behavior of autistic children[6] and the inappropriate table manners and eating habits of institutionalized retarded children,[7] as well as verbal and physical aggression of adolescents who were classified as delinquents,[8] disruptive social behaviors of adult psychiatric patients,[9] and alcohol consumption of chronic abusers.[10] The advantages of using time out in psychiatric hospitals have been described as follows.

> First, the procedure has clear-cut rules [that] can be easily followed and understood by patients and ward personnel. Second, there is avoidance of long and punitive isolation. The fact that the approach is only mildly aversive makes it acceptable to patients and staff. The

temporary inconvenience of a time out does not elicit the angry and resentful responses that other methods of behavioral control sometimes engender. Third, brief 5-minute time out provides up to 12 learning trials per hour. This permits repeated opportunities to test environmental contingencies in a relatively brief period of time and facilitates learning. Finally, the method requires little staff time and automatically provides objective data regarding the effectiveness of the therapeutic intervention.[11]

At least two factors seem to account for the effectiveness of time out from positive reinforcement. First, time out often removes reinforcers that are maintaining the undesired behavior (i.e., extinction). Second, being in a nonreinforcing environment is generally unpleasant.[12]

RESPONSE COST

Response cost involves removal of some valued item or privilege when an undesirable behavior is performed.[13] Traffic tickets and fines for tardiness (e.g., having points deducted for a class assignment turned in late) are familiar examples of response cost. When we misbehaved as children, we may have been deprived of being able to watch television, going to a friend's house, or having a special dessert. At school, violating rules may have resulted in loss of recess. An interesting example of the effectiveness of response cost in reducing undesirable behavior on a mass scale is that of telephone companies instituting a charge for local directory assistance (previously a free service). For example, in Cincinnati the use of local directory assistance calls was substantially reduced after customers began to be charged for them although long-distance directory assistance requests, which remained free, did not decline (see Figure 7-1).[14] In each case, there was a *cost* for the undesirable response. If the cost is high enough (which is an individual matter), then the frequency of the behavior on which the cost is contingent will decline.

Response cost is a relatively simple procedure that has been used in a variety of settings and with many different kinds of deceleration target behaviors. In one application, the feasibility of substantially reducing daily cash register shortages was demonstrated in a small pizza parlor.[15] After establishing that the average daily shortage over the course of a week was 4.02 percent of the daily receipts, the owner informed his employees that whenever the shortage exceeded 1 percent, the shortages would be deducted from their salaries. The threat of this response cost immediately reduced the shortages to an average of 0.43 percent. When the response cost conditions were temporarily removed, the shortages immediately increased almost ninefold, to 3.73 percent. When the response cost was again put into effect, the cash register shortages dropped to almost zero (0.04 percent).

The loss of valuables need not be permanent for response cost to be effective in decelerating undesirable behaviors. Ogden Lindsley, a pioneer in the use of consequential behavioral therapy, described the use of a "Sunday box" to

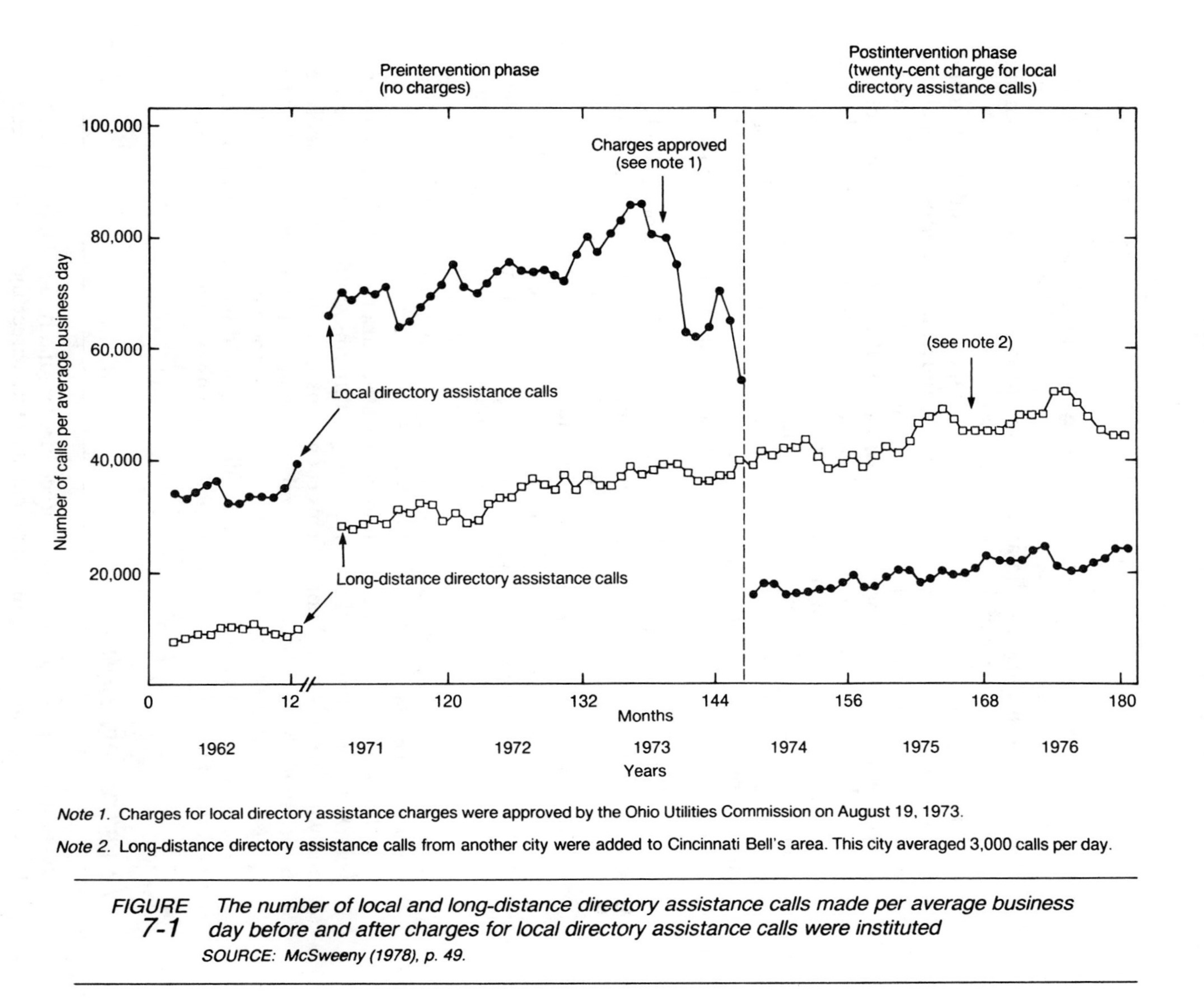

Note 1. Charges for local directory assistance charges were approved by the Ohio Utilities Commission on August 19, 1973.

Note 2. Long-distance directory assistance calls from another city were added to Cincinnati Bell's area. This city averaged 3,000 calls per day.

FIGURE 7-1 *The number of local and long-distance directory assistance calls made per average business day before and after charges for local directory assistance calls were instituted*

SOURCE: McSweeny (1978), p. 49.

reduce the number of personal items that his family members left lying around the house.[16] Whenever a misplaced item was found, it was put in a large box, and the owner was not permitted to retrieve it until the following Sunday. The power of this procedure was made clear to its inventor when Lindsley unthinkingly left his briefcase in an inappropriate location one day and couldn't get it back until the beginning of the next week.

In many cases, the *threat* of a potential response cost is a sufficient incentive to change a maladaptive behavior.[17] One procedure requires that a client give the therapist a number of valuable items that, according to an explicitly stated contract, the client will lose permanently if the terms of the contract are not fulfilled. The valuables might include favorite personal objects such as a ring, clock, pen, record, or book. The contract might state that the client is to stay on a specified diet for a week or spend a minimum number of hours per week in family activities. If the client does not fulfill the terms of the contract, the therapist automatically disposes of one of the client's valuables, by donating it to a charity organization or needy cause (which, ethically, is not the therapist!).

Sometimes a client deposits money, usually in the form of bank checks, with the therapist who contributes a prescribed sum to the client's *least* favorite cause whenever the deceleration target behavior is performed. In one such case, a black client who was addicted to amphetamines gave his therapist $50, which was to be forwarded to the the Ku Klux Klan if the client took the drugs. This potential response cost procedure was successful in keeping the client free of drugs for 15 months.[18] In actual practice, when the response cost is high, adult clients rarely violate their contracts with the therapist. In such instances, the client's appropriate behavior is negatively reinforced: the client successfully *avoids* the loss of valuables.

Response cost has been used to decelerate a variety of undesirable target behaviors, including smoking, overeating, stuttering, and psychotic speech, and with diverse clinical populations such as psychiatric patients, mentally retarded individuals, schoolchildren, and "predelinquent" boys. The effects of response cost often endure when the response cost contingency is removed, and some of the negative side effects typically associated with deceleration behavioral therapies (discussed later) do not occur with response cost.[19]

OVERCORRECTION

Overcorrection is a deceleration procedure originally developed by Richard Foxx and Nathan Azrin[20] in which clients first correct the harmful effects of their misbehavior and then intensively practice an appropriate alternative behavior.[21] The first phase involves *restitution*—making amends for the damage done—and occasionally even improving on the conditions that existed before the damage occurred. The second phase involves *positive practice* of a behavior appropriate to the situation, usually in an exaggerated fashion. Case 7-2 illustrates both phases of overcorrection.

CASE 7-2

*Elimination of Object Throwing Through Overcorrection**

A 62-year-old female psychiatric patient, who had been institutionalized for 43 years, began picking up objects from the floor and throwing them at other patients and staff members. Her behavior was not only inappropriate but was also potentially dangerous.

The restitution phase of the overcorrection procedure involved the patient's apologizing to individuals who had been hit. If the patient refused to apologize when she was requested to do so by a staff member, the staff member apologized in the patient's behalf and prompted her to nod in agreement.

Positive practice consisted of five minutes of picking up trash on the floor and putting it into a garbage can. If the patient refused to do the positive practice, the staff member physically guided her through the clean-up activity. This prompting was discontinued after several sessions because the patient began to voluntarily perform the overcorrection behavior.

Before the overcorrection procedure was instituted, the patient threw objects at other people an average of 13 times per day. After two weeks of overcorrection, the frequency of the target behavior decreased to less than an average of one incident per day and remained at or below that level for about four months, at which point observations were terminated.

Overcorrection is a relatively new behavioral therapy that appears to have much promise. Most evidence suggests that it is a highly effective treatment for eliminating certain classes of socially inappropriate and personally maladaptive behaviors.[22] In addition to its use in treating behaviors that harm or annoy other people and the environment, overcorrection effectively reduces or eliminates behaviors that have negative consequences primarily for the client, including self-injurious behaviors,[23] bedwetting,[24] and autistic behaviors.[25] In contrast to other techniques for decelerating undesirable behaviors, such as extinction, time out, and response cost, overcorrection has the distinct advantage of including procedures for accelerating an adaptive alternative behavior. This constructive rehabilitation orientation and the relative ease of implemention, should make overcorrection attractive to parents, teachers, and other nonprofessional therapeutic agents.

The overcorrection method is especially applicable to treating behaviors that infringe on the rights of others and violate the law, such as stealing.[26] Thus it is interesting to compare overcorrection with the typical strategies used by the courts to deal with such misconduct. Being jailed or paying a fine does not guarantee that offenders will continue to see the sentence as the result of their criminal actions. Occasionally a judge's sentence includes simple correction procedures (especially for juvenile first offenders), such as having the offender make restitution to the victim in the form of money or services. Overcorrection procedures would seem to be even more powerful as a deterrent of similar future crimes because the offender's sentence is closely associated with the crime. Furthermore, the victim, who is frequently ignored by the law, is com-

*Foxx & Azrin (1972).

pensated somewhat. Such a practice is consistent with some laws, as in the area of consumer protection, that automatically require the offender to pay the victim a settlement several times larger than the actual loss.

Although overcorrection has primarily been used with clients who function at a low level (e.g., individuals labeled mentally retarded or psychotic), the basic procedures could potentially be applied to a variety of maladaptive behaviors of normal children and adults. Overcorrection appears particularly suited for eliminating many common minor destructive acts of children such as throwing food on the floor and leaving toys and clothes strewn all over the house. Teachers might use overcorrection to reduce frequent errors in students' writing, such as misspelling, incorrect grammar, and typographical errors. Environmental pollution (e.g., littering) and energy waste (e.g., leaving lights on when they are not needed) also would seem to be appropriate targets for overcorrection procedures.

SATIATION

Recall that "prevent a client from satiating on the reinforcer(s) used to accelerate a target behavior" is one of the principles for administering positive reinforcers ("too much of a good thing can be bad"). However, if the objective is to eliminate an undesirable behavior, satiation can sometimes be used to advantage. **Satiation** as a consequential behavioral therapy for decelerating maladaptive behaviors essentially provides the client with an overabundance of an event (e.g., activities or commodities) that appears to be a reinforcer in order to reduce its potency in maintaining the behavior.

In **response satiation,** the client is asked to engage in the very behavior that is undesirable (i.e., the deceleration target behavior) and to do this repeatedly and in an exaggerated fashion. One application of response satiation is to eliminate the bizarre and/or ritualistic behaviors sometimes exhibited by psychiatric patients, as is illustrated in Case 7-3.

CASE 7-3

*Ritualistic "Circle Turning" Eliminated by Response Satiation**

A male chronic psychiatric patient in his mid-40s had the persistent habit of turning in circles when he was at a day treatment center during the day and in his supervised living home (a kind of half-way house) in the evenings and on weekends. The behavior was not only annoying and distracting to others, but it also effectively precluded his engaging in any meaningful social interactions.

To deal with the maladaptive habit, each time he was observed turning circles at the

*Spiegler & Agigian (1977).

day treatment center, a staff member would tell him to turn five more circles to his left, but in a location out of view of other patients (to reduce attention from other patients that might reinforce the ritualistic behavior). After he complied, he was then told to turn five circles to the right. The patient was also to turn circles each morning when he arrived at the day treatment center and every afternoon as he was leaving the center. At home the patient frequently turned circles in front of the television set, much to the chagrin of the other residents of the home. Whenever the supervised-home manager observed this behavior, he instructed the patient to go to the corner of the room out of sight of others and to turn circles there. The response satiation was supplemented with reinforcement for engaging in social activities (which were incompatible with circle turning) both at the day treatment center and at home. Extinction may also have been operative if the circle turning was at least partially maintained by social attention, because the client was always asked to perform the target behavior away from other people.

The patient's long-standing maladaptive behavior rapidly declined and then ceased altogether. During the more than a year and a half follow-up period after the termination of the treatment plan, no incidents of circle turning were reported.

Stimulus satiation involves providing a client with an overabundance of an item or very frequent access to an activity that is directly related to an undesirable behavior. Case 7-4 is a classic example of stimulus satiation.

CASE 7-4

*Reducing Hoarding Behavior by Stimulus Satiation**

A female psychiatric patient who had been hospitalized for nine years collected a large number of towels in her room. At any one time she had about 20 towels in her room. Repeated efforts by the ward staff to discourage this behavior had proved ineffective, and so twice a week towels had been collected from the patient's room.

Stimulus satiation involved staff members' bringing a towel to the patient when she was in her room at random times throughout the day; the staff members made no comments to the patient as they handed towels to her. The number of towels given to the patient rapidly increased so that in the first week of the program she was given an average of seven towels each day. By the third week, the number increased to 60 per day. No steps were taken to prevent the patient from collecting additional towels or to remove any towels from her room.

During the first weeks of stimulus satiation, the patient was observed "patting her cheeks with a few of the towels, apparently enjoying them." Later, when hundreds of towels were in her room, she was observed spending much of her time folding and stacking the towels. During the first week of stimulus satiation, the patient typically thanked the staff member for bringing her a towel. As the number of towels given to the patient rapidly in-

*Ayllon (1963).

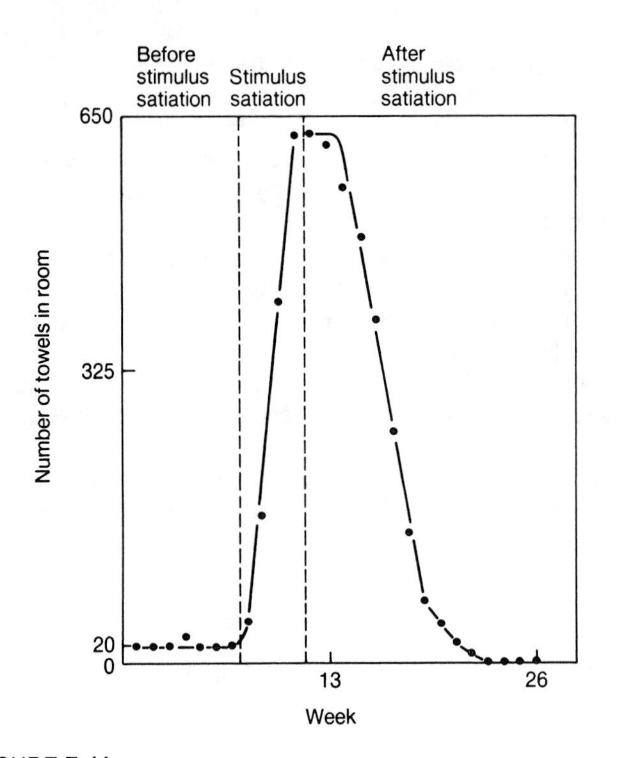

CASE FIGURE 7-4A

The number of towels found in the patient's room before, during, and after stimulus satiation *SOURCE: Adapted from Ayllon (1963), p. 57.*

creased, she began to protest (e.g., "Don't bring me no more towels. I've got enough.") In the third week a typical comment was "Take them towels away. . . . I can't sit here all night and fold towels."

Stimulus satiation was terminated after four weeks, and at that time there were 625 towels in the patient's room. A week later the patient began to remove the towels and continued to discard them so that by the twelfth week after the end of stimulus satiation she had an average of 1.5 towels in her room, a drastic reduction from the average of 20 towels she had kept in her room before the treatment was implemented. Case Figure 7-4A shows the average number of towels in the patient's room before, during, and after stimulus satiation. Follow-up observations for more than a year indicated that the patient's towel hoarding had been successfully eliminated.

Case 7-4 has interesting historical significance. Besides being an effective treatment of the patient's maladaptive behavior, it demonstrated that a behavioral therapy approach could successfully deal with psychotic behavior. It was carried out in the late 1950s, at which time few psychiatric hospital personnel were aware of the potential of behavioral therapies in treating psychotic behavior, and those personnel that had a passing familiarity with such therapies were highly skeptical of their efficiency. Hoarding behavior, for example, was viewed (psychoanalytically) as a sign of a deep-seated need for security and love, and it was presumed that the hoarding behavior could not be eliminated without first meeting the patient's underlying needs. The validity of this model of abnormal behavior was clearly not substantiated by the outcome of Case 7-4.

Rapid smoking is a combined response and stimulus satiation therapy that requires clients to smoke their usual brand of cigarettes at the rate of one puff every six seconds, to inhale normally, and to continue smoking this way until they cannot tolerate another puff. An early investigation of rapid smoking found that the decrease in smoking obtained lasted at least six months,[27] which is impressive because most smoking relapses occur in the first three months after treatment. There is also evidence that the long-term abstinence rates are somewhat superior to those obtained with other methods.[28] These results must be considered tentative, however, because more recent research has not consistently obtained comparable results.[29] Furthermore, rapid smoking appears to create some short-term stress to the cardiovascular system (e.g., increased pulse rate and blood pressure).[30] Therefore, people who, for health reasons, most need assistance in stopping smoking (e.g., people who are overweight and have a history of cardiovascular disease) are the very people who are at greatest risk for using rapid smoking.[31]

Satiation is used only occasionally, and most often after other behavioral therapies for eliminating undesirable behaviors have proved unsuccessful. This is probably due to the paradoxical nature of the procedure—to wit, encouraging the behavior that needs to be eliminated. This procedure is in basic opposition to the direct approach of behavioral therapy and, more importantly, has the potential to backfire and result in an acceleration of the deceleration target behavior.

PHYSICALLY AVERSIVE CONSEQUENCES

The final consequential behavioral therapy procedure used to decelerate undesirable behavior to be discussed is the direct administration of *physically aversive consequences*. Physically aversive consequences are either painful or unpleasant, but none are dangerous or result in permanent harm to the client. For example, lemon juice squirted in the mouth, which has been found to be an effective aversive consequence with some children,[32] is distinctly unpleasant but in no way harmful.

There is an obvious similarity between the use of physically aversive consequences being discussed here and the use of aversive events in substitution therapies, which was described in Chapter 5. In many cases, the physically aversive events are the same (e.g., mild shock or noxious odors). The major difference lies in the timing of the aversive event. In consequential therapy, the aversive event is applied as a *consequence* of (i.e., after) the deceleration target behavior; thus the client must perform the deceleration target behavior in order to employ the therapy. In substitution therapy, the aversive event can be *associated* with various environmental cues and covert behaviors such as thoughts or feelings related to the target behavior. The client need not perform the deceleration target behavior per se. In clinical practice, this fundamental theoretical difference may be obscured because employing a physically aversive event as a consequence often also results in its being associated with external and internal cues that are present when the deceleration target behavior is performed.

Physically aversive consequences can be a very effective and efficient means of decreasing an undesirable behavior, at least temporarily.* Nevertheless, the use of physically aversive consequences in behavioral therapy is generally a last resort, for several reasons. First, there are ethical and humanitarian objections to its use, even with voluntary clients. Some therapists find it distasteful to employ physically aversive consequences irrespective of their clients' reactions to them. This point is illustrated in the following quotation from the report of Case 7-5. "Observers of the sessions in which the shocks were applied reported that, on the basis of observable autonomic responses . . . the [client] recovered from the shock episodes much faster than the [therapist]."[35] A second, reason for using physically aversive consequences as a last resort is that they can have negative side effects (to be enumerated shortly). Third, many other behavioral therapies can be employed that do not have societal objections or potential limitations. Thus, in deciding to use physically aversive consequences, the therapist must determine whether this strategy is the most effective and efficient treatment, and, even if it is, whether the potential gains outweigh the potential drawbacks. This cost-benefit analysis is done in conjunction with the client, client's family, or guardian in the case of nonvoluntary clients. Therapists may also be required by laws and professional ethical codes to consult with a special board, composed of other professionals and sometimes laypeople, that reviews all therapeutic uses of physically aversive consequences.

Self-destructive behavior performed by some autistic, severely retarded, or psychotic patients has often been treated by contingent shock because such behavior tends to be highly resistant to other forms of therapy. (Overcorrection may prove to be an effective alternative therapy to physically aversive consequences in the treatment of self-destructive behavior.[36]) The large benefits (decreasing a potentially very harmful behavior) clearly outweigh the minimal cost (brief, moderate pain), as can be seen in Case 7-5.

*Historically,[33] physically aversive consequences were thought to be less effective in modifying behavior than reinforcement; thus they were largely neglected as a topic of scientific investigation until about 20 years ago. Our basic understanding of the use of physically aversive consequences as a behavioral therapy still lags far behind the large body of existing information concerning reinforcement, and this state of affairs is likely to persist because ethical constraints make it difficult to study scientifically the use of physically aversive consequences with humans.[34]

CASE 7-5

*Eliminating Self-Destructive Behavior by Using Contingent Shock**

The client was a 6-year-old girl who did not communicate verbally at all, was diagnosed as having diffuse brain damage, and was hyperactive. Her predominant behavior was climbing in high places (e.g., on furniture, window sills, trees), interspersed with sitting and rocking rhythmically. The girl's climbing was clearly a serious threat to her physical well-being and her life itself. For example, "her body bore multiple scars from past falls; her front teeth were missing, having been left imbedded in molding from which she had fallen while climbing outside the second story of her house."

From the initial behavioral assessment of the maintaining conditions of the child's climbing, it appeared that the behavior was being reinforced by her mother's attention. Time out from positive reinforcement was first attempted, and later extinction and social attention for behaviors that were incompatible with climbing (e.g., sitting at a table) were tried. When all these procedures failed to reduce the dangerous climbing behavior, the therapist, in consultation with the child's parents, decided to use contingent electric shock because of the extremely serious potential consequences of the target behavior.

CASE FIGURE 7-5A

Tracings from photographs (taken through a one-way mirror) showing the client dangerously climbing in the room in which the therapy was administered

SOURCE: Risley (1968), p. 23.

*Risley (1968). Quotations are from pp. 22 and 25.

The shock was delivered by a hand-held device (resembling a long flashlight) that was powered by seven 1.5-volt batteries that delivered an average voltage of 300–400 volts. "Subjectively, the shock produced a sharp, extremely painful sting, localized in the area of the body to which the contacts were touched, much like being struck with a vigorously applied willow switch. The pain terminated with the removal of the shock, with no after-effects such as redness, swelling of the skin, tingling, or aching."

The contingent electric shock was first carried out by the therapist in a controlled setting, a room with an 11-foot ceiling and a large one-way mirror that allowed the child's mother to observe the therapy from an adjacent room. The room contained a small table and chairs in the center. At one end of the room, next to the door, there was a ventilator frame that formed a 5-inch ledge six feet above the floor. A bookcase in front of the ventilator gave the child access to climbing onto the ledge and then onto the door, as shown in Case Figure 7-5A (on the previous page).

Each therapy session began with the therapist and child seated at the table. Whenever the child climbed on the bookcase, the therapist shouted "No!" Then he immediately ran over to her, took hold of one of her legs, touched the shock contacts to her calf or lower

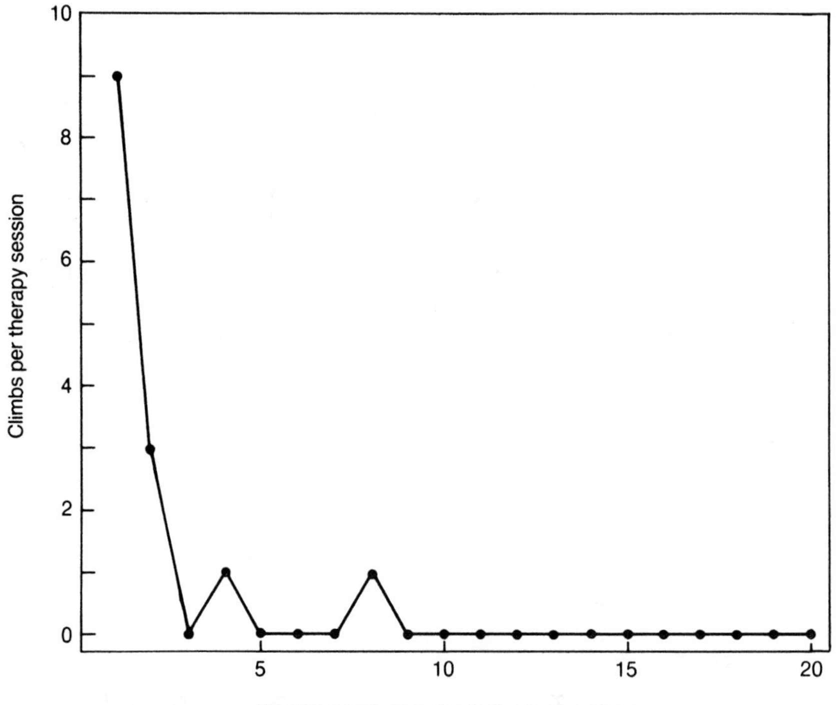

CASE FIGURE 7-5B

Graph illustrating the rapid decline of climbing behavior when mild shock was administered by the therapist as a consequence of climbing. Each dot represents one day.

SOURCE: Data from Risley (1968).

thigh, and pressed the switch for approximately one second. The therapist then returned to his chair.

As Case Figure 7-5B shows, the contingent electric shock rapidly reduced the client's climbing behavior. In the first therapy session in which contingent electric shock was used, the child climbed nine times. In the second session, climbing occurred only three times, and thereafter only twice in the subsequent 18 sessions.

Although the climbing had been successfully eliminated in the therapy sessions, the child's mother reported that it had not decreased at home. Thus, the treatment effects appeared to be specific to the therapy sessions. Furthermore, it was determined that treatment effects were predominantly associated with the therapist, the person who administered the shocks. Accordingly, the child's mother was instructed in the use of the shock apparatus so that the contingent electric shock therapy that had been successful in elim-

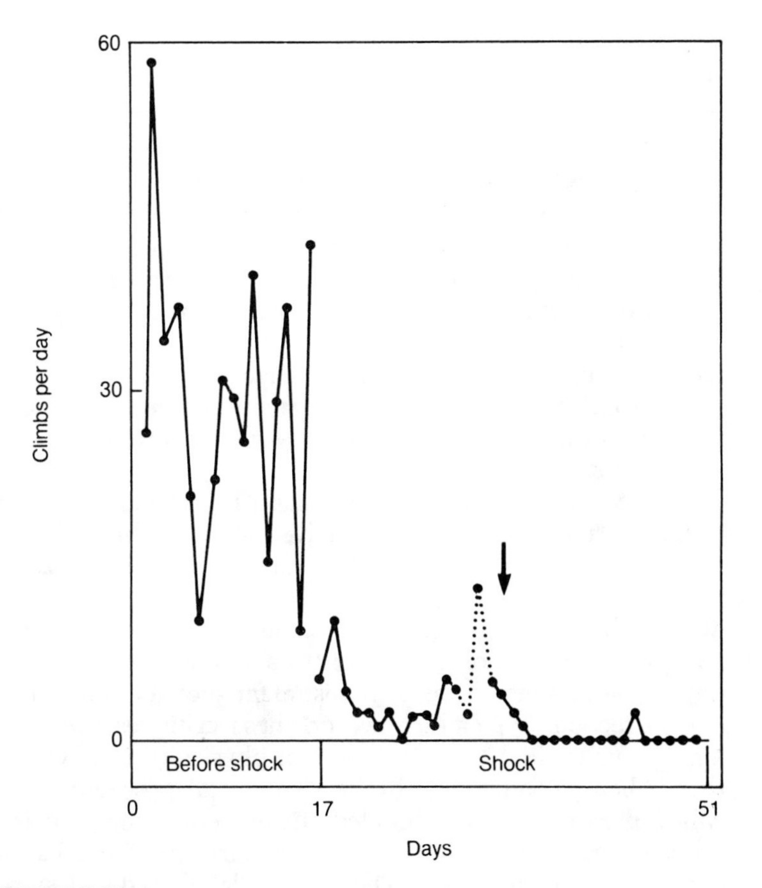

CASE FIGURE 7-5C

Graph showing the frequency of the child's climbing at home before and after mild shock was administered by the child's mother as a consequence of each incidence of climbing. Each dot represents one day. The dotted lines indicate the days on which the shock apparatus was malfunctioning, and the arrow indicates the day on which it was again operative. *SOURCE: Adapted from Risley (1968), p. 29.*

inating climbing in the therapy sessions could be used at home. The mother carried the shock device in her apron pocket. Whenever she saw the child climbing, the mother shouted "No!" Then she continued to scold the child as she approached her, applied the shock (as the therapist had done), and then immediately resumed whatever she was doing without further interaction with the child.

As Case Figure 7-5C (p. 163) shows, in the 16 days before the therapy was instituted at home, the mother observed the child climbing an average of 29 times per day. On Day 17, the mother began making electric shock a consequence of the girl's climbing, and within four days the rate of climbing was reduced to an average of twice a day. The shock apparatus malfunctioned for four days (Days 29–32), but after it was repaired (Day 33) the child's climbing rapidly decreased to zero, and, with one exception, did not recur in the next 15 days.

A WORD ABOUT PUNISHMENT

What is punishment? The use of physically aversive consequences in behavioral therapy is an example of punishment, as are all the consequential behavioral therapies designed to decelerate undesirable behaviors that have been discussed in this chapter. The technical definition of "punishment" in behavioral therapy is an empirical one that is parallel to the empirical definition of reinforcement (see Chapter 6). **Punishment** occurs whenever an event that follows a behavior (i.e., a consequence) *decreases* the likelihood that the behavior will recur. However, the generic term *punishment* has been deliberately deleted from the discussion thus far in an effort to describe very useful behavioral therapies without unfairly biasing the reader's evaluation of these procedures.

The word *punishment* is common in our culture and language and, especially in recent years, it has received some "bad press" in the popular media as well as in the professional literature. Various ethical objections concerning punishment have been raised, and are discussed in detail later in this book. Most of the serious and factual objections have been concerned with the use of *physically* aversive consequences. In fact, much of this criticism is not directly applicable to other forms of punishment such as time out, response cost, and overcorrection. Typically, however, these critiques use the term *punishment* ambiguously; although it is the use of physically aversive consequences per se that is being condemned, by implication all procedures that are technically called *punishment* are included. Even before the criticisms of the use of punishment in behavioral therapy, the term itself has had a host of negative connotations in our society. The name or label used to designate something can have a powerful influence on the way it is viewed by people. (Shakespeare's universal wisdom notwithstanding, punishment by any other name would not "smell" as sour.) Accordingly, in this book the term *punishment* is not used to label the general category of behavioral therapies that decelerate undesirable behaviors by changing their consequences.

ADMINISTERING AVERSIVE CONSEQUENCES

Consequential therapies that directly decelerate maladaptive behaviors generally make the consequences of performing the target behavior aversive (unpleasant or undesirable). As with reinforcers (which are often pleasant or desirable consequences), aversive consequences must be individually suited for each client. For instance, running laps around a track would not be a physically aversive consequence for an avid jogger. Case 7-5 gave a vivid example of how falling from a considerable height (which most people would find highly unpleasant, to say the least) was *apparently* not aversive to the 6-year-old child. We can only *assume* that falling was not aversive to the client because there is a lack of evidence to the contrary—specifically, the client continued to engage in behavior that resulted in falling. We *know*, however, that falling was not a consequence that reduced her climbing, regardless of whether or not she experienced falling as aversive.

In clinical practice, generalized aversive consequences are often tried before extensive assessment procedures are used to identify individualized aversive consequences. It is generally more difficult to identify potential aversive consequences than to identify potential reinforcers for a client. Aversive consequences are events that a person avoids, and unless their absence is conspicuous they cannot easily be observed.

Aversive consequences, like reinforcers, can be administered by other people, such as the therapist or a member of the client's family, by the client, or by the environment, as when touching a hot stove results in getting burned. Self-administration of aversive consequences is used in behavioral therapy less frequently than self-administered reinforcers because clients generally cannot be counted on to consistently subject themselves to unpleasant events, for obvious reasons. However, occasionally clients do successfully self-administer aversive consequences,[37] especially if the consequences are only moderately aversive and require little effort to administer. One easily self-administered mildly aversive consequence is snapping a large rubber band conveniently worn around the wrist whenever the client performs the deceleration target behavior. Generally, self-administered aversive consequences are most likely to be effective when the client is an adult who is highly motivated to eliminate a persistent maladaptive habit.

Guidelines for Administering Aversive Consequences

There are a number of generally agreed-on guidelines for effectively administering aversive consequences to decelerate an undesirable target behavior. Most of them parallel the guidelines for administering reinforcers (see Chapter 6).

Due to the limited research findings dealing with the effects and effectiveness of aversive consequences with humans noted earlier, the guidelines for administering aversive consequences listed here are primarily, although not exclusively, extrapolated from research involving nonhuman laboratory animals.[38] However, they are commonly used in the clinical practice of behavioral therapy and represent the best guidelines we have at present.

1. *The aversive consequence should occur immediately after the deceleration target behavior has been performed.* As with reinforcement, the closer the consequences are to the target behavior, the more likely it is that the client will associate performing the target behavior with the consequences.

2. *The aversive consequence should be administered every time* (i.e., on a continuous schedule) *the deceleration target behavior occurs* (or, where this is not feasible, as frequently as possible). This guideline should be contrasted with the general advantage of switching from continuous to intermittent schedules of reinforcement. In the case of aversive consequences, more persistent reduction of the target behavior seems to be facilitated by applying the consequences continously. A corollary of this guideline is that the aversive consequence should be inevitable—that is, the client should not be able to "escape" the consequence once he or she has performed the target behavior.

3. *The aversive consequence should be administered from the beginning at the maximum strength to be used in therapy and continued at this level* (rather than gradually increasing its potency). A relatively weak aversive consequence is likely to lose its effectiveness because the client becomes habituated (used to) it. The "maximum strength" of the aversive consequence is determined individually for each client, based on the client's subjective report that the consequence is as aversive as he or she can or is willing to tolerate.

4. *The aversive consequence should be administered contingent on a specific behavior, rather than on a class of behaviors* (e.g., on "eating high-calorie foods," rather than on "eating"). Target behaviors should be narrowly defined and highly specific.

5. *The client should be aware of the target behavior for which the aversive consequence is administered.* The client should be directly told about the contingency between the target behavior and the aversive consequence at the outset of the therapy and should be reminded of it at various times during therapy if necessary. Administering the aversive consequence immediately after the target behavior is performed also helps to make the contingency clear. Adhering to this guideline decreases the chances that the client will misconstrue the target of the aversive consequence, thereby rendering it ineffective in decelerating the target behavior. The following fable underlines this important point.

> Fed up with young Lulac's persistent use of profanities, a father wrote to the local newspaper advice column. The columnist's reply suggested the traditional "banishment to your room" procedure. Armed with this advice, the father awaited the first opportunity to see if it worked.
>
> Midway through dinner that evening, Lulac politely said, "Please pass the fuckin' carrots." Before any of the family members' hands could reach the relish tray to fulfill the request, the father immediately sent Lulac to his room.
>
> Some time later, when Lulac was permitted to return to the dinner table, his father calmly inquired, "What was it you wanted, dear?"
>
> "You bet your sweet ass it's not carrots," was Lulac's immediate reply.

6. *The administration of aversive consequences should not be closely followed by any reinforcer.* Adversive consequences should not be a signal to the client that a reinforcer is forthcoming because this may lead to an *increase* in the deceleration target behavior. This situation commonly occurs when a parent administers some form of aversive consequences for a young child's misbehavior (e.g., a scolding or spanking) and then, in response to the child's crying, comforts the child (e.g., with a hug and "I love you").

7. *A "warning" cue should be given before an aversive consequence is administered.* The cue is most often a verbal expression (e.g., "No!") or a gesture (e.g., shaking a pointed finger at the client). When the client learns that the aversive consequence is usually preceded by the cue (i.e., unless the client stops engaging in the deceleration target behavior immediately after the cue), then the cue by itself may decelerate the target behavior. The cue becomes a symbolic consequence, because it is associated with the actual aversive consequence. When a warning cue has this effect, the aversive consequence need be administered only occasionally (to renew the association between the cue and the aversive consequence).

The seven guidelines just described all directly deal with the administration of aversive consequences. Two other guidelines stress essential supplementary reinforcement procedures:

8. *The reinforcers that are maintaining the deceleration target behavior should be removed.* Events that are reinforcing the deceleration target behavior work against the aversive consequences being instituted to decrease the target behavior. If it is not possible or practical to remove the maintaining reinforcers, the client should have the opportunity to gain the same reinforcers for other behaviors. This choice is particularly important when the reinforcers are very attractive or essential to the client (e.g., the approval of close friends).

9. *An adaptive acceleration target behavior that is incompatible with the deceleration target behavior should be reinforced in conjunction with the application of aversive consequences.* This guideline is perhaps the single most crucial factor in assuring that the client will not revert back to performing the deceleration target behavior once it has been suppressed by the aversive consequences.

EVALUATION OF AVERSIVE CONSEQUENCES TO DECELERATE MALADAPTIVE BEHAVIORS

Taking as a group the various forms of consequential behavioral therapy that attempt to decelerate maladaptive behavior, what can be said of their effectiveness? Ample evidence now exists to support the statement that aversive consequences can, in some cases, decrease undesirable behaviors when properly applied (i.e., following the guidelines just outlined).[39] However, the suppression of the deceleration target behavior is often temporary. Long-term elimination or reduction of the deceleration target behavior is facilitated by simultaneously reinforcing an incompatible acceleration target behavior as well as by applying the therapy in the client's natural environment and using naturally occurring aversive consequences whenever possible so that the behavior change will be maintained after the therapy has ended. An example of a naturally occurring aversive consequence for a woman with a drinking problem might be friends' refusing to interact with her when she drank excessively.

Irrespective of the therapy's effectiveness, the use of aversive consequences can result in some undesirable side effects. First, although the aversive consequences are contingent on a particular target behavior, clients may associate the unpleasantness with various aspects of the therapy situation, such as the person administering the consequences, the setting in which the therapy takes place, and adaptive and desirable behaviors related to the target behavior. When this inappropriate overgeneralization occurs, the client actively avoids the stimuli (people, setting, objects, and related behaviors) associated with the aversive consequences. The client may come to dislike or even fear the therapist and the therapy situation. Appropriate behaviors closely related to the inappropriate deceleration target behavior may also acquire negative connotations. For example, an adolescent who must forfeit privileges (response cost) for fighting with younger siblings may avoid interacting with them altogether.

The amount and extent of such inappropriate overgeneralization can be reduced if the client remains aware of the specific purpose of the aversive consequences (see Guideline 5). The problem of the client's coming to dislike, fear, and avoid the therapeutic agent who administers the aversive consequences is decreased when the agent also provides pleasant consequences (reinforcers) for the client, so that the agent will not be viewed only as the bearer of bad consequences. This approach is especially important when the therapeutic agent must have continued and varied interactions with the client, as when parents, spouses, close friends, and teachers act as agents. It also helps to have the aversive consequences administered by several different people, again increasing the chances that the client will properly associate the aversive consequences with his or her misbehavior rather than with the presence of a particular individual.

A second possible negative side effect of the use of aversive consequences is that clients sometimes exhibit undesirable emotional responses such as crying, tantrums, and fear.[40] Related to this possibility is a third potential adverse side effect: inappropriate avoidance behavior, such as not attending therapy meetings and dropping out of treatment altogether.[41] For example, one therapy program had clients self-administer mild shock for taking a cigarette. Half the clients left the treatment, feeling that although they wanted to stop smoking they were unwilling to experience the shock to do so.[42]

Fourth, occasionally clients behave aggressively when aversive consequences are employed. The aggression may be toward the therapeutic agent administering the aversive consequences (e.g., hitting the therapist),[43] and sometimes it involves self-injurious behavior.[44]

Finally, clients (especially, but not limited to, children) may imitate the use of aversive consequences to control other people's behavior. This situation is likely to occur when the use of aversive consequences leads to an immediate, rapid, and dramatic decrease in the target behavior. The problem with such imitation is that the clients usually are not aware of the circumstances in which the use of aversive consequences is appropriate and are not familiar with the important guidelines for their administration. Misapplied therapeutic procedures always have the potential for disastrous outcomes, especially with aversive consequences.

To summarize, aversive consequences can be effective, especially in temporarily suppressing a target behavior. They are best used after other therapies have been attempted because other therapies (e.g., reinforcement therapies) are usually more effective (especially in the long run) and do not have some of the potential undesirable side effects and the ethical and humanitarian objections associated with the therapeutic use of aversive consequences. When aversive consequences are used, the guidelines for their administration must be carefully followed. Finally, the use of aversive consequences should be only one part of a treatment package that also includes the acceleration of an adaptive and appropriate behavior to take the place of the deceleration target behavior.

SUMMARY

Although the preferred strategy for decelerating behaviors is to accelerate alternative adaptive behaviors, it is sometimes necessary to first, or concurrently, directly decrease maladaptive behaviors. In extinction, the reinforcers that are maintaining the target behavior are withdrawn. Time out from positive reinforcement cuts off a client's access to positive reinforcers for a brief, specified time period. Response cost involves removal of some valued item or privilege when the client performs the deceleration target behavior (fines and traffic tickets are common examples). Overcorrection is a complex procedure in which the client first makes restitution for the harmful effects of an act (e.g., cleaning up after throwing objects around the room) and then practices an alternative, adaptive response in an exaggerated manner (e.g., straightening up the room over and over again). Satiation provides the client with an overabundance of a reinforcer in order to reduce its potency in maintaining a maladaptive behavior. Physically aversive consequences are sometimes used, usually after other methods have proved ineffective and in cases where immediate deceleration of a behavior is called for (especially self-destructive behavior).

A variety of guidelines for effectively administering aversive consequences of all kinds have been developed, including administering the consequences immediately, continously, at maximum strength, and contingent on a very specific behavior. Most importantly, an adaptive alternative behavior should be accelerated in conjunction with decelerating the maladaptive behavior. When the guidelines for effective use and ethical considerations are taken into account, using aversive consequences to decelerate behaviors can be effective and it has a role, albeit a minor one, in behavioral therapy.

REFERENCE NOTES

1. For example, Allen, Turner, & Everett, 1970; Neisworth & Moore, 1972.
2. For example, Bachman, 1972; Corte, Wolf, & Locke, 1971.
3. Barton, Guess, Garcia, & Baer, 1970.
4. For example, White, Nielson, & Johnson, 1972.
5. For example, Foxx & Shapiro, 1978; Mansdorf, 1977.
6. For example, Tate & Baroff, 1966.
7. For example, Barton, Guess, Garcia, & Baer, 1970.
8. For example, Kendall, Nay, & Jeffers, 1975.
9. Cayner & Kiland, 1974.
10. For example, Bigelow, Liebson, & Griffiths, 1974; Griffiths, Bigelow, & Liebson, 1974.
11. Cayner & Kiland, 1974, p. 145.
12. Leitenberg, 1965.
13. Kazdin, 1972.
14. McSweeny, 1978.
15. Marholin & Gray, 1976.
16. Lindsley, 1966.
17. For example, Mann, 1972, 1976.
18. Boudin, 1972.
19. Bellack & Hersen, 1977.
20. Foxx & Azrin, 1972.
21. Axelrod, Brantner, & Meddock, 1978; Ollendick & Matson, 1978.
22. Axelrod, Brantner, & Meddock, 1978; Ollendick & Matson, 1978.
23. For example, Harris & Romanczyk, 1976.
24. Azrin, Sneed, & Foxx, 1973.
25. Wells, Forehand, Hickey, & Green, 1977.
26. Azrin & Wesolowski, 1974.
27. Lichtenstein, Harris, Birchler, Wahl, & Schmahl, 1973.
28. Lichtenstein & Rodrigues, 1977.
29. Lando, 1975; Raw & Russell, 1980; Sutherland, Amit, Golden, & Rosenberger, 1975.
30. For example, Dawley & Dillenkoffer, 1975; Hauser, 1974; Horan, Hackett, Nicholas, Linberg, Stone, & Lukaski, 1977; Lichtenstein & Glasgow, 1977.
31. Poole, Sanson-Fisher, German, & Harker, 1980.
32. For example, Sajwaj, Libet, & Agras, 1974.
33. See Skinner, 1938; Solomon, 1964.
34. Baer, 1970.
35. Risley, 1968, p. 25.
36. See Ollendick & Matson, 1978.
37. See Thoresen & Mahoney, 1974.
38. Azrin & Holz, 1966.
39. For example, Kazdin, 1980; O'Leary, 1976; Rachman & Teasdale, 1969.
40. For example, Azrin & Wesolowski, 1975a; Doleys & Arnold, 1975; Matson & Ollendick, 1977; Tate & Baroff, 1966.
41. For example, Boren & Colman, 1970; Powell & Azrin, 1968.
42. Powell & Azrin, 1968.
43. For example, Foxx & Azrin, 1972; Knight & McKenzie, 1974; Mayhew & Harris, 1978.
44. For example, Azrin, Gottlieb, Hughart, Wesolowki, & Rahn, 1975; Rollings, Baumeister, & Baumeister, 1977.

CHAPTER

8 Token Economies

This chapter and the next are devoted to a detailed look at two applications of the consequential behavioral therapy procedures described in the previous two chapters. Chapter 8 examines the systematic use of token reinforcers to motivate groups of clients to perform a wide range of adaptive behaviors. Chapter 9 deals with the use of consequential behavioral therapy procedures to treat a variety of physical or medical disorders.

A *token economy* is a structured environment in which clients earn token reinforcers for performing acceleration target behaviors and exchange the tokens for desired commodities, activities, and privileges. This approach is most frequently employed with groups of clients, such as in classrooms, psychiatric wards, prisons, and half-way houses.[1] (Token systems are also employed with individual clients using the same general procedures for groups of clients described in this chapter.) Token economies are particularly useful in situations where there are a large number of clients and a small number of staff members, because they offer a technology whereby a few staff members are able to provide consistent reinforcement for the adaptive behaviors of many clients.

The token economy provides a systematic set of procedures for motivating people to behave in particular ways. There is a standard list of desirable adaptive behaviors for which people can earn tokens, and the number of tokens that can be earned for each behavior is specified in advance. The tokens can be spent on reinforcing events called **backup reinforcers** (e.g., a candy bar or watching an hour of television), each of which has a designated token cost. Thus, clients in the token economy know what they have to do to earn tokens and how they can spend them. Clients may exchange the tokens they earn for any of the backup reinforcers provided by the token economy. Usually a variety of backup reinforcers is available, which (1) allows for individual differences in events that are reinforcing and also (2) helps to prevent reinforcer satiation.

Tokens can be given immediately after a desirable behavior occurs, whereas many reinforcers are not readily available at the time the behavior is performed (e.g., watching a *specific* television program). At a later time, the person can exchange the tokens for backup reinforcers. The tokens become reinforcers because they can be exchanged for backup reinforcers, just as people come to value money, which is a type of token. The tokens are of two general types: *actual tokens* and *points*. Examples of actual tokens include poker chips (different colors may be used to designate different values), colored pieces of cardboard, slugs, metal washers, specially designed paper currency, trading stamps, and money itself. An alternative to tangible tokens is to use points that are recorded, such as on a card carried by the client or on a chart posted on the wall.

To illustrate the nature of a token economy, one particular token economy is here described in detail, and then other applications of token economies are briefly discussed.

AN EXAMPLE OF A TOKEN ECONOMY

The Community Training Center, a program for rehabilitating chronic psychiatric patients, is located at a Veterans Administration Hospital.[2] The basic goal of the program is to prepare the *trainees* (the name given to the patients in the program) for independent living in the community. Although all the trainees live outside the hospital and come to the Community Training Center during the day, most have been hospitalized for psychiatric problems for some time (an average of more than eight years). Most are male, and their average age is 45. The trainees are not able to live independent lives because they lack necessary skills in self-care, home management, interpersonal behavior, and community survival. To treat these behavioral deficits, the Community Training Center is run as a school in which a variety of classes dealing with daily living and social skills are conducted. To motivate learning and applying the skills, a token economy called the *credit system* is used.

Credits and Credit Cards

Credits are points that can be earned or spent. Each trainee has his or her own daily *credit card*, which is printed on a 3×5 index card. The credit card (see Figure 8-1) contains the trainee's name, the date, the cumulative credits earned to date, and the trainee's credit balance at the end of the previous day. Each time the trainee earns or spends credits, a description of the transaction is written in the "class/activity" column, the number of credits involved is indicated in the "earn" or "spend" column, and a new balance is recorded.

Trainees usually fill out their own credit cards, recording what they have done to earn credits or how they have chosen to spend them, along with the appropriate number of credits transacted and their new balance. By writing

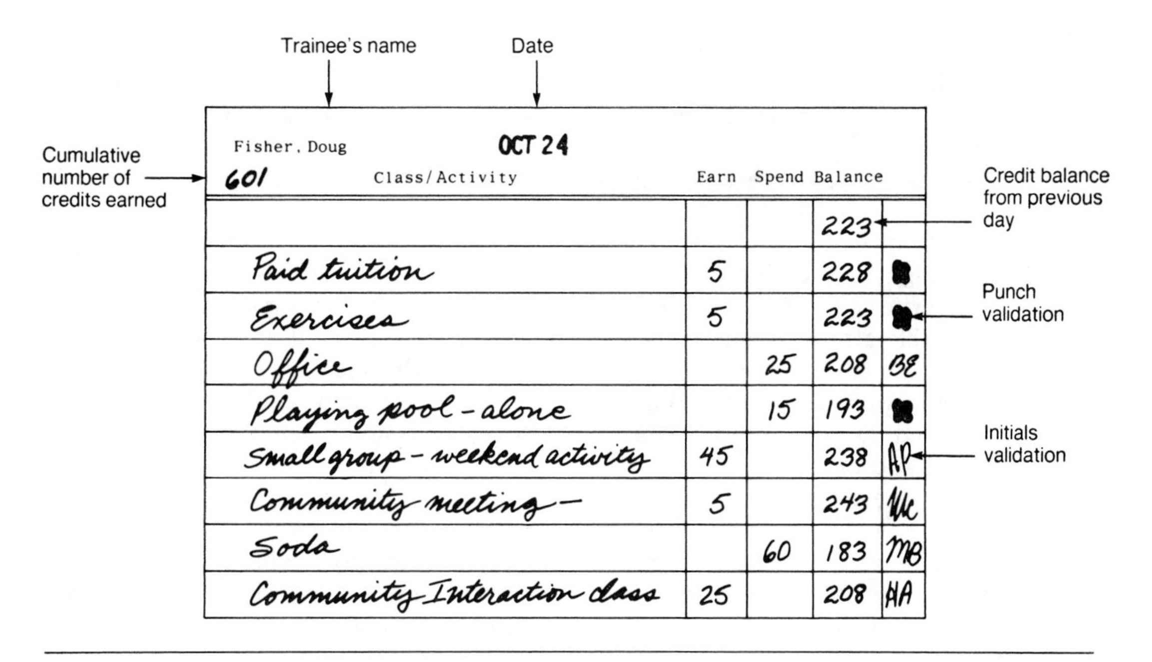

Trainee's name
Date
Cumulative number of credits earned
Fisher, Doug
OCT 24
601
Class/Activity
Earn
Spend
Balance
223
Paid tuition 5 228
Exercises 5 223
Office 25 208 BE
Playing pool - alone 15 193
Small group - weekend activity 45 238 AP
Community meeting - 5 243
Soda 60 183 MB
Community Interaction class 25 208 HA
Credit balance from previous day
Punch validation
Initials validation

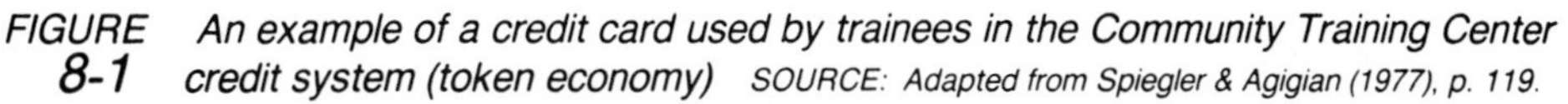
FIGURE 8-1 *An example of a credit card used by trainees in the Community Training Center credit system (token economy)* SOURCE: *Adapted from Spiegler & Agigian (1977), p. 119.*

down what they have done to earn credits and the number of credits earned, trainees become aware of the contingency between their behaviors and reinforcers. This procedure is also a form of self-reinforcement, an important skill necessary for independent living, where reinforcers frequently must be self-administered. Each credit transaction is validated by a staff member, either with the staff member's initials or a specially shaped punch in the last column of the credit card. The staff member also records the credits earned or spent in a master record, in much the same way as a separate record of charge account expenditures and credits are kept by a store or bank. Validating credit transactions and maintaining a master record of them essentially precludes trainees' awarding themselves unearned credits.

Earning Credits

Credits are earned primarily for learning and practicing skills that are relevant to independent living. In their classes, trainees earn credits for the amount and quality of their participation and for demonstrating learning on periodic assessments in the form of written and oral quizzes and on behavioral tests that usually involve role playing. Sometimes it is necessary to shape the class participation of new trainees by first giving credits for attendance only, then for a combination of attendance and participation, and finally for participation only.

Homework is an integral part of many of the classes, and trainees earn credits for doing homework. In a few classes, such as current events, a trainee may earn credits for bringing something tangible to class, such as a newspaper article or a written report. Usually, however, homework consists of community practice of skills learned in class (e.g., taking a friend to lunch at a restaurant).

Several principles have guided the development of procedures for dispensing reinforcers in the classroom. They stress the importance of (1) establishing clearly defined criteria for earning credits, (2) making trainees aware of the criteria (as by posting them in the classroom), (3) giving credits as soon as possible after a target behavior is performed, (4) pairing naturally occurring reinforcers (such as social reinforcers from the instructor and other class members) with credits, (5) making the contingency between the desired behavior and the reinforcers unambiguous and public, and (6) minimizing interruptions and distractions of ongoing activities when administering reinforcers.

The number of credits awarded for a specific behavior may vary from trainee to trainee, depending on the relative difficulty of that behavior for the individual trainee. For example, a trainee who rarely spoke to others would receive substantially more credits for commenting on another trainee's performance in class than would a trainee who had little difficulty with this task.

Backup Reinforcers

Trainees spend their credits on a variety of backup reinforcers, which fall into two major categories: activities and commodities. In the planning stages of the Community Training Center program, trainees were interviewed individually to determine the kinds of activities they would enjoy doing, and observations were made of the ways in which they spent their time during the day. Within the constraints of the physical facilities and the availability of equipment (e.g., table tennis and pool tables), a list of potentially reinforcing activities was constructed. Since then, activities purchased infrequently have been eliminated, and new activities suggested by trainees or staff empirically proven to be backup reinforcers (i.e., by being purchased) have been added. In addition to the standard list of backup reinforcers, trainees may request to spend their credits in some unique way, which is permitted if the request is reasonable and practical.

Some activities for which credits may be spent, along with their credit costs, are listed in Table 8-1. Note that the credit costs vary widely among different activities, which primarily reflects the relative therapeutic benefit of each activity. For example, reinforcing activities that involve interaction and conversation with other people (e.g., playing bridge) give trainees opportunities to practice social communication skills. The cost of activities that involve two or more trainees is frequently less than those done alone (e.g., playing solitaire). Trainees pay 15 credits to play pool alone; 10 credits to play with one or two other trainees, which often necessitates some conversation among them (e.g., "It's your turn"); and only 5 credits to play with three other trainees, which usually results in playing with partners and increases the opportunities for social interaction. In general, the more active an activity, the less it costs

TABLE 8-1 *Examples of Activities and Their Credit Costs*

ACTIVITY	CREDIT COST
Travel club	10/hour
Photography	10/hour
Short films	10/hour
Feature films	50/film
Pool	
Playing alone	15/game
Playing with 1 or 2 others	10/game
Playing with 3 others	5/game
Ping pong	
Singles	10/game
Doubles	5/game
Bowling	10/hour
Table games	10/hour
Ceramics	10/hour
Cooking	10/hour
Reading	15/hour
Sitting	25/hour

SOURCE: Adapted from Spiegler & Agigian (1977), p. 127.

(e.g., sitting is 25 credits per hour; reading is 15 credits per hour; table games are 10 credits per hour). More desirable activities—those in which trainees frequently spend their time—cost more than less desirable activities. For example, watching a feature film, which costs about 30 credits per hour, is more attractive to trainees than the Travel Club, which costs 10 credits per hour. Supply and demand as well as other economic considerations are taken into account in the operation of a token economy because it is a mini-economy, subject to many of the same principles and problems that affect major monetary economies.[3]

Trainees at the Community Training Center can also spend their credits on a variety of commodities. They are sold (for credits only) at a store named the Crediteria, which is open for business at various times during the day. A partial list of the items sold at the Crediteria appears in Table 8-2. Posters advertise items sold at the Crediteria to encourage trainees to spend their credits.

The Reinforcement Room at the Community Training Center is a large area in which trainees can partake in a variety of activities that are backup reinforcers (e.g., playing pool, darts, and pinball, watching television, listening to the radio or records, and reading). Because the Reinforcement Room serves to centralize reinforcing activities, trainees are exposed to other trainees engaging in pleasurable activities, and such modeling encourages them to participate in the activities. In the Reinforcement Room, reinforcers are purchased in two ways. Trainees may spend their credits for specific activities in a central location where each activity has its own cost. Or they may purchase a block of time

TABLE 8-2 *Examples of Items Sold at the Crediteria and Their Credit Costs*

ITEM	CREDIT COST
Coffee	20/6 oz.
First paper cup each day	5
Additional paper cups	50
Sugar	5
Cream	5
Soft drink	60/can
Sandwich	50
Candy	
Small	30
Large	60
Cookies	40/package
Potato chips	40/bag
Popcorn	40/bag
Ice cream (e.g., pops, cones)	50
Juice	20/cup
Canned dessert	50/can
Small notebook	100
Pen	50
Toothpaste	300
Razor blades	100
Toothbrush	200
After-shave lotion	300
Soap	200
Bubble bath	300
Model kit (e.g., airplanes, cars)	400

SOURCE: Spiegler & Agigian (1977), p. 129.

in the Reinforcement Room and engage in whatever activities they choose during that period.

This "flat rate" (e.g., 60 credits per hour) procedure is sometimes used in conjunction with an ongoing class. After successfully completing a class assignment, the trainee is awarded a specified number of credits, half of which can be saved for future spending and half of which must be spent immediately in the Reinforcement Room. Thus, directly after demonstrating competence in a particular behavior (often a small component of a complex skill), trainees are encouraged to reinforce themselves by engaging in some enjoyable activity of their own choosing. This procedure of immediately following a small unit of learning with a period of reinforcement may occur several times during a 50-minute class. Besides providing immediate, direct reinforcement, trainees get into the habit of spending their credits and reinforcing themselves for learning appropriate behavior. The procedure has proven to be highly successful both in teaching very basic skills and in working with trainees who are new to the program. By receiving both credits and direct reinforcers, the trainee is effectively exposed to the benefits of the credit system.

Decelerating Maladaptive Behaviors Using the Credit System

The major function of the credit system is to accelerate adaptive social and daily living skills by reinforcing them, first with credits and later with backup reinforcers. As might be expected, the trainees have a great many maladaptive behaviors, which are treated primarily by reinforcing alternative adaptive behaviors. Trainees must also pay credits for performing certain maladaptive behaviors. This procedure can be viewed in two ways. In most token economies, such payment is considered a fine, a type of response cost; clients are penalized for their undesirable behaviors. At the Community Training Center, however, trainees are considered to be paying for the *privilege* of engaging in the maladaptive behavior. There is an important difference between construing paying to perform maladaptive behaviors as a fine and as a privilege, a distinction that is more than semantic. "Fine" connotes something *imposed on* a person and implies that the person has no control over its occurrence. In contrast, "privilege" connotes something that the person has earned and therefore implies that the individual is *responsible* for it. Accordingly, trainees are encouraged to see that they make the free choice to engage in maladaptive behaviors and accept the consequences (i.e., paying credits) just as they perform alternative adaptive behaviors and reap the consequences (i.e., earning credits).

Examples of undesirable behaviors for which trainees pay credits are given in Table 8-3. Note that the credit costs for engaging in maladaptive behaviors are considerably higher than the credit costs for reinforcing activities listed in Table 8-1. The high credit cost for these undesirable privileges effectively discourages purchasing them. "Sleeping in class," for example, has rarely been purchased by trainees. And, in fact, trainees rarely sleep in classes because the rules of the credit system are operative during classes and all other aspects of the Community Training Center program (except during lunch). Trainees are often charged different amounts for performing the same maladaptive behaviors depending on the frequency with which they typically engage in the behavior. For example, a trainee who is late to most classes has to pay more for that "privilege" than a trainee who only occasionally comes late to a class.

Individualizing the Credit System

Although the credit system (and other token economies) is primarily designed so that the rules and procedures pertain to all trainees (clients), there is some individualization to meet the special needs of particular people. Two illustrations have already been given: (1) trainees requesting to spend their credits in unique ways and (2) credit costs being differentially determined depending on

TABLE 8-3 *Examples of Maladaptive Behaviors and the Average Credit Cost to Trainees for the Privilege of Engaging in Them*

MALADAPTIVE BEHAVIOR	AVERAGE CREDIT COST
Sleeping in class	75
Smoking in class	50
Leaving class early (unexcused)	50
Cutting class	100
Being late to class	15
Coming to class without having done the homework	50
Pacing in class	20
Having an unbalanced credit card	10
Making a mess (e.g., cigarette ashes on the floor)	25
Begging	20

Note: The credits charged for privileges usually vary with individual trainees and their particular problems with the maladaptive behavior.

SOURCE: Adapted from Spiegler & Agigian (1977), p. 132.

the trainee involved. Two additional examples of individualization within the credit system are discussed here.

Activities at the Community Training Center are classified as either for earning or for spending credits, and they are generally used for their respective purposes. However, occasionally a particular trainee is paid credits to engage in an activity for which most trainees pay credits. For example, some trainees do not know how to play table games, such as cards and checkers, or feel awkward playing these games. Because table games can easily and inexpensively be shared with friends at home, it is beneficial for some trainees to learn to play table games and to feel comfortable spending their time in this way. These trainees are paid credits to learn and play table games. As the naturally occurring reinforcers that come from this activity (e.g., winning and socializing) begin to influence the trainee's behavior, the number of credits for playing table games is faded and eventually the trainee is asked to pay credits for playing.

The foregoing example points to an important principle of token economy programs: *the token economy is a means to an end, not an end in itself.* Thus the treatment goals of the Community Training Center program are the *major* factor that dictates earning or spending activities, credits costs, and other details of operating the token economy.

Contingency Contracts

Often trainees have unique problems that cannot be adequately dealt with through the overall credit system. For example, one trainee needed to wear glasses to prevent eye strain during his classes at the Community Training Center, but he frequently left them at home and consequently had to be excused from classes. Because this problem is not common for trainees, having one's eyeglasses is not a standard behavior for which trainees earn credits. For such special problems, an individual agreement in the form of a contract is made with the client.

Agreements of this sort made in behavioral therapy are called **contingency contracts** because they spell out the specific consequences that are contingent on the client performing (or not performing) particular target behaviors.[4] The contingency contract for the client who frequently forgot his eyeglasses appears in Figure 8-2 and illustrates the major features of contingency contracts in general. Contingency contracts are often employed outside the context of a token economy, in which case the contingencies involve consequences other than tokens; otherwise, the features of the contingency contracts are the same.

To begin with, note that the contingency contract is very specific. For instance, it specifies the exact time period during which the agreement is in effect, that prior contracts are no longer valid, and the provisions for periodically reviewing the contract. The target behavior and the contingency for performing it are clearly spelled out. The contract not only indicates what the client is

INDIVIDUAL BEHAVIORAL CONTRACT BETWEEN TRAINEE A.
AND STAFF MEMBER B.

Effective Dates: the CTC quarter beginning July 1, 1976, and ending August 30, 1976.

This contract supersedes all previous contracts to which Trainee A. was a party. This contract will be reviewed every Monday.

Trainee A.'s Responsibilities	*Trainee A.'s Rewards*
1. Bring his eyeglasses with him to the CTC each day.	1. Trainee A. will earn 25 credits, to be paid by Staff Member B. at the CTC on the arrival of Trainee A. each morning.
2. Bring his eyeglasses to the CTC for one entire week, Monday through Friday.	2. Trainee A. will earn a bonus of 100 credits, to be paid by Staff Member B. at the CTC on the arrival of Trainee A. on Friday morning.

(signature)
______________________ Trainee A.

(signature)
______________________ Staff Member B.

FIGURE 8-2 An example of a contingency contract for accelerating a trainee's bringing his eyeglasses to the Community Training Center
SOURCE: Spiegler & Agigian (1977), p. 152.

required to do but also lists the responsibilities of the other party involved in implementing the contract. The contract is stated in simple, unambiguous language so that it is clearly understood, is put in writing, and is signed by all people involved. In contrast to informal, verbal agreements, written contracts have the advantage that they minimize disagreements about the terms. Signing the contract tends to make the parties more committed to fulfilling their roles.

Contingency contracts have been used to treat a wide range of target behaviors, including study behavior[5] and physical exercise[6] of college students, disruptive behavior of sixth-graders,[7] problem behaviors of juvenile offenders,[8] smoking,[9] overeating,[10] problem drinking,[11] and marital discord.[12]

OVERVIEW OF THE USES OF TOKEN ECONOMIES

The previous section examined the details of one token economy—a day treatment program for providing chronic psychiatric outpatients with skills necessary to live independently in the community. Token economies have been used to treat a variety of maladaptive behaviors and client populations, some of which are reviewed in this section.[13]

Token Economies in Treating Hospitalized Psychiatric Patients

Token economies have been used to motivate hospitalized psychiatric patients to adjust to hospital living and to engage in behaviors that will have some carryover to their lives when they leave the hospital. Examples are grooming, taking care of their clothes, making their beds, and doing "household" clean-up chores. For those psychiatric patients who have little hope of living independent lives outside the hospital (e.g., older patients or patients who are also severely mentally retarded), optimal adaptation to institutional living is a viable goal. In the case of patients who have the potential to be discharged from the hospital, ward maintenance programs are somewhat less efficacious and less justified. Still, these programs do reinforce many behaviors that are applicable outside the hospital and that are alternatives to maladaptive behaviors that seem to be fostered by institutionalization,[14] such as dependency and apathy.[15]

Token economies that focus on routine adaptive behaviors on the ward have led to improvement in patients' general cooperativeness, social interactions, and ability to communicate as well as decreased use of psychotropic medication.[16] The following description of one program[17] is typical of the changes observed on psychiatric wards run as token economies.

> The program has been quite successful in combating institutional behavior. Prior to the introduction of tokens most patients rarely left the ward. The ward and its surrounding grounds were dominated by sleeping patients. Little interest was shown in ward activities or parties. Before the tokens were introduced, the ward was cleaned and the clothing room operated by patients from "better" wards. [After the tokens were introduced,] the ward was cleaned and the clothing

room operated by the patients of this ward themselves. Now, no one stays on the ward without first earning tokens, and, in comparison to prior standards, the ward could be considered "jumping."

Increased discharge and lower readmission rates have also been reported for token economy programs as compared to custodial ward care.[18]

Token programs that reinforce adaptive ward behavior have reduced specific psychotic behaviors, such as hallucinations,[19] depression,[20] and inappropriate screaming.[21] This finding is important and interesting because the acceleration target behaviors (e.g., appropriate dress, eating habits, and routine work tasks) were not incompatible with the deceleration target behaviors (i.e., the psychotic behaviors). Nonetheless, the increase in adaptive ward behavior apparently replaces the maladaptive and inappropriate psychotic behaviors.

Token Economies in Training Mentally Retarded Individuals

Institutionalized mentally retarded individuals share many of the same behavioral deficits as institutionalized psychiatric patients, although the origins and some of the maintaining conditions of the deficiencies are different. For example, mentally retarded individuals frequently lack basic daily living and self-care skills, ranging from brushing their teeth and bathing to taking care of their clothes and dressing neatly and appropriately. Token economies have been successfully used to teach such skills and to motivate their consistent practice.[22] Various socially inappropriate and personally maladaptive behaviors among institutionalized retarded patients have also been controlled in token economies. One program[23] was primarily aimed at reducing disruptive behaviors, such as physical aggression and irrational speech, among institutionalized severely and profoundly retarded males (IQs below 35) between the ages of 14 and 34 years. Both tokens and social praise were administered for engaging in behaviors other than the deceleration target behaviors—usually behaviors that were partially incompatible with the undesirable behaviors (e.g., working productively in a sheltered workshop). The disruptive behaviors were also specifically decelerated by time-out, response cost (token fines), and overcorrection procedures.

Verbal behaviors have been important target behaviors for mentally retarded children and adolescents and sometimes adults.[24] Token reinforcers (exchangeable for items such as candy, soda, toys, books, grooming items, and pennies) in conjunction with social reinforcers have been used to teach and maintain a variety of language and speech skills. Because of the complexity of verbal behaviors, token reinforcement programs to accelerate verbal behaviors are usually administered individually to clients and generally involve modeling and shaping procedures.

A number of token economy programs have demonstrated that an increased amount of work as well as higher-quality work can be obtained using token reinforcement.[25] In one of the most sophisticated token programs for accelerating work-related behaviors, moderately retarded (IQs between 51 and 36) young adults earned tokens for a variety of jobs, which were divided into three levels.[26] The lowest level included janitorial-type tasks; the middle level consisted of jobs with more responsibility, such as using machines and checking attendance; and the highest level required more responsibility, independence, and skill, such as sorting and distributing mail and serving as a teacher's aide. The clients were able to progress through the levels by meeting specified performance criteria (in essence, a shaping process). Interestingly, no more tokens were earned for higher-level jobs, but more prestige was associated with higher-level work. The tokens were exchangeable for a variety of backup reinforcers, including tasty foods, money, and access to pleasurable activities. The program was successful in placing some of the third-level clients into jobs in the community.

The Ellwyn Institute in Philadelphia is a group home for mentally retarded adults that uses a token economy.[27] The residents receive tokens for various work tasks necessary for running the home as well as for social behaviors with other residents and staff. They also earn tokens for attending recreational activities in the community and for behaviors leading to gainful employment in the community, such as contacting prospective employers and going on job interviews. Once residents are working in the community, their employers are asked to participate in the token reinforcement program by providing the staff with feedback about the residents' performance on the job so that the patients can receive tokens for appropriate on-the-job behaviors.[28]

Token Economies in the Classroom

Token economies have been used in the classroom at all educational levels and with widely variant student populations (e.g., mentally retarded, "delinquent," and "normal" children). The two major categories of target behaviors have been conduct and academic performance. Some undesirable classroom behaviors modified by token economies are aggression toward other students, talking "out of turn," being out of one's seat, disregarding teachers' instructions, throwing objects, destroying property, and disturbing other students—all behaviors that interfere with classroom learning.

The basic strategies that have been employed to eliminate disruptive and inattentive behaviors include: (1) students earn tokens for appropriate classroom behavior, such as speaking at the proper time and remaining seated during a lesson (accelerating incompatible appropriate target behaviors), (2) students lose tokens for inappropriate classroom behavior (directly decelerating the inappropriate target behaviors by response cost), or (3) a combination of these two strategies. Backup reinforcers in classroom token economies have included commodities (e.g., toys, snacks, and school supplies) and attractive activities (e.g., having extended recess time and going on field trips).

Typically, token programs for decelerating inattention and disruptive acts in the classroom have applied individual contingencies—earning or losing tokens or both—to particular "problem" students. Group contingencies, which capitalize on peer pressure and competition, have also been used. In a **group contingency,** all members of a specified group must successfully perform the target behavior in order for any member to receive the reinforcer. One example is the "good behavior game," in which a class is divided into teams that compete with one another for earning the highest number of points for "good" conduct or losing the least number of points for misbehavior. The team with the most points gets the backup reinforcers.[29]

The ultimate purpose of increasing attentive and decreasing disruptive classroom behavior is to create optimal learning conditions. However, while attention and proper conduct in the classroom may be necessary conditions for learning, they are not likely to be sufficient conditions. In general, classroom token programs that focus on attention and conduct alone have not produced concomitant improvements in academic performance,[30] although there are exceptions.[31] Recently there has been a trend toward using token economies in the classroom to directly deal with academic behaviors,[32] which is more in keeping with the direct approach toward problem behaviors advocated by behavioral therapists.

Token economies have successfully increased the academic performance (both in terms of the quantity and quality of tasks completed) in basic subject areas, such as arithmetic and reading,[33] as well as more complex skills, such as creative writing. One token program was developed to increase writing skills of elementary school students who volunteered for a remedial class offered in the summer.[34] The children earned points for the number of *different* adjectives, verbs, and beginnings of sentences in stories that they wrote. The class was divided into two teams, and group contingencies were used, the backup reinforcers being candy and early recess. An increase in the number of different sentence parts was observed when, and only when, points were given for the specific sentence parts (e.g., adjectives), as can be seen in Figure 8-3. For example, the mean number of adjectives in the students' stories increased during the four days that only adjectives were reinforced with points, but not in the following four days when only verbs were reinforced. When all three sentence parts were reinforced, an increase in each part was observed. The most significant indication of the success of this project may be that people who were unfamiliar with the procedures used in the class rated the stories written during the token reinforcement days as more creative than those written during the baseline period when no token reinforcers were administered.

Achievement Place: A Token Economy for "Predelinquent" Youths

One of the most impressive applications of the token economy has been in home-style, residential rehabilitation programs for "predelinquent adolescents," defined as youths who have committed minor crimes (e.g., petty thefts or fighting). Achievement Place, the first of these family-style homes, was established in 1967 in Lawrence, Kansas,[35] under the direction of Elery Phillips, Montrose Wolf, and Dean Fixsen, and has served as a model for several dozen programs in the United States and Canada.[36] The residents of Achievement Place are six to eight lower socioeconomic boys between the ages of 10 and 16

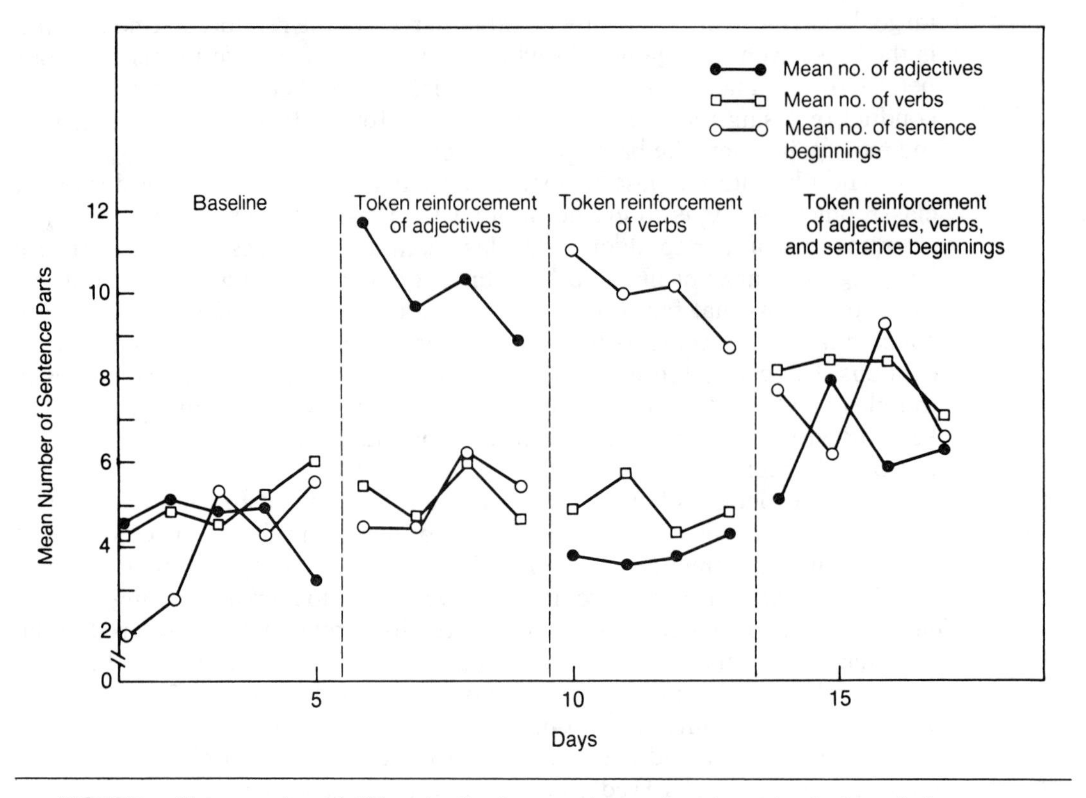

FIGURE 8-3 *Mean number of different adjectives, verbs, and sentence beginnings during baseline and token reinforcement phases in a class designed to increase elementary school students' writing skills*

SOURCE: Adapted from Maloney & Hopkins (1973), p. 429.

who have been referred by the courts. Achievement Place is located in the boys' local community and is run by "teaching parents," a married couple who have had graduate training in behavioral therapy.[37] Since the development of the first Achievement Place, similar programs have been set up for girls.[38] Because most Achievement Place programs are for boys (and consequently most published information is about those programs), the discussion here is limited to programs for boys.

The token economy at Achievement Place is a point system. Points are earned for a variety of appropriate social skills (e.g., proper manners), academic skills (e.g., good study behavior), and daily living skills (e.g., personal hygiene). Points are lost for inappropriate behaviors in these areas. Table 8-4 lists some examples of behaviors for which points are earned or lost. Backup reinforcers are primarily privileges naturally available in the home; Table 8-5 gives some examples under the daily and weekly point systems.

There are two basic levels within the Achievement Place token economy.

TABLE 8-4 *Examples of Behaviors and the Number of Points That They Earned or Lost at Achievement Place*

BEHAVIORS THAT EARNED POINTS	POINTS
Watching news on television or reading the newspaper	300 per day
Cleaning and maintaining neatness in one's room	500 per day
Keeping one's person neat and clean	500 per day
Reading books	5 to 10 per page
Aiding house-parents in various household tasks	20 to 1000 per task
Doing dishes	500 to 1000 per meal
Being well dressed for an evening meal	100 to 500 per meal
Performing homework	500 per day
Obtaining desirable grades on school report cards	500 to 1000 per grade
Turning out lights when not in use	25 per light
BEHAVIORS THAT LOST POINTS	**POINTS**
Failing grades on the report card	500 to 1000 per grade
Speaking aggressively	20 to 50 per response
Forgetting to wash hands before meals	100 to 300 per meal
Arguing	300 per response
Disobeying	100 to 1000 per response
Being late	10 per minute
Displaying poor manners	50 to 100 per response
Engaging in poor posture	50 to 100 per response
Using poor grammar	20 to 50 per response
Stealing, lying, or cheating	10,000 per response

SOURCE: Phillips (1968), p. 215.

TABLE 8-5 *Privileges That Could Be Earned with Points on the Daily and Weekly Point Systems at Achievement Place*

PRIVILEGE	PRICE IN POINTS	
	Weekly System	*Daily System*
Basics (hobbies and games)	3000	400
Snacks	1000	150
Television	1000	150
Allowance (per $1.00)	2000	300
Permission to leave Achievement Place (home, downtown, sports events)	3000	[a]
Bonds (savings for gifts, special clothing, etc.)	1000	150
Special privileges	Variable	[a]

[a] Not available.

SOURCE: Phillips, Phillips, Fixsen, & Wolf (1971), p. 46.

When a boy first enters the program, he is placed on a *daily system* in which the points he earns are exchangeable each day for backup reinforcers. This arrangement helps the boy learn how the token economy works—especially the contingency between appropriate and inappropriate behavior and earning and losing points, as well as the importance of having points in order to partake of the "good things in life." When a boy is familiar with the token economy, he is switched to a *weekly system,* in which the points earned are exchanged for backup reinforcers once a week. Most boys are on the weekly system for the 9 to 12 months they typically reside at Achievement Place. Because there are ample opportunities to earn points, the boys usually are able to buy all the privileges they desire.

When a boy's behavior indicates that he should be ready to leave Achievement Place in the near future, the use of points to motivate appropriate behavior is faded by placing him on the *merit system.* Under the merit system, no points are earned or lost and all backup reinforcers are free, but the boy must continue to demonstrate a high level of approproate social, academic, and daily living behaviors. The merit system prepares the youth for his return to his home environment, where no point system exists.[39]

A Day at Achievement Place

A typical weekday at Achievement Place begins when the boys rise at about 6:30 A.M., wash and dress, and clean their rooms. Each day one boy serves as manager and pays points to hold this prestigious position; the manager earns points according to how well the various household chores are performed by the other boys.[40] In the morning, the manager assigns clean-up jobs, supervises their completion, and awards points to the boys on the basis of how well they perform their jobs. Morning chores are followed by breakfast, and then the boys are off to school.

Academic achievement is stressed at Achievement Place. The boys attend the same school they were enrolled in before coming to Achievement Place, and the teachers and school administrators work closely with the Achievement Place teaching parents to remediate the youths' school-related problem behaviors. The teachers provide the teaching parents with systematic feedback about each boy's school performance through daily or weekly report cards, which the boy brings home to Achievement Place. Points are earned or lost depending on the boy's school performance.[41]

After school the boys return to Achievement Place, have a snack (purchased with points), and then begin their homework or other point-earning activities such as chores around the house. Later they engage in various recreational activities (e.g., bike riding and playing games) if these privileges have been earned.

After dinner, a family conference is held. Here the boys and the teaching parents discuss the events of the day, evaluate the manager's performance, consider problems in the program, and decide on consequences for specific rule violations. The rest of the evening is usually spent in group or individual activities, and bedtime is about 10:30 P.M.

Evaluation of Achievement Place

A number of carefully controlled studies have demonstrated the effectiveness of the Achievement Place token economy in increasing a variety of appropriate behaviors (such as keeping their belongings tidy, being on time, completing homework, saving money, and learning about current events) and in decreasing inappropriate behaviors (such as acting aggressively, using poor grammar, and making articulation errors).[42] The articulation errors were modified by other boys who earn points for serving as "speech therapists."[43]

The Achievement Place program has also been shown to result in more global changes than the specific target behaviors just mentioned. The most impressive and consistent findings have been the relatively low recidivism rates for the participants of the program.[44] Boys who have been court-committed to Achievement Place were compared with youths who had been committed to the Kansas Boys School (an institution for about 250 delinquent boys) and with youths who were placed on formal probation by the courts. The term *recidivism* was defined as having committed a delinquent act that resulted in a court action placing the youth in a correctional institution or sending him to adult court for prosecution. At the time recidivism data were collected, all youths had been out of their respective rehabilitation program for at least one year. The lower recidivism rates for participants in the Achievement Place program are shown in Figure 8-4.

As regards school attendance and performance, boys at Achievement Place were similar to boys in the other two groups (Boys School or on probation) before their respective treatments, but one to one and a half years after treatment the Achievement Place boys were somewhat more successful at staying in school, attending regularly, and receiving higher grades. (More long-term follow-up data indicate that these differences have not been totally maintained.)[45]

The attitudes of the Achievement Place program participants have also been examined by comparing them before, during, and after treatment with the attitudes of a comparable sample of nondelinquent boys. Compared to the nondelinquent youths, before treatment the Achievement Place boys had lower self-esteem, tended to be more fatalistic (believing that they had little control over what happened to them), and had lower achievement orientation (i.e., interest in accomplishing tasks and improving their life situation). When these attitudes were assessed after the boys were released from Achievement Place, large increases in self-esteem and the degree to which the boys believed they had control over their lives were observed. In fact, on both these measures the Achievement Place boys exhibited more favorable attitudes than did the boys in the comparison group. Achievement orientation also increased but still remained below the level of the comparison group.[46]

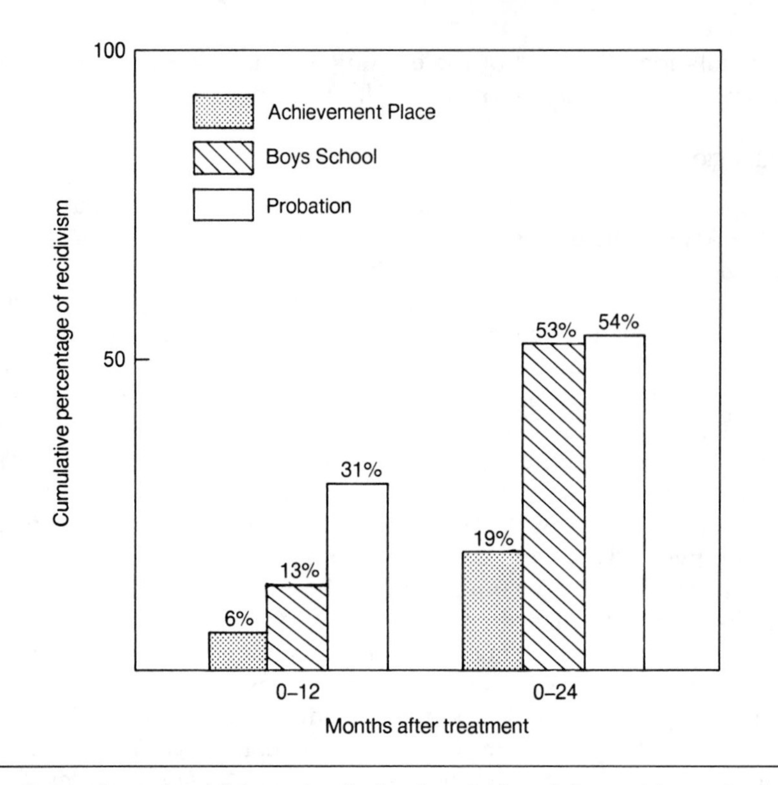

FIGURE 8-4 Comparison of recidivism rates for treatment of predelinquent boys at Achievement Place, at Boys School, and on probation

SOURCE: Data from Fixsen, Phillips, Phillips, & Wolf (1976).

EVALUATION OF TOKEN ECONOMIES

Examples of the evidence for the efficacy of token economies in the context of the specific applications were reviewed throughout this chapter. This section presents a brief overview of the effectiveness of token economies and discusses several criticisms of them.

Since the first major token economy was established more than 20 years ago at Anna State Hospital,[47] numerous token economies have been implemented in a wide variety of settings. According to the most comprehensive review of token economies, which was published several years ago,

> it is clear that no form of treatment seems to have been applied so generally as the token economy. There is no other technique that can claim such a widespread applicability across behaviors, settings, and populations, at least among treatment, rehabilitation, and educational techniques that have been empirically validated. Conse-

quently, there is no clear competing technique that has demonstrated empirically the breadth of changes that can be effected with token reinforcement.[48]

The effectiveness of many token economies has been systematically evaluated by periodically withdrawing the token reinforcement and then reinstating it, in what are called **reversal design** experiments. In most cases, the clients' behaviors deteriorate to approximately pretreatment baseline levels when the tokens are withheld and improve when the token reinforcement is resumed. Such repeated periodic withdrawal and reinstatement of the token economy provide impressive evidence that the token economy is responsible for the clients' therapeutic gains.

Even if token economies are successful in creating desirable changes in clients' behaviors, it is still important to ask how effective token economies are relative to other types of treatments and interventions (e.g., educational techniques). Although the number of comparative studies to date is fairly small, the following conclusions seem warranted, at least tentatively.

> Generally, the token economy has been shown to be more effective than standard treatments such as custodial care in psychiatric hospitals and traditional educational practices. Comparative studies with specific treatments suggest that the token economy fares better than insight-oriented and relationship therapy, milieu therapy, pharmacotherapy, and a few other techniques.[49]

Critics have objected to the use of token economies on ethical and humanitarian grounds. For example, there is the "popular" issue of bribery, which has already been discussed in the evaluation of positive reinforcement in Chapter 6. A related criticism has been that token economies are demeaning, especially for adults. Some people view token reinforcement as more appropriate for children than for adults, arguing that adults are "above" receiving tokens for their appropriate behavior. Interestingly, the same people who voice such an argument are somehow unwilling to part with the green paper tokens they carry in their wallets!

But the issue goes deeper than the fact that our economic system uses token reinforcers. It is necessary to examine how the dignity of the clients is affected by participating in a token economy. Token economies tend to increase clients' self-esteem, self-respect, pride, and sense of worth. For example, with regard to one token economy employed on a ward of a psychiatric hospital, it was concluded that "The program's most notable contribution to patient life is the lessening of staff control and putting the burden of responsibility, and thus more self-respect, on the patient."[50] Moreover, on a number of occasions and in different types of token economies, I have overheard comments of *adult* clients virtually identical to the remark made to me by a 40-year-old man of superior intelligence who was soon to graduate from the Community Training Center program (discussed earlier in the chapter). The man came over to me and, with obvious pride in what he had accomplished in his classes that day, said, "Doctor Spiegler, I earned 120 credits today." Although there is nothing extraordinary about this remark, it sounds very much like a salesperson telling her husband when she gets home from work, "I made three big sales today and earned a $120 bonus" or a college student telling roommates, "I got an 'A' on that paper I worked so hard on last week."

A not infrequent pitfall of treatment programs that involve a token economy is that the ultimate goals are ignored, or periodically forgotten, in favor of more pressing and pragmatic problems of maintaining order. Because token economies provide a means of efficiently "managing" a large number of clients, "management" sometimes can become the primary concern in token economies. This imbalance is understandable in that token economies are often employed in treatment settings that are overcrowded with clients and understaffed (e.g., psychiatric hospitals or institutions for the mentally handicapped). Nonetheless, this state of affairs needs to be corrected by altering the conditions of the treatment facility, not by reinforcing adaptive *institutional* behavior—which is rarely in the clients' best interest. Consider the example of token economies designed for hospitalized chronic psychiatric patients. The typical goals of these programs are to promote adequate self-care skills and reduce apathy. The fact that patients do not take care of their own basic needs and remain generally uninterested in their daily lives is at least partially due to the nature of most psychiatric hospitals. There are no incentives to stay clean and dress neatly because patients typically have little interaction with other people, especially those outside their ward (both fellow patients and staff). Apathy is an obvious consequence of having little that is interesting to do on the ward and little to even look forward to. Providing token reinforcers for self-care behaviors and interest in daily events ignores the fact that at least some of the maintaining conditions reside in the structure of the hospital and are independent of the clients per se. The problems might be more appropriately dealt with by changing conditions of the institution rather than by reinforcing the desired behaviors in settings that are generally unconducive to such behaviors.[51]

SUMMARY

Token economies are systems in which clients earn token reinforcers (such as points) for performing specified acceleration target behaviors and exchange the tokens for specified backup reinforcers (i.e., commodities or activities). They provide an efficient means of motivating a large group of clients (e.g., in a hospital ward) to engage in desirable behaviors, although they can be set up for individual clients. Token economies have been used to treat a large variety of maladaptive behaviors with diverse client populations, including treating psychiatric patients, training mentally retarded individuals, and dealing with problems in the classroom.

Contingency contracts are formal written agreements that spell out what a client must do in order to receive specific consequences (reinforcers or aversive consequences). They may be used as part of a token economy to deal with individual clients' problem behaviors.

In the treatment of "predelinquent" youths, Achievement Place has stood as a model token economy program for more than a decade. The program treats court-referred adolescents in a home-style residential setting where virtually all the youths' behaviors are motivated by earning and losing points exchangeable for privileges and desirable commodities.

Overall, token economies represent an effective and widely applicable treatment modality; not only do they accelerate desirable and adaptive behaviors and decelerate undesirable and maladaptive behaviors, but they also appear to increase clients' self-esteem and dignity.

REFERENCE NOTES

1. Kazdin, 1977b.
2. Spiegler & Agigian, 1977.
3. Winkler, 1971, 1973.
4. For example, DeRisi & Butz, 1975; Homme, Csanyi, Gonzales, & Rechs, 1969; Stuart. 1971.
5. For example, Bristol & Sloane, 1974.
6. For example, Wysocki, Hall, Iwata, & Riordan, 1979.
7. For example, White-Blackburn, Semb, & Semb, 1977.
8. For example, Stuart, 1971; Stuart & Lott, 1972.
9. For example, Spring, Sipich, Trimble, & Goeckner, 1978.
10. For example, Mann, 1972.
11. For example, Miller, 1972.
12. For example, Stuart, 1969.
13. Kazdin, 1977b.
14. For example, Ayllon & Azrin, 1968b; Carlson, Hersen, & Eisler, 1972; Gripp & Magaro, 1974.
15. For example, Atthowe & Krasner, 1968; Schaefer & Martin, 1966.
16. For example, Maley, Feldman, & Ruskin, 1973; Shean & Zeidberg, 1971.
17. Atthowe & Krasner, 1968, p. 41.
18. For example, Gorham, Green, Caldwell, & Bartlett, 1970; Heap, Boblitt, Moore, & Hord, 1970; Hollingsworth & Foreyt, 1975; Lloyd & Abel, 1970; McReynolds & Coleman, 1972; Rybolt, 1975.
19. For example, Anderson & Alpert, 1974.
20. Hersen, Eisler, Alford, & Agras, 1973.
21. O'Brien & Azrin, 1972.
22. For example, Girardeau & Spradlin, 1964; Horner & Keilitz, 1975; Hunt, Fitzhugh, & Fitzhugh, 1968; Lent, 1968; Spradlin & Girardeau, 1966.
23. Peniston, 1975.
24. For example, Baer & Guess, 1971, 1973; Brickes & Brickes, 1970; Guess, 1969; Guess & Baer, 1973; MacCubrey, 1971; Schumaker & Sherman, 1970.
25. For example, Hunt & Zimmerman, 1969; Zimmerman, Stuckey, Garlick, & Miller, 1969.
26. Welch & Gist, 1974.
27. "Asylum on the front porch," 1974; Clark, Bussone, & Kivitz, 1974; Clark, Kivitz, & Rosen, 1972; "A rehabilitation center for the mentally handicapped," 1972; Wilkie, Kivitz, Clark, Byer, & Cohen, 1968.
28. Clark, Bussone, & Kivitz, 1974.
29. For example, Barrish, Saunders, & Wolf, 1969; Harris & Sherman, 1973; Maloney & Hopkins, 1973; Medland & Stachnik, 1972.
30. For example, Ferritor, Buckholdt, Hamblin, & Smith, 1972; Harris & Sherman, 1974. See also O'Leary, 1972; Winett & Winkler, 1972.
31. Iwata & Bailey, 1974.
32. Kazdin, 1975.

33. For example, Ayllon & Roberts, 1974; Chadwick & Day, 1971; Dalton, Rubino, & Hislop, 1973; Glynn, 1970; Knapczyk & Livingston, 1973; Lahey & Drabman, 1974; Rosenfeld, 1972; Wilson & McReynolds, 1973.
34. Maloney & Hopkins, 1973.
35. Phillips, 1968.
36. Fixsen, Phillips, Phillips, & Wolf, 1976.
37. Phillips, Phillips, Fixsen, & Wolf, 1971.
38. For example, Minkin, Braukmann, Minkin, Timbers, Timbers, Fixsen, Phillips, & Wolf, 1976; Timbers, Timbers, Fixsen, Phillips, & Wolf, 1973.
39. Phillips, Phillips, Fixsen, & Wolf, 1971.
40. Phillips, Phillips, Wolf, & Fixsen, 1973.
41. Bailey, Wolf, & Phillips, 1970.
42. Bailey, Timbers, Phillips, & Wolf, 1971; Phillips, 1968.
43. Bailey, Timbers, Phillips, & Wolf, 1971.
44. Fixsen, Phillips, Phillips, & Wolf, 1976.
45. Fixsen, Phillips, Phillips, & Wolf, 1976.
46. Eitzen, 1975.
47. Ayllon & Azrin, 1965, 1968b.
48. Kazdin, 1977b, p. 202.
49. Kazdin, 1977b, p. 226.
50. Atthowe & Krasner, 1968, p. 41.
51. Krasner, 1976.

CHAPTER

9 Consequential Behavioral Therapies in the Treatment of Medical Disorders

Behavioral therapy procedures are increasingly being used to treat a wide array of physical or medical disorders. In fact, much of the work done in the new interdisciplinary field called *behavioral medicine*[1] relies on the principles and procedures of behavioral therapy. This chapter presents some examples of consequential behavioral therapy procedures used to deal with medical and health-related problems. Consequential therapy procedures have been used in the treatment of enuresis, pain, and seizures, and have helped promote compliance with prescribed medical procedures and the practice of health care behaviors. The chapter ends with a brief discussion of biofeedback for treating a variety of physical disorders, a topic that has received considerable attention in the popular press and among lay people.

Behavioral therapy procedures other than consequential therapies are also used in behavioral medicine. For example, systematic desensitization and deep muscle relaxation as well as flooding (discussed in previous chapters) have been used to treat a host of medical disorders. In cases where epileptic seizures are triggered by psychological stress, relaxation training and systematic desensitization for the stress-inducing events have effectively reduced the number of seizures.[2] Relaxation training is a widely used and often effective treatment for insomnia that is unrelated to physiological disorders such as drug dependence.[3] Systematic desensitization has also been used to reduce patients' fear of necessary medical procedures, such as receiving hypodermic injections[4] and hemodialysis.[5] There are initial indications that flooding may be an effective treatment for bulimia, a serious medical condition that involves periodic binge eating followed by vomiting. One maintaining condition of bulimia may be the reinforcing effect of anxiety reduction that apparently comes from vomiting. Flooding is employed to reduce the client's anxiety so that he or she need not resort to vomiting.[6]

Subsequent chapters describe other behavioral therapies that deal with medical and health problems. Examples include the reduction of fear of medical and dental procedures by modeling (Chapter 10), the treatment of overeating and insomnia through stimulus control procedures (Chapter 12), and the prevention of cardiovascular disease through a multiphasic intervention program on a community-wide basis (Chapter 15).

THE TREATMENT OF ENURESIS

Enuresis is the inability of people beyond the age of 3 to voluntarily control urination, when there is no known physical reason for this problem. Enuresis most frequently occurs when the person is asleep, in which case it is referred to as *nocturnal enuresis* or *bedwetting*, although it sometimes occurs while the person is awake and engaged in daily activities. It is a common problem among children—approximately 15 percent of all five-year-olds are enuretic,[7] and enuresis is a major problem in approximately 25 percent of all children who receive psychiatric treatment.[8] Neither traditional psychotherapy[9] nor drug therapy[10] has proved to be very effective in treating enuresis.

Urination is the natural response to bladder tension (the bladder filling up). When we are asleep, bladder tension awakens us, and we get out of bed and go to the bathroom. Bedwetters, however, are not awakened by bladder tension, resulting in a wet bed.

Bell-and-Pad Method

The **bell-and-pad method** of treating enuresis was developed by Hobart and Molly Mowrer in 1938,[11] and until recently it was the most successful form of treatment available. This method is a substitution behavioral therapy: awakening is substituted for urination as the predominant response to bladder tension while asleep. A specially prepared pad, containing two pieces of bronze screening separated by heavy cotton fabric, is placed under the bed sheet (see Figure 9-1). When urination begins, the urine seeps through the fabric and closes an electrical circuit that sounds a bell. Through repeated associations between bell and bladder tension, the tension alone becomes the stimulus that awakens the client before urination starts.

The first evaluation of the bell-and-pad method was done with 30 children who wet their beds each night.[12] Within two months, all 30 children had met the success criterion of 14 consecutive nights without bedwetting. The procedure has been used for over 40 years, and more recent studies indicate that it has been successful in 70 to 80 percent of cases. The relapse rate after six months has been about 32 percent, and the predominant reason for failure has been parents' unwillingness to carry out the procedures.[13]

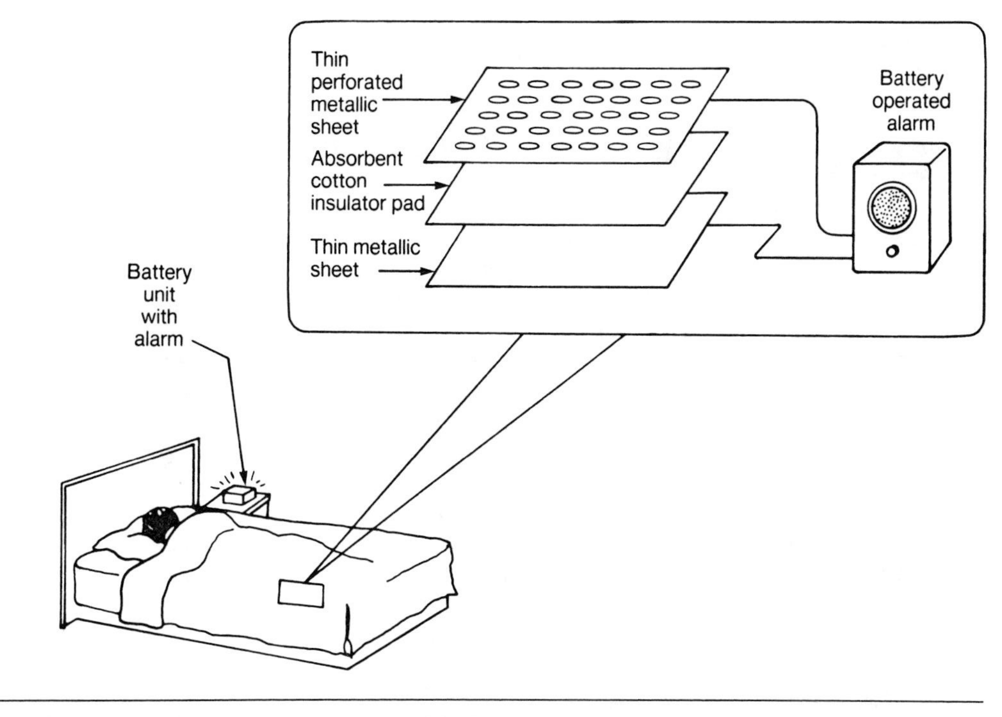

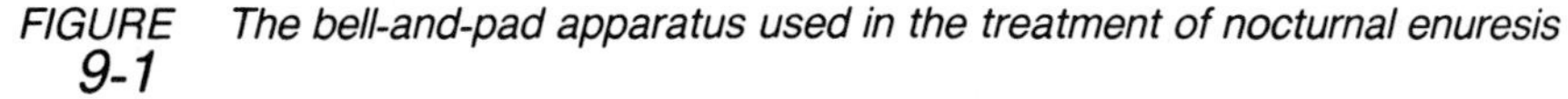

FIGURE 9-1 The bell-and-pad apparatus used in the treatment of nocturnal enuresis

Dry-Bed Training

Dry-bed training, developed by Nathan Azrin and his associates,[14] consists of a set of procedures based primarily on consequential behavioral therapy principles. This method appears to eliminate enuresis even more quickly and to last even longer than the bell-and-pad method.[15] The steps involved in dry-bed training are outlined in Table 9-1. The basic idea is to teach the child all the necessary behaviors involved in keeping the bed dry throughout the night by repeated practice and by using reinforcers to shape the complete repertoire of behaviors.

The treatment begins with one night of intensive training. The client is awakened every hour to urinate if necessary and to be praised for having a dry bed. When an accident occurs, the child goes through an overcorrection procedure composed of two phases: (1) *cleanliness training,* which involves changing nightclothes and wet sheets; and (2) 20 trials of *positive practice,* which consist of lying in bed for a count of 50, then hurrying to the bathroom and attempting to urinate, and finally returning to bed. In addition, during the day clients are given practice in holding their urine through a procedure called *retention control training,*[16] which involves shaping the retention of increasingly greater amounts of urine (created by frequent drinking of favorite beverages) for increasingly longer periods of time.

TABLE 9-1 *Outline of Dry-Bed Training Without the Use of a Bell-and-Pad Apparatus*

I. Training day
  A. Afternoon
    1. Parents and child [a boy, in this example] are informed of the entire procedure.
    2. Child is encouraged to drink his favorite beverage to increase urination.
    3. Child is requested to attempt initiation of urination every 0.5 hour.
      a. If child feels the need to urinate, he is asked to hold for increasingly longer periods of time.
      b. If child *has* to urinate, he is asked to lie in bed as if he were asleep, then jump up and go to the bathroom, role playing what he should do at night. He then is rewarded with a beverage and praise.
    4. Child is motivated to work at dry beds.
      a. Parents and child review inconveniences caused by bedwetting.
      b. Parents contract with the child for rewards to be given after first dry night and after a specified series of dry nights.
      c. Child specifies [people] he'd like to tell when he can keep dry.
      d. Child is given a chart to mark to show his progress posting this in a prominent spot.
  B. One hour before bedtime with parents watching
    1. Child is informed of all phases of . . . procedures.
    2. Child role plays cleanliness training [to be used if bedwetting occurs].
      a. Child is required to put on own pajamas.
      b. Child is required to remove sheets and put them back on.
    3. Child role plays positive practice in toileting [to be used if bedwetting occurs].
      a. Child lies down in bed as if asleep (lights out).
      b. Child counts to 50.
      c. Child arises and hurries to bathroom where he attempts urination.
      d. Child returns to bed.
      e. Steps a–d [are] repeated 20 times with parent counting trials.
  C. At bedtime
    1. Child repeats instructions on accident correction and nighttime awakenings to trainer.
    2. Child continues to drink fluids.
    3. Parents talk to child about rewards and their confidence in child.
    4. [Parents] comment on dryness of sheets.
    5. Child retires for the night.
  D. Hourly awakenings till 1 A.M. [by trainer]
    1. If child is dry
      a. Minimal prompt [light touching] is used to awaken [stronger prompt used if child doesn't wake].
      b. Child is asked what he should do.
        1. If can wait another hour
          i. Trainer praises his urinary control.
          ii. Child returns to bed.
        2. If must urinate
          i. Child goes to bathroom.
          ii. Trainer praises him for correct toileting.
          iii. Child returns to bed.
        3. Child feels bedsheets and comments on their dryness.

4. Trainer praises child for having dry bed.
5. Child is given fluids (after 11 P.M. discontinue beverages).
6. Child returns to sleep.

2. When an accident has occurred
   a. Parent awakens child and reprimands him for wetting.
   b. Parent directs child to bathroom to finish urinating.
   c. Child is given cleanliness training.
      1. Child changes nightclothes.
      2. Child removes wet sheets and places them in dirty laundry.
      3. Child obtains clean sheets and remakes bed.
   d. Positive practice in correct toileting (20 trials) is performed immediately after cleanliness training.
   e. Child is reminded that positive practice is necessary before bed the following evening.

E. Parents check the child 0.5 hour earlier [i.e., before normal waking time] the next morning [if bed is wet, go through steps II.B.].

II. Posttraining parental supervision
  A. If dry in the morning
    1. Point out to child 0.5 hour before his usual bedtime that he may stay up that extra 0.5 hour because he needn't practice . . . that night.
    2. Point out his chart to show his progress toward rewards.
    3. Tell visitors to the home how he is keeping his bed dry.
    4. Bring his success up at least three times a day.
  B. If wet in the morning
    1. Wake him 0.5 hour earlier, asking him what he should do and to feel his sheets.
    2. Child is required to change his bed and pajamas.
    3. Child does positive practice in correct toileting (20 trials).
    4. Child does positive practice (20 trials) 0.5 hour before bed that night.
    5. Child marks chart and is told we will try again tomorrow.
    6. Tell visitors to the home that the child is learning to keep his bed dry.

SOURCE: Adapted from Azrin & Thienes (1978).

Clients are given considerable responsibility for their own treatment, even in the case of children as young as 3 years old. For example, all the trainer's (therapist's) description and explanation of the procedures is done in the presence of both the child and parents. Indeed, in the most recent version of the dry-bed method (description follows),[17] the child is first instructed in the procedures, and then the child explains the procedures to the parents, requesting their help in carrying them out. The nature of the procedures emphasizes that it is the client who is developing the self-control skills and being rewarded for his or her accomplishments. When accidents do occur, the client assumes the responsibility of correcting them by cleaning up and then by practicing the behaviors required to prevent accidents in the future.

Dry-bed training has evolved in a number of respects over the past eight years, including streamlining the procedures by eliminating two features that were part of the original treatment package. A bell-and-pad apparatus had been used to signal accidents,[18] but research has demonstrated that it is not an essential component of the treatment.[19] It has also been shown that parents can assume responsibility for implementing the first night of intensive training (as well as subsequent nights of training), thereby eliminating the need for a therapist to spend an entire night at the child's home. Instead of observing the therapist perform the dry-bed training during the course of the first night of treatment,[20] parents are now taught to be trainers in a single office visit lasting about an hour and a half.[21]

A recent version of the dry-bed method (i.e., without bell-and-pad or therapist-trainer) illustrates the rapidity and long-lasting effectiveness of the treatment.[22] The clients were 44 children whose ages ranged from 3 to 15 years, with a mean age of 6.8. years. As Figure 9-2 shows, before dry-bed training the children were wetting their beds an average of 92 percent of the nights. On the first day after the intensive training, bedwetting was reduced to 18 percent, with gradual decreases thereafter to 4 percent after the fifth month of follow-up, a level that was maintained one year later.

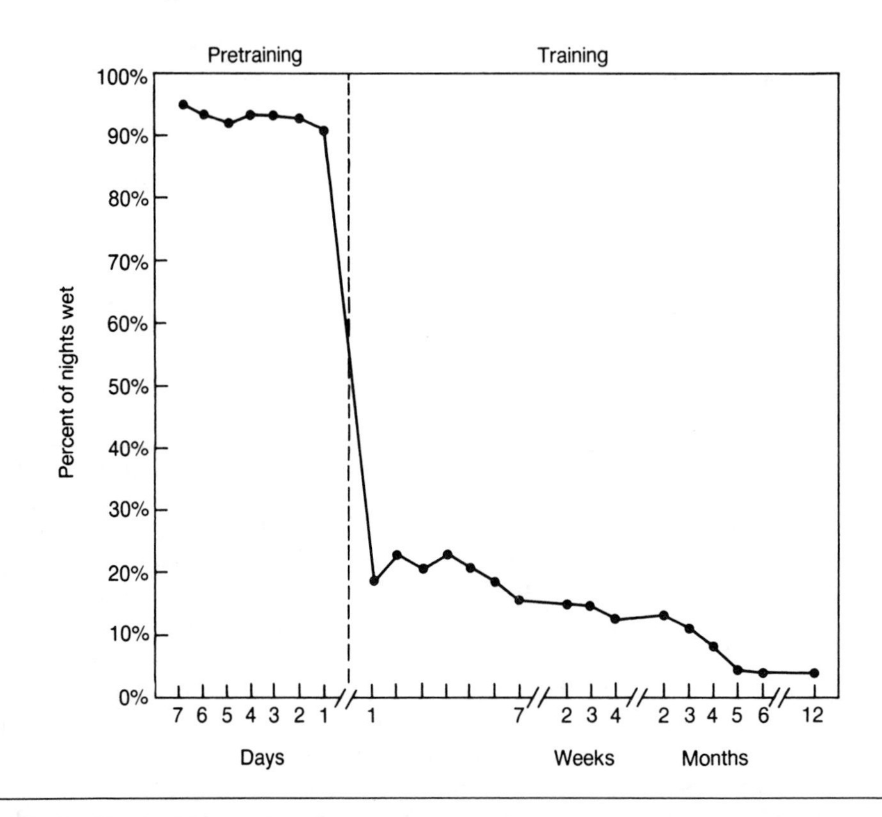

FIGURE 9-2 *Bedwetting by 44 enuretic children after office instruction given to children and parents in the dry-bed training method*

SOURCE: Azrin, Thienes-Hontos, & Besalel-Azrin (1979), p. 18.

Dry-Pants Toilet Training

The general principles of dry-bed training have been extended to normal day-time toilet training with very impressive results.[23] In the course of normal development, most children learn to appropriately use the toilet over a period of several months, and parental attempts to speed this process generally have proven to be of little benefit.[24] Several methods of intensive reinforcement training have been moderately successful in reducing training time to approximately one month.[25] In contrast, using the **dry-pants method** (the day-time version of the dry-bed method), children who ranged in age from 20 to 36 months were toilet trained in an average of four hours (an average of just over two hours was required for children older than 26 months). The number of toileting accidents were reduced from an average of more than six per day before training to about one per week within the first week after training, and this level was maintained through a four-month follow-up.[26]

THE TREATMENT OF PAIN

What is pain? Most people consider it a sensation that is "inflicted" on them, which implies that they have nothing to do with its presence (unless they are engaged in an activity known to result in pain, such as strenuous physical exercise). Furthermore, most people believe that they are relatively powerless to eliminate pain except through medical interventions such as pain medication. The behavioral approach to pain is quite different. Pain is viewed as a complex *behavior* that has both covert and overt components. The major covert behaviors are subjective feelings of intense discomfort. Examples of overt pain behaviors are moaning, screaming, grimacing, wincing, talking about the uncomfortable or unbearable sensations, moving in a guarded, unnatural manner that indicates discomfort (e.g., limping), and restricting activities that presumably would result in pain (e.g., staying in bed rather than getting up). The determinants of pain, as for any behavior, can be found in its antecedents and consequences.

Until recently, pain was viewed only in terms of its antecedents. In a medical or disease model, pain is considered to be the response to the activation of pain receptors by some underlying pathology, such as a viral infection or a fractured bone. Diagnosis involves finding the pathology, and treatment consists of removing it so that pain no longer occurs. When the diagnostic procedures fail to find pathological factors that account for the pain, it is assumed that the underlying causes are emotional or psychological, and the treatment then involves identifying and eliminating the psychological problems (e.g., intrapsychic conflicts). In either case, pain is conceptualized as resulting from antecedent events within the person, be they tissue or psychic. This traditional approach to pain is useful in many, but certainly not all, cases of pain.

It is now recognized that pain may also be *maintained* by its consequences (although it may originate in pathological antecedents). This perspective is particularly useful in cases of *chronic* pain that has proved intractable to medi-

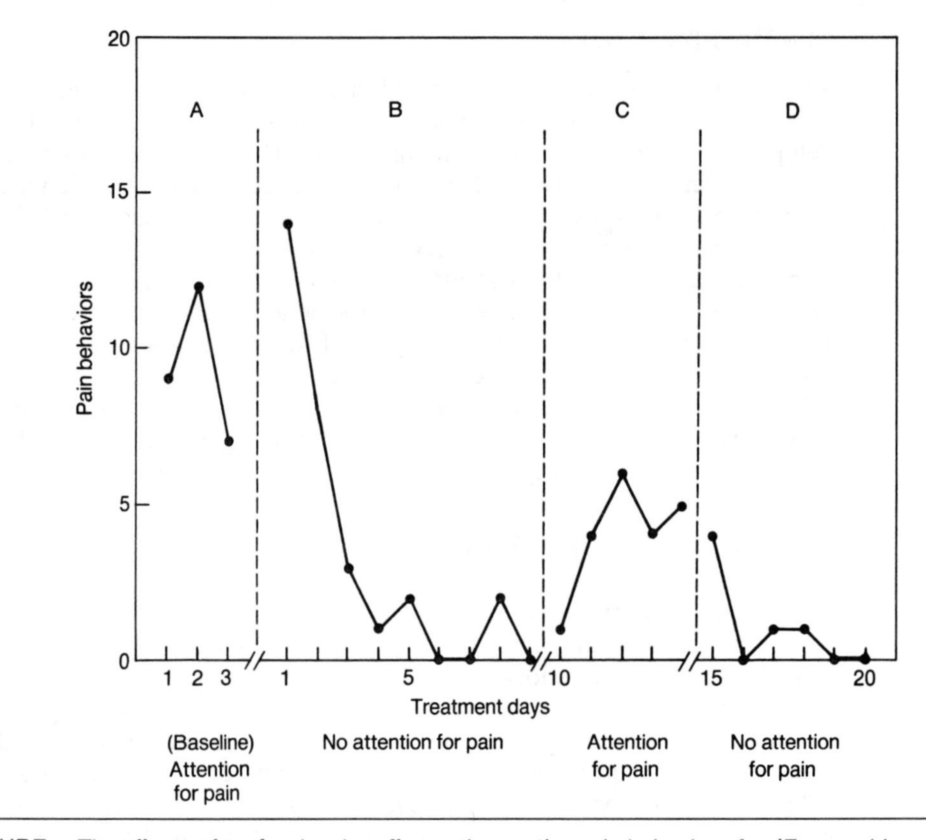

FIGURE 9-3 *The effects of professional staff attention on the pain behavior of a 47-year-old man with chronic low back pain* SOURCE: *Adapted from Fordyce (1976), p. 89.*

cal or surgical treatment. The consequences of a person's pain frequently reinforce the pain. For example, family members, friends, and even medical personnel usually respond to an individual's pain with concern, attention, sympathy, and a host of other behaviors aimed at comforting and assuming responsibilities for the patient. In one demonstration of the relationship between the responsiveness of the professional staff and pain (see Figure 9-3), the number of pain behaviors exhibited by a 47-year-old male patient with chronic low back pain was counted under four conditions: (A) normal conditions (baseline) in which the staff gave the patient attention when he displayed pain, (B) withdrawing staff attention for pain behavior, (C) again attending to the patient when he exhibited pain behavior, and finally (D) once more withholding attention in the presence of pain behavior. That staff attention was a reinforcer for pain is clearly seen in Figure 9-3: pain behaviors decreased when attention was withheld (B); they increased when attention was reinstated (C); and then they decreased when attention was once more withdrawn (D).[27]

Hospitalized patients are usually given pain medication only when they indicate that they are experiencing discomfort. Usually the consequence of a verbal complaint of discomfort—an overt pain behavior—is relief from the discomfort (brought about by the medication), which is a potent negative reinforcer for the patient's complaint. Receiving pain medication may also be reinforcing because it often produces pleasurable side effects (e.g., feeling "high" or calm). Furthermore, pain behaviors are frequently negatively reinforced by the patient being exempted from unpleasant activities, such as going to work, doing chores, and having to make decisions.

A Consequential Therapy Program for Pain

When pain behavior is being maintained by its reinforcing consequences, the treatment involves changing these consequences. Specifically, the pain behavior is extinguished by no longer reinforcing it. At the same time, abundant reinforcers are provided for alternative behaviors that are incompatible with pain (e.g., getting out of bed and engaging in normal activities). This approach is best illustrated by a comprehensive treatment program for certain cases of chronic, debilitating pain, begun more than 15 years ago by William Fordyce and his associates at the Pain Clinic of the University of Washington School of Medicine.[28]

Potential patients for the University of Washington Pain Clinic are carefully screened by physicians, psychologists, and social workers and must meet a number of criteria in order to be admitted to the program. These criteria are especially noteworthy because they address important treatment and ethical considerations. Accordingly, brief comments about these issues are included in parentheses after each of the following criteria.

1. The pain must be chronic and of long-standing duration and must not have been (and is not likely to be) responsive to traditional medical treatment. (These requirements are important because, given the experimental nature of the treatment, ethical considerations regarding the patient's welfare require that all established treatment procedures be attempted first.)

2. Behavioral assessment indicates the strong possibility that the pain behavior is being maintained by environmental consequences. (This criterion assures that the consequential behavioral therapy procedures are appropriate.)

3. Reinforcers can be identified for the patient, including those which can reasonably be controlled in the hospital while the individual is still an inpatient as well as in the patient's home environment. The latter includes pleasant activities in which the patient engaged in before the pain problem and which the patient would be likely to reestablish, assuming that the treatment were to result in the patient being physically capable of doing the activity. (This criterion ascertains that the proposed therapy is feasible because potent reinforcers, which are the *sine qua non* of the treatment, are available and can be used.)

4. The patient must be physically capable of walking. (Again, this criterion assures that the therapy is feasible, in this case because the patient is able to perform a behavior that the treatment will require.)

5. The patient agrees to participate in the program, and, whenever possible, the patient's spouse also agrees to be part of the patient's treatment. (Besides the obvious ethical consideration of patient consent, the patient's com-

mitment increases the chance of success. The spouse's cooperation is important because the spouse is usually the patient's primary reinforcing agent.)

Individualized target behaviors are established for each patient. The most frequent deceleration target behaviors include taking pain medication, moaning, talking about experiencing pain, making gestures or facial expressions that indicate discomfort, and reclining or sitting in order to ease pain. The specific acceleration target behaviors usually fall into several broad categories: exercises in physical therapy, physically demanding tasks in occupational therapy (e.g., weaving), walking on a measured course, and various work assignments.

Before patients begin the treatment program, baseline measurements of pain medication use and of activity levels are recorded. During this period, medication is given to the patient whenever it is requested (i.e., on an "as-needed" basis), and the dosage and frequency of medication are carefully noted. The amounts of time the patient spends in various active behaviors, such as standing and walking, are recorded. The patient is also given a number of performance tests to assess the amount of activity that can be tolerated. For example, in the case of patients with back pain, the number of sit-ups the patient can do is counted. The duration of uninterrupted exercise before pain or fatigue sets in is also measured.

The treatment program begins in the hospital and continues at home. Essentially, the treatment involves *extinguishing pain behaviors by removing their reinforcing consequences*—primarily attention, medication, and rest—and *reinforcing adaptive behaviors that are incompatible with pain.*

The most generalized reinforcer for pain behavior is the attention of people in the patient's environment. The major aspect of the treatment program involves encouraging all people who come in contact with the patient (including hospital personnel) to ignore or respond matter-of-factly to all types of pain behavior in an effort to extinguish them. At the same time, people are encouraged to reinforce, as with praise and attention, all instances of "well behavior" (i.e., nonpain behavior), such as verbal reports of feeling good and physical activities that are incompatible with pain behavior.

Medication is the most common means of alleviating chronic pain, and it is typically administered on an "as-needed" basis. When patients experience pain, they request or self-administer medication. Thus, among the consequences of pain are physical relief from the drugs and sometimes the attention of the person providing the medication, both of which are potentially powerful reinforcers. These reinforcers are withdrawn by making medication *time-contingent* rather than pain-contingent. Specifically, patients are given medication at fixed time intervals, whether or not they express a need for it. Initially the patient is given the same dosage of medication that he or she was taking prior to beginning the treatment program but now only at fixed time intervals (i.e., never on request) that are *shorter* than the patient's general pattern. This procedure assures that the patient does not experience pain and that the pain does not result in the reinforcing consequences associated with medication. Over the course of treatment, the dosage of medication is gradually reduced and eventually completely eliminated in most cases. The medication is always delivered in a *pain cocktail*, a liquid such as cherry syrup that masks the taste, color, and amount of medication it contains. This procedure eliminates some of the cues that indicate to patients whether or not they are actually receiving medication and, in some cases, what the approximate dosage is. (The patients are fully aware of the procedure.)

Rest, like medication, is another common consequence of pain. Pain becomes a signal to stop whatever activity one is doing and to sit or lie down to reduce the discomfort experienced. Because rest is often a reinforcer, the treatment program includes procedures for removing rest as a consequence for pain and instead making it a consequence of activity. The amount of work a patient is able to do before exhibiting pain behavior is established individually for a number of therapy activities (e.g., doing exercises). The initial amount of work that the patient is required to do at each activity is *less* than this tolerance limit. When this initial quota is reached, the patient is then allowed to rest before going on to the next activity. The patient also receives the attention and praise of the physical and occupational therapists for completing the performance quota. As the patient's tolerance limits increase, the work quotas required to rest are gradually increased.

Generalization and Maintenance of Treatment Gains

A critical part of the treatment program involves systematic procedures for assuring that the decrease in pain behaviors achieved in the hospital generalizes to the patient's home environment and persists over time. Suppose a patient's major treatment gain has been to substantially increase his or her ability to stand and walk for longer periods of time while engaging in physical therapy tasks. These new skills must generalize to the patient's natural environment so that, for example, he or she is now able to do routine tasks around the house, shop in stores for brief periods of time, and engage in limited social activities outside the home with family and friends. Although the basic motions for these activities may be the same as those practiced in physical therapy, they are now being used in very different settings. Also, it is essential that the patient at least maintain the degree of mobility he or she was capable of when he or she left the hospital.

Three basic strategies are employed in behavioral therapy to promote generalization (to the client's natural environments) and maintenance (over time), and examples of each have been given in previous chapters. One involves *training clients in self-control skills* so that they can take over as their own therapeutic agents, thereby "automatically" focusing behavioral changes in the natural environment and preparing clients to maintain their improvement.

A second strategy is to *structure the client's everyday living situation* so that therapy continues when the client terminates therapy. This strategy usually involves enlisting the aid of important people in the client's life to carry out therapeutic procedures (e.g., prompting and reinforcing adaptive behaviors) that are necessary for the client to make and maintain the required behavioral changes. Minimally, the people with whom the client is in frequent contact should be sufficiently knowledgeable about the client's treatment plan so that they do not inadvertently sabotage it, as by reinforcing maladaptive behavior with attention.

The third strategy for promoting generalization and maintenance of treatment gains is to *use treatment goals and procedures consistent with the client's natural environment*. In other words, rather than attempting to change the client's natural environment, the therapy realistically takes into account the already existing structure of the client's everyday life situation, including supports and limitations. For example, adaptive behaviors would be accelerated in therapy, using reinforcers that are available in the client's natural environment and that are most likely to be the consequences of the client's performing the target behaviors at home.

The University of Washington Pain Clinic program relies primarily on the second and third strategies for assuring generalization and maintenance of behavior changes. Spouses and others closely associated with the patient assume an integral role in the patient's therapy. They are made "partners" in the therapy from the outset, beginning with the explanation and description of the treatment program given to both the patient and the spouse. Spouses are asked to come on a regularly scheduled basis for training in the therapy procedures for which they will be responsible. They are taught to identify, observe, and record the patient's pain behaviors and "well behaviors." They are also taught to identify, observe, and record their own responses to the patient's pain behaviors. Next they learn to extinguish the patient's pain behavior, as by withdrawing attention for it, and to reinforce the patient's alternative adaptive behaviors. Finally, consideration is also given to assuring that the spouse's therapeutic endeavors on behalf of the patient are maintained by seeing that the spouse is adequately reinforced for helping the patient. Although a caring spouse no doubt receives some reinforcement by observing the patient's progress, this may not be sufficient to maintain the spouse's assistance, especially over a long period of time.

Part of the treatment program is designed to help patients reestablish activities in their lives that were reinforcing to them prior to the onset of their pain problem and to make these activities contingent on "well behaviors." For example, consider

> the pain patient who has been helped toward more walking, bending, stooping, and lifting, . . . activities usually required before one can get to a movie, a card party, or a big dinner. If the activities were not required . . . to do those other things, they [would] be programmed to become so. The new plan [would be] to walk instead of [drive] to the movie. The card party [would] be preceded by appropriate amounts of preparatory housework. The pleasant conversation about the day's activities [would] be reserved for a stroll rather than while sitting. In each instance, a naturally occurring reinforcer [would] become, at least in part, contingent on an activity targeted for increase in treatment.[29]

Evaluation of the Program

The effectiveness of the University of Washington Pain Clinic treatment program has been evaluated using 36 patients (26 female and 10 male) who exhibited chronic pain.[30] Their average age was 42, and most suffered from a form of back pain. They had experienced pain for an average of more than 7½ years and had been out of full-time employment for an average of almost 3½ years.

The consistent improvements shown by these patients on a variety of indices are impressive, especially because all the patients had long-standing pain that had proved to be intractable to traditional medical treatment. However, the results of this study can only be considered suggestive because the treatment program was not compared to appropriate control conditions. Before admission to the program, the patients spent an average of 9.1 hours per day in "up time" (standing, walking, or sitting, but not reclining). During the last week of their inpatient treatment, they were averaging 12.7 hours per day in "up time," and at follow-up (an average of 22 months after leaving the hospital) they were averaging 13.6 hours per day in "up time." Figure 9-4 shows the significant increases in patients' performance from the first to the last week of treatment (a span of four weeks) on the three most frequently prescribed activities during inpatient treatment. Finally, at the same time that the patients'

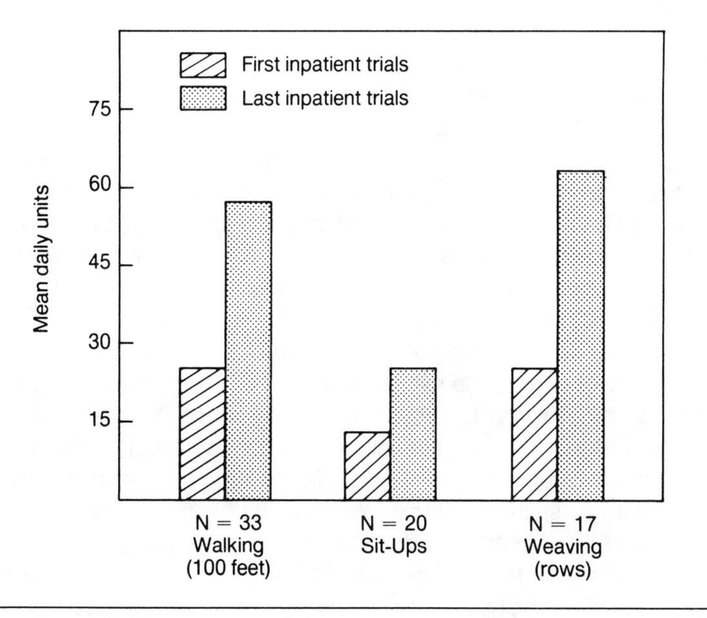

FIGURE 9-4 Significant changes in performance of the most frequently prescribed activities during inpatient treatment of chronic pain SOURCE: *Adapted from Fordyce, Fowler, Lehmann, Delateur, Sand, & Trieschman (1973), p. 405.*

activity level increased, the amount of pain medication the patients took significantly decreased, which indicates that the increased activity was not due to pain being masked by increased medication.

THE TREATMENT OF SEIZURES

Seizures, like pain, are sometimes maintained by environmental contingencies as well as physical abnormalities. In such instances, it may be possible to substantially reduce, or even eliminate, seizure behavior by modifying the maintaining antecedents and consequences in much the same way as pain behaviors are decreased (see previous section). Case 9-1 illustrates how the seizure behavior of a child was essentially eliminated by changing the typical consequences of that behavior.

CASE 9-1

Treatment of Psychogenic Seizures by Extinction and Reinforcement*

A 10-year-old girl was hospitalized after having a seizure. Physical tests were administered to ascertain the cause of her seizures, but the results were either negative or ambiguous. It was therefore concluded that her seizures were *psychogenic* (i.e., no identifiable organic cause). Analysis of the interactions among members of the girl's family did reveal several possible environmental antecedents and consequences for her seizures as well as for her temper tantrums and for various physical complaints associated with the seizures. For example, one possible antecedent of the client's seizure behavior may have been inadvertent modeling by the client's mother. Several months before the client's seizures began, "the mother had experienced a headache of such intensity that she 'rocked and banged' in pain and had to be taken to the hospital." The most probable maintaining condition of the client's seizure behavior appeared to be the attention she received from her parents for this behavior. Accordingly, treatment focused on changing those consequences.

The therapist met with the parents alone during three weekly counseling sessions. After an assessment of the probable maintaining conditions of the child's seizures and related behaviors, the following treatment plan was devised. The parents were to act "deaf and dumb" whenever their daughter had a seizure or exhibited other abnormal behaviors (temper tantrums and physical complaints). They were to reinforce her with attention for appropriate behaviors such as drawing, playing with siblings, and helping her mother.

Although no direct observations of the frequency of the client's temper tantrums and physical complaints were made prior to treatment, an approximate baseline was obtained by asking the parents to estimate their frequency during the two weeks prior to the child's hospitalization. (The therapist noted that "ethical and practical considerations militated against delaying treatment . . . until a more adequate baseline could be obtained.") The

*Gardner (1967).

treatment plan was begun as soon as the client was discharged from the hospital. The parents were contacted every two weeks (for 30 weeks) by telephone to check on the progress of the treatment. In the first two weeks, the frequency of the client's seizures dropped to zero, and her tantrums and somatic complaints decreased to approximately one-half of the estimated prehospitalization baseline. At the 26-week follow-up, the parents were asked to temporarily provide attention for the client's deviant behaviors in order to ascertain if these behaviors had, in fact, been maintained by parental attention and to clarify the differential diagnosis between psychogenic and organic seizures. Within 24 hours, the child's physical complaints drastically increased to about one per hour, and she had a seizure. At this point, the treatment contingencies were reinstated. Although no seizures followed the reinstatement of the treatment contingencies, there was a temporary increase in physical complaints and tantrums, which then dropped to the level maintained in the previous 26 weeks. At a one-year follow-up, the client's mother reported that no further seizures had occurred.

Patients who have seizures often exhibit a reliable idiosyncratic pattern of preseizure behaviors. One approach to treating seizures is therefore to interrupt the *chain* of antecedents and thereby prevent or postpone the final "link" in the chain, the seizure itself. Two consequential behavioral therapy procedures have proved effective in significantly decreasing seizures in mentally retarded children and teenagers by altering the consequences of preseizure behaviors.[31] With both procedures, the first step is to identify the behaviors that reliably occur before a seizure for each patient. One treatment then applies aversive consequences for one or more of the preseizure behaviors. When such a behavior occurs, the change agent (such as a teacher or parent) first shouts, "No!" loudly and sharply and then grasps the patient by the shoulders and vigorously shakes the patient once. Four patients were treated in this manner, with the result that seizures were substantially reduced in three of the four patients.

The other consequential procedure involved reinforcing behavior that was incompatible with one of the preseizure behaviors. (This technique is formally known as **differential reinforcement of other behavior**, and is frequently abbreviated **DRO**.) It was implemented with a 17-year-old girl whose seizures consisted of the following chain of behaviors: "(1) her body became tense and rigid, (2) she clenched her fists and raised her arms at a 90-degree angle from her body, (3) her head snapped back and a grimace appeared on her face, and (4) the major motor seizure ensued." The treatment procedure involved the following four steps: (1) as soon as the patient raised her arms (the second preseizure behavior), they were placed back at her sides, or in her lap if she were sitting; (2) a delay of five seconds was imposed; (3) she was praised effusively for having lowered her arms; and (4) she was given a piece of candy. The delay was imposed so that the patient would not associate the reinforcement with an inappropriate chain of behavior—namely, hands up followed by hands down. These procedures were effective in reducing the patient's average number of seizures per day from 16 before treatment to near-zero during treatment.

The use of consequential behavioral therapies to treat seizures is in its initial stages. However, the few reported cases have produced favorable results, and this form of treatment appears to be promising.

COMPLIANCE WITH MEDICAL PROCEDURES

Patients' failure to comply with medical procedures (e.g., taking prescribed medication or engaging in rehabilitative exercises) is a major problem for the medical profession,[32] and estimates indicate that it may occur as frequently as 50 percent of the time.[33] Obviously, the most potent therapeutic drug can be of no help to patients who do not take the medication prescribed by their physicians, and the best advice concerning changing one's health-related behaviors (e.g., bed rest and cutting down on cigarette smoking) cannot benefit patients whose behavior remains unchanged. Unfortunately, few useful guidelines for practicing health care professionals currently exist.[34] Part of the reason for this state of affairs is that until recently research on compliance to medical regimens has primarily focused on identifying the personal characteristics associated with noncompliance (e.g., age, sex, educational level, and personality traits). This line of research has not paid off because there appears to be little or no relationship between patient characteristics and noncompliance.[35] Recently, attention has shifted to viewing compliance as a *behavior* (rather than a trait)[36] and to developing procedures for accelerating specific compliance behaviors.

Behavioral therapies are just beginning to be used to promote compliance with medical regimens and, not surprisingly, reinforcement procedures are playing a major role in these applications.[37] Generally patients are capable of complying with medical regimens, in that they know how (or can easily learn) to follow prescribed procedures. The problem of noncompliance seems to be one of inadequate incentives for complying. With many medical regimens, the immediate consequences of "following the doctor's orders" are not likely to be positive (reinforcing) and may even be mildly aversive, such as the pain and fatigue resulting from doing prescribed physical rehabilitation exercises. It is only the long-term consequences that bring the patient substantial benefits in terms of improved health and even increased life span. (As with many long-term positive consequences, they often do not serve as effective reinforcers because the behaviors that led to the consequences are so far removed from them.)

One reason why compliance may be a major problem is that physicians typically give written or oral instructions that they expect patients to carry out at home on their own. This practice assumes (1) that instructions are effective in initiating and maintaining compliance behaviors and (2) that the effects of the instructions given in the office will generalize to the patient's home environment, where the compliance is relevant.[38] Both assumptions are very tenuous.

The results of several studies indicate that instructions alone are not likely to be sufficient to change patients' health-related behaviors,[39] whereas reinforcement procedures may be.[40] This finding is illustrated in Case 9-2. Furthermore, the treatment procedures used in the case were carried out by the patient's mother at home, which eliminated the problem of generalization.

CASE 9-2

*Increasing Compliance to a Medical Regimen with Token Reinforcement and Prompts**

Like many juvenile diabetics, Amy, who was 9 years old, had a history of failing to comply with her physician's self-care instructions. *Diabetes mellitus* is a serious inherited disease that has no cure but can be controlled by special diet, monitoring the sugar level in the urine, and personal hygiene (as well as insulin injections and exercise).

> The diet is essential because it provides a diabetic with a consistent intake of carbohydrates, fat, and protein that is carefully balanced in dosage and time with insulin injections (which lower the blood sugar). Urine tests are critical because they provide a diabetic with feedback on sugar level, allowing them to adjust exercise, insulin, or diet as needed. Personal hygiene, especially routine foot care, is also essential because diabetics tend to have poor circulation. Injuries are not healed quickly, and thus arteriosclerosis and the subsequent development of gangrene can occur. A loss of sensation in the feet can also occur, which is why the feet must be examined regularly or some injuries may not be discovered until they have become infected.
>
> Amy's physician had given Amy and her mother detailed verbal and written instructions on diet, insulin injections, urine testing, and skin care, but Amy was neglecting to test her urine or engage in foot care on a regular basis. She was also neglecting to eat at scheduled times or eat all of the food on her plate. [Therapy] took place in the child's home.
>
> A multiple baseline across three medical responsibilities, urine testing, dieting, and foot care, was used to evaluate the treatment procedures. Amy collected four urine samples per day: before breakfast, before lunch, before dinner, and before bedtime. She tested for concentration of glucose in the urine and for acetone (a by-product of the metabolism of fat). She was required to eat all of the food on her plate, eat at scheduled times that coincided with insulin injections, and cut down on snacks with a high sugar content. Amy was required to put on clean color-fast socks each day, wash her feet with mild soap, pat them dry, and inspect them for cuts and bruises every evening. Compliance to these behaviors was defined as the completion of a task at the prescribed time or within 15 minutes before or after that time. If she did not comply within the time allotted, a "no" was scored for compliance on a daily chart by her mother. For noncompliance, Amy's mother prompted her to complete the task.

Before treatment began, Amy was given a test to ascertain if she knew how to perform the required behaviors. She was taught those skills she did not know how to perform,

*Lowe & Lutzker (1979). Quotation is from pp. 58–59.

and she practiced them until she demonstrated competence. Amy's mother was trained to implement the therapy and assessment procedures so that the treatment could be carried out at home. In addition, to ascertain how reliably the mother recorded compliance behaviors, the older sister as well as the therapist also periodically recorded Amy's behavior. The reliability between their ratings proved to be quite acceptable (e.g., between Amy's mother and sister: 98 percent agreement for foot care, 95 percent agreement for urine testing, and 87 percent agreement for diet). (This interobserver reliability was calculated using the standard formula: number of agreements divided by total number of observations—i.e., number of agreements and disagreements—multiplied by 100.) Amy's mother collected baseline data for one week and then continued to record Amy's behavior during the treatment.

Two treatment procedures were used, and they were introduced in a "staggered" manner (see Case Figure 9-2A). The first involved providing Amy with a "memo" (written instructions) that described in detail and in easy-to-understand language the specific self-care procedures she was to carry out and when she was to do them. The second involved a

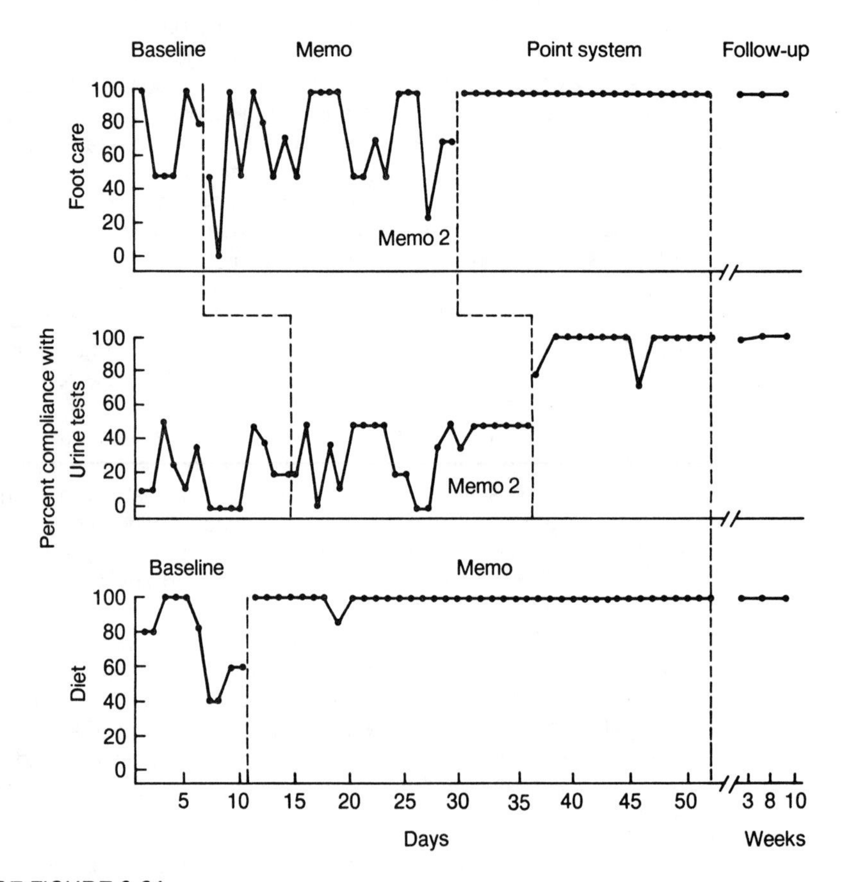

CASE FIGURE 9-2A

Percentage compliance to foot care, urine testing, and diet SOURCE: *Lowe & Lutzker (1979), p. 61.*

point system in which Amy could earn points for complying with the medical instructions; the points could be exchanged at a later time for daily and weekly backup reinforcers.

As Case Figure 9-2A indicates, the prompts provided by the memo were ineffective in increasing foot care: before therapy Amy was inconsistently complying with the prescribed foot care approximately 72 percent of the time, and this rate remained unchanged with the memo. With the introduction of the point system, Amy's compliance became perfect (i.e., 100 percent) and remained at that level. The memo was slightly effective in accelerating Amy's compliance with the urine tests, increasing from an average of 16 percent during baseline to an average of 35 percent with the memo, although her compliance was still quite inconsistent. Again the point system proved to be effective in accelerating Amy's compliance to a near perfect level (average of 97 percent). The memo was effective in accelerating Amy's compliance to the diet from an average of 72 percent (with considerable variability) before treatment to an average of 99 percent with the memo. Hence, there was no need to introduce the point system for this target behavior.

At the end of two and a half months, the therapist terminated formal contact with Amy and her family, but Amy's parents continued the treatment on their own. Ten weeks later, a follow-up indicated that Amy's consistently high level of compliance to all three medical responsibilities had been maintained. At this point, Amy's mother said that she planned to continue the therapy procedures.

The procedures used in Case 9-2 illustrate a number of elements important in producing compliance with medical regimens. First, the program was administered at home by the patient's parents rather than merely through consulting visits in the physician's office. Second, the compliance target behaviors were precisely and unambiguously defined, which made it possible to reliably assess if compliance was occurring and which probably facilitated the patient's performing the requisite behaviors. Third, immediate reinforcing consequences were provided for compliance behaviors rather than the program's relying on the long-range consequences of improved physical condition.

THE PRACTICE OF HEALTH CARE BEHAVIORS

Promoting the practice of various healthy behaviors is another major problem faced by the medical profession. The primary difference between fostering health care behaviors and creating compliance to medical regimens is that health care behaviors are generally recommended for the "prevention" of medical problems, whereas medical regimens are usually prescribed as treatment of a disorder. Because of the similarity of the two areas, only two examples of consequential behavioral therapy procedures to promote the practice of health care behaviors are discussed here.

As for compliance with medical treatments, providing individuals with potent incentives for performing the health-related behaviors is the most frequently employed procedure and also may prove to be the most effective. For example, one study compared the relative effectiveness and cost-efficiency of prompts and reinforcers to encourage low-income rural parents to seek dental care for their children.[41] The participants in this study were 35 families of 51 children who were identified, on the basis of a dental screening test administered at a local school, as needing immediate dental care. After being matched on such variables as children's school grade, parental educational and income levels, and severity of children's dental problems, the families were randomly assigned to one of three treatments, as follows.

> *One Prompt (note only).* In this treatment, parents received a single notification of the outcome of the dental screening in the form of a note. Notes were typed on school letterhead stationery and sent home with children in sealed envelopes. . . .
>
> *Three Prompts (note, telephone call, home visit).* Subjects in this treatment received three notifications in the following sequence: (1) note (identical to that with One-Prompt group sent home with child), (2) telephone contact by school staff, and (3) home visit by dental hygienist. . . .
>
> *One Prompt plus $5 Incentive.* Parents in this treatment were notified of the results of the dental screening in the form of a note identical in form and content to the one used in the two previous groups with one addition: it included a "Dental Coupon" as shown in Figure 9-5. To receive the value of the coupon, $5, parents were instructed to complete the following steps: make a dental appointment for their child, take the child for a complete dental examination, obtain the signature of the dentist on the coupon, and, finally, mail the coupon in the stamped, addressed envelope that was included.[42]

Looking at the comparison outcome data for these three treatments, which appear in Table 9-2, the "one prompt plus $5 incentive" procedure clearly was the most effective procedure. It resulted in the highest percentage of families making at least one visit to a dentist, in the most follow-up visits, and in the highest percentage of families that completed dental care. The prompt-incentive technique was more expensive than the one-prompt procedure, but substantially less than the three-prompt procedure. Overall, the combination of a single prompt and a small monetary incentive thus appears to maximize effectiveness and to minimize cost.

A second example of using consequential behavioral therapy procedures to promote healthy behaviors involved an experimental project to increase the food consumed by children in a Head Start program.[43] The problem was that the 6-year-old black children, who came from rural and economically impoverished families, were refusing to eat the meals served at the program, and thus during the day they were not getting proper nutrition. They were not getting proper nutrition at home either, because the average body weight of the children was from four to six pounds below the minimum standard for height and age. (Their diet at home consisted largely of cornbread, beans, bread, lard, and collard greens, which, obviously, is not a balanced diet.) Thus, getting the youngsters to eat nutritious meals while at the Head Start program could significantly affect their health.

DENTAL HEALTH COUPON

[This Coupon Worth $5.00]

[Expires 4/28/75]

Pay to the Order of (Child's Name/Address) ____________________

FIVE DOLLARS 00/100 ____________ DOLLARS

I certify that ____________ (child's name) has made a dental visit to our office.

Date of Visit ____________
Dentist's Sign. ____________

	Yes	No	
Treatment Unwarranted	___	___	
Treatment Initiated	___	___	
Additional Visits Required	___	___	Approx. # ___

- -

To Receive $5.00 Mail To: School Psychological Services
925 Miccosukee Rd. Tall., Fla.
Att: Maxin Reiss

FIGURE 9-5 The Dental Health Coupon used as an incentive to encourage parents to seek dental care for their children SOURCE: Reiss, Piotrowski, & Bailey (1976), p. 391.

Two possible maintaining conditions for the children's refusal to eat the foods provided were identified. On the antecedent side, the children were unaccustomed to eating the so-called common nourishing foods served to them. This fact was determined by visits to the children's homes, which included observations of the food they ate at home. On the consequence side, no positive incentives existed for the children eating the unfamiliar food, and various punitive measures were sometimes used to get children to eat the food. For example, in one instance, a school employee attempted "to pour milk down the throat of a child" for the youngster's "own good." It was decided to attempt to modify the consequences of eating the food offered in the Head Start program through reinforcement procedures.

Reinforcement I (approval). The four teachers who were working with the children were instructed to circulate around the cafeteria praising and giving sugar-coated cereal to children contingent upon

TABLE 9-2 *Comparison of Three Procedures for Encouraging Dental Care*

	ONE PROMPT	THREE PROMPTS	ONE PROMPT PLUS $5 INCENTIVE
Number of families in group	13	10	12
Percent of families making at least one visit	23% (3 of 13)	60% (6 of 10)	67% (8 of 12)
Number of follow-up visits	6	1	18
Percent of families completing dental treatment	8% (3 of 13)	10% (1 of 10)	42% (5 of 12)
Cost per student[a]	$0.20	$11.58	$4.14
Cost per participating student[b]	$0.88	$19.75	$6.21

[a]Includes all children whose families were contacted.

[b]Includes all children who actually were taken to the dentist.

SOURCE: Data from Reiss, Piotrowski, & Bailey (1976).

> engaging in eating behavior. Teachers were reminded to "catch the children being good" and pair immediate treats with verbal praise. The teachers used such praise comments as "You're eating well today, Johnny; here is a treat for putting your food in your mouth"; "Sally, you're tasting those eggs this morning; that's very good; here's a treat"; "William, it makes me proud and I'll bet you feel proud, too, when you drink your milk like that; here's a treat"; "Children, look at Suzy, she gets a treat for eating her bacon." Another aspect of the approval phase involved giving a special reward to each child who finished the entire meal. This procedure was explained to the children, and they were told that the students who finished all the food would receive five small candies. Students were also given verbal praise paired with the candy (e.g., "Al, you finished, that's a big boy, here's your candy").[44]

These procedures were instituted after a baseline of the children's eating behaviors and amount of food consumed was obtained.

The relatively simple reinforcement procedures employed were successful. The praise and treats offered the children for eating increased the average percent of children observed eating from 20 percent during baseline to 33 percent when the reinforcers were administered. The proportion of the meals consumed also increased from an average of 76 percent during baseline to an average of 93 percent during reinforcement. All except one of the 46 children increased his or her consumption of food with the reinforcement, and 78 percent increased their consumption by more than 10 percent. The four children who had been eating less than half of their meals before reinforcement increased their food consumption by more than 40 percent. The overall changes in the amounts of food the children ate were probably significant enough to make an impact on their health if one considers that the average child was eating nearly 20 percent more when reinforcers were provided.

The aim of this experimental project was merely to demonstrate the feasibility and effectiveness of using simple reinforcement procedures to increase the children's consumption of unfamiliar nutritious foods, and it was run for only 15 days. Although the aim of the project was met, the question of the maintenance of the increased food consumption remains. Because the children reported during the last week of the project that they "liked" the food, it is quite possible that the special food reinforcers and teachers' praise could be faded as the food became a naturally occurring reinforcer. Further investigation would be necessary to assess that possibility.

MODIFYING BODILY FUNCTIONS THROUGH BIOFEEDBACK

Interest in modifying our internal bodily functions is certainly not new. It has been reported for hundreds of years, for example, that yogis in India have successfully slowed their heart rate, increased their body temperature, and stayed alive for long periods of time with relatively little oxygen. There have also been reports that people in deep hypnotic trances have been able to create blisters, remove warts, and modify physiological functions such as blood sugar level and salivation.

Over the past two decades, there has been considerable investigation of the voluntary control of many different internal bodily functions. This area of study has been called **biofeedback** because the control of one's bodily processes is aided by information (feedback) about the rate or level of the particular function (e.g., heart rate or degree of muscle tension). To provide such precise information, the person is "hooked up" to a device, such as a polygraph, that monitors one or more internal bodily states and translates this information into feedback the person can use. Usually the feedback is in the form of a signal, such as a tone or light flash, which indicates when the person is appropriately changing the internal state (e.g., decreasing blood pressure). The feedback is a reinforcer for modifying the internal state in the desired direction.

Biofeedback is necessary because most people, at least in Western cultures, are not aware of changes in many of their bodily states. People in Eastern cultures may be more attuned to their internal bodily states (undoubtedly because more attention is paid to them, as in meditation), as suggested in the opening paragraph of this section.

Biofeedback has been used to treat a variety of diseases and physical disorders, including hypertension, cardiac arrhythmias, migraine and tension headaches, epilepsy, and stomach acidity in ulcer patients. Successful treatment of these problems has been found for some, but certainly not all, of the clients who were given relevant biofeedback treatment. There appear to be large individual differences in people's ability to modify bodily processes using biofeedback.[45]

People also differ in the rapidity with which they can gain control over their bodily functions through biofeedback training as well as in the amount of physiological change they are capable of making. Although most people are able to effect measurable changes in physiological functions, often the changes are not large enough to have any meaningful impact on their physical disorders. For example, a patient suffering from hypertension (high blood pressure) might learn to consistently lower her systolic blood pressure from 200 to 190 but such a decrease would not make a significant impact on the condition and its complications.

Training People to Drink in Moderation

Because it has been widely assumed that people with drinking problems (so-called alcoholics) cannot control their alcohol consumption and function as "social drinkers," the usual treatment goal is total abstinence.[46] However, a relatively recent and controversial new approach to the treatment of alcohol addiction or dependency uses biofeedback to train clients to drink in moderation.

In the first test of this form of treatment, adults with drinking problems (ages 22–25 years) were taught to discriminate the concentration of alcohol in their blood (from zero to 0.08 percent).[47] Feedback was provided by a large meter that indicated the blood alcohol concentration, as determined by a breathalyzer test. The clients were instructed to associate their present subjective feelings with the meter readings. In the second phase of treatment, clients drank alcohol and received mild shocks if their blood alcohol concentration exceeded 0.06 percent, which is the average level reached when drinking two to three martinis over the course of an hour at a cocktail party.

Treatment consisted of 6 to 12 two-hour sessions (the number of sessions depended on each client's progress) using the procedures just described. Individual progress in maintaining controlled drinking was followed for periods ranging from 16 to 60 weeks. Seventy-five percent of the clients were able to drink in moderation, exceeding 0.07 percent blood alcohol concentration only rarely. Another 11 percent were drinking less than before treatment and exceeded the 0.07 percent level once or twice per week.

A number of subsequent studies have confirmed that *some* people with drinking problems can learn to drink in moderation with the aid of biofeedback treatment.[48] There is some reasonable doubt, however, that most people can continue to maintain acceptable blood alcohol levels without receiving occasional "refresher" biofeedback sessions.[49] Dependency on biofeedback apparatus for maintaining changes in bodily processes in one's everyday environment is a major problem in this new area of treatment. Nevertheless, for some people with a drinking problem, learning to drink in moderation through biofeedback, even with the inconvenience of periodic booster sessions, may be a more reasonable alternative than total abstinence. Because drinking alcoholic beverages is so much a part of our social customs, it is extremely difficult for a person to avoid situations in which drinking is expected (e.g., at parties; before, during, and after dinner; and while entertaining business clients and associates). If people could learn to control their drinking, they might be able to function in our "drinking culture" without having to drastically change their social and even work habits, which has obvious advantages.

Skeletal Muscle Training

Biofeedback training has been found to be most effective in controlling various skeletal muscles.[50] Using electromyographic (EMG) feedback to retrain skeletal muscles in paralyzed patients is a prime example of this treatment. The electromyograph monitors muscle contraction from electrodes placed either directly into the muscle or attached to the skin over the muscle.

The success of EMG feedback training in the rehabilitation of hemiplegia (paralysis on one side of the body, as from a stroke) is most impressive. For example, one group of 20 hemiplegic patients had shown no muscle movement on the affected side of the body for one year despite traditional neuromuscular rehabilitation therapy. Remarkably, 17 of these patients were trained to produce strong, voluntary arm movements in a single five-minute EMG feedback session.[51]

Biofeedback training that includes some sort of home practice has been found to be particularly effective.[52] As an example of this approach, a group of 10 hemiplegic patients first received EMG feedback training in the hospital and then used a portable EMG device with surface electrodes at home.[53] Five of these patients learned to move their paralyzed legs to an extent that permitted removal of the leg braces they had been forced to wear since the onset of their hemiplegia, which is an impressive clinical improvement. Those patients who appeared to be poorly motivated for treatment dropped out of therapy early and received little benefit from it; motivation is an important factor accounting for the success of biofeedback therapy (or any behavioral therapy) with some clients and not with others.

One of the earliest applications of EMG biofeedback was for the treatment of subvocal speech, which is common during silent reading and which seriously interferes with reading speed. Rapid and long-lasting cessation in subvocal speech of high school and college students has been achieved using auditory feedback from the laryngeal muscles.[54] Interestingly, one study found that the absence of subvocal speech was maintained only by high school students who were above average in intelligence.[55] Although there is no evidence that eliminating subvocalization increases reading speed, students who have undergone biofeedback training report that they are less fatigued after several hours of reading than they were before training.

The two other major areas in which EMG feedback has been attempted are in deep muscle relaxation training and in relieving tension headaches. There is no clear-cut evidence that EMG feedback facilitates learning deep muscle relaxation. There is evidence that a combination of EMG feedback training and the practice of relaxation at home can relieve tension headaches (by relaxing the forehead muscles). However, the contribution of the biofeedback component of the treatment package has yet to be established.[56]

The Current Status of Biofeedback Therapy

In the past few years, biofeedback techniques have been the subject of numerous articles in popular magazines, newspapers, and books written for the general public. Indeed, the term *biofeedback* has some meaning for most people today, unlike less than a decade ago. Generally, highly exaggerated claims have been made for the effectiveness of biofeedback for curing all sorts of ills, improving one's concentration, providing inner peace, and more! Biofeedback courses, programs, and entire centers have been developed primarily by business people rather than by professionals trained in administering and monitoring the techniques. Biofeedback devices for measuring heart rate, blood pressure, skin temperature, GSR (galvanic skin response, a common indicator of anxiety), EEG (electroencephalogram, of brain waves), EMG, and even ESP (extrasensory perception) can be purchased through the mail and "over the counter." Yet, in many ways, the promise of biofeedback as a therapeutic technique is still largely unfulfilled.

In this brief review of biofeedback uses, a number of cautions and problems have been noted. There is the consistent finding that some people seem to benefit from biofeedback training whereas others do not. Even when individuals are able to reliably modify their bodily processes using biofeedback, the magnitude of these changes is often clinically negligible. (This has frequently been the case in modifying autonomic functions, such as blood pressure and respiration rate, which is why these potentially important applications of biofeedback have not been discussed.) Also, effects of biofeedback training often do not generalize to the clients' natural environments, where biofeedback is generally not available.

Moreover, many studies that have demonstrated the effectiveness of biofeedback training have serious methodological flaws, which leaves open questions such as "Is biofeedback training an effective treatment?" Many studies fail to control adequately for placebo effects, or for factors other than the biofeedback per se. For example, clients' beliefs that the biofeedback *will* be effective (undoubtedly heightened by the impressive apparatus employed and the aura of sophisticated science in operation) may account in part for the changes obtained during biofeedback training. Another problem with biofeedback studies is their failure to separate adequately the contribution of various treatment components when biofeedback training is employed with other procedures. For example, evidence suggests that EMG biofeedback procedures are no more effective than standard tension-release instructional procedures for inducing deep muscle relaxation[57] (see Chapter 4). If additional research substantiates this finding, then the obvious question is "Why use elaborate, expensive biofeedback apparatus?"

Therefore, we must exercise considerable caution regarding the general efficacy of biofeedback. It is clearly not a panacea. At the same time, biofeedback may well prove to be an extremely effective treatment for *certain* disorders and with *particular* clients. Such cautious optimism seems to be warranted given the potential merits of biofeedback therapy. In the treatment of medical problems, biofeedback would be preferable to medication that may have negative side effects or to surgical procedures, which always pose some risk to the patient. Also, controlling one's own bodily functions to alleviate psychological as well as physical problems is part of the general trend in behavioral therapy to teach clients self-control skills.

SUMMARY

Consequential behavioral therapies are increasingly being used to treat medical disorders. For example, until recently the most successful treatment of enuresis (bedwetting) was a substitution therapy called the bell-and-pad method. Dry-bed training, which has been found to be even more effective, is a complex treatment package involving prompting, reinforcement, overcorrection, and shaping. Also, when pain is conceptualized as a behavior that is at least partially maintained by its consequences (e.g., attention from sympathizers), it can be significantly reduced by applying appropriate extinction and reinforcement procedures. The successful treatment program at the University of Washington Pain Clinic illustrates this therapy for pain. Seizures (like pain) can be maintained in part by environmental consequences, and they can be reduced by extinction and reinforcement procedures. Another approach to treating seizures is to interrupt the chain of antecedent behaviors that typically occur before a seizure by using aversive consequences and differential reinforcement of other (incompatible) behaviors.

Medical patients frequently do not benefit from effective treatment procedures because they fail to comply with "doctors' orders," and reinforcement procedures have been successful in promoting compliance. Similarly, the use of potent reinforcers has been helpful in fostering the practice of important health care behaviors (e.g., eating nutritional food, obtaining needed dental work). A final example of the use of consequential therapy procedures in the treatment of medically related disorders is the use of biofeedback to monitor and modify bodily functions.

REFERENCE NOTES

1. Agras, 1979; Schwartz & Weiss, 1977.
2. For example, Parrino, 1971.
3. For example, Borkovec, 1977.
4. For example, Nimmer & Kapp, 1974; Turnage & Logan, 1974.
5. Katz, 1974.
6. Rosen & Leitenberg, 1982.
7. Yates, 1970.
8. Kanner, 1972.
9. For example, Deleon & Mandell, 1966; Werry & Cohrssen, 1965; Yates, 1970.
10. For example, Kardish, Hillman, & Werry, 1968; Yates, 1970.
11. Mowrer & Mowrer, 1938.
12. Mowrer & Mowrer, 1938.
13. Deleon & Sacks, 1972; Doleys, 1977.
14. Azrin, Sneed, & Foxx, 1973.

15. Azrin, Sneed, & Foxx, 1974.
16. Kimmel & Kimmel, 1970; Paschalis, Kimmel, & Kimmel, 1972.
17. Azrin, Thienes-Hontos, & Besalel-Azrin, 1979.
18. Azrin, Sneed, & Foxx, 1973, 1974.
19. Azrin & Thienes, 1978.
20. Azrin, Sneed, & Foxx, 1974
21. Azrin, Thienes-Hontos, & Besalel-Azrin, 1979.
22. Azrin, Thienes-Hontos, & Besalel-Azrin, 1979.
23. Foxx & Azrin, 1973a, 1973b.
24. For example, Madsen, Hoffman, Thomas, Karopsak, & Madsen, 1969.
25. For example, Madsen, 1965; Madsen, Hoffman, Thomas, Karopsak, & Madsen, 1969; Mahoney, VanWagenen, & Meyerson, 1971; Pumroy & Pumroy, 1965.
26. Foxx & Azrin, 1973a.
27. Fordyce, 1976.
28. Fordyce, 1976.
29. Fordyce, 1976, p. 98.
30. Fordyce, Fowler, Lehmann, DeLateur, Sand, & Trieschmann, 1973.
31. Zlutnick, Mayville, & Moffat, 1975.
32. For example, Gentry, 1977; Zifferblatt, 1975.
33. Gillum & Barsky, 1974.
34. Blackwell, 1973; Marston, 1970; Sackett & Haynes, 1976.
35. Marston, 1970; Sackett & Haynes, 1976.
36. For example, Kasl, 1975; Zifferblatt, 1975.
37. For example, Baile & Engel, 1978; Dunbar & Agras, 1978.
38. Irvin, 1976.
39. Katz & Lutzker, 1976; Lutzker & Drake, 1976.
40. Miller, Hersen, & Eisler, 1974.
41. Reiss, Piotrowski, & Bailey, 1976.
42. Reiss, Piotrowski, & Bailey, 1976, pp. 389–390.
43. Madsen, Madsen, & Thompson, 1974.
44. Madsen, Madsen, & Thompson, 1974, p. 260.
45. Miller, 1978.
46. Pattison, 1966.
47. Lovibond & Caddy, 1970.
48. For example, Silverstein, Nathan, & Taylor, 1974; Sobell & Sobell, 1973, 1976; Vogler, Compton, & Weissbach, 1975.
49. Silverstein, Nathan, & Taylor, 1974.
50. Blanchard & Young, 1974.
51. Andrews, 1964.
52. Blanchard & Young, 1974.
53. Johnson & Garton, 1973.
54. For example, Aarons, 1971; Hardyck & Petrinovich, 1969; Hardyck, Petrinovich, & Ellsworth, 1966, 1967.
55. Hardyck & Petrinovich, 1969.
56. Blanchard & Young, 1974.
57. Alexander & Smith, 1979.

CHAPTER 10 Modeling Therapies

Modeling therapies capitalize on the well-known phenomenon of **observational learning,** the process by which people are influenced by observing (i.e., seeing, hearing about, reading about) someone else's behavior. Much of our behavior is acquired and maintained through observational learning. In fact, most of us are probably unaware of the degree to which this process takes place in our lives, because it is so prevalent that we do not pay much attention to it. Observational learning is not a newly discovered phenomenon: people have probably always used the behavior of others as guides for their own behavior. In the past two decades, however, observational learning has been examined extensively and scientifically. A major offshoot of these studies has been the development of behavioral therapies that use the principles and procedures of modeling to alleviate practical human problems.

MODELING AND IMITATION: BASIC CONCEPTS

The term **model** is reserved for the exemplar, the person who demonstrates the behavior that the observer observes. A model may actually be present or may be observed indirectly. The term **live modeling** refers to observing a model in the flesh, so to speak, whereas **symbolic modeling** involves observing a model indirectly, as in the movies, on television, by reading, through an oral description of someone's behavior, or even by imagining a model's behaviors.

Observing a model does not necessarily mean that the observer will imitate the model's behavior. We are exposed to countless models during the course of even a single day, yet we select only a few as guides for our own behavior—that is, imitate them. A variety of factors influence whether or not we imitate a model we have observed. The degree to which we remember what the model did is obviously a prerequisite for imitation. How appropriate the model is as an exemplar for us is also important. Experts rarely imitate novices, for example, and, in fact, much of an expert's behavior is usually inappropriate for novices to imitate. Another important factor influencing imitation is what we observe happen to the model as a consequence of the model's behavior. Such vicarious consequences tend to affect the observer in much the same way as if the consequences had occurred to the observer directly.

Imitating a model sometimes involves copying exactly what the model did as best we can. More often, however, our subsequent behavior is influenced more indirectly by suggesting acceptance of a more general *class* of behaviors of which the model's behavior is perceived to be an example. Consider 5-year-old Doug, who sees his parents regularly donate money to a variety of charities; subsequently Doug may become more willing to share his toys with his friends or to divide a piece of chocolate cake with his sister.

FOUR FUNCTIONS OF MODELING

Modeling generally has four distinguishable effects on observers.[1] First, modeling may serve a *learning* function by providing observers with examples of new behaviors (behaviors that the person did not previously know how to perform). Over the years we have acquired much of our everyday behaviors, including such complex behavior patterns as language, by observing others perform the behaviors, in contrast to being told how to perform the behavior (direct instruction). Second, modeling often has an *eliciting* effect by providing people with cues that prompt them to engage in actions they already know how to perform. Social conformity, such as applauding when others clap and wearing faddish clothes, is a common example of how modeling elicits behavior. Third, modeling can have a *disinhibiting* effect by facilitating behaviors that the person knows how to perform but is not performing because doing so evokes anxiety or other negative reactions. When we see another person *safely* (with no aversive consequences) engage in a behavior that has seemed threatening to us, we tend to "lose our inhibitions" and imitate the model. For example, parents help their children overcome their fear of getting on a swing in the playground by pointing out the other children who are enjoying swinging. Finally, the fourth function of modeling involves *inhibiting* behavior that the person knows how to perform. When we observe that a model's actions result in aversive consequences, we are often less likely to engage in similar behavior. For example, a child may initially become fearful of going on a swing after having seen another child fall off the swing. Each of the four functions served by modeling has been applied therapeutically.

Accelerating New Adaptive Behaviors

There is some truth in the old adage that a picture is worth a thousand words. Modeling is an extremely efficient means of teaching a person how to perform a large variety of behaviors. Its efficiency can be seen by contrast with reinforcement procedures, the other major behavioral therapy procedure used to accelerate new behaviors. Because the new behavior must occur before it can be reinforced, reinforcement by itself is rarely sufficient to establish a behavior never before performed. Prompts are often required to get the client to perform the behavior (or an approximation of it) so that it can be reinforced. Prompts, in turn, usually involve modeling, as when a therapist describes how a person (a symbolic model) would perform the behavior or when the therapist (a live model) directly demonstrates the behavior for the client. Modeling and reinforcement are frequently combined in behavioral therapy.

Behavior rehearsal is a therapy technique in which real-life situations are role played within the therapy session. Behavior rehearsal is used both to assess how a client deals with problematic life situations and to help the client develop adaptive behaviors. In the case of assessment, clients are asked to role play the way they typically behave so that the therapist can determine what behaviors the client needs to learn or perfect. When behavior rehearsal is used to teach people adaptive behaviors, (1) the therapist models the behavior for the client, (2) the client then attempts to imitate the therapist, and (3) the therapist critiques the client's performance and shapes the client's behavior by selectively reinforcing those components of the total behavior that the client performed well. Both applications of behavior rehearsal are illustrated in Case 10-1.

CASE 10-1

Developing Dating Skills by Modeling and Reinforcement for Imitation*

Joe was a 17-year-old high school junior with very limited heterosexual social experience. Until a recent growth spurt, his physical development had been somewhat retarded. Whereas formerly he described himself as a "skinny midgit," now his height and build were at least average for his age, and he began to think of himself as physically attractive. A month before entering therapy, Joe was asked to a party by a girl he liked. Although he was flattered at the invitation, he did not have a good time at the party because he "seemed out of it and didn't know what to do or say." He wanted to start dating and participating in social activities, and a close male friend suggested that he talk to the school psychologist about his problem.

An initial assessment determined that Joe's infrequent dating and social behavior were probably maintained by a social skills deficit. During their weekly meetings, Joe and the school psychologist worked on developing specific social skills primarily through modeling. An excerpt from the session devoted to "calling for a date" illustrates the general procedures used.

Psychologist: Suppose you wanted to ask Helen to attend a dance at school. What might you say?

*From the author's files.

Joe: Well, I'm not exactly sure. I guess I'd just ask her if she wanted to go.

Psychologist: Why don't you pretend that you are calling Helen and actually say what you might say on the phone to her?

Joe: OK, but don't expect much.

Psychologist: Remember, we are only practicing. Just give it a try.

Joe: "Hello, Helen, this is Joe. How ya doin? Listen, if you've got nothing better to do, would you want to go to the dance with me?"

Psychologist: That's a reasonable start. Let's see if we can make it even better. For one thing, you don't want to make it sound like going to the dance with you is a last resort. Let me model one possible way you might start off the conversation after you've said hello. Listen and see if you can tell the difference: "There's a dance at school next Saturday, and I'd like to take you if you're not busy."

Joe: Yeah, I can hear the difference.

Psychologist: Why don't you try to say something like that?

Joe: "I saw the sign about the dance next weekend at the gym, and I was wondering if you'd like to go with me."

Psychologist: Very good. That's much better. No apologies; just a straightforward statement of what you'd like.

Behavior rehearsal was continued until Joe was able to comfortably and skillfully ask for a date in an appropriate manner during the practice sessions with the psychologist. The next step was to have Joe actually call a girl for a date and report back to the therapist as to how the conversation went. The psychologist reinforced Joe's appropriately asking for a date (not his having secured a date). When a difficulty arose in actually using the newly acquired social skill, modeling, behavior rehearsal, and reinforcement for imitation were again used in the therapy session.

The procedures employed in Case 10-1 are typical of those used to assist clients in developing new adaptive behaviors. Rather than being asked to merely mimic the psychologist's demonstration of "asking for a date," Joe was instructed to imitate the general approach the psychologist had modeled (making a direct and nonapologetic request). This instruction allowed Joe to use his own words and style, which made his asking for a date more natural and appropriate for him.

Behavior rehearsal provided the client with an opportunity to perfect the skill of asking for a date in a nonthreatening atmosphere. Then he was given a homework assignment to actually ask for a date. The psychologist reinforced Joe's appropriately *asking for* the date rather than *getting* the date because the latter depends on factors other than Joe's behavior, such as the girl's interest and availability.

When we observe a model, we observe not only what the model has done but also what happens as a result of the model's acts. The consequences of a model's behavior are important because they indicate the consequences we may receive for imitating the model.

Because the consequences of a model's behavior influence observers indirectly, they are called **vicarious consequences.** The term **vicarious reinforcement** refers to instances in which the consequences of the model's behavior increase the likelihood that observers will imitate, and **vicarious aversive consequences** refer to the instances in which the consequences of the model's acts decrease the chances that observers will imitate. The use of vicarious reinforcement to accelerate a new adaptive behavior can be seen in Case 10-2.

CASE 10-2

*Accelerating Question Asking by Disadvantaged Children, Through Televised Modeling and Vicarious Reinforcement**

The ability to ask questions to obtain information is an important intellectual skill that, along with many forms of language, is primarily learned through observational learning. Appropriate models for asking questions do not exist in the Papago Indian subculture of Arizona because asking questions is not promoted as a way of obtaining information in that culture. However, because Papagos must deal with English-speaking governmental and educational bureaucracies, Papago parents want their children to develop English-language skills.

To meet this need, three 10-minute videotaped modeling sequences were made depicting "Papago adult females interacting with costumed animal characters adapted from Papago folklore and legends." The models asked a large variety of causal questions ("why" and "how" questions) and were reinforced for this behavior. To ascertain whether the children could learn causal questions by viewing these modeling sequences, half the children were shown the modeling tapes and half were shown three 10-minute tapes "depicting interesting activities unrelated to the target behavior."

Four-year-old children who were attending a Head Start program were tested for their use of causal questions before viewing the videotapes, after viewing them, and five to ten days after the posttest to see if the children retained their newly developed language skill. The children were shown a set of 20 color drawings dealing with Papago life and, in a game format, were asked to make up a question about each picture. Two points were given for each causal question (e.g., "Why is the boy opening the box?"), one point for each noncausal question (e.g., "What is the boy doing?"), and no points for each statement (e.g., "The boy is opening the box") or for no response.

The results are depicted in Case Figure 10-2A. The children who viewed the modeling sequences substantially increased the number of causal questions they asked after the modeling treatment and maintained this gain approximately one week later. In contrast, the children who saw videotapes unrelated to causal questions showed no increase in asking this type of question.

*Henderson, Swanson, & Zimmerman (1975).

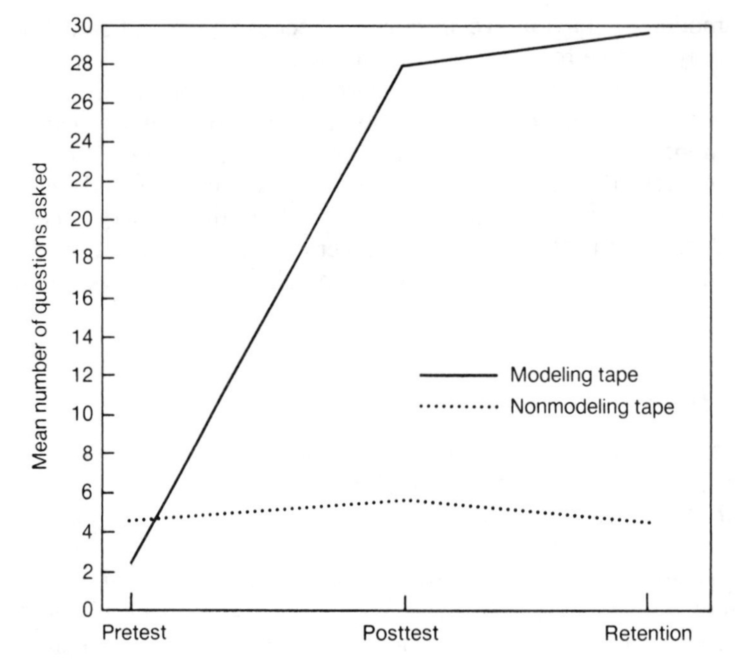

CASE FIGURE 10-2A

The mean number of questions asked by those Papago children who saw and did not see videotaped models asking questions and being rewarded for that behavior

SOURCE: Data from Henderson, Zimmerman, Swanson, & Bergan (1974).

The effectiveness of modeling to teach Papago children to ask questions is impressive for two reasons. First, questions about causal relations are considered relatively mature for children aged 4¼ years old (the mean age of the children in this study) who have been raised in the predominant English-speaking culture, which promotes question asking. Thus, the present test of the effectiveness of modeling to teach causal questions to "educationally disadvantaged" youngsters was a particularly stringent one. Second, the children who saw the modeling sequences did not merely mimic the models they observed. There is evidence that these children abstracted a linguistic rule (i.e., the general form of questions dealing with causal relations) and generalized it to a different situation. The scenes in the modeling videotape were very different from the circumstances of the test situation, so direct copying of modeled questions was not possible. Furthermore, when the children were tested they asked a large variety of specific questions, most of which the models had not asked.

Eliciting Behaviors a Client Already Knows How to Perform

In the majority of cases in which a client's problem is being maintained by a skill deficit, the client knows how to perform the requisite behaviors but is doing so (1) too infrequently, (2) too weakly, (3) for too short a time (to be effective) or (4) at inappropriate times. The approach taken in therapy is to provide such clients with antecedents that will result in their performing the behaviors appropriately. Modeling can provide such cues relatively simply. Much of our behavior is elicited and facilitated by being in the presence of other people performing the appropriate behavior. For example, it is easier to study in the library, where other people are studying, than in the cafeteria. Case 10-3 illustrates how modeling alone (i.e., without reinforcement) can elicit the performance of a target behavior that the client already knew how to perform but was not performing.

CASE 10-3

*Accelerating a Prescribed Oral Hygiene Practice by Modeling**

Julie was a 25-year-old married woman who had recently had oral surgery for a serious and progressive gum condition. The dentist instructed Julie to use a Water Pik, a device that cleans between the teeth by squirting water, on a daily basis, and warned Julie that if she did not use the Water Pik, her gum condition would worsen and probably would result in the loss of her natural teeth.

Several months after Julie's surgery, her husband, Art, noticed that Julie was not using the Water Pik and mentioned this to her. Julie said that she would start using it. Another month passed, and the Water Pik still remained unused. Art became increasingly concerned about his wife's negligence and began to remind Julie about using the Water Pik. His reminders became more frequent and more forceful when his wife did not heed them. Julie became extremely annoyed at Art's "playing parent" and emphatically told Art to stop bothering her about *her* teeth.

Art was very concerned about his wife's dental condition and called their dentist. The dentist recommended that Art speak to a behavioral therapist with whom he had worked in the past for treating patients' fears of dental procedures. The behavioral therapist suggested that Art come in with his wife to discuss the problem, but that course of action was abandoned when Art said that he was sure that Julie would refuse.

The therapist then outlined a treatment in which Art would serve as a model for his wife. Because even people with normal teeth and gums can benefit from the regular use of the Water Pik, the therapist suggested that Art use the device on a daily basis and record the times that his wife used the Water Pik to see if his modeling made a difference. Art was cautioned not to discuss the use of the Water Pik with his wife nor to reinforce her using it (e.g., by verbal praise and encouragement), if and when she did. These restrictions were established to avoid reinstating any negative feelings Julie might have had about Art's exhortations to use the Water Pik.

The results of this modeling procedure were striking. As can be seen in Case Figure 10-3A, Julie had never used the Water Pik in the 30 weeks prior to Art's modeling. During the first week of modeling, Julie used the Water Pik six days out of seven; the next week she

*From the author's files.

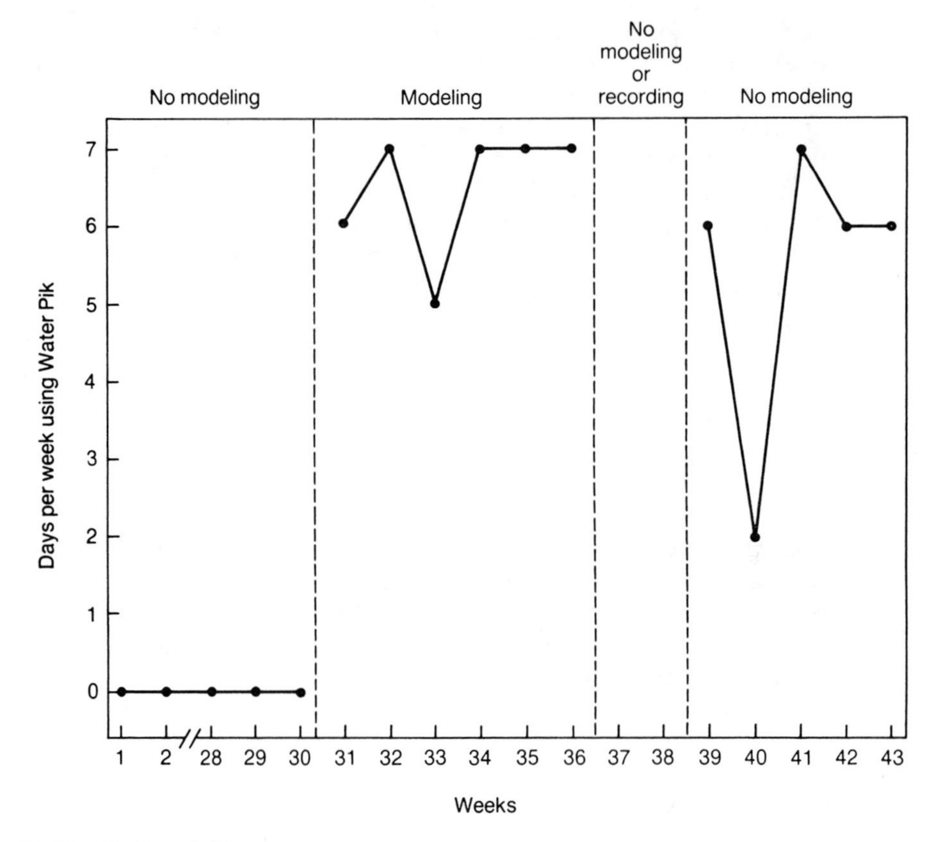

CASE FIGURE 10-3A
Number of times the Water Pik was used each week

used it every day; and after a drop to five times per week in the third week of modeling, she used the Water Pik every day for the next three weeks.

Art was out of town on business during the next two weeks, so it was not possible for him to either model the target behavior or record its occurrence. The day he returned from his trip, he called the behavioral therapist to report on what had transpired during the previous two months. The therapist suggested that Art discontinue his modeling and just record how often Julie used the Water Pik. As shown in Case Figure 10-3A, during the next five weeks Julie used the Water Pik about 5½ times per week. This rate was not only a vast improvement over the pretreatment period, but it was also also sufficient for Julie's dental hygiene needs.

The subtlety of modeling in teaching and eliciting adaptive behaviors can in *some* instances make it easier for the client to accept and benefit from the treatment, such as when clients resist change because they want to initiate the change themselves rather than have it imposed on them. Children frequently resist their parents' explicit instructions *just because* they are being told what to do, the "Mother, I'd rather do it myself" phenomenon. The same type of resistance can occur with adults, as in Case 10-3. The husband's modeling the target behavior for his wife probably constituted a less intrusive, although not necessarily a less influential, form of therapy than if the husband had made various reinforcers, such as his approval, contingent on his wife's using the Water Pik. Modeling provided Julie with an alternative behavior, and it was her choice to imitate.

Disinhibiting Target Behaviors

Anxiety or other negative emotions frequently keep people from engaging in adaptive behaviors that they are fully capable of performing. Sometimes people have experienced aversive consequences when they engaged in the threatening behavior, but usually people have had no direct negative experiences. Rather, they anticipate aversive outcomes. For example, most people who are afraid of swimming and water sports have never come close to drowning; in fact, they have never been in the water! And therein may lie the maintaining conditions of their fear of the water. Because they have never been in the water, they have not tested the reality of the situation, which is that most people do not drown. If they had been exposed to the feared situation and had found that nothing disastrous or frightening occurred, their fear would have been extinguished. But people with intense *unrealistic* fears of various situations do not place themselves in the threatening situations—which, of course, is understandable despite its being maladaptive.

Various behavioral therapy procedures have been developed to gradually expose clients to threatening events so that their fear can extinguish. Recall that one advantage of using systematic desensitization in imagination, rather than *in vivo,* is that clients who are severely afraid are exposed to the threatening events more indirectly (they are imagining the events rather than actually being in them). Modeling treatments of fear also have this advantage because clients observe someone else in the threatening situation and are not themselves directly exposed to it. This procedure is referred to as **vicarious extinction** because when a client observes that nothing aversive happens to a model who is performing in the threatening situation, the client's own fear tends to extinguish.

Chapter 1 noted an early use of modeling to vicariously extinguish 3-year-old Peter's fear of furry animals and objects in general, and of white rabbits in particular. Recall that part of Peter's treatment involved exposing him to fearless peer models. During daily play sessions, Peter interacted with three other children who had shown that they were unafraid of furry animals. A rabbit was put in the room for part of each of these play sessions, and the other children played with the rabbit. Initially, Peter avoided going near the rabbit, but at the end of seven play sessions, Peter had progressed from "almost complete terror at the sight of the rabbit to a completely positive response with no signs of disturbance."[2] Because modeling therapies have been particularly effective in helping people overcome their unrealistic fears, some recent examples will be described in detail later in the chapter.

Inhibiting Maladaptive Target Behaviors

Just as observing that a model is reinforced for her or his actions increases the likelihood that an observer will imitate the model, observing a model receive negative consequences reduces the likelihood of subsequent imitation. For example, a motorist who sees a car skid on a bridge 200 yards down the road is able to learn from the negative experience of the other driver and can slow down and drive cautiously over the bridge. Parents frequently discourage their children from engaging in misbehavior by pointing to the negative outcomes that peers have incurred for those acts (e.g., "Remember what happened to Mike when he threw the snowball at Barney's car"). Obviously there is a distinct advantage to being exposed to vicarious aversive consequences rather than receiving aversive consequences oneself; the former is generally a far less painful way to learn not to perform certain behaviors. However, vicarious aversive consequences have been employed infrequently in behavioral therapy to decelerate maladaptive target behaviors.[3]

ACCELERATING INTERPERSONAL BEHAVIORS THROUGH MODELING

Modeling is frequently used to teach and elicit interpersonal behaviors. The distinction between these two functions of modeling is often clouded: to what extent is the client's skill deficit due to an inability to perform the requisite behaviors and/or to a failure to engage in the behaviors at the appropriate time and place. In most cases, especially with adult clients, both functions are usually served by modeling. How modeling is used to teach clients very basic social skills is described first and then how modeling is used to foster a more complex set of interpersonal skills, namely assertive behavior, is discussed.

Basic Social Skills

Modeling, in combination with reinforcement for imitation, is a highly efficient and effective means of teaching basic social skills such as interacting with other people, offering and responding to appropriate greetings, and engaging in minimal social conversation. For modeling of social behaviors to be effective in reducing a client's social skills deficit, obviously the client must imitate appropriate models. Although some early theories of observational learning considered imitation to be innate, most contemporary accounts view imitation as a learned behavior.[4] Imitation is a very basic social skill that is a prerequisite for learning many other social and nonsocial behaviors people typically acquire through observational learning. Although most children learn to imitate by being reinforced for emulating the behavior of adults and peers in the course of their normal development, a small percentage of children do not learn to imitate (e.g., because they have minimal contact with models, or because they are not reinforced for imitation). This latter group of children must be taught **generalized imitation,** the basic social skill of emulating others' behavior, before they can acquire behaviors through observational learning.[5] Generalized imitation is often taught by prompting and shaping the imitation of very simple responses that may have little or no social usefulness. For example, a child may be taught to touch her head: the model demonstrates that behavior, prompts the behavior (e.g., the model says, "Touch your head"), and reinforces successive approximations of the behavior until the entire behavior is performed. Then other simple behaviors are modeled and prompted, and imitation is reinforced—eventually the child learns the general class of behaviors being reinforced; namely, imitation of the model. The use of modeling to increase the social interaction of a young child who was extremely socially withdrawn and had a deficit in generalized imitation skills is presented in Case 10-4. The case provides an excellent example of how a general problem is translated into precisely defined target behaviors and then how their frequency is carefully measured by direct observations of the client before and after therapy.

CASE 10-4

Extreme Social Withdrawal Treated by Live and Symbolic Modeling*

The client was a 6-year-old boy (called Sam here, for convenience) who was enrolled in a preschool because his extreme social withdrawal from peers had delayed his enrolling in public school. The prospect of any social interaction seemed to result in considerable distress and fear, as is illustrated in the following incident.

> Two children tried to join [Sam] when he was sitting alone in a packing crate. The children temporarily blocked the only exit from the crate, and in less than 20 seconds [Sam's] face became flushed and he perspired, trembled, and cried out to the teacher in a panic-stricken voice.

Two target behaviors were pinpointed for therapy. The acceleration target behavior was social interaction, which was defined as "any verbal or nonverbal behavior directed toward another child (or children) that involved a *reciprocal* quality." Examples included standing, sitting, or walking next to another child in response to an invitation to do so, exchanging a glance or smile with another child, and working, playing, or talking to another child. Sam was observed for 15 randomly selected five-minute periods over the course of two weeks. During these pretreatment observations, Sam interacted with his peers only 5 percent of the time. To have a basis for evaluating the client's improvement after therapy, the five oldest boys in the preschool who were judged by the teacher to be socially competent were also observed for the same period of time as Sam. They were found to spend an average of 55 percent of their time in social interaction.

The deceleration target behavior was "avoidance behavior," which was defined in terms of specific avoidance responses such as lowering eyes to avoid looking at another child, suddenly abandoning a solitary activity when a peer arrived, turning away when an-

*Ross, Ross, & Evans (1971). Quotations are from pp. 275 and 277.

other child initiated conversation, and hiding during group activities. Sam was observed for 10 randomly selected 15-minute periods, during which time he exhibited a total of 52 avoidance responses.

Sam avoided interpersonal relations to such an extent that he would not attend to potential peer models. His avoidance of verbal or visual contact even extended to not viewing symbolic presentations (e.g., television or movies) in which young children appeared. Therefore, before modeling therapy could be used the child had to be given generalized imitation training.

> To do this, M. [the model, who was a male undergraduate] was paired with a variety of tangible and social rewards; was positive and demonstrative to [Sam] and rewarded him for imitative responses; and was immediately responsive to [Sam's] bids for attention, help and approval. When M. was absent, [the therapist] encouraged [Sam] to reproduce M.'s behaviors and rewarded him for imitative responses. By the end of this phase [of therapy] . . . [Sam] was strongly attached to M.: he talked constantly about M. . . . , reproduced many of M.'s verbal and nonverbal behaviors, and waited eagerly at the door of the preschool for M. to come.

It was now possible to employ modeling as the major component of a multiphasic treatment plan to accelerate Sam's social interaction and decelerate avoidance behavior. The seven basic therapeutic procedures employed were as follows:

1. *Observation of a live model.* The model interacted with children in Sam's presence so that Sam could observe that being with the children was "safe" (vicarious extinction). At first Sam would not even watch the model, so the therapist had to verbally describe to Sam what was taking place.

2. *Observation of symbolic models.* In the context of short presentations of pictures, stories, and movies, the therapist or the model discussed the rewarding aspects of young children with Sam. Despite the brevity of these presentations, for the first six sessions Sam wanted to leave. With this therapy procedure and all others, the procedure was terminated before Sam became so upset that he left.

3. *Live modeling and vicarious reinforcement.* The model exhibited considerable reluctance about interacting with peers and then asked the therapist humorous and somewhat fearful questions, which enabled the therapist to reassure the model. Sam merely observed these modeling sequences.

4. *Live modeling and behavior rehearsal.* The therapist and the model demonstrated appropriate social behavior for Sam in the context of arguing about funny, hypothetical social situations. Sam was induced to join these interactions on the pretext that the model needed him to help win the argument.

5. *Participant modeling.* Sam accompanied the model as the model interacted with other children. As Sam began to participate in the social interactions, the model stayed close by. (Participant modeling is discussed in greater detail later.)

6. *Modeling and behavior rehearsal of skills necessary for peer interactions.* The model demonstrated behaviors necessary for successfully interacting with peers, such as playing various games, engaging in standard rituals, and using appropriate slang expressions.

7. *Graduated* in vivo *practice.* In a nearby playground, Sam was asked to mingle with

children whom he did not know, while the therapist observed. As Sam became more competent and confident, he was encouraged to engage in increasingly longer and closer social interactions. These sessions were also used to assess Sam's progress during therapy and provided information about behaviors that required modeling and behavior rehearsal.

At the conclusion of seven weeks of treatment, Sam had increased his social interaction to approximately the level of children who were judged socially competent. For example, in the posttreatment assessment Sam was observed to be interacting with peers 48 percent of the time (recall that he did so only 5 percent before treatment) and exhibited only 4 avoidance responses (as compared to 52 before treatment). Two months after treatment, Sam was given a generalization test in a playground setting that was significantly different from the protected nursery school setting. He "was able to join ongoing play groups, initiate verbal contacts, and sustain effective social interactions, all with children who were complete strangers to him. Furthermore [he] accomplished these tasks competently, unhesitatingly, with obvious pleasure, and with no adult intervention whatsoever."

With nursery school children who rarely interacted with their peers, but whose social withdrawal was less extreme than the child discussed in Case 10-4, brief exposure to filmed modeling proved to be a highly potent treatment.[6]

> [A 23-minute film] portrayed a sequence of 11 scenes in which children interacted in a nursery school setting. In each of these episodes, a child is shown first observing the interaction of others and then joining in the social activities, with reinforcing consequences ensuing. The other children, for example, offer him play material, talk to him, smile, and generally respond in a positive manner to his advances into the activity. The scenes were graduated on a dimension of threat in terms of the vigor of the social activity and the size of the group. The initial scenes involve very calm activities such as sharing a book or toy while two children are seated at a table. In the terminal scenes, as many as six children are shown gleefully tossing play equipment around the room.[7]

After viewing this film only once, the previously socially withdrawn children were soon engaging in as many or more social interactions as were children who had not been socially withdrawn in the first place (see the posttest comparison of the solid and dotted lines in Figure 10-1). A follow-up at the end of the school year disclosed that five of the six treated children continued to be socially active, while socially withdrawn children who were not treated by viewing the film were still rated as extremely isolated.

These results were replicated by comparing the same modeling film treatment with a shaping procedure that involved approximately five hours of praise and attention from an adult, contingent on performing successive approximations to social interaction. The modeling treatment was found to be superior to the shaping procedure, and the addition of shaping to the modeling treatment did not enhance its effectiveness. Furthermore, this finding is even

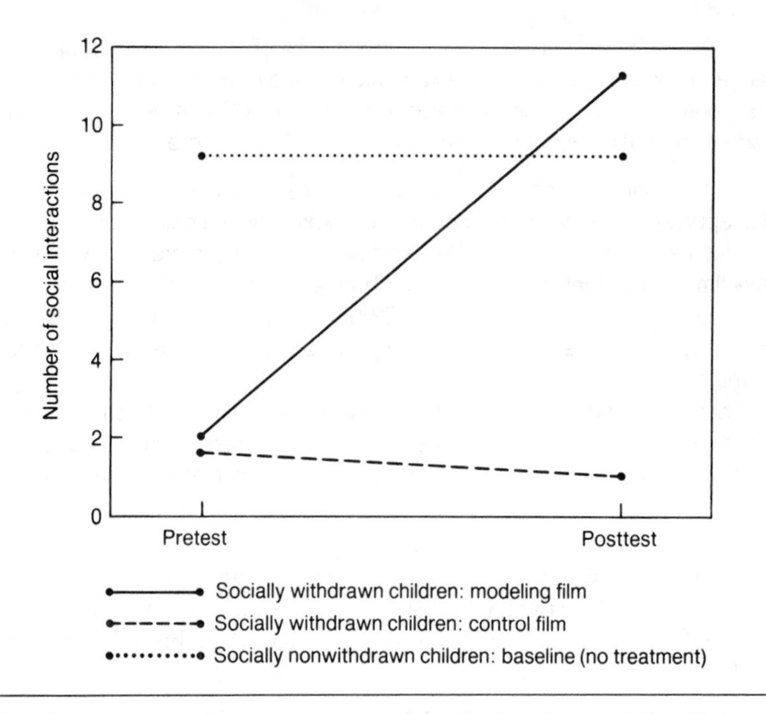

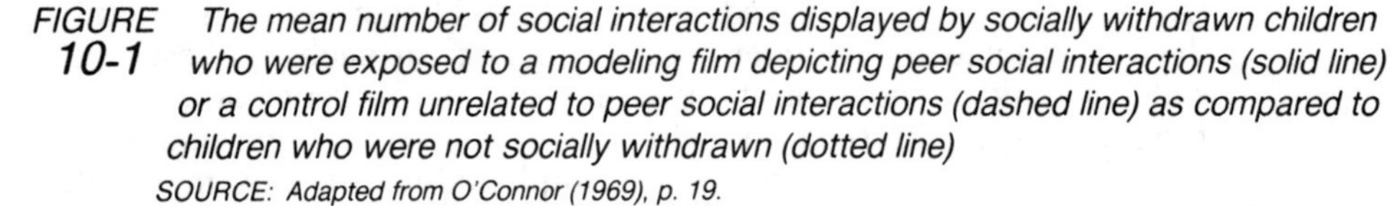

FIGURE 10-1 *The mean number of social interactions displayed by socially withdrawn children who were exposed to a modeling film depicting peer social interactions (solid line) or a control film unrelated to peer social interactions (dashed line) as compared to children who were not socially withdrawn (dotted line)*

SOURCE: Adapted from O'Connor (1969), p. 19.

more impressive if one considers the relative efficiency of the two treatments. Whereas shaping necessitated five hours of an adult's time for each child, a group of children were simultaneously treated by having them view the modeling film, which was 13 times faster!

One factor that often enhances imitation is similarity of the model to the observer: the more similar they are, generally the more likely it is that the observer will imitate the model. This similarity is maximized by **self-modeling,** in which clients serve as their own models. The use of self-modeling to modify inappropriate social behavior is illustrated in Case 10-5.

CASE 10-5

*Modifying Inappropriate Social Behavior by Self-Modeling**

Ten-year-old Chuck was a resident of a treatment center for patients with intractable bronchial asthma. Chuck spent most of his time alone, and his peers usually rebuffed his attempts to interact with them by calling him a "boob" or a "baby." He would respond by

*Creer & Miklich (1970).

retreating to his room and throwing a temper tantrum. Chuck also displayed inappropriate behavior with adults, such as giggling constantly, attempting to tickle them, and jumping into their laps during interviews. In addition, Chuck usually overslept, failed to make his bed or keep his room tidy, and did not show up on time for his medication.

To deal with these problems, a self-modeling videotape was prepared. Chuck and two other boys were asked to take part in a television film (a request that was not considered extraordinary because the public relations personnel who frequently visited the center sometimes made similar requests). In one of the self-modeling sequences, Chuck appropriately approached two boys who were playing a game and asked if he could play with them; in the other sequence, Chuck came into an adult's office and seated himself in an appropriate chair (rather than his customary jumping onto the adult's lap).

In the two weeks following the making of the videotape sequences, no changes were observed in Chuck's behavior. (Change could have resulted from the behavior rehearsal involved in making the videotape.) At this point Chuck was taught to operate the videotape recorder and monitor, and he viewed the appropriate self-modeling tape daily for four weeks. This exposure resulted in a substantial increase in socially appropriate behavior in his daily interactions. After treatment ended, Chuck maintained his appropriate social behavior for the remaining six months that he was a resident at the center. Significantly, many reports of Chuck's improved behavior came from staff members who were unaware that Chuck had undergone the self-modeling treatment.

Children are not the only people in our society who exhibit basic social skill deficits. Many socially marginal individuals, such as people who are institutionalized, also do not engage in some fundamental social behaviors, either because the behaviors are no longer reinforced (as is often the case in total institutions such as prisons and psychiatric hospitals) or, in some cases, because the behaviors were never learned in the first place.[8] Videotaped modeling sequences have been used to teach such people basic social skills.[9]

In one instance, chronic psychiatric patients (who had been hospitalized, on the average, for more than 21 years) viewed a series of modeling videotapes in which models demonstrated appropriate responses to social overtures and the initiation of social interactions.[10] Each videotape first presented the entire sequence of an interaction and then broke the sequence down into its components. After each interaction, the patient was instructed (by the therapist in the videotape) to imitate the model's behavior during a 15-second gap in the videotape. One example of an interaction component was as follows:

Therapist: Hello, may I sit down?

Model: Sure, have a seat.

Therapist: [to camera] Now you do that—offer me a seat when I ask you.

The modeling treatment was found to significantly increase the patients' general level of functioning in the hospital.

Assertive Behavior

The term *assertive behavior* refers to a broad category of behaviors that all involve acting in a manner that assures one of not having one's legitimate rights violated and of securing those things to which one is rightfully entitled. Examples of specific assertive behaviors include making one's reasonable desires explicitly known (e.g., to a sexual partner), appropriately expressing one's opinions and feelings (e.g., even when they are unpopular), refusing unreasonable requests (e.g., when a freind asks to borrow money one can't spare), asking for what one is entitled to (e.g., when receiving incorrect change), and not allowing oneself to be taken advantage of (e.g., when a person steps ahead in a line). Obviously, there are many different forms of assertive behavior. Furthermore, these behaviors appear to be relatively situation-specific; that is, a person may act assertively in some circumstances and not in others. Therefore, it is a mistake to refer to an individual as an "assertive" or "unassertive" *person,* although one can correctly characterize an individual's *behavior* in a particular situation as assertive or unassertive.

Assertive behavior is not always appropriate or adaptive. In any situation, we must assess the potential consequences for ourselves and others for acting assertively. For example, suppose you are on a vacation away from home, and you meet someone who invites you to dinner at his house. When you arrive for dinner, you find your host busily cooking a lavish meal, and during dinner he mentions that he has been preparing the meal since lunch time. As it turns out, your host is a very poor cook. When the host asks you after dinner how you liked the meal, what do you say? Expressing your honest opinion would be the assertive reply, but this would undoubtedly make your host feel terrible. The meal is now over, and you are not likely to have to subject yourself to such an ordeal again. Thus, the consequences for your evading the question or even saying that it was delicious are not negative for you and are positive for your host. In this case, expressing your honest opinion would probably not be appropriate, although it would be assertive. Or consider the situation in which you have just received the check at a restaurant and you must rush off to an appointment. You quickly add up the check and see that a small error has been made: rather than $8.92, the total should be $8.72. The assertive behavior in this case would be to point out the mistake to the waiter. However, your waiter is quite busy, and he is not likely to be back to collect your money for several minutes. So you decide that it is not worth 20 cents to be late for your appointment, and you pay the bill as it stands.

It is important to distinguish between assertive and aggressive behavior. The essential difference lies in the *means* by which the same basic aim of securing what one is entitled to is attained. Assertive behavior does this forcefully but without violating another person's rights, whereas aggressive behavior may accomplish the same goal but at someone else's expense. The difference between assertive, aggressive, and nonassertive responses to the same situation can be seen in the examples in Table 10-1.

Assertive behavior and **assertion training** (procedures for teaching people to act assertively) have become "hot" contemporary topics in popular psychology, as witnessed by a number of books recently written for the general public, including, for example, "treatises . . . on the 'technique' of how, when, and why to say no; what to say no to; and why you should not feel guilty in saying no."[11] Courses in assertion training have also burgeoned in the past few years. This popularity is no doubt correlated with a variety of "rights" movements that emerged in the 1970s. Because people are becoming more aware of the advantages of acting assertively and because nonassertive behavior is frequently a maintaining condition of interpersonal problems (e.g., marital discord), assertion training is frequently called for in therapy. Interestingly, in recent years assertion training has been used as part of many different kinds of psychotherapy (e.g., psychoanalysis and sensitivity training), although assertion training is clearly a behavioral therapy.

Behavioral Assessment of Assertive Behavior

A thorough assessment of the problem behavior and its maintaining conditions is the first step in assertion training (as in any form of behavioral therapy). Lack of overt assertive responses may be maintained by one of three conditions or by a combination of them: (1) a *skill deficit*—the person does not know how to act assertively in particular situations; (2) a *motivational deficit*—the person is not reinforced for acting assertively (there is no "payoff" for doing so, or the person fears retaliation, correctly or not); and/or (3) a *discrimination deficit*—the person does not know when it is appropriate to act assertively.

Two general approaches to assessing assertive behavior have been used: behavioral observations and self-report inventories. Behavioral observations may be carried out in a natural situation that potentially calls for an assertive response. A parent might observe her son playing with his friends to see if he is behaving assertively (e.g., expressing his choices about what games to play). Such naturalistic observations are generally difficult to make, however, because they require a relatively unobtrusive observer to be present at critical moments in specific situations. Because assertive behavior tends to be situation-specific, one cannot assume that a person who acts assertively in one situation will do so in other situations.

Practically, then, most behavioral observations to assess a client's assertive behavior involve contrived situations where the client is asked to role play a hypothetical situation, such as the following.

> The client is told to sit in a chair and imagine that he or she has come to a lecture early in order to get a good seat in the front row. The therapist (or an assistant), playing the part of another person who has come to the lecture, walks up to the seated client and says, "I sat in this seat last week. Would you mind taking another seat?"

TABLE 10-1 Comparison of Assertive, Aggressive, and Nonassertive Responses to Common Situations

SITUATION	**ASSERTIVE RESPONSE**	AGGRESSIVE RESPONSE	NONASSERTIVE RESPONSE
You don't drink alcoholic beverages, and at a party someone offers you a mixed drink.	**"No, thank you."**	"No! I don't want any alcohol. Just get it away from me."	"Oh . . . thanks but . . . I guess it won't hurt me."
You come to a professor to get help with an assignment you don't understand. The professor tells you that she doesn't have time to help you.	**"I realize you are busy, but the assignment is due soon and I don't want to turn it in late. Might you have a few minutes later today or early tomorrow?"**	"How do you expect me to do the assignment when I don't understand it? You could find the time if you wanted to. You just don't give a damn."	"Oh, OK. I guess I'll just do the best I can."
You are rushing off to class and don't want to be late. A friend stops you to ask you to help him move some furniture in his room right then.	**"Sorry, I'm on my way to class. If you still need help this evening, let me know."**	"You must be kidding! I'm on my way to class. Find someone else."	"Well, I'm on my way to class, but I guess I could give you a hand for just a few minutes."
You have just parked your car next to a car that has a dented fender. As you get out of your car, the owner of the other car comes up to you and accuses you of denting the fender.	**"I just pulled in, and I am sure that I didn't hit your car."**	"Hey, watch who you are accusing! I didn't touch your car, buddy."	"I didn't do that. I didn't hit your car, honest. Why do you think I did it?"

Like all role-played assessment, this type of evaluation has the limitation that the client is only acting and therefore may behave differently in the actual situation. Nevertheless, much important information can be gathered from role playing. When the client is asked only to react to a situation and is not told how to behave, observers can see whether the client acts assertively or not. Furthermore, the degree and quality of assertiveness can also be measured. Assertive behavior involves a number of components including both *what* a person does and says as well as *how* the behavior is performed. Frequently the way in which an assertive response is made is even more important than the content of the message. Some stylistic components of assertive behavior are listed in Table 10-2 and are compared with nonassertive and aggressive counterparts. Scales have been developed for observers to rate clients on these components, either as the clients are role playing or at a later time if the client's behavior during role playing is recorded, as on videotape.[12]

There are two general types of written self-report inventories for assessing a client's assertive behavior. One asks clients to rate the degree to which statements concerning assertive behavior are characteristic of them, on a numerical scale that ranges from "very characteristic of me" to "very uncharacteristic of me."[13] Examples of such statements are "I don't argue over prices with salespeople," "I avoid asking questions because I don't want to appear stupid," and "When I am asked to do something, I must know why." An example of this first type of self-report inventory of assertive behavior appears in Participation Exercise 10-1. By responding to the inventory, you will "experience" this type of assessment procedure, and you may also learn something about your own assertive behavior.

TABLE 10-2 Some Physical and Verbal Stylistic Components of Assertive, Nonassertive, and Aggressive Behaviors

COMPONENT	**ASSERTIVE**	NONASSERTIVE	AGGRESSIVE
Eye contact	**Looking at person while talking**	Looking away from person while talking	Intently staring at person while talking
Facial expression	**Appropriate to message**	Sheepish or expressionless	Hostile no matter what the message is
Gestures	**Moderate; appropriate to message**	None or inappropriate to message	Excessive; overenthusiastic
Body posture	**Erect; at an appropriate distance; leaning slightly toward the person**	Slouched; a bit too far from the person; leaning away from the person	Erect; either too close or too far from person; exaggerated leaning in either direction
Voice quality	**Firm (confident); appropriately loud; appropriate expression**	Apologetic; whisper; monotone	Overzealous; shouting; "soap-box" speech

PARTICIPATION EXERCISE 10-1

Assessing Assertive Behavior by a Self-Report Inventory

This participation exercise gives an example of a self-report inventory* that is used to assess clients' assertive behavior. Follow the instructions for completing the inventory.

INSTRUCTIONS

Using the following scale, respond to each item by writing down the number of the item that best describes how typical the statement is for you. There are no right or wrong answers. Respond to each item honestly.

0 = No or never
1 = Somewhat or sometimes
2 = Average
3 = Usually or a good deal
4 = Practically always or entirely

1. When someone is very unfair to me, I call it to the person's attention.
2. I find it difficult to make decisions.
3. I speak up when someone steps ahead of me in line.
4. I avoid situations or people for fear of embarrassment.
5. When a salesperson tries hard to sell me something that I really do not want or need, I find it difficult to say no.
6. When a latecomer is waited on before me, I say something about it.
7. I freely speak up in discussions and debates.
8. If a person has borrowed something from me (such as money, or a book, or a piece of clothing) and is late in returning it, I say something to the person.
9. I express my positive feelings to others.
10. I express my negative feelings to others.
11. If someone is talking during a movie (or play, concert, lecture) and it is interfering with my hearing or concentration, I ask the person to be quiet.
12. I look directly at the person I am talking to.
13. If some dish I have ordered in a restaurant is served improperly, I ask to have it corrected.
14. I return merchandise that I find to be defective.
15. I am able to refuse unreasonable requests made of me.
16. I am able to easily compliment or praise others.
17. If someone is disturbing me, I say something to the person.
18. When I first meet someone I do not know, I introduce myself and initiate a conversation.
19. When I am not receiving service to which I am entitled, I ask for it.

Besides giving you experience in responding to a behavioral self-report inventory, your responses may increase your awareness of how you deal with situations that frequently call

*Adapted from Alberti and Emmons Assertiveness Inventory (1978).

for assertive behavior. This inventory should not be considered a standardized test. There are no "correct" answers, and there are no formal scoring procedures. (For example, because assertive behavior is generally considered situation-specific, as discussed in the text, it is *not* appropriate to add the numbered responses to the items to obtain a total assertiveness score.) You could evaluate your behavior, however, to see if you behave the way you would like to in the situations listed.

The other type of self-report assessment device asks clients to indicate how they would respond to a situation (described in writing) by choosing one of several alternative responses. An example of this type of self-report measure is the Conflict Resolution Inventory,[14] which measures one type of assertive behavior, the ability to refuse unreasonable requests. One situation and the alternative responses from the Conflict Resolution Inventory are given here:

> A person *you do not know very well* is going home for the weekend. He or she has some books that are due at the library and asks if you would take them back so they won't be overdue. From where you live, it is a 25-minute walk to the library, the books are heavy, and you hadn't planned on going near the library that weekend.
> 1. I would *refuse* and would not feel uncomfortable about doing so.
> 2. I would *refuse* but would feel uncomfortable doing so.
> 3. I would *not refuse* but would feel uncomfortable because I didn't.
> 4. I would *not refuse* even though I might prefer to, but would not feel particularly uncomfortable because I didn't.
> 5. I would *not refuse,* because it seems to be a reasonable request.[15]

Assertion Training

The details of assertion training vary with each client's specific problem regarding assertive behavior. In most cases, modeling and behavior rehearsal are the major components of the therapy. The following is a general outline of the procedures used in assertion training.

First, a situation that may be appropriate for assertive behavior is described. The therapist and the client discuss the situation to determine what type of behavior is most appropriate and why. Next, the therapist models an assertive response to the situation. This modeling is sometimes supplemented with instructions concerning the essential elements of the assertive response, such as an emphasis on certain words, voice intonation, body posture, and so on. Then the client is asked to imitate the therapist's assertive behavior. The imitation need not be an exact copy of the model's behavior. In fact, once clients learn the essential elements of the particular assertive response, they are encouraged to use their own variations on the basic theme, to fit their own personal styles and preferences. The therapist gives the client feedback on his or her response, and reinforces the client for successively more assertive responses.

This sequence of steps is repeated until the client is skilled at making appropriate assertive responses to the situation while role playing with the therapist. The client is then given homework assignments to try out the assertive behaviors in the natural environment. This experimentation is done gradually, beginning with simple interactions that are relatively nonthreatening and nonconsequential and gradually progressing to more complex interactions that may be threatening because they involve important consequences for the client. Thus, situations in the client's life that call for assertive behaviors are practiced in a hierarchical order (see Table 10-3).

Once a client knows *how* to be assertive and *when* it is appropriate to be assertive, these skills need to be reinforced in order for them to become a permanent part of the client's behavioral repertoire. The therapist reinforces the client for acting assertively, not for obtaining a favorable outcome from actions that may be out of the client's control (e.g., a student who appropriately asks a professor to explain the grading of an examination question, but the professor refuses to do so).

Ultimately, however, the assertive behavior must be maintained by the naturally occurring *intermittent* reinforcers that are a consequence of appropriate assertive behavior. Such reinforcement may come from the favorable results of the assertive behavior, as when people obtain something to which they are entitled. It may also come from the good feelings of accomplishment, independence, and increased self-esteem that tend to be consequences of assertive behaviors. Or it may come from avoiding the reduced self-esteem and feelings of failure that tend to be the consequences of passive, nonassertive behavior.

Although appropriate assertive behavior generally meets with favorable outcomes, that is not always the case. The client must be prepared for the latter possibility through modeling and behavior rehearsal of situations in which assertive responses result in negative consequences (e.g., a client asks a friend for a reasonable favor and is turned down).

The procedures for assertion training described so far have involved live

TABLE 10-3 Prototype of a Hierarchy of Assertive Behaviors Practiced by a Client Having Difficulty with Refusing Unreasonable Requests (in descending order)

9. Refusing an unreasonable request from a close friend when the request is very important to the friend
8. Refusing an unreasonable request from a close friend when the request is moderately important to the friend
7. Refusing an unreasonable request from an acquaintance when the request is very important to the acquaintance
6. Refusing an unreasonable request from an acquaintance when the request is moderately important to the acquaintance
5. Refusing an unreasonable request from a close friend when the request is unimportant to the friend
4. Refusing an unreasonable request from an acquaintance when the request is unimportant to the acquaintance
3. Refusing an unreasonable request from a stranger when the request is very important to the stranger
2. Refusing an unreasonable request from a stranger when the request is moderately important to the stranger
1. Refusing an unreasonable request from a stranger when the request is unimportant to the stranger

Note: The rank ordering is an individual matter and will vary from client to client.

modeling. Symbolic forms of modeling have also been successfully applied, and two such applications will be briefly discussed. Tape-recorded assertion training packages have been developed to teach specific assertive behaviors to particular client populations.[16] One such program was designed to teach high school students to refuse unreasonable requests.[17] The students listened to a tape-recorded description of a situation in which an unreasonable request was made and heard a role-played interaction in which a model responded to the request with an appropriate refusal. Then the situation was described again, and this time the students practiced their own response to the situation in their minds, a technique called **covert behavior rehearsal.** Here is an example of one situation presented to the students:

> You are in the middle of doing your homework when a friend phones you and says she doesn't have much to do and would like to come over for a while. Now listen to how such a situation might be handled by two people.
>
> *[Friend:]* "Hi, I don't have much to do. Mind if I come over for a while?"
>
> *[Model:]* "I'm doing my homework, and I can't take a break now. But I'd like to do it some other time."
>
> Now listen to the same situation again. This time you will be asked to respond. You are in the middle of doing your homework when a friend phones you and says, "Hi, I don't have much to do. Mind if I come over for a while?" What would you say? (15-second pause).[18]

Covert modeling is a form of symbolic modeling in which clients are exposed to modeling sequences in their imaginations.[19] The client is asked to imagine scenes described by the therapist in which a model of the same sex and approximate age as the client behaves assertively. The presentation of each scene consists of a description of (1) the situation in which the assertive behavior is appropriate; (2) the model making an assertive response; and (3) the model receiving positive consequences for the assertive behavior. Examples of typical scenes appear in Table 10-4. Covert modeling can be an effective form

TABLE 10-4 Examples of Covert Modeling Scenes Used to Accelerate Assertive Behavior

SITUATION	MODELED ASSERTIVE BEHAVIOR	VICARIOUS REINFORCEMENT
1. A woman is eating in a restaurant with friends. She orders a salad and tells the waiter to put the dressing on the side. When the salad arrives, it has the dressing directly on it.	The woman immediately turns to the waiter and says, "I asked for my salad with the dressing on the side. Please bring me another salad without dressing and the dressing in a separate dish.	A few minutes later the waiter returns with the salad correctly prepared and says that he is very sorry for the error and hopes that the woman enjoys the salad.
2. A man who has a drinking problem is at a party where drinks are being served. The host offers him a cocktail.	The man says to the host, "No, thank you, but I would like a soft drink if you have one."	The host replies, "I sure do. I'll be right back with it."

of assertion training[20] and in some cases is as effective as overt symbolic modeling.[21]

Participation Exercise 10-2 gives you a chance to engage in an assertive training procedure that uses symbolic modeling, behavior rehearsal, and feedback to teach appropriate refusals of unreasonable requests.

PARTICIPATION EXERCISE 10-2

Assertion Training for Refusing Unreasonable Requests by Symbolic Modeling, Behavior Rehearsal, and Feedback

This participation exercise deals with one type of assertive behavior: refusing unreasonable requests. In each of the seven hypothetical situations described in Exercise Table 10-2A, a letter makes a request of the recipient. Assume that you have received the letter and, with the specific circumstances in mind, write a brief reply (two or three sentences should suffice) ***refusing the writer's unreasonable request.*** After you have written your reply, turn the page to Exercise Table 10-2B and read the modeling letter and the brief explanatory

EXERCISE TABLE 10-2A
Situations and Letters

SITUATION	LETTER TO RESPOND TO
1. You are invited to a party by a student you met briefly in a class you took during the summer. He (or she) asks you to pick up someone whom you hardly know at all, 30 miles out of your way.	Dear ________________, How's it going? We're having a little party at my house next Thursday, and I'd like you to come. My cousin was coming but he's having trouble getting a ride down. Do you think you can give him a lift? He lives about 45 minutes out of town so I've enclosed a map. See you on Thursday. Regards, Classmate
2. You have plans to go away for the weekend, and you will need your car. You receive a letter from a close relative.	Dear ________________, I am coming into town this coming weekend and am looking forward to seeing you. I am coming by bus so I'll need transportation to get around. I realize that it's short notice, but do you think I might borrow your car for the weekend? I'll have it back to you first thing Monday morning. Thanks, Cousin Avis

SITUATION	LETTER TO RESPOND TO
3. A record company you recently joined has sent you four albums you never ordered. In fact, you have promptly returned the order card stating that you didn't want any albums sent to you.	Dear Record Club Member: We have, up to this time, sent you four albums for a total of $26.96. We have not received any payment, however. Please send full payment immediately, including shipping and handling costs, as indicated on the enclosed bill. Thank you, President, Ripoff Records, Inc.
4. You are taking a course the second semester, and you receive a letter during the Christmas break from the professor who will be teaching the course.	Dear Student, You are registered for Psychology 988 this coming semester. Due to the extensive background required to understand the material, I am asking students to return four days early for brief introductory sessions. I will be expecting you unless I hear from you before then. Sincerely, Professor Broozer
5. You receive a letter from a religious organization you have never heard of and know nothing about, asking for a contribution.	Dear Neighbor, In order for our organization to grow and to build new places of worship, it is essential that we receive financial backing from people like you. Please open up your heart and send your check today. Return this card with your contribution so that we can continue sending you news and information. Most sincerely, President, United Affluent Church
6. A close friend of yours writes to you asking if you would pick up an important package for him at the local post office and pay the delivery charge. You pass by the post office daily on your way to work.	Dear ______________, I won't be in the city until some time next week, but I'm expecting an important package to arrive at the main post office. I would really appreciate it if you could pick it up for me and pay the delivery charge. It should only be a few dollars. I'll pay you back when I get back. Thanks, Your Friend

EXERCISE TABLE 10-2B

Model Letters and Explanatory Notes

MODEL LETTER	EXPLANATORY NOTE
1. Dear Classmate, Thanks for the invitation to the party. I'll sure be there, but I really won't be able to pick up your cousin. Thirty miles is just too far for me to go out of my way. I'm looking forward to seeing you at the party.	Polite and friendly; states what you will and will not do; ends on an upbeat
2. Dear Cousin Avis, Nice to hear from you. I am going away this weekend, so I won't be able to lend you my car for the weekend. Sorry that I'll miss your visit and that I can't help with transportation. Hope you have a pleasant visit.	Clearly says no; explains reasons (briefly without ***unnecessary*** details or elaboration), which is appropriate for someone you are close to; genuine expression of regret is acceptable and sometimes desirable (here, too, it is brief and to the point); pleasant wishes close out polite refusal
3. Dear President: I did not order any of the four albums you have sent me. In each case, I promptly returned the order cards and checked off that I did not want the record. Therefore, I refuse to pay for them, although I will return them at your company's expense.	Clearly explains situation; categorically says no; adds a compromise that demonstrates good faith (i.e., you just don't want to keep records)
4. Dear Professor Broozer, I'm sorry, but I will not be able to return to school four days early as you requested. I have made plans for these days. I would be willing to make up the class sessions I miss on returning, if this is possible.	Clearly says "I can't" do what has been requested; gives a simple explanation (i.e., no elaboration); demonstrates an appreciation of the problem by proposing an alternative means of handling it, which may be prudent given your future relationship with the professor
5. Dear President: I am not interested in your organization or in receiving any further news or information.	Very brief, formal reply, appropriate for the impersonal, form letter received; unequivocally states your position
6. Dear Friend, I'll be glad to pick up the package for you. Give me a call when you get back in town, and we'll arrange for you to pick it up.	Request is ***reasonable*** in this case

notes that accompany each letter, to get feedback on your letter. Your reply need not be a copy of the modeled letter, but it should contain most of the essential elements and generally make the same type of impact made by the modeled letter. Repeat the same steps for each situation and letter. To get the most benefit from the feedback provided in Exercise Table 10-2B, refer to it after writing each letter and before writing the next letter.

Here are some general guidelines you should keep in mind as you write your letters of refusal. Following them will help make your letters ***appropriately*** assertive.

1. Be polite.
2. Be direct; say what you mean. For example, if you mean that you ***don't want*** to do something, say that directly (and politely) and don't say that you are "not sure" if you can do something. The former reply would be honest and unambiguous, while the latter response would be dishonest (given your motivation) and ambiguous.
3. Do not apologize (but it might be appropriate to wish the writer luck in getting a positive response from others).
4. Tailor the letter to the degree of unreasonableness of the request (e.g., a mildly unreasonable request should not be responded to with a very strong reply, such as "You've got your nerve!").
5. Consider the relationship you have with the writer and any future relationships you might want. The closer you are, the harder it generally is to refuse a request.
6. In some cases, but certainly not all, a compromise may be called for—in effect, making the request more reasonable so that you feel comfortable ***partially*** doing what the writer has requested.
7. Remember: You are "entitled" to refuse unreasonable requests (and even reasonable ones) just as you are "entitled" to make them yourself.

TREATING FEAR AND ANXIETY BY MODELING

Modeling is a particularly efficient and effective treatment for clients who will not engage in activities because they are fearful or anxious about doing them. Two factors are associated with such negative affect. One is a real or perceived skill deficit: the client is relatively incompetent at the behavior, or thinks she or he is incompetent. The other is real or perceived negative consequences: the client fears that something unpleasant or otherwise aversive will occur if he or she engages in the behavior, whether or not this has any basis in reality. Modeling provides clients both with a demonstration of how to perform the behavior and with examples of another person successfully engaging in the behavior without incurring negative consequences (i.e., vicarious extinction).

Filmed Modeling for Minor Fears

The use of symbolic modeling in the form of brief films is particularly applicable to treating mild fears that are experienced by a large number of people, which justifies the time and expense of producing standard, permanent films for this purpose. When fears are more extreme and debilitating, individual therapy using live modeling is often required.

To illustrate the basic approach of filmed modeling to reduce minor fears, the use of a 14-minute color movie to reduce fear of nonpoisonous snakes will be discussed.[22] A brief description of the film follows.

> Betty is a 20-year-old woman who is afraid of snakes and comes to Mrs. Dunlap, an older woman who is an expert on snakes, to learn about snakes and overcome her fear. In successive scenes of the film, Betty gradually learns to approach and handle several snakes by following Mrs. Dunlap's demonstration of each behavior. As the film progresses, Betty, who initially appeared fearful, becomes noticeably more confident in handling the snakes and seems to be enjoying doing so more and more. While wearing gloves, Betty learns to stroke and pick up a small snake and then repeats this procedure with a large snake. Next, Betty removes the gloves and repeats these successively more difficult tasks barehanded. Toward the end of the film, Betty is shown confidently holding the larger snake. An accompanying narration describes what the film depicts and also includes information about snakes and their handling.

Several features of this film are worth noting because they illustrate general principles of modeling.[23] Two models appear in the movie. Mrs. Dunlap is a prime example of a **mastery model,** an expert who models a high degree of competence and confidence. Mrs. Dunlap adeptly handles the snakes and shows absolutely no fear in doing so. Betty, on the other hand, exemplifies a **coping model,** a novice at the behavior who is initially somewhat incompetent and ill at ease but gradually becomes more competent and comfortable performing the behavior—that is, she learns to cope effectively. At first Betty is somewhat fearful about handling snakes, but over the course of the film she overcomes these feelings by successfully learning to handle snakes and finding that no harm comes to her when she does. In general, coping models are preferable for helping clients overcome fears.[24] For one thing, a coping model is more like the fearful client than is a mastery model, which presumably makes the coping model more appropriate for the client. Furthermore, and perhaps of greater importance, a coping model demonstrates adaptive coping behaviors, the exact behavior that the client needs to imitate.[25]

A second feature of the modeling just described is that it includes *modeling of imitation;* in other words, part of what the model does is to imitate another model. Betty watches Mrs. Dunlap handle the snakes and then imitates this behavior. Thus the client sees an example of what he or she will be expected to do. A third important feature of the film is that viewers are exposed to the threatening situation in gradual, hierarchical steps, as in many behavioral therapies.[26]

One problem in dealing with a client's emotional reactions, such as fear or anxiety, is that such reactions are difficult to measure objectively—not surprisingly, because they are subjective experiences. Accordingly, behavioral therapists find overt behavioral anchors for the covert behaviors by observing what people do when they report that they are experiencing the emotions (see Chapter 2). When people are afraid of performing some behavior or being in a particular situation, they tend to avoid it. *Avoidance behavior* is frequently used as an overt behavioral anchor for fear because it can be measured objectively.

To assess the effectiveness of the modeling film just described, before and after viewing the modeling film clients were given a **behavioral avoidance test,** a standardized measure of the degree to which the person avoids a situation. Clients were taken to a room that contained a glass cage with a snake at one end. The floor was marked off in feet, so that the distance a client was able to walk toward the cage could be measured. Clients were asked to perform as many of the following steps as they felt comfortable doing: (1) enter a room containing a caged 2-foot water snake, (2) walk to the cage (a distance of about 15 feet), (3) put on a pair of gloves, (4) remove the lid of the cage and look in, (5) reach into the cage and stroke the snake, (6) pick up the snake, (7) remove the gloves, (8) stroke the snake, and finally (9) hold the snake barehanded. One measure of improvement was being able to perform more of the steps in the behavioral avoidance test after viewing the film than before.

Initially the film was tested on college students who reported mild fear of snakes, and their avoidance behavior significantly decreased after viewing the film just once. This is an example of *analogue research*: the students' "fear" of snakes was mild; in fact, their reactions to snakes would more accurately be described as distaste or unpleasantness rather than fear. Although they were likely to avoid interacting with snakes in most instances, they would not tend to go to extremes in this regard (e.g., never walking through the grass where snakes might be lurking). Furthermore, their negative reactions toward snakes interfered little, if at all, with their daily lives and customary activities. However, because this film was experimental in nature, it was prudent to use these analogue "clients" to pilot test its effectiveness in reducing negative reactions toward snakes before it was used with actual clients. Had the filmed modeling treatment been ineffective with the mildly fearful analogue "clients," then it would not have been used with actual clients whose fear was significantly greater and for whom fear of snakes had genuine negative consequences in their lives. Of course, that the treatment was effective in the analogue situation does not necessarily mean that it will be effective under actual clinical conditions, and thus the latter effectiveness must be empirically tested.

The same film was used to treat a group of older adults whose fear of snakes specifically interfered with some portion of their lives. For instance, one client who had been an avid water skier had not skied in several years, since having seen a water snake while skiing. Another client would not go on camping trips with his family because he feared that he might encounter a snake. A third client had spent considerable time gardening until she saw a small, harmless garter snake one day. Even with the more severe fear exhibited by these clients, watching the film a single time led to a significant decrease in their fear (as measured by the behavioral avoidance test), and a second viewing led to a further reduction in fear. These clients also benefited from engaging in deep muscle relaxation while viewing the film.

The efficiency of this treatment for reducing people's fear of snakes is particularly impressive. Viewing a 12-minute film, even several times, takes very little time. Because a modeling film was used instead of live modeling, and because deep muscle relaxation was taught by audiotaped instructions made by the therapist, the clients were able to meet in groups run by nonprofessional therapeutic assistants.

Participant Modeling for Severe Fears

Live modeling is usually somewhat more effective (although often less efficient) than symbolic modeling in reducing fear and anxiety, particularly when the client's fear is severe. In such cases, an "in-the-flesh" therapist-model may make the client feel more comfortable, which in turn is likely to increase the effectiveness of the modeling treatment. Also, it is sometimes helpful or necessary for the therapist to prompt a client's imitation. In **participant modeling,** the therapist models the anxiety-evoking behavior for the client and then encourages and guides the client through the behavior.[27] This behavioral therapy is also known as *contact desensitization*[28] and as *guided participation,*[29] for reasons that will become apparent as the procedures are described.

1. The therapist first models the anxiety-evoking behavior for the client.
2. The client is then asked to imitate the therapist, while the therapist assists the client in performing the behavior through verbal and physical prompts (e.g., actually holding a client's hand as he or she uses a scalpel to dissect a frog). The contact between the therapist and client reassures and calms the client (a form of *in vivo* desensitization). When a client's level of anxiety is moderate, this guided participation facilitates the client's practicing the anxiety-evoking behavior. When a client's anxiety level is severe, the procedure may be absolutely necessary if the client is to perform the behavior at all.
3. The therapist gradually fades the prompts. After a while the client performs the behavior with only the therapist's presence (i.e., no physical contact) as a source of support, and finally that too is gradually faded.
4. The behaviors that are modeled and practiced are arranged in a hierarchy. The treatment proceeds from the least to the most anxiety-evoking behaviors, with the rate of exposure being controlled by the client's level of anxiety (as in systematic desensitization). All these steps are illustrated in Case 10-6.

CASE 10-6

*Severe Fear of Crossing Streets Treated by Participant Modeling**

Mrs. S. was a 49-year-old widow who had been profoundly afraid of crossing streets for the past 10 years. During that time she had tried individual and group insight therapy, but these approaches did not alleviate her intense fear. Her fear had caused her to withdraw almost

*Ritter (1969a). Quotation is from pp. 170–171.

completely, and because of her despair she had attempted suicide. The following description of the first therapy session using participant modeling illustrates the basic procedures of the client's treatment.

> A low-traffic location in which a narrow street intersected with a moderately wide street was chosen. The counselor walked across the narrow street for about one minute while Mrs. S. watched. Then the counselor firmly placed her arm around Mrs. S.'s waist and walked across with her. This was repeated a number of times until Mrs. S. reported she was fairly comfortable at performing the task. . . . Street crossing was then continued while physical contact between counselor and Mrs. S. was gradually reduced until the counselor only lightly touched the back of Mrs. S.'s arm as she walked slightly behind her. Contact was then eliminated completely, with the counselor first walking alongside Mrs. S. as the street was crossed and then slightly behind her. The counselor subsequently followed Mrs. S. approximately three-fourths of the way across the street and allowed her to go the remaining distance alone. Gradually the counselor reduced the distance she accompanied Mrs. S. until eventually Mrs. S. was able to cross the street entirely alone.

These procedures were then applied on increasingly wider and more heavily traveled streets. Four specific treatment goals had been set by the client, including independently crossing the four streets of a busy intersection. The client was also given increased responsibility for the therapy, including planning and carrying out her own homework practice. All four goals were accomplished within a period of 47 days.

Symbolic Modeling for Fear of Medical and Dental Procedures

Fear of medical and dental procedures can have far-reaching consequences in that it can keep people from seeking regular health checkups and obtaining necessary treatment. Symbolic modeling has been quite successful in reducing such fear and avoidance behavior.

Barbara Melamed and her associates have developed a 16-minute modeling film to reduce the anxiety of children facing hospitalization for elective surgery (e.g., hernia operations and tonsillectomies).[30] Entitled *Ethan Has an Operation,* the film depicts the experiences of a 7-year-old boy who has been hospitalized for a hernia operation.

> This film . . . consists of 15 scenes showing various events that most children encounter when hospitalized for elective surgery from the time of admission to time of discharge including the child's orientation to the hospital ward and medical personnel such as the surgeon and anesthesiologist; having a blood test and exposure to standard hospital equipment; separation from the mother; and scenes in the operating and recovery rooms. In addition to explanations of the hospital procedures provided by the medical staff, various scenes are narrated by the child, who describes his feelings and concerns that he had at each stage of the hospital experience. Both the child's behavior and verbal remarks exemplify the behavior of a

coping model so that while he exhibits some anxiety and apprehension, he is able to overcome his initial fears and complete each event in a successful and nonanxious manner.[31]

To test the effectiveness of the modeling film, it was shown to a group of children (ranging in age from 4 to 12) who were being hospitalized for elective surgery but who had never been in the hospital before. Anxiety was assessed by self-report inventories, behavioral observations, and a physiological measure the night before surgery and three to four weeks after surgery. The children who saw the modeling film exhibited a significant pre- to postoperative reduction of anxiety as compared to children who saw a control film. (All the children also had received extensive preoperative instructions from the hospital staff, which may have contributed to the reduction in fear.) The control film presented the experiences of a preadolescent boy on a nature trip in the country and had an interest value similar to that of the modeling film but was unrelated to hospitalization or surgery. Furthermore, parents reported a significant posthospitalization increase in behavior problems for children who had seen the control film, whereas such problems were less frequent among those who saw the modeling film.[32]

Related work has shown that a realistic modeling film depicting a child receiving an injection can reduce the apparent pain that children experience from actual injections.[33] An 18-minute film showed a series of boys and girls receiving injections from a nurse. Each child was first shown playing or reading in a hospital bed. A nurse then entered the room carrying a syringe and needle on a tray. After talking to the child for a short time, the nurse gave the child the injection. At the moment the injection was given, a close-up of the child's upper body and face showed the child wincing, exclaiming "Ouch," and frowning (a moderate and realistic reaction to the injection). Then the nurse put a Bandaid on the spot of the injection, said goodbye to the child, and left the room. The film was made in the pediatric ward in which the children (aged 4 to 9 years) were to be hospitalized for minor surgery requiring a preoperative injection. The children viewed the film in their homes approximately 36 hours before receiving their preoperative injections.

Children who saw the movie just described, which showed realistic coping models, were compared with other groups of children. One group saw the same basic movie except that at the moment of the injection the patient-models did not show any pain or discomfort, which is unrealistic behavior because injections usually do hurt, at least slightly. A second, comparison group of children saw no movie at all. Children who had viewed the realistic pain movie appeared to experience the least pain when they received their injections, whereas children who had viewed the unrealistic no-pain movie seemed to experience the most pain.[34]

Films are not the only form of symbolic modeling therapy that can be used to alleviate fears of medical procedures. Books and pamphlets found in physicians' offices or available commercially that describe various diagnostic and treatment procedures usually involve modeling in that the experiences of

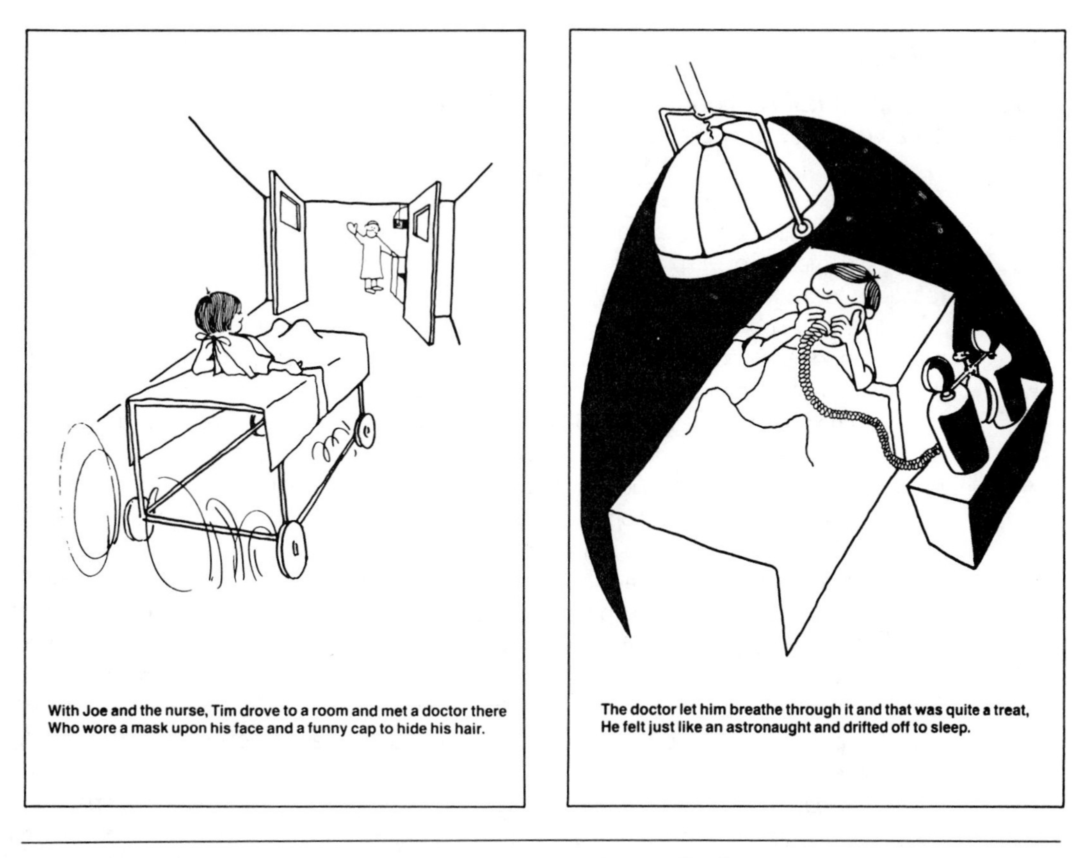

With Joe and the nurse, Tim drove to a room and met a doctor there
Who wore a mask upon his face and a funny cap to hide his hair.
The doctor let him breathe through it and that was quite a treat,
He felt just like an astronaught and drifted off to sleep.

FIGURE 10-2 *Illustrative pages from* My Tonsillectomy Coloring Book *SOURCE: Bob Knight & Associates (1969).*

actual or hypothetical patients are presented. Information in the form of picture books has been prepared for young children. For example, *My Tonsillectomy Coloring Book* is a large, soft-cover book that uses pictures with rhyming captions to tell the story of a young boy, named Cowboy Tim, who goes to the hospital to have his tonsils removed (see Figure 10-2).

A number of successful applications of modeling have also reduced children's fear of dentistry, paralleling the techniques for reducing fear of surgery and related procedures just described. However, children are not the only ones who suffer from such fear. Adults also avoid medical and dental care due to fear, and, in fact, may do so more than children because they are less likely to be "forced" to get needed care and treatment, such as by a parent. According to one estimate, as much as 6 percent of the population suffers from excessive fear of dental procedures.[35] Case 10-7 describes a treatment package for reducing fear and avoidance of dental procedures in adults and illustrates its application with a client who had not seen a dentist in 13 years.

CASE 10-7

Treatment of Dental Avoidance in Adults by Symbolic Modeling, Graduated Exposure, and Self-paced *In Vivo* Practice*

The treatment package used . . . included symbolic modeling, graduated exposure (a variant of systematic desensitization), and self-paced *in vivo* practice. It was described to clients as a means of helping them to [reduce] fear and learn new and more adaptive reactions to dentistry.

In the *symbolic modeling* segments, clients viewed a 20-minute videotape in which a patient (model) telephones a dentist for an appointment, drives to the office, sits in the waiting room, and then undergoes an oral examination.

During the examination, the dentist finds a cavity, which he offers to fill. The patient reluctantly agrees, and the procedure is carried out. The model displays initial apprehension, but with reassurance by the dentist, and through verbalized attempts to demonstrate self-control over the situation, becomes more relaxed and confident. Two versions of the tape were shown, one with a female and one with a male model. Clients were instructed to observe the model, to be aware of physical and cognitive reactions experienced, and to relax when needed. The modeling tape served several purposes: (1) it made the client more aware of his [or her] own reactions to specific elements of dentistry, (2) it provided information concerning dental examination and treatment procedures, (3) it modeled elements of patient control (e.g., asking dentist to stop briefly; asking questions about what will happen), and (4) it provided an opportunity to attempt control over stress reactions to the vicariously experienced situation.

Graduated exposure presented hierarchically arranged, 10-second videotaped segments of a dental procedure, as viewed from the patient's perspective. The clients viewed these segments while in a relatively relaxed state brought about by therapist-guided relaxation instructions. This procedure was carried out in a manner similar to systematic desensitization in that, if anxiety was experienced, the scene was terminated until the client became relaxed again. Progress to the next item on the hierarchy occurred when the client could view two consecutive presentations of a given segment while remaining relaxed.

In the *self-paced practice* component of treatment, the clients were aided in setting up a convenient time to simply sit in the waiting room of a cooperating dentist. They were told to relax and attend to the sights and sounds of the office. Following the waiting room experience, clients scheduled a time (e.g., at lunch or between regular dental patients) to explore the dental operatory equipment (including the handpiece, or drill) and relax in the dental chair. A dental assistant was present to demonstrate various pieces of equipment and explain their functions. . . .

CASE

Mr. R., a 38-year-old [man] was referred to us by a local dental practitioner. An attempted oral examination by the referring dentist had resulted in such extreme anxiety and avoidance

*Reprinted from Kleinknecht & Bernstein (1979), pp. 311–313.

that the client could not be treated. That examination was the client's first dental contact in 13 years, and was prompted only by pressure from his wife.

Mr. R. reported that his present reaction to dentists resulted from numerous early contacts with a dentist described as "rough and unsympathetic." His last dental contact (prior to being referred) was with an army dentist nicknamed "The Butcher." The main reason for avoidance was that drilling was extremely aversive, especially on posterior (back) teeth, which the client felt were difficult or impossible to completely anesthetize.

During the pretreatment interview, Mr. R. was unable to describe any specific physical reactions to dentistry other than "general tenseness." During the first viewing of the modeling film, the client was asked to attend carefully to his physical reactions to each sequence. Following this initial showing, Mr. R. was able to describe more specific reactions such as stomach and upper body tenseness and increased respiration rate. The client's subjective involvement in the tape was suggested by the fact that, on several occasions he sat back in his chair when the model sat back, and sat forward as the model did so. Also, when the explorer [instrument], needle, or drill were placed in the model's mouth, the client placed a hand over his own mouth, removing it only as the instrument was withdrawn from the model's mouth.

A second modeling session took place three days after the first. The client listened to five minutes of relaxation instructions before the tape was played and was encouraged to attempt to relax if he felt any tenseness. During this second viewing, the client reported less anxiety than in the first session. A third modeling session (four days later) resulted in moderate reactions to the drilling sequence only. At the fourth session, graduated-exposure segments involving drilling were presented, first at very low sound intensity, then at gradually increased volume until the client was able to remain relaxed while watching and listening. After the client successfully completed segmented graduated exposure, he was shown a continuous sequence of taped items, including an examination, injection, and simple restoration (filling). All graduated exposure procedures were completed in two sessions.

The client was then instructed to visit a dentist's office in his own time, simply to sit in the waiting room, relax, and attend to the various sights and sounds for 30 minutes. The client reported actually staying one hour, having fallen asleep. He was then asked to schedule a 30-minute period during the lunch hour in which he was to sit in a vacant dental chair, relax, and manipulate the drill and other implements until he felt comfortable with them. (A dental assistant was present to provide information about the instruments and other equipment.) The client reported being able to accomplish this last task with no anxiety. . . .

On the first posttreatment questionnaire, the client reported that his fear of dentistry since treatment was "better" and that he planned to see a dentist on a regular basis. This, in fact, occurred. He saw an oral surgeon on his own within two months following treatment and had two wisdom teeth removed. His six-month posttreatment report revealed that he still rated his reactions to dentistry as "better," but that he had no dental work done since the extractions, although he planned to seek continued dental treatment. At 12 months posttreatment, the client continues to rate his reaction to dentistry as "better" and reported two additional dental visits, one for an examination and cleaning and a subsequent one in which three teeth were filled. These reported dental contacts were verified by dental records. The dentist also noted that Mr. R. had two additional appointments scheduled to continue his dental treatment.

The treatment package described in Case 10-7 is noteworthy because of its relative brevity and efficiency. The total therapist contact time was 3½ hours, considerably less than the 8 to 10 hours typically required for systematic desensitization, which also is an effective form of treatment for dental fear.[36] The use of standard videotapes for the symbolic modeling and graduated exposure phases of treatment helped in this regard. Moreover, less therapist time was required because clients conducted the *in vivo* practice on their own.

OVERVIEW AND EVALUATION OF MODELING THERAPIES

Modeling therapies are based on the simple principle that clients can benefit from the experience of other people. Modeling can help clients learn new skills, can elicit desirable behaviors that they already know how to perform, can reduce disruptive anxiety or fear and resultant maladaptive avoidance behavior, and can appropriately inhibit clients from engaging in maladaptive behaviors. The modeling therapies developed to fulfill these therapeutic goals have, for the most part, been validated by well-controlled experimental studies. In general, modeling therapies have been shown to be at least as effective as other behavioral therapies in treating particular target behaviors, and with a number of specific applications modeling procedures have been found to be more effective.[37] However, much evidence for the effectiveness of modeling therapies is based on analogue research. Although a number of impressive case studies report successful treatment in which a variety of modeling therapies were employed with actual clients and clinical problems, case studies cannot be considered substitutes for experimental investigations that control for the effects of influences other than the therapy procedures themselves (e.g., clients' expectations regarding improvement).[38] Case studies rarely provide such necessary controls. Thus, definitive statements about the efficacy of modeling therapies with actual clients and problems await further appropriate studies.

Modeling therapies are most noteworthy for their relative efficiency in terms of time required for successful treatment and for their cost-effectiveness. Compared to other behavioral therapies for the same target behavior, modeling therapies frequently bring about therapeutic changes more quickly, which has obvious advantages for the distressed client as well as for the behavioral therapist, who can treat more clients. One factor that may account for the general rapidity of modeling therapies is that they often incorporate principles and techniques found in other behavioral therapies, such as (vicarious) reinforcement and gradual exposure to a threatening or difficult situation. This incorporation is, no doubt, a natural outcome of the fact that modeling therapies have been developed more recently than substitution and consequential behavioral therapies, and behavioral therapists prudently have adapted techniques and principles already proven effective to modeling therapies.

Symbolic modeling is especially efficient. Modeling films, videotapes, and reading material can be presented to many clients at once and do not require professional therapists to administer the treatment. Therefore, many people who would normally not have access to behavioral therapy can benefit from modeling therapy. For example, modeling films to reduce fear of dental procedures are now routinely shown in some dentists' offices. However, prepared symbolic modeling presentations have two potential drawbacks. First, they are costly to produce initially (although they prove to be very economical in the long run). Second, standard symbolic modeling presentations are aimed at an "average" client and thus inevitably there is some loss of effectiveness because the therapy is not individualized. This symbolic modeling can be supplemented with individualized live modeling, in which case the live modeling may not need to be as extensive and time consuming because the client has also been exposed to the symbolic modeling.

Another way in which modeling can be used efficiently as part of therapy involves the use of **naturally occurring models.** In our daily lives, we encounter many people who exhibit behaviors we could potentially imitate if that were appropriate. Clients can use these readily available models by observing them on their own time and at their own pace.[39] For example, a woman who is having difficulty making casual conversation with men in a social setting could go to a bar or a party and inconspicuously observe other women interact with men. Not only would the client see what the other women did and hear what they said, but she would also see the immediate consequences of their actions. For instance, if one of the models makes a fool of herself with the man she is talking to, then the client may save herself a similar fate by avoiding the particular behavior the model engaged in.

For naturally occurring models to be effective in influencing a client's behavior, the models must be *appropriate* for the client. The behavioral therapist directs the client to the type of models that would be most suitable, given the client's particular problem and personal characteristics. For instance, usually the model should be someone who is likely to display adaptive behaviors at a level of competence and confidence somewhat above the level at which the client is functioning (but not too far above). The therapist may also suggest people whom the client will want to avoid using as models (except as models of what not to do). Such a warning is often needed when a specific person in the client's everday life situation is a negative model, such as a parent who drinks excessively or a close friend who copes with frustration by acting violently.

Besides their direct use in treating problem behaviors, modeling procedures serve an important function in teaching behavioral therapy skills to both professional therapists and nonprofessional change agents, including clients themselves. Consider, for example, the important role of modeling in programs designed to instruct parents in modifying the deviant behaviors of children who have been diagnosed autistic. In learning to shape appropriate behaviors, therapists first model shaping procedures for the parents, using other staff members as their subjects. Later, parents practice shaping each other's behavior while the remaining parents in the group observe the procedure. After this training is completed, the therapist goes to individual homes and demonstrates how and in which circumstances the principles taught in the group sessions can be applied. Note that such training exposes the parents to both mastery models (the therapists) and coping models (other parents in training).

Recently behavioral therapists have begun to explore the possibility of using the principles and procedures of behavioral therapy to *prevent* problem behaviors.[40] Modeling has a great potential for preventing many of the problems it is so effective in treating. This is especially true for symbolic forms of modeling that can easily be reproduced and made available on a mass scale. For example, common fears of medical and dental procedures are often based on faulty information and on exaggerated or otherwise unrealistic expectations about the procedures. Rather than treat the fears once they have developed, symbolic modeling presentations could be produced to give children at an early age (when many of the fears originate) realistic information about medical and dental treatments. Similarly, social skills deficits could be prevented by routinely teaching these skills to people through symbolic forms of modeling. These and other possibilities for behavioral prevention are discussed in the final chapter of this book.

SUMMARY

Modeling therapies all involve learning by observing the behavior of others (models). Modeling can involve live or symbolic (e.g., in films) examples of behavior. Whether or not an observer imitates a model depends on a number of factors, including the appropriateness of the model and the consequences to the model (vicarious consequences). Modeling serves four basic functions. First, modeling can teach clients new behaviors, and numerous examples of modeling procedures to teach basic and complex social skills to children and adults exist. A prime example of a complex social skill taught via modeling is assertive behavior, and behavioral therapy procedures for assessing and training assertive responses have been developed. Second, modeling can prompt clients to engage in appropriate behaviors they already know how to perform, such as performing important health-related behaviors (e.g., engaging in regular exercise). Third, modeling may make it possible for people to perform behaviors that make them anxious (or to which they have other negative reactions) by exposing them to models who are successful at the behaviors and who experience no negative consequences (vicarious extinction). Participant modeling is a live modeling procedure that combines direct therapist support and resembles *in vivo* systematic desensitization. Fourth, modeling occasionally is used to inhibit maladaptive behaviors by exposing clients to models who incur aversive consequences for performing the behaviors. Modeling therapies are extremely efficient in terms of the speed with which they bring about therapeutic changes; with symbolic modeling such as in films, the number of clients that can benefit from the treatment is potentially very large. Modeling also serves the important function of training behavioral therapy skills to professionals and nonprofessionals (including clients themselves).

REFERENCE NOTES

1. Bandura, 1971, 1977b.
2. Jones, 1924.
3. See, for example, Kellam, 1969.
4. Bandura, 1971.
5. Metz, 1965.
6. O'Connor, 1969.
7. O'Connor, 1969, p. 18.
8. Spiegler & Agigian, 1977.
9. For example, Hersen & Bellack, 1976b; Hersen, Eisler, & Miller, 1974.
10. Jaffe & Carlson, 1976.
11. Franks & Wilson, 1976, p. 148.
12. For example, Eisler, Hersen, & Miller, 1973; Hersen, Eisler, Miller, Johnson, & Pinkston, 1973; McFall & Lillesand, 1971; McFall & Twentyman, 1973; Prince, 1975.
13. For example, Gambrill & Richey, 1975; Rathus, 1973.
14. McFall & Lillesand, 1971.
15. McFall & Lillesand, 1971, p. 315.
16. For example, McFall & Lillesand, 1971; McFall & Twentyman, 1973.
17. Prince, 1975.
18. Prince, 1975, p. 193.
19. For example, Kazdin, 1973, 1974a, 1974b, 1974c, 1974d, 1976; Rosenthal & Reese, 1976.
20. For example, Kazdin, 1974d, 1976; Rosenthal & Reese, 1976.
21. For example, Rosenthal & Reese, 1976.
22. Spiegler, Liebert, McMains, & Fernandez, 1969.
23. Spiegler, Liebert, McMains, & Fernandez, 1969.
24. For example, Bruch, 1975; Meichenbaum, 1971; Melamed & Siegel, 1975.
25. Kornhaber & Schroeder, 1975.
26. Spiegler, Liebert, McMains, & Fernandez, 1969.
27. For example, Bandura, 1975; Bandura, Jeffery, & Gajdos, 1975; Bandura, Jeffery, & Wright, 1974; Blanchard, 1970.
28. Ritter, 1968a, 1968b, 1969a, 1969b, 1969c.
29. For example, Bandura, Blanchard, & Ritter, 1969.
30. Melamed & Siegel, 1975.
31. Melamed & Siegel, 1975, p. 514.
32. Melamed & Siegel, 1975.
33. Vernon, 1974.
34. Vernon, 1974.
35. Friedson & Feldman, 1958.
36. See Klepac, 1975; Shaw & Thoresen, 1974.
37. For example, Rachman & Wilson, 1980.
38. Paul, 1969a.
39. Spiegler, 1970.
40. Spiegler, 1980.

CHAPTER 11

Cognitive Behavioral Therapies

During the past decade, behavioral therapists have increasingly recognized the need to deal *directly* with clients' cognitive processes, such as thoughts, attitudes, beliefs, attributions, and expectations. Cognitions may be target behaviors themselves, as when a client complains of recurrent disturbing thoughts (e.g., "I am responsible for my wife's dying of cancer" or "I'll never get my work done on time"). More often, cognitions are maintaining conditions of target behaviors, as when students' negative expectations about their performance on tests not only make them feel anxious but also result in a self-fulfilling prophecy—actually doing poorly on exams. The term **cognitive behavioral therapies** refers to interventions based on the principles and techniques of behavioral therapy that are used to change clients' cognitions *directly.* Other forms of behavioral therapy are used to modify cognitions indirectly, by changing overt behaviors that are observable behavioral anchors (see Chapter 2) for unobservable covert cognitions (e.g., how a client acts toward someone indicates the client's attitude toward that person).

The use of cognitions in behavioral therapy is not new, the most obvious example being the use of imagery in therapies such as systematic desensitization and covert sensitization. In these applications, however, cognitive processes are used as vehicles for changing maladaptive behaivors rather than being the target behaviors of therapy. The definition of cognitive behavioral therapy will be restricted to procedures that aim at directly modifying cognitions.

A central premise of cognitive behavioral therapies is that *the way we view or interpret events in our environment influences how we behave.* In other words, the *meaning* we place on events, people, and things, and our beliefs and expectations about them, play significant roles in determining our behavior. The following example illustrates how people's attitudes and expectations about the outcome of an event can significantly affect both their feelings and actions. A young woman has just graduated from college and is going out on her first interview for a job. If she views the interview *optimistically*—as an opportunity to demonstrate her skills and knowledge—she is likely to appear relaxed and confident, to express herself well in the interview, and to do as well as she is capable of on the achievement test she is given. On the other hand, if she views the interview *pessimistically*—thinking about all the ways she may "blow" this golden opportunity—she is likely to come across as tense and dubious about her abilities, to speak hesitatingly and ambiguously during the interview, and even to perform below her potential on the achievement test. Suppose also that, while waiting for her appointment with the personnel manager, she notices that her heart is beating a bit faster than normal. With an optimistic attitude, the woman could easily attribute this phenomenon to excitement, but with a pessimistic mental set she is more likely to consider it nervousness.

Cognitive behavioral therapy does not negate the important influence of environmental factors on behavior. Instead, it recognizes another step in the influence process—namely, that cognitions often mediate the environment's effect on our behavior. We attribute meaning to events in the environment, which in turn affects how the environmental events influence our behavior. For instance, only if we view the consequences of a behavior as pleasant or desirable are we likely to engage in the behavior. Thus, the maintaining conditions of our behavior may be environmental factors or our view (belief, expectation) of environmental factors, and in most cases they include both. Abnormal behaviors—the problems that clients present in therapy—often involve distorted, unrealistic, or illogical perceptions of environmental events. When a client's abnormal behavior is maintained by faulty cognitions, cognitive behavioral therapies can be used to directly modify the cognitions so that they no longer maintain the maladaptive behavior.

At this point, you may well wonder how behavioral therapists—who are known for their emphasis on concrete, observable, and measurable phenomena—deal with such abstract, amorphous phenomena as thoughts, beliefs, and ideas. As will be shown in a moment, behavioral therapists have found a reasonably reliable and valid way to operationalize cognitive processes, which makes it possible for them to work with cognitions in much the same way as they work with overt behaviors. However, before this solution is discussed, do Participation Exercise 11-1, which takes only about three minutes.

PARTICIPATION EXERCISE 11-1

Thinking Out Loud

To do this short participation exercise, you will need a pencil, paper, and a minor problem. Think of a specific, minor problem that you have to solve in the next few days, such as when to find time to take your clothes to the cleaners, what to get a friend for a birthday present, or what you should do this weekend.

Once you've identified a specific problem, think about it for a couple of minutes. As you think about it, write down your thoughts. Alternatively, you can think out loud, listening carefully to what you are saying. The objective is to become aware of your thoughts and particularly of the form they take. Now return to reading the text.

Exactly what have you written or said in doing Participation Exercise 11-1? What form did your written or spoken thoughts take? You probably used words, phrases, and perhaps full sentences. In fact, much of our thinking and other cognitive processes involve the use of language. (Obviously not all our thoughts are in the form of language; thoughts can also exist as images or pictorial representations.) We are usually not aware of this, however, because thinking is more or less an automatic process, and we do not typically give much thought to our thoughts. We do tend to think the way we talk; often when we are thinking, we are essentially talking to ourselves much as we would to others. And therein lies the way in which behavioral therapists deal with their clients' cognitions.

SELF-TALK

Cognitions can be operationally defined as terms of **self-talk:** what people say to themselves when they are thinking, believing, evaluating, and interpreting. Behavioral therapists learn about their clients' cognitions by asking them to verbalize out loud what they are saying to themselves. The pervasiveness and importance of "inner speech" in our lives is succinctly stated by Carlos Castaneda's Don Juan:* "The world is such and such or so-and-so only because we tell ourselves that that is the way it is. . . . You talk to yourself. You're not unique at that. Every one of us does that. We carry on internal talk. . . . In fact we maintain our world with our internal talk."[2] And, in a more scientific mode, inner speech has been described as

> [the] soundless, mental speech, arising at the instant we think about something, plan or solve problems in our mind, recall books read or conversations heard, read and write silently. In all such instances, we think and remember with the aid of words which we articulate to ourselves. Inner speech is nothing but speech to oneself, or concealed verbalization, which is instrumental in the logical processing of sensory data, in their realization and comprehension within a definite system of concepts and judgments. The elements of inner speech are found in all our conscious perceptions, actions, and emotional experiences, where they manifest themselves as verbal sets, instructions to oneself, or as verbal interpretation of sensations and perceptions. This renders inner speech a rather important and universal mechanism.[3]

*This quotation and the extracts that follow were originally noted by Meichenbaum.[1]

Clients are only sometimes aware of their self-talk, and probably not everyone engages in self-talk.

> Because of the habitual nature of one's expectations or beliefs, it is likely that such thinking processes become automatic and seemingly involuntary. . . . Moreover . . . maladaptive cognitions may take a pictorial form instead of or in addition to verbal form. . . . For example, a woman with a fear of walking alone found that her spells of anxiety followed images of her having a heart attack and being left helpless.[4]

Whether clients engaged in self-talk or were aware of it prior to being in cognitive behavioral therapy is less critical than whether or not they are willing to view behavior "*as if* it were affected by self-statements and modifiable by them."[5] Accordingly, clients who do not conceptualize their thought processes in terms of inner speech are asked to do so. For example, they could ask themselves the following question when they are thinking about a particular situation: "If I were talking to myself, what might I be telling myself about the situation, about how I feel about it, and about what it means to me?"

A variety of cognitive behavioral therapies have been developed; most involve some form of **cognitive restructuring**—that is, modifying clients' views and ideas that are maintaining maladaptive and disturbing behaviors. Several representative cognitive behavioral therapies are described in this chapter, and additional examples are given in the next chapter on self-control behavioral therapies, which rely heavily on cognitive behavioral therapy procedures.

THOUGHT STOPPING

Thought stopping was one of the earliest cognitive behavioral therapies to be developed.[6] As the name implies, it is used to eliminate unwanted thoughts, such as obsessive ruminations (e.g., constantly worrying about being contaminated by germs), depressive ideas (e.g., "I can't seem to make friends"), and self-degrading thoughts (e.g., "I'm just no good for anything").

Thought stopping is a self-control therapy, because clients usually implement it on their own—whenever disturbing thoughts occur. To teach the client how to stop thoughts, the therapist tells the client to concentrate on the unwanted thoughts and may suggest that the client close her or his eyes to fully focus attention on the upsetting thoughts. The client is instructed to signal the therapist, as by raising a finger, when the thoughts are clearly in mind. As soon as the client signals, the therapist shouts, "Stop!" The client is then asked what just happened, and inevitably the client reports that the thoughts did indeed stop. After repeating this procedure, several times, the client is instructed to try the technique on his or her own, first by shouting "Stop!" out loud and then subvocally. With a little practice (often only a few minutes), clients can easily learn to momentarily eliminate distressing thoughts in their daily lives.

But what happens once the momentary disrupting effect of the thought-stopping procedure passes? To just *not think about* the disturbing thoughts won't work; as we all know, that tactic usually results in thinking about them even more! The individual needs to be actively thinking about something else. Therefore, in the second phase of thought stopping the client is instructed to follow the subvocalization of "Stop!" with thoughts that are incompatible with the disturbing thoughts. The client makes a list of incompatible thoughts and memorizes several so that they are readily available to use when disturbing thoughts occur. The nature of the incompatible thoughts varies with the specific upsetting thoughts. For example, thoughts of succeeding are appropriate substitutes for thoughts of failing, just as thoughts of being healthy are good substitutes for ruminations about disease and death.

Initially, clients must remember to stop their disturbing thoughts whenever they occur. After a while, however, the technique becomes almost automatic, perhaps because the act of thought stopping is reinforced by the cessation of the unpleasant thoughts as well as the introduction of pleasant thoughts that the client substitutes.

In some instances clients can abruptly disrupt the upsetting thoughts and, without substituting other thoughts, not have the upsetting thoughts return a short time later. Many clients, however, find it helpful or necessary to focus on incompatible thoughts. As a two-phase procedure, thought stopping is a substitution behavioral therapy similar to aversion-relief therapy (see Chapter 5) because it combines decelerating an undesirable target behavior with accelerating an alternative (substitute) desirable target behavior. Case 11-1 illustrates the use of thought stopping to deal with jealous thoughts.

CASE 11-1

*Eliminating Jealousy by Thought Stopping**

A 27-year-old unmarried man discovered that the woman with whom he believed he was having an exclusive sexual relationship had had sexual relations with another man a few weeks before. After an initial period of feeling intensely hurt and angry, the man resolved to forget the incident, having been convinced that the woman's feelings for him had not changed. However, he frequently remembered the woman's sexual affair and became extremely upset whenever he thought of the woman being sexually intimate with the other man. These thoughts were not only uncomfortable, but they prevented him from concentrating on whatever he was doing at the time.

Several years previously the man had had a similar problem for which he sought the help of a behavioral therapist. He had been taught thought stopping and had learned to apply it successfully. Recalling the procedure, he applied thought stopping to his present distressing and disruptive thoughts. Whenever he found himself ruminating about the woman's affair, he yelled "Stop!" to himself and then began to imagine one of two prearranged pleasant thoughts. One pleasant thought was directly related to the woman; it involved her acting in a loving way toward him and otherwise demonstrating her desire to continue their relationship. The other pleasant thought was completely unrelated to the woman or their relationship; it concerned his playing a good game of tennis, an activity he

*From the author's files.

enjoyed and that he took pride in doing well. Either pleasant thought successfully kept him from returning to thoughts of the woman's affair.

Before thought stopping, the distressing thoughts had lasted from several minutes to as long as an hour and had occurred on the average of 10 times each day. Thought stopping had the immediate and dramatic effect of reducing the duration of the intrusive thoughts to only a few seconds. Within a week, the man was just subvocalizing "Stop!" (without substituting a pleasant thought), which was sufficient to completely erase the unpleasant thought and allow him to immediately return to whatever he had been thinking about when the unpleasant thought intruded. The frequency of the thoughts gradually declined, over the course of the first week of the self-implemented treatment, to no more than twice a day. By the end of the second week, the thoughts were occurring about five times per week; and after a month, they occurred no more than once a week. Three months later, the man reported being completely free of the disturbing thoughts.

Evaluation of Thought Stopping

Thought stopping is a straightforward procedure that clients can learn very quickly and can easily apply on their own with little or no supervision from a behavioral therapist. Clients can experience relief from their disturbing thoughts in just a few trials of thought stopping, and they readily accept the technique and are enthusiastic about using it. Thought stopping enjoys widespread clinical use, although there is very little controlled research to validate its effectiveness.[7] It would be important to evaluate the effectiveness of thought stopping independent of other therapies with which it is often combined (e.g., aversive consequences for the disturbing thoughts),[8] the interaction of the therapies, and the role of placebo effects. **Placebo effects** are factors other than the therapy itself that can lead to changes in the target behavior (e.g., the therapist's encouragement or the client's belief that the treatment will work). However, until the necessary studies are done, there seems to be no danger in clients' using thought stopping.

RATIONAL-EMOTIVE THERAPY

Rational-emotive therapy, the most well-known form of cognitive restructuring, was developed by psychologist Albert Ellis more than 20 years ago.[9] The name *rational-emotive therapy* comes from the basic assumption that so-called emotional disorders or negative emotions, such as anxiety, depression, anger, and guilt, are directly caused by faulty or irrational thoughts.

The Theory Behind Rational-Emotive Therapy

Ellis's theory of emotional reactivity involves three steps: (1) some real external event occurs in a person's life, (2) the person thinks about and interprets the event, and (3) the person feels and behaves in a manner consistent with these thoughts and beliefs. Take a simple example, with which most readers will be able to identify. You do poorly on an examination, and you subsequently feel extremely depressed and worthless. The most obvious and also the simplest explanation for your negative emotions is that they are the direct result of your poor test performance. But consider, for a moment, what the consequences of doing poorly on a test actually are. They include such possibilities as your ending up with a lower course grade than you would have liked, your having to study harder for the next exam or do an extra credit assignment you hadn't planned on, your parents being displeased, and so on. If you examine these and any other realistic consequences *objectively*, you will find that none of them *per se* can directly cause you to feel very depressed and worthless. In other words, depression and feelings of worthlessness are not inevitable or even logical consequences of poor test performance. Admittedly, you might be upset or annoyed, but the actual consequences would not be of a magnitude to justify your extreme emotional reactions. Why, then, do you feel so depressed and demoralized? From the standpoint of rational-emotive therapy, and cognitive behavioral therapies in general, the intense negative emotions are the direct result of your thoughts and beliefs about doing poorly on the examination. Although you may not have been aware of them at the time, the odds are good that you were making such self-statements as "How could I have blown that test?—I must be really dumb!"; "I guess I'm not as smart as I thought I was"; "I'm just a 'C' student"; or "I'll never do well in that course (on that type of exam, in college, or even, at anything)." These evaluations and beliefs about yourself are directly responsible for your feelings of depression. Only when you *interpret* poor test performance as indicative of your self-worth and competence can your test performance play an *indirect* role in your experiencing such extreme negative emotions.

Self-statements that result in negative emotions and maladaptive behaviors have several distinctive characteristics. First, they are *illogical,* in the sense that they do not necessarily follow from the precipitating events. Doing poorly on an examination or any other task does not mean that one is worthless, incompetent, or stupid. There just is no evidence to support such a conclusion. Of course, if a student did poorly on *every* exam, then it might be concluded that the student has not been successful in taking examinations. But one still could not conclude that the person would never do well on exams, that the person was a poor student, and certainly not that the person was (generally) incompetent or stupid.

Second, self-statements that lead to abnormal behavior and disturbing emotions are *irrational* because they are based on faulty assumptions. For example, to conclude that poor test performance indicates stupidity is just not supported by evidence. Intelligence is one of many factors that contribute to high test performance; other factors include knowledge of the subject matter, test-taking skills, motivation, and emotional state at the time of the examination. Furthermore, to conclude that doing poorly on a test means one is worthless (or worth less than if one had done well) is irrational for another reason. The implicit assumption that test performance and self-worth are causally related is *not empirically verifiable:* it is not possible to gather evidence for or

TABLE 11-1 *Common Irrational Beliefs Identified by Ellis*

1. It is a dire necessity for an adult to be loved by everyone for everything she or he does.
2. Certain acts are awful or wicked, and people who perform such acts should be severely punished.
3. It is horrible when things do not go the way we would like them to.
4. Human misery is externally caused and is forced on us by outside people and events.
5. If something is or may be dangerous or fearsome, one should be terribly upset by it.
6. It is easier to avoid than to face life difficulties.
7. We need something greater than ourselves on which to rely.
8. We should be completely competent, intelligent, and achieving in all possible respects.
9. Because something once strongly affected someone's life, it should affect it indefinitely.
10. One must have certain and perfect control over things.
11. Human happiness can be achieved by inertia and inaction.
12. We have virtually no control over our emotions, and we cannot help feeling certain things.

SOURCE: Ellis (1970).

against that assumption, because an individual's personal worth is not measurable.

A third characteristic of self-statements that cause people problems is that they frequently involve a *sense of duty:* they implicitly or explicitly include such words as "must," "should," "ought," and "have to." For example, a student's depression about doing poorly on a test might be the result of the irrational belief that a student *must* do well on examinations. In general, people feel guilty when they do not act in ways that they think they *should,* or when they act in ways that they believe they *should not.* Virtually all statements that use such words are irrational because, in fact, there are only a few behaviors that we *must* do, if we want to stay alive. (People are reminded of this occasionally when they are temporarily incapacitated by physical illness and are unable to engage in normal activities. At such times, all the tasks that *had* to get done do not get accomplished and somehow the consequences are never catastrophic.) You may find it interesting to observe how often "ought," "should," "must," and "have to" are used in everyday speech. The frequency is quite high for most people.

Ellis has identified 12 irrational beliefs that are commonly held by people in Western cultures and that are frequently at "the root of most emotional disturbance."[10] These "core irrational ideas," listed in Table 11-1, are irrational because they either are not or cannot be supported by empirical evidence. (It may be possible to support one or more of these ideas by other sources of evidence, however, such as on the basis of *faith,* which is a form of evidence used to support religious doctrine.)

The Process of Rational-Emotive Therapy

Three basic operations are involved in rational-emotive therapy. First, the therapist helps the client identify the precipitating external events of the problem. Although rational-emotive therapy does not deal with these events directly, it is important to identify them because they are the focus of the client's irrational self-statements and beliefs. This first task is usually accomplished by a detailed interview in which the therapist directs the client to recall the immediate antecedents of the problem.

Second, the therapist helps the client (1) to discover the specific self-statements he or she is making about the external event and then (2) to identify the irrational beliefs that underlie these self-statements. In particular the client and therapist look for self-statements that contain any of the following: (1) "must" or "should" (e.g., "I should like my father"); (2) the idea that something is awful, terrible, or catastrophic (e.g., "Living without my wife is the worst thing that ever happened to me"); (3) the idea that something is unbearable (e.g., "I absolutely can't stand being ignored"); or (4) damning or blaming oneself or others (e.g., "It is *all* my fault").[11]

Once the underlying irrational beliefs have been identified, clients must come to realize that their faulty beliefs (embodied in self-statements) are maintaining their problems, not external events. At this stage in rational-emotive therapy, clients may be given a homework assignment: to record their self-talk whenever their problem behavior occurs so as to make explicit the relationship that exists between the self-statements and the problem. Figure 11-1 presents

	REAL-LIFE SITUATION	CLIENT'S SELF-TALK ABOUT SITUATION	CLIENT'S EMOTIONAL REACTION
BEFORE THERAPY	Failed course	(Unaware of or not focusing on self-talk)	Angry, depressed
DURING THERAPY	Failed course	1. "This is horrible." 2. "My parents will hit the roof." 3. "I am just plain stupid."	Angry, depressed
AFTER THERAPY	Failed course	1. "This sure won't help my average." 2. "My parents aren't going to be pleased, but they'll get over it." 3. "It's not the end of the world; I can make up the course."	Upset, disappointed

FIGURE 11-1 An example of how (1) the client's understanding of (self-talk about) the causal sequence of events leads to emotional reactions and how (2) the resulting emotional reactions change in rational-emotive therapy

an example of the typical changes in clients' understanding of the causal sequence of events leading to their problems, and of the resulting changes in their emotional reactions.

In the third basic operation of rational-emotive therapy, the therapist helps the client (1) to identify and analyze illogical self-statements and (2) to substitute appropriate logical self-statements. The therapist models this process for the client by (1) identifying an illogical self-statement the client has made, (2) analyzing why it is illogical, and finally (3) replacing it with a logical statement that objectively follows from the precipitating external event and that is not based on irrational beliefs. For example, suppose a client who has been turned down when asking for a date verbalizes the following self-statement: "I feel awful because Carol said she didn't want to go out with me. I don't seem to attract women that I am attracted to." The therapist might model the following thought process for the client: "That doesn't make any sense. I'm blowing up the situation. I didn't feel great when Carol said no, but it wasn't terrible. And just because Carol isn't interested in me doesn't mean I can't be attractive to other women I like. So, I don't like being turned down, but there are other women who might like to go out with me."

Case 11-2 is an excerpt from an initial rational-emotive therapy session.

CASE 11-2

Treatment of Depression by Rational-Emotive Therapy*

The client was in his first year of college at a highly prestigious university. He had graduated from a small high school where he had encountered little competition from his fellow students and got very high grades with little effort. On entering therapy, the client described himself as apathetic and depressed. The following is an excerpt from the client-therapist dialogue during the first session of rational-emotive therapy. The dialogue is annotated to note the general principles of rational-emotive therapy being illustrated. In the annotation, T stands for therapist, C for client.

Therapist: How long have you had these feelings of depression?

Client: Ever since the beginning of this quarter, I think.

Therapist: Can you tell me what is bothering you?

Client: Everything is . . . I don't know . . . a bunch of shit. I don't seem to care about anything anymore. I don't even care about school anymore, and that used to mean a lot to me.

Therapist: How are you doing in school, gradewise?

Client: Lousy. This quarter I've studied a total of two hours.

T elicits potential precipitating external events.

Therapist: Let's see. Fall quarter was your first at Stanford? How were your grades then?

Client: Shitty; had a 2.3 average. "C" average. And I worked hard, too. I feel like shoving the whole thing.

Therapist: Maybe this is part of what is getting you down. How did you do in high school?

*Rimm & Masters (1974). Dialogue is from pp. 421–424.

Client: Graduated with almost a 4.0. I thought I'd set the world on fire at Stanford, and I'm doing rotten.

Therapist: What does that make you, in your eyes?

T inquires about C's view of external events.

Client: I'm a failure. . . . I'll never get accepted to a decent medical school with grades like that. I'll probably end up pumping gas in Salinas . . . that's all I'm good for. I feel worthless.

Therapist: Sounds like you've been saying to yourself, "I'm a failure . . . I'm worthless" on account of your "C" average last quarter. That would be enough to depress anybody.

T introduces idea of self-talk.

Client: It's true. I've got to do well and I'm not.

C uses "must."

Therapist: So, you believe that in order for you to consider yourself a worthwhile person, you've got to succeed at something . . . like making "A's" at Stanford?

Client: A person's got to be good at something to be worth a damn. School was the only thing I was ever much good at in the first place.

C holds one of Ellis's common irrational beliefs.

Therapist: I'd like to point out that you're competing against some of the best students in the country, and they don't care very much about grading on the curve there. An average performance among outstanding people isn't really average, after all, is it?

T introduces rational ideas to counter C's irrational ones.

Client: I know what you are getting at, but that doesn't help too much. Any decent medical school requires at least a "B+" average, and I've got to get into medical school. That's been my goal ever since I was a kid.

C uses more "musts."

Therapist: Now, wait a minute! You say you *have* to go to medical school. Sounds like you think not going to medical school is against the law. Is that so?

Client: Well, not exactly. You know what I mean.

Therapist: I'm not sure. Do you really mean that you want very much to go to medical school? Because that is very different from believing that you *must* go to medical school. If you think you have to go to medical school, you are going to treat it like it's a life or death thing, which it isn't. But you believe that it is, and that is likely to be a major reason why you're depressed.

T challenges validity of "must."

Client: I can see your point, but even if I agreed with you, there's my family. They wouldn't agree with you.

Therapist: What do you mean?

Client: They are big on my being successful. All my life my parents have been telling me that the whole family is counting on my being a doctor.

Therapist: OK, but that is their belief. Does it have to be yours?

Client: I just can't let them down.

Therapist: What would happen if you did?

Client: They'd be hurt and disappointed. Sometimes I almost think they wouldn't like me any more. That would be awful!

C is catastrophizing.

Therapist: Well, the worst possible thing that could happen if you don't go to medical school is that your father and mother wouldn't like you, and might even reject you. You aren't even sure this would happen.

Therapist: But, even if they did, does it follow that it would be awful? Could you prove that, logically, I mean?

T models logical analysis of C's thoughts and beliefs.

Client: It's lousy when your own family rejects you.

Therapist: I still can't see the logical connection between their rejecting you and things being awful or even lousy. I would agree that it wouldn't exactly be a pleasant state of affairs. You are equating rejecting with catastrophe, and I'd like you to try and convince me one follows from the other.

T continues to challenge C's illogical thoughts.

Client: They wouldn't even want me around . . . like I was a worthless shit. And that would be rotten.

Therapist: Well, there you go again, telling yourself that because they would reject you, which means they wouldn't want you around, you are a worthless shit. Again, I don't see the logic.

Client: It would make me feel that way.

Therapist: No, I emphatically disagree . . . it's *you* who would make you feel that way. By saying those same things to yourself.

Note T's direct confrontation.

Client: But I believe it's true.

Therapist: I'm still waiting for some logical basis for your belief that rejection means you are worthless, or not going to medical school means you're a shit.

Client: OK, I agree about the medical school bit. I don't *have* to go. But about my parents . . . that's heavy. As far as reasons are concerned . . . (long pause) . . . I started to say I need them for emotional support but, as I think about it, I get a hell of a lot more from a couple of good buddies here at school than I ever got from them. They are pretty cold, especially Mom.

C begins to imitate logical analysis of his thoughts.

Therapist: OK. . . . What else might be terrible about being rejected by your parents?

Client: I was thinking . . . where would I go over the holidays? But I don't spend that much time at home anyway, come to think of it. But, there is money . . . this place is damned expensive and I don't have a scholarship. If they cut off funds, that would be a disaster.

Therapist: There you go again . . . catastrophizing. Prove to me that it would be a disaster.

Client: Well, maybe I was exaggerating a bit. It would be tough, though I suppose I could apply for support, or get a job maybe. In fact, I know I could. But then it would take longer to get through school, and that would be shitty.

Therapist: Now you are beginning to make a lot of sense. I agree that it would be shitty . . . but certainly not terrible.

Client: You know, for the first time in weeks I think I feel a little better. Kind of like there is a load off my mind. Is that possible?

Therapist: I don't see why not, but I'm wondering what would happen if you'd start feeling depressed tonight or tomorrow . . . how would you deal with it?

Behavior rehearsal of identifying and challenging irrational self-talk will be used at this point (see text).

Case 11-2 is typical of a rational-emotive therapy session and illustrates the basic three operations involved in rational-emotive therapy. It is not uncommon for clients to begin to view events in their lives more logically and rationally in the very first session, because the therapist generally provides many examples that challenge the validity of self-statements and encourages the client to do this from the outset of therapy. Obviously, for this adaptive mode of thinking and reasoning to be useful to the client, the client will have to continue it at home without therapist assistance. To prepare clients to challenge their irrational self-statements on their own, behavior rehearsal in the therapy session is used. For example, in the therapist's last question in Case 11-2, the therapist was assessing how the client would deal with feelings of depression if and when they occurred. In other words, would the client examine what he was saying to himself when he felt depressed, determine if his self-statements were logical and rational, challenge those statements that were illogical and irrational, and finally substitute logical and rational self-statements?

Evaluation of Rational-Emotive Therapy

Despite its public notoriety and current popularity among practicing clinical psychologists,[12] rational-emotive therapy has several important limitations. First, although it has been used clinically for 20 years, relatively few adequately controlled studies of its effectiveness have been performed.[13] In short, the available studies

> do not provide adequate information on which to reach firm conclusions about the efficacy of RET [rational-emotive therapy] as a treatment method. Evidence on the long-term efficacy of RET is lacking. Encouragingly, the evidence suggests that RET is more effective than no treatment or placebo influences on some measures, in most studies. However, it is not possible to conclude that RET is superior to alternative treatment methods such as systematic desensitization, prolonged exposure, or behavioral rehearsal.[14]

Second, although some evidence shows that irrational self-statements are related to maladaptive emotional reactions to life situations,[15] the precise nature of this relationship is as yet unknown. Available data do not support Ellis's basic contention that abnormal behaviors are *caused* by irrational beliefs. The data only indicate that abnormal behaviors and irrational beliefs are correlated.[16] Furthermore, there is little support for clients' irrational beliefs being restricted to or even including one or more of Ellis's 12 core irrational ideas (Table 11-1).[17] Clinicians have reported that two of these core irrational beliefs—"Everyone must love me" and "I must be perfect in everything I do"—appear to be held by many clients with anxiety-related problems.[18] Still, such irrational ideas are too global and imprecise to be applicable to individual clients.[19] For example, it is doubtful that many clients actually believe that *everyone* must love them. Instead, clients are more likely to believe that a few key individuals in their lives should love them.

A third limitation of rational-emotive therapy is that it tends to be very direct and confrontive. This approach is not well suited to clients who tend to resist change when they are "coerced" into modifying their beliefs[20] or who prefer an approach to dealing with their problems that is somewhat less therapist directed.

BECK'S COGNITIVE THERAPY

Psychiatrist Aaron Beck has developed procedures he calls **cognitive therapy**[21] that are very similar to Ellis's rational-emotive therapy, although the two therapists apparently developed their theories and techniques independently. Because of the similarity in the two approaches, the discussion of Beck's cognitive therapy only briefly highlights some features that add to what has already been discussed in relation to rational-emotive therapy.

Cognitive therapy has been used primarily to treat depression, although other target behaviors have included phobic behavior, obsessions, psychosomatic disorders, and schizophrenic behavior.[22] Beck has analyzed the maladaptive thought patterns of depressed clients and has found three common themes: (1) interpreting external events negatively, (2) disliking oneself, and (3) viewing the future negatively. Such distorted perceptions and interpretations are the result of making logical errors, and Beck has identified specific errors that are frequently made by depressed clients (see Table 11-2).

The therapist's task in cognitive therapy is (1) to make clients aware of the logical errors they are making in interpreting events in their lives, (2) to help clients challenge the basic premises of their illogical thoughts, and (3) to relabel the events more accurately. Clients are encouraged to distinguish their ideas from the events they symbolize and to view their beliefs as hypotheses

TABLE 11-2 Logical Errors That Depressed Clients Often Make

LOGICAL ERROR	DEFINITION	EXAMPLE
Arbitrary inference	Drawing conclusions without sufficient evidence, or when the evidence is actually contradictory	Believing that one has been laid off from a job because of personal incompetence, although the company has gone out of business
Overgeneralization	Drawing a general conclusion on the basis of a single incident	Concluding that one will never succeed after failing on the first attempt
Selective abstraction	Attending to a detail while ignoring the total context	Feeling rejected because a friend who was rushing to catch a bus did not stop to talk
Personalization	Erroneously attributing an external event to oneself	Thinking that people who are laughing are laughing at oneself
Polarized thinking	Thinking in extremes, in a black-or-white or all-or-none fashion	Believing that one is a pauper after having lost one's wallet (assuming that not all of one's fortune was in the wallet)

SOURCE: Beck (1963).

(rather than established facts) that they are capable of empirically testing. For example, a woman who believes that men will not want to date her unless she "jumps into bed" with them on the first date would be encouraged to check out this hypothesis by going out on dates and not having sex immediately. This approach does not say that the woman's hypothesis is incorrect, just that it is a hypothesis she can validate empirically.

A variety of specific cognitive therapy techniques have been developed to accomplish the basic aims just mentioned. For example, early in therapy for depression the therapist and the client may compile a list of daily activities to elevate the client's mood, a technique called **activity schedule making.** Similarly, in **mastery and pleasure therapy,** the client keeps a running account of daily activities and writes an "M" beside each mastery experience and a "P" beside each pleasure experience. "The purpose of this procedure is to penetrate the 'blindness' of depressed patients to situations in which they are successful and their readiness to forget situations that do bring them some satisfaction."[23]

Alternative therapy is used for two different purposes. One is to entertain alternative explanations of experiences to help clients recognize their negative and distorted biases and substitute more accurate interpretations for them. The other is to consider alternative ways of dealing with problems. While discussing different means of solving problems, clients may discover solutions to problems they had considered insoluble as well as may recognize that solutions previously discarded may indeed be viable. Alternative therapy can be especially valuable for clients who are contemplating suicide because they believe there is no way out of their dilemma.

Cognitive therapy includes some procedures directly aimed at modifying client's overt behavior, which in turn is expected to influence the client's thoughts and beliefs. (In this regard, the term *cognitive* therapy is a misnomer.) Such procedures are often employed with clients who are so severely depressed that they do not perform even the most mundane and routine behaviors (e.g., getting dressed, feeding themselves, and going to the bathroom). Furthermore, such individuals frequently view themselves as losers, believing that they cannot succeed at anything they attempt. Getting such clients to engage in even a minimal amount of activity and to experience some success in doing so may be a necessary first step in therapy. To accomplish these goals, **graded task assignments** may be used. In this technique, the client is asked to perform a series of tasks beginning with very brief and simple behaviors, ones that the therapist is certain that the client can do, and gradually increasing in complexity and duration as the client succeeds at each task. For example, a man who did not feel capable of preparing his own meals first might be given the task of making a cup of tea. When the client successfully did this, he and the therapist would design a slightly more complex task until the client's behavior was shaped so that he was preparing an entire meal on his own. Case 11-3 illustrates the impact that graded task assignments can have on a client whose activity level has been minimal. The therapist was Beck himself.

CASE 11-3

Using Graded Task Assignments to Accelerate Walking in a Severely Depressed Client*

The patient was a 52-year-old man who had spent over a year in a hospital without moving away from his bed. He had had many trials of antidepressant medications without any improvement. I saw him for only one visit. At this time, the patient was sitting in a chair next to his bed. After preliminary introductions and general social interchanges, the interview proceeded thus:

Therapist: I understand that you haven't moved away from your bedside for a long time. Why is that?
Patient: I can't walk.
Therapist: Why is that? . . . Are your legs paralyzed?
Patient: [irritated] Of course not! I just don't have the energy.
Therapist: What would happen if you tried to walk?
Patient: I'd fall on my face, I guess.
Therapist: What would you say if I told you that you were capable of walking any place in the hospital?
Patient: I'd say you were crazy.
Therapist: How about testing that out?
Patient: What's that?
Therapist: Whether I'm crazy.
Patient: Please don't bother me.
Therapist: You said you don't think you could walk. Many depressed people believe that, but when they try it they find they do better than they expected.
Patient: I *know* I can't walk.
Therapist: Do you think you could walk a few steps?
Patient: No, my legs would cave in.
Therapist: I'll bet you can walk from here to the door [about 5 yards].
Patient: What happens if I can't do it?
Therapist: I'll catch you.
Patient: I'm really too weak to do it.
Therapist: Suppose I hold your arm. [The patient then took a few steps supported by the therapist. He continued to walk beyond the prescribed five yards—without further assistance. He then walked back to his chair, unassisted.]
Therapist: You did better than you expected.
Patient: I guess so.
Therapist: How about walking down to the end of the corridor [about 20 yards]?
Patient: I know I don't have the strength to walk that far.
Therapist: How far do you think you can walk?
Patient: Maybe to the next room [about 10 yards].

The patient easily walked to the next room and then continued to the end of the corridor. The therapist continued to propose specific goals and to elicit the patient's re-

*Reprinted from Beck (1976), pp. 284–286.

sponses to the goals. After successful completion of each task, a greater distance was proposed.

Within 45 minutes, the patient was able to walk freely around the ward. He was thereby able to "reward" himself for his increased activity by being able to obtain a soda from the vending machine. Later, when he extended the range of his activities, he was able to walk to different points in the hospital and gain satisfaction from various recreational activities. Within a few days, he was playing ping-pong and going to the hospital snack bar and, in less than a week, he was able to walk around the hospital grounds and enjoy seeing the flowers, shrubs, and trees. Another automatic reward was the favorable response he received from members of the hospital staff and from the other patients. The patient began to speak about himself in positive terms and to make concrete plans for leaving the hospital permanently—a goal he reached in a month.

Not only were the graded task assignments useful in getting the patient to be more active, but they also resulted in success experiences for the client. In turn, his success helped him to change his view of himself from being sick and weak to being healthy and capable of functioning. Before the therapy session, the client believed that he was too weak to walk. By getting him to walk, the therapist set up an experience that provided the client with data refuting his hypothesis about himself.

Evaluation of Cognitive Therapy

Because of the similarity between cognitive therapy and rational-emotive therapy, cognitive therapy will be evaluated by comparing and contrasting it with rational-emotive therapy. Cognitive therapy fares somewhat better than rational-emotive therapy with respect to the three specific limitations of rational-emotive therapy discussed earlier. First, as with rational-emotive therapy, relatively few outcome studies of cognitive therapy exist. However, recently the amount and quality of that research has increased. For example, two well-controlled studies of cognitive therapy for depression have demonstrated that cognitive therapy was superior to traditional drug therapy[24] and to a treatment package to increase clients' social skills so that they could obtain more social reinforcers (which tend to be sparse for depressed clients).[25] Incidently, research evaluating the effectiveness of cognitive therapy is facilitated by the fact that cognitive therapy techniques are quite precisely defined and described, so that different researchers can be reasonably sure that they are employing the same procedures. In contrast, rational-emotive therapy procedures are generally not specifically delineated, so one cannot know exactly how the therapy was carried out in each study.

A second advantage of cognitive therapy, in contrast with rational-emotive therapy, is that no assumptions are made about the existence of a common set of irrational beliefs held by all clients. Instead, cognitive therapists assume that each client has idiosyncratic "automatic thoughts" that are distorted interpretations of events. This approach is consistent with the behavioral therapy emphasis that each client's problem is unique and must be treated by an individualized therapy strategy.

Third, cognitive therapy tends to be less confrontive than rational-emotive therapy. The Socratic dialogue approach in cognitive therapy is more conducive to clients' discovering for themselves the distortions and inaccuracies in their self-talk. This self-discovery approach is consistent with another basic emphasis of behavioral therapy: having clients assume responsibility for their therapy.

SELF-INSTRUCTION

When we are faced with a difficult or threatening situation, we tell ourselves things about the situation and our ability to handle it. Often these self-statements are maladaptive, in that they focus on the negative aspects of the external events and our personal inadequacies for coping with them. **Self-instruction** is a cognitive behavioral therapy developed by Donald Meichenbaum[26] to teach people to make useful, positive self-statements when they encounter problems—in other words, to instruct themselves in how to effectively cope with the situation. Self-instruction therapy has been used to treat such problems as (1) deficits in problem solving among children[27] and the elderly,[28] (2) performance anxiety[29] and lack of creative thinking[30] of college students, and (3) bizarre thoughts and speech of patients diagnosed as schizophrenic.[31] Self-instruction is a treatment package in which the major components are **cognitive modeling** (the model verbalizes adaptive thoughts) and **cognitive behavior rehearsal** (the client mentally practices a behavior, such as thinking about what one is going to say before making a telephone call). Several applications of self-instruction are described here.

Self-instruction therapy was first used to decelerate impulsive behavior of children.[32] Children who act impulsively do not think before acting, a pattern that often has undesirable consequences for them as well as for other people. The general goal of self-instruction therapy for impulsive behavior is to train the children to think and plan before acting—or, in terms that children are more likely to understand, to "stop, look, and listen" (see Figure 11-2). Self-instructional training for impulsive behavior involves five steps:

1. An adult model performs a task while verbalizing out loud an adaptive, counterimpulsive strategy (cognitive modeling). For example, while engaging in a task involving copying line patterns, the model might say,

> OK, what is it I have to do? You want me to copy the picture with the different lines. I have to go slowly and carefully. OK, draw the line down, down, good; then to the right, that's it; now down some more and to the left. Good, I'm doing fine so far. Remember, go slowly. Now back up again. No, I was supposed to go down. That's OK. Just erase the line carefully. . . . Good. Even if I make an error I can go on slowly and carefully. I have to go down now. Finished. I did it![33]

FIGURE 11-2 *Pictures used to encourage and remind children to employ self-instructions to reduce impulsive behavior* SOURCE: *Palkes, Stewart, & Kahana (1968), p. 819.*

This brief cognitive modeling includes a number of important skills usually absent in children who tend to act impulsively: "(1) problem definition ('What is it I have to do?'); (2) focusing attention and response guidance ('carefully . . . draw the line down'); (3) self-reinforcement ('Good, I'm doing fine'); and (4) self-evaluative coping skills and error-correcting options ('That's OK. . . . Even if I make an error I can go on slowly')."[34]

2. The child then performs the task as the model verbalizes the instructions out loud (cognitive participant modeling).

3. Next the child performs the task while verbalizing the instructions out loud (overt self-instructions).

4. Now the child performs the task while whispering the instructions (fading the overt self-instructions).

5. Finally the child performs the task while saying the instructions to her- or himself (covert self-instructions).

Using this sequence of activities, the child is first given practice with brief and simple perceptual motor tasks, such as coloring figures within boundaries. Gradually the length and complexity of the tasks are increased.[35]

Similar procedures have been used to teach children basic problem-solving skills—specifically, thinking of alternative ways to do a task and considering the potential consequences. The training emphasizes *how* (not what) to think about problems. It is presented to the children as a game and often includes pictorial prompts to remind the child to use self-instructions, such as the cue cards illustrated in Figure 11-3. Self-instruction in problem solving is applicable even with young children. For example, preschool children have been taught to use self-instructions to resolve interpersonal conflicts with their peers by first learning to solve cognitive problems and gradually, over the course of training, shifting to interpersonal problems.[36]

Psychiatric patients diagnosed as schizophrenic frequently have difficulty attending to the task at hand or to the situation they are in. Self-instructional training has been useful in teaching such patients attentional and task-relevant skills.[37] The training begins by teaching the patients to monitor their own thoughts and actions and to observe others' reactions to their behavior, in order to identify inappropriate thoughts and overt behaviors. When they find that they are thinking or acting inappropriately, such as engaging in bizarre, incoherent, or irrelevant actions or speech, they are instructed to use this feedback as a cue to apply self-instructions "to be relevant and coherent, to make myself understood."[38]

The therapist models self-statements that will help the patient meet this goal, and then the patient rehearses them first overtly and then covertly. An example of statements the therapist might model is as follows:

> I have to figure out how a bird and a flower are alike. A bird and a flower. [Pause.] A bird is small and a flower is small. I got it, the bird can eat the flower. [Pause.] No that doesn't help. That doesn't tell me how they are alike. I have to see how they are alike. Go slowly and think this one out. Don't just say the first thing that comes to mind. [Pause, while the model thinks.] I want to give the best answer I can. Let me imagine in my mind the object . . . bird, flower . . . out in the fresh air. They both need air to live. That's it: they are both living things. Good, I figured it out. If I take my time and just think about how the two objects are alike, I can do it.[39]

Self-instruction is initially applied to performing simple and highly structured tasks (e.g., copying figures) that do not involve interpersonal interactions that

FIGURE 11-3 *Cue cards used to prompt children to use self-instructions in solving problems*
SOURCE: Camp, B. W., & Bash, M. A. S. Think Aloud: Increasing social and cognitive skills—A problem-solving program for children (Primary Level). *Champaign, Ill.: Research Press, 1981. Reprinted by permission.*

the patient might find threatening. Cognitively more complex tasks (e.g., interpreting proverbs) and interpersonal tasks (e.g., being interviewed) are introduced as a patient becomes more competent at making task-relevant self-statements. A more detailed description of the use of self-instruction (to decelerate schizophrenic speech) is presented in Case 11-4.

CASE 11-4

*Using Self-Instructions to Decelerate Schizophrenic Speech**

The patient was a single 47-year-old male who had been hospitalized for a psychiatric condition seven times in the previous 11 years. His presenting abnormal behavior was described as "generalized inappropriate verbal behaviors. In conversation he appeared highly anxious and often responded to questions with irrelevant repetitious answers. Inappropriate verbal behavior was often accompanied by inattention to the environment."

Self-instructional therapy was carried out in six semiweekly sessions, each of which lasted approximately 45 minutes. The following self-instructions were given to the patient cumulatively, at the rate of one or two per session:

1. Don't repeat an answer.
2. I must pay attention to what others say. What did they ask me?
3. The only sickness is talking sick. I mustn't talk sick.
4. I must speak slowly.
5. People think it's crazy to ramble on. I won't ramble on.
6. Remember to pause after I say a sentence.
7. That's the answer. Don't add anything on.
8. I must stay on the topic.
9. Relax, take a few deep breaths.

> The procedure for the treatment sessions was as follows. The therapist was asked a question (e.g., How do you like the weather?) by a staff member not involved with the case. The therapist then verbalized the target self-instruction followed by the appropriate answer (e.g., Don't repeat an answer. [Pause] I like it very much.). After three such demonstrations, the [patient] was instructed to imitate the therapist's performance. This continued until the [patient] reached a criterion of three consecutive appropriate performances. The therapist then modeled whispering the self-instructions and verbalizing the appropriate answer. The [patient] again imitated this to a criterion of three consecutive appropriate performances. Finally, the therapist presented the self-instructions covertly and then verbalized the appropriate response. After each trial the therapist emphasized that he had actually repeated the instruction to himself. Again the [patient] imitated this performance to criterion. [He] was given feedback on all trials, and praise was delivered for correct imitations. The [patient] was instructed to practice self-instructions between sessions.

Before self-instruction training, an average of 65.5 percent of the patient's speech was inappropriate. This figure dropped to 16.5 percent during treatment (most of the inap-

*Meyers, Mercatoris, & Sirota (1976). Quotations are from pp. 480 and 481.

propriate speech occurred in the early sessions). To ascertain whether the training generalized to other people than the therapist, the patient was observed interacting with other people following therapy, during which times only 8.4 percent of his speech was inappropriate. Based on this vast improvement, the ward staff decided to discharge the patient from the hospital. He moved into a half-way house in the community and received training in social and community living skills in an outpatient program (the Community Training Center; see Chapter 8). At a six-month follow-up, the patient had maintained a low rate of inappropriate speech, was holding a part-time job at a fast food restaurant, and was otherwise functioning well. The patient's continued success may well have been due to factors other than the self-instruction training alone (e.g., the outpatient treatment program). However, he did report that one factor he believed contributed to his improvement was the " 'new self-instructions that stop me from talking like a crazy man,' " and he also reported that he was continuing to use the self-instructions (e.g., during his successful job interview for the restaurant job).

The use of self-instruction to teach college students creative problem solving serves as a final illustration of the technique.[40] The basic aim of this training is to eliminate self-talk that interferes with creative problem solving and to replace it with enhancing self-talk. First students are taught to be aware of countercreativity self-statements they make when confronted with a problem to be solved (e.g., "There is only one way to fix it, and that won't work"). Then students are taught to substitute creativity-enhancing self-statements (e.g., "Right now I can think of only one way to fix it, but maybe there are other ways"). The trainer models creativity-enhancing self-statements, which the students imitate and rehearse. The following example shows how a trainer cognitively modeled a practice task. The task involved listing innovative ways to change a toy monkey so that children could have more fun with it.

> I want to think of something no one else will think of, something unique. Be freewheeling, no hangups. I don't care what anyone thinks; just suspend judgment. I'm not sure what I'll come up with; it will be a surprise. The ideas can just flow through me. OK, what is it I have to do? Think of ways to improve a toy monkey. Toy monkey. Let me close my eyes and relax. Just picture a monkey. I see a monkey, now let my mind wander; let one idea flow into another. I'll use analogies. Let me picture myself inside the monkey. . . . Now let me do the task as if I were someone else.[41]

After presenting this general strategy, the trainer then listed aloud possible answers to the problem and frequently modeled the use of verbal self-reinforcement (e.g., "That's a good idea; this is fun!"). The trainer also modeled self-instructions students could use to cope with not being able to generate any ideas and with feeling frustrated (e.g., "Take it easy . . . the ideas will come, but I can't force them . . . just relax, take a break, go slowly"). The self-instructional training program was individualized: each student's notions about creativity were assessed, and the self-instructions modeled for each student reflected these ideas. Self-instructional training significantly increased the students' originality and flexibility on tests of divergent thinking and increased their preference for complex thinking. Moreover, students reported that they were applying the self-instructional creativity training on their own to solve personal and academic problems.

Evaluation of Self-Instruction

Considerable research has demonstrated that self-instructional training can modify a variety of target behaviors in both children and adults. However, because more than half of the studies have involved relatively minor problems (e.g., mild to moderate test anxiety in college students) and there have been few long-term follow-ups, the clinical significance of much of the research must be considered only suggestive. Still, a recent review of the evidence concluded that

> the overall pattern of results across the thirty-four studies [reviewed] is encouraging. SIT [self-instructional training] was compared with various control conditions and alternative forms of treatment including systematic desensitization, behaviour rehearsal, EMG biofeedback, and [consequential behavioral therapy] procedures. The findings suggest that SIT was significantly superior to control conditions in most studies and equaled or outperformed comparison treatments in others.[42]

Also, it appears that self-instruction may be more effective with some target behaviors (such as children's impulsive behavior) than other target behaviors (such as adults' schizophrenic speech).[43]

Self-instructional training shares with cognitive therapy many of the characteristics that contrast it favorably with rational-emotive therapy. Self-instructional training consists of structured and clearly delineated treatment procedures. It does not rely on high-pressure persuasion by the therapist to change clients' cognitions. Finally, self-instruction, like cognitive therapy, places a greater emphasis on behavioral therapy procedures such as modeling, behavior rehearsal, and graduated *in vivo* practice by clients.

Most of the cognitive behavioral therapies described in this chapter involve cognitive restructuring—that is, substituting positive, adaptive self-statements for negative, maladaptive self-statements. Participation Exercise 11-2 will give you some first-hand experience with cognitive restructuring.

PARTICIPATION EXERCISE 11-2

Cognitive Restructuring

Most cognitive behavioral therapies involve a form of cognitive restructuring: substituting positive, adaptive self-statements for negative, maladaptive self-statements. In this participation exercise, you have a chance to practice this skill by finding positive self-statements for some examples of negative self-statements. You have seen many examples of this process in this chapter, and doing the participation exercise will help you apply what you have read about, as well as demonstrate your understanding of how cognitive restructuring works. You will also be practicing a coping skill that you may find useful in dealing with difficult or stressful situations in your daily life.

The exercise presents a brief description of a situation and an example of a negative self-statement someone faced with that situation might make. These self-statements are maladaptive because they present the consequences of the situation as so terrible that nothing can be done to cope with what is, in reality, an unfortunate, but not necessarily disastrous, situation. Your task is to think of self-statements that are more positive, optimistic, and adaptive. The statements should also be realistic. For example, if one's new car is stolen, it would be unrealistic to say to oneself, "I didn't need the car," because that is not likely to be true.

For each situation and negative self-statement, list on a separate sheet of paper two possible alternative self-statements that are positive and adaptive. Then compare your self-statements with the examples given in Appendix B.

Situation	*Negative Self-Statements*
1. Having to hand in a long, difficult assignment the next day	1. "No way will I ever get this work done for tomorrow."
2. Getting into an automobile accident	2. "Oh no, my father will kill me."
3. Being asked to a dance but not being a skillful dancer	3. "I can't go; I'll make a fool of myself."
4. Losing one's job	4. "I'll never get another job."
5. Moving to a new home away from family and friends	5. "Everything I have is left behind."
6. Having a roommate you don't get along with	6. "I'll never get along with her/him. What a horrible year this is going to be!"
7. Breaking up with the person you are in love with	7. "He/She was everything to me . . . my whole life. I have nothing else to live for anymore."
8. Not getting into graduate school	8. "I guess I'm just too dumb. I don't know what I'll do."
9. Having to participate in class discussions	9. "Everyone else knows more than I do so I'd better not say anything."
10. Reading latest issue of favorite magazine for two hours instead of completing assignments due the next day	10. "Oh, hell. I just blew a couple of hours. If I had only worked for those two hours . . . that really makes me mad. Why am I so dumb? I do this all the time."

OVERVIEW AND STATUS OF COGNITIVE BEHAVIORAL THERAPY

The advent of cognitive behavioral therapy over the past decade is a clear recognition by behavioral therapists of the central role that cognitive processes such as thoughts, beliefs, and attitudes play in human behavior. The 1968 suggestion made by a group of prominent behavioral therapists that "current [behavioral therapy] procedures should be modified and new procedures developed to capitalize upon the human organism's unique capacity for cognitive control"[44] has clearly been followed. This chapter has described representative examples of cognitive behavioral therapies. Thought stopping is a very specific technique with an important but limited application. Self-instruction is a more general therapeutic procedure that provides clients with a means of influencing cognitions, which in turn influence client behavior. Both rational-emotive therapy and cognitive therapy are broad approaches to dealing with clients' maladaptive cognitions.

These cognitive behavioral therapies differ somewhat in their emphases and specific therapeutic techniques, but they share several key common elements. First, cognitive behavioral therapies are all based on the recognition that clients' cognitive processes—operationalized as self-talk—often play a critical role in maintaining abnormal behaviors. Second, the self-talk that maintains abnormal behavior is assumed to involve interpretations of actual external events that are somehow distorted (exaggerated or out of context) and irrational (emotional and illogical reactions rather than accurate and logical deductions from and representations of the existing objective facts). Third, clients are taught to become aware of the maladaptive self-talk associated with their problems. Fourth, clients learn to examine, and challenge when appropriate, the validity and rationality of their views of external events and to substitute more adaptive, accurate, rational, and logical interpretations, thus changing the maintaining conditions of problem behaviors.

The Place of Cognitive Behavioral Therapy in Behavioral Therapy

Cognitive behavioral therapy has developed in the past 10 years and has not been around long enough to comment on its permanent place in the broader field of behavioral therapy. In fact, some behavioral therapists believe that cognitive processes in general and cognitive-related therapy techniques in particular have no place in behavioral therapy, which traditionally emphasizes overt behavior.[45] Despite the heated arguments over this issue that have been (and still are being) waged, cognitive behavioral therapy seems to be here to stay. However, at least for the present, it is probably most useful to consider cognitive behavioral therapies as a subset of behavioral therapies. This subset employs both cognitive *and* behavioral techniques to change clients' cognitions as the maintaining conditions of target behaviors (or, in a minority of cases, to change the target behaviors themselves, such as obsessive thoughts).

For most target behaviors, cognitive techniques alone are often not sufficient treatments; overt behavioral or performance-based techniques are required as well. (In contrast, behavioral therapy procedures can, as noted in previous chapters, stand on their own as effective treatments.) At the same time, in some instances a cognitive behavioral perspective is clearly indicated and may even be necessary for successful treatment. Consider the case of a woman, Mrs. H., who was extremely anxious about venturing outside her house.[46] Participant modeling had led to an initial improvement but then no further progress was made.

> Observation of her behavior during a behavioral assignment to approach a feared situation then revealed that Mrs. H. was sustaining her participation in activities she had previously avoided by telling herself that "it would soon be over," "a few more minutes and then I can retire to safety," and statements to that effect. In short, although she had shown some behavioral change she had not ceased representing the situation as dangerous, as a place she could (and should) soon withdraw from. Although her repeated exposure to the fear-producing situation satisfied the operations . . . of extinction, her subjective representation of these conditions seemed to negate the usual effects of [extinction]. Complementing these graded behavioral tasks with [self-instructional training] directed at modifying her view of the situation was associated with marked improvement.[47]

This example illustrates that, in some cases in which cognitions are maintaining conditions of a client's problem, successful treatment requires assessing and dealing with client's cognitions. The cognitive behavioral approach has made an important contribution to behavioral therapy by (1) alerting behavioral therapists to this possibility, (2) making them aware of the important role cognitive processes play in human behavior, and (3) providing therapy procedures for directly changing maladaptive cognitions.

Cognitive behavioral therapies teach clients to become aware of their self-talk and to make it more adaptive. In other words, clients learn to gain self-control over their cognitions, which in turn influence their overt behaviors. Because clients potentially have direct control over their cognitions (as long as they are aware of them) and because cognitions affect overt behavior, a major strategy for providing clients with self-control of their behavior is through cognitive behavioral therapy procedures, as shown in the next chapter.

SUMMARY

Cognitive behavioral therapies involve interventions based on behavioral principles and procedures that directly change clients' cognitions (e.g., thoughts, attitudes, and expectations). They are based on the notion that the way we view environmental events influences our behavior. Cognitions are operationally defined as self-talk (i.e., what we say to ourselves when we think). A fundamental procedure of cognitive behavioral therapies involves cognitive restructuring, in which clients modify their self-talk that is maintaining their problem behaviors. In thought stopping, clients interrupt disturbing thoughts and then substitute incompatible, pleasant thoughts. Rational-emotive therapy involves (1) identifying maladaptive self-statements (which are often irrational or illogical) a client makes about real external events, (2) challenging these self-statements (on logical and rational grounds), and (3) substituting rational and logical adaptive self-statements. Cognitive therapy is similar to rational-emotive therapy and has been used primarily to treat depressive behavior. Both rational-emotive therapy and cognitive therapy also use a variety of behavioral therapy procedures (e.g., modeling, behavior rehearsal, and overt behavioral homework assignments) in addition to cognitive restructuring. Self-instruction teaches clients to make adaptive self-statements when they encounter difficulties in their lives—essentially to instruct themselves to cope with the situations. It involves cognitive modeling and cognitive behavior rehearsal and has been used to treat impulsive behavior, schizophrenic talk, and creative thought deficits. Although cognitive behavioral therapies are relatively new, and somewhat controversial, their results so far have been encouraging.

REFERENCE NOTES

1. Meichenbaum, 1977.
2. Castaneda, 1972, pp. 218–219.
3. Sokolov, 1972, p. 1.
4. Meichenbaum, 1977, pp. 188–189.
5. Meichenbaum, 1977, p. 189, emphasis added.
6. Wolpe, 1958.
7. Tyron, 1979.
8. For example, Dengrove, 1972; Wolpe, 1973.
9. Ellis, 1962.
10. Ellis, 1970.
11. Ellis, 1970.
12. Garfield & Kurtz, 1976.
13. For example, Mahoney, 1974; Mahoney & Arnkoff, 1978.
14. Rachman & Wilson, 1980, p. 207.
15. For example, Goldfried & Sobocinski, 1975.
16. For example, Goldfried & Sobocinski, 1975.
17. Rachman & Wilson, 1980.
18. Goldfried & Davison, 1976.
19. Wilson & O'Leary, 1980.
20. See Beck, 1976; Goldfried, 1977.
21. Beck, 1963, 1976.
22. Beck, 1976.
23. Beck, 1976, p. 272.
24. Rush, Beck, Kovacs, & Hollon, 1977.
25. Shaw, 1977.
26. Meichenbaum & Goodman, 1971.
27. For example, Bash & Camp, 1975; Camp & Bash, 1981; Camp, Blom, Herbert, & VanDoorwick, 1976; Spivack & Shure, 1974.

28. For example, Labouvie-Vief & Gonda, 1976; Meichenbaum, 1974.
29. For example, Meichenbaum, Gilmore, & Fedoravicius, 1971.
30. For example, Meichenbaum, 1975.
31. For example, Meichenbaum, & Cameron, 1973; Meyers, Mercatoris, & Sirota, 1976.
32. Meichenbaum & Goodman, 1971.
33. Meichenbaum & Goodman, 1971, p. 117.
34. Meichenbaum, 1977, p. 32.
35. Meichenbaum, 1977.
36. Spivack & Shure, 1974.
37. Meichenbaum & Cameron, 1973.
38. Meichenbaum, 1977.
39. Meichenbaum & Cameron, 1973, p. 525.
40. Meichenbaum, 1975.
41. Meichenbaum, 1977, p. 62.
42. Rachman & Wilson, 1980, p. 217.
43. See Margolis & Shemberg, 1976.
44. Davison, D'Zurilla, Goldfried, Paul, & Valins, 1968.
45. See Ledwidge, 1978, 1979; Locke, 1979; Mahoney & Kazdin, 1979; Meichenbaum, 1979.
46. Wilson, 1978a.
47. Wilson, 1978a, p. 22.

CHAPTER 12 Self-Control Therapies: Clients as Their Own Change Agents

The term **self-control,** as used in this book, refers to the training of clients to initiate, conduct, and evaluate their own therapy.* All types of psychotherapy aim at eliminating the need for treatment, but the way in which this goal is achieved varies with different types of psychotherapy. Increasingly, behavioral therapies are incorporating general strategies and specific techniques for preparing clients to function, to varying degrees, as their own change agents.[1] To properly distinguish between professional behavioral therapists and clients (or people in clients' lives, such as parents, spouses, and teachers) who assume therapeutic roles, the term *therapist* is reserved here for professionals, and **change agent** for nonprofessionals. Clients in behavioral therapy (and many other psychotherapies) are always necessary partners in their treatment, because they provide the therapist with information and cooperate in the treatment procedures. However, self-control requires that the client become the *primary* agent of change, the person who is most directly responsible for administering therapeutic procedures and thus for the success of therapy.

Examples of self-control approaches and specific self-control procedures have already been given in previous chapters. For example, cognitive behavioral therapies, such as thought stopping and self-instruction, are self-control procedures because only clients have direct control over their thoughts. Furthermore, these therapies are designed to be used when the troublesome thoughts or difficult situations naturally occur in the clients' lives. When clients

*A more restricted definition of "self-control" concerns delay of gratification: forgoing an immediate reward in order to obtain a more attractive but delayed reward (e.g., missing a late television movie in order to be rested the next day). Such self-regulatory behavior is only one type of self-control. This chapter uses the broad definition of self-control, referring to any processes in which clients take primary responsibility for their therapy.

are given significant roles in the therapeutic process, as is common in behavioral therapy, then they can apply the procedures on their own either as an adjunct to the regular therapy sessions or when problems recur after therapy has terminated. Recall, for example, Case 5-4 in which a college student, treated for his sadistic sexual fantasies by orgasmic reconditioning and covert sensitization, was able to successfully reinstitute these therapy techniques on his own when his fantasies returned later.

To appreciate the nature of self-control behavioral therapies, consider two different models of systematic desensitization used today: a passive substitution model versus an active self-control model. Systematic desensitization was originally viewed as a passive substitution process for eliminating the anxiety associated with various situations or objects,[2] and that is how systematic desensitization was presented in Chapter 4. An alternative conceptualization of systematic desensitization, spearheaded by Marvin Goldfried, involves actively teaching the client a skill (usually deep muscle relaxation) that the client can use to reduce feelings of anxiety whenever they occur.[3] The differences between this active self-control model and the traditional passive substitution model can be seen in a comparison of the basic procedures used in the various phases of systematic desensitization, summarized in Table 12-1.

To begin with, there is a difference in the rationale clients are given regarding the purpose of the procedure used to reduce their anxiety. Using the substitution model, the therapist explains that relaxation (or another adaptive alternative response) is repeatedly paired with the anxiety-evoking situation so that eventually relaxation, rather than anxiety, is associated with the situation. In self-control desensitization, clients are informed that they will be learning a *coping skill* that they can use to reduce anxiety.

TABLE 12-1 Comparison of the Emphases in Passive Substitution and Active Self-Control Systematic Desensitization

PHASE	PASSIVE SUBSTITUTION MODEL	ACTIVE SELF-CONTROL MODEL
Rationale	Replace anxiety with relaxation.	Learn the skill of relaxation to cope with anxiety.
Relaxation training	Differentiate feelings of tension and relaxation.	Use tension as a cue to relax (as well as differentiate between tension and relaxation).
Hierarchy construction	Common theme exists in each hierarchy.	No common theme is necessary.
Dealing with tension during scene presentation	Stop visualizing scene, and relax.	Continue visualizing scene, and use tension as a cue to relax.
Practice outside therapy sessions	Practice deep muscle relaxation.	Use relaxation to reduce tension that occurs in life situations (as well as practice relaxation).

Relaxation training is basically the same for both techniques, except that in self-control desensitization clients are instructed to use their feelings of tension as cues to relax the affected muscles. Thus, clients gain self-control over relaxation in contrast to relaxation achieved by following the therapist's instructions.

Although anxiety hierarchies are constructed in both techniques, there is no need for a common theme in the self-control desensitization hierarchy. In the substitution model, the relaxation response becomes associated with particular anxiety-evoking scenes that make up the hierarchy. In the self-control model, relaxation becomes associated with muscular tension, not with any particular external situation. Thus, the scenes in the self-control anxiety hierarchy need only elicit progressively greater degrees of anxiety and do not have to be related to one another in content. For example, one scene might have to do with the client's fear of people in authority, and another with the client's aversion to having dental work done.

A critical distinction between the substitution and the self-control models occurs during the desensitization process itself. With the substitution model, the client must visualize hierarchy scenes only while relaxed, to associate relaxation (never muscular tension) with the previously anxiety-evoking scene. The substitution of relaxation for muscle tension takes place while visualizing scenes. Accordingly, clients are instructed to stop visualizing a scene as soon as they begin to experience muscular tension. In contrast, with the self-control model the purpose of imagining the scenes is to give the client an opportunity to *practice the skill of relaxation.* Thus, if the client signals the therapist that muscle tension is being experienced while visualizing a scene, the client is instructed to continue imagining the scene and to relax while doing so—in other words, to actively *cope* with the difficult scene rather than avoid it.

Finally, the practice that the clients do outside the therapy session is somewhat different in each model. In both approaches, clients must practice muscle relaxation. Clients treated by self-control desensitization are also asked to use their newly acquired skill of relaxation in their daily lives whenever they feel excessive muscular tension (which involves additional training in differential relaxation).

There appear to be several advantages to employing self-control desensitization rather than substitution desensitization. In the substitution model, treatment takes place during the therapy sessions, takes place in the client's imagination, and only applies to the target situations. Thus, the substitution treatment occurs in a setting different from that in which it is intended to be applicable, and it specifically deals with a narrow range of life situations. By comparison, in the self-control model at least part of the treatment occurs outside the therapy sessions, in the actual (rather than imagined) anxiety-evoking situations, and to any situation that causes anxiety. Furthermore, self-control desensitization involves direct training in a skill that is practiced in the settings in which it will be used and that is applicable to many different situations. The self-control model has been demonstrated to be at least as effective as the substitution model in reducing anxiety, and it appears that self-control procedures can generalize to situations other than the one specifically treated in therapy.[4]

Self-control techniques can be classified in terms of three major functions: assessment, changing antecedents, and changing consequences. This chapter first examines procedures dealing with each of these functions: self-monitoring, stimulus control, and self-reinforcement, respectively. Then it turns to a discussion of two broad self-control therapies that train clients to use a variety of self-coping skills to deal with stress (stress inoculation) and problems or conflicts (problem-solving therapy) in their lives.

SELF-MONITORING

Self-monitoring involves observing and recording one's own behavior, and sometimes the antecedent and consequent conditions associated with it. You have already had an opportunity to attempt this task in Participation Exercise 3-2. To teach clients how to self-monitor their behaviors, the therapist models self-monitoring, and the client then practices self-monitoring as the therapist observes and provides feedback. The accuracy of self-monitoring varies considerably, depending on the client's skill, the behavior being observed, the situation in which the observation is taking place, and the specific self-monitoring procedures used. For example, self-monitoring tends to increase the more discrete the target behavior and the simpler the method of recording is.[5] Self-monitoring often is the first step in developing a self-control treatment plan, and it is a continuous process throughout treatment so that progress, or lack of it, toward one's treatment goals can be assessed.

Recall that one potential problem of self-monitoring as an assessment procedure is that merely recording the behavior one wishes to change may inadvertently result in change, usually in the desired direction, before any treatment is begun (the problem of reactivity discussed in Chapter 3).[6] Reactivity is a problem if the therapist and client are interested in getting an accurate baseline (i.e., pretreatment level) of the target behavior so that changes due to therapy can be assessed. Such assessment is always desirable when the therapy has the dual function of helping the client and providing general information about the effectiveness of the therapy being employed. On the other hand, if the aim is only to modify the client's behavior, as often occurs in private practice, then reactivity is advantageous in that the self-monitoring may function as the treatment itself. The following example illustrates this.

A 26-year-old woman sought help to eliminate her nailbiting, a habit she had had for as long as she could recall. In order to assess the nature of the problem, the therapist asked the woman to record the number of times and the circumstances in which her nail biting occurred over the next two weeks. When the client returned two weeks later, she had no record to show, because after the first few days of recording she was no longer biting her nails at all. The therapist suggested that the woman resume recording her nail biting if the behavior recurred, and "therapy" was terminated. When the therapist happened to meet the woman two and a half years later, she reported that she had never gone back to her previously long-standing habit, and the therapist's casual glance at her stylishly long fingernails substantiated her self-report. In this case, self-monitoring was instituted for the purpose of assessment rather than treatment, but it was so successful in decelerating the client's unwanted habit that no treatment procedures were necessary.[7]

Self-monitoring is usually employed as an assessment technique. As a change procedure, self-monitoring often produces changes that are relatively small and short-lived.[8] Consequently, self-monitoring is generally employed as one of several components of a treatment package.[9] Case 12-1 is an exception[10] in which two self-monitoring procedures constituted the only treatment used to eliminate intrusive ruminative thoughts.

CASE 12-1

*Self-Monitoring as a Treatment for Ruminative Thoughts**

J. was a 25-year-old woman of superior intelligence who was married and had two children. She complained of upsetting ruminative thoughts that had been increasing in frequency and intensity over the previous six years. The thoughts concerned cancer of the breast or stomach, and each episode lasted about 15 minutes. J. had no other significant problems and generally functioned well.

During the first phase of therapy, J. was instructed simply to tally and then graph each episode of ruminative thinking. This procedure led to a rapid decline in the frequency of her ruminative episodes over the first week, which stabilized at about two episodes per day (compared to 13 per day initially), as can be seen in Case Figure 12-1A. Although this represented an impressive improvement, even two episodes per day were upsetting to J.

To further reduce the frequency of the episodes, a more intensive self-monitoring system was instituted. Besides continuing to count and graph the frequency of her ruminative thoughts, J. was also asked to record seven variables related to the episodes: date, time of day, antecedent thoughts, antecedent overt behaviors, content of each episode, consequent events, and a rating of the severity of the episode. This intensive self-monitoring further reduced the rate of ruminative thoughts (see Case Figure 12-1A): only five episodes occurred in the last 25 days of recording. At this point all self-monitoring was stopped except for 10 consecutive days of keeping a simple frequency count (the procedure used in the first phase of treatment) each month for six months of follow-up. The rate of ruminative thoughts continued to decline, and no episodes were reported during the last four months of follow-up (see Case Figure 12-1A).

*Frederiksen (1975).

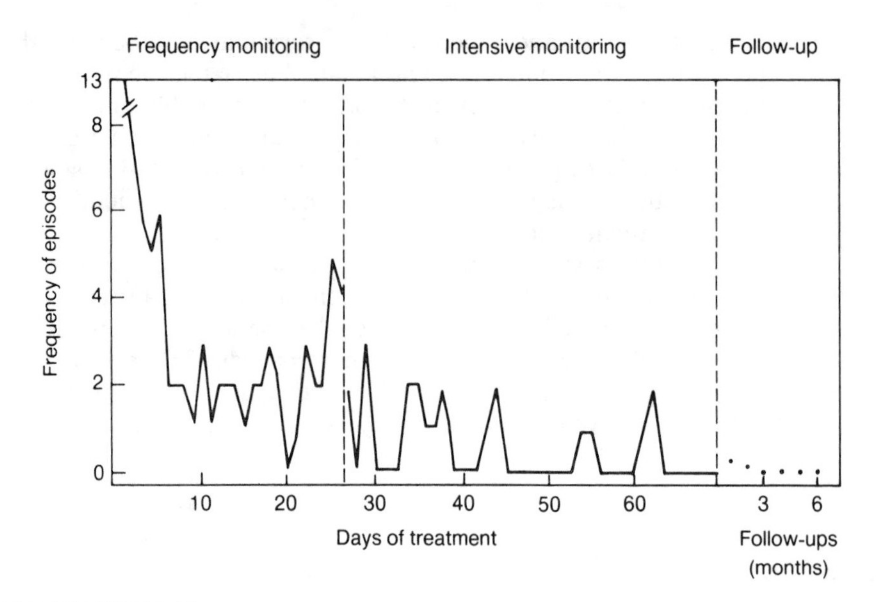

CASE FIGURE 12-1A

The frequency of ruminative thought episodes during two forms of self-monitoring treatment and monthly follow-up assessments SOURCE: *Adapted from Frederiksen (1975), p. 258.*

There are at least two reasons why self-monitoring may alter the behavior being recorded.[11] First, in the case of deceleration target behaviors, the individual may find it annoying and bothersome to record each instance of a target behavior, and thus self-monitoring may function as an aversive consequence. This effect seems to have occurred in Case 12-1, because the intensive monitoring procedure was more effective than merely recording the frequency of upsetting thoughts. Second, when acceleration target behaviors are being self-monitored, the record may serve as positive feedback (a reinforcer).

STIMULUS CONTROL

Many everyday behaviors are maintained by stimuli or cues that indicate to us that such behaviors are appropriate (see Chapter 2). For instance, seeing another person smoking or drinking a cup of coffee (two events frequently associated with cigarette smoking) may prompt a smoker to light up. It is possible to change problem behaviors that are maintained by environmental stimuli by altering the stimuli that elicit them. This form of self-control is called **stimulus control.**

Overeating

Eating is frequently influenced by environmental cues such as being in the kitchen or near a food-dispensing machine, by noting that it is mealtime (e.g.,

12 to 1 P.M. is the typical lunch hour), and by having food in front of you (e.g., having a plate of chocolate cookies on the table at which you are working). Self-control of the environmental cues that elicit eating behaviors is one of the most successful means of treating obesity.[12] To decelerate overeating (the behavior most frequently responsible for obesity), the range and frequency of the eliciting cues are progressively restricted by asking clients to follow rules such as the following:[13]

1. Eat in one place (e.g., the kitchen) and only at specified times (no between-meal snacks).
2. Separate eating from other activities (e.g., reading the newspaper or watching television).
3. Reduce the availability of high-calorie foods (e.g., do not buy them).
4. Reduce the accessibility of all foods, as by shopping on a day-to-day basis (and only after a meal), buying foods that require preparation, and storing food in places that are not easily accessible (e.g., on the top shelf in the pantry rather than on the kitchen counter).
5. Prepare and/or serve individual portions (e.g., put a slice of bread on the plate rather than half a loaf on the table).
6. Eat slowly, putting utensils down between bites and taking another bite only after the previous one has been swallowed, and taking planned, periodic breaks from eating during a meal (e.g., pushing the plate aside for five minutes).

These self-control procedures are effective in reducing the amount of food eaten (the deceleration target behavior) and in producing weight losses (the treatment goal). The classic program in which stimulus control procedures constituted the major treatment component was designed by Richard Stuart.[14] As is typical in behavioral therapy programs for weight control, the treatment package also included self-monitoring and self-reinforcement as well as reinforcement from others (e.g., therapist or spouse). Covert sensitization was also used with two of the clients. Eight overweight women (ages 21 to 43) attended 30-minute therapy sessions, three times per week for four to five weeks, during which they were taught the self-control techniques. They were also given additional "maintenance" sessions as needed. The results at the end of the year were impressive: each of the women had lost between 26 and 47 pounds. In addition, seven clients reported that the range of their social activities had increased, and three of the five married clients indicated more satisfying relations with their husbands. It is particularly noteworthy that three clients who were heavy smokers reported that they had adapted the self-control procedures they had learned in therapy to their smoking and had either substantially reduced or completely eliminated smoking. The success obtained by this program fostered a host of other programs involving stimulus control strategies for the treatment of overeating. Although subsequent behavioral therapy treatment programs that involve stimulus control procedures have consistently resulted in clients' losing weight, the weight losses have typically been less than those obtained in Stuart's initial program and have averaged 11 to 12 pounds, maintained for a year.[15]

Long-term maintenance (e.g., over a period of years) of weight loss probably requires major lifestyle changes (e.g., learning to undereat to compensate for inevitable overeating and generally avoiding high-calorie foods, such as those high in fats). Such changes are not possible in programs that last no more than several months, which is generally the maximum length of most behavioral therapy treatments for obesity.[16]

Insomnia

Insomnia, or chronic difficulty in sleeping, is a common problem; it is estimated that between 25 and 30 million people in the United States alone suffer from insomnia in one form or another.[17] Sleeping medication—the most common treatment—has a variety of drawbacks, including disruption of normal sleep patterns, dependence on drugs for sleeping, and the body's developing an increased tolerance to the medication so that larger and larger doses are required to achieve an effect. Behavioral therapies have provided alternative forms of treatment, and one or a combination of three behavioral therapies are typically employed: systematic desensitization, deep muscle relaxation (sometimes aided by biofeedback), and stimulus control. The stimulus control procedures are similar to those used to treat overeating. Their basic aim is to establish a client's bed as a clear-cut cue for sleep and only sleep (an exception being made for more arousing activities also typically associated with beds). Clients are instructed to follow several rules:[18]

1. Lie down [in bed] intending to go to sleep *only* when you are sleepy.
2. Don't use your bed for anything except sleep. [For example, do not read, watch television, or eat in bed.] Sexual activity is the only exception to this rule—unless it leaves you agitated and awake rather than pleasantly contented and tired [in which case sex should be engaged in somewhere else].
3. If you find yourself unable to fall asleep, get up and go into another room. Stay up as long as you wish and then return to the bedroom to sleep. . . . If you are in bed more than about 10 minutes without falling asleep and have not gotten up, you are not following this instruction.
4. If you still cannot fall asleep, repeat Step 3.
5. Get up at the same time every morning. [This routine allows your body to establish a regular sleep rhythm, and should be followed regardless of what time you go to sleep. Establishing a regular time to go to sleep is also helpful.]

6. Do not nap. [Napping can disrupt the regular sleep rhythm and make it harder to fall asleep at night.]

SELF-REINFORCEMENT

Self-administered reinforcers can be of any kind, including access to pleasant activities and desired commodities. Self-reinforcement of adaptive behaviors has some advantages over external reinforcement (i.e., reinforcement from others). The likelihood of reinforcement occurring may increase because the client is always available to administer the reinforcer. Moreover, when the target behavior is covert, usually only the client is aware that a reinforcer has been earned. Self-praise (e.g., thinking, "I sure did that well!") is an especially useful reinforcer because it can be easily administered immediately after the target behavior occurs.

Self-reinforcement as a self-control procedure has potential problems, however. For example, clients must be taught to discriminate the appropriate times for reinforcement and to reinforce themselves only when appropriate. If a person's target behavior is to complete all the morning's work before going to lunch (the reinforcer), leaving for a restaurant after only half the work is finished will not reinforce completing it (in fact, it is likely to reinforce *partially* completing work).

Another potential problem is that it may be difficult to get a client to administer self-reinforcers. This problem may seem a bit peculiar. After all, the client is not being asked to self-administer aversive consequences,* and we all enjoy patting ourselves on the back, treating ourselves, and so forth—don't we?

Unfortunately the answer is no. Clients often have difficulty setting realistic goals and then feeling good about meeting them. This problem is prominent in depressive behavior and is illustrated in Case 12-2, which also describes the general procedures of self-reinforcement as applied to self-control behavioral therapy. Depressive behaviors are often associated with a substantial reduction in the frequency and amount of reinforcers a person is receiving.[19] Consequently, self-reinforcement is one of the behavioral therapies used to treat depressive behavior.

While reading Case 12-2, try to answer these three questions: (1) What are the probable maintaining conditions of the client's depressive behavior? (2) How does the self-reinforcement therapy alter these maintaining conditions? and (3) What would be the similarities and differences between the self-reinforcement therapy as used in this case and a cognitive restructuring approach such as cognitive therapy or rational-emotive therapy? These questions are discussed after the case is presented.

*The self-administration of aversive consequences can also be used as a self-control procedure. However, it is not used nearly as frequently as self-reinforcement because it has all the drawbacks associated with the external administration of aversive consequences discussed in Chapter 7, as well as the problem that clients may understandably be reluctant to expose themselves to painful or distasteful events.

CASE 12-2
Treatment of Depression by Self-Reinforcement*

[L.M. was a 22-year-old married woman who, over the previous two years, had seen several therapists because of her feelings of depression and worthlessness, general inactivity, and frequent self-denigrating statements. The prior therapeutic attempts were aimed at giving L.M. insight into why she was depressed and at getting her involved in activities. Although she received some relief from these procedures, her depressive behaviors always returned.]

Raised as an only child, she [had received] countless lectures and negative comparisons by her mother with other children her age, the predominant theme being her deficient love and respect toward her mother. She perceived her father as being somewhat benign but he would not defend her from her mother's tirades. Her academic achievement was consistently above average. . . . According to her husband's accounts, she was a meticulous housekeeper and an excellent cook but nevertheless had an alacrity to criticize her [own] performance around the house. When asked to evaluate her achievement, "objectively" she realized that she did a number of things comparable to or better than her peers.

It was patent that L.M. was extremely harsh with herself to the point of restricting herself from pleasurable experiences. Her activities were carried out in a quasimechanical manner with an apparent unfavorable distortion [of] feedback in terms of considerable sensitivity only to unacceptable performances. [Recall Beck's analysis of the cognitive distortions of depressed clients discussed in Chapter 11.] When questioned about rewarding experiences she gave herself, she was quick to reply that this definitely contradicted her upbringing; thus, self-managed consequences were predominately aversive. . . .

It was decided to select a task that she performed frequently and considered important and to elaborate a self-reinforcement pattern for it. While reviewing her activities, she enumerated relating to people, housekeeping, reading, talking to her husband, watching television and drawing. When asked to assess them in terms of frequency and their importance to her she chose housekeeping as the first behavior to monitor and she was given three records to keep daily, assessing them at about the same time each evening (between 9–10 P.M.). She was instructed to record the total amount of time per day spent on washing and drying dishes, and dusting. Second, she was asked to rate her depression according to her own criteria on a 10-point scale, 10 being very depressed. She was to record the number of rewards she gave herself throughout the day for housekeeping. A reward was defined as "praising yourself, doing something you like, or feeling contented as a consequence for doing housework." . . .

During the second interview the role of positive self-reinforcement was explained in detail to her, especially in maintaining behaviors for which positive social reinforcement is available only intermittently. She was asked to take each chore *separately* and define what she wanted to accomplish in terms of the task and the amount of time estimated to complete it. . . .

At first it was necessary for the therapist to lower the goals that L.M. had set for herself thus increasing the probability of her attaining success. To provide later reference, each goal was written down specifying the performance before starting the task. When she had completed the task, she was told to assess what she had done in light of what she had

*Reprinted from Jackson (1972), pp. 302–304.

set out to do. If she judged that she had matched or surpassed her goals she was told to do something positive or pleasant immediately, such as compliment herself, have a cigarette or telephone an interesting friend. To concretize these operations at first, she was given a box of poker chips and told to take as many as she thought she deserved up to 10 and then record the number she took. The inclusion of the chips was to promote her dispensing consequences [for] her performance. During the interview the process was modeled by the therapist and then rehearsed by L.M. until she had it mastered.

Beginning the eleventh day, she was instructed to reinforce herself positively contingent upon her evaluation of her activity and was asked to continue monitoring her behaviors. [Case Figure 12-2A] indicates an increase in positive self-reinforcement and a corresponding decline in the self-rated depression. . . . Additionally, she spent less time doing housework, which she attributed to increased efficiency plus a more easygoing attitude toward it. One early outcome was a generalization of gains to other areas such as socializing. Independently she applied the procedure to behaviors associated with the role of hostess, deciding what behaviors she wanted to manifest, evaluating her performance, and then rewarding herself. This innovation received strong approval from the therapist. Interviews were held on the fifteenth and twenty-first days, at which time her progress was

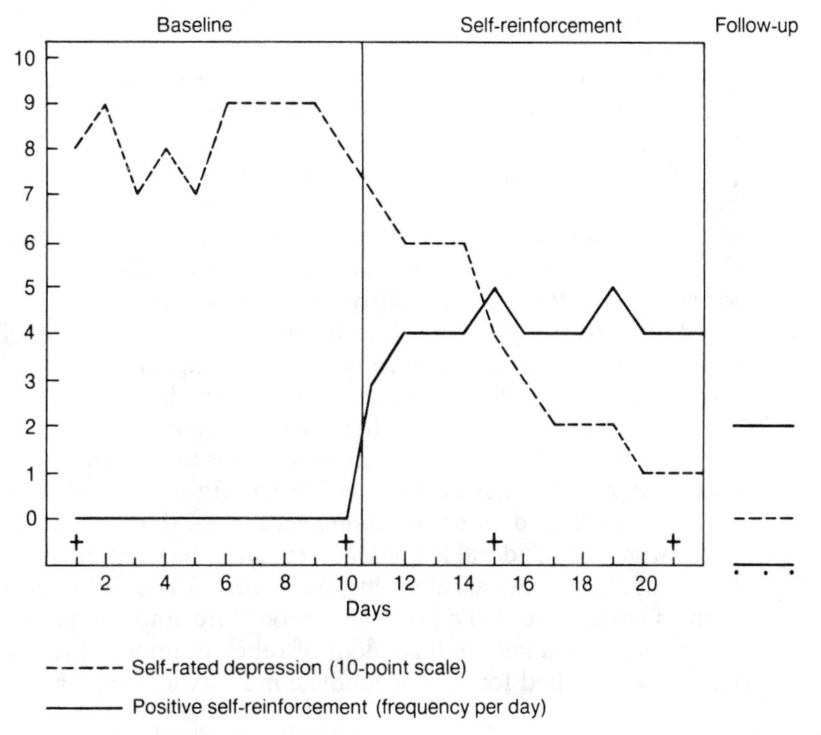

CASE FIGURE 12-2A

Daily records of self-rated depression and frequency of positive reinforcement

SOURCE: Adapted from Jackson (1972), p. 304.

reviewed and new tasks were assigned. During the fourth interview, Day 21, L.M. reported that her depression had subsided and she ceased the observing and recording but continued the self-reinforcement program. Approximately two months later, she was asked to resume [for several days] the monitoring of frequency of positive self-reinforcement [and] depression. . . . The results are shown in [Case Figure 12-2A]. The positive self-reinforcement now took the form of content or satisfaction in contrast to the initial feeling of "it still isn't good enough."

Even from the brief information provided in Case 12-2, it is not difficult to identify the probable maintaining conditions of L.M.'s depressive behavior: a negative and distorted view of her own capabilities.* Such a self-concept would account for L.M.'s employing unrealistically high standards for evaluating her own behavior. For instance, L.M. was critical of her domestic activities although her husband considered her an excellent homemaker (a good example of what Beck calls an arbitrary inference—see Table 11-2). The goal of the self-reinforcement therapy was to change L.M.'s negative self-concept (the probable maintaining conditions of her depressive behavior) by having her reward herself for performing tasks well, according to "objective" standards—that is, standards not distorted by her unduly critical self-evaluations. Note that the goal of self-reinforcement therapy in this particular case is the same as the goal of cognitive restructuring—namely, to get the client to view her behavior realistically. However, the ways in which the two different therapeutic approaches would achieve such a goal differ. Cognitive restructuring involves monitoring self-statements and substituting realistic statements for unrealistic ones. This purely cognitive therapy approach is aimed at directly modifying the client's covert behavior—that is, self-statements evaluating her own behavior (i.e., her self-concept). Self-reinforcement, on the other hand, involves rewarding objectively worthwhile behaviors; the client's beliefs about herself were indirectly modified by directly changing her overt behavior. In other words, appropriately rewarding herself for things she did well indirectly changed L.M.'s evaluations of her own behavior.

Although self-reinforcement procedures appear to be effective, as demonstrated in case studies dealing with a variety of target behaviors,[20] there are few well-controlled outcome studies on self-reinforcement with actual clinical populations. (Considerable analogue research has demonstrated the potency of self-reinforcement in accelerating behaviors.[21]) Thus, at present, self-reinforcement is best considered a promising procedure, and definitive statements about its efficacy (especially independent of other treatment factors, which are typically uncontrolled for in case studies) must await further investigations.

*The probable *origin* of L.M.'s view of herself is also obvious: as a child, L.M.'s mother repeatedly evaluated L.M.'s behavior negatively, especially in comparison to her peers. (Ellis hypothesizes that many of our irrational and illogical thoughts arise from repeated indoctrinations, beginning in childhood, about how we *should* behave or the way things *ought to be* in the world.)

STRESS INOCULATION

Stress inoculation prepares clients to deal with stressful situations by teaching them self-control coping skills and then by having them rehearse these skills while being exposed to a variety of stressors.[22] This approach is a behavioral analogue of biological immunization—the process by which a person's defenses against a microorganism are enhanced by exposing the individual to low doses of the microorganism. The therapy is divided into three phases.

The first phase of stress inoculation involves *cognitive preparation.* Clients are provided with an adaptive way to view and understand their negative reactions, such as fear or anger. Basically, the rationale offered clients is similar to that used in cognitive behavioral therapies—namely, negative emotions associated with a stressful situation are influenced by the way the people view the situation and the courses of action they take in relation to it, not by the situation per se. Accordingly, clients are told that they can learn coping skills that will allow them to reconceptualize and deal with such situations without becoming emotionally upset. To counter possible feelings of being overwhelmed by the task, the client is encouraged to view the task as a five-stage process:

1. *Preparing* for the stressful situation
2. *Confronting and coping* with the situation
3. *Dealing with temporary difficulties* in coping
4. *Assessing* one's performance in handling the situation
5. *Reinforcing oneself* for adaptive behaviors

In the second phase of stress inoculation training, the client learns various *coping skills.* Cognitive restructuring is the major coping skill employed in stress inoculation. Clients are taught to monitor their negative, maladaptive thoughts when faced with stressful situations and to replace them with incompatible coping self-statements at each of the five stages. Examples of possible coping self-statements applicable to different target behaviors are listed in Table 12-2.

The other specific coping skills taught depend, in part, on the target behavior being treated. For example, in the case of fear, the client might gather information about the feared situation or object, develop skills that would make the feared situation less threatening (e.g., learning to initiate and maintain conversations, in the case of interpersonal anxieties), and learn deep muscle relaxation to alleviate tension. As a self-control coping skill, differential deep muscle relaxation is useful in many situations—in fact, whenever a person feels unnecessary muscle tension that is uncomfortable and interferes with performing the task at hand (compare with self-control systematic desensitization). For instance, it is not uncommon for the muscles of the forehead and around the eyes to tense up when we are deep in thought or concentrating intently on some mental activity. A furrowed brow does not enhance performance and is likely to create fatigue, eyestrain, and a headache. Clients are

TABLE 12-2 *Examples of Coping Self-Statements Used in Stress Inoculation for Fear or Anxiety, Anger, and Pain*

STAGE OF COPING	FEAR OR ANXIETY	ANGER	PAIN
1. Preparing	What do I have to do? I can develop a plan to deal with it. Just think about what I can do about it. That is better than getting anxious. Maybe what I think is anxiety is eagerness to confront the situation.	What do I have to do? This is going to upset me, but I know how to deal with it. I can manage the situation. I know how to regulate my anger. Easy does it. Remember to keep your sense of humor.	What is it I have to do? Just think about what I can do about it. Don't worry: worrying won't help anything. I have lots of different strategies I can call on.
2. Confronting and Coping	One step at a time: I can handle the situation. Don't think about fear, just think about what I have to do. Stay relevant. This anxiety is what the doctor said I would feel. It's a reminder to use my coping exercise. Relax; I'm in control. Take a slow deep breath. Ah, good.	Think of what you want to get out of this. There is no point in getting mad. I'm not going to let him (or her) get to me. Look for the positives. Don't assume the worst or jump to conclusions.	I can meet the challenge. Don't think about the pain, just what I have to do. This tenseness can be an ally, a cue to cope. Just relax, breathe deeply and use one of the coping strategies.
3. Dealing with Temporary Difficulties	When fear comes, just pause. Keep the focus on the present; what do I have to do? I should expect my fear to rise. Don't try to eliminate fear totally; just keep it manageable.	My muscles are starting to feel tight. Time to relax and slow things down. I have a right to be annoyed, but let's keep the lid on. My anger is a signal of what I need to do. Time to instruct myself. Try to reason it out. Treat each other with respect.	When pain comes, just pause; keep focusing on what I have to do. Just remember, there are different strategies; they'll help me stay in control. When the pain mounts I can switch to a different strategy; I'm in control. Don't try to eliminate the pain totally; just keep it manageable.

STAGE OF COPING	FEAR OR ANXIETY	ANGER	PAIN
4. and 5. Assessing and Self-Reinforcement	*Partially Successful Coping* I didn't handle that as well as I could, but I'll get better. That's better than before. I used coping skills, so I'm making some progress. Don't give up; I'll do better the next time.	*Partially Successful Coping* These are difficult situations, and they take time to straighten out. I'll get better at this as I get more practice. Can I laugh about this? It's probably not so serious.	*Partially Successful Coping* I didn't cope with pain as well as I could, but I'll get better. That's better than before. I used coping skills, so I'm making some progress. Don't give up; I'll do better the next time.
	Successful Coping It worked, I did it. I made more out of my fear than it was worth. Wait until I tell my therapist about this.	*Successful Coping* I handled that one pretty well. It worked. I actually got through that without getting angry. That wasn't as hard as I thought.	*Successful Coping* Good, I did it. I knew I could do it. Wait until I tell my therapist about which procedures worked best.

SOURCE: Adapted from (Fear or Anxiety column) Meichenbaum (1974), (Anger) Novaco (1975), and (Pain) Turk (1975).

frequently taught deep muscle relaxation by listening to audiotapes or records on their own at home, and it is even possible to learn this useful coping skill by following written instructions. If you are interested in learning, Participation Exercise 12-1, which is at the end of this section, provides instructions.

When clients have mastered a number of coping skills, they are ready to practice applying them in the third and final phase of stress inoculation training. Clients are *exposed to stressful situations* and use their newly acquired coping skills to handle them. The stress-inducing circumstances might be receiving unpredictable electric shock, submerging one's arm in near-freezing water, imagining a stressful situation, or seeing a stressful film (e.g., of a bloody surgical operation). As an example, the following instructions were given to clients who were about to be exposed to a series of 10 electric shocks.

> Sometime in the next two or three minutes, maybe in a few seconds, maybe after three minutes, maybe somewhere in between, you will receive a shock. Just exactly how intense and exactly when you receive the shock depends on a random predetermined schedule. Try to cope with the anxiety and tenseness elicited by the situation by means of the coping techniques you have learned.[23]

Although such contrived stress-inducing procedures are not encountered in real life, they do allow the client to rehearse the coping skills learned in the safe environment of the therapy session before using them to deal with common stress-evoking situations. Furthermore, stress inoculation teaches the client *general* coping skills applicable in a wide range of stressful situations. The stress-evoking situations used during behavior rehearsal need not be the same as the ones clients will encounter in their natural environment (again, compare with the self-control model of systematic desensitization).

Stress inoculation was originally developed to treat fear or anxiety,[24] and the procedures have been expanded to deal with controlling maladaptive anger[25] and tolerating physical pain.[26] The major differences in stress inoculation training for anxiety, anger, and pain occur in the second phase, where coping skills are customized to the target behavior. As Table 12-2 shows, some coping self-statements are general enough to be used with almost any stressful situation. To control anger, clients are taught to view potential provocations as problems that require solution rather than as threats that require attack, and clients rehearse alternative strategies for solving the problem at hand. One coping skill clients are taught for tolerating pain is refocusing their attention, such as imagining scenes unrelated to the pain-producing experience and the physical sensations of pain.[27]

Stress inoculation is a relatively new self-control behavioral therapy, and preliminary research so far indicates that it can be an effective treatment procedure. This is encouraging, because interventions to help people deal with the ever-increasing stresses in our complex society are certainly needed.

Participation Exercise 12-1 follows; as noted earlier, it provides a guide to learning differential deep muscle relaxation.

PARTICIPATION EXERCISE 12-1

*Learning Differential Deep Muscle Relaxation and Using It as a Self-Control Procedure**

Differential deep muscle relaxation as a self-control behavioral therapy technique can be used in a wide variety of situations in which a person experiences muscle tension.† Recall that differential deep muscle relaxation involves totally relaxing those skeletal muscles that are not directly in use at a given time. It is also possible to ***partially*** relax those muscles that are essential to one's ongoing motoric activities by contracting the essential muscles just enough to perform the required function, without any excess tension.

In this participation exercise, you will be given instructions for teaching yourself deep muscle relaxation. With sufficient practice, you should be able to relax any tense muscle in your body within a few seconds. The application of this skill as a self-control procedure merely involves using tension in your muscles as a cue to begin relaxing those muscles. Obviously, if you are to use muscle tension as a cue to relax, you need to become aware of

*Writing of this participation exercise was facilitated by Bernstein and Borkovec's *Progressive Relaxation Training* (1973).

†Sherman (1975).

what tension in your muscles feels like, especially at moderate-to-low levels of tension. By alternately tensing and relaxing various muscle groups in the first phase of deep muscle relaxation training, you can become more finely tuned to recognizing tension in your muscles.

PREPARATION

First, read over the list of muscle groups and tensing instructions in Exercise Table 12-1A several times, so that you become familiar with the order in which the muscle groups will be relaxed and the specific means of tensing each individual muscle group. This preparation will allow you to practice tensing and relaxing with a minimum of disruption.

You will practice relaxation by lying on a relatively hard surface such as your bed (if it is firm) or a rug. You can also practice sitting in a comfortable, overstuffed chair (such as a recliner), but the instructions for tensing your muscles may have to be adapted slightly. No changes are necessary for practicing relaxation only in Phase 2.

The practice location should be relatively free of distraction, such as from noise or interruption. You may want to take the phone. You can also practice sitting in a comfortable, overstuffed chair (such as a recliner), but the instructions for tensing your muscles may have to be adapted slightly. No changes are necessary for practicing relaxation only (in Phase 2).

The practice location should be relatively free of distraction, such as from noise or interruption. You may want to take the phone off the hook and place a "Do not disturb" sign on your door during practice. It is not critical if your practice is interrupted, however; if this should happen, just resume where you left off.

Before you begin practicing, make yourself comfortable by loosening any tight clothing, taking off your shoes, and removing any articles of clothing or jewelry that might interfere with the exercises described in Exercise Table 12-1A.

LEARNING DEEP MUSCLE RELAXATION

You will learn deep muscle relaxation in two phases. In the first you will tense each muscle group before relaxing it, and in the second you will only relax each muscle group.

Phase 1: Tensing and Relaxing Muscles

After you have done the preparation just described, lie flat on your back with your legs slightly parted and your arms at your sides. Get comfortable (which may require wriggling around a bit until you are in a comfortable position). Take a few deep breaths and close your eyes lightly (to remove visual distractions).

Begin with the first of the 16 muscle groups (A1; see Exercise Table 12-1A, Part A). ***Tense those muscles for about five seconds*** (you may wish to count to yourself, "one-thousand-one, two-thousand-two," and so on). You should tense the muscles tightly, but do ***not*** strain your muscles; you should be very much aware of the tension but it should not hurt. As you tense the muscles, concentrate on the sensations you feel.

After about five seconds of tension, say the word ***relax*** to yourself and ***gradually*** relax the muscles you have just tensed. Make your muscles loose, smoothing them out. Continue relaxing your muscles for about 30 seconds or until they feel totally relaxed. As you relax, carefully focus on the sensations of relaxation and ***note the difference between tension and relaxation.***

Now repeat the tension-relaxation sequence for the same muscle group (A1).

EXERCISE TABLE 12-1A

Muscle Groups and Tensing Instructions for Learning Deep Muscle Relaxation

A: 16 MUSCLE GROUPS	
Muscle Group	*Tensing Instructions*
A1. Dominant hand and forearm (right hand if you're righthanded)	A1. Make a tight fist.
A2. Dominant biceps	A2. Push your elbow down against the floor (or bed), and simultaneously pull the elbow inward toward your body.
A3. Nondominant hand and forearm	A3. Do A1.
A4. Nondominant biceps	A4. Do A2.
A5. Upper part of face (forehead and scalp)	A5. Lift your eyebrows as high as you can. (Alternate: Make an exaggerated frown.)[a]
A6. Central part of face (upper cheeks and nose)	A6. Squint your eyes tightly, and simultaneously wrinkle up your nose.
A7. Lower part of face (jaw and lower part of cheeks)	A7. Bite your teeth together, and pull the corners of your mouth back. ***Caution:*** Do not clench your teeth very hard. Do this just enough to feel tension in your jaw and cheeks.
A8. Neck and throat	A8. Pull your chin down toward your chest, and simultaneously try to keep your chin from touching your chest. (You should feel a small amount of trembling or shaking in your neck.) (Alternate: Press your head against the floor [or bed].)[a]
A9. Chest, shoulders, and upper back	A9. Take a deep breath and hold it; at the same time pull your shoulders back as if you were trying to make your shoulderblades touch. (Alternate: Pull your shoulders upward as if you were trying to touch your shoulderblades to your ears. It may help to imagine that puppet strings are attached to your shoulders and are being pulled upward.)[a]
A10. Abdomen	A10. Make your stomach hard, as if you were bracing before being hit in the stomach. (Alternates: Pull your stomach in as far as it will go. Or, push your stomach out as far as it will go.)[a]
A11. Dominant thigh (upper leg)	A11. Keeping your leg straight, lift it a few inches off the floor.
A12. Dominant calf (lower leg)	A12. Pull your toes upward toward your head (without moving your legs).
A13. Dominant foot	A13. Point your toes, turn your foot inward, and curl your toes downward (as if you were burying them in the sand). ***Caution:*** Do not tense these muscles very hard or very long—just enough to feel the tightness under your arch and the ball of your foot for about 3–5 seconds. (You may also feel some tension in your calf.)
A14. Nondominant thigh	A14. Do A11.
A15. Nondominant calf	A15. Do A12.
A16. Nondominant foot	A16. Do A13.

B: SEVEN MUSCLE GROUPS	
Muscle Group	*Tensing Instructions*
B1. Dominant hand, forearm, and biceps	B1. Hold your arm out in front of you with your elbow bent at about 45 degrees while making a fist. (Alternate: Leave your arm supported on the floor [or bed]. Bend your arm at the elbow [about 45 degrees], make a fist, and press your elbow down and/or in toward your body.)[a]
B2. Nondominant hand, forearm, and biceps	B2. Do B1.
B3. Face	B3. At the same time, raise your eyebrows (or frown), squint your eyes, wrinkle up your nose, bite down, and pull the corners of your mouth back.[b]
B4. Neck and throat	B4. Do A8.
B5. Chest, shoulders, upper back, and abdomen	B5. Take a deep breath and hold it, pull your shoulderblades back and together, and make your stomach hard (or pull it in or push it out).
B6. Dominant thigh, calf, and foot	B6. Lift your leg up off the floor (or bed) a few inches, point your toes, and turn your foot inward.
B7. Nondominant thigh, calf, and foot	B7. Do B6.

C: FOUR MUSCLE GROUPS	
Muscle Group	*Tensing Instructions*
C1. Both hands, forearms, and biceps	C1. Do both B1 and B2 at the same time.
C2. Face and neck	C2. Do both B3 and B4 at the same time.
C3. Chest, shoulders, back, and abdomen	C3. Do B5.
C4. Both thighs, calves, and feet	C4. Do both B6 and B7 at the same time.

[a]Use the alternate tensing strategy only when the first one presented does not create tension in the appropriate muscle group.

[b]This procedure may be a bit difficult at first, but a few practice sessions will make simultaneous tensing of all the facial muscles relatively easy.

After you have tensed and relaxed the first muscle group (A1), proceed to the next muscle group (A2) and do the tension-relaxation sequence twice. Continue until you have gone through all of the 16 muscle groups (i.e., A1–A16). (This should take 35–45 minutes at first, and less as you become familiar with the procedures and become more proficient at relaxing your muscles quickly.) When you have tensed and relaxed each of the muscle groups (A1–A16) twice, remain in a relaxed state for several minutes. During this period, if you feel tension in any of your muscles, try to relax that tension away, by making your muscles loose and smooth.

To end your practice session, slowly count backward from 4 to 1, following these instructions for each number:

At "4" begin to move your legs and feet.

At "3" move your arms and hands.

At "2" move your head and neck.

At "1" open your eyes.

When you reach "1," you should feel relaxed and calm, as if you had just awakened from a nap. Sit up slowly, and then, after a moment or two, stand up.

Two points of caution. During your practice, ***concentrate on the sensations of tension and relaxation*** and do not let your mind wander to other thoughts. ***Do not fall asleep*** while practicing (which can happen if you are tired or if you become deeply relaxed). (You may, however, wish to practice relaxing shortly before retiring in order to help you fall asleep faster.)

You should devote at least three practice sessions to tensing and relaxing each of the 16 muscle groups (A1–A16) and more if you are still feeling tension in any of your muscles. Next follow the same instructions just described for the 7 muscle groups (i.e., B1–B7; see Exercise Table 12-1A, Part B) and do this for at least two sessions. Finally spend at least two sessions tensing and relaxing each of the 4 muscle groups (i.e., C1–C4; see Exercise Table 12-1A, Part C). Then proceed to Phase 2.

Phase 2: Relaxation Only

After making the necessary preparations for practice, begin with the first muscle group listed in Exercise Table 12-1A, Part A (16 muscle groups), and relax those muscles as deeply as possible. Recall the feelings you had when you released the tension in those muscles in Phase 1, and let your muscles get looser and looser, more and more comfortably relaxed. Even when you think that your muscles are completely relaxed, it is always possible to relax them a bit more. Go through each of the 16 muscle groups (A1–A16), relaxing them for at least 60 seconds or until they are completely relaxed. When you have relaxed all of these 16 muscle groups, follow the same procedure as in Phase 1 for concluding the practice session—that is, remain totally relaxed for a few moments and then count backward from 4 to 1 while slowly getting up. Remember, in Phase 2 you are ***only relaxing*** your muscles (do ***not*** first tense them).

Spend a minimum of two sessions relaxing each of the 16 muscle groups, then at least two sessions relaxing each of the 7 muscle groups, and finally at least two sessions relaxing each of the 4 muscle groups. Learning deep muscle relaxation takes time, so don't be impatient. Also, most people find that a few muscle groups are more difficult to relax than the others, and you will need to spend more time practicing relaxing your "troublesome" muscles.

PRACTICING DIFFERENTIAL RELAXATION

When you have completed the two phases of learning deep muscle relaxation, you are ready to practice relaxing your muscles whenever you feel unnecessary tension. You should do this during your daily activities, such as while driving your car, eating a meal, standing in line, or sitting in class. When you become aware of any unneeded tension, use that tension as a signal to relax. You may find it helpful to say the word ***relax*** (an example of a self-instruction) at the first sign of muscle tension and then proceed to relax the muscles that are beginning to tense. As you practice recognizing signs of muscle tension and relaxing away the tension, you will probably note that particular muscles seem to tense up more often than others. You may want to devote some additional Phase 2 practice to these specific muscles.

PROBLEM-SOLVING THERAPY

We are all confronted with various problems in our everyday lives. Some are minor and are handled in an almost automatic fashion (e.g., choosing what to order on a menu); others may present us with considerable challenge and difficulty (e.g., deciding which college to attend).

> Obviously, people differ greatly in how they can handle problems, no matter what their degree of complexity or seriousness. Much of what we view clinically as "abnormal behavior" or "emotional disturbance" may be more usefully construed as *ineffective behavior,* with its negative consequences, such as anxiety, depression, and the creation of secondary problems. A problem-solving approach can prove to be a useful means of dealing with many situational challenges. As used in the present context, *problem solving* is defined as a behavioral process, whether overt or cognitive, which (1) provides a variety of potentially effective responses to the problem situation, and (2) increases the likelihood of selecting the most effective response from among these various alternatives.[28]

Because the primary goal of problem solving is to identify the best solution to one's problem, problem-solving therapy can be the first step in a therapeutic process that then proceeds to implement the solution. If a client's major difficulty were *deciding* on a course of action, problem-solving therapy may be the only intervention required. Because problem-solving therapy teaches clients a broadly applicable coping skill, it often serves the dual purpose of (1) treating the immediate problem for which therapy was sought and (2) preparing clients to deal on their own with future problems when they arise.

An Example of Problem-Solving Therapy

Thomas D'Zurilla and Marvin Goldfried have developed an approach to problem-solving therapy[29] that involves five interrelated procedures: (1) general orientation, (2) problem definition and formulation, (3) generation of alternatives (strategies for solving the problem and tactics for implementing the strategies), (4) decision making (about the best strategy and tactic), and (5) action and assessment. These procedures are used in a seven-stage progression, illustrated schematically in Figure 12-1. The stages are cumulative, and the successful completion of each stage depends on skills and information learned in the previous stage(s). Accordingly, as the dashed lines in Figure 12-1 suggest, if difficulty is encountered in later stages it is sometimes necessary to return to previous stages before proceeding.

In the *general orientation* stage, the therapist explains the purpose and rationale of problem-solving therapy and outlines the procedures to be used. A major objective of this phase of therapy is to provide the client with certain attitudes or cognitive sets conducive to independent problem-solving behavior. These include understanding (1) that problems are a normal part of everyone's life and that people can learn to cope with them, (2) that it is important to

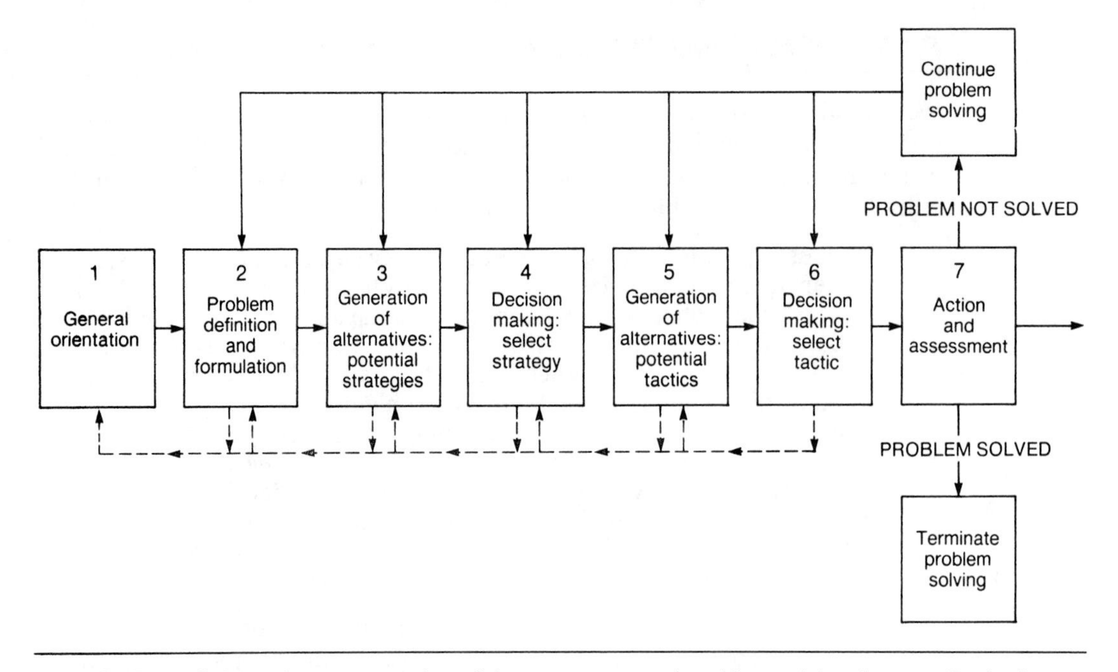

FIGURE 12-1 *Schematic representation of the seven steps of problem-solving therapy. Dashed lines indicate the possibility that difficulties at one stage may necessitate returning to a prior stage.* SOURCE: *Adapted from Goldfried & Davison (1976), p. 192.*

identify problems when they occur so that appropriate action can be taken, and (3) that effective problem solving involves carefully assessing alternative courses of action (one must avoid acting without prior deliberation).

In the second stage, the therapist helps the client to concretely *define* the problem situation, which involves pinpointing the critical events that surround the dilemma. This process closely resembles the tasks a behavioral therapist generally performs in making an initial behavioral assessment of clients' complaints; however, in problem-solving therapy clients are trained to do this on their own. When a precise definition of the problem situation has been made, clients must *formulate* their major goals regarding the problem situation as well as the issues or conflicts that make the situation problematic. Starting with this second stage of therapy, a checklist, such as the example in Figure 12-2, may be used to help clients formalize the problem-solving skills they are learning. Figure 12-2, Number 1, shows how the checklist is used in the definition and formulation stage.

The purpose of the third stage of problem-solving therapy is to *generate alternative strategies* or general approaches that might solve the problem. The objective is to come up with as many alternatives as possible so as to maximize the chances of finding the best available solution. This goal is primarily reached by "brainstorming," a procedure in which clients list all the strategies they can think of without censoring any possibilities, even if the strategies appear impractical or outlandish. The results of such brainstorming can be seen in Figure 12-2, Number 2.

In the fourth stage (*decision making*), the alternative strategies are evaluated to determine which one is most likely to solve the problem. Clients are taught to ask themselves "If this strategy worked, what would be the most probable consequences?" and to consider both immediate and long-range consequences, for themselves and for other people in their lives. Note that the checklist (Figure 12-2, Number 3) includes a formal rating system that facilitates the decision-making process.

Once a general course of action has been chosen, a tactic or specific means of implementing the strategy must be found. To do this (the fifth stage), *alternative tactics are generated,* employing the same procedures used in the third stage to generate alternative problem-solving strategies. In a sixth stage, the best tactic is chosen in a manner parallel to the *decision making* in the fourth stage except that the criterion here is the likelihood that the tactic will effectively and efficiently implement the strategy (see Numbers 4–5 and 6–7 in Figure 12-2).

In the seventh (final) stage of problem-solving therapy, clients *act* on the decisions they have made in the fourth and sixth stages and then they *assess* the effectiveness of their actions. Specifically, a client implements the specific tactic chosen and observes whether or not it results in a satisfactory solution to the problem. If the problem is solved, therapy is terminated. If the problem has not been resolved, then the client must return to one of the earlier stages and repeat the procedures in that stage and subsequent stages. For example, if the overall strategy for solving the problem still seems the most viable, then the difficulty may lie in not having chosen an adequate tactic for implementing the strategy. If the list of alternative tactics contains others that have a high probability of working, then one of these may be selected. If not, the client returns to the previous stage and generates additional alternative tactics.

A variety of behavioral therapy procedures are used in problem-solving therapy, including modeling, prompting, and reinforcement. In the early stages, the therapist may employ cognitive modeling to demonstrate the required problem-solving skills. For example, the therapist might model brainstorming for a hypothetical problem, to illustrate the uninhibited, open-ended process that is required, as the following verbal scenario indicates:

> How am I going to get my thesis finished by the June deadline? I could put in more hours, which would mean giving up my daily jogging and watching television . . . even sleeping. I could hire a typist to make my rough drafts more readable so I could rewrite more quickly. Maybe I could get an English grad student to help with my gramma and spellin. Of course, I could buy a thesis from one of those companies that sells them. . . .

When alternatives are being generated, the therapist reminds the client of the rules of brainstorming and praises the client's silly or obviously infeasible ideas as well as the practical, creative ones, to encourage the process of brainstorming. If the client has difficulty with brainstorming, the procedure may

PROBLEM-SOLVING CHECKLIST

1. Problem Definition and Formulation

   a. Definition of situation, including important details:

   Background: Although most of my courses at college are in the afternoon, I have one required course that meets at 8:00 in the morning. After the first few weeks of school, I began attending this class less and less regularly. I have gotten into the habit of studying late, and have a lot of trouble getting up to meet the class.

   Specific Problem Situation: It's halfway through the semester, and I've missed two weeks of my 8:00 class - about six consecutive class meetings. I'm really afraid to go back, because I feel I will be too far behind in the work and might not understand what's going on.

   b. Formulation of conflicts or issues:

Should return to class	vs.	Might not understand what's going on
Study late at night	vs.	Have to get up for early morning class
	vs.	

2. Brainstorming general courses of action (strategies):

3. Deciding on a strategy (or strategies) (++ = very good; + = good; 0 = neutral; - = bad; -- = very bad)

		Consequences of Strategy		
		For self	For others	Final Selection
a.	Return to class and try to catch up on course work on my own.	a. --	0	
b.	Return to class and get help from others in catching up with course work.	b. +	0	✓
c.	Continue as I am, but try to fake my way through the exams.	c. -	0	
d.	Ask some friends what they think I should do.	d. -	0	
e.	Return to class and make sure I don't miss any future classes.	e. +	0	✓
f.	Drop the course.	f. --	-	
g.	Try to keep up with course work and take final exam, but not actually attend classes.	g. --	-	
h.		h.		

FIGURE 12-2 *An example of a problem-solving checklist* SOURCE: Goldfried & Davison (1976), pp. 200–202.

4. Brainstorming specific ways of carrying out strategy "b"

5. Deciding on specific ways of carrying out strategy
(++ = very good; + = good; 0 = neutral; - = bad; -- = very bad)

	Brainstorming		For self	For others	Final Selection
			Consequences of Specific Behaviors		
a.	Look for a tutor.	a.	+	0	
b.	Ask the instructor if he would give me extra help in the course.	b.	0	-	
c.	Ask the instructor how he thinks I might best make up the material.	c.	++	0	√
d.	Ask some friends to explain the material I missed.	d.	+	-	
e.	Borrow some notes from a friend and try to catch up before returning to class.	e.	-	-	
f.	Borrow some notes from a friend but return to class immediately.	f.	+	-	
g.	Sneak into the instructor's office and steal his lecture notes.	g.	--	-	
h.	Find someone who has taken the course and borrow his lecture notes.	h.	+	0	
i.		i.			

6. Brainstorming specific ways of carrying out strategy "e"

7. Deciding on specific ways of carrying out strategy
(++ = very good; + = good; 0 = neutral; - = bad; -- = very bad)

	Brainstorming		For self	For others	Final Selection
			Consequences of Specific Behaviors		
a.	Completely rearrange my study habits so as to get to bed earlier.	a.	+	0	
b.	Get to bed earlier only on the nights before the early morning class.	b.	++	0	√
c.	Switch to a section that meets later in the day.	c.	0	0	
d.	Put my alarm clock on the other end of the room so I can make sure I get up on time.	d.	+	-	
e.	Get a friend to wake me up on time to get to class.	e.	+	-	
f.	Study through the night so that I can be sure to be awake early in the morning.	f.		-	
g.	Have a friend taperecord the lecture for me.	g.	+	-	
h.		h.			

need to be shaped. The therapist also teaches and encourages the client to self-reinforce appropriate problem-solving behaviors. When the client is ready to implement and test a tactic for solving the problem in the final stage, it may be necessary to employ various behavioral therapy procedures to facilitate the client's actions. For example, if the client feels anxious or inhibited in asking a friend for help, this difficulty needs to be alleviated first, as by systematic desensitization and assertion training.

Case 12-3 illustrates the use of problem-solving therapy to reduce a client's anxiety in examinations and in stressful interpersonal situations, which interfered with her studies. Initially, the treatment focused on decelerating her test anxiety through self-control systematic desensitization. When this approach proved ineffective, problem-solving therapy was employed to help the client identify and find solutions to her interpersonal problems.

CASE 12-3

*Treatment of Examination and Interpersonal Anxiety by Problem-Solving Therapy**

G. W., a 32-year-old female university student, originally entered therapy requesting treatment for test anxiety. It was subsequently determined that the area of most concern was not the test situation itself but anxiety associated with being prevented from studying for tests. This anxiety, which she felt was uncontrollable, occurred as a result of domestic and personal pressures [that] interfered with her studying.

The client, at time of treatment, had no difficulty in performing well on tests. She believed that her ability to study and write tests was more than sufficient since she had successfully completed two university degrees with high grades without experiencing these debilitating anxiety attacks. However, during the previous year she had become pregnant, and the birth of her child (in the summer) had increased her domestic responsibilities. It was during the following school year that G. W. began to complain of an inability to cope with home pressure and responsibilities, even those she had previously dealt with successfully. She maintained that the feelings of being overwhelmed and the high anxiety level were interfering with her ability to study. This, she believed, was the cause of the anxiety attacks since the maintenance of a high academic record was of utmost importance to her. During baseline evaluations, she reported that the feelings of being overwhelmed, and the subsequent feelings of panic occurred an average of five times a day. These feelings of panic were characterized by extreme nervousness, uncontrollable shaking, insomnia and nausea coupled with an inability to eat. These symptoms increased in intensity as a test or exam approached.

During the initial session, G. W. described her problems as a fear of taking examinations. At that time she indicated that her anxiety was strictly related to examination pressures. . . . Further questioning about the nature of her domestic and social pressures revealed that G. W. had difficulty identifying ways of coping with situations that interfered with her studying, getting to the university for classes, or taking exams. In other words, although the problem situations evoked anxiety, the anxiety persisted because she was

*Reprinted from Mayo & Norton (1980), pp. 287–289.

unable to identify effective strategies [that] would alter the problematic situations. For example, if her babysitter called saying she couldn't care for the baby the next day, G. W. would become very anxious and would have difficulty identifying solutions [that] would allow her to attend classes.

G. W. was taught a variant of systematic problem solving [after self-control systematic desensitization proved ineffective] to assist her in identifying effective alternatives for coping with situations producing anxiety. She was instructed in a brainstorming process that allowed her to identify a number of potential strategies to cope with problem situations. The problem situations for which alternative solutions were derived were based on items from the hierarchy [used in the unsuccessful desensitization]. After a number of possible solutions had been identified, G. W. was asked to evaluate these strategies by determining the costs and the benefits (to herself and others) of each strategy and select the solutions that seemed to have the most benefits and fewest costs. Training in problem solving occurred in one session. During the next week, G. W. was instructed to apply the problem-solving procedure to the remaining hierarchy items and, when appropriate, to use the chosen strategies in actual problem situations such as an unexpected visit from relatives, which interfered in her attempts to study.

When G. W. returned for her next session, she was asked to reevaluate the SUDs [subjective units of disturbance] for each hierarchy item. Although the remaining hierarchy items evoked little anxiety, further practice in applying the problem-solving skills was provided by having G. W. imagine herself coping with the stressful situations. This occurred during the remaining sessions. These sessions were directed at reducing any residual anxiety associated with certain hierarchical items. . . .

Sessions were approximately one hour in length and were held once a week. There was a total of 17 sessions. . . .

Following training and one week of home practice in systematic problem solving, G. W. reevaluated the SUDs level of all hierarchy items. Prior to treatment, Items 10–20 evoked 50–100 SUDs. After problem-solving training, only the last five items continued to evoke anxiety (20–50 SUDs); however, these items specified situations that G. W. had difficulty controlling. Hierarchy Item 19 for example read, "the babysitter does not show up, necessitating missing an exam." Even though the hierarchy items evoked little anxiety, G. W. was asked to imagine each situation and to imagine herself coping with the situation by using her problem-solving skills. This was done in an attempt to reduce her residual anxiety. After completing the hierarchy in this fashion, none of the items produced more than 10–15 SUDs.

G. W. was able to apply successfully the anxiety management procedures to her domestic and academic situations. She reported that she was able to arrange her environment so that she was able to prepare for examinations with minimal anxiety. In addition, she reported that insomnia, nervousness, and shaking were no longer problems. Her anxiety attacks decreased from approximately five per day during baseline to less than one per week.

During an interview with G. W. approximately six months after treatment, she indicated that she was still successfully using the problem-solving strategies to reduce anxiety related to schoolwork. In addition, she reported that she had successfully coped with the anxiety of separating from her husband by applying the skills she had acquired during treatment.

Evaluation of Problem-Solving Therapies

Problem-solving behavioral therapies (of which the model just described is one representative example) have been used to treat a variety of target behaviors with a wide range of clients, including helping kindergarten and grade school children learn to cooperate with peers,[30] facilitating mutual decision making between youths classified as "predelinquent" and their parents,[31] decreasing college students' overdependency on other people for personal decisions,[32] and enhancing harmony among family members.[33] Problem-solving therapies are particularly suited for clients facing major life decisions, where the consequences of an ineffective choice or course of action can be very serious. Examples would include marriage, divorce, changing jobs, and even the contemplation of suicide. In the last example, problem solving could help someone consider alternative solutions—besides ending one's life—to a seemingly untenable situation.[34]

Overall, the initial results of problem-solving therapies are quite promising. Problem-solving therapies in many ways epitomize the advantages of the self-control approach to behavioral therapy. In problem solving, behavioral therapists share their expertise with clients so that the clients learn to function as their own change agents. Not only does problem-solving therapy give clients a specific coping skill that they can apply on their own to many different target behaviors, but it also teaches clients general strategies such as precisely defining problems, weighing the consequences of one's actions, and evaluating the effectiveness of one's actions.[35]

STATUS AND APPRAISAL OF SELF-CONTROL BEHAVIORAL THERAPIES

The development of specific self-control behavioral therapies, such as those discussed in this chapter, is relatively recent (although involving clients as active participants in their treatment has been a consistent theme in behavioral therapy for a long time). Overall, the initial data available regarding the effectiveness of self-control behavioral therapies are positive, and self-control behavioral therapies appear to have some important advantages. Before examining them, however, several words of caution are in order.

Self-control therapies are clearly not suited for all clients and every problem. Because self-control therapies are implemented by clients on their own, clients must be capable of and willing to do this. Capability may be a limitation with clients of very low intelligence, and willingness might be a limitation with nonvoluntary clients (e.g., a teenager who is "forced" to be in treatment by her or his parents). A number of potential dangers also arise when nonprofessionals are taught and given license to use therapeutic skills. Because laypeople have only limited knowledge and experience, they may encounter situations for which their self-control skills are not appropriate. This problem diminishes when more general self-control skills are taught (e.g., self-reinforcement of appropriate behaviors) and when the therapist emphasizes the client's understanding of the rationale and principles that underlie specific techniques. Still, clients must be made aware of the limitations of the self-control procedures, and must learn when it is appropriate to seek direct professional assistance (and be willing to do so).

The potential advantages of self-control therapies appear to outweigh the potential limitations. Self-control therapies are able to meet two major challenges faced by all forms of psychotherapy: (1) *generalization* of treatment gains from the therapy situation to the client's natural environment and (2) long-term *maintenance* of treatment gains. Generalization is not a problem when self-control therapies are used, because the therapy is carried out in the client's everyday life situation and because the primary therapeutic agent is the client rather than the therapist. The chances of treatment gains being maintained over time are increased with self-control therapies, because clients can continue the therapy begun under the supervision of a professional therapist on their own (with minimal therapist consultation, if necessary). If the problem behavior recurs in the future, clients who have been treated via self-control therapies may be able to reinstate the therapy procedures rather than have to return to a therapist for assistance.

An obvious benefit of self-control behavioral therapies is that professional therapists can spend less time with clients and thus have time to work with more individuals. L.M., whose depressive behavior was alleviated by self-reinforcement (Case 12-2), met with the therapist only four times. Furthermore, because the self-control procedures are generally applicable to a variety of problem behaviors other than the specific one for which therapy was originally sought, clients often report that they have adapted and successfully used self-control techniques to alleviate other problems. Recall, for example, that several of the clients who had been trained to use self-administered stimulus control techniques to decelerate overeating generalized these techniques on their own to significantly reduce cigarette smoking. Another example was L. M.'s (Case 12-2) initiating the use of the self-reinforcement for socializing, which was another problem area in her life but one for which she had not received any treatment.

Several indirect benefits may accrue to the increased use of self-control behavioral therapies. First, some evidence suggests that clients who attribute therapeutic improvement to their own efforts maintain that improvement longer than clients who credit their gains to external sources, such as the therapist or luck.[36] Second, clients who show improvement in one problematic area of their lives often also exhibit, as an indirect consequence, general positive growth in other areas, including the way they view themselves (e.g., increased self-esteem). Clients whose problem behaviors are treated by self-control therapies may receive more of an "ego boost," because they are responsible for their therapeutic improvement, than clients whose therapy is primarily therapist controlled. Finally, because self-control behavioral therapies squarely place the knowledge and technology of modifying human behavior "in the hands" of the client, they foster personal freedom. As is discussed in the next chapter, the power of behavioral therapy techniques cannot be used against people—as some critics of behavioral therapy fear—if that power is given to the people, which is the essence of self-control behavioral therapies.[37]

SUMMARY

Self-control behavioral therapies train clients to initiate, conduct, and evaluate their own therapy. Some behavioral therapies are readily adapted, with minor changes, to a self-control model, such as systematic desensitization. The three basic functions of self-control procedures are assessment, changing antecedents, and changing consequences. An example of the assessment function is self-monitoring, which involves clients' observing and recording their own behaviors. Self-monitoring can also inadvertently change the target behaviors being measured, and it is sometimes used directly to modify behaviors. Stimulus control procedures change antecedent conditions that are maintaining target behaviors—specifically, environmental cues. Overeating and sleep difficulties are often amenable to modification through stimulus control. Self-reinforcement procedures exemplify changing consequences that are maintaining target behaviors. Stress inoculation is a complex treatment package that prepares clients to deal with stressful situations by teaching them coping skills and then having them rehearse the skills in simulated stressful situations. The major target behaviors that stress inoculation has been used to treat are anxiety or fear, anger, and pain. Problem-solving therapy is another complex self-control treatment package that aims at helping clients find solutions to almost any problem. The particular model of problem-solving therapy described in this chapter includes five interrelated procedures: (1) general orientation, (2) problem definition, (3) generation of solutions and ways of implementing them, (4) decision making about the best solution and way of implementing it, and (5) implementation of the solution and assessment of its effects. Although self-control therapies are not applicable or effective in all cases, they are often extremely efficient and effective, especially in terms of generalizing therapeutic gains and maintaining them over time.

REFERENCE NOTES

1. For example, Goldfried & Merbaum, 1973; Mahoney & Arnkoff, 1978; Mahoney & Thoresen, 1974; Thoresen & Mahoney, 1974; Watson & Tharp, 1977.
2. Wolpe, 1958.
3. Goldfried, 1971.
4. For example, Denney & Rupert, 1977; Spiegler, Cooley, Marshall, Prince, Puckett, & Skenazy, 1976; Zemore, 1975.
5. Mahoney & Arnkoff, 1978.
6. Thoresen & Mahoney, 1974.
7. From the author's files.
8. Thoresen & Mahoney, 1974.

9. For example, Rutner & Bugle, 1969.
10. See also, for example, Maletzky, 1974.
11. Kazdin, 1974e.
12. Stunkard & Mahoney, 1976.
13. Ferster, Nurnberger, & Levitt, 1962; Stuart, 1967; Stuart & Davis, 1972.
14. Stuart, 1967.
15. Jeffery, Wing, & Stunkard, 1978.
16. Spiegler, 1981, 1982.
17. Coates & Thoresen, 1977.
18. Coates & Thoresen, 1977, p. 154.
19. For example, Costello, 1972; Ferster, 1973; Lazarus, 1968; Lewinsohn, 1974; Lewinsohn & Graf, 1973.
20. Mahoney & Arnkoff, 1978.
21. Bandura, 1977b.
22. Meichenbaum, 1977.
23. Meichenbaum, 1977, p. 156.
24. Meichenbaum & Cameron, 1972.
25. Navaco, 1975, 1977a, 1977b.
26. Turk, 1975, 1976.
27. Turk, 1975.
28. Goldfried & Davison, 1976, pp. 186–187.
29. D'Zurilla & Goldfried, 1971; Goldfried & Davison, 1976.
30. Schneider & Robin, 1975; Shaftel & Shaftel, 1967; Spivak & Shure, 1974.
31. Kifer, Lewis, Green, & Phillips, 1974.
32. Goldfried & Davison, 1976.
33. Blechman, 1974; Blechman, Olson, & Hellman, 1976; Blechman, Olson, Schornagel, Halsdorf, & Turner, 1976.
34. Goldfried & Davison, 1976.
35. Mahoney & Arnkoff, 1978.
36. For example, Davison, Tsujimoto, & Glaros, 1973; Davison & Valins, 1969.
37. London, 1969.

CHAPTER 13 Ethical Issues in the Practice of Behavioral Therapy

In the practice of behavioral therapy, questions such as what behavior is to be changed, by whom, and for what purpose confront both therapist and client. These ethical and moral issues, already mentioned in previous chapters, are discussed in detail in this chapter. Before reading further, take a few minutes to do Participation Exercise 13-1.

PARTICIPATION EXERCISE 13-1

A Prereading Assessment of Your Opinions About Ethical Issues Related to Behavioral Therapy

The purpose of this brief participation exercise is to assess your opinions about some of the ethical issues that are discussed in this chapter, as well as to start you thinking about them. List the numbers 1 through 11 on a lined sheet of paper. Then, using the following scale, choose the letter(s) that best represents your opinion about each statement and write it next to the number of the statement. There are *no right or wrong answers.*

AA = Strongly Agree
A = Moderately Agree
a = Slightly Agree
d = Slightly Disagree
D = Moderately Disagree
DD = Strongly Disagree

1. Behavioral therapy poses ethical and moral problems that do ***not*** exist with other forms of therapy.
2. The practice of behavioral therapy is mechanistic and impersonal.
3. The therapist determines the goals of behavioral therapy for the client.
4. Behavioral therapy treats each client's problem as unique.
5. Behavioral therapy procedures tend to increase clients' personal freedom.
6. People have little control over the environmental events that influence their behavior.
7. Behavioral therapy makes clients conform to behaviors that society considers appropriate and acceptable.
8. Treatments that involve pain or discomfort to a client are unethical.
9. Many nonvoluntary clients (e.g., children or committed psychiatric patients) are capable of making informed decisions about their own treatment.
10. Behavioral therapy techniques can be used for harmful purposes.
11. One way of assuring that behavioral therapy techniques will ***not*** be used against people is to restrict knowledge of the techniques only to professional behavioral therapists.

In preparation for reading this chapter, you may find it useful to think about the arguments you would make if you were asked to substantiate your opinion about each of the preceding statements. When you have finished this participation exercise, save the sheet of paper on which you rated the statements, because you will be asked to use it later.

PLACING ETHICAL ISSUES CONCERNING BEHAVIORAL THERAPY IN PERSPECTIVE

At the outset it is essential to have a realistic and fair perspective from which to examine the ethical challenges faced by behavioral therapy. Behavioral therapy is ethically *neutral* in that it does not dictate whose behavior or what behaviors should be changed. Behavioral therapy only specifies *how* to change behaviors when this is appropriate—that is, when a behavioral therapist's services have been solicited.

Furthermore, although ethical and moral questions are germane to behavioral therapy, behavioral therapists have no special expertise in answering them, because ethics and morality are philosophical and not scientific or clinical in nature. However, this position does not mean that behavioral therapists have abdicated their responsibility for dealing with ethical issues that arise in their clinical practice. Indeed, behavioral therapists have been among the most outspoken critics of ethical abuses of behavioral therapy[1] and have been hard at work to protect clients from potential violations of their ethical and moral rights.[2]

It is also important to keep in mind that ethical and moral issues are inherent in *any* therapeutic or other influential process (e.g., in education, religion, law, and mass media)—that is, whenever one person's (client's) behavior is to be changed directly or indirectly by another person (therapist). Yet, from the frequent "bad press" to which behavioral therapy has been subjected in the 1970s, it would appear that behavioral therapy is considered especially vulnerable to ethical dilemmas. This distorted impression is the result of many factors. For example, by coincidence behavioral therapy has emerged at a time of heightened concern about external control (e.g., by governments), the invasion of personal privacy (e.g., through "bugging" and computer storage of personal information), and the abuse of civil liberties (e.g., of institutionalized psychiatric patients and prisoners). "Reacting to the seemingly unchecked growth of these influences, many citizens have come to adopt positions that are highly critical of any and all behavior influence efforts."[3]

Another factor that accounts, in part, for the disproportionate attack on behavioral therapy is a confusion about what *is* and what *is not* behavioral therapy. This problem has occurred most frequently when the term *behavior modification* is used (rather than behavioral therapy). Although *behavior modification* has a specific meaning (essentially synonymous with *behavioral therapy;* see Chapter 1), it has been mistakenly confused with *any* procedure that modifies behavior, including psychosurgery (e.g., lobotomies and implanting electrodes in the brain), electroconvulsive shock therapy (ECT), drugs, so-called brainwashing, sensory deprivation, and even torture.[4] A survey of articles indexed under "behavior modification" in the New York *Times* over a five-year period revealed that the term was incorrectly applied approximately half of the time.[5] In some cases, the treatment procedures had absolutely no relationship to any form of behavioral therapy. For example, the use of a drug causing a brief period of paralysis of the muscles (including those of the respiratory system) as punishment for prisoners has been *erroneously* described as behavior modification.[6]

The extent to which the name of a therapy procedure can influence people's perceptions of it was revealed in an investigation entitled "A Rose by Any Other Name . . . : Labeling Bias and Attitudes toward Behavior Modification."[7] In this study, undergraduate and graduate students evaluated a videotape of a teacher using reinforcement procedures in a special education class of an elementary school. The students were divided into two groups for the study. All the students saw the same videotape, except that in one group the videotape was described as illustrating "behavior modification" while in the other group it was labeled as "humanistic education." Not surprisingly, "when the events on the videotape were described as illustrative of humanistic education, (1) the teacher received significantly more favorable ratings and (2) the teaching method was seen as significantly more likely to promote academic learning and emotional growth."[8]

With respect to the issues of freedom and control, there is yet another potential explanation for behavioral therapy being viewed as more controlling than traditional psychotherapies. Historically, the image of healer has been that of an authoritarian, all-knowing agent who administers treatment to a passive and naive client. This model was carried over into psychoanalysis (the modern prototype of psychotherapy), and some people have mistakenly assumed that these are the roles of client and therapist in behavioral therapy. This erroneous assumption leads to the *false* conclusion that the behavioral therapist decides what behavior is to be changed and how to change it, and that the client passively submits to the therapist's decisions. It is not hard to see how such images would generate fear of an authoritarian therapist controlling the behavior of a powerless client. However, this picture is far from the reality of the roles played by client and therapist in behavioral therapy, where the client usually decides on treatment goals and actively shares the behavioral therapist's knowledge and skills in order to achieve the goals.

All this is not to say that ethical problems do not arise in behavioral therapy. They do, but the discussion of them that follows here focuses only on what behavioral therapy actually *is,* not on what has sometimes, and erroneously, been called, or attributed to, behavioral therapy.

The discussion begins with a close examination of the often-heard criticism that behavioral therapy is mechanistic (machinelike, impersonal) and therefore is dehumanizing. Then it considers the criticisms that behavioral therapy manipulates and controls clients as well as deprives them of their personal freedom. Next the discussion deals with the use of aversive procedures, and then the treatment of nonvoluntary clients (e.g., institutionalized patients and children), two particular areas that have justifiably raised vital ethical issues. The coverage of ethical issues concludes by examining the dangers of and safeguards for potent behavioral therapy procedures.

IS BEHAVIORAL THERAPY MECHANISTIC AND IMPERSONAL?

The erroneous conception of behavioral therapy as mechanistic and impersonal stems, in part, from the early history of this approach. As described in Chapter 1, behavioral therapy has its roots (but not its "maintaining conditions") in learning theory and laboratory experiments concerning the learning of nonhuman animals. However, the connection between actual clinical practices of behavioral therapy and learning experiments in the laboratory is at best analogous or metaphorical. Yet many behavioral therapists continue to rely on learning theory terminology, which has pejorative connotations to some people—terms such as *conditioning, stimulus, response,* and *shaping.* Some behavioral therapists still explain their procedures in terms of training laboratory animals. This tendency is unfortunate because behavioral therapies can be accurately described in terms of the procedures they entail (an operational description), as the preceding chapters show. Moreover, nonhuman animal analogues do not account for the complexity and sophistication of human behavior. Consider how the consequences of people's behavior influence its subsequent performance:

> Contrary to the mechanistic metaphors—in which reinforcers supposedly alter conduct automatically and unconsciously—people are not much affected by response consequences if they are unaware of what is being reinforced. When they know what they are being reinforced for, they may respond in accommodating or oppositional ways depending upon how they value the incentives, the influencers, and the behavior itself, and how others respond. Thus, reinforcers serve mainly as incentive motivators rather than as mechanical or insidious controllers of conduct. Consequences alter behavior through the intervening influence of thoughts and valuations.[9]

Another source of evidence against the argument that behavioral therapies are mechanistic and impersonal is the fundamental practice within behavioral therapy of considering each case as unique and of designing a treatment plan specific to the client's individual problem. Before any behavioral therapy can begin, the maintaining conditions of the target behavior(s) are assessed. No universal assumptions (e.g., "unresolved Oedipus complex" or "failure to self-actualize") are made about the cause of the problem. Although no doubt similarities exist among people who have similar problems, each problem behavior is considered to be the product of a set of conditions special to the particular client. Critics of behavioral therapy often are ignorant of the importance of individualizing behavioral treatment plans, as the following true incident illustrates.

One of my clinical psychology graduate students, who was learning to do behavioral therapy, wanted to work with adolescents at a local psychiatric hospital. Initially the staff flatly refused her request, expressing serious skepticism about the effectiveness of behavioral therapy with their clients. However, the student therapist finally convinced the staff to allow her to work with Brian, a 14-year-old boy who presented multiple problems to the staff and with whom all treatment efforts had proved ineffective. Over the course of two weeks, the student therapist met with Brian on several occasions to discuss his view of "his" problems and to observe Brian in a variety of settings. The student therapist then selected one of Brian's problem behaviors and designed a contingency contract for changing the behavior. Brian agreed to the contract, because it specified that special privileges would be available to him contingent on his performing the required acceleration target behavior. The student therapist was able to get the cooperation of several staff members in administering the contract. Much to the surprise and delight of the staff, the contingency contract was successful in substantially changing Brian's behavior. In fact, the staff members were so impressed with the effectiveness of the contingency contract that they prepared to use it for another client by merely crossing out "Brian" and substituting "Jeff"! Obviously, the important fact that in behavioral therapy a contingency contract—or any treatment plan—is specifically designed for a particular client and for that client *alone* (which may have been one factor responsible for its success with Brian) had not been understood by the staff.

Behavioral therapy cannot be implemented in a rigid, robotlike fashion, as some critics have argued. (This is true even though behavioral therapy procedures are usually clearly and precisely delineated.) On the contrary, successful behavioral therapy requires a good therapeutic (client-therapist) relationship, one in which there is rapport, trust, and caring.[10] However, the therapeutic relationship assumes a different role in behavioral therapy from the role it assumes in many traditional modes of psychotherapy (e.g., client-centered or Rogerian therapy and psychoanalysis) in which the relationship between client and therapist is a major vehicle for helping the client. In behavioral therapy, the therapeutic relationship *facilitates* implementing the primary therapeutic procedures, which directly influence the maintaining conditions of the target behavior. Thus, a good therapeutic relationship is a necessary but not sufficient condition for effective behavioral therapy.[11]

The first way in which a good therapeutic relationship facilitates behavioral therapy concerns the receptivity of the client to therapy. Not only is it important for the client to cooperate with the therapy procedures, but the client's positive expectations about the effectiveness of the treatment can play an important role in actually making therapy effective.[12] Second, the initial assessment of target behaviors and maintaining conditions involves mutual trust between the therapist and the client. Clients need to believe that they are gathering and reporting important information, that it will be held in confidence by the therapist, and that it will be used to benefit them. The therapist, in turn, must trust that the client is providing accurate self-reports. Third, to be able to design a treatment plan that is appropriate for a client, the therapist must understand the client's problem from the *client's* perspective (empathic understanding), and this goal requires a close relationship with the client. Fourth, because much behavioral therapy is actually implemented by the client at home, the therapist must often motivate the client to do homework assignments. One potentially potent source of such motivation is the therapist's approval, and in order for therapist approval to become a social reinforcer for the client, a good relationship between the therapist and client must exist. Fifth, behavioral therapists frequently model adaptive behaviors for clients, and imitation is enhanced when the client views the therapist positively.[13]

ON CONTROL AND FREEDOM IN BEHAVIORAL THERAPY

Many ethical criticisms of behavioral therapy are related to claims that its practices manipulate or control clients and therefore rob them of their personal freedom. This section explores these claims with respect to *voluntary clients*—people who themselves seek help with their problems and who are essentially free to terminate therapy at any time. A later section discusses *non-voluntary clients*—people who do not necessarily want to be treated and who are to some degree externally constrained to remain in therapy.

Freedom involves having *alternatives* from which to choose. One becomes more free as one's options increase. In a very real sense, all behavioral therapies provide clients with alternative ways of behaving and thus enhance their personal freedom. This effect is most obvious for techniques that accelerate desirable behaviors. For instance, when modeling and reinforcement procedures are used to provide clients with skills formerly unavailable to them, the clients' freedom is increased. This effect is equally true for the mentally retarded child who learns to ask questions in order to obtain assistance, and for the business executive who learns appropriate assertive behavior to be applied in complex social interactions. In each case, *after successful behavioral therapy the client has more ways of behaving than before therapy.*

Deceleration behavioral therapies also provide clients with increased alternatives. A woman whose drinking problem has been helped by covert sensitization is now more free, because she has many more options, such as being able to hold a job and engage in activities that can be impaired by intoxication (e.g., sports, social contacts, and sexual intercourse). A man whose intense fear of leaving the security of his home has been alleviated through participant modeling can now engage in many activities previously unavailable to him (e.g., going to the movies, friends' houses, stores, and restaurants).

Behavioral therapy provides the procedures for achieving various therapeutic goals but does not specify the specific goals. *The goals of behavioral therapy are chosen by the clients;* clients are the "final authority" for deciding for themselves what is desirable or undesirable, adaptive or maladaptive. The behavioral therapist's role in goal setting is to help the client (1) clarify goals for therapy and (2) specify the goals so that they are unambiguous, measurable, and realistic. Often clients initially do not know what their goals are, or come for therapy with ambiguous and conflicting goals. In such cases, the therapist helps the client to clarify goals, which often involves exploring their consequences. In the final analysis, however, the client decides what the goals of therapy are to be.

Most goals in behavioral therapy involve increasing socially desirable behaviors and decreasing socially undesirable behaviors. Does this statement mean that behavioral therapy fosters social conformity? To the extent that clients are provided with prosocial alternatives, social conformity becomes possible but not inevitable. In other words, just because a client develops a new way of behaving that happens to conform to norms of social acceptability does not mean that the client will choose to act that way. The consequences of social conformity or social deviance for the particular client will determine how the client will behave. But it is important to recognize that most problems that necessitate therapy involve too little of some socially desirable behavior (e.g., problem solving when frustrated) and/or too much of a socially undesirable behavior (e.g., physical aggression when frustrated). By providing clients with socially desirable alternative behaviors, clients are able to engage in behaviors they were not capable of before therapy.

Whereas clients are in the best position to evaluate what goals are right for them, the behavioral therapist is the expert in the methods used to attain those goals. (Otherwise, the client would not seek the assistance of a therapist.) But even in the area of goal attainment, clients in behavioral therapy play a role in the decision to use a particular therapeutic procedure. Before any treatment is begun, the behavioral therapist describes the proposed therapy procedures to the client in language that the client can fully understand. The therapist frequently explains the underlying rationale of the procedures and gives the client some information about their advantages and general success rate. Clients are made aware of the role they will play in the therapy and possible negative consequences of the procedures. In short, clients are informed about the proposed treatment so that they are able to question and even refuse the treatment suggested. Of course, because clients assume that the therapist is more knowledgeable about the appropriateness of therapy procedures than they are, in practice clients frequently rely heavily on the therapist's suggestions and advice.

Occasionally a therapist presents alternative treatments to a client, outlines the advantages and disadvantages of each, and asks the client to decide which procedure seems most desirable. For example, in order to eliminate an annoying habit, both response cost and extinction may be potentially useful. The therapist points out that response cost is likely to decelerate the target behavior more quickly but that response cost could also be less desirable in that the client might have to forfeit personal valuables (e.g., money deposited with the therapist). Armed with such information, the client is able to make a personal cost-benefit analysis and decide which therapy seems most desirable or appealing.

The explicit nature of behavioral therapy practices is another factor that fosters clients' freedom. Clients can know the details of their treatment because behavioral therapy procedures are clearly delineated, unlike some other forms of psychotherapy (e.g., in psychoanalysis, successful treatment requires that patients gain insight about their problems—but "insight" can only be vaguely defined). The results of behavioral treatment can also be explicit because the goals are stated in clear-cut, measurable terms. Therefore, both client and therapist are aware of how therapy is proceeding as well as of when the goals have been met and therapy is no longer necessary. In behavioral therapy, measurements of treatment goals dictate whether therapy is effective, rather than the subjective judgment of the therapist (as is frequently the case in other forms of therapy). The client's goals, the details of the therapy procedures, and the criteria for success are typically spelled out in some formal client-therapist agreement. Such openness not only enhances the clients' personal freedom but also may increase the power of the therapy procedures. People who are actively involved in the processes influencing them tend to be more receptive to changing.[14]

THE ETHICS OF AVERSIVE PROCEDURES

Of all the behavioral therapies, aversive procedures have been criticized most strongly as being unethical. At least part of the public outcry is based on two widespread misconceptions. First, many people believe that aversive procedures are extensively used in behavioral therapy, and some people even think of aversive procedures as being synonymous with behavioral therapy. In fact, *aversive procedures constitute a small proportion of behavioral therapy techniques, and they tend to be used infrequently.* A second and related misconception is that aversive procedures are highly effective and therefore constitute a threat to clients in behavioral therapy. The fact is that aversive procedures *in general* are relatively weak behavioral therapies in that their effects tend to be temporary, which is a major reason for their limited use.

The myth of aversive behavioral therapy procedures as powerful and evil forces has been spurred by exaggerated and inaccurate representations, such as in the popular film and book *A Clockwork Orange.* In the story, a young hoodlum who has been committing a series of sadistic and brutal attacks on innocent people is taken to a prison hospital for treatment. Strapped to a chair with his eyelids pinned open, he is "forced" to watch films of violence while feeling nausea and panic induced by a drug he has been given. After a few such treatments, even the thought of violence makes him extremely anxious, and he is considered to be "cured" of his antisocial behavior. Unfortunately, the "public at large has no ready way of knowing that there are major inaccuracies in the [story], and consequently it became one of the rallying points for emotionally engendered misconceptions."[15]

It should also be recognized that aversive control of human behavior was not invented by behavioral therapists. For years, parents have spanked, teachers have given failing grades, employers have reprimanded, and police have issued tickets. Furthermore, there is nothing inherently unethical about aversive procedures simply because they involve pain or discomfort. After all, we do not consider it unethical to have teeth drilled at the dentist or to receive an injection to prevent or cure a disease.

Having placed the use of aversive procedures in behavioral therapy in its proper perspective, let us examine their ethicality. Recall that there are two major categories of aversive behavioral therapy procedures: (1) aversion therapies, which substitute negative reactions for positive reactions (Chapter 5), and (2) the use of aversive consequences, which decelerate maladaptive behaviors (Chapter 7). The remarks in this section are relevant to both categories.

Aversive techniques are usually employed as a last resort, when alternative therapy procedures have failed to decelerate serious debilitating behaviors. In each case, a cost-benefit analysis must be made: Does the potential outcome of therapy—reduction of a serious, maladaptive behavior—outweigh the potential negative effects of the aversive procedure (e.g., temporary pain or discomfort)? Consider the two general classes of deceleration target behaviors for which aversive procedures have been employed. One is the self-destructive behavior of autistic or severely mentally retarded children.[16] The following account dramatically illustrates the ethical dilemmas that arise when aversive behavioral therapies are used.

> A colleague . . . showed us a deeply moving film. The heroine was an institutionalized primary-grade girl. She was a head-banger, so a padded football helmet was put on her head. Because she could take it off, her hands were tied down in her crib. She kept tossing her neck and tore out her hair at every opportunity. She accordingly had a perpetually bruised face on a hairless head, with a neck almost as thick as that of a horse. She was nonverbal.
>
> My colleague and his staff carefully planned a program for her, using all kinds of reinforcers. She was remanded to their program, but persisted in her typical behavior. In desperation, the ultimate weapon was unwrapped. When she tossed her head, my colleague yelled "Don't!" simultaneously delivering a sharp slap to her cheek. She subsided for a brief period, tossed again, and the punishment was delivered. My colleague reports that less than a dozen slaps were ever delivered and the word "Don't!" yelled even from across the room was effective. Its use was shortly down to once a week and was discontinued in a few weeks. In the meantime, the football helmet was removed and the girl began to eat at the table. She slept in a regular bed. Her hair grew out, and she turned out to be a very pretty little blond girl with delicate features and a delicate neck. In less than a year, she started to move toward joining a group of older girls whose behavior, it was hoped, she would [imitate]. She smiled often.
>
> The initial institution and her parents discovered that she had been slapped. They immediately withdrew her from the custody of my colleague's staff. The last part of the film shows her back at the institution. She is strapped down in her crib. Her hands are tied to a side. She is wearing a football helmet. Her hair is torn out, her face is a mass of bruises and her neck is almost as thick as that of a horse.[17]

The other major category of target behaviors for which aversive techniques are used is socially inappropriate or personally maladaptive habits that seriously interfere with normal life. Examples include sexual deviations (e.g., exhibitionistic and pedophilic behaviors), addictions (e.g., to drugs or food), and criminal acts (e.g., shoplifting). Aversive procedures can be an important *part* of a comprehensive treatment plan for such undesirable behaviors when the major treatment techniques accelerate alternative, socially desirable behaviors. The brief discomfort from aversion therapy is minimal, compared to the repeated institutionalization, extensive interference with work and family life, social ostracism, and self-depreciation that result from long-standing socially unacceptable behaviors.[18]

Aversive stimuli need not be physically painful to be effective. Covert sensitization (which uses unpleasant imagery in association with the deceleration target behavior) and procedures that temporarily deprive a client of reinforcers (such as time out and response cost) are also technically aversive behavioral therapy procedures.

Misuse and abuse of aversive procedures do occur. Misuse is usually perpetrated by inexperienced individuals who have learned only some of the information and skill required to ethically and effectively apply the techniques. For example, aversive consequences often need only be applied for a short while to be effective,[19] but through ignorance they may be continued long after they have had their desired effect. Such misuse is likely to produce no decrease, sometimes produces an increase in the deceleration target behavior, and certainly is overly harsh treatment. More than with most acceleration therapies, deceleration therapies, especially those which involve aversive techniques, require the expertise of a professional behavioral therapist.

Abuses of aversive techniques usually arise when the deceleration target behavior is annoying to others, such as a student throwing spit-balls at classmates, or an institutionalized psychiatric patient disturbing ward activities with inappropriate outbursts. For the individuals who are responsible for maintaining order in these situations, it is likely to be easier to devise some aversive consequence to immediately stop the annoying behavior than to think of and then accelerate alternative prosocial behaviors that would successfully compete with the disruptive behavior.

A variety of guidelines have been proposed to promote the ethical use of aversive procedures and include the following (these guidelines for the ethical use of aversive procedures should be considered a required supplement to the guidelines for the *effective use* of aversive procedures outlined in Chapter 7):

1. Aversive procedures should be considered only after a detailed evaluation indicates that other alternatives are not possible or would be ineffective or inefficient.
2. Informed consent must be obtained from the client or the client's advocate (see also next section).
3. The procedures should be implemented only by a competent professional.
4. Whenever possible, non-physically-aversive techniques should be tried before physically painful stimuli are employed.
5. Aversive techniques should always be used in conjunction with procedures that simultaneously accelerate behaviors that are alternatives to the ones being eliminated.
6. Clear-cut measures of the target behavior should be collected before and after therapy to document its effectiveness (or ineffectiveness).

These guidelines should be closely monitored by special committees composed of both competent professionals and laypeople from the community who are concerned with the welfare of clients and the concerns of the public.[20]

Most questions about the ethicality of aversive methods are germane to nonvoluntary clients, as the examples discussed in this section imply. With clients who freely volunteer to receive aversive procedures no real ethical problems arise; for example, few people would consider it unethical for consenting adults to subject themselves to a series of mild shocks in order to eliminate their desire to drink alcohol. On the other hand, ethical issues are prominent in the treatment of nonvoluntary clients, and the dilemmas raised are especially acute when aversive methods are employed.

NONVOLUNTARY CLIENTS AND COERCION

Nonvoluntary clients have little or no choice about the treatment they receive, either because they are considered incapable of making these decisions or because they reside in institutions, which makes them especially vulnerable to coercion. Children are examples of clients who are limited by their inability to make certain decisions. Prison inmates, on the other hand, are usually capable of making their own decisions, but their decision making may be subject to coercion by prison authorities. Institutionalized psychiatric patients and mentally retarded individuals are limited by both restrictions. In considering the ethical issues that pertain to nonvoluntary clients, remember that these issues are relevant to all forms of psychotherapy and not just behavioral therapy.

Informed consent of clients regarding both the goals and methods of treatment is one of the major safeguards against unethical practices. With nonvoluntary clients, however, informed consent becomes a tricky and complicated problem. In cases where it is assumed that clients are incapable of making prudent decisions about what is in their best interest, who is to make these decisions? Usually this responsibility is legally delegated to the client's guardian, such as a parent for a child or a relative for an adult institutionalized patient. Part of the responsibility is likely to fall on the institutional staff as well because lay guardians look to professionals for guidance in making decisions about treatment for the client.

Guardians and institutional staff have interests and needs of their own, which may be at variance with the client receiving the best possible treatment. For instance, there are burdens involved in serving as the guardian of an institutionalized person. At the very least, these include expenditure of time and the weighty responsibility of having to make decisions for another human being. In many cases, a family is placed under financial and emotional strain when one of their members is institutionalized. The net result of these forces is all too often that guardians' decisions about clients are influenced by the guardians' own self-interests. Parents, for example, may decide to have their child institutionalized because this approach is less expensive and burdensome than day treatment and home care. Similarly, because institutions in which nonvoluntary clients reside are usually understaffed and have inadequate facilities, staff members may be more interested in meeting the clients' basic needs and in maintaining decorum as efficiently as possible than in providing needed treatment. This description of what often occurs is not a condemnation of either guardians or institutional staff. Any blame should be placed on the societal forces that have brought about this situation.

Some of these problems could be mitigated, although not eliminated, if nonvoluntary clients were given more say about their treatment. The basic assumption that nonvoluntary clients are totally incompetent to make informed choices about their own welfare is only useful for a *small minority* of nonvoluntary clients, such as severely brain-damaged individuals who merely exist as biological organisms, young children who have minimal communication skills, and mute, unresponsive psychotic patients. A substantial majority of nonvoluntary clients may well be capable of contributing vital information about their needs and desires, which can be used, along with the judgments of guardians and professionals, to reach more ethically justifiable decisions about their treatment.

Misleading assumptions about nonvoluntary clients' reasoning, comprehension, and decision-making capabilities may be the result of labeling. Just because the law considers 12-year-old children "minors" does not mean that they are *unable* to make informed decisions about themselves any more than calling someone an "adult" automatically implies that he or she is capable of decision making. Due to preconceived notions about children's abilities (or lack of them), children are rarely given an opportunity to demonstrate their true capabilities. Similarly, it is typically assumed that a hospitalized psychiatric patient with a diagnosis of "schizophrenia" is "out of contact with reality." Most patients who exhibit schizophrenic behaviors (e.g., talking to "voices") have periods when they are definitely "in contact" and able to communicate well enough to allow them to speak in their own behalf. Thus, it may be possible to elicit and then use a nonvoluntary client's wishes regarding treatment, which can be considered *partial informed consent.*

Informed consent, however, does not necessarily mean *voluntary consent.* Nonvoluntary clients always have less power than their caretakers, who unfortunately sometimes use their superior power to exert undue influence over nonvoluntary clients to consent to certain treatments. For example, consider prison inmates who may be told by the warden that they may take part in a therapeutic program if they wish to but that they do not have to. At the same time, the inmates know that pleasing the warden may lead to special privileges or a favorable recommendation for parole. Thus, even when nonvoluntary clients are capable of providing informed consent for treatment, they may be restricted in their ability to consent voluntarily.

On a more optimistic note, there are ways in which nonvoluntary clients can exercise their freedom *not* to change their behavior. Successful behavioral therapy relies heavily on the client's active participation. A prison inmate, for example, who only "went through the motions" of being in treatment in order to be viewed favorably by the guards and warden could retain his or her individual freedom not to change. A second way in which a nonvoluntary client is free not to change is illustrated by the manner in which courts deal with sexually deviant behavior that threatens the welfare of others (e.g., pedophilic behavior): the offender is given the choice between treatment or incarceration.

Granted, incarceration is not a very attractive alternative to therapy, but it is an alternative, which means that the client cannot be forced to submit to treatment.

Despite the obviously unsolved ethical predicaments surrounding the treatment of nonvoluntary clients, behavioral therapists have proposed and used a variety of procedures and guidelines that provide some safeguards for the rights of such clients. Some of these safeguards are as follows:

1. The nonvoluntary client should be consulted about the goals and methods of therapy, as much as is possible.
2. Explicit written treatment contracts should be used. They should specify in detail (a) the target behaviors, (b) the therapy procedures to be employed, and (c) the procedures for keeping accurate measurements of changes in the target behaviors during treatment (so that an objective index of successful treatment is available). The contract should be signed by the therapist(s), the client's guardian(s), and whenever possible, the client.
3. Extraordinary care should be taken if aversive procedures are employed as part of the treatment plan, because the risk of abuse and exploitation is much greater with nonvoluntary clients than with voluntary clients.
4. Special committees should be established to monitor all treatment of nonvoluntary clients. They should be made up of both professionals and concerned laypeople who are competent to evaluate treatment ethicality and legality.[21] Also, it has been suggested that for institutionalized clients "an ombudsman system, independent of the administration chain of command, could be instituted to ensure that inmates' complaints were receiving due consideration."[22]

These guidelines for the ethical treatment of nonvoluntary clients in behavioral therapy are only a beginning toward solving the dilemmas discussed in this section. At the root of these complicated problems are our society's general attitudes and specific means of dealing with a host of socially marginal and powerless people,[23] a topic that clearly is beyond the scope of this discussion.

THE MIXED BLESSING OF POTENT THERAPIES: DANGERS AND SAFEGUARDS

In the early 1960s, when behavioral therapies were just becoming accepted as alternative methods of treatment, critics argued that the procedures were too superficial and would have little impact. As it became increasingly clear that behavioral therapy procedures could in fact result in major changes in behavior and as the mental health profession in general became increasingly aware of the need to safeguard clients' rights, critics of behavioral therapy changed their tune. Now they began to worry about the misuse or abuse of admittedly *potent* behavioral therapies. The moral of this historical account is simple: only potentially powerful procedures need be feared.

Dangers: Illusory and Real

Although there is substantial evidence supporting the potency of many behavioral therapies, they are far from panaceas. For example, exaggerated claims that behavioral therapy can, under any circumstances, produce radical changes in people's behavior are erroneous and highly misleading. (Such claims are sometimes made by critics who "generously" impart undeserved omnipotent powers to behavioral therapy in order to place it in an unfavorable light.) As mentioned previously, a now-classic example of such exaggeration occurs in *A Clockwork Orange.* The treatment that the hero is forced to undergo to "cure" him of his savage, sadistic acts is very much science *fiction!* In reality, it is extremely difficult, and often impossible, to change a person's behavior when the individual does not want to change.[24]

Behavioral principles and procedures (much like atomic energy) can either help or harm. The methods of behavioral therapy are independent of the aims toward which they are put: there is nothing unethical (or ethical, for that matter) in the principles of reinforcement, shaping, or modeling. Questions of ethicality become germane only when the end products of these means are specified. Then, whether a goal is considered ethical or unethical depends on one's values. For instance, most readers would not consider it ethically wrong to teach a child to read or write through modeling and shaping. It is conceivable, however, that in an economically impoverished culture parents might object to a child spending time in school learning to read and write when the child might be learning skills that would enable the child to contribute to the family's income and resources (e.g., mechanical and manual labor skills).

All forms of therapy exert influence and control over clients. But several factors have placed behavioral therapy under closer scrutiny in this regard. First, as already mentioned, some behavioral therapies, such as reinforcement procedures, have been found to be especially potent in changing people's behavior. The ability to exert an influence is the primary prerequisite for potential misuse.

Second, the methods of behavioral therapy are explicit and fully open to inspection by clients, the public, and critics. In fact, behavioral therapists consider this openness to be one of the advantages of their approach to treatment. The steps involved in the procedures are spelled out so that novice therapists can learn them, other therapists can use them, and clients can understand and apply them on their own. At the same time, the explicit nature of behavioral therapy makes it obvious that influence is being exerted to change a client's behavior, and this explicitness serves to heighten people's defenses against possible abuses. When therapy procedures are presented in vague, general terms (e.g., "gaining insight about one's behavior"), then they typically are considered somehow less suspect.

In a related vein, a third factor that may account for the greater suspicion surrounding behavioral therapy is the presence of a treatment plan. Behavioral therapy stresses the importance of carefully planning treatment, based on a detailed assessment of the conditions maintaining the target behavior. Non-behavioral therapies often rely on the evolving process of therapy to dictate subsequent interventions. The point here is not which approach is better, but rather the attitudes that each evokes. People tend to be more suspicious of careful planning than of a capricious, free-flowing approach.[25] It is not clear why this should be the case. One possibility is that if control is viewed as dangerous, then planned control is even more threatening; in an analogous way, premeditated murder is a more serious crime than accidental murder.

All this is not to say that behavioral therapy cannot be misused or abused. In fact, one problem is that everyone has access to the *rudiments* of behavioral therapy. Even if the goals at which the elementary procedures are aimed are in the best interest of the recipient, lack of professional training and experience in behavioral therapy could produce more harm than good. As the old adage states, "A little knowledge is a dangerous thing." The problem of proliferating behavioral therapy procedures becomes a definite danger when the procedures are used unethically or for malevolent purposes. There are a small number of well-documented incidents of such misuse, most of which have been perpetuated against people who have little or no influence over their environment—institutionalized individuals and prison inmates.[26] Behavioral therapists have been actively concerned with preventing similar incidents from occurring in the future, such as by devising guidelines for the ethical use of behavioral therapies. For example, in 1977 the Association for Advancement of Behavior Therapy adopted a checklist of ethical issues that should be considered whenever therapeutic procedures are applied.[27] These issues, each presented as a question, are listed in Table 13-1, along with some preliminary comments concerning the development and use of the checklist.

Safeguards Through Countercontrol

Making people aware and knowledgeable about behavioral therapy may be the major safeguard against its potential abuse. Individuals who are aware that they are being controlled and understand how this control is being exerted are less easily influenced by others. Moreover, knowledge of behavioral therapy procedures enables individuals to exert *countercontrol.* In fact, people who are controlled by behavioral techniques can exert influence over their controllers by the very same techniques! However, such countercontrol becomes difficult when people are ignorant or uninformed as well as in situations where there is disproportionate power.

Disproportionate power exists in any situation in which certain parties have authority over others. A typical example is when teachers exert more power over students than the reverse. But if students are taught effective means of influencing their teachers' behavior, countercontrol is possible, as Case 13-1 illustrates.

TABLE 13-1 Checklist of Ethical Issues for Human Services

Rather than recommending a list of prescriptions and proscriptions, the committee agreed to focus on critical ethical issues of central importance to human services.

On each of the issues described below, ideal interventions would have maximum involvement by the person whose behavior is to be changed, and the fullest possible consideration of societal pressures on that person, the therapist, and the therapist's employer. The committee recognizes that the practicalities of actual settings sometimes require exceptions, and that there certainly are occasions when exceptions can be consistent with ethical practice. Even though some exceptions may eventually be necessary, the committee feels that each of these issues should be explicitly considered.

The questions related to each issue have deliberately been cast in a general manner that applies to all types of interventions, and not solely or specifically to the practice of behavior therapy. The committee felt strongly that issues directed specifically to behavior therapists might imply erroneously that behavior therapy was in some way more in need of ethical concern than non-behaviorally-oriented therapies.

In the list of issues, the term *client* is used to describe the person whose behavior is to be changed; *therapist* is used to describe the professional in charge of the intervention; *treatment* and *problem,* although used in the singular, refer to any and all treatments and problems being formulated with this checklist. The issues are formulated so as to be relevant across as many settings and populations as possible. Thus, they need to be qualified when someone other than the person whose behavior is to be changed is paying the therapist, or when that person's competence or the voluntary nature of that person's consent is questioned. For example, if the therapist has found that the client does not understand the goals or methods being considered, the therapist should substitute the client's guardian or other responsible person for *client,* when reviewing the issues below.

A. Have the goals of treatment been adequately considered?
   1. To ensure that the goals are explicit, are they written?
   2. Has the client's understanding of the goals been assured by having the client restate them orally or in writing?
   3. Have the therapist and client agreed on the goals of therapy?
   4. Will serving the client's interests be contrary to the interests of other persons?
   5. Will serving the client's immediate interests be contrary to the client's long-term interest?

B. Has the choice of treatment methods been adequately considered?
   1. Does the published literature show the procedure to be the best one available for that problem?
   2. If no literature exists regarding the treatment method, is the method consistent with generally accepted practice?
   3. Has the client been told of alternative procedures that might be preferred by the client on the basis of significant differences in discomfort, treatment time, cost, or degree of demonstrated effectiveness?
   4. If a treatment procedure is publicly, legally, or professionally controversial, has formal professional consultation been obtained, has the reaction of the affected segment of the public been adequately considered, and have the alternative treatment methods been more closely reexamined and reconsidered?

C. Is the client's participation voluntary?
   1. Have possible sources of coercion on the client's participation been considered?
   2. If treatment is legally mandated, has the available range of treatments and therapists been offered?
   3. Can the client withdraw from treatment without a penalty or financial loss that exceeds actual clinical costs?

D. When another person or an agency is empowered to arrange for therapy, have the interests of the subordinated client been sufficiently considered?
   1. Has the subordinated client been informed of the treatment objectives and participated in the choice of treatment procedures?
   2. Where the subordinated client's competence to decide is limited, have the client as well as the guardian participated in the treatment discussions to the extent that the client's abilities permit?

Continued

TABLE 13-1 Continued

3. If the interests of the subordinated person and the superordinate persons or agency conflict, have attempts been made to reduce the conflict by dealing with both interests?

E. Has the adequacy of treatment been evaluated?
   1. Have quantitative measures of the problem and its progress been obtained?
   2. Have the measures of the problem and its progress been made available to the client during treatment?

F. Has the confidentiality of the treatment relationship been protected?
   1. Has the client been told who has access to the records?
   2. Are records available only to authorized persons?

G. Does the therapist refer the clients to other therapists when necessary?
   1. If treatment is unsuccessful, is the client referred to other therapists?
   2. Has the client been told that if dissatisfied with the treatment, referral will be made?

H. Is the therapist qualified to provide treatment?
   1. Has the therapist had training or experience in treating problems like the client's?
   2. If deficits exist in the therapist's qualifications, has the client been informed?
   3. If the therapist is not adequately qualified, is the client referred to other therapists, or has supervision by a qualified therapist been provided? Is the client informed of the supervisory relation?
   4. If the treatment is administered by mediators, have the mediators been adequately supervised by a qualified therapist?

SOURCE: "Ethical issues for human services" (1977), pp. v–vi.

CASE 13-1

Students as Change Agents in an Experimental Program to Improve Teachers' Interaction with Students*

The setting for this experimental program was a school that was known for its hostility toward students in special education classes, particularly adolescent minority children. Attempts to reintegrate special education children into the mainstream of the school had been largely unsuccessful. Although teachers were specifically directed by their supervisors to treat all students equally, regular class teachers continued to scapegoat special education children.

> Seven children with an age range of 12 to 15 were selected as behavior engineers. Two children were Caucasian, two were black and three were Chicanos. Each engineer was assigned two clients (teachers), and each had the responsibility of accelerating praise rates and decelerating negative comments and punishment by the teachers.
>
> Instruction and practice in behavior modification theory and techniques were given during one period a day by the special class teachers. Initially, instruction was on a one-to-one basis, but later the whole class worked together on practicing their newly learned skills. The children were told that they were going to

*Graubard, Rosenberg, & Miller (1974). Quotation is from pp. 422–423.

participate in an experiment. Scientific accuracy was stressed as being extremely important. Students were directed to record all the client teacher's remarks during the pilot period of two weeks. Through consensual validation of the class and special education staff, these comments were sorted into positive or negative groups.

Techniques taught to the children included making eye contact with teachers and asking for extra help and, further, children were taught to make reinforcing comments such as "Gee, it makes me feel good and work so much better when you praise me" and "I like the way you teach that lesson." They also were taught to use reinforcing behavior, such as sitting up straight and nodding in agreement as teachers spoke. These techniques and phrases were used contingent upon teacher performance.

Pupils were also taught to break eye contact with the teacher during a scolding, to ignore a teacher's provocation, to show up early for class, and to ask for extra assignments. These techniques were explicitly taught and practiced repeatedly.

When the student behavior engineers had mastered the consequential behavioral therapy skills, a nine-week experiment to assess their effectiveness in changing teachers'

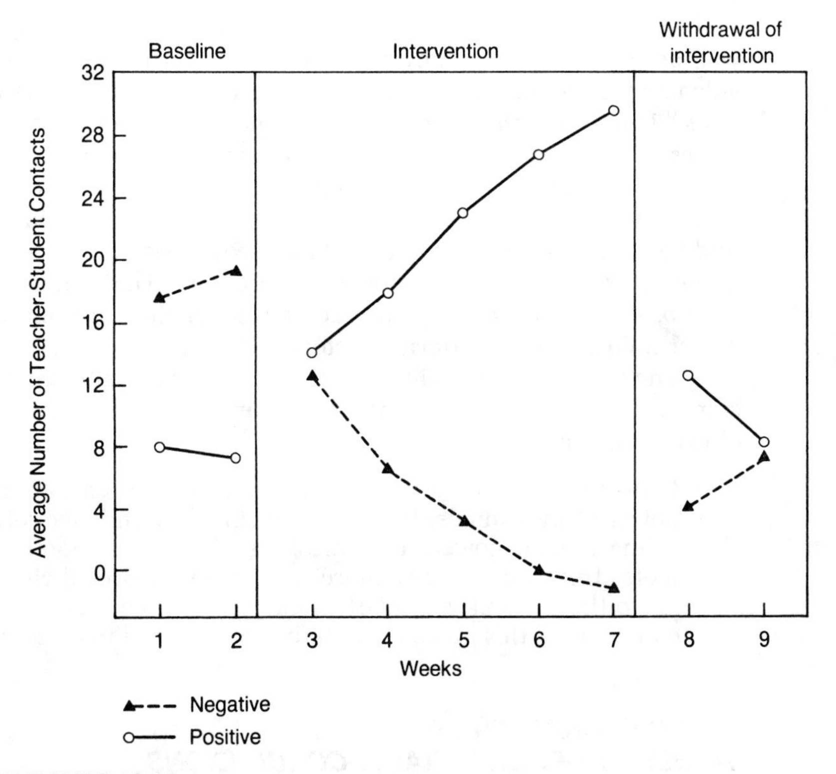

CASE FIGURE 13-1A

The average number of positive and negative teacher-student contacts during baseline, student intervention, and withdrawal of student intervention *SOURCE: Adapted from Graubard, Rosenberg, & Miller (1974), p. 425.*

behaviors was conducted. The students recorded both positive and negative contacts that teachers made with them, and the accuracy of these observations was checked periodically by an independent observer in the classroom.

The impressive success the students had in modifying their teachers' behavior can be seen in Case Figure 13-1A (p. 341) which shows the average number of positive and negative teacher-student contacts over the nine weeks. The first two weeks were for baseline observations. Starting with the first week of intervention (Week 3), teachers' positive contacts significantly increased and teachers' negative contacts significantly decreased. This trend continued over the next four weeks of intervention. During the last two weeks, the interventions were stopped in order to assess whether the students' interventions were responsible for the change in the teachers' behaviors. The decrease in positive contacts and increase in negative contacts observed during this period clearly indicate that the students had successfully modified their teachers' interactions with them by using appropriate consequential behavioral therapy procedures. These findings suggest the possibility of diffusing disproportionate power by providing the "weaker" members of our society with behavioral therapy skills to alter the behavior of more powerful individuals.

It is a "fact of life" that we are constantly influenced by other people as well as by our physical environment. This idea is unsettling for many individuals who would like to think of themselves as the "captains of their own fates." However, although our behavior may be determined by various external forces in our lives, this does not mean that we cannot, in turn, affect those forces. As Skinner has aptly observed, "We cannot choose a way of life in which there is no control. We can only change the controlling conditions."[28] And by changing controlling conditions people assume an active role in determining their own fates, as shown by Case 13-1. This action is an example of *reciprocal determinism:* external factors influencing our behavior and our behavior influencing the external factors.[29]

The recent emphasis in behavioral therapy on self-control may well have come at an opportune time, when people are becoming more aware and fearful of external control.[30]

> In order to defend individual freedom, it is necessary to enhance the power of individuals. *If* behavior technology endangers freedom by giving refined powers to controllers, then the antidote which promotes freedom is to give more refined power over their own behavior to those who [would be] endangered. Since everyone [could be] endangered, this means facilitating self-control in everyone.[31]

ETHICAL CHALLENGES TO BEHAVIORAL THERAPY: CONCLUSIONS

This chapter has examined the major ethical challenges faced by behavioral therapy. In order to counter ethical criticisms of behavioral therapy, evidence has been presented concerning what behavioral therapies are and how they are used to help people. First, behavioral therapy pays special attention to the uniqueness of each client, which makes its approach personal and intimate (rather than mechanistic and detached). Second, behavioral therapy fosters personal freedom by providing clients with alternative ways of behaving, which allows them to make choices in their lives (rather than being constrained). And, third, behavioral therapy teaches clients how to control their own behavior by assessing and influencing the factors in their lives that govern their behavior (so that they are not victims of external control).

Many behavioral therapists, including myself, believe that such practices make behavioral therapy not only an ethical endeavor but also a distinctly humanizing approach to treatment. Specifically, behavioral therapy promotes such humanistic goals as (1) individuality; (2) increased awareness of oneself (as a unique human being) and the factors that influence one's behavior; (3) the ability to transcend the constraints of the immediate situation and to create new environments consistent with one's personal goals, potential, and aspirations; and thus (4) becoming a self-determining, responsible person.

Before reading this chapter, you were asked to assess your opinions about some of the ethical issues to be discussed in the chapter. Now, you may wish to reassess your opinions by doing Participation Exercise 13-2.

PARTICIPATION EXERCISE 13-2

A Postreading Assessment of Your Opinions About Ethical Issues Related to Behavioral Therapy

After reading this chapter, have your opinions about ethical issues related to behavioral therapy changed? You can check this possibility out by assessing your present opinions of the 11 statements you rated before you read the chapter (in Participation Exercise 13-1). For the moment, do ***not*** refer to the sheet of paper containing your prereading opinions. Take another sheet of paper, and list the numbers 1 through 11. Using the following scale, write the letter(s) that best represents your ***present*** opinion about each statement listed. Note that because the statements are listed in descending order, you will ***start at the bottom of your answer sheet with number 11 and work up.***

AA = Strongly Agree
A = Moderately Agree
a = Slightly Agree
d = Slightly Disagree
D = Moderately Disagree
DD = Strongly Disagree

11. One way of assuring that behavioral therapy techniques will ***not*** be used against people is to restrict knowledge of the techniques only to professional behavioral therapists.
10. Behavioral therapy techniques can be used for harmful purposes.

9. Many nonvoluntary clients (e.g., children and committed psychiatric patients) are capable of making informed decisions about their own treatment.
8. Treatments that involve pain or discomfort to a client are unethical.
7. Behavioral therapy makes clients conform to behaviors that society considers appropriate and acceptable.
6. People have little control over the environmental events that influence their behavior.
5. Behavioral therapy procedures tend to increase clients' personal freedom.
4. Behavioral therapy treats each client's problem as unique.
3. The therapist determines the goals of behavioral therapy for the client.
2. The practice of behavioral therapy is mechanistic and impersonal.
1. Behavioral therapy poses ethical and moral problems that do ***not*** exist with other forms of therapy.

Now compare the ratings you made in Participation Exercises 13-1 and 13-2. Have your opinions shifted on any of the statements? If so, how have they changed? What new information or ideas changed your opinions?

SUMMARY

Behavioral therapy is essentially ethically neutral—it does not specify whose behavior or what behavior is to be changed, only how change is to be implemented. Still, ethical issues arise in any form of therapy. Some ethical criticisms of behavioral therapy are not warranted, because they are addressed to an erroneous conception of the nature of contemporary behavioral therapy, such as that it is mechanistic and impersonal. In fact, behavioral therapy is individualized for each client, and a good therapeutic relationship is necessary for effective behavioral therapy. Concerning the issue of freedom and control, clients in behavioral therapy directly choose their own treatment goals; clients indirectly choose their therapy in that behavioral therapists explain therapy procedures to clients ahead of time and typically enter into contractual agreements in this regard; the fact that behavioral therapy often teaches clients adaptive behaviors enhances their freedom by providing them with increased alternatives from which to choose. The use of aversive therapy procedures raises sensitive ethical issues. Although in practice aversive procedures are used relatively infrequently in behavioral therapy, and usually as a last resort, special precautions must be taken when they are employed. In each individual case, a cost-benefit analysis must be made to determine if the aversive procedures are warranted. Nonvoluntary clients present particular ethical problems because they are subject to coercion in that they often have little say about their treatment. However, there are many ways in which nonvoluntary clients can have at least partial say about their treatment. To the extent that behavioral therapies are potent, the possibility of their abuse, such as against people for harmful purposes, exists, although few actual instances of such abuse have occurred. The best safeguard against potential abuse is to make clients (and people in general) knowledgeable about behavioral therapy so they can either resist being influenced or exert countercontrol using the same techniques that are being used to influence them.

REFERENCE NOTES

1. For example, Bandura, 1975; Davison, 1976; Davison & Stuart, 1975.
2. For example, Stolz, 1977.
3. Davison & Stuart, 1975, p. 756.
4. Franks & Wilson, 1978, p. 26.
5. Turkat & Feuerstein, 1978.
6. Reimringer, Morgan, & Bramwell, 1970.
7. Woolfolk, Woolfolk, & Wilson, 1977.
8. Woolfolk, Woolfolk, & Wilson, 1977, p. 184.
9. Bandura, 1975, p. 14.
10. For example, Morris & Suckerman, 1974a, 1974b; Wilson & Evans, 1977.
11. Parloff, Waskow, & Wolfe, 1978.
12. Goldfried & Davison, 1976.
13. Bandura, 1969.
14. Bandura, 1969.
15. Franks & Wilson, 1975, pp. 3–4.
16. For example, Lovaas & Simmons, 1969.
17. Goldiamond, 1974, pp. 62–63.
18. Bandura, 1969.
19. For example, Lovaas & Simmons, 1969.
20. For example, Risley & Twardosz, 1974.
21. Kassirer, 1974.
22. Bootzin, 1975, p. 152.
23. See Spiegler & Agigian, 1977.
24. Bandura, 1969.
25. Kanfer & Phillips, 1970.
26. For example, Cotter, 1967.
27. "Ethical issues for human services," 1977.
28. Skinner, 1974, p. 190.
29. Bandura, 1977b; Mahoney, 1974.
30. See London, 1969; Skinner, 1971.
31. London, 1969, pp. 213–214.

CHAPTER 14

The Status of Contemporary Behavioral Therapy

Having discussed the basic principles of behavioral therapy and its major therapeutic approaches, it is now appropriate to evaluate behavioral therapy by reviewing the current status of the field. This chapter begins with an appraisal of the effectiveness of behavioral therapies, and then turns to some important issues concerning the comprehensiveness of behavioral therapy. The chapter concludes with an examination of the major strengths and weaknesses of behavioral therapy.

HOW EFFECTIVE ARE BEHAVIORAL THERAPIES?

It makes little sense to pose the broad question "How effective is behavioral therapy?" because there is no single technique of behavioral therapy. Appropriate questions focus on the relative efficacy of specific behavioral therapies—that is, how effective is a particular therapy procedure compared to other behavioral or nonbehavioral therapies, to appropriate control conditions (e.g., for placebo effects), and to no treatment. It is well known that clients may improve without any formal therapeutic intervention (a phenomenon called *spontaneous remission*), and it is therefore necessary to ascertain whether a specific therapy leads to more improvement than no treatment at all.

Even more meaningful questions are concerned with the effectiveness of particular behavioral therapies for specific problem behaviors. Because there are dozens of behavioral therapies and far more problem behaviors, a complete review of research that attempts to answer such questions is not feasible. But the findings on the effectiveness of various behavioral therapies discussed in this book for some of the more prevalent problem behaviors can be briefly summarized. Much of the following review is based on Kazdin and Wilson's 1978 book, *Evaluation of Behavior Therapy*.[1] The review is based on research data available through 1980.

Anxiety-Related Target Behaviors

In the treatment of avoidance (phobic) behaviors, behavioral therapies have been shown to be particularly effective; and participant modeling and *in vivo* flooding are the most effective therapies.[2] Systematic desensitization, the technique used most frequently to date, is also effective but tends to take more time and is likely to generalize less well to the client's natural environment. Participant modeling and *in vivo* flooding appear to be the only consistently effective treatments for obsessive-compulsive behaviors[3] such as repetitive, ritualistic acts (e.g., checking, 18 times each night, to see that one's front door is locked). This finding is significant, because obsessive-compulsive behaviors have been especially difficult to treat by a variety of traditional treatments, such as verbal psychotherapy, drugs, and psychosurgery,[4] as well as by other behavioral therapies, such as systematic desensitization.

Marital and Sexual Problems

Marital discord and sexual dysfunction are complex and often related problems, and behavioral therapies have shown considerable promise in their treatment. Because of the multifaceted nature of these problems, treatment packages are usually employed, rather than single therapies. For example, typical target behaviors for marital discord—such as improved communication, reciprocal reinforcement of needs, and problem solving—are treated by a combination of direct instruction, modeling, behavior rehearsal, and contingency contracting.[5] The success of Masters and Johnson-type treatment of sexual dysfunction, which includes many behavioral components such as modeling, feedback, shaping, and *in vivo* desensitization, is unprecedented, compared with the complete lack of evidence supporting other forms of treatment. Although problems of sexual deviation (e.g., exhibitionistic and fetishistic behaviors) tend to be highly resistant to change, substitution aversion therapies such as covert sensitization have been used with some success where traditional treatments have failed.[6]

Addictive Behaviors

Substance addictions have also not typically responded well to any type of treatment. Alcohol abuse has sometimes been successfully treated by aversion therapy when the aversive stimulus is a drug that makes the client nauseous (e.g., Antabuse), but not when the aversive stimulus is mild shock.[7] Because the antecedents and consequences of alcohol abuse and addiction are complex (including familial, occupational, peer, and personal stress factors), it is not surprising that the most successful therapeutic approaches have involved treatment packages. For example, with a client addicted to alcohol, a combination of (1) a community reinforcement program including job, family, and social counseling with (2) an incentive program for self-administering Antabuse was found to be more successful than was routine hospital treatment. Two years after treatment, this behavioral therapy treatment package had significantly decreased the amount of time clients spent drinking and being in an institution and increased the time they spent on the job and at home.[8] Teaching clients to discriminate the amount of alcohol in their blood in order to allow them to drink in moderation (as opposed to total abstinence) is a promising but controversial procedure (see Chapter 9).[9] Although in a few individual cases behavioral therapy has been used with some success to treat "hard" drug addiction, there are no controlled-outcome studies of such applications, making it impossible to conclude that behavioral therapy is superior to any other treatment approach to drug addiction.[10]

With a fair number of exceptions, behavioral therapy procedures have not had much success in decelerating cigarette smoking. Although therapies such as systematic desensitization, stimulus control, contingency contracting, and aversion therapies have all resulted in temporary reductions in smoking, their effectiveness does not tend to last.[11] (This finding is not surprising given the massive symbolic modeling of cigarette smoking that continues to appear in advertisements, despite the established causal relationship between cigarette smoking and a host of debilitating and fatal diseases.)

Obesity is another health-related problem for which behavioral therapy procedures have had only limited success. Treatment packages have focused on self-control skills such as self-monitoring, self-reinforcement, stimulus control, and contingency contracting. Such behavioral treatment packages are clearly superior to other approaches (e.g., traditional psychotherapy, drugs, or social pressure) in the *short term*, but the weight losses obtained do not tend to be maintained over long periods of time.[12]

Adult Psychotic Behaviors

The treatment of psychotic behavior is certainly one of the most significant contributions made by behavioral therapy. Although there is evidence that many psychotic behaviors have biological bases, medical treatments have proven to be only partially effective. For example, major tranquilizers or antipsychotic medications can be useful in reducing bizarre behaviors (e.g., hallucinations and delusional thoughts), but as with any deceleration procedure, they do not foster alternative adaptive behaviors. Modeling and reinforcement therapies have been quite successful in teaching and instigating such behaviors.[13]

Token economies have primarily been used to accelerate adaptive behaviors (e.g., self-care and basic social skills) in institutional settings. Yet there is evidence that such programs promote generalization to behaviors that are desirable outside the institution, including decreasing the dependent behavior and apathy typically associated with institutionalization, as well as depression, screaming, ritualistic behaviors, and dependence on medication. Increased adaptive ward behaviors have also been associated with increases in cooperation, communication skills, social interactions, and positive mood.[14] A few token economy programs, such as the Community Training Center (see Chapter 8), have directly promoted adaptive behaviors that patients must be able to perform if they are to leave the institution and successfully live independently in the community.[15]

In addition to token economy programs on wards of institutionalized patients, individualized reinforcement programs (often in the form of contingency contracts) have been used to accelerate a variety of adaptive behaviors (e.g., social and communication skills) and to decelerate maladaptive behaviors by accelerating incompatible adaptive behaviors. These procedures have been shown to be more effective than general ward care (e.g., custodial care or activities "therapy") and specific nonbehavioral treatment alternatives (e.g., individual verbal psychotherapy and milieu therapy).[16]

Childhood and Adolescent Problem Behaviors

Behavioral therapies have been useful in dealing with a variety of childhood and adolescent problems. Minor problems—the sort all children seem to have, such as not paying attention to parents, failure to do chores, and fighting with peers—often have been effectively treated by training parents and teachers to use various consequential behavioral therapies to alter the problem behaviors of the children.[17] More severe problems—such as stealing, truancy, and destroying property—that are referred to mental health or law enforcement agencies have been successfully modified by changing environmental contingencies in the home and at school.[18] Problem behaviors that result in juvenile court ajudication are typically dealt with by institutionalizing the youth in a "training school." Home-style behavioral therapy programs such as Achievement Place have been shown to be more effective than institutionalization or probation (see Chapter 8).

Other childhood problem behaviors that have been treated by behavioral therapies include enuresis, hyperactivity, and psychotic behavior. For treatment of enuresis—a relatively minor but frequent problem—the bell-and-pad method and dry-bed training are the most effective therapies ever developed (see Chapter 9).

The diagnostic label *hyperactivity* (or *hyperkinesis*) refers to a set of behaviors that includes constant activity, restlessness, distractibility, and short attention span. It occurs in approximately 10 percent of schoolchildren, and a large percentage (as much as 50 percent) of referrals to therapy in elementary school children present this problem.[19] Hyperactive behavior generally has been treated with medication, but recently behavioral therapy involving reinforcing behaviors incompatible with constant activity has provided a possible alternative to drug therapy.[20]

Psychotic behavior of children (often labeled *infantile autism* or *childhood schizophrenia*) is characterized by aloofness, lack of communicative speech, intolerance for change in routine or in surroundings, and repetitive and self-stimulatory behavior. Whereas psychoanalytic treatment of these behaviors has shown no success (compared to no treatment), behavioral therapy procedures—such as modeling, use of positive and negative consequences, prompting, and shaping—have led to significant changes in this extremely deviant behavior.[21] These procedures have reduced repetitive, self-stimulatory, and self-destructive behaviors and increased social interactions, communication, and language skills. The most extensive treatment program for childhood psychotic behavior was spearheaded by Ivar Lovaas and his colleagues at the University of California at Los Angeles Neuropsychiatric Clinic. In contrast to many other behavioral therapy programs, Lovaas's treatment program for childhood psychotic behavior involves intensive therapy for a relatively long period of time, and thus the number of children who can benefit is very small. The other major problem with this treatment is that the changes do not easily generalize beyond the specific treatment setting. Not surprisingly, when the contingencies that existed in the program (e.g., reinforcement for correct communicative speech) change at home or in a regular school (e.g., reinforcement in the form of attention when children fail to communicate), the children quickly return to their psychotic behaviors.[22] Recently parents have become involved in the training program so that the appropriate contingencies can be continued outside the clinic.[23]

Problem Behaviors Associated with Mental Retardation

People who are intellectually handicapped and labeled "mentally retarded" present a variety of problem behaviors for which behavioral therapy procedures have proved highly effective.[24] Besides their intellectual deficits, these individuals often lack adequate self-care, communication, and social skills and may engage in various socially inappropriate behaviors (e.g., disrobing in public) that limit their functioning outside of institutions. The major behavioral therapies used to alleviate these problems are modeling and a variety of consequential procedures.[25] Self-care skills that have been successfully taught include dressing, feeding, grooming, exercising, personal hygiene, and toileting. Dry-pants training (see Chapter 9) is perhaps the most impressive self-care treatment package developed; even with institutionalized retarded children, toilet training can be completed in less than one day[26] and is maintained at least several months after treatment.[27] The particular verbal and language skills taught vary with the individuals' degree of intellectual impairment and have ranged from naming objects and asking simple questions (in severely retarded children)[28] to discussing current events (in borderline retarded individuals).[29] Similarly, a wide range of social skills has been taught, from simple greetings[30] to peer and play behavior.[31] Behavioral therapies have also successfully suppressed a number of behaviors that interfere with learning and engaging in "normal" activities, including public disrobing,[32] sprawling on the floor,[33] screaming and crying,[34] and eating trash and feces.[35]

Conclusions

The preceding review has summarized the research regarding the efficacy of behavioral therapies for some of the most common problems treated by psychotherapists. Evaluating treatment effectiveness is among the most complicated and difficult areas of research because of a host of methodological, practical, and ethical limitations.[36] Behavioral therapists have always had a serious commitment to evaluating their therapies, and generally speaking they have tended to have a higher level of training and skill in doing evaluation research than do many non-behaviorally-oriented therapists. Nonetheless, many studies that assess the efficacy of behavioral therapies have serious inadequacies limiting the conclusions that can be drawn. Behavioral therapists have been among the loudest and most stringent critics of this research.[37] Still, it is important to place behavioral therapy outcome research in proper perspective:

> Few therapy techniques or set of techniques have as strong an empirical base demonstrating behavior change with *clinical populations* and in examining the *generality and durability* of these changes as have behavior therapy techniques. Moreover, behavior therapy is distinguished by its breadth of applications to a wide range of clients (e.g., preschool children, nursing home residents), treatment populations (e.g., psychotics, neurotics, delinquents), and problem areas (e.g., seizures, hypertension, anxiety, delusions).[38]

Compared to alternative approaches, behavioral therapies clearly are at least as effective and frequently more effective. Furthermore, even if behavioral therapies were only no *less* effective than other forms of psychotherapy, they would still be preferable in many instances because they are usually more efficient. Changes in behavioral therapy are frequently achieved in a relatively short time span, compared to alternative treatments, such as most verbal psychotherapies. For example, although there is some evidence that the proportion of clients who are successfully treated for sexually deviant behavior may be similar for both behavioral therapies[39] and psychoanalysis,[40] the average duration of the most effective behavioral therapy is six to seven hours, compared to a minimum of 150 hours for psychoanalytic treatment. Moreover, the use of nonprofessionals, such as parents and teachers, and clients themselves, as change agents in some behavioral therapy programs is more cost-effective than approaches that require total participation of professional therapists.

The obviously favorable picture of the efficacy of behavioral therapies does *not* mean that they are panaceas. Furthermore, to say that a particular behavioral therapy is more effective than other forms of treatment is not to say that optimal treatment effectiveness exists. In other words, "better than" (more effective than) is not necessarily the same as "good" (effective). For example, in the case of several problem behaviors that are extremely difficult to modify, such as sexually deviant behavior and psychotic behaviors, behavioral therapies are the best available treatments, but the absolute degree of improvement and especially its maintenance over time are still far too low.

THE COMPREHENSIVENESS OF BEHAVIORAL THERAPIES

Critics have contended that behavioral therapy is a superficial form of treatment. Their arguments have concerned the degree to which behavioral therapies treat only the surface manifestations of deep, underlying problems as well as the extent to which behavioral therapies are capable of treating complex human problems and so-called nonbehavioral problems.

The Issue of Symptom Substitution and Side Effects

The notion of symptom substitution is based on the psychoanalytic argument that a problem behavior indicates a complex, intrapsychic conflict of which the target behavior may be only one possible manifestation. This argument implies that unless the underlying conflict is treated, the conflict will continue to affect the client. Thus, if the problem behavior is successfully eliminated another problem behavior (symptom) will appear in place of (as a substitute for) the one eliminated—to wit, *symptom substitution*. This argument has been refuted by behavioral therapists on both theoretical and empirical grounds. First, behavioral therapists do not adhere to the basic theoretical assumption of underlying intrapsychic causes and multiple symptoms, because these theoretical assumptions have not been empirically validated.[41] Second, there is no empirical support for symptom substitution actually occurring when behavioral therapy successfully eliminates a deceleration target behavior.[42] Studies specifically designed to detect negative side effects of behavioral therapy have failed to find evidence of symptom substitution.[43]

Even if one rejects the basic (psychodynamic) theoretical assumptions that predict symptom substitution and accepts the fact that empirical data do not support symptom substitution, there is still the related issue of side effects. Recently, behavioral therapists have addressed the important question of whether changes in a target behavior are associated with changes in nontreated behaviors. The evidence clearly indicates that such influences frequently occur,[44] which is not surprising, because an individual's behaviors are interrelated. It would be expected, for example, that a teenage girl who has learned to cope with frustration by problem solving, rather than outbursts of anger, would as an indirect result of therapy, show improvements in other aspects of her interpersonal relations with peers and adults. Although the secondary effects of behavioral therapy on nontreated behaviors can be positive[45] or negative,[46] fortunately they are almost always positive.[47]

The Complexity of Target Behaviors

The criticism that behavioral therapy is only effective with discrete and simple behaviors arose in the late 1950s when behavioral therapists were attempting to gain recognition for their new approach as a viable alternative to traditional modes of therapy. At that time, narrow target behaviors were modified in order to dramatically demonstrate the effectiveness of behavioral procedures or to develop and refine new behavioral therapies.[48] The field of behavioral therapy has come a long way from this important initial work, however. Behavioral therapy is no longer (if indeed it ever was) restricted to the treatment of monosymptomatic phobic behaviors and simple maladaptive habits, as is evident from the examples used in this book.

The practice of behavioral therapy may *seem* to be concerned only with simple behaviors because it deals with target behaviors. To review, complex and multifaceted problem behaviors are dealt with in behavioral therapy by systematically treating one or two very specific (target) behaviors that are aspects of the overall problem(s). When satisfactory improvement is achieved with the initial target behaviors, therapy proceeds to treat additional discrete target behaviors. Using this strategy, it is possible to bring about behavioral changes rapidly, which usually has two effects. The client receives some relief, and, as a consequence of experiencing improvement, the client becomes more motivated to work on other target behaviors. Moreover, improvement in even a single target behavior frequently has positive carryover to other aspects of the client's problem behavior(s), as was discussed in the previous section. Thus, treating discrete narrow behaviors may have the net result of creating beneficial changes in related, much broader, and more complex behaviors.

The Treatment of "Nonbehavioral" Problems

How does behavioral therapy deal with problems that do not *appear* to involve specific problem behaviors? A case in point are so-called existential crises, in which the client's chief complaints are not experiencing any meaning in life and finding activities and interpersonal relationships boring and worthless. One of the behavioral therapist's first tasks in treating such a problem is to work with the client to translate vague complaints into clear-cut, measurable target behaviors. Getting the client to be specific is not always possible, however. People who have the general feeling that life is worthless often experience difficulty thinking concretely and focusing on specific aspects of their lives. Therefore, the target behaviors may have to be the vague feelings, which can be measured in loose terms, such as rating one's feelings of self-worth on a scale ranging from 1 to 10. Even such a gross self-report measure can be useful in assessing changes in the problem behavior.

Next a thorough behavioral assessment would be made of the client's problematic feelings to find their probable maintaining conditions. Important questions include "When did the feelings first begin and what was happening in the client's life at that time? How often do they occur? Under what circumstances are they more severe and when less severe? What are the consequences of these feelings for the client and important people in the client's life?"

The answers to such questions enable the therapist and the client to formulate a treatment plan to change some of the probable conditions maintaining the client's feelings of worthlessness. Often a client's vague negative emotions are related to problematic life situations, although this connection may not be apparent to the client. Such situations may include problems in the client's social life (e. g., marital conflict, lack of dates, and few or no satisfactory relationships), or work life (e.g., dissatisfaction with one's job, being less productive or making less money than one would like, and doing poorly in one's schoolwork). If one or more major problems are occurring in the client's life, they may be the maintaining conditions of the client's negative self-thoughts and feelings. Solving a client's concrete problems is likely to have some positive side effects on the client's attitudes and emotions and therefore may alleviate the "existential crisis." This approach does not work in all cases of existential-type problems but it does work in some cases, and it illustrates the general approach that might be used in behavioral therapy to treat such "nonbehavioral" problems.

The Limits of Behavioral Therapy

What are the limits of behavioral therapy? Are there any problem behaviors for which behavioral therapies are not applicable? Despite the fact that behavioral therapy probably has a greater diversity of application than any other school of psychotherapy, it is not a universal remedy. There are problem behaviors for which behavioral therapy has not been shown to be effective at all or for which it is effective only in conjunction with other modes of treatment. Prime examples are problem behaviors maintained by basic biological factors that cannot be altered by behavioral therapy procedures. Specifically, certain disorders seem to be maintained by chemical imbalances and seem to be affected only by medical treatments, such as medication. Some types of depressive behavior (notably psychotic depression and bipolar affective disorders which are characterized by alternating episodes of depressive and manic behavior) have been successfully alleviated only with medical treatments.

In other cases in which biological factors are maintaining the problem behavior, behavioral therapy may be useful as a component of the total treatment package. For example, patients diagnosed as "schizophrenic" typically show extreme deficits in social and daily living skills. Such deficits can be treated with behavioral therapy procedures. However, other aspects of schizophrenic behavior, such as bizarre thoughts and hallucinations, may interfere with learning and practicing these skills. Therefore, it may be necessary first to reduce these intrusive behaviors (which may be partially maintained by chemical imbalances) with antipsychotic medication so that the patients can learn social and daily living skills.

The major limiting factor on the applicability of behavioral therapy is the nature of the maintaining conditions, not the nature of the target behavior. In the preceding examples of depressive and schizophrenic behaviors, no behavioral therapies can alter the chemical imbalances that are at least partially maintaining these problem behaviors. On the other hand, certain problem behaviors have physiological maintaining conditions that can be treated by behavioral therapy, such as anxiety due to muscular tension. Also, a number of physiological disorders have been successfully treated by behavioral therapies, such as some types of chronic pain and seizures maintained by the consequences of the patient's behaviors, and enuresis, which is frequently maintained by antecedents and consequences that can be changed through behavioral therapy procedures (see Chapter 9).

An important direction in which the field of behavioral therapy is advancing has been in developing therapies capable of changing maintaining conditions previously untreatable through behavioral principles and procedures. For example, cognitive behavioral therapies now make it possible to directly alter target behaviors maintained by thoughts, beliefs, and attitudes.

Behavioral therapy is not suitable for all people and all therapeutic goals. For example, the straightforward, directive style of behavioral therapy is not suitable for clients who prefer a more nondirective, laissez-faire approach or a more confrontive approach, as might be obtained from client-centered (Rogerian) therapy and Gestalt therapy, respectively. Likewise, the emphasis in behavioral therapy on alleviating actual problem behaviors as directly as possible is not appropriate for clients who are concerned with understanding the origins of their present problems and delving into their early childhood experiences and relationships, as is done in psychoanalysis.

MAJOR STRENGTHS AND WEAKNESSES OF BEHAVIORAL THERAPY

Most issues presented in this examination of the major assets and liabilities of the behavioral approach to therapy have already been specifically discussed or alluded to at various points throughout the book. This broad perspective of the nature of behavioral therapy and knowledge of its specifics provides the background for the following overview of the field's primary strengths and weaknesses.

Major Strengths

Six significant strengths of behavioral therapy will be discussed: (1) the success in creating therapeutic changes, (2) the breadth of application, (3) the precise specification of therapeutic goals and procedures, (4) the sophistication of behavioral assessment, (5) the commitment to empiricism, and (6) the emphasis on research.

Success in Creating Therapeutic Changes

Foremost among the strengths of behavioral therapy is its *effectiveness*. Behavioral therapies vary in their efficacy, depending on the target behavior, the type of client, and the setting in which the therapy is implemented. But the evidence supports the broad statement that behavioral therapies in general have a relatively high rate of success. Compared to many traditional forms of psychotherapy, behavioral therapies are also significantly more *efficient* in terms of both the length of time required for treatment and the cost of professional services. The efficiency is due in part to the occasional use of nonprofessionals as therapists and to the use of clients as their own change agents.

Breadth of Application

The breadth of application of behavioral therapy can be seen in the wide variety of clients, problem behaviors, and settings that have been used to illustrate behavioral therapy in this book alone, and these examples are far from exhaustive. Behavioral therapy has met the needs of certain groups of clients with whom many traditional psychotherapies have been inappropriate and therefore ineffective, including infants and young children and people with low intelligence. Clients who cannot afford expensive, long-term therapy have benefited from relatively efficient and therefore less costly behavioral therapies. In contrast to many other psychotherapies that are limited to treating certain kinds of disorders, behavioral therapy has made inroads into the treatment of many problem behaviors that were previously not helped by psychotherapy, such as psychotic behaviors and some medical problems (e.g., pain and enuresis). Behavioral therapy has also been implemented in settings in which psychotherapy has not typically been employed, including the home, schools, industry, and the community.

Precise Specification of Therapeutic Goals and Procedures

The advantages of defining therapy goals in unambiguous, measurable terms have been stressed throughout this book. This specification not only provides both client and therapist with objective criteria for successful therapy but also enables researchers to objectively evaluate the effects of behavioral therapies. When the specifics of a therapeutic procedure have been spelled out, it is possible to perform independent tests of its efficacy. If the effectiveness of the therapy is primarily based on its procedures and not on the skill of the therapist, then therapists in different settings should find comparable success rates using the therapy for similar clients and target behaviors. A clear, detailed description of therapeutic procedures also is invaluable in training behavioral therapists.

Sophistication of Behavioral Assessment

A related strength of behavioral therapy is the *relative* precision and sophistication of the assessment procedures employed to evaluate the problem behaviors and to measure changes in target behaviors and their maintaining conditions. Behavioral assessment is not without its limitations. Nonetheless, it is superior to many traditional methods of assessment that tend to be highly subjective and inferential. Direct observation of overt behavior is more reliable and valid than are indirect assessment procedures such as projective techniques (e.g., the Rorschach inkblots) used in psychodynamic therapies. In contrast to traditional self-report procedures, behavioral self-reports require little or no inference because clients are asked directly about the information desired (see

Chapter 3). Structured interviews used in behavioral assessment elicit samples of behavior and tend to be better predictors of the way clients actually act in their natural environments than are the open-ended interview procedures used in conjunction with many traditional therapies.[49] In sum, one strength of behavioral therapy is that new methods of assessment have been developed, many of which are superior to traditional personality assessment procedures.

Commitment to Empiricism

The heavy reliance on empirical data to validate procedures is one of the strongest assets of behavioral therapy. Simply stated, procedures that have been demonstrated to be effective are used in behavioral therapy, and those which fail to demonstrate effectiveness are rejected. The criteria for effectiveness are pragmatic (e.g., Does the therapy result in desired changes and are the changes maintained over time? Does it do so more quickly and less expensively than other therapies?). Such empirically verifiable questions tend to be asked about behavioral therapy, in contrast to theoretical questions concerning the degree to which therapy procedures are consistent with conceptualizations of the nature of abnormal behavior, how it develops, and how it can be modified (which are typically asked about many other forms of therapy).

Emphasis on Research

A tremendous amount of research on behavioral therapy has been carried out over the past two decades—far more than on any other form of psychotherapy. Although many of these studies have methodological and practical flaws, in general the level of scientific rigor (e.g., precision and control) tends to be much higher than with research carried out on other modes of therapy. For example (as already noted), behavioral therapies usually are described in detail, enabling their replication in subsequent studies. This is frequently not true of research on traditional therapies, in which the therapeutic procedures are often stated in very general terms (often by just naming the therapy, such as "insight-oriented therapy" or "nondirective counseling"). The outcome measures of behavioral therapy are relatively clear-cut and objective, in contrast to the measures of effectiveness of traditional psychotherapies, which tend to be general and subjective (e.g., therapist's judgment of the client(s) as "much improved," "somewhat improved," or "not improved"). Finally, compared to research on traditional therapies, investigations of behavioral therapy include a much higher proportion of experimental studies. Because experimental studies have a greater degree of control over extraneous factors that could possibly affect changes in target behaviors while clients are undergoing therapy, they provide the best basis for evaluating the effects of a therapeutic procedure.[50]

The general commitment of behavioral therapy to a scientific approach has not only placed behavioral therapy on firmer ground as an effective treatment strategy, but it also has probably had a favorable influence on nonbehavioral therapies.[51] Behavioral therapy has served as a model of the specification of therapeutic procedures and outcome, the development of innovative and more reliable and valid assessment procedures, and the commitment to evaluation of therapy in terms of empirical data from scientifically rigorous investigations.

Major Weaknesses and Directions for Future Development

The following discussion of the major weaknesses of behavioral therapy is more extensive than that of its major strengths. Such emphasis is appropriate because the strengths of behavioral therapy have been the focus of this book. Besides serving as a critique of contemporary behavioral therapy, this section indicates areas for future development, refinement, and research.

Ever since behavioral therapy established itself as a viable and growing field in the early 1970s, many behavioral therapists have felt secure enough to become strong critics and responsible monitors of their own practices. Just as behavioral therapists have been among the most stringent critics of research evaluating the effectiveness of behavioral therapy, they have also waged heated arguments among themselves about such issues as the appropriateness of specific therapeutic procedures, the definition and nature of the field, and particular limitations and shortcomings. The following discussion is consistent with the tradition of healthy skepticism and critical self-evaluation that has characterized behavioral therapy.

Lack of a Unified Theory

Behavioral therapy, unlike many other psychotherapies, is not based on any unified theory that explains and predicts how its change procedures work. Although many behavioral therapists state that their endeavors are based on "modern learning theory,"[52] this claim is more illusion than reality. There is no single theory of learning; rather, there exist many different, and often conflicting, theories. Furthermore, as noted in Chapter 1, there is little evidence to support the contention that behavioral therapy procedures are derived from or even consistent with various theories of learning. In fact, critics of behavioral therapy have accurately commented that some behavioral therapy procedures existed long before the development of modern learning theories, which partially refutes the blanket claim that "learning theory has been necessary or . . . very important in *developing* the specific techniques."[53] Rather, behavioral therapy is based on a "nontheoretical amalgamation of pragmatic principles,"[54] which can be predicted from and explained by a variety of theoretical perspectives.

What would be the advantages of having a unified theory of behavioral therapy? Such a theory would explain the mechanisms or principles that underlie behavioral therapy procedures, as well as predict and explain their successes and failures. Presently, without such a theory it is difficult to decide on optimal treatment procedures for each unique combination of client, problem, and setting. Formulas for selecting the best treatment can be discovered empirically, but this is usually a lengthy process that involves countless studies and many years of work.

The field of behavioral therapy also lacks a unified theory to explain and predict the conditions that are generally responsible for people developing abnormal behaviors. Those behavioral theories that do exist tend to be incomplete and to conflict with one another.[55] However, because behavioral therapy is concerned with changing abnormal behaviors, a theory of the development of these behaviors is less important than a theory of how the treatment works.

Because of the diversity of treatment procedures that comprise behavioral therapy, there is the possibility that no single, comprehensive theory of change processes can exist.[56] Recently, however, Albert Bandura has formulated a *theory of perceived self-efficacy* that is the first major attempt to provide a unified theoretical explanation of behavioral therapy procedures (as well as of other approaches to psychotherapy).[57] The term *self-efficacy* refers to an individual's belief or expectation that he or she can master a situation and bring about desired outcomes by personal efforts. According to self-efficacy theory, a common cognitive mechanism mediates the effects of all psychological change procedures. Specifically, psychotherapeutic procedures, of any form, are postulated to be effective because they create and strengthen a client's expectations of personal efficacy.

> In this conceptual system, expectations of personal mastery affect both initiation and persistence of coping behavior. The strength of people's convictions in their own effectiveness is likely to affect whether they will even try to cope with given situations. At this initial level, perceived self-efficacy influences choice of behavioral settings. People fear and tend to avoid threatening situations they believe exceed their coping skills, whereas they get involved in activities and behave assuredly when they judge themselves capable of handling situations that would otherwise be intimidating.
>
> Not only can perceived self-efficacy have directive influence on choice of activities and settings, but, through expectations of eventual success, it can affect coping efforts once they are initiated. Efficacy expectations determine how much effort people will expend and how long they will persist in the face of obstacles and aversive experiences. The stronger the perceived self-efficacy, the more active the efforts. Those who persist in subjectively threatening activities that are in fact relatively safe will gain corrective experiences that reinforce their sense of efficacy, thereby eventually eliminating their defensive behavior. Those who cease their coping efforts prematurely will retain their self-debilitating expectations and fears for a long time.[58]

Support for the theory of perceived self-efficacy is beginning to accumulate rapidly, although much of the research evidence is based on analogue studies.[59] So far the data indicate a correlation between overt behavioral improvements, such as coming closer to a feared situation (as measured on a behavioral avoidance test), and clients' perceived self-efficacy (as assessed by self-report measures).[60] The theory has been the subject of much scrutiny and discussion among behavioral therapists in the past few years, and, not surprisingly, it has been criticized as well as praised.[61] Although self-efficacy theory could eventually provide a general theoretical explanation of diverse behavioral therapy procedures, it is still too rudimentary to come close to meeting that worthwhile goal. More than likely, perceived self-efficacy will turn out, at best, to be a viable theory of a narrow range of behavioral therapies—most notably, performance-based procedures such as participant modeling for the treatment of specific avoidance behaviors.

Problems with Behavioral Assessment

One problem with current behavioral assessment is that it relies too much on self-report measures when other assessment procedures are possible. Certain behaviors, particularly covert behaviors, can only be assessed by self-report. For such behaviors, reliable and valid self-report measures are necessary. Because self-reports are easy to obtain, however, behavioral therapists too often rely on self-report measures of behaviors that could be more accurately assessed in other ways. At the very least, self-report measures should be supplemented with other assessment procedures, such as direct observation by others, for the purpose of cross-validation.

Direct observation of behavior in the client's natural environment also has drawbacks. It frequently requires considerable time of one or more observers who first must be trained to accurately and reliably measure the target behaviors. To avoid having observation affect the client's behavior and thereby result in an unrepresentative sample, the observer(s) must remain unobtrusive, and this is sometimes difficult. For instance, no matter how accustomed a family becomes to an observer in its home at dinner time, the interactions among the family members are bound to be somewhat different from when they are alone.

Contrived situational tests resembling the natural situations in which a client is having difficulties are more economical than direct observations in the client's natural surroundings. However, clients may not provide an accurate sample of their behavior, because they feel under pressure to perform or because they know that they are in a "safe" environment where the consequences of their behavior are negligible. When behavior rehearsal is used to obtain a sample of a client's typical behavior, there is always the possibility that such role playing will involve different abilities from those needed in the corresponding life situation. Finally, situational tests may not be "lifelike" enough to give the therapist a valid indication of the client's customary behavior. For example, a client who demonstrates the ability to refuse an unreasonable request made by the therapist in a role-played assessment may still be unable to use these assertive behaviors when confronted with an unreasonable request from a boss or spouse. Indeed, such a possibility would be predicted by the situational specificity emphasis of the behavioral approach (see Chapter 2).[62]

Physiological measurements are beset with a host of technical limitations. The primary problem is that accurate and inexpensive portable monitoring devices have yet to be developed, and such devices are essential for assessing a client's physiological responses in the natural situations in which the problem occurs. Even when physiological measurements are taken in a therapist's office to assess a client's internal responses to ongoing treatment (e.g., relaxation therapy), they may provide inaccurate information because of malfunctioning equipment that goes undetected or extraneous factors (e.g., body movement) that result in distorted measurements.

Inadequate Generalization and Maintenance of Treatment Gains

In evaluating the effectiveness of psychotherapy, three different phases of treatment must be examined: (1) the *initial induction* of change, (2) the *generalization* or transfer of this change to the client's natural environment, and (3) the *maintenance* or durability of the change over time. In general, behavioral therapies have been successful in inducing short-term therapeutic changes in the therapy setting (i.e., the first phase of treatment). Far less success can be claimed for the generalizability and durability of changes initially produced by behavioral therapies. This statement does not mean that behavioral therapies that successfully modify a client's problem behavior in the short term and within the confines of the treatment setting are ineffective. Instead, the decreased effectiveness of behavioral therapies in the second and third phases may be due to the fact that the different phases of treatment are influenced by different factors and therefore require different intervention procedures.[63] Behavioral therapists have, in fact, devoted most of their efforts to developing, evaluating, and refining procedures for the *initial induction* of therapeutic change. Until recently, this strategy has been appropriate, because only after a treatment has proved to be effective at inducing change is it relevant to pursue its generalization and maintenance. But now that many behavioral therapies are effective in changing target behaviors, behavioral therapists must devote more attention to ensuring that the treatment effects transfer to the client's natural environment and endure over time.

Behavioral therapists have been aware of this need and are increasingly developing interventions to increase the generalization and maintenance of their therapies. Some of the procedures for generalizing therapeutic changes to the client's natural environment that have been illustrated in previous chapters include (1) implementing the therapy in the client's natural environment(s); (2) involving important people in the client's life in the treatment (e.g., parents, spouses, employers, and teachers); (3) establishing therapeutic goals and using treatment procedures consistent with the client's natural environment(s); (4) employing naturally occurring contingencies to accelerate and decelerate target behaviors; (5) changing the client's natural environment(s) so that the critical factors that influenced the initial therapeutic gains also will occur outside the therapy setting; and (6) having more than one person administer the treatment (e.g., therapist and parent) and varying the settings in which the treatment is provided so that the client does not associate the therapeutic change with a single person or setting.

Examples of behavioral therapy procedures that tend to maintain the treatment effects over time include (1) using self-control procedures so that the primary change agent, the client, is always present; (2) employing intermittent reinforcement to increase the chances that the client will continue to perform reinforced behaviors; (3) administering periodic "booster" treatments (as is frequently done with aversion therapies); and (4) in the case of deceleration target behaviors, providing the client with alternative behaviors that the client will be able to continue after treatment.

Obviously there is a partial reciprocal relationship between generalization and maintenance of therapeutic gains. Maintenance is enhanced by changes in the target behavior occurring in a variety of settings, and if the changes are sustained over time, they are more likely to occur in different settings.

Despite the specific behavioral therapy procedures that have been employed to promote generalization and maintenance of treatment gains, the success of these efforts has been less than satisfactory in many instances. (Note that generalization and maintenance of treatment gains is a critical issue for *all* forms of psychotherapy.) A number of factors interfere with implementing generalization and maintenance procedures and with assessing their effectiveness. The farther a client gets from the therapist, both in terms of physical distance and time, the more difficult it becomes for the therapist to have sufficient influence over the client's life to assure generalization and maintenance and to continue to assess the target behavior. For example, typically clients' motivation to continue therapy or assessment procedures declines in the absence of regular and frequent contact with (and encouragement from) the therapist. Consequently, procedures for sustaining treatment gains are often diluted (or abandoned completely) to the point where they become ineffective.

Although the weighty problems involved in the generalization and maintenance of treatment gains must be recognized, they should not be taken as signs for surrender. Rather, it behooves behavioral therapists to accept the difficult challenge of assuring that the often impressive changes behavioral therapies bring about are not lost when treatment terminates. The importance of this challenge cannot be overemphasized—if changes that occur in therapy do not transfer to the client's natural environment(s) where the problems are occurring and do not continue after therapy, the effectiveness of the treatment procedures is substantially diminished. Generalization and maintenance of therapeutic changes cannot be taken for granted. In most cases, specific interventions beyond those employed in the initial induction of change must be instituted to assure widespread and lasting effects.

Problems with Behavioral Therapy Research

The state of the art in behavioral therapy research is far from ideal and certainly can and should be improved. Two important criticisms concern the heavy reliance on analogue research and the general lack of follow-up studies.

Analogue research uses conditions that resemble, but are not the same as, actual clinical circumstances. The differences between the analogue situation and the clinical situation can include one or more variables. The individuals studied may not be "real" clients inasmuch as they have not sought or been referred for treatment of a problem behavior but instead have been recruited for the specific purpose of investigating a therapeutic procedure. Such research participants often lack some characteristics of actual clients, including motivation for and expectations about therapy. The target behaviors treated may be "subclinical" in the sense that they are mild forms of actual problem behaviors. Minor fears of small animals, such as nonpoisonous snakes, dogs, and white rats, have frequently been used to investigate treatments to decelerate fear. The subjects in these analogue studies might be mildly apprehensive about or dislike dogs, for example, but these feelings would not interfere with their normal functioning (e.g., they would not cross the street every time they saw a dog farther down the block or avoid visiting friends who had dogs).

Analogue studies may also be carried out in nonclinical settings. For instance, the treatment might be administered in a research room in a department of psychology rather than in a clinic, and the therapist may be relatively inexperienced (e.g., a graduate student learning to do therapy). Obviously such a setting is likely to alter people's expectations about and reactions toward the treatment being administered.

Analogue studies usually deal with narrow, clearly defined research questions under carefully controlled conditions. Their ultimate goal is to provide information that can be generalized to and implemented in actual therapy conditions. Analogue research plays an important role in the development of treatment procedures, but its major limitation is the extent to which findings can be generalized to treatment of "real" clients, with "genuine" problems under actual clinical conditions. Accordingly, analogue research must always be considered an initial step, followed by actual clinical research.[64]

Unfortunately, too much empirical research support for the efficacy of behavioral therapies is based primarily on analogue studies. Research in actual clinical settings is difficult, costly, and plagued with significant practical and ethical problems. But the challenge of clinical research must be met in order to make definitive claims about the efficacy of behavioral therapy.

A second major limitation of behavioral therapy research is that most studies do not collect follow-up data.[65] Assessing maintenance effects after therapy is always difficult and sometimes impossible, even for the most conscientious investigator.[66] Keeping track of clients who leave therapy and securing their cooperation for follow-up assessments present monumental practical problems (which increase with the length of time before the follow-up) and also raise some important ethical questions, such as interference with a client's right to privacy and anonymity. In those few cases where follow-up data are collected, data may be assessed by procedures of questionable reliability and validity. For example, when clients have moved from the immediate area in which the therapy occurred, the only feasible way to collect follow-up data may be through self-report measures collected by questionnaires and telephone interviews.[67]

The Dangers of Teaching Behavioral Therapy to Nonprofessionals

On many occasions in this book, it has been pointed out that behavioral therapists openly share their expertise with their clients by explaining in detail (on a level the client can understand) the nature of the treatment to be used and its underlying rationale. The purpose of this practice is to make clients active and knowledgeable partners in their therapy, to enhance treatment success. With self-control behavioral therapies, clients become their own change agents under the supervision of the professional behavioral therapist. Similarly, significant people in the client's life, such as a spouse, parent, or friend, may be taught basic therapy procedures so that they can help administer the therapy in the client's home environment.

Along with numerous advantages of these practices, there are potential hazards. As the old adage predicts, "a little knowledge can be dangerous" if it is mistaken for a great deal of knowledge. As long as clients or nonprofessionals understand the limits of their expertise in behavioral therapy, the danger is minimal. However, there is always the possibility that instruction in *some* of the principles and a *few* of the procedures of behavioral therapy will be construed by laypeople as qualifying them to apply this limited knowledge to other people or to substantially different target behaviors or circumstances. (Parallel dangers are involved in providing brief introductory workshops in behavioral therapy procedures for professional therapists who have had little or no previous experience in or understanding of behavioral therapy.[68])

Awareness of these potential hazards and specific precautionary measures is important. First, behavioral therapists should emphasize to nonprofessionals the *limitations* of the latter's knowledge and skills. They should include a warning that nonprofessionals are not qualified to use their behavioral therapy skills with other people. Second, it is important that nonprofessionals be taught the basic *principles* or orienting concepts that underlie the therapy procedures so that they are less likely to be "technique-bound."[69] For example, in using reinforcement therapies it is essential to understand (1) that reinforcers vary from person to person and at different times and circumstances with the same person and (2) that an event is only a reinforcer if it accelerates the behavior it follows. Otherwise, reinforcers used for a particular client at a specific time may be considered universally applicable. Third, therapists should assess whether nonprofessionals understand the limitations and principles that have been explained to them. Fourth, any treatment program using nonprofessional therapeutic agents should include periodic supervision and assessment of progress and problems.

Insufficient Attention to the Acceptability of Therapies to Clients

Effectiveness in producing therapeutic changes is, and should be, the major criterion for evaluating behavioral therapies. A number of secondary criteria, including efficiency and cost-effectiveness, also are increasingly being considered in designing and evaluating behavioral therapies.

Acceptability or attractiveness of behavioral therapy procedures to clients is another important standard of evaluation that has been given too little attention. All other things being equal, clients would be expected to seek out the most effective treatment that requires the least amount of time, effort, and money. But acceptability is another factor that can influence the particular therapy a client chooses and will stick with and that may override the criterion of effectiveness or efficiency.[70] This situation is particularly true for therapies that have some aversive or distasteful aspects. For example, flooding may be more effective than systematic desensitization for the treatment of some types of fear, but clients may prefer desensitization to flooding because the direct confrontation with the feared events in flooding is more upsetting than gradually imagining the feared events in desensitization.[71]

Because of the reluctance of many people to seek treatment for their problems, and because of the difficulties of motivating clients to remain in treatment, the issue of the acceptability of behavioral therapies is critical. Even the most effective treatments are useless if clients are unwilling to undergo them.

Thus, the attractiveness and palatability of therapy procedures need to be considered in developing new therapy procedures and in selecting appropriate treatments for individual clients. Acceptability of a treatment procedure is ultimately an individual matter and must be decided independently for each client, given the client's goals for therapy and personal attitudes and preferences. The manner in which therapy procedures are presented to clients can influence the general acceptability of therapies. For example, the words used to describe a procedure can make the client more or less amenable to trying it. (Recall the discussion in Chapter 7 on the adverse affects of the label *punishment*.)

Because acceptability is only beginning to be recognized as a significant criterion for evaluating behavioral therapies, we lack information about features of therapies that make them desirable or undesirable to clients. Measures of "consumer satisfaction" should be routinely collected from clients in various behavioral therapies; the initial attempts to obtain such data have provided useful information.[72]

It is also important to investigate the acceptability of various behavioral therapies to therapists. The effectiveness of therapies may well be enhanced by factors that make their implementation more pleasant or satisfying to the therapist. Some initial studies concerning the preferences that nonprofessionals have for administering various behavioral therapies have already been made.[73]

In the late 1950s, behavioral therapy successfully survived its "birth traumas," which involved harsh rejection by the established psychotherapeutic community. During its childhood (1960s), it began to cope with the realities of the problems with which it was conceived to deal. Behavioral therapy established its own identity, while still maintaining some of the naive idealism and braggadocio often characteristic of precocious children. In its adolescence (1970s), it exhibited a great growth spurt, developing new techniques and expanding its areas of competence, while refining and testing the limits of the procedures it had established in its childhood. Behavioral therapy is now in its early adulthood, and is giving up some of the wide-eyed idealism it tended to have in adolescence, replacing idealism with a more realistic and mature self-evaluation of limitations as well as strengths, and taking specific actions to overcome the former and to capitalize on the latter.

SUMMARY

Behavioral therapies have been successful in treating anxiety-related problems, marital and sexual problems, addictive behaviors, adult psychotic behaviors, childhood and adolescent problem behaviors, and problem behaviors associated with mental retardation. Overall, behavioral therapies have been highly successful with some problems and have fared at least as well as and often somewhat better than other treatments with more intractable problems.

There are four major issues regarding the comprehensiveness of behavioral therapy. First, although behavioral therapies do not lead to symptom substitution, they often have side effects, which are largely positive. Second, behavioral therapies successfully treat complex human problems by treating relatively simple target behaviors related to the problem. Third, so-called nonbehavioral problem behaviors (e.g., "existential crises") can be treated with behavioral therapy by defining specific target behaviors, and then changing their maintaining conditions. Fourth, behavioral therapy can potentially treat a vast array of problems, although it is not applicable for all problems and clients.

The major strengths of behavioral therapy are (1) success in creating therapeutic changes; (2) breadth of application; (3) precise specification of goals and procedures; (4) sophistication of behavioral assessment procedures; (5) commitment to empiricism; and (6) emphasis on research. Its major weakness are (1) lack of unified theory; (2) overreliance on self-report assessment, low validity of some situational tests, and inability to monitor physiological responses in natural environments; (3) inadequate generalization and maintenance of treatment gains; (4) heavy reliance on analogue studies and inadequate follow-ups; (5) potential dangers of using nonprofessional change agents; and (6) poor acceptability of certain behavioral therapies to clients.

REFERENCE NOTES

1. Kazdin & Wilson, 1978.
2. Kazdin & Wilson, 1978; Rachman & Wilson, 1980.
3. Marks, Rachman, & Hodgson, 1975; Rachman & Hodgson, 1980; Roper, Rachman, & Marks, 1975.
4. For example, Goodwin, Guze, & Robins, 1969; Kringlen, 1965.

5. Kazdin & Wilson, 1978.
6. Kazdin & Wilson, 1978; O'Leary & Wilson, 1975.
7. Rachman & Wilson, 1980.
8. Azrin, 1976.
9. Sobell & Sobell, 1976.
10. Callner, 1975; Götestam, Melin, & Öst, 1976.
11. Bernstein & McAlister, 1976; Hunt & Matarazzo, 1973.
12. Kazdin & Wilson, 1978.
13. Bellack & Hersen, 1977.
14. Kazdin, 1977b.
15. For example, Henderson & Scoles, 1970; Spiegler & Agigian, 1977.
16. Kazdin & Wilson, 1978.
17. For example, Tharp & Wetzel, 1969; Yen & McIntire, 1976.
18. For example, Patterson, 1974; Patterson, Cobb, & Ray, 1973; Patterson & Reid, 1973.
19. Freedman, Kaplan, & Sadock, 1976.
20. Ayllon, Layman, & Kandel, 1975; Christensen, 1975.
21. Lovaas & Newsom, 1976.
22. Lovaas, Koegel, Simmons, & Long, 1973.
23. See Lovaas, Koegel, Simmons, & Long, 1973; Patterson & Bechtel, 1970.
24. Kazdin & Wilson, 1978.
25. Birnbrauer, 1976; Thompson & Grabowski, 1977.
26. Azrin & Foxx, 1974.
27. Foxx & Azrin, 1973b.
28. For example, Twardosz & Baer, 1973.
29. For example, Keilitz, Tucker, & Horner, 1973.
30. For example, Stokes, Baer, & Jackson, 1974.
31. For example, Knapczyk & Yoppi, 1975.
32. Foxx, 1976.
33. Azrin & Wesolowski, 1975b.
34. Webster & Azrin, 1973.
35. Foxx & Martin, 1975.
36. For example, Bergin & Strupp, 1972; Gottman & Markman, 1978; Strupp, 1978.
37. For example, Franks & Wilson, 1973, 1974, 1975, 1976, 1977, 1978, 1979; Kazdin & Wilson, 1978; Paul, 1969a; Yates, 1975.
38. Kazdin & Hersen, 1980, p. 289.
39. Bancroft, 1974.
40. Bieber, Dain, Dince, Drellich, Grand, Gundlach, Kremer, Rifkin, Wilbur, & Bieber, 1962.
41. For example, Ullmann & Krasner, 1965; Yates, 1958.
42. For example, Bandura, 1969; Yates, 1970.
43. See Mahoney, Kazdin, & Lesswing, 1974.
44. For example, Bandura, 1969; Cahoon, 1968; Kazdin & Wilson, 1978.
45. For example, Bennett & Maley, 1973; Gripp & Magaro, 1971; Maley, Feldman, & Ruskin, 1973; Shean & Zeidberg, 1971.
46. For example, Balson, 1973; Becker, Turner, & Sajwaj, 1978; Meyer & Crisp, 1966; Sajwaj, Twardosz, & Burke, 1972.
47. Kazdin & Wilson, 1978.
48. Ullmann & Krasner, 1965.
49. For example, Mischel, 1972.
50. Liebert & Spiegler, 1982.
51. Kazdin & Hersen, 1980.
52. For example, Wolpe, 1973.
53. Breger & McGaugh, 1966, p. 171.
54. Weitzman, 1967, p. 303.
55. Kazdin & Wilson, 1978.

56. Compare with Lazarus, 1976.
57. Bandura, 1977a, 1978.
58. Bandura, 1977a, pp. 193–194.
59. For example, Bandura & Adams, 1977; Bandura, Adams, Hardy, & Howells, 1980; Bandura & Schunk, 1981; Chambliss & Murray, 1979a, 1979b; Condiotte & Lichtenstein, 1981; DiClemente, 1981; Gauthier & Ladouceur, 1981; Gould & Weiss, 1981; Schunk, 1981; Weinberg, Yukelson, & Jackson, 1980.
60. For example, Bandura, Adams, & Beyer, 1977.
61. For example, Rachman, 1978.
62. Liebert & Spiegler, 1978.
63. For example, Kazdin & Wilson, 1978.
64. Compare with Borkovec & Rachman, 1979.
65. For example, Keeley, Shemberg, & Carbonell, 1976.
66. For example, Meltzoff & Kornreich, 1970.
67. For example, Spiegler & Agigian, 1977.
68. Ott, 1980.
69. See Anastasi, 1972.
70. Kazdin & Wilson, 1978.
71. Crowe, Marks, Agras, & Leitenberg, 1972.
72. Kazdin & Wilson, 1978.
73. For example, Porterfield, Herbert-Jackson, & Risley, 1976; Rosenbaum, O'Leary, & Jacob, 1975.

CHAPTER 15

The Future of Behavioral Therapy

This book has examined behavioral therapy as practiced today, and it is fitting to conclude with a view of the future. From all indications, behavioral therapy as a general approach to viewing and treating problem behaviors is here to stay, although many of its specific procedures are likely to change as they are continually reevaluated and refined, and as new and more effective procedures are developed to overcome existing limitations.

Behavioral therapy appears to be a major therapeutic approach of the future rather than a passing fad. Faddish therapies are characterized by a rapid and prolific development of new treatment techniques. Evaluation of such therapies tends to be unsystematic and to rely heavily on unsubstantiated testimonials by leaders of the therapeutic movement as well as by "cured and converted" clients. The leaders of such movements are often charismatic figures who spend considerable time proselytizing, especially in the public (rather than professional) media, such as by writing popular books (which tend to sell well) and appearing on television talk shows. Almost as suddenly as fads arise as "front-page stories," they become soon-forgotten "obituaries."

In contrast, behavioral therapy has exhibited none of these characteristics. Behavioral therapy developed rather slowly over a period of about 25 years, and from its inception has systematically evaluated its procedures through empirical research. Interestingly, the field of behavioral therapy has had few charismatic leaders (neither B. F. Skinner nor Joseph Wolpe, who are most likely to be considered the parents of contemporary behavioral therapy, would be considered charismatic). Until the past few years, most information about behavioral therapy was available only in professional journals and books or at professional conferences. Finally, far from fading into oblivion, there are many indications that the field of behavioral therapy is burgeoning, including the continued increase in the number of (1) new therapy procedures, (2) new applications of existing therapies, (3) empirical research studies and new journals in which to publish them, (4) new behavioral therapy professional organizations and members in these and in existing organizations, (5) behavioral therapists, and (6) nonbehavioral therapists who recognize behavioral therapy as a viable alternative approach to treatment.[1]

Although any discussion of the future of behavioral therapy is speculative, it is possible to make plausible predictions on the basis of the current state of behavioral therapy. This look into the future of behavioral therapy is divided into three areas, which become progressively more speculative because the current information becomes increasingly less substantial. First some important ways in which contemporary behavioral therapy can and should be refined and improved are reviewed. Next the discussion focuses on several current trends in behavioral therapy that appear to be gaining increasing empirical and social support, signs that portend their continued growth in the future. Finally, the application of behavioral therapy principles to new areas that have particular social significance is considered.

FUTURE REFINING OF CONTEMPORARY BEHAVIORAL THERAPY

The major weaknesses of behavioral therapy, which were discussed in the previous chapter, certainly require improvement, which will occupy the efforts of behavioral therapists for some time to come. Of these weaknesses, the most pressing problem appears to be the development of procedures that promote (1) generalization beyond the therapy situation and (2) maintenance of treatment effects long after therapy has terminated. Some of these procedures already exist and must be refined and applied on a regular basis; other techniques for generalization and maintenance need to be devised. Improvements in behavioral assessment and research, which are also problematic areas, are necessary for the development of effective generalization and maintenance strategies. For example, more objective and reliable measures of change may be required to assess a client's behavior in natural environmental settings where the assessment must be made by a variety of individuals, many of whom have had little training in the observation and recording of behavior. In order to evaluate lasting effects of treatment, follow-up studies of actual clinical cases (not analogue research) will have to be carried out.

The need for theoretical formulations of behavioral change procedures will become increasingly important in the future. For instance, factors that should facilitate generalization or maintenance of therapeutic changes could be predicted from such theory. Also, because the number and diversity of behavioral therapies will probably increase in the future as areas of application widen, a comprehensive theory of underlying change mechanisms will enable useful matches among clients, problems, and therapies.

CURRENT TRENDS WITH FUTURE POTENTIAL

Several current trends within behavioral therapy are continuing to grow in breadth of application, refinement of techniques, and empirical support, and therefore will probably be prominent in the future. Because all have been given extensive coverage in previous chapters, they are mentioned only briefly here.

Self-control is the most pervasive current trend, because it is applicable to a wide variety of behavioral therapies. Not only was an entire chapter (12) devoted to self-control techniques, but examples of the basic premise of self-control—clients' assuming responsibility for their own treatment—appear in all the chapters that describe therapy procedures. With many therapies, clients can take complete charge of their treatment (under the supervision of the therapist). With virtually all behavioral therapies, at least some responsibilities for treatment can be assumed by most clients. In addition to efficiency in terms of minimizing professional therapists' time, self-control procedures are well suited for generalization and maintenance of therapeutic change, because the change agent (the client) is always available.

In cases where it is necessary or better for the primary change agent to be someone other than the client, it has often been possible to use *nonprofessionals* (e.g., parents and teachers). This practice is a long-standing tradition in behavioral therapy and continues to be effective. Indeed, some related developments in behavioral therapy indicate a possible increase in the use of laypeople as therapeutic agents. One development is the trend within behavioral therapy to provide treatment in the client's natural environment, which is the setting where nonprofessionals play their major roles. The second is the increasing specificity of techniques, which makes it possible to train laypeople to competently administer narrow, well-defined aspects of therapy.

Recently there has been an increase in the development of "over-the-counter" treatment packages that clients and/or nonprofessional change agents can apply with minimal or no professional supervision for the amelioration of common behavioral problems such as overeating,[2] enuresis,[3] toilet training,[4] muscle tension,[5] and lack of assertive behavior.[6] The treatment packages are contained in books, on cassette tapes, or in brief courses. Despite the dangers and limitations of prepackaged nonspecific behavioral therapies, their cost-effectiveness for a majority of clients probably means that they will be designed for more and more common target behaviors in future years.

The avent of *cognitive behavioral therapies* marks a major turning point in the field because it has formalized and legitimized the practice of dealing behaviorally with target behaviors and maintaining conditions that are not fully or even totally in the external environment. Although many behavioral therapists have for a long time recognized the importance of cognitive processes in the maintenance of problem behaviors, until recently few behavioral therapies existed for directly treating them. Cognitive behavioral therapies have provided a variety of procedures that deal with thoughts, attitudes, beliefs, and expectations within the confines of the basic principles of behavioral therapy. From all indications, cognitive behavioral therapy will continue to grow during the next decade. Besides the proliferation of cognitive behavioral therapy techniques and research in the area (including a new journal entitled *Cognitive Therapy and Research*), there are other signs of enthusiastic acceptance of cognitive behavioral therapy. These signs include annual conferences and numerous workshops exclusively devoted to cognitive therapies, as well as an increased demand for clinical training in these new techniques.[7]

A final prediction of current trends in behavioral therapy that appear to be destined to play significant roles in the future is the general area of *behavioral medicine*, which involves the application of behavioral therapy principles and procedures to treating as well as preventing (see the next section) medical disorders. Behavioral medicine is one of the "hottest" topics both in behavioral therapy and in medicine. Some examples of behavioral medicine applications discussed in previous chapters include treatment of muscle tension, headaches, obesity, pain, enuresis, drug addiction, insomnia, and paralysis. The following commentary predicts a bright future for behavioral medicine:

> From all appearance, the development of behavioral medicine represents more than just another substantive area within the broad confines of [behavioral therapy]. Rather, it reflects a more fundamental coming together of behavioral and biomedical scientists [and clinicians] in an endeavor that has potentially far-reaching consequences for both.[8]

NEW DIRECTIONS WITH FUTURE POTENTIAL

Two areas could greatly benefit from the application of behavioral principles. One involves direct intervention for major societal problems, and the other concerns prevention of various problem behaviors and physical disorders. Both are significant areas that clearly require attention, and in both cases there are initial indications that behavioral therapy principles and procedures may prove useful.

The Potential of Behavioral Interventions for Societal Problems

Some potential applications of behavioral therapy principles and procedures to societal problems involve unemployment, neighborhood problems, racial integration, and ecological problems.

Unemployment

Although the problems of unemployment are largely due to the state of the economy, in many individual cases people are unemployed because they lack essential skills for securing and holding employment. Initial work has begun on using behavioral therapy procedures to help unemployed people find jobs.[9] One effort involved a job-finding club in which members (1) were given training in finding sources of employment (e.g., asking friends and contacting former employers), (2) role-played job interviews, (3) learned about appropriate dress, (4) practiced writing resumes, and (5) increased their interests in various jobs to enhance the likelihood of finding employment. In addition, club members were given partners to provide support to one another. An evaluation of the program showed that club members obtained employment more quickly and secured higher-paying jobs than did a comparable group of nonmembers. Three months after the training program, 92 percent of the members had jobs, as compared to 60 percent of the nonmembers.[10]

Neighborhood Problems

It has been observed that "the cynicism, apathy, and feelings of helplessness which often typify citizens' attitudes toward the possibility of exerting any degree of control over their larger social systems . . . are realistic [attitudes] because most people lack even the most rudimentary knowledge of how to effect changes in [these] systems."[11] An initial demonstration of the applicability of behavioral therapy procedures to community organization and action found that welfare recipients could be motivated to attend neighborhood self-help meetings by providing tangible reinforcers for attendance.[12] In another project, lower-socioeconomic-class adolescents and adults attended weekly neighborhood meetings to identify and attempt to solve community problems, such as securing health care, arranging for repairs to a community center, organizing social events, and finding and distributing social welfare resources. Participants were taught problem-solving skills through modeling, behavior rehearsal, and social reinforcement, and subsequently they demonstrated improved skills in solving problems.[13]

Racial Integration

Racial integration is a complex social problem, typically dealt with by attempting to change attitudes along with legally enforcing integration. The difficulty with modifying attitudes is that corresponding changes in overt behaviors, such as interracial social interactions, may not follow.[14] The possibility of increasing racial integration through positive reinforcement was explored in a program designed to integrate five black children with the majority of white children in a first-grade classroom. Pretreatment observations showed that the children separated themselves along racial lines during all activities involving social interactions. To accelerate interracial social interactions, the children were reinforced with tokens (redeemable for after-lunch snacks) and praise for "sitting with new friends at lunch." (This target behavior required interracial combinations of children, although the children were not specifically told this.) The reinforcement procedures did increase the amount of interracial interaction during lunch and, even more significantly, the social integration generalized to a free-play period immediately after lunch even though the children received no reinforcers for interracial interactions at that time. Unfortunately, when the experimental program ended and the children no longer received reinforcers for racial integration during lunch, the effects were not maintained.[15] However, this finding is not surprising, given the typical problems with maintenance of behavior change after treatment is terminated. The experimental project at least demonstrated that racial integration can be influenced by reinforcement procedures.

Ecological Problems

During the past decade, people have become more and more aware of ecological issues such as environmental pollution and energy conservation. A number of experimental programs using the principles of consequential behavioral therapy have shown promising results in dealing with some of these problems. Most programs have employed prompts (in the form of instructions and reminders) and positive reinforcers for the appropriate ecological behaviors.[16] Although the prompts indicate what the appropriate behaviors are and in some cases how to perform them, prompts alone generally have little effect on changing people's behaviors in relation to the environment. For example, the use of signs, pamphlets, and television commercials have not been successful in reducing littering[17] or conserving energy.[18] The most critical factor in all the programs that have resulted in people engaging in ecologically sound behaviors appears to be the use of potent reinforcers.

A number of experimental programs have demonstrated that both children and adults will cooperate in depositing trash in cans or bags as well as in picking up and properly disposing of trash if they are given tangible incentives. These programs have been carried out in diverse settings, including a movie theater,[19] wilderness recreational areas,[20] a zoo,[21] and the yards in a low-income urban housing development.[22] Money is most frequently used as the incentive for the clean-up behavior, but tickets for admission to movies and for soft-drinks as well as attractive items for young children (e.g., a Smokey the Bear patch and a comic book) have also been used.

The essential role of reinforcers in promoting antilitter behavior is clearly seen in a study that compared six different procedures for encouraging children to pick up litter and dispose of it properly in neighborhood movie theaters.[23] The procedures were (1) giving litterbags to the children as they entered the theater and telling them to use them while they are in the theater, (2) handing out litterbags as just described with an additional announcement during intermission telling the children to put their trash in the bags and deposit them in the cans in the lobby before leaving, (3) placing extra trash cans in conspicuous places around the theater, (4) showing an antilitter cartoon before the regular show, (5) providing litterbags and giving dimes for returning them with trash before leaving, and (6) providing litterbags and giving free tickets to a special children's movie for returning them. As Figure 15-1 shows, the two incentive procedures resulted in far more trash removal than any of the other procedures.

Another approach to the control of pollution caused by litter involves inducing people to recycle products such as paper and bottles.[24] For example, response cost and reinforcement are the primary components of a large-scale program for promoting the recycling of beverage bottles in Oregon. By law,

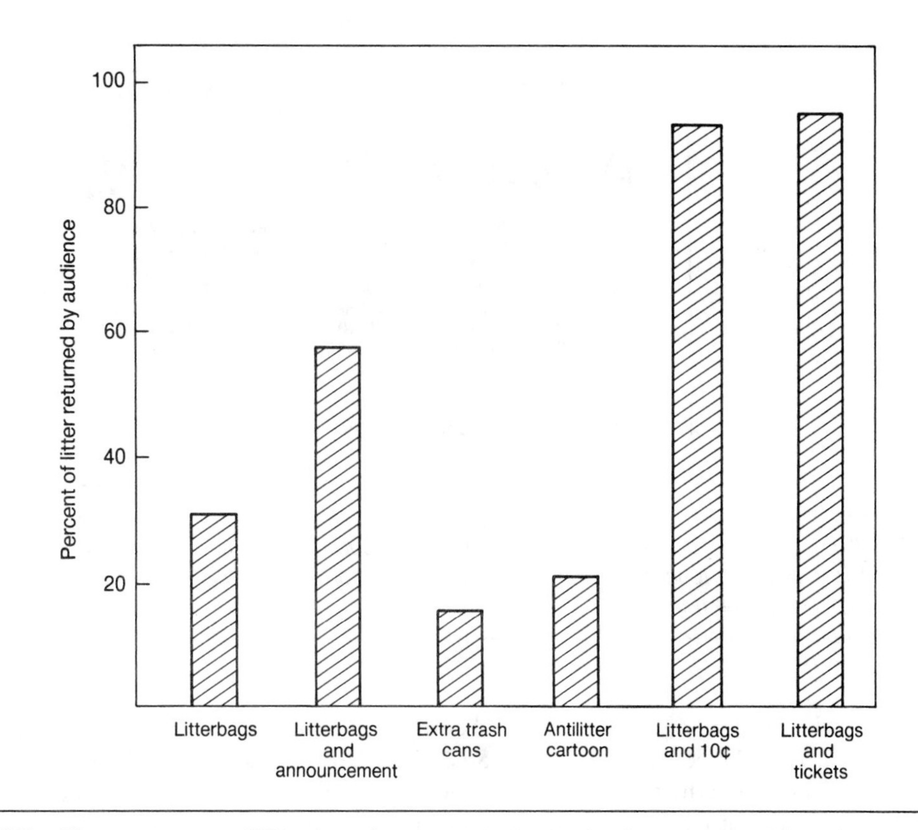

FIGURE 15-1 *The percentage of litter deposited in movie theater trash cans when different antilitter procedures were in effect. The percentage of litter was determined by comparing the weight of the litter deposited in the trash cans with all the litter in the theater after the show (including litter left on the floor and picked up by the staff).* SOURCE: *Data from Burgess, Clark, & Hendee (1971).*

only returnable bottles are sold in Oregon, and a substantial deposit is paid when beverages are purchased and refunded when the bottles are returned. Also, heavy fines are imposed for public littering. Research conducted by the Oregon Environmental Council indicates that littering has been substantially reduced, and significant savings in energy have been achieved (because disposal containers are not produced and disposed of).[25]

Energy conservation is the other major ecological problem that has been dealt with by behavioral therapy procedures. Small experimental programs have demonstrated that families can be induced to conserve electricity, both by lowering the total consumption[26] and by decreasing "peaking" (using high rates of electricity for brief periods of time, which results in the inefficient use of power generating facilities).[27] Monetary incentives have proved to be the most potent means of creating conservation, although feedback alone has led to some conservation. In some cases the reduction in electricity usage has been quite substantial. For example, one program gave residents in married student housing at a West Virginia university weekly cash payments in proportion to

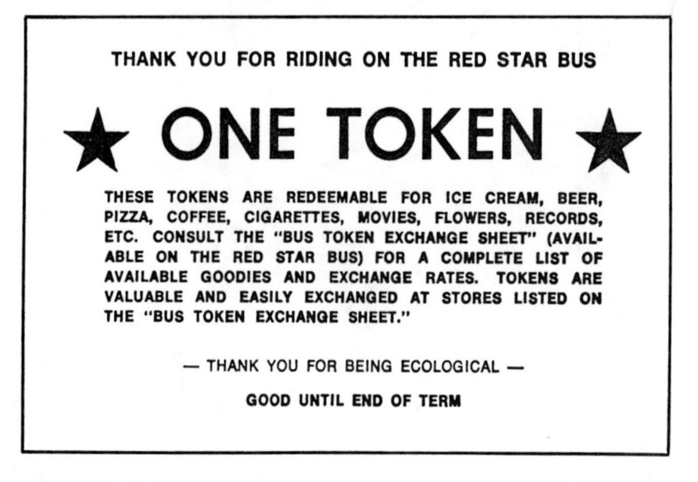
THANK YOU FOR RIDING ON THE RED STAR BUS

★ ONE TOKEN ★

THESE TOKENS ARE REDEEMABLE FOR ICE CREAM, BEER, PIZZA, COFFEE, CIGARETTES, MOVIES, FLOWERS, RECORDS, ETC. CONSULT THE "BUS TOKEN EXCHANGE SHEET" (AVAILABLE ON THE RED STAR BUS) FOR A COMPLETE LIST OF AVAILABLE GOODIES AND EXCHANGE RATES. TOKENS ARE VALUABLE AND EASILY EXCHANGED AT STORES LISTED ON THE "BUS TOKEN EXCHANGE SHEET."

— THANK YOU FOR BEING ECOLOGICAL —

GOOD UNTIL END OF TERM

FIGURE 15-2 *A sample token given for riding a special public bus as part of an experimental program to increase the use of public transportation* SOURCE: Everett, Hayward, & Meyers (1974), p. 2.

the amount of electricity saved compared to individual baseline rates ($3.00 for a 10 to 19 percent reduction, $6.00 for a 20 to 29 percent reduction, and so on). This procedure resulted in reductions in electricity consumption that ranged from 26 to 46 percent, with a mean of 33 percent.[28]

Various approaches to conserving gasoline have been attempted in experimental programs. One is to induce people to drive fewer miles in cars, primarily by providing reinforcers for reduction in miles driven and also by having people keep an accurate record of the miles they drive (i.e., self-monitoring). Two studies demonstrated a reduction of 20 percent in college students' nonessential driving when the students were given money or other reinforcers (e.g., car servicing or a university parking sticker) for driving fewer miles.[29] Another approach to gasoline conservation is to get people to use more economical forms of transportation.[30] For example, during an eight-day period, usage of a specially marked bus in a university community was increased by 150 percent when the riders were given tokens (shown in Figure 15-2) exchangeable for a variety of backup reinforcers, including a free bus ride, a cheeseburger, candy, potato chips, and having one's name in the newspaper for being an "eco-hero."[31]

The Potential for a Technology of Behavioral Prevention

So far, the predictions about the future of behavioral therapy have been that present treatment procedures will be refined and that behavioral therapy will expand its applications to help alleviate additional individual and societal problems. An even more worthwhile goal would be to use behavioral therapy procedures to prevent the problem behaviors they are now used to treat. There are a number of indications that behavioral principles hold considerable promise for prevention, but as yet this is largely a matter of speculation.

Prevention, which involves measures taken to forestall the occurrence of a problem behavior, should be distinguished from treatment or therapy that involves procedures to alleviate a problem behavior after it has occurred. A distinction is often made among *primary prevention* (actions taken to prevent a problem from occurring), *secondary prevention* (early treatment of a problem once it has occurred), and *tertiary prevention* (rehabilitation after treatment to minimize the long-term effects of the problem).[32] This section deals only with primary prevention because, in fact, such prevention is truly prevention, whereas secondary and tertiary "prevention" are more accurately referred to as *treatment* and *rehabilitation*, respectively.[33]

Prevention is indicated for people who have a high risk or vulnerability for developing the problem behavior. Determining if preventive measures are called for is generally a matter of predicting the probability that an individual will, at some future time, develop a particular problem behavior. This approach is most economical, because it can be expensive and wasteful to provide prevention for those who do not need it. On the other hand, identifying people who are likely to develop a particular problem behavior and those who are not likely to can be extremely difficult as well as costly, and it represents a major obstacle to prevention programs of any kind. An alternative strategy is to administer preventive services to all people (e.g., in a school system or neighborhood community). This approach is expensive, but it eliminates the difficulty of accurately identifying potentially "at-risk" people as well as the deleterious effects of singling out certain people and stigmatizing them with a negative label (e.g., "predelinquent").

Four basic models of behavioral prevention can be distinguished: immunization, coping skills, coping skills plus immunization, and environmental structuring.[34]

The Immunization Model

Ernest Poser of McGill University first proposed the possibility of immunizing people to stressful situations that result in problem behaviors, rather like the way people are immunized against microorganisms that cause physical diseases.[35] "Behavioral immunology"[36] involves exposing people to stressful situations in small doses and in a safe environment (e.g., a therapist's office) before they encounter the stressful situations in real life. Presumably individuals preexposed to stressful situations devise coping strategies *on their own*, which are then available to them when they encounter future stress. However, in the immunization model the primary component is *graded preexposure* to stressful events, and no direct attempt is made to teach people ways of coping with the stress (as in the coping skills model to be discussed later).

In an early test of the immunization model, young children who had never seen a dentist before were preexposed on several occasions to the dentist's office and were given a mock dental examination that involved no actual dental work. When these children and a comparable group of children who had no preexposure came for their actual dental visits, videotape recordings were made of the first three minutes of each visit. Raters who had no knowledge of which children had been preexposed were able to reliably differentiate between the preexposed and nonpreexposed children on the basis of the videotapes of the first visit (but not in subsequent visits). Furthermore, the dentist, who also was unaware of which children had been preexposed, was able to differentiate between the two groups of children.[37]

In practice, it is frequently difficult to distinguish between prevention and treatment. For example, although the children who were preexposed to dental procedures had never been to a dentist's office before, they are likely to have known something about the aversive features of dental treatment (e.g., pain and numbness) from hearing about the experiences of peers or adults (an example of naturally occurring vicarious aversive consequences). Thus the preexposure may have served both as therapy for minimal apprehension about dental treatment and as prevention of more extensive adverse reactions to dental procedures.

The same type of confounding of prevention and treatment probably occurred in the program for reducing fear of medical procedures through symbolic modeling, discussed in Chapter 10. Recall that the children who saw the film *Ethan Has an Operation* prior to entering the hospital for surgery had never been hospitalized before, but it is likely that they had some fears related to hospitalization and surgery. However, there was specific evidence of prevention that was an indirect result of the modeling treatment. Children who had not seen the film exhibited a significant increase in the frequency of behavioral problems after they left the hospital, unlike children who had seen the film.[38]

One investigation of the use of symbolic modeling to prevent future avoidance behavior used extensive selection procedures to assure that the participants were not initially fearful.[39] Only first-grade children "who had never encountered a live snake, could handle a lifelike toy snake and gave no behavioral 'cognitive' indication of being snake-phobic"[40] were included in this analogue study of preventing avoidance behavior. Two basic modeling films were used, one in which child actors interacted with snakes in a fearless manner (mastery modeling) and the other in which child actors initially exhibited some fear and avoidance of the snakes and then gradually became more comfortable (coping modeling). In general, children who viewed the mastery modeling showed less fear and avoidance of snakes and had lower levels of physiological arousal when they first encountered a live snake as compared (1) to children who viewed the coping modeling, (2) to children who viewed a control film about snakes that did not include modeling, and (3) to children who viewed no film. It is noteworthy that the mastery modeling was consistently more effective than the coping modeling, a finding that is the reverse of what is typically found in *treating* fears through modeling films.[41] A possible broad implication of this finding is that, whereas the basic procedures and principles of behavioral therapy may prove to be applicable to prevention, the specific techniques may require some modification when extrapolating from treatment to prevention.

The initial success of symbolic modeling in preventing behavioral problems is heartening because symbolic modeling is an ideal procedure for mass prevention. Once the symbolic modeling sequence, such as a film, is produced, it can be economically shown to large groups. However, before such mass inoculations are attempted, the effects of the modeling sequences must be carefully evaluated not only to ascertain that they will have beneficial effects, but also to assure that there will be no direct or indirect negative effects of viewing the films. For example, some components of films designed to prevent maladaptive fear may actually make some observers more fearful (a sensitization rather than a "desensitization" effect).[42]

The Coping Skills Model

In contrast to the immunization model, the coping skills model of prevention gives individuals direct training in skills that will help them deal with difficult or stressful situations in the future or that will otherwise prevent the development of disabling disorders. A prime example of this approach (and a classic study in behavioral medicine) is the Stanford Three Community Study, a multifaceted program for preventing cardiovascular disease, such as premature heart attack and stroke.[43]

> The aims of the intervention were to increase a person's awareness of the probable causes of cardiovascular disease and of the specific behaviors that may reduce risk. People were to be provided with the information and skills necessary to achieve the recommended changes to help them become self-sufficient in the maintenance of the new health habits and skills. They were advised to follow dietary habits that would lead to the prevention of weight gain or to a reduction in weight for those who were overweight. An increase in physical activity was advised for all, and cigarette smokers were educated on the need for ceasing or reducing their cigarette consumption and the ways to achieve these goals. Methods for self-assessment or self-scoring of risk-related habits were presented to provide a basis for self-directed behavior modification.[44]

A mass-media campaign and a face-to-face intensive instruction program were used to accomplish these aims. The mass-media campaign was carried out in two northern California communities, and high-risk individuals in one of the communities received intensive instruction. A third community, which received no prevention measures, served as a control. All three communities had comparable populations of approximately 14,000.

The two-year mass-media campaign included television and radio programs and spots, weekly newspaper columns, newspaper stories and advertisements, printed materials sent by mail, and posters in buses, stores, and places of employment. The campaign was designed "to take into account the participants' media habits and the specific behavioral changes the townspeople would have to make as indicated by the baseline survey. Care was taken to produce media items that would illustrate behavioral skills as well as inform and motivate the adult population."[45]

The intensive instruction program was provided for a random sample of people in one of the communities who, it was determined, had a high risk of developing cardiovascular disease. The program lasted for 10 weeks and in virtually all cases also involved the participation of spouses of the high-risk individuals. Approximately 60 percent of the participants were provided intensive instruction in small groups, and 40 percent received individual sessions in their homes.

> The behavior modification principles applied in the intensive instruction program follow these five general steps: (1) an analysis of the participants' behavior, (2) modeling of the new behaviors, (3) guided practice in the new behaviors, (4) artificial reinforcement in the new behaviors from instructions, and (5) maintenance of the new habits without artificial reinforcement. Individuals were given instructions that were specific to their own particular risk factors: smokers who were lean and had what were considered to be normal plasma cholesterol or triglyceride values were given supplemental instruction only about how to stop smoking. Individuals who had elevated blood pressure levels were given special instruction in salt restriction and weight loss, whereas individuals with elevated levels of plasma lipids were given supplemental instruction in qualitative dietary changes.[46]

Both the mass-media campaign and the intensive instruction were successful in (1) increasing participants' knowledge about cardiovascular disease and the important risk factors, (2) decreasing specific behaviors that increase the risk of cardiovascular disease, such as eating high-cholesterol foods and smoking cigarettes, and (3) decreasing the estimated risk of cardiovascular disease. The intensive face-to-face intervention in combination with the mass-media campaign was the most effective strategy for high-risk participants. These are exciting findings because they indicate that it may be possible to prevent a major health problem on a *mass scale* by using behavioral therapy procedures and principles.

Considerable attention has been paid to skills training as a basic behavioral therapy procedure, which is understandable because the maintaining conditions of many problem behaviors lie in skill deficits. Yet very little has been done to use skills training to prevent problem behaviors. This state of affairs may be due to some of the major obstacles with which efforts to prevent behavioral problems must contend. First, the usual approach to prevention involves identifying people who have a high risk of developing the particular problem, and this task is generally complex and difficult. Second, it is often very difficult to convince people that preventive measures could be beneficial, because the target behaviors are not present. When a client has a problem, the need and desire to treat it is much easier to comprehend. Third, prevention efforts must be carried out *before* problem behaviors occur, which may mean that, for many problem behaviors, they must be implemented relatively early in people's lives.

The Coping Skills Plus Immunization Model

A third model of behavioral prevention involves immunizing people to future stress in the context of teaching them coping skills. Stress inoculation is a prototype of this approach: people learn self-control coping skills (e.g., cognitive restructuring and relaxation) and rehearse them while being exposed to a variety of stressors. In fact, any procedure that teaches coping skills and allows the client to practice them in contrived and actual stressful situations fits this model of prevention. As another example consider the active, self-control approach to systematic desensitization in which clients learn to successfully cope with anxiety by practicing relaxation while visualizing themselves handling an anxiety-evoking event. In contrast, systematic desensitization as a passive, substitution procedure involves only graded exposure to stressful events and thus fits the immunization model of prevention. Although both approaches to systematic desensitization have been shown to be effective for *treating* anxiety, it may be that only the coping skill approach will prove successful in *preventing* anxiety.[47]

One program has compared an immunization prevention procedure (substitution systematic desensitization) to a coping skills plus immunization procedure (cognitive rehearsal) for the prevention of public speaking anxiety in ninth-grade girls.[48] Although the participants were not highly anxious about public speaking (so that treatment was not indicated), they were considered to be vulnerable to public speaking anxiety because of their age, sex, not having taken a speech course, and scoring in the mid-range on a self-report measure of confidence as speakers. The participants knew that they would be asked to deliver a short speech (at least four minutes long) in front of a live audience after the program ended. One group of girls was given six sessions of group systematic desensitization (substitution model) in which the girls visualized 18 hierarchy scenes concerning public speaking while relaxed (e.g., the first scene was a teacher announcing in class that an oral report would have to be given in two weeks). Girls in a second group were given six sessions of group cognitive rehearsal, which involved visualizing themselves in each of the same 18 scenes and actively coping with the situation, using one of three coping strategies presented for each scene. For example, the three suggested coping strategies for "losing one's place while giving a speech" (the next to the highest hierarchy item) were "(1) I handle this step by taking a deep breath and remaining calm, (2) I handle this by looking down at my notes and taking as much time as I need to find my place, [and] (3) I cope with this by looking for my place while realizing how calm I feel."[49] In comparison to a third group of girls who received no preventive interventions, only the cognitive rehearsal group showed reduced susceptibility to public speaking anxiety (as measured by their reported self-confidence about making the speech one week after the program ended). During the actual speech, no differences among the groups were found in overt behavioral signs of anxiety, such as lack of eye contact, deadpan expression, and restrained hands. Note that these behaviors might also have indicated the girls' lack of appropriate public speaking training. Thus, if the coping skills training had also included public speaking skills, a greater degree of prevention might have been obtained.[50]

The potential of combining coping skills with immunization would seem to be a more potent means of preventing behavioral problems than either approach alone. Although coping skills procedures that include immunization (or graded preexposure) exist and have been demonstrated to be effective treatments, their use for prevention is as yet only a promising possibility.

The Environmental Structuring Model

The fourth general approach to prevention of problem behaviors is to structure people's environments so that they facilitate adaptive behaviors or deter maladaptive behaviors. Ideally, this restructuring should be done on a mass scale, such as establishing working conditions that minimize stress. Various proposals have even been made for utopian societies that are arranged to maximize adaptive and healthy behavior among all individuals using behavioral therapy principles and procedures.[51] In the immediate future, however, prevention of behavioral problems through environmental structuring will need to focus on narrow target behaviors with individuals or small groups of people. To illustrate this model of behavioral prevention, consider the following two limited projects, which employed very different procedures.

Shoplifting is one of the most frequent crimes in the United States.[52] The two general approaches to preventing shoplifting are aimed either at making shoppers aware of the consequences of stealing merchandise (e.g., by signs indicating that shoplifters will be prosecuted) or at increasing the threat of detecting shoplifting (e.g., with closed-circuit television). Both approaches are examples of stimulus control in that they use environmental cues to indicate that certain behaviors will result in aversive consequences. The effectiveness of the two approaches was evaluated in a clothing section of a small department store. During an initial baseline period, the amount of shoplifting was measured, but no prevention procedures were instituted. The first prevention procedure involved posting signs indicating that shoplifting was stealing, was a crime, increases inflation, and so on. The second prevention procedure involved posting signs that stated, "ATTENTION SHOPPERS & SHOPLIFTERS—The items you see marked with a red star are items that shoplifters frequently take." Red stars, approximately five inches from point to point, were mounted on racks holding the targeted clothing items. Although the general signs partially reduced shoplifting, the use of signs and stars to identify frequently taken items virtually eliminate shoplifting. It appears that the more specific the prompts, the more effective is the effort to prevent shoplifting.[53]

A second example of structuring the environment to prevent behavioral problems focused on changing family interactions to decrease the likelihood that children would engage in juvenile delinquent behavior. One approach to the treatment of juvenile delinquent behavior has been to deal directly with maladaptive family interactions that are possible maintaining conditions of the individual juvenile's problem behaviors.[54] A short-term, behavioral, family systems intervention program has been shown to significantly reduce court referrals of the identified delinquent clients 6 to 18 months after treatment.[55] The behavioral, family systems therapy involved

> a set of clearly defined therapist interventions focused on family interaction patterns in the direction of greater clarity and precision of communication, increased reciprocity of communication and social reinforcement, and contingency contracting emphasizing equivalence of rights and responsibilities for all family members.[56]

Because the goal of this therapy is to modify the interactions among family members so that the members become more effective in solving problems, it might also be expected to *prevent* problem behaviors in *younger* siblings. And indeed it does. When the court records for siblings of the initially referred juvenile offenders were examined approximately three years after the family therapy had terminated, it was found that significantly fewer families who had received the behavioral treatment (20 percent) had subsequent court contacts for siblings than families who had received no treatment (40 percent) or two nonbehavioral treatments (59 percent and 63 percent).[57]

Behavioral Prevention in Perspective

Of the four models of behavioral prevention, teaching coping skills plus providing immunization appears to be the most promising and feasible at present. Behavioral therapies already include a variety of procedures that teach clients coping skills and provide immunization in the course of learning them. Although immunization probably results in developing coping skills as one is exposed to stressful situations, directly teaching coping skills with proven effectiveness is a more prudent approach than leaving such learning to chance. Interestingly, one advantage of having people spontaneously develop their own ways of coping with stress is that the coping skills they use may be more individualized than if standard skills were taught. However, it is possible to take into account individual differences in coping styles, such as by providing a number of alternative coping strategies and encouraging people to adapt them to their unique needs and inclinations. If both the immunization model and the coping skills model prove to be effective prevention strategies, their combination should be more potent than either model alone.

Based on what we presently know, what would be an optimal yet practical prototype for preventing problem behaviors? It might be a prevention package that teaches coping skills through symbolic modeling, such as videotapes and books, and includes specific provisions for people practicing, on their own, the coping skills in progressively more stressful situations. The efficiency and economy of symbolic modeling for providing information and teaching skills to many people have already been mentioned. In prevention, more so than in treatment, efficiency and economy must be prime considerations because prevention is always aimed at a much higher proportion of the population than is treatment (because only some of the people who receive preventive measures would be expected to develop the target problem behaviors).

In the long run, restructuring the environment probably has the greatest potential for mass prevention of behavioral problems. However, except on a small scale, making substantial modifications in our existing environments to prevent problems from arising will require such major efforts as extensive funding, involvement of governmental agencies, enactment of new legislation, and, of course, changes in people's attitudes and possibly social customs. These undertakings are lengthy and costly, and are not likely in the near future. Nevertheless, it is important to develop a behavioral technology of environmental structuring to promote desirable behaviors and discourage undesirable behaviors in small projects, such as the two described in the previous section. This approach not only would help prevent problem behaviors in small segments of the population, but would also bring us closer to a goal of general environmental planning to prevent problem behaviors.

It is clear from this discussion that behavioral prevention is largely based on the assumption that effective therapy procedures can be readily translated into effective prevention procedures. As mentioned earlier, the assumption of commonality between behavioral therapy and behavioral prevention is likely to prove useful in general; it is in the specific details of the two enterprises that differences are likely to appear.

The objective of behavioral therapy is to alleviate the human suffering resulting from a host of problem behaviors that interfere with people's personal lives, make them unhappy, and create major societal problems. Although its efforts are noteworthy in achieving this aim, behavioral therapy procedures and principles could make an even greater contribution by preventing the problem behaviors from occurring in the first place. The obstacles to designing and implementing prevention programs notwithstanding, using the general principles and procedures of contemporary behavioral therapy in the service of prevention could be the most challenging and worthwhile endeavor of all.

The first task you were asked to do in reading this book was to examine your thoughts about behavioral therapy. It is fitting, then, that your last active participation in learning about contemporary behavioral therapy is to reconsider those thoughts in Participation Exercise 15-1.

PARTICIPATION EXERCISE 15-1

Afterthoughts About Contemporary Behavioral Therapy

You began your introduction to contemporary behavioral therapy in Chapter 1 by indicating whether you thought each of 17 statements about behavioral therapy was true or false (Participation Exercise 1-1). All the statements were false because they all were common misconceptions about behavioral therapy. At this point, having read the entire book, you should know why each of the statements is false. As a final review of contemporary behavioral therapy, read each of the 17 statements again and jot down specific reasons for each of them being false. Then compare your reasons with those given in Appendix B.

1. Behavioral therapy is the application of well-established laws of learning.

2. Behavioral therapy directly treats symptoms.
3. A trusting relationship between client and therapist is not important in behavioral therapy.
4. Behavioral therapy cannot deal with problems of feelings, such as depression and low self-esteem.
5. There is generally little verbal interchange between therapist and client in behavioral therapy.
6. The cooperation of a client is not necessary for successful behavioral therapy.
7. Most patients in behavioral therapy can be successfully treated in less than five sessions.
8. Behavioral therapy is not applicable to problems that involve cognitions, such as obsessional thoughts and undesirable attitudes.
9. Positive reinforcement works better with naive children than with sophisticated adults.
10. Behavioral therapy has been adopted as the primary mode of treatment in most psychiatric hopsitals and mental health centers.
11. Behavioral therapists do not use assessment techniques but rather focus immediately on treatment.
12. Much behavioral therapy involves the use of painful or aversive stimulation.
13. Behavioral therapy cannot begin until the client has well-defined goals for therapy.
14. Behavioral therapy is primarily applicable to dealing with relatively simple problem behaviors, such as phobias (e.g., fear of snakes) or undesirable habits (e.g., smoking).
15. Behavioral therapy includes biological treatments such as drugs and psychosurgery (e.g., lobotomies).
16. In behavioral therapy, the therapist determines the goals for the client.
17. In behavioral therapy, the therapist is directly responsible for the success of therapy.

SUMMARY

What speculations can be made about the future of behavioral therapy? Indications are that behavioral therapy is not a fad and that its general approach to viewing and treating problem behaviors is here to stay. Its specific procedures are likely to change as the field is evaluated and refined. In particular, several of the major limitations of behavioral therapy discussed in Chapter 14—promoting generalization and maintenance of treatment gains, improving behavioral assessment, and developing theoretical underpinnings—are likely to be focused on in the near future. Some of the current trends in behavioral therapy that are likely to continue are the emphasis on self-control procedures, the use of nonprofessional change agents, the development of "over-the-counter" treatment packages, the use of cognitive behavioral therapy procedures, and the growth of behavioral medicine. A relatively new direction in the field that appears to have considerable future potential is the application of behavioral therapy principles and procedures to deal with societal problems, such as unemployment, neighborhood problems, racial integration, and ecological issues. Initial experimental projects in these areas have provided promising results. Perhaps the most worthwhile use of behavioral therapy principles and procedures would be for prevention. Four basic models of behavioral primary prevention can be distinguished: immunization, coping skills, coping skills plus immunization, and environmental structuring. Little actual implementation of these models to prevention has been carried out thus far, and prevention has a whole set of practical problems beyond those encountered with treatment. Given the potential benefits of preventing problem behaviors and physical disorders, behavioral primary prevention should be an important future goal for the field.

REFERENCE NOTES

1. For example, Wachtel, 1977.
2. For example, Stuart & Davis, 1972.
3. For example, Houts, Liebert, & Liebert, 1979.
4. For example, Azrin & Foxx, 1974.
5. For example, Wenrich, Dawley, & General, 1976.
6. For example, Alberti & Emmons, 1978; Bower & Bower, 1976.
7. Franks & Wilson, 1978.
8. Franks & Wilson, 1978, p. 303.
9. For example, Jones & Azrin, 1973.
10. Azrin, Flores, & Kaplin, 1975.
11. Spiegler & Agigian, 1977, pp. 320–321.
12. Miller & Miller, 1970.
13. Briscoe, Hoffman, & Bailey, 1975.
14. For example, Mann, 1959.
15. Hauserman, Walen, & Behling, 1973.
16. See Kazdin, 1977a; Nietzel, Winett, MacDonald, & Davidson, 1977.
17. Kazdin, 1977a; Kohlenberg & Phillips, 1973.
18. For example, Hayes & Cone, 1977; Kohlenberg, Phillips, & Proctor, 1976; Winett & Nietzel, 1975.
19. For example, Burgess, Clark, & Hendee, 1971.
20. For example, Clark, Burgess, & Hendee, 1972; Powers, Osborne, & Anderson, 1973.
21. For example, Kohlenberg & Phillips, 1973.
22. Chapman & Risley, 1974.
23. Burgess, Clark, & Hendee, 1971.
24. For example, Geller, Chaffee, & Ingram, 1975; Geller, Wylie, & Farris, 1971; Reid, Luyben, Rawers, & Bailey, 1976; Witmer & Geller, 1976.
25. *Oregon's Bottle Bill, the 1977 Report*, 1977.
26. For example, Hayes & Cone, 1977.
27. For example, Kohlenberg, Phillips, & Proctor, 1976.
28. Hayes & Cone, 1977.
29. Foxx & Hake, 1977; Hake & Foxx, 1978.
30. For example, Deslauriers & Everett, 1977; Everett, Haywood, & Meyers, 1974.
31. Everett, Hayward, & Meyers, 1974.

32. Caplan, 1964.
33. For example, Kessler & Albee, 1975.
34. Spiegler, 1980.
35. Poser, 1970; Poser & King, 1975, 1976.
36. Poser & King, 1975.
37. Poser & King, 1975.
38. Melamed & Siegel, 1975.
39. Poser & King, 1975.
40. Poser & King, 1975, p. 288.
41. King, 1975.
42. See Poser & King, 1975; Spiegler, Liebert, McMains, & Fernandez, 1969.
43. Maccoby, Farquhar, Wood, & Alexander, 1977.
44. Maccoby, Farquhar, Wood, & Alexander, 1977, p. 104.
45. Maccoby, Farquhar, Wood, & Alexander, 1977, p. 104.
46. Maccoby, Farquhar, Wood, & Alexander, 1977, p. 106.
47. Poser & King, 1976.
48. Cradock, Cotler, & Jason, 1978.
49. Cradock, Cotler, & Jason, 1978, p. 392.
50. Cradock, Cotler, & Jason, 1978.
51. See Skinner, 1948, 1971, 1974.
52. Weinstein, 1974.
53. McNees, Egli, Marshall, Schnelle, & Risley, 1976.
54. For example, Alexander & Parsons, 1973; Parsons & Alexander, 1973.
55. Alexander & Parsons, 1973.
56. Klein, Alexander, & Parsons, 1977, p. 471.
57. Klein, Alexander, & Parsons, 1977.

APPENDIX A Guidelines for Choosing a Behavioral Therapist*

[The following guidelines can help a prospective client choose a behavioral therapist—a sometimes difficult task for the nonprofessional, particularly for someone who is feeling confused and perhaps frightened. The guidelines have been published by the Association for the Advancement of Behavior Therapy.]

After the decision to seek therapy has been made, an individual may feel unsure about how to choose a therapist. Persons seeking therapy often find that they have no standards to use in evaluating potential therapists. There are many competent therapists of varying theoretical persuasions. The purpose of this guide is to provide you with information that might be useful in selecting a behavior therapist. No guideline can provide strict rules for selecting the best therapist for a particular individual. We can, however, suggest questions you might ask and areas of information you might want to cover with a potential behavior therapist before you make a final decision. On the following pages, we will discuss these areas:

What is behavior therapy?

Qualifications and training necessary for particular mental health professionals.

How to get the names of behavior therapists.

Practical information about therapists.

Questions to ask when deciding on a therapist.

What to do if you are dissatisfied with your therapist.

*The "Guidelines" were written by Marsha Linehan, Ph.D. (University of Washington, Seattle), during her tenure as Membership Chairperson of the Association for Advancement of Behavior Therapy, with a committee consisting of Richard Bootzin, Ph.D., Joseph Cautela, Ph.D., Perry London, Ph.D., Morris Perloff, Ph.D., Richard Stuart, D.S.W., and Todd Risley, Ph.D.

WHAT IS BEHAVIOR THERAPY?

There is no single definition of behavior therapy. Although some common points of view are shared by most behavior therapists, there is a wide diversity among those persons who call themselves behavior therapists. The definition that follows is meant to give you a general idea of what behavior therapy is. It is not, however, an absolute definition. The particular behavior therapist you select may agree with some parts of it and disagree with other parts. The following definition is adapted from "Behavior Modification: Perspective on a Current Issue," published by the National Institute of Mental Health:

> Behavior therapy is a particular kind of therapy that involves the application of findings from behavioral science research to help individuals change in ways they would like to change. There is an emphasis in behavior therapy on checking up on how effective the therapy is by monitoring and evaluating the individual's progress. Most behaviorally-oriented therapists believe that the current environment is most important in affecting the person's present behavior. Early life experiences, long time intrapsychic conflicts, or the individual's personality structure are considered to be of less importance than what is happening in the person's life at the present time. The procedures used in behavior therapy are generally intended to improve the individual's self-control by expanding the person's skills, abilities, and independence.

QUALIFICATIONS AND TRAINING NECESSARY FOR PARTICULAR MENTAL HEALTH PROFESSIONALS

Behavior therapy can be done by a number of different mental health professionals. Competent behavior therapists are trained in many different disciplines, and the distinction between different types of mental health professions can sometimes be confusing. Therefore, we have listed below a brief description of the training received by different types of professionals who may offer behavior therapy.

Psychiatric Social Workers

A psychiatric social worker must have a college degree, plus at least two years of graduate training in a program accredited by the Council on Social Work Education. A psychiatric social worker who is certified by the Academy of Certified Social Workers (ACSW) must have a master's or doctoral degree in Social Work (MSW or DSW) from a program approved by the Council on Social Work Education, two years of post-degree experience in the practice of social work, and membership in the National Association of Social Workers. In addition, the certified psychiatric social worker must pass a written exam and submit several professional references. Licensing procedures vary from state to state.

Psychologists

Psychologists usually have doctoral degrees (Ph.D., Ed.D., Psy.D.) from graduate programs approved by the American Psychological Association. The *National Register of Health Service Providers in Psychology* lists psychologists who have a doctoral degree from a regionally accredited university, have at least two years of supervised experience in health services, one of which is postdoctoral, and are licensed or certified by the state for the independent practice of psychology. After five years of post-doctoral experience, a psychologist may apply for credentials from the American Board of Professional Psychology. This involves a review by the Board of the applicant's experience and an examination that the applicant must pass. Licensing or certification procedures vary from state to state.

Psychiatrists

A psychiatrist must have a medical degree. Although technically an individual can practice psychiatry having had four years of medical school and a one-year medical internship, most psychiatrists continue their training in a three-year residency program in psychiatry. Psychiatrists who have Board certification have had two years of post-residency experience in practicing psychiatry and must have passed an examination given by the American Board of Psychiatry and Neurology.

PRACTICAL INFORMATION ABOUT THERAPISTS

You have the right to obtain the following information about any potential therapist. This information may be obtained from the referral person, over the phone with the therapist, or at your first visit with the therapist. Although you may not feel that all this information is relevant, you will need a substantial amount of it in order to evaluate whether a particular therapist would be good for you.

Your first session with a therapist should always be a consultation. This session does not commit you to working with the therapist. The goals in the first session should be to find out whether therapy would be useful for you and whether this particular therapist is likely to be helpful to you. During this session you may want to discuss with your therapist any values which are particularly important to you. If your therapist's views are very different from yours, you may want to find a therapist more compatible with you. An important aspect of therapy for you will be the relationship between you and the therapist. This first session is a time for you to determine whether you will feel comfortable and confident working with this particular therapist.

The following are things you need to know about a prospective therapist:

Training and Qualifications

An earlier section of this guide gives a description of the qualifications and amount of training necessary for an individual to obtain a particular mental health-related degree. You should find out whether the individual therapist is licensed or certified by your state. If the person is not licensed or certified by your state, you may want to ask whether the person is being supervised by another mental health professional.

Because behavior therapists vary in types of training, there are no set rules on which professional qualifications would be best for any given person. It is common, though, for clients to want to know about the training, experience, and other professional qualifications of a potential therapist. Good therapists will not mind being asked questions about their qualifications and will freely give you any professional information which you request. If a therapist does not answer your questions, you should consult another therapist.

Fees

Many people feel uncomfortable asking about fees. However, it is important information which a good therapist will be quite willing to give a potential client. The following are financial questions you may want to cover with a therapist. This information may be obtained over the phone or during your first visit. You will want to know:

1. How much does the therapist charge per session?
2. Does the therapist charge according to income (sliding scale)?
3. Does the therapist charge for the initial session? (Since many therapists *do* charge for the initial session, you should get this information before your first visit.)
4. Is there a policy concerning vacations and missed or cancelled sessions? Is there a charge?
5. Will your health insurance cover you if you see this therapist?
6. Will the therapist want you to pay after each session, or will you be billed periodically?

Other Questions

The following are other questions you may want to ask a potential therapist:

1. How many times a week will the therapist want to see you?
2. How long will each session last?
3. How long does the therapist expect treatment to last? (Some therapists only do time-limited therapy, whereas others set no such limits.)
4. What are some of the treatment approaches likely to be used?
5. Does the therapist accept phone calls at the office or at home?

6. When your therapist is out of town or otherwise unavailable, is there someone else you can call if an emergency arises?
7. Are there any limitations on confidentiality?

QUESTIONS TO ASK WHEN DECIDING ON A THERAPIST

A behavior therapist will devote the first few sessions to assessing the extent and causes of the concerns which you have. Generally, your therapist will be asking quite specific questions about the concerns or problems causing you distress and about when and where these occur. As the assessment progresses, you can expect that you and your therapist will arrive at mutually agreeable goals for how you want to change. If you cannot agree on the goals of therapy, you should consider finding another therapist.

Once the initial goals are decided upon, you can expect the therapist to discuss with you one or more approaches for helping you reach your goals. As you continue therapy, you can expect your therapist to continually evaluate with you your progress toward these goals. If you are not progressing, or if progress is too slow, your therapist will most likely suggest modifying or changing the treatment approach. At each of these points you may want to ask yourself the following questions:

1. Do you understand what the therapist has asked you to do?
2. Do the therapist's instructions seem relevant to your objectives?
3. Do you believe that following these instructions is likely to help you make significant progress?
4. Has the therapist given you a choice of alternative therapy approaches?
5. Has the therapist explained possible side effects of the therapy?
6. Do you know what the therapist's own values are, to the extent that they are relevant to your problem?

WHAT TO DO IF YOU ARE DISSATISFIED WITH YOUR THERAPIST

Talk with Your Therapist

People often feel angry or frustrated at times about their therapy. If you do, you should discuss these concerns, dissatisfactions, and questions with the therapist. A good therapist will be open to hearing them and discussing your dissatisfactions with you.

Get a Second Opinion

If you feel that the issues and problems you have raised with your therapist are not being resolved, you may want to consider asking for a consultation with another professional. Usually the therapist you are seeing can suggest someone you can consult. If your therapist objects to your consulting another professional, you should change to another therapist who will not object.

Consider Changing Therapists

Many people feel that it is never acceptable to change therapists once therapy has begun. This is simply not true. Good therapists realize that they might not be appropriate for every person.

The most important thing you need to ask yourself when deciding to continue with a particular therapist is "Am I changing in the direction I want to change?" If you do not feel that you are improving, and if, after discussing this with your therapist, it does not appear likely to you that you will improve with this therapist, you should consult another therapist.

HOW TO GET THE NAMES OF BEHAVIOR THERAPISTS

If you don't already have the name of a therapist, you might try some of the following suggestions:

1. Ask for recommendations from your family physician, friends, and relatives.
2. Look through the Association for Advancement of Behavior Therapy Membership Directory. AABT is not a certifying organization, and not all members listed offer behavior therapy. However, you might call persons listed in the directory to ask for a referral. Members are listed by city and state, as well as alphabetically.
3. Call your state psychological association or district psychiatric association, and ask for a referral. You can locate your state psychological association by writing or calling the American Psychological Association, 1200 17th Street, Northwest, Washington, DC 20036, phone (202) 833–7600. Only certified or licensed persons will be referred by these organizations. District psychiatric associations can be found by calling or writing the American Psychiatric Association, 1700 18th Street, Northwest, Washington, DC 20009, phone (202) 232–7878.
4. Call the university psychology, social work or medical school psychiatry departments in your area and ask for a referral. Ask to speak with someone in clinical or counseling psychology, the chairperson of the social work department, or the chairperson of the department of psychiatry.
5. Call your local community mental health clinic. The clinic may have a behavior therapist on the staff or be able to give you a referral.
6. Look in the directories of the American Psychological Association and the American Psychiatric Association. Copies of these directories should be in your public library. Members in these organizations will often be able to give you a referral.

7. Look in the *National Register of Health Service Providers in Psychology* published by the Council of National Health Service Providers in Psychology, 1200 17th Street, Northwest, Washington, DC 20036. Persons listed might be able to give you a referral.

8. Look in the National Association of Social Workers' *Register of Clinical Social Workers* published by the National Association of Social Workers, 1425 "H" Street, Northwest, Washington, DC 20005. Persons listed might be able to give you a referral.

APPENDIX B Answers for Participation Exercises

P.E. 2-1 Distinguishing Between Traits and Behaviors

1. T	5. T	9. T	13. B	17. T
2. B	6. T	10. B	14. T	18. T
3. B	7. B	11. T	15. T	19. T
4. B	8. T	12. B	16. B	20. B

P.E. 2-2 Translating Trait Descriptions into Behaviors

Sociable
- Attending social events
- Meeting new people
- Inviting people to your house
- Talking with strangers
- Going places where people often gather
- Being with other people rather than being alone

Hostile
- Criticizing someone slanderously
- Striking a person
- Spreading rumors about someone
- Fighting
- Defacing someone's property

Helpful
- Giving a hitchhiker a lift
- Tutoring a student
- Lending money to a friend
- Doing volunteer work
- Changing a flat tire for a stranger
- Giving someone good advice

Thrifty
- Budgeting your money
- Using a car pool
- Making your own clothes
- Sharing an apartment
- Shopping at sales

Dependable
- Being on time
- Keeping a promise
- Adhering to a schedule
- Paying back borrowed money

Smart
- Getting good grades in school
- Scoring high on an I.Q. test
- Reading difficult books
- Writing a book
- Speaking several languages fluently
- Solving complex problems

Patient
- Sticking to a long frustrating task until it is completed
- Answering a rude customer politely
- Cheerfully waiting for a late person
- Tutoring a "slow" student
- Calmly teaching a beginning driver
- Sitting attentively through a boring lecture

Healthy
- Exercising regularly
- Eating nutritional foods
- Sleeping an appropriate number of hours each night
- Passing a physical examination
- Attending a health spa
- Bringing blood pressure to normal

P.E. 2-3 Distinguishing Between Overt and Covert Behavior

1. O	5. O	9. C	13. O	17. C
2. C	6. C	10. O	14. C	18. O
3. O	7. C	11. C	15. O	19. C
4. C	8. O	12. C	16. O	20. O

P.E. 2-4 Thinking Overt Behavior

Silent reading
- Looking at a page of a book (for a reasonable time)
- Eyes moving across lines of page
- Lip movements while looking at page
- Turning pages (at reasonable time intervals)

Worrying
- Pacing
- Saying you are worried
- Biting your finger nails
- Sweating
- Tensing your muscles
- Chain smoking

Feeling happy
- Smiling
- Laughing
- Saying you are happy
- Telling jokes
- Playing
- "Jumping for joy"

Being interested
- Looking at person talking to you
- Taking courses on subject
- Reading about a subject
- Asking questions about subject
- Working in field of interest
- Talking about the interest

Listening (to speaker)
- Looking directly at speaker
- Taking notes on what speaker is saying
- Verbally disagreeing with speaker
- Asking questions about the talk
- Telling others about what speaker had to say

Liking (a person)
- Often speaking with the person
- Smiling in the company of the person
- Giving presents to the person
- Saying you like the person
- Inviting the person to do things
- Often writing to the person
- Being affectionate toward the person

P.E. 2-5 Identifying Antecedents and Consequences of Behaviors

Behavior	*Antecedents*	*Consequences*
1. Running		
	Wanted to lose weight	Lost 12 pounds
	Heard of health benefits of running	Breathing improved
	Saw neighbors running	Felt more energetic
	Doctor recommended it	Better able to concentrate
		Wife began running
2. Calling the police		
	Hot evening	Reported the crime
	Sitting in her apartment	Was thanked by police
	Looking out window	Police rushed to the scene
	Saw attack	
3. Attending a party		
	Cousin was graduating	Saw many old friends
	Received an invitation	Met interesting new people
	Accepted invitation	Found a golf partner
4. Going to a play		
	Play was in town	Earned extra credits
	Jackie read about play	Was disappointed
	Play received good reviews	Felt she wasted her time
	Got a pass for the play	Her grade was boosted
	Jackie expected to earn extra credits	
5. Getting up too late		
	Got to bed very late	Missed the bus to work
	Was intoxicated	Missed two important clients
	Forgot to set the alarm	
6. Cooking a fancy meal		
	Parents coming for visit	Her kitchen was messed up
	Barbara wanted to make a good impression	The dish was a success
	Perfect situation for trying new recipe	Parents enjoyed her meal
	She enjoyed preparing fancy meals	Barbara enjoyed the meal
		Barbara felt satisfied
7. Writing a letter		
	Parents' request to answer brother's letter	Felt relieved
	Got out some stationery	Expected brother to be pleased
	Looked up the address	Hoped it might alleviate dispute
		Received a letter from her brother
		Made her brother happy

	Antecedents	Consequences
8. Joining a car pool		
	Saw an ad in newspaper	Conserved energy
	Rising price of gas	Reduced pollution
	Poor condition of his car	
9. Shopping for new clothes		
	Jane needed new clothes	She felt good
	Saved enough money to go shopping	People complimented her
	Took family car	
	Obtained directions to shopping mall	
10. Pulling a fire alarm box		
	Saw alarm box	Ran from scene
	Wanted to impress his friends	Fire trucks came
	Thought of the excitement if he pulled the alarm	Crowd gathered
	Read the instructions	Fire chief was angry
	Saw no one was around	Chief announced it was false alarm
		Investigation
		Crowd dispersed
		Trucks left

P.E. 3-1 Finding Acceleration Target Behaviors That Are Incompatible with Deceleration Target Behaviors

Deceleration	*Acceleration*
Eating junk food between meals	Eating only fruits between meals
	Only drinking between meals
	Only eating at mealtime
	Buying only healthy foods
Cramming for exams	Studying 2 hours per day a week before exam
	Putting all books away at 11 P.M. the night before exam
	Scheduling nonstudy activities the night before exam
"Blowing" entire paycheck	Immediately depositing part of check into bank account
	Sticking to a budget
	Have paycheck automatically deposited
	Have someone else hold your money for you
	Immediately paying off all bills

Deceleration	*Acceleration*
Using foul language	Using only decent language Using a nonsense word when angry Counting to 10 when frustrated Stamping feet instead of swearing
Leaving lights on when not in use	Shutting lights off immediately after use Only turning lights on when needed Working with daylight only Shutting lights off when leaving room
Wasting time	Have more planned than you can complete Following a schedule Having activity prepared for free times Carry a portable hobby (e.g., reading, knitting)
Being late for classes	Arriving 5 minutes early to class Camping out the night before in classroom
Speeding	Driving 5 miles below the speed limit Having someone else drive Taking a bus Using the automatic speed control in your car
Procrastinating in paying bills	Paying all bills within 3 days of receipt Having someone pay all bills for you Paying cash for transactions
Littering	Using garbage cans Carrying litter bag with you Using nondisposable items (e.g., glasses instead of paper cups)

P.E. 11-2 Cognitive Restructuring

1. "If I work real hard I may be able to get it all done for tomorrow."
   "This is going to be tough but it is still possible to do it."
   "It will be a real challenge finishing this assignment for tomorrow."
   "If I don't get it finished, I'll just have to ask the teacher for an extension."
2. "What's done is done; I'll just have to make the best of it."
   "I'll just have to figure out a way that I can pay for this."
   "This is going to cost me, but thank God no one was injured."
   "Maybe my father will understand if I explain it to him calmly."

3. "I'm sure there are others who aren't great dancers either."
"Hey, it's all for fun. So what if I don't dance well."
"There's still time to learn. I'll ask my cousin to give me a few quick lessons."
"I'll just do what everyone else does. Maybe no one will even notice."
4. "I'll just have to look harder for another job."
"There will be rough times ahead, but I've dealt with rough times before."
"Hey, maybe my next job will be a better deal altogether."
"There are agencies that can probably help me get some kind of a job."
5. "I'll miss everyone, but it doesn't mean we can't stay in touch."
"Just think of all the new people I'm going to meet."
"I guess it will be kind of exciting moving to a new home."
"Now I'll have two places to call home."
6. "Maybe I'll find he (or she) is not so bad a person after all."
"Just because we are roommates doesn't mean we have to be friends."
"If it doesn't work out maybe I can find a way to switch roommates."
"Maybe if I act friendly toward him (or her) he (or she) will act better toward me."
"Just because I don't get along with my roommate doesn't mean my whole year is going to be bad."
7. "I really thought our relationship would work, but it's not the end of the world."
"Maybe we can try again in the future."
"I'll just have to try to keep myself busy and not let it bother me."
"It sure is hard to accept, but I'll just have to live with it."
"If I met him (her), there is no reason why I won't meet someone else someday."
8. "I'll just have to reapply next year."
"There are things I can do with my life other than going to grad school."
"I guess a lot of good students get turned down. It's just so damn competitive."
"I can still get a half decent job I can enjoy."
"This could be a good thing for me. It will give me time to think about my future."
"Perhaps there are a few other programs that I could apply to."
9. "I have as much to say as anyone else in the class."
"My ideas may be different, but they're still valid."
"It's OK to be a bit nervous; I'll relax as I start talking."
"I might as well say something; how bad could it sound?"
"I may as well speak up. I'm sure half the class feels the same way I do."
10. "Now I'm really behind. I'll just have to put in a few extra hours later to make it up."
"Hey, I enjoyed reading the magazines. I think it was almost worth falling behind."
"There will be time in the morning to finish my work. I'll just have to get up a little earlier."
"Just because I blew those two hours doesn't mean I have to give up and blow the next two."
"I should know better, but I guess I don't. So I'll just get into the work now."

P.E. 15-1 Afterthoughts About Contemporary Behavioral Therapy

Note: The following explanations are overviews only; see appropriate parts of the text for full explanations.

1. A diversity of theories of learning exists (and they are often in conflict with one another); at present there are no "well-established laws of learning." Behavioral therapy procedures do use various principles of learning (e.g., reinforcement, shaping, extinction). However, behavioral therapy is much more accurately viewed as the application of procedures that have been empirically demonstrated to change the maintaining conditions of problem behaviors.
2. Behavioral therapy directly treats the ***maintaining conditions*** of problem behaviors (symptoms), thereby indirectly changing the problem behaviors.
3. A trusting relationship is very important in behavioral therapy so that the client will cooperate fully with the therapist's directives and so that the therapist can have confidence that the client is implementing them. However, in contrast to some other forms of therapy (e.g., psychoanalysis), the trusting relationship is not the major means of bringing about therapeutic change but rather facilitates the therapy.
4. Both emotional states, such as depression and anxiety, and cognitions, such as self-evaluations, are considered covert behaviors that are both directly (Chapter 11) and indirectly treated by behavioral therapy.
5. Verbal interchange is usually the major means by which client and behavioral therapist communicate. However, behavioral therapy is an action-oriented therapy that involves much more than just talking about the client's problems.
6. It is rarely possible for any form of therapy to be effective without the cooperation of the client. Furthermore, behavioral therapy generally involves the active participation of clients in their therapy.
7. Behavioral therapy usually brings about changes in problem behaviors in considerably fewer therapy sessions than many other forms of psychotherapy (especially insight-oriented therapies) but generally not in as few as five sessions.
8. Cognitive behavioral therapies directly deal with clients' cognitions that are either maintaining (overt) problem behaviors or are themselves (covert) problem behaviors.
9. Reinforcement procedures work as well with adults as with children. The types and sources of reinforcers differ for children and adults, but adults' behaviors are as much influenced by reinforcers as are children's behaviors.
10. Although behavioral therapy is becoming widely accepted, it still is probably not the major mode of therapy employed for treating abnormal behaviors in general. The predominant mode of psychotherapy is still one of many variations of insight-oriented, verbal psychotherapy.
11. Because behavioral therapy treats the maintaining conditions of a problem behavior, the initial step in treatment always must be an ***assessment*** of the maintaining conditions. Additionally, the success of behavioral therapy is judged by comparing pretherapy measures of the target behavior with during-therapy and posttherapy measures.
12. Aversive procedures are used in a small minority of cases and usually after nonaversive procedures have been tried and have failed. Furthermore, because aversive procedures are used to decelerate target behaviors, they must be supplemented with acceleration procedures, which comprise the vast majority of behavioral therapy procedures.
13. In practice, clients often do not have well-defined goals. Thus, frequently before treatment can begin, behavioral therapists must first help clients decide on realistic and clearly delineated goals for therapy.

14. Behavioral therapy treats a wide array of complex human problems, as is amply illustrated in this book. The complex problem behaviors are treated by successively changing target behaviors, which are relatively simple components of the more complex behavior, until the entire complex problem behavior has been successfully treated.
15. Biological treatments, such as drug therapy and psychosurgery, are ***not*** part of behavioral therapy.
16. The client (and/or the client's legal guardian in the case of a nonvoluntary client) decides on her or his own goals for therapy. The therapist may assist the client to formulate realistic goals, but the client (and/or guardian) has the final say regarding treatment goals.
17. Clients in behavioral therapy are actively involved in their therapy and often directly institute therapeutic procedures in their home environments (under a therapist's supervision). Thus, the client, rather than the therapist, is most responsible for the success of behavioral therapy (although, obviously, the therapist assumes ***some*** of the responsibility).

References

Aarons, L. Subvocalization: Aural and EMG feedback in reading. *Perceptual and Motor Skills*, 1971, *33*, 271–306.

Agras, W. S. President's message. *Behavioral Medicine Update*, 1979, *1*, 3.

Alberti, R. E., & Emmons, M. L. *Your perfect right: A guide to assertive behavior* (3rd ed.). San Luis Obispo, Calif.: Impact Publishers, 1978.

Alexander, A. B., & Smith, D. D. Clinical applications of EMG biofeedback. In R. J. Gatchel & K. P. Price (Eds.), *Clinical applications of biofeedback: Appraisal and status*. New York: Pergamon, 1979. Pp. 112–133.

Alexander, J. F., & Parsons, B. V. Short-term behavioral intervention with delinquent families: Impact on family process and recidivism. *Journal of Abnormal Psychology*, 1973, *81*, 219–225.

Allen, K. E., Turner, K. K., & Everett, P. M. A behavior modification classroom for Head Start children with problem behaviors. *Exceptional Children*, 1970, *37*, 119–127.

Anant, S. S. The use of verbal aversion (negative conditioning) with an alcoholic: A case report. *Behaviour Research and Therapy*, 1968, *6*, 695–696.

Anastasi, A. The cultivation of diversity. *American Psychologist*, 1972, *27*, 1091–1099.

Anderson, L. T., & Alpert, M. Operant analysis of hallucination frequency in a hospitalized schizophrenic. *Journal of Behavior Therapy and Experimental Psychiatry*, 1974, *5*, 13–18.

Andrews, J. M. Neuromuscular re-education of the hemiplegic with the aid of the electromyograph. *Archives of Physical Medicine and Rehabilitation*, 1964, *45*, 530–532.

Anton, W. D. An evaluation of outcome variables in the systematic desensitization of test anxiety. *Behaviour Research and Therapy*, 1976, *14*, 217–224.

Arkowitz, H., Lichtenstein, E., McGovern, K., & Hines, D. The behavioral assessment of social competence in males. *Behavior Therapy*, 1975, *6*, 3–13.

Ashem, B., & Donner, L. Covert sensitization with alcoholics: A controlled replication. *Behaviour Research and Therapy*, 1968, *6*, 7–12.

Asylum on the front porch: II. Community life for the mentally retarded. *Innovations*, 1974, *1*, 11–14.

Atthowe, J. M., Jr., & Krasner, L. Preliminary report on the application of contingent reinforcement procedures (token economy) on a "chronic" psychiatric ward. *Journal of Abnormal Psychology*, 1968, *73*, 37–43.

Axelrod, S., Brantner, J. P., & Meddock, T. D. Overcorrection: A review and critical analysis. *Journal of Special Education*, 1978, *12*, 367–391.

Ayllon, T. Intensive treatment of psychotic behavior by stimulus satiation and food reinforcement. *Behaviour Research and Therapy*, 1963, *1*, 53–61.

Ayllon, T. Some behavioral problems associated with eating in chronic schizophrenic patients. In L. P. Ullmann & L. Krasner (Eds.), *Case studies in behavior modification*. New York: Holt, Rinehart & Winston, 1965.

Ayllon, T., & Azrin, N. H. The measurement and reinforcement of behavior of psychotics. *Journal of the Experimental Analysis of Behavior*, 1965, *8*, 357–383.

Ayllon, T., & Azrin, N. H. Reinforcer sampling: A technique for increasing the behavior of mental patients. *Journal of Applied Behavior Analysis*, 1968, *1*, 13–20. (a)

Ayllon, T., & Azrin, N. H. *The token economy: A motivational system for therapy and rehabilitation*. New York: Appleton-Century-Crofts, 1968. (b)

Ayllon, T., Layman, D., & Kandel, H. J. A behavioral-educational alternative to drug control of hyperactive children. *Journal of Applied Behavior Analysis*, 1975, *8*, 137–146.

Ayllon, T., & Michael, J. The psychiatric nurse as a behavioral engineer. *Journal of the Experimental Analysis of Behavior*, 1959, *2*, 323–334.

Ayllon, T., & Roberts, M. D. Eliminating discipline problems by strengthening academic performance. *Journal of Applied Behavior Analysis*, 1974, *7*, 71–76.

Azrin, N. H. Improvements in the community-reinforcement approach to alcoholism. *Behaviour Research and Therapy*, 1976, *14*, 339–348.

Azrin, N. H., Flores, T., & Kaplan, S. J. Job-finding club: A group-assisted program for obtaining employment. *Behaviour Research and Therapy*, 1975, *13*, 17–27.

Azrin, N. H., & Foxx, R. M. *Toilet training in less than a day*. New York: Simon & Schuster, 1974.

Azrin, N. H., Gottlieb, L., Hughart, L., Wesolowski, M. D., & Rahn, T. Eliminating self-injurious behavior by educative procedures. *Behaviour Research and Therapy*, 1975, *13*, 101–111.

Azrin, N. H., & Holz, W. C. Punishment. In W. K. Honig (Ed.), *Operant behavior: Areas of research and application*. New York: Appleton-Century-Crofts, 1966.

Azrin, N. H., & Powell, J. Behavioral engineering: The reduction of smoking behavior by a conditioning apparatus and procedure. *Journal of Applied Behavior Analysis*, 1968, *1*, 193–200.

Azrin, N., Rubin, H., O'Brien, F., Ayllon, T., & Roll, D. Behavioral engineering: Postural control by a portable operant apparatus. *Journal of Applied Behavior Analysis*, 1968, *1*, 99–108.

Azrin, N. H., Sneed, T. J., & Foxx, R. M. Dry bed: A rapid method of eliminating bedwetting (enuresis) of the retarded. *Behaviour Research and Therapy*, 1973, *11*, 427–434.

Azrin, N. H., Sneed, T. J., & Foxx, R. M. Dry-bed training: Rapid elimination of childhood enuresis. *Behaviour Research and Therapy*, 1974, *12*, 147–156.

Azrin, N. H., & Thienes, P. M. Rapid elimination of enuresis by intensive learning without a conditioning apparatus. *Behavior Therapy*, 1978, *9*, 342–354.

Azrin, N. H., Thienes-Hontos, P., & Besalel-Azrin, V. Elimination of enuresis without a conditioning apparatus: An extension by office instruction of the child and parents. *Behavior Therapy*, 1979, *10*, 14–19.

Azrin, N. H., & Wesolowski, M. D. Theft reversal: An overcorrection procedure for eliminating stealing by retarded persons. *Journal of Applied Behavior Analysis*, 1974, *7*, 577–581.

Azrin, N. H., & Wesolowski, M. D. Eliminating habitual vomiting in a retarded adult by positive practice and self-correction. *Journal of Behavior Therapy and Experimental Psychiatry*, 1975, *6*, 145–148. (a)

Azrin, N. H., & Wesolowski, M. D. The use of positive practice to eliminate persistent floor sprawling by profoundly retarded persons. *Behavior Therapy*, 1975, *6*, 627–631. (b)

Bachman, J. A. Self-injurious behavior: A behavioral analysis. *Journal of Abnormal Psychology*, 1972, *80*, 211–224.

Baer, D. M. A case for the selective reinforcement of punishment. In C. Neuringer & J. L. Michael (Eds.), *Behavior modification in clinical psychology*. New York: Appleton-Century-Crofts, 1970.

Baer, D. M., & Guess, D. Receptive training of adjectival inflections in mental retardates. *Journal of Applied Behavior Analysis*, 1971, *4*, 129–139.

Baer, D. M., & Guess, D. Teaching productive noun suffixes to severely retarded children. *American Journal of Mental Deficiency*, 1973, *77*, 498–505.

Baile, W. F., & Engel, B. T. A behavioral strategy for promoting treatment compliance following myocardial infarction. *Psychosomatic Medicine*, 1978, *40*, 413–419.

Bailey, J. S., Timbers, G. D., Phillips, E. L., & Wolf, M. M. Modification of articulation errors of pre-delinquents by their peers. *Journal of Applied Behavior Analysis*, 1971, *4*, 265–281.

Bailey, J. S., Wolf, M. M., & Phillips, E. L. Home-based reinforcement and the modification of pre-delinquents' classroom behavior. *Journal of Applied Behavior Analysis*, 1970, *3*, 223–233.

Balson, P. M. Encopresis: A case with symptom substitution. *Behavior Therapy*, 1973, *4*, 134–136.

Bancroft, J. H. *Deviant sexual behavior*. Oxford, England: Oxford University Press, 1974.

Bandura, A. *Principles of behavior modification*. New York: Holt, Rinehart & Winston, 1969.

Bandura, A. (Ed.). *Psychological modeling: Conflicting theories*. Chicago: Aldine-Atherton, 1971.

Bandura, A. Effecting change through participant modeling. In J. D. Krumboltz & C. E. Thoresen (Eds.), *Counseling methods*. New York: Holt, Rinehart & Winston, 1975.

Bandura, A. Self-efficacy: Toward a unifying theory of behavioral change. *Psychological Review*, 1977, *84*, 191–215. (a)

Bandura, A. *Social learning theory*. Englewood Cliffs, N.J.: Prentice-Hall, 1977. (b)

Bandura, A. Reflections on self-efficacy. In S. Rachman (Ed.), *Advances in behaviour research and therapy* (Vol. 1). Oxford, England: Pergamon, 1978.

Bandura, A., & Adams, N. E. Analysis of self-efficacy theory of behavioral change. *Cognitive Therapy and Research*, 1977, *1*, 287–308.

Bandura, A., Adams, N. E., & Beyer, J. Cognitive process mediating behavioral change. *Journal of Personality and Social Psychology*, 1977, *35*, 125–139.

Bandura, A., Adams, N. E., Hardy, A. B., & Howells, G. N. Tests of the generality of self-efficacy theory. *Cognitive Therapy and Research*, 1980, *4*, 39–66.

Bandura, A., Blanchard, E. B., & Ritter, B. The relative efficacy of desensitization and modeling approaches for inducing behavioral, affective, and cognitive changes. *Journal of Personality and Social Psychology*, 1969, *13*, 173–199.

Bandura, A., Jeffery, R. W., & Gajdos, E. Generalizing change through participant modeling with self-directed mastery. *Behaviour Research and Therapy*, 1975, *13*, 141–152.

Bandura, A., Jeffery, R. W., & Wright, C. L. Efficacy of participant modeling as a function of response instruction aids. *Journal of Abnormal Psychology*, 1974, *83*, 56–64.

Bandura, A., & Schunk, D. H. Cultivating competence, self-efficacy, and intrinsic interest through proximal self-motivation. *Journal of Personality and Social Psychology*, 1981, *41*, 586–598.

Bandura, A., & Walters, R. H. *Social learning and personality development*. New York: Holt, Rinehart & Winston, 1963.

Barlow, D. H. Increasing heterosexual responsiveness in the treatment of sexual deviation: A review of the clinical and experimental evidence. *Behavior Therapy*, 1973, *4*, 655–671.

Barlow, D. H. Behavioral assessment in clinical settings: Developing issues. In J. D. Cone & R. P. Hawkins (Eds.), *Behavioral assessment: New directions in clinical psychology*. New York: Brunner/Mazel, 1977.

Barlow, D. H., & Abel, G. G. Recent developments in assessment and treatment of paraphilias and gender-identity disorders. In W. E. Craighead, A. E. Kazdin, & M. J. Mahoney (Eds.), *Behavior modification: Principles, issues, and applications* (2nd ed.). Boston: Houghton Mifflin, 1981. Pp. 337–356.

Barlow, D. H., Leitenberg, H., & Agras, W. S. Experimental control of sexual deviation through manipulation of the noxious scene in covert sensitization. *Journal of Abnormal Psychology*, 1969, *74*, 597–601.

Barrett, B. H. Reduction in rate of multiple tics by free operant conditioning methods. *Journal of Nervous and Mental Disease*, 1962, *135*, 187–195.

Barrish, H. H., Saunders, M., & Wolf, M. M. Good behavior game: Effects of individual contingencies for group consequences on disruptive behavior in a classroom. *Journal of Applied Behavior Analysis*, 1969, *2*, 119–124.

Barton, E. S., Guess, D., Garcia, E., & Baer, D. M. Improvement of retardates' mealtime behaviors by timeout procedures using multiple base-line techniques. *Journal of Applied Behavior Analysis*, 1970, *3*, 77–84.

Bash, M., & Camp, B. *Think aloud program: Group manual*. Unpublished manuscript, University of Colorado Medical School, 1975.

Beck, A. T. Thinking and depression. *Archives of General Psychiatry*, 1963, *9*, 324–333.

Beck, A. T. *Depression: Causes and treatment*. Philadelphia: University of Pennsylvania Press, 1972.

Beck, A. T. *Cognitive therapy and the emotional disorders*. New York: International Universities Press, 1976.

Beck, A. T., Ward, C. H., Mendelsohn, M., Mock, J., & Erbaugh, J. An inventory for measuring depression. *Archives of General Psychiatry*, 1961, *4*, 561–571.

Becker, J. V., Turner, S. M., & Sajwaj, T. E. Multiple behavioral effects of the use of lemon juice with a ruminating toddler-age child. *Behavior Modification*, 1978, *2*, 267–278.

Becker, W. *Parents are teachers: A child management program*. Champaign, Ill.: Research Press, 1971.

Bellack, A. S., & Hersen, M. *Behavior modification: An introductory textbook*. Baltimore: Williams & Wilkins, 1977.

Bennett, P. S., & Maley, R. S. Modification of interactive behaviors in chronic mental patients. *Journal of Applied Behavior Analysis*, 1973, *6*, 609–620.

Bergin, A. E., & Lambert, M. J. The evaluation of therapeutic outcomes. In S. L. Garfield & A. E. Bergin (Eds.), *Handbook of psychotherapy and behavior change: An empirical analysis* (2nd ed.). New York: Wiley, 1978. Pp. 139–189.

Bergin, A. E., & Strupp, H. H. (Eds.). *Changing frontiers in the science of psychotherapy*. Chicago: Aldine-Atherton, 1972.

Bernstein, D. A., & Borkovec, T. D. *Progressive relaxation training: A manual for the helping professions*. Champaign, Ill.: Research Press, 1973.

Bernstein, D. A., & McAlister, A. The modification of smoking behavior: Progress and problems. *Addictive Behaviors*, 1976, *1*, 89–102.

Bieber, I., Dain, H. J., Dince, P. R., Drellich, M. G., Grand, H. G., Gundlach, R. H., Kremer, M. W., Rifkin, A. H., Wilbur, C. B., & Bieber, T. B. *Homosexuality: A psychoanalytic study*. New York: Basic Books, 1962.

Bigelow, G., Liebson, I., & Griffiths, R. Alcoholic drinking: Suppression by a brief time-out procedure. *Behaviour Research and Therapy*, 1974, *12*, 107–115.

Bijou, S. W. Methodology for an experimental analysis of child behavior. *Psychological Reports*, 1957, *3*, 243–250. (a)

Bijou, S. W. Patterns of reinforcement and resistance to extinction in young children. *Child Development*, 1957, *28*, 47–54. (b)

Bijou, S. W. Operant extinction after fixed-interval schedules with young children. *Journal of the Experimental Analysis of Behavior*, 1958, *1*, 25–29.

Bijou, S. W., & Oblinger, B. Responses of normal and retarded children as a function of the experimental situation. *Psychological Reports*, 1960, *6*, 447–454.

Bijou, S. W., & Orlando, R. Rapid development of multiple-schedule performances with retarded children. *Journal of the Experimental Analysis of Behavior*, 1961, *4*, 7–16.

Birnbrauer, J. S. Mental retardation. In H. Leitenberg (Ed.), *Handbook of behavior modification and behavior therapy*. Englewood Cliffs, N.J.: Prentice-Hall, 1976.

Blackwell, B. Patient compliance. *New England Journal of Medicine*, 1973, *289*, 249–253.

Blanchard, E. B. The relative contributions of modeling, informational influences, and physical contact in the extinction of phobic behavior. *Journal of Abnormal Psychology*, 1970, *76*, 55–61.

Blanchard, E. B., & Young, L. D. Clinical applications of biofeedback training: A review of evidence. *Archives of General Psychiatry*, 1974, *30*, 573–589.

Blechman, E. A. The family contract game: A tool to teach interpersonal problem solving. *Family Coordinator*, 1974, *23*, 269–281.

Blechman, E. A., Olson, D. H. L., & Hellman, L. D. Stimulus control over family problem-solving behavior: The family contract game. *Behavior Therapy*, 1976, *7*, 686–692.

Blechman, E. A., Olson, D. H. L., Schornagel, C. Y., Halsdorf, M., & Turner, A. J. The family contract game: Technique and case study. *Journal of Consulting and Clinical Psychology*, 1976, *44*, 449–455.

Bootzin, R. R. *Behavior modification and therapy: An introduction*. Cambridge, Mass.: Winthrop, 1975.

Boren, J. J., & Colman, A. D. Some experiments on reinforcement principles within a psychiatric ward for delinquent soldiers. *Journal of Applied Behavior Analysis*, 1970, *3*, 29–37.

Borkovec, T. D. Insomnia. In R. B. Williams & W. D. Gentry (Eds.), *Behavioral approaches to medical treatment*. Cambridge, Mass.: Ballinger, 1977.

Borkovec, T. D., & Rachman, S. The utility of analogue research. *Behaviour Research and Therapy*, 1979, *17*, 253–262.

Boudewyns, P. A., Tanna, V. L., & Fleischman, D. J. A modified shame aversion therapy for compulsive obscene telephone calling. *Behavior Therapy*, 1975, *6*, 704–707.

Boudin, H. M. Contingency contracting as a therapeutic tool in deceleration of amphetamine use. *Behavior Therapy*, 1972, *3*, 602–608.

Bower, S. A., & Bower, G. H. *Asserting yourself: A practical guide for positive change*. Reading, Mass.: Addison-Wesley, 1976.

Breger, L., & McGaugh, J. L. Learning theory and behavior therapy: A reply to Rachman and Eysenck. *Psychological Bulletin*, 1966, *65*, 170–173.

Brickes, W. A., & Brickes, D. D. Development of receptive vocabulary in severely retarded children. *American Journal of Mental Deficiency*, 1970, *74*, 599–607.

Briscoe, R. V., Hoffman, D. B., & Bailey, J. S. Behavioral community psychology: Training a community board to problem solve. *Journal of Applied Behavior Analysis*, 1975, *8*, 157–168.

Bristol, M. M., & Sloane, H. N. Effects of contingency contracting on study rate and test performance. *Journal of Applied Behavior Analysis*, 1974, *7*, 271–285.

Bruch, M. Influence of model characteristics on psychiatric inpatients' interview anxiety. *Journal of Abnormal Psychology*, 1975, *84*, 290–294.

Burgess, R. L., Clark, R. N., & Hendee, J. C. An experimental antilitter procedure. *Journal of Applied Behavior Analysis*, 1971, *4*, 71–75.

Buss, A. H., Plomin, R., & Willerman, L. The inheritance of temperaments. *Journal of Personality*, 1973, *41*, 513–524.

Cahoon, D. D. Symptom substitution and the behavior therapies: A reappraisal. *Psychological Bulletin*, 1968, *69*, 149–156.

Callahan, E. J., & Leitenberg, H. Aversion therapy for sexual deviation: Contingent shock and covert sensitization. *Journal of Abnormal Psychology*, 1972, *81*, 60–73.

Callner, D. A. Behavioral treatment approaches to drug abuse: A critical review of the research. *Psychological Bulletin*, 1975, *82*, 143–164.

Camp, B. W., & Bash, M. A. S. *Think aloud: Increasing social and cognitive skills—A problem-solving program for children (primary level)*. Champaign, Ill.: Research Press, 1981.

Camp, B., Blom, G., Herbert, F., & VanDoorwick, W. *"Think aloud": A program for developing self-control in young aggressive boys*. Unpublished manuscript, University of Colorado Medical School, 1976.

Caplan, G. *Principles of preventive psychiatry*. New York: Basic Books, 1964.

Carlson, C. G., Hersen, M., & Eisler, R. M. Token economy programs in the treatment of hospitalized adult psychiatric patients. *Journal of Nervous and Mental Disease*, 1972, *155*, 192–204.

Cartwright, D. E. Effectiveness of psychotherapy: A critique of the spontaneous remission argument. *Journal of Counseling Psychology*, 1955, *2*, 290–296.

Castaneda, C. *A separate reality: Further conversations with Don Juan*. New York: Pocket Books, 1972.

Cautela, J. R. Treatment of compulsive behavior by covert sensitization. *Psychological Record*, 1966, *16*, 33–41.

Cautela, J. R. Covert sensitization. *Psychological Reports*, 1967, *20*, 459–468.

Cautela, J. R. The use of covert sensitization in the treatment of alcoholism. *Psychotherapy: Theory, Research and Practice*, 1970, *7*, 86–90.

Cautela, J. R. Covert sensitization for the treatment of sexual deviations. *Psychological Record*, 1971, *21*, 37–48.

Cautela, J. R. Rationale and procedures for covert conditioning. In R. D. Rubin, H. Fensterheim, J. D. Henderson, & L. P. Ullmann (Eds.), *Advances in behavior therapy*. New York: Academic Press, 1972. Pp. 85–96.

Cautela, J. R., & Kastenbaum, R. A reinforcement survey schedule for use in therapy, training, and research. *Psychological Reports*, 1967, *20*, 1115–1130.

Cautela, J. R., & Wisocki, P. A. The use of male and female therapists in the treatment of homosexual behavior. In R. D. Rubin & C. M. Franks (Eds.), *Advances in behavior therapy*. New York: Academic Press, 1969.

Cayner, J. J., & Kiland, J. R. Use of brief time out with three schizophrenic patients. *Journal of Behavior Therapy and Experimental Psychiatry*, 1974, *5*, 141–145.

Chadwick, B. A., & Day, R. C. Systematic reinforcement: Academic performance of underachieving students. *Journal of Applied Behavior Analysis*, 1971, *4*, 311–319.

Chambliss, C. A., & Murray, E. J. Cognitive procedures for smoking reduction: Symptom attribution versus efficacy attribution. *Cognitive Therapy and Research*, 1979, *3*, 91–96. (a)

Chambliss, C. A., & Murray, E. J. Efficacy attribution, locus of control, and weight loss. *Cognitive Therapy and Research*, 1979, *3*, 349–354. (b)

Chapman, C., & Risley, T. R. Antilitter procedures in an urban high-density area. *Journal of Applied Behavior Analysis*, 1974, *7*, 377–383.

Christensen, D. E. Effects of combining methylphenidate and a classroom token system in modifying hyperactive behavior. *American Journal of Mental Deficiency*, 1975, *80*, 266–276.

Christophersen, E. R. *Little people—Guidelines for common sense child rearing*. Lawrence, Kan.: H & H Enterprises, 1977.

Clark, G. R., Bussone, A., & Kivitz, M. S. Elwyn Institute's community living program. *The Challenge*, 1974, *17*, 14–15.

Clark, G. R., Kivitz, M. S., & Rosen, M. From research to community living. *Human Needs*, 1972, *1*, 25–28.

Clark, R. N., Burgess, R. L., & Hendee, J. C. The development of antilitter behavior in a forest campground. *Journal of Applied Behavior Analysis*, 1972, *5*, 1–5.

Coates, T. J., & Thoresen, C. E. *How to sleep better: A drug-free program for overcoming insomnia*. Englewood Cliffs, N.J.: Prentice-Hall, 1977.

Condiotte, M. M., & Lichtenstein, E. Self-efficacy and relapse in smoking cessation programs. *Journal of Consulting and Clinical Psychology*, 1981, *49*, 648–658.

Conrad, S. R., & Wincze, J. P. Orgasmic reconditioning: A controlled study of its effects upon sexual arousal and behavior of adult male homosexuals. *Behavior Therapy*, 1976, *7*, 155–166.

Corte, H. E., Wolf, M. M., & Locke, B. J. A comparison of procedures for eliminating self-injurious behavior of retarded adolescents. *Journal of Applied Behavior Analysis*, 1971, *4*, 201–213.

Costello, C. G. Depression: Loss of reinforcers or loss of reinforcer effectiveness? *Behavior Therapy*, 1972, *3*, 240–247.

Cotharin, R. L., & Mikulas, W. L. Systematic desensitization of racial emotional responses. *Journal of Behavior Therapy and Experimental Psychiatry*, 1975, *6*, 347–348.

Cotter, L. H. Operant conditioning in a Vietnamese mental hospital. *American Journal of Psychiatry*, 1967, *124*, 23–28.

Cradock, C., Cotler, S., & Jason, L. A. Primary prevention: Immunization of children for speech anxiety. *Cognitive Therapy and Research*, 1978, *2*, 389–396.

Craighead, W. E., Kazdin, A. E., & Mahoney, M. J. *Behavior modification: Principles, issues, and applications*. Boston: Houghton Mifflin, 1976.

Creer, T. L., & Miklich, D. R. The application of a self-modeling procedure to modify inappropriate behavior: A preliminary report. *Behaviour Research and Therapy*, 1970, *8*, 91–92.

Crowe, M. J., Marks, I. M., Agras, W. S., & Leitenberg, H. Time limited desensitization, implosion and shaping for phobic patients: A crossover study. *Behaviour Research and Therapy*, 1972, *10*, 319–328.

Cunningham, C. E., & Linscheid, T. R. Elimination of chronic infant ruminating by electric shock. *Behavior Therapy*, 1976, *7*, 231–234.

Daley, M. F. The "Reinforcement Menu": Finding effective reinforcers. In J. D. Krumboltz & C. E. Thoresen (Eds.), *Behavioral counseling: Cases and techniques*. New York: Holt, Rinehart & Winston, 1969. Pp. 42–45.

Dalton, A. J., Rubino, C. A., & Hislop, M. W. Some effects of token rewards on school achievement of children with Down's syndrome. *Journal of Applied Behavior Analysis*, 1973, *6*, 251–259.

Davison, G. C. Case report: Elimination of a sadistic fantasy by a client-controlled counter-conditioning technique. *Journal of Abnormal Psychology*, 1968, *73*, 84–90.

Davison, G. C. Homosexuality: The ethical challenge. *Journal of Consulting and Clinical Psychology*, 1976, *44*, 157–162.

Davison G. C. Personal communication, May 28, 1982.

Davison, G. C., D'Zurilla, T. J., Goldfried, M. R., Paul, G. L., & Valins, S. In M. R. Goldfried (Chair), *Cognitive processes in behavior modification*. Symposium presented at the meeting of the American Psychological Association, San Francisco, August 1968.

Davison, G. C., & Stuart, R. B. Behavior therapy and civil liberties. *American Psychologist*, 1975, *30*, 755–763.

Davison, G. C., Tsujimoto, R. N., & Glaros, A. G. Attribution and the maintenance of behavior change in falling asleep. *Journal of Abnormal Psychology*, 1973, *82*, 124–133.

Davison, G. C., & Valins, S. Maintenance of self-attributed and drug-attributed behavior change. *Journal of Personality and Social Psychology*, 1969, *11*, 25–33.

Dawley, H. H., & Dillenkoffer, R. L. Minimizing the risks in rapid smoking treatment. *Journal of Behavior Therapy and Experimental Psychiatry*, 1975, *6*, 174.

Deleon, G., & Mandell, W. A comparison of conditioning and psychotherapy in the treatment of functional enuresis. *Journal of Clinical Psychology*, 1966, *22*, 326–330.

Deleon, G., & Sacks, S. Conditioning functional enuresis: A four-year follow-up. *Journal of Consulting and Clinical Psychology*, 1972, *39*, 299–300.

Dengrove, E. Thought-block in behavior therapy. *Behavior Therapy*, 1972, *3*, 344–346.

Denney, D. R., & Rupert, P. A. Desensitization and self-control in the treatment of test anxiety. *Journal of Counseling Psychology*, 1977, *24*, 272–280.

DeRisi, W. J., & Butz, G. *Writing behavioral contracts: A case simulation practice manual*. Champaign, Ill.: Research Press, 1975.

Deslauriers, B. C., & Everett, P. B. The effects of intermittent and continuous token reinforcement on bus ridership. *Journal of Applied Psychology*, 1977, *62*, 369–375.

DiClemente, C. C. Self-efficacy and smoking cessation maintenance, *Cognitive Therapy and Research*, 1981, *5*, 175–187.

Doleys, D. M. Behavioral treatment of nocturnal enuresis in children: A review of the recent literature. *Psychological Bulletin*, 1977, *84*, 30–54.

Doleys, D. M., & Arnold, S. Treatment of childhood encopresis: Full cleanliness training. *Mental Retardation*, 1975, *13*, 14–16.

Donner, L., & Guerney, B. G. Automated group desensitization for test anxiety. *Behaviour Research and Therapy*, 1969, *7*, 1–13.

Dubey, D. R., Kent, R. N., O'Leary, S. G., Broderick, J., & O'Leary, K. D. Reactions of children to classroom observers: A series of controlled investigations. *Behavior Therapy*, 1977, *8*, 887–897.

Dunbar, J., & Agras, W. S. *A controlled investigation of a behavioral intervention with poor adherers to a medication regimen*. Unpublished manuscript, Stanford University, 1978.

D'Zurilla, T. J., & Goldfried, M. R. Problem solving and behavior modification. *Journal of Abnormal Psychology*, 1971, *78*, 107–126.

Eisler, R. M., Hersen, M., & Miller, P. M. Effects of modeling on components of assertive behavior. *Journal of Behavior Therapy and Experimental Psychiatry*, 1973, *4*, 1–6.

Eisler, R. M., Hersen, M., & Miller, P. M. Shaping components of assertive behavior with instructions and feedback. *American Journal of Psychiatry*, 1974, *131*, 1344–1347.

Eisler, R., Hersen, M., Miller, D. M., & Blanchard, E. B. Situational determinants of assertive behaviors. *Journal of Consulting and Clinical Psychology*, 1975, *43*, 330–340.

Eitzen, D. S. The effects of behavior modification on the attitudes of delinquents. *Behaviour Research and Therapy*, 1975, *13*, 295–299.

Ellis, A. *Reason and emotion in psychotherapy*. New York: Lyle Stuart Press, 1962.

Ellis, A. *The essence of rational psychotherapy: A comprehensive approach in treatment*. New York: Institute for Rational Living, 1970.

Epstein, L. H. Psychophysiological measurement in assessment. In M. Hersen & A. S. Bellack (Eds.), *Behavioral assessment: A practical handbook*. Oxford, England: Pergamon Press, 1976. Pp. 207–232.

Epstein, L. H., Hersen, M., & Hemphill, D. P. Music feedback in the treatment of tension headache: An experimental case study. *Journal of Behavior Therapy and Experimental Psychiatry*, 1974, *5*, 59–63.

Epstein, L. H., & Masek, B. J. Behavioral control of medicine compliance. *Journal of Applied Behavior Analysis*, 1978, *11*, 1–9.

Erwin, E. *Behavior therapy: Scientific, philosophical, and moral foundations*. New York: Cambridge University Press, 1978.

Ethical issues for human services. *Behavior Therapy*, 1977, *8*(5), v–vi.

Evans, P. D., & Kellam, A. M. P. Semi-automated desensitization: A controlled clinical trial. *Behaviour Research and Therapy*, 1973, *11*, 641–646.

Everett, P. B., Hayward, S. C., & Meyers, A. W. The effects of a token reinforcement procedure on bus ridership. *Journal of Applied Behavior Analysis*, 1974, *7*, 1–9.

Eysenck, H. J. The effects of psychotherapy: An evaluation. *Journal of Consulting Psychology*, 1952, *16*, 319–324.

Ferritor, D. E., Buckholdt, D., Hamblin, R. L., & Smith, L. The noneffects of contingent reinforcement for attending behavior on work accomplished. *Journal of Applied Behavior Analysis*, 1972, *5*, 7–17.

Ferster, C. B. A functional analysis of depression. *American Psychologist*, 1973, *28*, 857–870.

Ferster, C. B., Nurnberger, J. I., & Levitt, E. B. The control of eating. *Journal of Mathetics*, 1962, *1*, 87–109. (Reprinted in M. R. Goldfried & M. Merbaum (Eds.), *Behavior change through self-control*. New York: Holt, Rinehart & Winston, 1973. Pp. 195–212.)

Fixsen, D. L., Phillips, E. L., Phillips, E. A., & Wolf, M. M. The teaching-family model of group home treatment. In W. E. Craighead, A. E. Kazdin, & M. J. Mahoney, *Behavior modification: Principles, issues, and applications*. Boston: Houghton Mifflin, 1976. Pp. 310–320.

Fordyce, W. E. *Behavioral methods for chronic pain and illness*. St. Louis: Mosby, 1976.

Fordyce, W. E., Fowler, R. S., Lehmann, J. F., DeLateur, B. J., Sand, P. L., & Trieschmann, R. B. Operant conditioning in the treatment of chronic pain. *Archives of Physical Medicine and Rehabilitation*, 1973, *54*, 399–408.

Foxx, R. M. The use of overcorrection to eliminate the public disrobing (stripping) of retarded women. *Behaviour Research and Therapy*, 1976, *14*, 53–61.

Foxx, R. M., & Azrin, N. H. Restitution: A method of eliminating aggressive-disruptive behavior of retarded and brain damaged patients. *Behaviour Research and Therapy*, 1972, *10*, 15–27.

Foxx, R. M., & Azrin, N. H. Dry pants: A rapid method of toilet training children. *Behaviour Research and Therapy*, 1973, *11*, 435–442. (a)

Foxx, R. M., & Azrin, N. H. *Toilet training the retarded: A rapid program for day and night time independent toileting*. Champaign, Ill.: Research Press, 1973. (b)

Foxx, R. M., & Hake, D. F. Gasoline conservation: A procedure for measuring and reducing the driving of college students. *Journal of Applied Behavior Analysis*, 1977, *10*, 61–74.

Foxx, R. M., & Martin, E. D. Treatment of scavenging behavior (coprophagy and pica) by overcorrection. *Behaviour Research and Therapy*, 1975, *13*, 153–162.

Foxx, R. M., & Shapiro, S. T. The timeout ribbon: A nonexclusionary timeout procedure. *Journal of Applied Behavior Analysis*, 1978, *11*, 125–136.

Franklin, B. (B. F. Skinner). Operant reinforcement of prayer. *Journal of Applied Behavior Analysis*, 1969, *2*, 247.

Franks, C. M. Behavior therapy, the principles of conditioning and the treatment of the alcoholic. *Quarterly Journal of Studies on Alcohol*, 1963, *24*, 511–529.

Franks, C. M. (Ed.). *Behavior therapy: Appraisal and status*. New York: McGraw-Hill, 1969. (a)

Franks, C. M. Introduction: Behavior therapy and its Pavlovian origins: Review and perspectives. In C. M. Franks (Ed.), *Behavior therapy: Appraisal and status*. New York: McGraw-Hill, 1969. (b)

Franks, C. M., & Wilson, G. T. (Eds.). *Annual review of behavior therapy: Theory and practice* (Vol. 1). New York: Brunner/Mazel, 1973.

Franks, C. M., & Wilson, G. T. (Eds.). *Annual review of behavior therapy: Theory and practice* (Vol. 2). New York: Brunner/Mazel, 1974.

Franks, C. M., & Wilson, G. T. (Eds.). *Annual review of behavior therapy: Theory and practice* (Vol. 3). New York: Brunner/Mazel, 1975.

Franks, C. M., & Wilson, G. T. (Eds.). *Annual review of behavior therapy: Theory and practice* (Vol. 4). New York: Brunner/Mazel, 1976.

Franks, C. M., & Wilson, G. T. (Eds.). *Annual review of behavior therapy: Theory and practice* (Vol. 5). New York: Brunner/Mazel, 1977.

Franks, C. M., & Wilson, G. T. (Eds.). *Annual review of behavior therapy: Theory and practice* (Vol. 6). New York: Brunner/Mazel, 1978.

Franks, C. M., & Wilson, G. T. (Eds.). *Annual review of behavior therapy: Theory and practice* (Vol. 7). New York: Brunner/Mazel, 1979.

Frederiksen, L. W. Treatment of ruminative thinking by self-monitoring. *Journal of Behavior Therapy and Experimental Psychiatry*, 1975, *6*, 258–259.

Freedman, A. M., Kaplan, H. I., & Sadock, B. J. *Modern synopsis of comprehensive psychiatry/II* (2nd ed.). Baltimore: Williams & Wilkins, 1976.

Friedson, E., & Feldman, J. J. The public looks at dental care. *Journal of the American Dental Association*, 1958, *57*, 325–335.

Galassi, J. P., DeLo, J. S., Galassi, M. D., & Bastien, S. The College Self-Expression Scale: A measure of assertiveness. *Behavior Therapy*, 1974, *5*, 165–171.

Gambrill, E. D., & Richey, C. A. An assertion inventory for use in assessment and research. *Behavior Therapy*, 1975, *6*, 550–561.

Gardner, J. E. Behavior therapy treatment approach to a psychogenic seizure. *Journal of Consulting Psychology*, 1967, *31*, 209–212.

Garfield, S. L., & Kurtz, R. Clinical psychologists in the 1970s. *American Psychologist*, 1976, *31*, 1–9.

Gauthier, J., & Ladouceur, R. The influence of self-efficacy reports on performance. *Behavior Therapy*, 1981, *12*, 436–439.

Geer, J. H. The development of a scale to measure fear. *Behaviour Research and Therapy*, 1965, *3*, 45–53.

Geller, E. S., Chaffee, J. L., & Ingram, R. E. Promoting paper recycling on a university campus. *Journal of Environmental Systems*, 1975, *5*, 39–57.

Geller, E. S., Wylie, R. G., & Farris, J. C. An attempt at applying prompting and reinforcement toward pollution control. *Proceedings of the 79th Annual Convention of the American Psychological Association*, 1971, *6*, 701–702 (Summary).

Gentry, W. D. Noncompliance to medical regimen. In R. B. Williams & W. D. Gentry (Eds.), *Behavioral approaches to medical treatment*. Cambridge, Mass.: Ballinger, 1977.

Gershman, L. Case conference: A transvestite fantasy treated by thought-stopping, covert sensitization, and aversive shock. *Journal of Behavior Therapy and Experimental Psychiatry*, 1970, *1*, 153–161.

Gillum, R. R., & Barsky, A. J. Diagnosis and management of patient noncompliance. *Journal of the American Medical Association*, 1974, *12*, 1563–1567.

Girardeau, F. L., & Spradlin, J. E. Token rewards in a cottage program. *Mental Retardation*, 1964, *2*, 345–351.

Glynn, E. L. Classroom applications of self-determined reinforcement. *Journal of Applied Behavior Analysis*, 1970, *3*, 123–132.

Goldfried, M. R. Systematic desensitization as training in self-control. *Journal of Consulting and Clinical Psychology*, 1971, *37*, 228–234.

Goldfried, M. R. The use of relaxation and cognitive relabeling as coping skills. In R. B. Stuart (Ed.), *Behavioral self management*. New York: Brunner/Mazel, 1977.

Goldfried, M. R., & Davison, G. C. *Clinical behavior therapy*. New York: Holt, Rinehart & Winston, 1976.

Goldfried, M. R., & Kent, R. N. Traditional versus behavioral personality assessment: A comparison of methodological and theoretical assumptions. *Psychological Bulletin*, 1972, *77*, 409–420.

Goldfried, M. R., & Merbaum, M. (Eds.). *Behavior change through self-control*. New York: Holt, Rinehart & Winston, 1973.

Goldfried, M. R., & Sobocinski, D. Effect of irrational beliefs on emotional arousal. *Journal of Consulting and Clinical Psychology*, 1975, *43*, 504–510.

Goldfried, M. R., & Sprafkin, J. N. *Behavioral personality assessment*. Morristown, N.J.: General Learning Press, 1974.

Goldiamond, I. Self-control procedures in personal behavior problems. *Psychological Reports*, 1965, *17*, 851–868.

Goldiamond, I. Toward a constitutional approach to social problems: Ethical and constitutional issues raised by applied behavior analysis. *Behaviorism*, 1974, *2*, 1–79.

Goodwin, D. W., Guze, S. B., & Robins, E. Follow-up studies in obsessional neurosis. *Archives of General Psychiatry*, 1969, *20*, 182–187.

Gorham, D. C., Green, L. W., Caldwell, L. R., & Bartlett, E. R. Effect of operant conditioning techniques on chronic schizophrenics. *Psychological Reports*, 1970, *27*, 223–234.

Götestam, K. G., Melin, L., & Öst, L. Behavioral techniques in the treatment of drug abuse: An evaluation review. *Addictive Behaviors*, 1976, *1*, 205–226.

Gottman, J. M., & Markman, H. J. Experimental designs in psychotherapy research. In S. L. Garfield & A. E. Bergin (Eds.), *Handbook of psychotherapy and behavior change: An empirical analysis* (2nd ed.). New York: Wiley, 1978. Pp. 23–62.

Gould, D., & Weiss, M. Effect of model similarity and model self-talk on self-efficacy in muscular endurance. *Journal of Sport Psychology*, 1981, *3*, 17–29.

Graubard, P. S., Rosenberg, H., & Miller, M. B. Student applications of behavior modification to teachers and environments or ecological approaches to social deviancy. In R. Ulrich, T. Stachnik, & J. Mabry (Eds.), *Control of human behavior* (Vol. 3). Glenview, Ill.: Scott, Foresman, 1974. Pp. 421–436.

Green, L. Temporal and stimulus factors in self-monitoring of obese persons. *Behavior Therapy*, 1978, *9*, 328–341.

Griffiths, R., Bigelow, G., & Liebson, I. Suppression of ethanol self-administration in alcoholics by contingent time-out from social interactions. *Behaviour Research and Therapy*, 1974, *12*, 327–334.

Gripp, R. F., & Magaro, P. A. A token economy program evaluation with untreated control ward comparison. *Behaviour Research and Therapy*, 1971, *9*, 137–149.

Gripp, R. F., & Magaro, P. A. Token economy program in the psychiatric hospital: Review and analysis. *Behaviour Research and Therapy*, 1974, *12*, 205–228.

Guess, D. A functional analysis of receptive and productive speech: Acquisition of the plural morpheme. *Journal of Applied Behavior Analysis*, 1969, *2*, 55–64.

Guess, D., & Baer, D. M. An analysis of individual differences in generalization between receptive and productive language in retarded children. *Journal of Applied Behavior Analysis*, 1973, *6*, 311–329.

Hagen, R. L., Craighead, W. E., & Paul, G. L. Staff reactivity to evaluative behavioral observations. *Behavior Therapy*, 1975, *6*, 201–205.

Hake, D. F., & Foxx, R. M. Prompting gasoline conservation: The effects of reinforcement schedule, a leader, and self-recording. *Behavior Modification*, 1978, *2*, 339–369.

Harbert, T. L., Barlow, D. H., Hersen, M., & Austin, J. B. Measurement and modification of incestuous behavior: A case study. *Psychological Reports*, 1974, *34*, 79–86.

Hardyck, C. D., & Petrinovich, L. F. Treatment of subvocal speech during reading. *Journal of Reading*, 1969, *1*, 1–11.

Hardyck, C. D., Petrinovich, L. F., & Ellsworth, D. W. Feedback of speech muscle activity during silent reading: Rapid extinction. *Science*, 1966, *154*, 1467–1468.

Hardyck, C. D., Petrinovich, L. F., & Ellsworth, D. W. Feedback of speech muscle activity during silent reading: Two comments. *Science*, 1967, *157*, 581.

Harris, S. L., & Romanczyk, R. G. Treating self-injurious behavior of a retarded child by overcorrection. *Behavior Therapy*, 1976, *7*, 235–239.

Harris, V. W., & Sherman, J. A. Use and analysis of the "Good Behavior Game" to reduce disruptive classroom behavior. *Journal of Applied Behavior Analysis*, 1973, *6*, 405–417.

Harris, V. W., & Sherman, J. A. Homework assignments, consequences, and classroom performance in social studies and mathematics. *Journal of Applied Behavior Analysis*, 1974, *7*, 505–519.

Hauser, R. Rapid smoking as a technique of behavior modification: Caution in selection of subjects. *Journal of Consulting and Clinical Psychology*, 1974, *42*, 625.

Hauserman, N., Walen, S. R., & Behling, M. Reinforced racial integration in the first grade: A study in generalization. *Journal of Applied Behavior Analysis*, 1973, *6*, 193–200.

Hayes, S. C., & Cone, J. D. Reducing residential electrical energy use: Payments, information, and feedback. *Journal of Applied Behavior Analysis*, 1977, *10*, 425–436.

Heap, R. F., Boblitt, W. E., Moore, C. H., & Hord, J. E. Behavior-milieu therapy with chronic neuropsychiatric patients. *Journal of Abnormal Psychology*, 1970, *76*, 349–354.

Hedberg, A. G., & Campbell, L. A comparison of four behavioral treatments of alcoholism. *Journal of Behavior Therapy and Experimental Psychiatry*, 1974, *5*, 251–256.

Henderson, J. D., & Scoles, P. E. A community-based behavioral operant environment for psychotic men. *Behavior Therapy*, 1970, *1*, 245–251.

Henderson, R. W., Swanson, R., & Zimmerman, B. J. Inquiry response induction of preschool children through televised modeling. *Developmental Psychology*, 1975, *11*, 523–524.

Henderson, R. W., Zimmerman, B. J., Swanson, R., & Bergan, J. R. *Televised cognitive skill instruction for Papago Native American children*. Final report on Children's Bureau grant number 0-0CD-CD-479. Tucson, Ariz.: Arizona Center for Educational Research and Development, 1974.

Hermann, J. A., deMontes, A. I., Dominguez, B., Montes, F., & Hopkins, B. L. Effects of bonuses for punctuality on the tardiness of industrial wo~kers. *Journal of Applied Behavior Analysis*, 1973, *6*, 563–570.

Hersen, M., & Bellack, A. S. A multiple-baseline analysis of social-skills training in chronic schizophrenics. *Journal of Applied Behavior Analysis*, 1976, *9*, 239–245. (a)

Hersen, M., & Bellack, A. S. Social skills training for chronic psychiatric patients: Rationale, research findings, and future directions. *Comprehensive Psychiatry*, 1976, *17*, 559–580. (b)

Hersen, M., Eisler, R. M., Alford, G. S., & Agras, W. S. Effects of token economy on neurotic depression: An experimental analysis. *Behavior Therapy*, 1973, *4*, 392–397.

Hersen, M., Eisler, R. M., & Miller, P. M. An experimental analysis of generalization in assertive training. *Behaviour Research and Therapy*, 1974, *12*, 295–310.

Hersen, M., Eisler, R. M., Miller, P. M., Johnson, M. B., & Pinkston, S. G. Effects of practice, instructions, and modeling on components of assertive behavior. *Behaviour Research and Therapy*, 1973, *11*, 443–451.

Hollingsworth, R., & Foreyt, J. P. Community adjustment of released token economy patients. *Journal of Behavior Therapy and Experimental Psychiatry*, 1975, *6*, 271–274.

Homme, L. E. *How to use contingency contracting in the classroom*. Champaign, Ill.: Research Press, 1971.

Homme, L. E., Csanyi, A., Gonzales, M., & Rechs, J. *How to use contingency contracting in the classroom*. Champaign, Ill.: Research Press, 1969.

Horan, J. J., Hackett, G., Nicholas, W. C., Linberg, S. E., Stone, C. I., & Lukaski, H. C. Rapid smoking: A cautionary note. *Journal of Consulting and Clinical Psychology*, 1977, *45*, 341–343.

Horner, R. D., & Keilitz, I. Training mentally retarded adolescents to brush their teeth. *Journal of Applied Behavior Analysis*, 1975, *8*, 301–309.

Houts, A. C., Liebert, D. E., & Liebert, R. M. *Parent guide*. Suffolk County, N.Y.: Suffolk Enuresis Clinic, 1979.

Hunt, J. G., Fitzhugh, L. C., & Fitzhugh, K. B. Teaching "exit-ward" patients appropriate personal appearance by using reinforcement techniques. *American Journal of Mental Deficiency*, 1968, *73*, 41–45.

Hunt, J. G., & Zimmerman, J. Stimulating productivity in a simulated sheltered workshop setting. *American Journal of Mental Deficiency*, 1969, *74*, 43–49.

Hunt, W. A., & Matarazzo, J. D. Three years later: Recent developments in the experimental modification of smoking. *Journal of Abnormal Psychology*, 1973, *81*, 107–114.

Irvin, W. *The effects of facilitative packaging and verbal reinforcement upon compliance with medical regimens by psychiatric outpatients*. Unpublished master's thesis, University of the Pacific, 1976.

Isaacs, W., Thomas, I., & Goldiamond, I. Application of operant conditioning to reinstate verbal behavior in psychotics. *Journal of Speech and Hearing Disorders*, 1960, *25*, 8–12.

Itard, J. M. G. *The wild boy of Aveyron*. New York: Appleton-Century-Crofts, 1962.

Iwata, B. A., & Bailey, J. S. Reward versus cost token systems: An analysis of the effects on students and teacher. *Journal of Applied Behavior Analysis*, 1974, *7*, 567–576.

Jackson, B. Treatment of depression by self-reinforcement. *Behavior Therapy*, 1972, *3*, 298–307.

Jacobs, M., Thompson, L. A., & Truxaw, P. The use of sexual surrogates in counseling. *Counseling Psychologist*, 1975, *1*, 73–77.

Jacobson, E. *Progressive relaxation*. Chicago: University of Chicago Press, 1938.

Jaffe, P. G., & Carlson, P. M. Relative efficacy of modeling and instructions in eliciting social behavior from chronic psychiatric patients. *Journal of Consulting and Clinical Psychology*, 1976, *44*, 200–207.

Janda, L. H., & Rimm, D. C. Covert sensitization in the treatment of obesity. *Journal of Abnormal Psychology*, 1972, *80*, 37–42.

Jeffery, R. W., Wing, R. R., & Stunkard, A. J. Behavioral treatment of obesity: The state of the art, 1976. *Behavior Therapy*, 1978, *9*, 189–199.

Johnson, H. E., & Garton, W. H. Muscle re-education in hemiplegia by use of electromyographic device. *Archives of Physical Medicine and Rehabilitation*, 1973, *54*, 320–325.

Johnson, S. M., & Bolstad, O. D. Methodological issues in naturalistic observation: Some problems and solutions for field research. In L. A. Hamerlynck, L. C. Handy, & E. J. Mash (Eds.), *Behavior change: Methodology, concepts, and practice*. Champaign, Ill.: Research Press, 1973.

Jones, M. C. A laboratory study of fear: The case of Peter. *Pedagogical Seminar*, 1924, *31*, 308–315.

Jones, R. J., & Azrin, N. H. An experimental application of a social reinforcement approach to the problem of job-finding. *Journal of Applied Behavior Analysis*, 1973, *6*, 345–353.

Kallman, W. M., Hersen, M., & O'Toole, D. H. The use of social reinforcement in a case of conversion reaction. *Behavior Therapy*, 1975, *6*, 411–413.

Kanfer, F. H., & Phillips, J. S. *Learning foundations of behavior therapy*. New York: Wiley, 1970.

Kanner, L. *Child psychiatry*. Springfield, Ill.: Thomas, 1972.

Kaplan, H. S. *The new sex therapy: Active treatment of sexual dysfunctions*. New York: Brunner/Mazel, 1974.

Kaplan, H. S. *The illustrated manual of sex therapy*. New York: Quadrangle, 1975.

Kardish, S., Hillman, E., & Werry, J. Efficacy of imipramine in childhood enuresis. *Canadian Medical Association Journal*, 1968, *99*, 263–266.

Kasl, S. V. Issues in patient adherence to health care regimens. *Journal of Human Stress*, 1975, *1*, 5–17.

Kassirer, L. B. Behavior modification for patients and prisoners: Constitutional ramifications of enforced therapy. *Journal of Psychiatry and Law*, 1974, *2*, 245–302.

Katchadourian, H. A., & Lunde, D. T. *Fundamentals of human sexuality*. New York: Holt, Rinehart & Winston, 1972.

Katz, R. C. Single session recovery from a hemodialysis phobia: A case study. *Journal of Behavior Therapy and Experimental Psychiatry*, 1974, *5*, 205–206.

Katz, R. C., & Lutzker, J. R. *A comparison of three methods for training time-out*. Paper presented at the meeting of the American Psychological Association, Washington, D. C., September 1976.

Kazdin, A. E. Response cost: The removal of conditioned reinforcers for therapeutic change. *Behavior Therapy*, 1972, *3*, 533–546.

Kazdin, A. E. Covert modeling and the reduction of avoidance behavior. *Journal of Abnormal Psychology*, 1973, *81*, 87–95.

Kazdin, A. E. Comparative effects of some variations of covert modeling. *Journal of Behavior Therapy and Experimental Psychiatry*, 1974, *5*, 225–231. (a)

Kazdin, A. E. Covert modeling, model similarity, and reduction of avoidance behavior. *Behavior Therapy*, 1974, *5*, 325–340. (b)

Kazdin, A. E. The effect of model identity and fear-relevant similarity on covert modeling. *Behavior Therapy*, 1974, *5*, 624–635. (c)

Kazdin, A. E. Effects of covert modeling and modeling reinforcement on assertive behavior. *Journal of Abnormal Psychology*, 1974, *83*, 240–252. (d)

Kazdin, A. E. Reactive self-monitoring: The effects of response desirability, goal setting, and feedback. *Journal of Consulting and Clinical Psychology*, 1974, *5*, 704–716. (e)

Kazdin, A. E. Characteristics and trends in applied behavior analysis. *Journal of Applied Behavior Analysis*, 1975, *8*, 332.

Kazdin, A. E. Effects of covert modeling, multiple models, and model reinforcement on assertive behavior. *Behavior Therapy*, 1976, *7*, 211–222.

Kazdin, A. E. Extensions of reinforcement techniques to socially and environmentally relevant behaviors. In M. Hersen, R. M. Eisler, & P. M. Miller (Eds.), *Progress in behavior modification* (Vol. 4). New York: Academic Press, 1977. (a)

Kazdin, A. E. *The token economy: A review and evaluation*. New York: Plenum, 1977. (b)

Kazdin, A. E. *History of behavior modification: Experimental foundations of contemporary research*. Baltimore: University Park Press, 1978.

Kazdin, A. E. *Behavior modification in applied settings* (Rev. ed.). Homewood, Ill.: Dorsey, 1980.

Kazdin, A. E., & Hersen, M. The current status of behavior therapy. *Behavior Modification*, 1980, *4*, 283–302.

Kazdin, A. E., & Wilcoxon, L. A. Systematic desensitization and nonspecific treatment effects: A methodological evaluation. *Psychological Bulletin*, 1976, *83*, 729–758.

Kazdin, A. E., & Wilson, G. T. *Evaluation of behavior therapy: Issues, evidence, and research strategies*. Cambridge, Mass.: Ballinger, 1978.

Keeley, S. M., Shemberg, K. M., & Carbonell, J. Operant clinical intervention: Behavior management or beyond? Where are the data? *Behavior Therapy*, 1976, *7*, 292–305.

Keilitz, I., Tucker, D. J., & Horner, R. D. Increasing mentally retarded adolescents' verbalizations about current events. *Journal of Applied Behavior Analysis*, 1973, *6*, 621–630.

Kellam, A. M. P. Shop lifting treated by aversion to a film. *Behaviour Research and Therapy*, 1969, *7*, 125–127.

Keller, F. S. "Good-bye, teacher. . . ." *Journal of Applied Behavior Analysis*, 1968, *1*, 79–89.

Kendall, P. C., Nay, W. R., & Jeffers, J. Timeout duration and contrast effects: A systematic evaluation of a successive treatments design. *Behavior Therapy*, 1975, *7*, 609–615.

Kent, R. N., & Foster, S. Direct observational procedures: Methodological issues in naturalistic settings. In A. R. Ciminero, K. S. Calhoun, & H. E. Adams (Eds.), *Handbook of behavioral assessment*. New York: Wiley, 1977.

Kessler, M., & Albee, G. W. Primary prevention. In M. R. Rosenzweig & L. P. Porter (Eds.), *Annual review of psychology*. Palo Alto, Calif.: Annual Review, 1975.

Kifer, R. F., Lewis, M. A., Green, D. R., & Phillips, E. L. Training predelinquent youths and their parents to negotiate conflict situations. *Journal of Applied Behavior Analysis*, 1974, *7*, 357–364.

Kimmel, H. D., & Kimmel, E. An instrumental conditioning method for treatment of enuresis. *Journal of Behavior Therapy and Experimental Psychiatry*, 1970, *1*, 121–124.

King, M. C. *Prevention of maladaptive avoidance responses through observational learning: An analogue study*. Unpublished doctoral dissertation, McGill University, 1975.

Klein, N. C., Alexander, J. F., & Parsons, B. V. Impact of family systems intervention on recidivism and sibling delinquency: A model of primary prevention and program evaluation. *Journal of Consulting and Clinical Psychology*, 1977, *45*, 469–474.

Kleinknecht, R. A., & Bernstein, D. A. Short term treatment of dental avoidance. *Journal of Behavior Therapy and Experimental Psychiatry*, 1979, *10*, 311–315.

Klepac, R. K. Successful treatment of avoidance of dentistry by desensitization or by increasing pain tolerance. *Journal of Behavior Therapy and Experimental Psychiatry*, 1975, *6*, 307–310.

Knapczyk, D. R., & Livingston, G. Self-recording and student teacher supervision: Variables within a token economy structure. *Journal of Applied Behavior Analysis*, 1973, *6*, 481–486.

Knapczyk, D. R., & Yoppi, J. O. Development of cooperative and competitive play responses in developmentally disabled children. *American Journal of Mental Deficiency*, 1975, *80*, 245–255.

Knight, M. F., & McKenzie, H. S. Elimination of bedtime thumbsucking in home settings through contingent reading. *Journal of Applied Behavior Analysis*, 1974, *7*, 33–38.

Koebel, P., & Crist, R. The use of fading to reduce an aversion to snoring. *Behavior Therapy*, 1977, *8*, 94–95.

Kohlenberg, R. J. Operant conditioning of human anal sphincter pressure. *Journal of Applied Behavior Analysis*, 1973, *6*, 201–208.

Kohlenberg, R., & Phillips, T. Reinforcement and rate of litter depositing. *Journal of Applied Behavior Analysis*, 1973, *6*, 391–396.

Kohlenberg, R., Phillips, T., & Proctor, W. A behavioral analysis of peaking in residential electrical energy consumers. *Journal of Applied Behavior Analysis*, 1976, *9*, 13–18.

Kolvin, I. "Aversive imagery" treatment in adolescents. *Behaviour Research and Therapy*, 1967, *5*, 245–248.

Kornhaber, R. C., & Schroeder, H. E. Importance of model similarity on extinction of avoidance behavior in children. *Journal of Consulting and Clinical Psychology*, 1975, *43*, 601–607.

Krapfl, J. E. *Differential ordering of stimulus presentation and semi-automated versus live treatment in the systematic desensitization of snake phobia*. Unpublished doctoral dissertation, University of Missouri, 1967.

Krasner, L. Behavior modification: Ethical issues and future trends. In H. Leitenberg (Ed.), *Handbook of behavior modification and behavior therapy*. Englewood Cliffs, N. J.: Prentice-Hall, 1976. Pp. 627–649.

Krasner, L., & Ullmann, L. P. *Behavior influence and personality: The social matrix of human action*. New York: Holt, Rinehart & Winston, 1973.

Kringlen, E. Obsessional neurotics: A long-term follow-up. *British Journal of Psychiatry*, 1965, *111*, 709–722.

Labouvie-Vief, G., & Gonda, J. Cognitive strategy training and intellectual performance in the elderly. *Journal of Gerontology*, 1976, *31*, 327–332.

Lahey, B., & Drabman, R. Facilitation of the acquisition and retention of sight word vocabulary through token reinforcement. *Journal of Applied Behavior Analysis*, 1974, *7*, 307–312.

Lando, H. A. A comparison of excessive and rapid smoking in the modification of chronic smoking behavior. *Journal of Consulting and Clinical Psychology*, 1975, *43*, 350–355.

Lang, P. J. The mechanics of desensitization and the laboratory study of fear. In C. M. Franks (Ed.), *Behavior therapy: Appraisal and status*. New York: McGraw-Hill, 1969.

Lang, P. J. The application of psychophysiological methods to the study of psychotherapy and behavior modification. In A. E. Bergin & S. L. Garfield (Eds.), *Handbook of psychotherapy and behavior change: An empirical analysis*. New York: Wiley, 1971.

Lang, P. J. Physiological assessment of anxiety and fear. In J. D. Cone & R. P. Hawkins (Eds.), *Behavioral assessment: New directions in clinical psychology*. New York: Brunner/Mazel, 1977. Pp. 178–195.

Lang, P. J., Melamed, B. G., & Hart, J. A. A psychophysiological analysis of fear modification using an automated desensitization procedure. *Journal of Abnormal Psychology*, 1970, *76*, 220–234.

Lavin, N. I., Thorpe, J. G., Barker, J. C., Blakemore, C. B., & Conway, C. G. Behaviour therapy in a case of transvestism. *Journal of Nervous and Mental Disease*, 1961, *133*, 346–353.

Lawson, D. M., & May, R. B. Three procedures for the extinction of smoking behavior. *Psychological Record*, 1970, *20*, 151–157.

Lazarus, A. A. Group therapy of phobic disorders by systematic desensitization. *Journal of Abnormal and Social Psychology*, 1961, *63*, 505–510.

Lazarus, A. A. Learning theory and the treatment of depression. *Behaviour Research and Therapy*, 1968, *6*, 83–89.

Lazarus, A. A. *Behavior therapy and beyond*. New York: McGraw-Hill, 1971.

Lazarus, A. A. *Multimodal behavior therapy*. New York: Springer, 1976.

Lazarus, A. A., & Abramovitz, A. The use of "emotive imagery" in the treatment of children's phobias. *Journal of Mental Science*, 1962, *108*, 191–195.

Lazarus, A. A., & Davison, G. C. Clinical innovations in research and practice. In A. E. Bergin & S. L. Garfield (Eds.), *Handbook of psychotherapy and behavior change: An empirical analysis*. New York: Wiley, 1971.

Lazarus, A. A., Davison, G. C., & Polefka, D. A. Classical and operant factors in the treatment of a school phobia. *Journal of Abnormal Psychology*, 1965, *70*, 225–229.

Ledwidge, B. Cognitive behavior modification: A step in the wrong direction? *Psychological Bulletin*, 1978, *85*, 353–375.

Ledwidge, B. Cognitive behavior modification: A rejoiner. *Cognitive Therapy and Research*, 1979, *3*, 133–140.

Lee, E. S. Negro intelligence and selective migration: A Philadelphia test of the Klineberg hypothesis. *American Review*, 1951, *16*, 227–232.

Leitenberg, H. Is time-out from positive reinforcement an aversive event? A review of the experimental evidence. *Psychological Bulletin*, 1965, *64*, 428–441.

Leitenberg, H. Behavioral approaches to treatment of neuroses. In H. Leitenberg (Ed.), *Handbook of behavior modification and behavior therapy*. Englewood Cliffs, N.J.: Prentice-Hall, 1976. Pp. 124–167. (a)

Leitenberg, H., Agras, W. S., Thomson, L., & Wright, D. E. Feedback in behavior modification: An experimental analysis in two phobic cases. *Journal of Applied Behavioral Analysis*, 1968, *1*, 131–137.

Lent, J. R. Mimosa Cottage: Experiment in hope. *Psychology Today*, 1968, *2*(1), 50–58.

Lewinsohn, P. M. A behavioral approach to depression. In R. J. Freidman & M. M. Katz (Eds.), *The psychology of depression: Contemporary theory and research*. New York: Wiley, 1974.

Lewinsohn, P. M., & Graf, M. Pleasant activities and depression. *Journal of Consulting and Clinical Psychology*, 1973, *41*, 261–268.

Lewinsohn, P. M., & Libet, J. Pleasant events, activity schedules, and depression. *Journal of Abnormal Psychology*, 1972, *79*, 291–295.

Libb, J. W., & Clements, C. B. Token reinforcement in an exercise program for hospitalized geriatric patients. *Perceptual and Motor Skills*, 1969, *28*, 957–958.

Liberman, R. P. Behavior therapy in psychiatry: New learning principles for old problems. In J. P. Brody & H. K. H. Brody (Eds.), *Controversy in psychiatry*. Philadelphia: Saunders, 1978.

Lichtenstein, E., & Glasgow, R. E. Rapid smoking: Side effects and safeguards. *Journal of Consulting and Clinical Psychology*, 1977, *45*, 815–821.

Lichtenstein, E., Harris, D. E., Birchler, G. R., Wahl, J. M., & Schmahl, D. P. Comparison of rapid smoking, warm, smoky air and attention-placebo in the modification of smoking behavior. *Journal of Consulting and Clinical Psychology*, 1973, *40*, 92–98.

Lichtenstein, E., & Rodrigues, M. R. P. Long-term effects of rapid smoking treatment for dependent cigarette smokers. *Addictive Behaviors*, 1977, *2*, 109–112.

Lick, J. R., & Katkin, E. S. Assessment of anxiety and fear. In M. Hersen & A. S. Bellack (Eds.), *Behavioral assessment: A practical handbook*. Oxford, England: Pergamon, 1976. Pp. 175–206.

Liebert, R. M., & Spiegler, M. D. *Personality: Strategies and issues* (3rd ed.). Homewood, Ill.: Dorsey, 1978.

Liebert, R. M., & Spiegler, M. D. *Personality: Strategies and issues* (4th ed.). Homewood, Ill.: Dorsey, 1982.

Lindsley, O. R. Operant conditioning methods applied to research in chronic schizophrenia. *Psychiatric Research Reports*, 1956, *5*, 118–139.

Lindsley, O. R. Characteristics of the behavior of chronic psychotics as revealed by free-operant conditioning methods. *Diseases of the Nervous System* (Monograph Supplement), 1960, *21*, 66–78.

Lindsley, O. R. Free-operant conditioning and psychotherapy. *Current Psychiatric Therapies*, 1963, *3*, 47–56.

Lindsley, O. R. An experiment with parents handling behavior at home. *Johnstone Bulletin* (Johnstone Training Center, Bordentown, N. J.), 1966, *9*, 27–36.

Lindsley, O. R. A reliable wrist counter for recording behavior rates. *Journal of Applied Behavior Analysis*, 1968, *1*, 77–78.

Lloyd, K. E., & Abel, L. Performance on a token economy psychiatric ward: A two-year summary. *Behaviour Research and Therapy*, 1970, *8*, 1–9.

Locke, E. A. Behavior modification is not cognitive and other myths: A reply to Ledwidge. *Cognitive Therapy and Research*, 1979, *3*, 119–126.

London, P. *Behavior control*. New York: Harper & Row, 1969.

London, P. The end of ideology in behavior modification. *American Psychologist*, 1972, *27*, 913–920.

Lovaas, O. I. *The autistic child: Language development through behavior modification*. New York: Irvington, 1977.

Lovaas, O. I., Koegel, R., Simmons, J. Q., & Long, J. S. Some generalization and follow-up measures on autistic children in behavior therapy. *Journal of Applied Behavior Analysis*, 1973, *6*, 131–166.

Lovaas, O. I., & Newsom, C. D. Behavior modification with psychotic children. In H. Leitenberg (Ed.), *Handbook of behavior modification and behavior therapy*. Englewood Cliffs, N.J.: Prentice-Hall, 1976.

Lovaas, O. I., & Simmons, J. Q. Manipulation of self-destruction in three retarded children. *Journal of Applied Behavior Analysis*, 1969, *2*, 143–157.

Lovibond, S. H., & Caddy, G. Discriminated aversive control in the moderation of alcoholics' drinking behavior. *Behavior Therapy*, 1970, *1*, 437–444.

Lowe, K., & Lutzker, J. R. Increasing compliance to a medical regimen with a juvenile diabetic. *Behavior Therapy*, 1979, *10*, 57–64.

Lubetkin, B. S., & Fishman, S. T. Electrical aversion therapy with a chronic heroin user. *Journal of Behavior Therapy and Experimental Psychiatry*, 1974, *5*, 193–195.

Lubin, B. *Manual for the Depression Adjective Check List*. San Diego, Calif.: Educational and Industrial Testing Service, 1967.

Luborsky, L. A note on Eysenck's article "The effects of psychotherapy: An evaluation." *British Journal of Psychology*, 1954, *45*, 129–131.

Lutzker, J. R., & Drake, J. A. *A comparison of trainer-training techniques to produce rapid toilet training*. Paper presented at the meeting of the American Psychological Association, Washington, D.C., September 1976.

Maccoby, N., Farquhar, J. W., Wood, P. D., & Alexander, J. Reducing the risk of cardiovascular disease: Effects of a community-based campaign on knowledge and behavior. *Journal of Community Health*, 1977, *3*, 100–114.

MacCubrey, J. Verbal operant conditioning with young institutionalized Down's syndrome children. *American Journal of Mental Deficiency*, 1971, *75*, 676–701.

MacPhillamy, D., & Lewinsohn, P. M. *The Pleasant Events Schedule*. Eugene: University of Oregon, 1971. (Mimeo)

Madsen, C. H. Positive reinforcement in the toilet training of a normal child. In L. P. Ullmann & L. Krasner (Eds.), *Case studies in behavior modification*. New York: Holt, Rinehart & Winston, 1965. Pp. 305–307.

Madsen, C. H., Hoffman, M., Thomas, D. R., Koropsak, E., & Madsen, C. K. Comparison of toilet training techniques. In D. M. Gelfand (Ed.), *Social learning in childhood*. Monterey, Calif.: Brooks/Cole, 1969.

Madsen, C. H., Jr., Madsen, C. K., & Thompson, F. Increasing rural Head Start children's consumption of middle-class meals. *Journal of Applied Behavior Analysis*, 1974, *7*, 257–262.

Madsen, C. K., Greer, R. D., & Madsen, C. H. *Research in music behavior: Modifying music behavior in the classroom*. New York: Teachers College Press, Columbia University, 1975.

Mahoney, K., VanWagenen, R. K., & Meyerson, L. Toilet training of normal and retarded children. *Journal of Applied Behavior Analysis*, 1971, *4*, 173–181.

Mahoney, M. J. *Cognition and behavior modification*. Cambridge, Mass.: Ballinger, 1974.

Mahoney, M. J., & Arnkoff, D. Cognitive and self-control therapies. In S. L. Garfield & A. E. Bergin (Eds.), *Handbook of psychotherapy and behavior change: An empirical analysis* (2nd ed.). New York: Wiley, 1978. Pp. 689–722.

Mahoney, M. J., & Kazdin, A. E. Cognitive behavior modification: Misconceptions and premature evacuation. *Psychological Bulletin*, 1979, *86*, 1044–1049.

Mahoney, M. J., Kazdin, A. E., & Lesswing, N. J. Behavior modification: Delusion or deliverance. In C. M. Franks & G. T. Wilson (Eds.), *Annual review of behavior therapy: Theory and practice* (Vol. 2). New York: Brunner/Mazel, 1974.

Mahoney, M. J., & Thoresen, C. E. *Self-control: Power to the person*. Monterey, Calif.: Brooks/Cole, 1974.

Malamuth, N., Wanderer, Z. W., Sayner, R. B., & Durrell, D. Utilization of surrogate partners: A survey of health professions. *Journal of Behavior Therapy and Experimental Psychiatry*, 1976, *7*, 149–150.

Maletzky, B. M. "Assisted" covert sensitization in the treatment of exhibitionism. *Journal of Consulting and Clinical Psychology*, 1974, *42*, 34–40.

Maletzky, B. M. "Assisted" covert sensitization in the treatment of exhibitionism. In D. J. Cox & R. J. Daitzman (Eds.), *Exhibitionism: Description, assessment and treatment*. New York: Garland Press, 1980.

Maley, R. F., Feldman, G. L., & Ruskin, R. S. Evaluation of patient improvement in a token economy treatment program. *Journal of Abnormal Psychology*, 1973, *82*, 141–144.

Maloney, K. B., & Hopkins, B. L. The modification of sentence structure and its relationship to subjective judgments of creativity in writing. *Journal of Applied Behavior Analysis*, 1973, *6*, 425–433.

Mann, J. H. The effect of inter-racial contact on sociometric choices and perceptions. *Journal of Social Psychology*, 1959, *50*, 143–152.

Mann, R. A. The behavior-therapeutic use of contingency contracting to control an adult behavior problem: Weight control. *Journal of Applied Behavior Analysis*, 1972, *5*, 99–109.

Mann, R. A. The use of contingency contracting to facilitate durability of behavior change: Weight loss maintenance. *Addictive Behaviors*, 1976, *1*, 245–249.

Mansdorf, I. J. Reinforcer isolation: An alternative to subject isolation in time-out from positive reinforcement. *Journal of Behavior Therapy and Experimental Psychiatry*, 1977, *8*, 391–393.

Margolis, R. B., & Shemberg, K. M. Cognitive self-instruction in process and reactive schizophrenics: A failure to replicate. *Behavior Therapy*, 1976, *7*, 668–671.

Marholin, D., II, & Gray, D. Effects of group response cost procedures on cash shortages in a small business. *Journal of Applied Behavior Analysis*, 1976, *9*, 25–30.

Marks, I. Behavioral psychotherapy of adult neurosis. In S. L. Garfield & A. E. Bergin (Eds.), *Handbook of psychotherapy and behavior change: An empirical analysis* (2nd ed.). New York: Wiley, 1978. Pp. 493–547.

Marks, I. M., Rachman, S., & Hodgson, R. Treatment of chronic obsessive-compulsive neurosis by in-vivo exposure. *British Journal of Psychiatry*, 1975, *127*, 349–364.

Marquis, J. N. Orgasmic reconditioning: Changing sexual object choice through controlling masturbation fantasies. *Journal of Behavior Therapy and Experimental Psychiatry*, 1970, *1*, 263–271.

Marquis, J. N. An expedient model for behavior therapy. In A. A. Lazarus (Ed.), *Clinical behavior therapy*. New York: Brunner/Mazel, 1973.

Marquis, J. N., Morgan, W. G., & Piaget, G. W. *A guidebook for systematic desensitization* (2nd ed.). Palo Alto, Calif.: Veterans' Workshop, Veterans Administration Hospital, 1971.

Marston, M. V. Compliance with medical regimens: A review of the literature. *Nursing Research*, 1970, *19*, 312–323.

Masters, W. H., & Johnson, V. E. *Human sexual inadequacy*. Boston: Little, Brown, 1970.

Matson, J. L., & Ollendick, T. H. Issues in toilet training normal children. *Behavior Therapy*, 1977, *8*, 549–553.

Mayhew, G. L., & Harris, F. C. Some negative side effects of a punishment procedure for stereotyped behavior. *Journal of Behavior Therapy and Experimental Psychiatry*, 1978, *9*, 245–251.

Mayo, L. L., & Norton, G. R. The use of problem solving to reduce examination and interpersonal anxiety. *Journal of Behavior Therapy and Experimental Psychiatry*, 1980, *11*, 287–289.

McFall, R. M., & Lillesand, D. B. Behavior rehearsal with modeling and coaching in assertion training. *Journal of Abnormal Psychology*, 1971, *77*, 313–323.

McFall, R. M., & Marston, A. R. An experimental investigation of behavior rehearsal in assertive training. *Journal of Abnormal Behavior*, 1970, *76*, 295–303.

McFall, R. M., & Twentyman, C. T. Four experiments on the relative contributions of rehearsal, modeling, and coaching to assertion training. *Journal of Abnormal Psychology*, 1973, *81*, 199–218.

McNees, M. P., Egli, D. S., Marshall, D. S., Schnelle, R. S., Schnelle, J. F., & Risley, T. R. Shoplifting prevention: Providing information through signs. *Journal of Applied Behavior Analysis*, 1976, *9*, 399–405.

McReynolds, W. T., & Coleman, J. Token economy: Patient and staff changes. *Behaviour Research and Therapy*, 1972, *10*, 29–34.

McSweeny, A. J. Effects of response cost on the behavior of a million persons: Charging for directory assistance in Cincinnati. *Journal of Applied Behavior Analysis*, 1978, *11*, 47–51.

Medland, M. B., & Stachnik, T. J. Good-behavior game: A replication and systematic analysis. *Journal of Applied Behavior Analysis*, 1972, *5*, 45–51.

Meichenbaum, D. Examination of model characteristics in reducing avoidance behavior. *Journal of Personality and Social Psychology*, 1971, *17*, 298–307.

Meichenbaum, D. Self-instructional training: A cognitive prosthesis for the aged. *Human Development*, 1974, *17*, 273–280.

Meichenbaum, D. Enhancing creativity by modifying what subjects say to themselves. *American Educational Research Journal*, 1975, *12*, 129–145.
Meichenbaum, D. *Cognitive-behavior modification: An integrative approach*. New York: Plenum Press, 1977.
Meichenbaum, D. Cognitive behavior modification: The need for a fairer assessment. *Cognitive Therapy and Research*, 1979, *3*, 127–132.
Meichenbaum, D., & Cameron, R. *Stress inoculation: A skills training approach to anxiety management*. Unpublished manuscript, University of Waterloo, 1972.
Meichenbaum, D., & Cameron, R. Training schizophrenics to talk to themselves: A means of developing attentional controls. *Behavior Therapy*, 1973, *4*, 515–534.
Meichenbaum, D., Gilmore, B., & Fedoravicius, A. Group insight *vs.* group desensitization in treating speech anxiety. *Journal of Consulting and Clinical Psychology*, 1971, *36*, 410–421.
Meichenbaum, D., & Goodman, J. Training impulsive children to talk to themselves: A means of developing self-control. *Journal of Abnormal Psychology*, 1971, *77*, 115–126.
Melamed, B. G., & Siegel, L. J. Reduction of anxiety in children facing hospitalization and surgery by use of filmed modeling. *Journal of Consulting and Clinical Psychology*, 1975, *43*, 511–521.
Meltzoff, J., & Kornreich, M. *Research in psychotherapy*. New York: Atherton, 1970.
Mercatoris, M., & Craighead, W. E. The effects of nonparticipant observation on teacher and pupil classroom behavior. *Journal of Educational Psychology*, 1974, *66*, 512–519.
Metz, J. R. Conditioning generalized imitation in autistic children. *Journal of Experimental Child Psychology*, 1965, *2*, 389–399.
Meyer, R. G. A behavioral treatment of sleepwalking associated with test anxiety. *Journal of Behavior Therapy and Experimental Psychiatry*, 1975, *6*, 167–168.
Meyer, V., & Crisp, A. H. Some problems in behaviour therapy. *British Journal of Psychiatry*, 1966, *112*, 367–381.
Meyers, A., Mercatoris, M., & Sirota, A. Use of covert self-instruction for the elimination of psychotic speech. *Journal of Consulting and Clinical Psychology*, 1976, *44*, 480–483.
Miller, H. R., & Nawas, M. M. Control of aversive stimulus termination in systematic desensitization. *Behaviour Research and Therapy*, 1970, *8*, 57–61.
Miller, L. K., & Miller, O. L. Reinforcing self-help group activities of welfare recipients. *Journal of Applied Behavior Analysis*, 1970, *3*, 57–64.
Miller, N. E. Biofeedback and visceral learning. *Annual Review of Psychology*, 1978, *29*, 373–404.
Miller, P. M. The use of behavioral contracting in the treatment of alcoholism: A case report. *Behavior Therapy*, 1972, *3*, 593–596.
Miller, P. M., Hersen, M., & Eisler, R. Relative effectiveness of instructions, agreements, and reinforcement in behavioral contracts with alcoholics. *Journal of Abnormal Psychology*, 1974, *83*, 19–24.
Minkin, N., Braukmann, C. J., Minkin, B. L., Timbers, G. D., Timbers, B. J., Fixsen, D. L., Phillips, E. L., & Wolf, M. M. The social validation and training of conversational skills. *Journal of Applied Behavior Analysis*, 1976, *9*, 127–139.
Mischel, W. *Personality and assessment*. New York: Wiley, 1968.
Mischel, W. Direct versus indirect personality assessment: Evidence and implications. *Journal of Consulting and Clinical Psychology*, 1972, *3*, 319–324.
Mischel, W. On the empirical dilemmas of psychodynamic approaches: Issues and alternatives. *Journal of Abnormal Psychology*, 1973, *82*, 335–344.
Moore, N. Behavior therapy in bronchial asthma: A controlled study. *Journal of Psychosomatic Research*, 1965, *9*, 257–276.
Morgan, W. G. The shaping game: A teaching technique. *Behavior Therapy*, 1974, *5*, 271–272.

Morganstern, K. P. Implosive therapy and flooding procedures: A critical review. *Psychological Bulletin*, 1973, *79*, 318–334.

Morganstern, K. P. Behavioral interviewing: The initial stages of assessment. In M. Hersen & A. S. Bellack (Eds.), *Behavioral assessment: A practical approach*. Oxford, England: Pergamon Press, 1976. Pp. 51–76.

Morris, R. J. , & Suckerman, K. R. The importance of the therapeutic relationship in systematic desensitization. *Journal of Consulting and Clinical Psychology*, 1974, *42*, 147. (a)

Morris, R. J., & Suckerman, K. R. Therapist warmth as a factor in automated systematic desensitization. *Journal of Consulting and Clinical Psychology*, 1974, *42*, 244–250. (b)

Mowrer, O. H., & Mowrer, W. M. Enuresis: A method for its study and treatment. *American Journal of Orthopsychiatry*, 1938, *8*, 436–447.

Nathan, P. E. Alcoholism. In H. Leitenberg (Ed.), *Handbook of behavior modification and behavior therapy*. Englewood Cliffs, N.J.: Prentice-Hall, 1976. Pp. 3–44.

Navaco, R. *Anger control: The development and evaluation of an experimental treatment*. Lexington, Mass.: Heath, 1975.

Navaco, R. A stress-inoculation approach to anger management in the training of law enforcement officers. *American Journal of Community Psychology*, 1977, *5*, 327–346. (a)

Navaco, R. Stress inoculation: A cognitive therapy for anger and its application to a case of depression. *Journal of Consulting and Clinical Psychology*, 1977, *45*, 600–608. (b)

Nawas, M. M., Welsch, W. V., & Fishman, S. T. The comparative effectiveness of pairing aversive imagery with relaxation, neutral tasks and muscular tension in reducing snake phobia. *Behaviour Research and Therapy*, 1970, *6*, 63–68.

Neisworth, J. T., & Moore, F. Operant treatment of asthmatic responding with the parent as therapist. *Behavior Therapy*, 1972, *3*, 95–99.

Nelson, R. O., Kapust, J. A., & Dorsey, B. L. Minimal reactivity of overt classroom observations on student and teacher behaviors. *Behavior Therapy*, 1978, *9*, 695–702.

Nesbitt, E. B. An escalator phobia overcome in one session of flooding *in vivo*. *Journal of Behavior Therapy and Experimental Psychiatry*, 1973, *4*, 405–406.

New tool: "Reinforcement" for good work. *Business Week*, December 18, 1971, pp. 76–77.

Nietzel, M. T., Winett, R. A., MacDonald, M. L., & Davidson, W. S. *Behavioral approaches to community psychology*. New York: Pergamon, 1977.

Nimmer, W. H., & Kapp, R. A. A multiple impact program for the treatment of injection phobias. *Journal of Behavior Therapy and Experimental Psychiatry*, 1974, *5*, 257–258.

O'Brien, F., & Azrin, N. H. Behavioral engineering: Control of posture by informational feedback. *Journal of Applied Behavior Analysis*, 1970, *3*, 235–240.

O'Brien, F., & Azrin, N. H. Symptom reduction by functional displacement in a token economy: A case study. *Journal of Behavior Therapy and Experimental Psychiatry*, 1972, *3*, 205–207.

O'Connor, R. D. Modification of social withdrawal through symbolic modeling. *Journal of Applied Behavior Analysis*, 1969, *2*, 15–22.

O'Leary, K. D. The assessment of psychopathology in children. In H. C. Quay & J. S. Werry (Eds.), *Psychopathological disorders of childhood*. New York: Wiley, 1972.

O'Leary, K. D., & Wilson, G. T. *Behavior therapy: Application and outcome*. Englewood Cliffs, N.J.: Prentice-Hall, 1975.

O'Leary, S. G. *The use of punishment with normal children*. Paper presented at the meeting of the Association for Advancement of Behavior Therapy, New York, December 1976.

Ollendick, T. H., & Matson, J. L. Overcorrection: An overview. *Behavior Therapy*, 1978, *9*, 830–842.

Oregon's bottle bill, the 1977 report. State of Oregon Department of Environmental Quality, 1977.

Ott, B. D. Advocacy and instruction in behavior therapy: Examination of productivity in current directions. *the Behavior Therapist*, 1980, *3*, 23–24.

Palkes, H., Stewart, M., & Kahana, B. Porteus maze performance after training in self-directed verbal commands. *Child Development*, 1968, *39*, 817–826.

Parloff, M. B., Waskow, I. E., & Wolfe, B. E. Research on therapist variables in relation to process and outcome. In S. L. Garfield & A. E. Bergin (Eds.), *Handbook of psychotherapy and behavior change: An empirical analysis* (2nd ed.). New York: Wiley, 1978. Pp. 233–282.

Parrino, J. J. Reduction of seizures by desensitization. *Journal of Behavior Therapy and Experimental Psychiatry*, 1971, *2*, 215–218.

Parsons, B. V., & Alexander, J. F. Short-term family intervention: A therapy outcome study. *Journal of Consulting and Clinical Psychology*, 1973, *41*, 195–201.

Paschalis, A. P., Kimmel, H. D., & Kimmel, E. Further study of diurnal instrumental conditioning in the treatment of enuresis nocturna. *Journal of Behavior Therapy and Experimental Psychiatry*, 1972, *3*, 253–256.

Patel, C. H. Yoga and biofeedback in the management of hypertension. *Lancet*, 1973, *2*, 1053–1055.

Patel, C. H. Twelve-month follow-up of yoga and biofeedback in the management of hypertension. *Lancet*, 1975, *1*, 62–64. (a)

Patel, C. H. Yoga and biofeedback in the management of "stress" in hypertensive patients. *Clinical Science and Molecular Medicine*, 1975, *48*, 171–174. (b)

Patel, C. H., & North, W. R. S. Randomized controlled trial of yoga and biofeedback in management of hypertension. *Lancet*, 1975, *2*, 93–99.

Patterson, G. R. Interventions for boys with conduct problems: Multiple settings, treatments, and criteria. *Journal of Consulting and Clinical Psychology*, 1974, *42*, 471–481.

Patterson, G. R. *Families: Applications of social learning to family life*. Champaign, Ill.: Research Press, 1975.

Patterson, G. R., & Bechtel, G. G. Formulating the situational environment in relation to states and traits. In R. B. Cattell (Ed.), *Handbook of modern personality study*. Chicago: Aldine, 1970.

Patterson, G. R., Cobb, J. A., & Ray, R. S. A social engineering technology for retraining families of aggressive boys. In H. E. Adams & I. P. Unikel (Eds.), *Issues and trends in behavior therapy*. Springfield, Ill.: Thomas, 1973.

Patterson, G. R., & Gullion, M. E. *Living with children: New methods for parents and teachers*. Champaign, Ill.: Research Press, 1976.

Patterson, G. R., & Reid, J. B. Intervention for families of aggressive boys: A replication study. *Behaviour Research and Therapy*, 1973, *11*, 1–12.

Pattison, E. M. A critique of alcoholism treatment concepts, with special reference to abstinence. *Quarterly Journal of Studies in Alcoholism*, 1966, *27*, 49–71.

Paul, G. L. *Insight vs. desensitization in psychotherapy*. Stanford, Calif.: Stanford University Press, 1966.

Paul, G. L. Insight vs. desensitization in psychotherapy two years after termination. *Journal of Consulting Psychology*, 1967, *31*, 333–348.

Paul, G. L. Behavior modification research: Design and tactics. In C. M. Franks (Ed.), *Behavior therapy: Appraisal and status*. New York: McGraw-Hill, 1969. (a)

Paul, G. L. Outcome of systematic desensitization. II: Controlled investigations of individual treatment, technique variations, and current status. In C. M. Franks (Ed.), *Behavior therapy: Appraisal and status*. New York: McGraw-Hill, 1969. (b)

Paul, G. L., & Lentz, R. J. *Psychosocial treatment of chronic mental patients: (Milieu vs. social learning programs)*. Cambridge, Mass.: Harvard University Press, 1977.

Paul, G. L., & Shannon, D. T. Treatment of anxiety through systematic desensitization in therapy groups. *Journal of Abnormal Psychology*, 1966, *71*, 124–135.

Pedalino, E., & Gamboa, V. U. Behavior modification and absenteeism: Intervention in one industrial setting. *Journal of Applied Psychology*, 1974, *59*, 694–698.

Peniston, E. Reducing problem behaviors in the severely and profoundly retarded. *Journal of Behavior Therapy and Experimental Psychiatry*, 1975, *6*, 295–299.

Peterson, D. R. *The clinical study of social behavior*. New York: Appleton-Century-Crofts, 1968.

Phillips, D., Fischer, S. C., & Singh, R. A children's reinforcement survey schedule. *Journal of Behavior Therapy and Experimental Psychiatry*, 1977, *8*, 131–134.

Phillips, E. L. Achievement Place: Token reinforcement procedures in a home-style rehabilitation setting for "pre-delinquent" boys. *Journal of Applied Behavior Analysis*, 1968, *1*, 213–223.

Phillips, E. L., Phillips, E. A., Fixsen, D. L., & Wolf, M. M. Achievement Place: Modification of the behaviors of pre-delinquent boys within a token economy. *Journal of Applied Behavior Analysis*, 1971, *4*, 45–59.

Phillips, E. L., Phillips, E. A., Wolf, M. M., & Fixsen, D. L. Achievement Place: Development of the elected manager system. *Journal of Applied Behavior Analysis*, 1973, *6*, 541–561.

Pineda, M. R., Barlow, D. H., & Turner, B. B. Treatment of a severe speech disorder by behavior modification: A case study. *Journal of Behavior Therapy and Experimental Psychiatry*, 1971, *2*, 203–207.

Pitts, C. E. Behavior modification—1787. *Journal of Applied Behavior Analysis*, 1976, *9*, 146.

Poole, A. D., Sanson-Fisher, R. W., German, G. A., & Harker, J. The rapid-smoking technique: Some physiological effects. *Behaviour Research and Therapy*, 1980, *18*, 581–586.

Porterfield, J. K., Herbert-Jackson, E., & Risley, T. R. Contingent observation: An effective and acceptable procedure for reducing disruptive behavior of young children in a group setting. *Journal of Applied Behavior Analysis*, 1976, *9*, 55–64.

Poser, E. G. Toward a theory of behavioral prophylaxis. *Journal of Behavior Therapy and Experimental Psychiatry*, 1970, *1*, 39–43.

Poser, E., & King, M. Strategies for the prevention of maladaptive fear responses. *Canadian Journal of Behavioral Science*, 1975, *7*, 279–294.

Poser, E. G., & King, M. C. Primary prevention of fear: An experimental approach. In I. G. Sarason & C. D. Spielberger (Eds.), *Stress and anxiety, III*. New York: Hemisphere, 1976. Pp. 325–344.

Powell, J., & Azrin, N. The effects of shock as a punisher for cigarette smoking. *Journal of Applied Behavior Analysis*, 1968, *1*, 63–71.

Powers, R. B., Osborne, J. G., & Anderson, E. G. Positive reinforcement of litter removal in the natural environment. *Journal of Applied Behavior Analysis*, 1973, *6*, 579–586.

Premack, D. Reinforcement theory. In D. Levine (Ed.), *Nebraska symposium on motivation*. Lincoln: University of Nebraska Press, 1965. Pp. 123–180.

Prince, H. T., II. *The effects of covert behavioral rehearsal, modeling, and vicarious consequences in assertive training*. Unpublished doctoral dissertation, University of Texas at Austin, 1975.

Pumroy, D. K., & Pumroy, S. S. Systematic observation and reinforcement technique in toilet training. *Psychological Reports*, 1965, *16*, 467–471.

Rachman, S. Studies in desensitization. II: Flooding. *Behaviour Research and Therapy*, 1966, *4*, 1–6. (a)

Rachman, S. Studies in desensitization. III: Speed of generalization. *Behaviour Research and Therapy*, 1966, *4*, 7–15. (b)

Rachman, S. (Ed.). *Advances in behaviour research and therapy* (Vol. 1). Oxford, England: Pergamon, 1978.

Rachman, S., & Hodgson, R. *Obsessions and compulsions*. Englewood Cliffs, N.J.: Prentice-Hall, 1980.

Rachman, S., & Teasdale, J. *Aversion therapy and behaviour disorders: An analysis*. Coral Gables, Fla.: University of Miami Press, 1969.

Rachman, S. J., & Wilson, G. T. *The effects of psychological therapy* (2nd enlarged ed.). Oxford, England: Pergamon, 1980.

Rathus, S. A. A 30-item schedule for assessing assertive behavior. *Behavior Therapy*, 1973, *4*, 398–406.

Raw, M., & Russell, M. A. H. Rapid smoking, cue exposure and support in the modification of smoking. *Behaviour Research and Therapy*, 1980, *18*, 363–372.

A rehabilitation center for the mentally handicapped. *Hospital & Community Psychiatry*, 1972, *23*, 311–314.

Reid, D. H., Luyben, P. L., Rawers, F. A., & Bailey, J. S. The effects of prompting and proximity of containers on newspaper recycling behavior. *Environment and Behavior*, 1976, *8*, 471–482.

Reimringer, M. J., Morgan, S. W., & Bramwell, P. F. Succinylcholine as a modifer of acting-out behavior. *Clinical Medicine*, 1970, *77*, 28–29.

Reiss, M. L., Piotrowski, W. D., & Bailey, J. S. Behavioral community psychology: Encouraging low-income parents to seek dental care for their children. *Journal of Applied Behavior Analysis*, 1976, *9*, 387–397.

Richardson, F. C., & Suinn, R. M. A comparison of traditional systematic desensitization, accelerated massed desensitization, and anxiety management training in the treatment of mathematics anxiety. *Behavior Therapy*, 1973, *4*, 212–218.

Rimm, D. C., deGroot, J. C., Boord, P., Heiman, J., & Dillow, P. V. Systematic desensitization of an anger response. *Behaviour Research and Therapy*, 1971, *9*, 273–280.

Rimm, D. C., & Masters, J. C. *Behavior therapy: Techniques and empirical findings*. New York: Academic Press, 1974.

Risley, T. R. The effects and side effects of punishing the autistic behaviors of a deviant child. *Journal of Applied Behavior Analysis*, 1968, *1*, 21–34.

Risley, T. R. Behavior modification: An experimental-therapeutic endeavor. In L. A. Hamerlynck, P. O. Davidson, & L. E. Acker (Eds.), *Behavior modification and ideal mental health services*. Alberta, Canada: University of Calgary Press, 1969. Pp. 103–127.

Risley, T. R., & Twardosz, S. *Suggesting guidelines for the humane management of the behavior problems of the retarded*. Unpublished manuscript, Johnny Cake Child Study Center, January 1974.

Ritter, B. Effect of contact desensitization on avoidance behavior, fear ratings, and self-evaluative statements. *Proceedings of the American Psychological Association*. Washington, D.C.: American Psychological Association, 1968. (a)

Ritter, B. The group desensitization of children's snake phobias using vicarious and contact desensitization procedures. *Behaviour Research and Therapy*, 1968, *6*, 1–6. (b)

Ritter, B. Eliminating excessive fears of the environment through contact desensitization. In J. D. Krumboltz & C. E. Thoresen (Eds.), *Behavioral counseling: Cases and techniques*. New York: Holt, Rinehart & Winston, 1969. Pp. 168–178. (a)

Ritter, B. Treatment of acrophobia with contact desensitization. *Behaviour Research and Therapy*, 1969, *7*, 41–45. (b)

Ritter, B. The use of contact desensitization, demonstration-plus-relaxation and demonstration alone in the treatment of acrophobia. *Behaviour Research and Therapy*, 1969, *7*, 157–164. (c)

Rollings, J. P., Baumeister, A. A., & Baumeister, A. A. The use of overcorrection procedures to eliminate the stereotyped behaviors of retarded individuals: An analysis of collateral behaviors and generalization of suppressive effects. *Behavior Modification*, 1977, *1*, 29–46.

Roper, G., Rachman, S., & Marks, I. M. Passive and participant modeling in exposure treatment of obsessive-compulsive neurotics. *Behaviour Research and Therapy*, 1975, *13*, 271–279.

Rosen, G. M., Glasgow, R. E., & Barrera, M. A controlled study to assess the clinical efficacy of totally self-administered systematic desensitization. *Journal of Consulting and Clinical Psychology*, 1976, *44*, 208–217.

Rosen, J. C., & Leitenberg, H. Bulimia nervosa: Treatment with exposure and response prevention. *Behavior Therapy*, 1982, *13*, 117–124.

Rosenbaum, A., O'Leary, K. D., & Jacob, R. G. Behavioral intervention with hyperactive children: Group consequences as a supplement to individual contingencies. *Behavior Therapy*, 1975, *6*, 315–323.

Rosenfeld, G. W. Some effects of reinforcement on achievement and behavior in a regular classroom. *Journal of Educational Psychology*, 1972, *63*, 189–193.

Rosenthal, R. Interpersonal expectations: Effects of the experimenter's hypothesis. In R. Rosenthal & R. L. Rosnow (Eds.), *Artifact in behavioral research*. New York: Academic Press, 1969.

Rosenthal, T. L., & Reese, S. L. The effects of covert and overt modeling on assertive behavior. *Behaviour Research and Therapy*, 1976, *14*, 463–470.

Ross, D. M., Ross, S. A., & Evans, T. A. The modification of extreme social withdrawal by modeling with guided participation. *Journal of Behavior Therapy and Experimental Psychiatry*, 1971, *2*, 273–279.

Rush, A. J., Beck, A. T., Kovacs, M., & Hollon, S. Comparative efficacy of cognitive therapy and pharmacotherapy in the treatment of depressed outpatients. *Cognitive Therapy and Research*, 1977, *1*, 17–37.

Rushall, B. S., & Siedentop, D. *The development and control of behavior in sport and physical education*. Philadelphia: Lea & Febiger, 1972.

Rutner, I. T. & Bugle, C. An experimental procedure for the modification of psychotic behavior. *Journal of Consulting and Clinical Psychology*, 1969, *33*, 651–653.

Rybolt, G. A. Token reinforcement therapy with chronic psychiatric patients: A three-year evaluation. *Journal of Behavior Therapy and Experimental Psychiatry*, 1975, *6*, 188–191.

Sachs, D. A. Behavioral techniques in a residential nursing home facility. *Journal of Behavior Therapy and Experimental Psychiatry*, 1975, *26*, 123–127.

Sackett, D. L., & Haynes, R. B. (Eds.). *Compliance with therapeutic regimens*. Baltimore: Johns Hopkins University Press, 1976.

Sajwaj, T., Libet, J., & Agras, S. Lemon-juice therapy: The control of life-threatening rumination in a six-month-old infant. *Journal of Applied Behavior Analysis*, 1974, *7*, 557–563.

Sajwaj, T., Twardosz, S., & Burke, M. Side effects of extinction procedures in a remedial preschool. *Journal of Applied Behavior Analysis*, 1972, *5*, 163–172.

Saunders, D. G. A case of motion sickness treated by systematic desensitization and in vivo relaxation. *Journal of Behavior Therapy and Experimental Psychiatry*, 1976, *7*, 381–382.

Scarr, S. Genetic factors in activity motivation. *Child Development*, 1966, *37*, 663–673.

Schaefer, H. H., & Martin, P. L. Behavioral therapy for "apathy" of hospitalized schizophrenics. *Psychological Reports*, 1966, *19*, 1147–1158.

Schneider, M., & Robin, A. *Turtle manual.* Unpublished manuscript, State University of New York at Stony Brook, 1975.

Schnelle, J. F., Kirchner, R. E., Macrae, J. W., McNees, M. P., Eck, R. H., Snodgrass, S., Casey, J. D., & Uselton, P. H. Police evaluation research: An experimental and cost-benefit analysis of a helicopter patrol in a high crime area. *Journal of Applied Behavior Analysis*, 1978, *11*, 11–21.

Schnelle, J. F., Kirchner, R. E., McNees, M., & Lawler, J. M. Social evaluation research: The evaluation of two police patrolling strategies. *Journal of Applied Behavior Analysis*, 1975, *8*, 353–365.

Schubot, E. D. *The influence of hypnotic and muscular relaxation in systematic desensitization of phobic behavior.* Unpublished doctoral dissertation, Stanford University, 1966.

Schumacher, S., & Lloyd, C. W. Assessment of sexual dysfunction. In M. Hersen & A. S. Bellack (Eds.), *Behavioral assessment: A practical handbook.* Oxford, England: Pergamon, 1976. Pp. 419–435.

Schumaker, J., & Sherman, J. A. Training generative verb usage by imitation and reinforcement procedures. *Journal of Applied Behavior Analysis*, 1970, *3*, 273–287.

Schunk, D. H. Modeling and attributional effects on children's achievement: A self-efficacy analysis. *Journal of Educational Psychology*, 1981, *73*, 93–105.

Schwartz, G. E., & Weiss, S. M. What is behavioral medicine? *Psychosomatic Medicine*, 1977, *39*, 377–381.

Schwitzgebel, L. Survey of electromechanical devices for behavior modification. *Psychological Bulletin*, 1968, *70*, 444–459.

Schwitzgebel, L., & Schwitzgebel, K. *Psychotechnology: Electronic control of mind and behavior.* New York: Holt, Rinehart & Winston, 1973.

Serber, M. Shame aversion therapy. *Journal of Behavior Therapy and Experimental Psychiatry*, 1970, *1*, 213–215.

Serber, M. Shame aversion therapy with and without heterosexual retraining. In R. D. Rubin, H. Fensterheim, J. D. Henderson, & L. P. Ullmann (Eds.), *Advances in behavior therapy.* New York: Academic Press, 1972. Pp. 115–119.

Shaftel, F. R., & Shaftel, G. *Role-playing for social values: Decision-making in the social studies.* Englewood Cliffs, N.J.: Prentice-Hall, 1967.

Shapiro, M. B. An experimental approach to diagnostic psychological testing. *Journal of Mental Science*, 1951, *97*, 748–764.

Shapiro, M. B. Experimental studies of a perceptual anomaly. II. Confirmatory and explanatory experiments. *Journal of Mental Science*, 1952, *98*, 605–617.

Shapiro, M. B. Experimental method in the psychological description of the individual psychiatric patient. *International Journal of Social Psychiatry*, 1957, *3*, 89–102.

Shapiro, M. B. A method of measuring psychological changes specific to the individual psychiatric patient. *British Journal of Medical Psychology*, 1961, *34*, 151–155. (a)

Shapiro, M. B. The single case in fundamental clinical research. *British Journal of Medical Psychology*, 1961, *34*, 255–262. (b)

Shapiro, M. B. The single case of clinical-psychological research. *Journal of General Psychology*, 1966, *74*, 3–23.

Shaw, B. F. Comparison of cognitive therapy and behavior therapy in the treatment of depression. *Journal of Consulting and Clinical Psychology*, 1977, *45*, 543–551.

Shaw, D. W., & Thoresen, C. E. Effects of modeling and desensitization in reducing dental phobia. *Journal of Counseling*, 1974, *21*, 415–420.

Shean, J. D., & Zeidberg, Z. Token reinforcement therapy: A comparison of matched groups. *Journal of Behavior Therapy and Experimental Psychiatry*, 1971, *2*, 95–105.

Sherman, A. R. Two-year follow-up training in relaxation as a behavioral self-management skill. *Behavior Therapy*, 1975, *6*, 419–420.

Shipley, R. H., & Boudewyns, P. A. Flooding and implosive therapy: Are they harmful? *Behavior Therapy*, 1980, *11*, 503–508.

Shorkey, C., & Himle, D. P. Systematic desensitization treatment of a recurring nightmare and related insomnia. *Journal of Behavior Therapy and Experimental Psychiatry*, 1974, *5*, 97–98.

Silverstein, S. J., Nathan, P. E., & Taylor, H. A. Blood alcohol level estimation and controlled drinking by chronic alcoholics. *Behavior Therapy*, 1974, *5*, 1–15.

Sipich, J. F., Russell, R. K., & Tobias, L. L. A comparison of covert sensitization and "nonspecific" treatment in the modification of smoking behavior. *Journal of Behavior Therapy and Experimental Psychiatry*, 1974, *5*, 201–203.

Skeels, H. M. Adult status of children with contrasting early life experiences. *Monographs of the Society for Research in Child Development*, 1966, *31* (Whole No. 3).

Skinner, B. F. *The behavior of organisms*. New York: Appleton-Century-Crofts, 1938.

Skinner, B. F. *Walden Two*. New York: Macmillan, 1948.

Skinner, B. F. *Science and human behavior.* New York: Macmillan, 1953.

Skinner, B. F. A new method for the experimental analysis of the behavior of psychotic patients. *Journal of Nervous and Mental Disease*, 1954, *120*, 403–406.

Skinner, B. F. *Beyond freedom and dignity.* New York: Knopf, 1971.

Skinner, B. F. *About behaviorism.* New York: Knopf, 1974.

Skinner, B. F., Solomon, H. C., & Lindsley, O. R. *Studies in behavior therapy. Metropolitan State Hospital, Waltham, Massachusetts, Status Report I*, November 30, 1953.

Skinner, B. F., Solomon, H. C., Lindsley, O. R., & Richards, M. E. *Studies in behavior therapy. Metropolitan State Hospital, Waltham, Massachusetts, Status Report II*, May 31, 1954.

Sloane, R. B., Staples, F. R., Cristol, A. H., Yorkston, N. H., & Whipple, K. *Psychotherapy versus behavior therapy.* Cambridge, Mass.: Harvard University Press, 1975.

Smith, M. L., & Glass, G. V. Meta-analysis of psychotherapy outcome studies. *American Psychologist*, 1977, *32*, 752–760.

Smith, R. E. The use of humor in the counterconditioning of anger responses: A case study. *Behavior Therapy*, 1973, *4*, 576–580.

Smith, R. E., & Gregory, P. B. Covert sensitization by induced anxiety in the treatment of an alcoholic. *Journal of Behavior Therapy and Experimental Psychiatry*, 1976, *7*, 31–33.

Sobell, M. B., & Sobell, L. C. Alcoholics treated by individualized behavior therapy: One year treatment outcome. *Behaviour Research and Therapy*, 1973, *11*, 599–618.

Sobell, M. B., & Sobell, L. C. Second year treatment outcome of alcoholics treated by individualized behavior therapy: Results. *Behaviour Research and Therapy*, 1976, *14*, 195–215.

Sokolov, A. N. *Inner speech and thought.* New York: Plenum Press, 1972.

Solomon, R. L. Punishment. *American Psychologist*, 1964, *19*, 239–253.

Solomon, R. W., & Wahler, R. G. Peer reinforcement control of classroom problem behavior. *Journal of Applied Behavior Analysis*, 1973, *6*, 49–56.

Spiegler, M. D. A modeling approach. In J. Schwartz (Chair), *Alternatives within behavior modification.* Symposium presented at the meeting of the California State Psychological Association, Monterey, January 1970.

Spiegler, M. D. Behavioral primary prevention: Introduction and overview. In M. D. Spiegler (Chair), *Behavioral primary prevention: A challenge for the 1980s.* Symposium presented at the meeting of the Association for Advancement of Behavior Therapy, New York, November 1980.

Spiegler, M. D. *The nature and treatment of avoidance behavior in obese persons.* Paper presented at the Grand Canyon International Conference on the Treatment of Addictive Behaviors, Grand Canyon, Arizona, November 1981.

Spiegler, M. D. *The role of avoidance behaviors in the treatment of obesity.* Paper presented at the Fourteenth Banff International Conference on Behavior Sciences: Advances in Clinical Behavior Therapy, Banff, Alberta, Canada, March 1982.

Spiegler, M. D., & Agigian, H. *The community training center: An educational-behavioral-social systems model for rehabilitating psychiatric patients.* New York: Brunner/Mazel, 1977.

Spiegler, M. D., Cooley, E. J., Marshall, G. J., Prince, H. T., II, Puckett, S. P., & Skenazy, J. A. A self-control versus a counterconditioning paradigm for systematic desensitization: An experimental comparison. *Journal of Counseling Psychology*, 1976, *23*, 83–86.

Spiegler, M. D., & Liebert, R. M. Some correlates of self-reported fear. *Psychological Reports*, 1970, *26*, 691–695.

Spiegler, M. D., Liebert, R. M., McMains, M. J., & Fernandez, L. E. Experimental development of a modeling treatment to extinguish persistent avoidance behavior. In R. D. Rubin & C. M. Franks (Eds.), *Advances in behavior therapy, 1968.* New York: Academic Press, 1969.

Spivack, G., & Shure, M. B. *Social adjustment of young children.* San Francisco: Jossey-Bass, 1974.

Spradlin, J. E., & Girardeau, F. L. The behavior of moderately and severely retarded persons. In N. R. Ellis (Ed.), *International review of research in mental retardation* (Vol. 1). New York: Academic Press, 1966.

Spring, F. L., Sipich, J. F., Trimble, R. W., & Goeckner, D. J. Effects of contingency and noncontingency contracts in the context of a self-control-oriented smoking modification program. *Behavior Therapy*, 1978, *9*, 967–968.

Stampfl, T. G., & Levis, D. J. Essentials of implosive therapy: A learning-theory-based psychodynamic behavioral therapy. *Journal of Abnormal Psychology*, 1967, *72*, 496–503.

Stampfl, T. G., & Levis, D. J. *Implosive therapy: Theory and technique.* Morristown, N.J.: General Learning Press, 1973.

Steinmark, S. W., & Borkovec, T. D. Active and placebo treatment effects on moderate insomnia under counterdemand and positive demand instructions. *Journal of Abnormal Psychology*, 1974, *83*, 157–163.

Stewart, M. A. Psychotherapy by reciprocal inhibition. *American Journal of Psychiatry*, 1961, *118*, 175–177.

Stokes, T. F., Baer, D. M., & Jackson, R. L. Programming the generalization of a greeting response in four retarded children. *Journal of Applied Behavior Analysis*, 1974, *7*, 599–610.

Stolz, S. B. Why no guidelines for behavior modification? *Journal of Applied Behavior Analysis*, 1977, *10*, 349–367.

Stolz, S. B., & Associates. *Ethical issues in behavior modification: Report of the American Psychological Association Commission.* San Francisco: Jossey-Bass, 1978.

Strupp, H. H. *Who needs intrapsychic factors in clinical psychology?* Paper presented at the Albert Einstein College of Medicine, New York, 1966.

Strupp, H. H. Psychotherapy research and practice: An overview. In S. L. Garfield & A. E. Bergin (Eds.), *Handbook of psychotherapy and behavior change: An empirical analysis* (2nd ed.). New York: Wiley, 1978. Pp. 3–22.

Stuart, R. B. Behavioral control of overeating. *Behaviour Research and Therapy*, 1967, *5*, 357–365.

Stuart, R. B. Operant-interpersonal treatment for marital discord. *Journal of Consulting and Clinical Psychology*, 1969, *33*, 675–682.

Stuart, R. B. Behavioral contracting with the families of delinquents. *Journal of Behavior Therapy and Experimental Psychiatry*, 1971, *2*, 1–11.

Stuart, R. B., & Davis, B. *Slim chance in a fat world: Behavioral control of obesity.* Champaign, Ill.: Research Press, 1972.

Stuart, R. B., & Lott, L. A., Jr. Behavioral contracting with delinquents: A cautionary note. *Journal of Behavior Therapy and Experimental Psychiatry*, 1972, *3*, 161–169.

Stunkard, A. J., & Mahoney, M. J. Behavioral treatment of the eating disorders. In H. Leitenberg (Ed.), *Handbook of behavior modification and behavior therapy.* Englewood Cliffs, N.J.: Prentice-Hall, 1976. Pp. 45–73.

Sue, D. The effect of duration of exposure on systematic desensitization and extinction. *Behaviour Research and Therapy*, 1975, *13*, 55–60.

Sutherland, A., Amit, Z., Golden, N., & Rosenberger, Z. Comparison of three behavioral techniques in the modification of smoking behavior. *Journal of Consulting and Clinical Psychology*, 1975, *43*, 443–447.

Swan, G. E., & MacDonald, M. L. Behavior therapy in practice: A national survey of behavior therapists. *Behavior Therapy*, 1978, *9*, 799–807.

Tate, B. G., & Baroff, G. S. Aversive control of self-injurious behavior in a psychotic boy. *Behaviour Research and Therapy*, 1966, *4*, 281–287.

Taylor, D. W. A. A comparison of group desensitization with two control procedures in the treatment of test anxiety. *Behaviour Research and Therapy*, 1971, *9*, 281–284.

Tharp, R. G., & Wetzel, R. J. *Behavior modification in the natural environment.* New York: Academic Press, 1969.

Thomas, D. R., Becker, W. C., & Armstrong, M. Production and elimination of disruptive classroom behavior by systematically varying teacher's behavior. *Journal of Applied Behavior Analysis*, 1968, *1*, 35–45.

Thompson, T., & Grabowski, J. (Eds.). *Behavior modification of the mentally retarded* (2nd ed.). New York: Oxford University Press, 1977.

Thoresen, C. E., & Mahoney, M. J. *Behavioral self-control.* New York: Holt, Rinehart & Winston, 1974.

Thorpe, J. G., Schmidt, E., Brown, P. T., & Castell, D. Aversion-relief therapy: A new method for general application. *Behaviour Research and Therapy*, 1964, *2*, 71–82.

Timbers, G. D., Timbers, B. J., Fixsen, D. L., Phillips, E. L., & Wolf, M. M. *Achievement Place for pre-delinquent girls: Modification of inappropriate emotional behaviors with token reinforcement and instructional procedures.* Paper presented at the meeting of the American Psychological Association, Montreal, Canada, 1973.

Tooley, J. T., & Pratt, S. An experimental procedure for the extinction of smoking behavior. *Psychological Record*, 1967, *17*, 209–218.

Turk, D. *Cognitive control of pain: A skills training approach for the treatment of pain.* Unpublished master's thesis, University of Waterloo, 1975.

Turk, D. *An expanded skills training approach for the treatment of experimentally induced pain.* Unpublished doctoral dissertation, University of Waterloo, 1976.

Turkat, I. D., & Feuerstein, M. Behavior modification and the public misconception. *American Psychologist*, 1978, *33*, 194.

Turnage, J. R., & Logan, D. L. Treatment of hypodermic needle phobia by in vivo systematic desensitization. *Journal of Behavior Therapy and Experimental Psychiatry*, 1974, *5*, 67–69.

Twardosz, S., & Baer, D. M. Training two severely retarded adolescents to ask questions. *Journal of Applied Behavior Analysis*, 1973, *6*, 655–661.

Tyron, G. S. A review and critique of thought stopping research. *Journal of Behavior Therapy and Experimental Psychiatry*, 1979, *10*, 189–192.

Ullmann, L. P., & Krasner, L. *Case studies in behavior modification.* New York: Holt, Rinehart & Winston, 1965.

Ventis, W. L. Case history: The use of laughter as an alternative response in systematic desensitization. *Behavior Therapy*, 1973, *4*, 120–122.

Vernon, D. T. A. Modeling and birth order in responses to painful stimuli. *Journal of Personality and Social Psychology*, 1974, *29*, 794–799.

Voegtlin, W. L., Lemere, F., Broz, W. R., & O'Hollaren, P. Conditioned reflex therapy of chronic alcoholism. *Quarterly Journal of Studies on Alcohol*, 1941, *2*, 505–511.

Vogler, R. E., Compton, J. V., & Weissbach, T. A. Integrated behavior change techniques for alcoholics. *Journal of Consulting and Clinical Psychology*, 1975, *43*, 233–243.

Wachtel, P. L. *Psychoanalysis and behavior therapy: Toward an integration.* New York: Basic Books, 1977.

Wagner, M. K., & Bragg, R. A. Comparing behavior modification approaches to habit decrement—smoking. *Journal of Consulting and Clinical Psychology*, 1970, *34*, 258–263.

Wahler, R. G. Oppositional children: A quest for parental reinforcement control. *Journal of Applied Behavior Analysis*, 1969, *2*, 159–170.

Wahler, R. G., Winkel, G. H., Peterson, R. F., & Morrison, D. C. Mothers as behavior therapists for their own children. *Behaviour Research and Therapy*, 1965, *3*, 113–124.

Walker, C. E., Hedberg, A., Clement, P. W., & Wright, L. *Clinical procedures for behavior therapy.* Englewood Cliffs, N.J.: Prentice-Hall, 1981.

Walton, D., & Mather, M. D. The relevance of generalization techniques to the treatment of stammering and phobic symptoms. *Behaviour Research and Therapy*, 1963, *1*, 121–125.

Watson, D., & Friend, R. Measurement of social-evaluative anxiety. *Journal of Consulting and Clinical Psychology*, 1969, *33*, 448–457.

Watson, D. L., & Tharp, R. G. *Self-directed behavior: Self-modification for personal adjustment* (2nd ed.). Monterey, Calif.: Brooks/Cole, 1977.

Watson, J. B. *Behavior: An introduction to comparative psychology.* New York: Holt, 1914.

Webster, D. R., & Azrin, N. H. Required relaxation: A method of inhibiting agitative-disruptive behavior of retardates. *Behaviour Research and Therapy*, 1973, *11*, 67–78.

Weidner, F. *In vivo* desensitization of a paranoid schizophrenic. *Journal of Behavior Therapy and Experimental Psychiatry*, 1970, *1*, 79–81.

Weinberg, R. S., Yukelson, D., & Jackson, A. Effect of public and private efficacy expectations on competitive performance. *Journal of Sport Psychology*, 1980, *2*, 940–949.

Weinstein, G. W. The truth about teenage shoplifting. *Parents Magazine*, April 1974, 42–43, 60–61.

Weitzman, B. Behavior therapy and psychotherapy. *Psychological Review*, 1967, *74*, 300–317.

Welch, M. W., & Gist, J. W. *The open token economy system: A handbook for a behavioral approach to rehabilitation.* Springfield, Ill.: Thomas, 1974.

Wells, K. C., Forehand, R., Hickey, K., & Green, K. D. Effects of a procedure derived from the overcorrection principle on manipulated and non-manipulated behaviors. *Journal of Applied Behavior Analysis*, 1977, *10*, 679–687.

Wenrich, W. W., Dawley, H. H., & General, D. A. *Self-directed systematic desensitization: A guide for the student, client and therapist.* Kalamazoo, Mich.: Behaviordelia, 1976.

Werry, J. S., & Cohrssen, J. Enuresis—an etiological and therapeutic study. *Journal of Pediatrics*, 1965, *67*, 423–431.

White, G. D., Nielson, G., & Johnson, S. M. Timeout duration and the suppression of deviant behavior in children. *Journal of Applied Behavior Analysis*, 1972, *5*, 111–120.

White-Blackburn, G., Semb, S., & Semb, G. The effects of a good-behavior contract on the classroom behaviors of sixth-grade students. *Journal of Applied Behavior Analysis*, 1977, *10*, 312.

Wickramasekera, I. Aversive behavior rehearsal for sexual exhibitionism. *Behavior Therapy*, 1976, *7*, 167–176.

Wilkie, E. A., Kivitz, M. S., Clark, G. R., Byer, M. J., & Cohen, J. S. Developing a comprehensive rehabilitation program within an institutional setting. *Mental Retardation*, 1968, *6*, 35–38.

Willerman, L. Activity level and hyperactivity in twins. *Child Development*, 1973, *44*, 288–293.

Willerman, L. *The psychology of individual and group differences.* San Francisco: W. H. Freeman, 1979.

Willerman, L., & Plomin, R. Activity level in children and their parents. *Child Development*, 1973, *44*, 854–858.

Williams, C. D. The elimination of tantrum behavior by extinction procedures: Case report. *Journal of Abnormal and Social Psychology*, 1959, *59*, 269.

Wilson, G. T. Cognitive behavior therapy: Paradigm shift or passing phase? In J. P. Foreyt & D. P. Rathjen (Eds.), *Cognitive behavior therapy: Research and application.* New York: Plenum Press, 1978. Pp. 7–32. (a)

Wilson, G. T. On the much discussed nature of the term "behavior therapy." *Behavior Therapy*, 1978, *9*, 89–98. (b)

Wilson, G. T., & Davison, G. C. Processes of fear reduction in systematic desensitization: Animal studies. *Psychological Bulletin*, 1971, *76*, 1–14.

Wilson, G. T., & Evans, I. M. The therapist–client relationship in behavior therapy. In R. S. Gurman & A. M. Razin (Eds.), *The therapist's contribution to effective psychotherapy: An empirical approach.* New York: Pergamon, 1977.

Wilson, G. T., & O'Leary, K. D. *Principles of behavior therapy.* Englewood Cliffs, N.J.: Prentice-Hall, 1980.

Wilson, G. T., & Tracey, D. A. An experimental analysis of aversive imagery versus electrical aversive conditioning in the treatment of chronic alcoholics. *Behaviour Research and Therapy*, 1976, *14*, 41–51.

Wilson, M. D., & McReynolds, L. V. A procedure for increasing oral reading rate in hard of hearing children. *Journal of Applied Behavior Analysis*, 1973, *6*, 231–239.

Winett, R. A., & Nietzel, M. T. Behavioral ecology: Contingency management of consumer energy use. *American Journal of Community Psychology*, 1975, *3*, 123–133.

Winett, R. A., & Winkler, R. C. Current behavior modification in the classroom: Be still, be quiet, be docile. *Journal of Applied Behavior Analysis*, 1972, *5*, 499–504.

Winkler, R. C. The relevance of economic theory and technology to token reinforcement systems. *Behaviour Research and Therapy*, 1971, *9*, 81–88.

Winkler, R. C. An experimental analysis of economic balance, savings, and wages in a token economy. *Behavior Therapy*, 1973, *4*, 22–40.

Witmer, J. F., & Geller, E. S. Facilitating paper recycling: Effects of prompts, raffles, and contests. *Journal of Applied Behavior Analysis*, 1976, *9*, 315–322.

Wolpe, J. *Psychotherapy by reciprocal inhibition.* Stanford, Calif.: Stanford University Press, 1958.

Wolpe, J. *The practice of behavior therapy* (2nd ed.). New York: Pergamon, 1973.

Wolpe, J., & Lang, P. J. A fear survey schedule for use in behavior therapy. *Behaviour Research and Therapy*, 1964, *2*, 27–30.

Wolpe, J., & Lazarus, A. A. *Behavior therapy techniques: A guide to the treatment of neurosis.* New York: Pergamon, 1966.

Woolfolk, A. E., Woolfolk, R. L., & Wilson, G. T. A rose by another name . . . : Labeling bias and attitudes toward behavior modification. *Journal of Consulting and Clinical Psychology*, 1977, *45*, 184–191.

Wright, J. C. A comparison of systematic desensitization and social skill acquisition in the modification of a social fear. *Behavior Therapy*, 1976, *7*, 205–210.

Wysocki, T., Hall, G., Iwata, B., & Riordan, M. Behavioral management of exercise: Contracting for aerobic points. *Journal of Applied Behavior Analysis*, 1979, *12*, 55–64.

Yates, A. J. Symptoms and symptom substitution. *Psychological Review*, 1958, *65*, 371–374.

Yates, A. J. *Behavior therapy.* New York: Wiley, 1970.

Yates, A. J. *Theory and practice in behavior therapy* (2nd ed.). New York: Wiley, 1975.

Yen, S., & McIntire, R. W. (Eds.). *Teaching behavior modification.* Kalamazoo, Mich.: Behaviordelia, 1976.

Yule, W., Sacks, B., & Hersov, L. Successful flooding treatment of a noise phobia in an eleven-year-old. *Journal of Behavior Therapy and Experimental Psychiatry*, 1974, *5*, 209–211.

Zemore, R. Systematic desensitization as a method of teaching a general anxiety reducing skill. *Journal of Consulting and Clinical Psychology*, 1975, *43*, 157–161.

Zifferblatt, S. M. Increasing patient compliance through the applied analysis of behavior. *Preventive Medicine*, 1975, *4*, 173–182.

Zimmerman, J., Stuckey, T. E., Garlick, B. J., & Miller, M. Effects of token reinforcement on productivity in multiple handicapped clients in a sheltered workshop. *Rehabilitation Literature*, 1969, *30*, 34–41.

Zlutnick, S., Mayville, W. J., & Moffat, S. Modification of seizure disorders: The interruption of behavioral chains. *Journal of Applied Behavior Analysis*, 1975, *8*, 1–12.

Name Index

Page numbers followed by *n* refer to footnotes.

Subject Index

Note: Page numbers for definitions are in italics. Page numbers followed by *n* refer to footnotes. Index includes illustrations.

Continued from page iv

P. 185 (bottom) From "Achievement Place: Modification of the Behaviors of Pre-Delinquent Boys Within a Token Economy," by E. L. Phillips, E. A. Phillips, D. L. Fixen, and M. M. Wolf, *Journal of Applied Behavior Analysis*, 1971, 4, p. 46. Copyright © 1971 by the Society for the Experimental Analysis of Behavior, Inc.

P. 196 From "Rapid Elimination of Enuresis by Intensive Learning Without a Conditioning Apparatus" by N. H. Azrin and P. M. Thienes from *Behavior Therapy*, 9, 1978, pp. 342–354.

P. 198 From "Elimination of Enuresis Without a Conditioning Apparatus: An Extension by Office Instruction of the Child and Parents" by N. H. Azrin, P. Thienes-Hontos, and V. Besalel-Azrin from *Behavior Therapy*, 10, 1979, p. 18.

P. 200 From Wilbert E. Fordyce, *Behavioral Methods for Chronic Pain and Illness*, St. Louis, 1967, The C. V. Mosby Co.

P. 205 From "Operant Conditioning in the Treatment of Chronic Pain" by W. E. Fordyce, R. S. Fowler, J. F. Lehmann, B. J. DeLauteur, P. L. Sand, and R. B. Trieschmann, *Archives of Physical Medicine and Rehabilitation*, 1973, p. 54.

P. 209 From "Increasing Compliance to a Medical Regimen with a Juvenile Diabetic" by K. Lowe and J. R. Lutzker, *Behavior Therapy*, 1979, 10, pp. 57–64.

P. 213 From "Behavioral Community Psychology: Encouraging Low-Income Parents to Seek Dental Care for Their Children" by M. L. Reiss, W. D. Piotrowski, and J. S. Bailey, *Journal of Applied Behavior Analysis*, 1976, 9, p. 391. Copyright © 1976 by the Society for the Experimental Analysis of Behavior, Inc.

P. 234 "Modification of Social Withdrawal Through Symbolic Modeling" by R. D. O'Connor, *Journal of Applied Behavior Analysis*, 1969, 2, p. 19. Copyright © 1969 by the Society for the Experimental Analysis of Behavior, Inc.

P. 254 Reprinted with permission from *Journal of Behavior Therapy and Experimental Psychiatry*, 10, R. A. Kleinknecht and D. A. Bernstein, "Short Term Treatment of Dental Avoidance." Copyright © 1979 by Pergamon Press, Ltd.

P. 270 From *Behavior Therapy: Techniques and Empirical Findings* by D. C. Rimm and J. C. Masters. Reprinted by permission of Academic Press and the author.

Pp. 274, 276 From "Cognitive Therapy and the Emotional Disorders" by A. T. Beck. Copyright © 1976 by International Universities Press.

P. 279 Used with the permission of Helen Palkes, Associate Professor of Psychology, The Edward Mallinckrodt Department of Pediatrics, Division of Pediatric Psychology, Washington University School of Medicine, Director, Psychology Laboratory, St. Louis Children's Hospital.

P. 281 From *Think Aloud: Increasing Social and Cognitive Skills—A Problem-Solving Program for Children* by B. W. Camp and M. A. S. Bash. Research Press, 1981. Reprinted by permission.

P. 295 Reprinted with permission from *Journal of Behavior Therapy and Experimental Psychiatry*, 6, L. W. Frederiksen, "Treatment of Ruminative Thinking by Self-Monitoring." Copyright © 1975 by Pergamon Press, Ltd.

P. 300 From "Treatment of Depression by Self-Reinforcement" by B. Jackson, *Behavior Therapy*, 1972, 3, pp. 302–304. Reprinted by permission of Academic Press and the author.

Pp. 312, 314–15 From *Clinical Behavior Therapy* by Marvin R. Goldfried and Gerald C. Davison. Copyright © 1976 by Holt, Rinehart and Winston. Reprinted by permission of Holt, Rinehart and Winston, CBS College Publishing.

P. 316 Reprinted with permission from *Journal of Behavior Therapy and Experimental Psychiatry*, 11, L. L. Mayo and G. R. Norton, "The Use of Problem Solving to Reduce Examination and Interpersonal Anxiety." Copyright © 1980 by Pergamon Press, Ltd.

P. 340 (top) From "Ethical Issues for Human Services by Association for Advancement of Behavior Therapy" from *Behavior Therapy*, 3, 1977.

P. 340 (bottom) From "Student Applications of Behavior Modification to Teachers and Environments or Ecological Approaches to Social Deviancy" by P. S. Graubard, H. Rosenberg, and M. B. Miller, in R. Ulrich, T. Stachnik, and J. Mabry (eds.), *Control of Human Behavior*, vol. 3, Glenview, Ill.: Scott, Foresman, 1974, pp. 421–436.

P. 391 *Guidelines for Choosing a Behavioral Therapist* reprinted with permission from Association for Advancement of Behavior Therapy.